The Complete Works of Rosa Luxemburg

The Complete Works of Rosa Luxemburg

VOLUME IV, POLITICAL WRITINGS 2:
ON REVOLUTION—1906–1909

Edited by Peter Hudis
and Sandra Rein

*Translated by Jacob Blumenfeld,
Nicholas Gray, Henry Holland,
Zachary King, Manuela Kölke,
and Joseph Muller*

Verso would like to express its gratitude to Rosa Luxemburg Stiftung for help in publishing this book

The publisher also gratefully acknowledges the assistance of Dietz Verlag, publisher of Rosa Luxemburg's *Gesammelte Werke*, the German source of all English translations herein

This paperback edition first published by Verso 2023
First published by Verso 2022
Translation © Jacob Blumenfeld, Nicholas Gray, Henry Holland, Zachary King, Manuela Kölke, and Joseph Muller 2021, 2023

All rights reserved

The moral rights of the authors have been asserted

1 3 5 7 9 10 8 6 4 2

Verso
UK: 6 Meard Street, London W1F 0EG
US: 388 Atlantic Avenue, Brooklyn, NY 11217
versobooks.com

Verso is the imprint of New Left Books

ISBN-13: 978-1-80429-040-8
ISBN-13: 978-1-78873-810-1 (US EBK)
ISBN-13: 978-1-78873-809-5 (UK EBK)

British Library Cataloguing in Publication Data
A catalogue record for this book is available from the British Library

Library of Congress Cataloging-in-Publication Data
A catalog record for this book is available from the Library of Congress

Typeset in Minion Pro by MJ&N Gavan, Truro, Cornwall
Printed and bound by CPI Group (UK) Ltd, Croydon CR0 4YY

Dedicated to the memory of George Shriver (1936–2020)
Translator, friend, and revolutionary

Contents

Acknowledgments ix
Editorial Foreword xi
Introduction: Rosa Luxemburg's Concept of Revolution
    by Peter Hudis and Sandra Rein xv
Abbreviations xxxv

1902
Social Reform and Social Revolution 3
On the Day after the Social Revolution 7

1906
The Russian Revolution 13
Armed Revolt in Moscow 17
What Do We Want? A Commentary on the Program of the Social
    Democracy of the Kingdom of Poland and Lithuania 23
Critique in the Workers' Movement 65
The Historical Services of the Polish Bourgeoisie and Mr. Świętochowski 69
The Year of the Revolution 75
"Through Fiery Smoke, in a Haze of Brothers' Blood ..." 83
The Program of "National" Trickery 87
Boycotting the Tsar's Duma 91
Under the Workings of Revolution 95
The Tactics of Revolution 99
In a Revolutionary Hour, What Next? [April 1905] 105
In a Revolutionary Hour, What Next? [May 1905] 115
In a Revolutionary Hour, What Next? [March–April 1906] 131
Traitors of Poland 151
The June Days of 1848: A Page from the History of the Workers'
    Struggle for Bread and Freedom 155
Blanquism and Social Democracy 169
Why Does the Revolution Not Break Out? 175
Organization and Disorganization 179
The Nationalists Declare Revolutionaries Outlaws 183
The Practice of Revolution 189
The Mass Strike, the Political Party, and the Trade Unions 193
Party Congress of the Social Democratic Party of Germany in
    Mannheim [September 23–29, 1906] 263
The Russian Revolution [September 25, 1906] 269

General Strike and German Social Democracy 273
The Mass Strike in Court 281

1907
The Lockout of Textile Workers in Łódź 289
The May Day Celebrations 293
For May 1, 1907 297
Speeches at the 1907 Congress of the Russian Social Democratic
    Labor Party 299

1908
Liquidation (Part I) 325
Liquidation (Part II) 347
The Epic of Łódź 369
Lessons from the Three Dumas 375
The Cancan of the Counterrevolution 395
The Black Card of the Revolution 411
Speech about May Day as a Day of Working-Class Struggle 417

1909
May 1 and the Class Struggle 423
Revolutionary Hangover 427
The May Day Celebrations before the Decision 439
The Funeral of the May Day Celebrations 443
Excerpts and Notes from Books and Studies on the English Revolution 449

A Glossary of Personal Names 479
Index 521

Acknowledgments

This volume would not have been possible without the tireless efforts of numerous scholars who have done monumental work over the past several decades to bring Rosa Luxemburg's manuscripts, unsigned essays and articles, and other previously unknown or inaccessible writings to light. We are especially indebted to Annelies Laschitza (1934–2018), who devoted decades of her life to unearthing, collecting, and analyzing the full expanse of Luxemburg's writings, as well as the Japanese Luxemburg scholar Narihiko Ito (1931–2017) and the Polish historian Feliks Tych (1929–2015). Our work is indebted to them.

This volume in particular would also not have been possible without the advice and support of Evelin Wittich and Jörn Schütrumpf of the Rosa Luxemburg Foundation, who have assisted us at each step of this project of issuing the *Complete Works*—from helping to select the materials in this volume to finding the original documents, as well as providing invaluable encouragement and assistance in all phases of our work. We wish to especially thank Luxemburg scholar and historian Ottokar Luban for his guidance and encouragement throughout the project, as well as Holger Politt for his translations into German of many of Luxemburg's writings originally composed in Polish.

We wish to especially thank Sebastian Budgen and Jacob Stevens of Verso Books for remaining true to the project of issuing these volumes of the *Complete Works*, despite unexpected delays and difficulties along the way.

A special thanks to our translators—Jacob Blumenfeld, Nicholas Gray, Henry Holland, Zachary King, Manuela Kölke, and Joseph Muller—who overcame many obstacles in performing a labor of love to bring alive Luxemburg's voice.

Particular thanks go to Rory Castle for his assistance in the early stages of working on this volume, as well as Dana Mills, who assisted in the editing of Luxemburg's "Notes on the English Revolution." Loren Balhorn of the Rosa Luxemburg Foundation has also provided valuable advice and assistance.

A special shout-out to the editorial board of *The Complete Works of Rosa Luxemburg*, who helped make this volume possible by carefully reviewing the manuscript, offering invaluable suggestions, and keeping us focused: Paul Le Blanc, Andrew Bonnell, Ankica Čakardić, Julia Damphouse, Jason Dawsey, Sebastian Engelmann, Henry Holland, Manuela Kölke, Ewa Majewska, Dana Mills, Helen Scott, David Norman Smith, Lori Turner, Rida Vaquas, and Joshua Wavrant.

Most of all, we wish to thank the Rosa Luxemburg Foundation in Berlin, which covered the cost of many of the translations, as well as the individuals who made this volume possible through their contributions to the Toledo Fund, which also helped cover translation costs.

Sadly, our colleague and friend George Shriver—who translated much of the material found in the first three volumes of this series as well as the entirety of *The Letters of Rosa Luxemburg* (London and New York: Verso, 2011)—died in April 2020. He passed only weeks before a new generation of activists took to the streets in the United States and around the world demanding social and racial justice—causes to which George devoted his life. His work as translator and colleague will be sorely missed, but we will not forget his many contributions. We devote this volume to his memory.

Editorial Foreword

Rosa Luxemburg is widely considered one of the most outstanding theorists of socialism, and her influence has extended far and wide since she joined the Marxist movement at the end of the nineteenth century. While her writings have inspired generations of revolutionaries, a great deal of her work has remained unavailable in English. When we began this project of issuing her *Complete Works* a decade ago, we estimated that close to 80 percent of her writings (essays, articles, speeches, manuscripts, and letters) had never appeared in English. Since then, several thousand more pages of material by her have been discovered or identified in German, and thousands more remain to be translated from Polish—her native language. Our aim is to make all of these writings available in at least seventeen volumes, newly translated and carefully annotated.

Rosa Luxemburg was born in Zamość, Poland, in 1871 and moved to Warsaw with her family in 1873. She faced a childhood illness that left her with a permanent disability; however, this did not prevent her from attending an all-girls school in Warsaw (which was rarely accessed by Polish Jewish children) or from becoming politically active, even at a young age. As a result of her political activities, she was forced to leave Poland for Switzerland in 1889. Exile in Switzerland allowed her the opportunity to study at the University of Zurich. Her doctoral dissertation, *The Industrial Development of Poland*, was presented in 1897, and her doctoral degree of law was conferred in that year. Luxemburg was one of very few women to hold a PhD from a major university at the time. While in Switzerland, she continued her political work, often in conjunction with Leo Jogiches, in co-founding the Social Democracy of the Kingdom of Poland (SDKP) and later the Social Democracy of the Kingdom of Poland and Lithuania (SDKPiL). She moved to Berlin in 1898 and lived there until her death in 1919.

The Social Democratic Party of Germany (SPD) was the leading socialist party in Europe, and Luxemburg became a leading figure in it. Her reputation was built on her critiques of reformism and the failing leadership of the SPD, as well as her organizational abilities among the proletariat. When revolution broke out in Russia in 1905–06, she returned to Poland to support the efforts of the SDKPiL and to report on the progress of the revolution to the SPD and the international movement more broadly. Her analyses, made in the moment of revolution, are the focus of this volume. In March 1906 she was apprehended by Polish authorities in Warsaw and imprisoned, and was not released until July. As part of analyzing the lessons from the Russian experience, she wrote *The Mass Strike, the Political Party, and the Trade Unions*.

Following her return to Germany in 1906, Luxemburg continued to represent the positions of the SDKPiL while active in the SPD. In these years, she taught at the SPD's party school, faced periods of further incarceration, and completed one of her most significant theoretical works, *The Accumulation of Capital*. As Luxemburg found herself in increasing conflict with the SPD leadership—over theoretical positions but also, most significantly, over her opposition to militarism and imperialism—she (along with Karl Liebknecht, Clara Zetkin, and Franz Mehring) founded the Spartacus Group in 1916. As a result of her antiwar activities, she was again imprisoned in 1915 for three and a half years. After her release in 1918, she participated in the German Revolution and helped co-found the Communist Party of Germany (KPD). In early January 1919, with the acquiescence of the SPD, Luxemburg and Liebknecht were apprehended by the Freikorps and then summarily executed. Luxemburg's body, dumped in the Landwehr Canal, was not recovered until four months later.

While many efforts were made after her death to preserve and collect her multitudinous writings, it is only now that an effort is underway to make all of her writings available in English.

The Complete Works of Rosa Luxemburg is organized into three categories: (1) Economic Writings (Volumes 1 and 2, published in 2013 and 2015), (2) Political Writings (Volumes 3 to 12), and (3) Complete Correspondence (Volumes 13 to 17). The political writings are divided into various themes: "On Revolution," "Debates on Revolutionary Strategy and Organization," "The National Question," "Colonial Policy and Imperialism," and "On Literature."

This is the second of three volumes on the revolutions she observed and participated in during her lifetime: Russia 1905–1906, Russia 1917, and Germany 1918–19. The first volume of "On Revolution" (Volume 3 of the *Complete Works*, published in 2019) contains her writings on the subject to the end of 1905. This fourth volume of the *Complete Works* contains her writings "On Revolution" from 1906 to 1909. The forthcoming Volume 5 will contain her writings on the Russian Revolution of 1917 and the German Revolution of 1918–19.

In separating her political writings into specific themes, we do not imply that Luxemburg's concern for revolution is restricted to the three volumes devoted to this subject. All of her work—from her economic theory to political writings on spontaneity, organization, nationalism, imperialism, and democracy—has the concept of revolution at its core. The materials in this volume *directly* address *actual* revolutions: the period leading up to them, the revolutions themselves, and the period immediately following them. Of central importance are her writings on the 1905 Russian Revolution, one of the most outstanding revolutionary upheavals of modern times, in which she directly participated and on which she drew repeatedly in developing her distinctive contributions to revolutionary theory. This volume also contains her recently discovered "Notes on the English Revolution" of the 1640s.

With a handful of exceptions (such as "The Mass Strike, the Political Party, and the Trade Unions" and "Speeches at the 1907 Congress of the Russian Social

Democratic Labor Party"), almost all of the writings in this volume appear in English for the first time.

The German-language pamphlets, essays, articles, and speeches in this volume are translated from Volumes 2, 6, 7.1, and 7.2 of her *Gesammelte Werke*; the Polish- and Russian-language documents are translated from the original newspapers, journals, and transcripts of meetings in which they first appeared.

All footnotes in the text, unless otherwise indicated, are by the editors and/or translators. We have greatly benefited from consulting the editorial apparatus and footnotes provided by the editors of the *Gesammelte Werke*, as well as Holger Pollitt's footnotes and introduction to the German-language collection of some of Luxemburg's Polish writings, in *Arbeiterrevolution 1905/06: Polnische Texte* (Berlin: Dietz Verlag, 2015). The editors have also produced the name glossary. In all areas of our work, we are indebted to the many outstanding scholars on Luxemburg—from Germany, Poland, and Japan in particular—without which our work would not be possible.

Introduction: Rosa Luxemburg's Concept of Revolution

Rosa Luxemburg continues to capture the imagination of activists and scholars worldwide; in fact, today interest in her life and works is enjoying a veritable renaissance. This is no small feat for an individual whose intellectual and activist life reached its height in the early twentieth century. It is no small feat for a woman of her generation. And it is no small feat for a disabled Polish Jewish émigré (or exile, depending on your perspective) in Germany. But, on balance, Rosa Luxemburg was not a socialist who thought small or acted small. Although she faced many forms of exclusion in her time, it was impossible for socialists to ignore her clear-minded analysis and single-minded commitment to social change.

So why does it become especially difficult to ignore her today, even though she lived in a period so different from ours and the issues she discussed are so rooted in the particularity of her era? It is because of the rise of a whole series of spontaneous grassroots movements for freedom around the world since the global economic recession of 2008, which reached its sharpest and most creative expression in 2020 with the response to the glaring inequities exposed by the COVID-19 pandemic and mass protests against police abuse and for racial justice. These protests and movements—which that spring and summer occurred in over 2,400 US towns and cities and in dozens of countries around the world—were the product of a new generation of activists seeking a *liberatory* alternative to existing society. As the ongoing growth of interest in socialist ideas continues—and all signs indicate it will, in light of the depth of today's economic, political, and ecological crisis—it is only to be expected that many will be drawn anew to exploring the contributions of one of the most independent figures in the Marxist tradition.

This is not to suggest that there is a direct connection between the subject of this volume—the 1905 Russian Revolution—and today's movements against racism, sexism, class inequality, and environmental degradation. Far from it! However, those who have experienced the travail as well as exhilaration of the massive protests that erupted in the United States and around the world over the police murder of George Floyd may find Luxemburg's response to the revolution more relevant than they expect. The 1905 Revolution was completely unanticipated, occurring in one of the most hierarchical and repressive countries on earth; and yet, seemingly out of nowhere, the most downtrodden, neglected, and marginalized sections of the populace poured into the streets demanding democracy, better living conditions, and an end to militarism in a series of actions lasting well over a year. Luxemburg caught the spirit of this new development from its moment of inception and argued that it heralded a new revolutionary era—that it demanded a *reorganization of thought* on the part of anyone who believed that either piecemeal reforms or putschist actions taken behind the backs of the masses were no longer adequate. A new kind of revolt, she argued, was now before us, whose lessons needed to be *internalized*—not just by those in Russia,* but throughout the world. What was thought impossible now began to become possible.

Over the past several decades, many held that the development of an alternative to both capitalism and the failed efforts to surmount it by "socialist" revolutions of the past one hundred years was likewise impossible. Or if not impossible, it was at least implausible that any movement in that direction would occur within the United States, dominated as it was in 2020 by the most egregious form of political retrogression in its history. It may be too early to tell whether the movement for Black lives and for social justice shows that a new anti-capitalist movement is being born in the US and elsewhere; but the events of that spring and summer, and their ongoing reverberations, indicate that at least the possibility of a movement in that direction has arisen. And in a land of new possibilities, the expansive vision provided by the writings of Rosa Luxemburg provides vital direction.

THE SCOPE OF THIS VOLUME

This fourth volume of *The Complete Works of Rosa Luxemburg* takes up her writings on the Russian Revolution, beginning the year after its outbreak and ending c. 1909. It includes a variety of pamphlets, essays, newspaper articles, speeches at party congresses, and court transcripts. The "red thread" that ties all of these together is Luxemburg's deep commitment to revolutionary transformation from below and the need for Social Democratic† parties to help provide enlightenment and social consciousness to the oppressed. This was combined with an understanding that failures in the struggle for revolution must also be

---

* Throughout this introduction we refer to "Russia" as a synonym for the Russian Empire—almost half of which was comprised of *non*-Russians, such as Poles, Georgians, Finns, Armenians, Ukrainians, etc. A large percentage of the participants in the revolutionary movement of the time were members of these ethnic minorities. Since Luxemburg opposed calls for national self-determination by such groupings, when she refers to "Russia" she includes these non-Russian lands as well. Our usage here conforms to the nomenclature commonly used by her and others in the period but should not be read as ignoring the distinct ethnic differences within the tsarist empire or endorsing her specific position on the national question.

† "Social Democracy" was the term used to describe orthodox Marxism in the socialist movement prior to the outbreak of World War I in 1914. Although the Social Democratic movement contained reformist as well as revolutionary tendencies, Luxemburg often equates it to revolutionary Marxism in her writings of this period. From 1914 onward, when most socialist parties supported their respective governments during World War I, she emphasized the *crisis* of Social Democracy and helped co-found, in December 1918, the Communist Party of Germany (KPD).

acknowledged, and that they mark an important moment for the proletariat in setting the stage for future movements that rethink and rearticulate their demands.

But who exactly was Luxemburg addressing? Was she addressing the same or multiple audiences? The writings in this volume are more or less equally divided between those composed in German and Polish, with several others written for a Russian audience. Although all of her work is addressed in one way or another to revolutionary socialists, her writings in these respective languages often have a different register and purpose from one another.

Most of her writings in this volume that were composed in German consist of an effort to convince the German Social Democratic Party (SPD)—the largest socialist party that had ever existed up to that time—to learn from the Russian Revolution by adopting the strategy of the mass strike. This is famously expressed in her pamphlet *The Mass Strike, the Political Party, and the Trade Unions* (newly translated for this volume by Nicholas Gray), but it is also the theme of many other writings in this volume, such as speeches at party congresses, articles, writings on May Day, and so on.

An attentive reader will note that Luxemburg attaches many different adjectives to the word "strike"—in fact, there are more than fifteen types of strikes that can be identified in these writings. And it is important to recognize that the attachment of different adjectives is intended by Luxemburg to highlight the different modes of organization and differing political demands embedded in the various kinds of strikes. However, as she puts it, the key to understanding the significance of the *mass strike* lies in understanding the role it plays—that is, its particular form:

> Political and economic strikes, mass strikes and partial strikes, strikes as a form of demonstration and militant strikes, general strikes in individual branches and general strikes in individual cities, peaceful wage struggles and street battles and struggles on the barricades—all these phenomena crisscross each other, run parallel to each other, intersect with each other, flow into each other; this is a perpetually moving, fluctuating sea of manifestations. And the law of motion of these phenomena becomes evident; it lies neither in the mass strike itself, nor in the latter's technical peculiarities, but rather in the political and social relation of forces within the revolution.*

The mass strikes of the Russian Revolution, she held, constitute a *new form* that compels Social Democracy and the labor unions to rethink their relationship both to the masses and to each other. As against the prevailing notion in Germany that the Russian workers were "backward" because they lacked trade

---

* See "The Mass Strike, the Political Party, and the Trade Unions," p. 221, below.

unions or legal political parties, she argued that the mass strike showed they were actually in advance of the "organized" German socialists. She sought to shake up the German party (and the Second International as a whole) from its staid reliance on legal forms of political action and parliamentarism by utilizing the militant tactics employed in Russia.

Success for Luxemburg is not defined merely by the achievements of any particular strike action or the total reconstitution of society. Success may be measured in the raising of consciousness among the working classes, the clarity of purpose that arises in collective action, and some of the so-called small victories—such as reduced working hours, improved conditions of work, and reduction in tax burden for working people. The "end" of violent uprisings or strikes marks neither the "end" of the revolution nor its failure. These peaceful periods are important moments for the consolidation of consciousness and for the party and other worker organizations to understand the historical importance of what has transpired.

But in her Polish writings, Luxemburg addresses a different audience facing a different set of issues. In the German party, she had become recognized by 1906 as one of its leading theoreticians, thanks to her role in exposing and condemning (from 1898) the "revisionist" reformism of Eduard Bernstein and his followers. However, she held no official leadership role in the party and encountered entrenched resistance from many of her male co-leaders—including those who claimed to oppose Bernstein but who were in fact much closer to his political position than hers.* She composed her Polish writings, on the other hand, while serving as the foremost leader of a political party—the Social Democracy of the Kingdom of Poland (SDKP, from 1893 to 1900) and later the Social Democracy of the Kingdom of Poland and Lithuania (SDKPiL, from 1900 onward). Whereas she often had to fight to get her voice heard within the German party, her voice in the Polish party was largely uncontested.† In the latter, she fought relentlessly to achieve organizational hegemony at the expense of other revolutionary groupings, such as the Polish Socialist Party (PPS) and its various factions. While she fought for *inclusion* in the German party, when it came to her work in the Polish movement, she fought to *exclude* parties other than her own from Social Democracy.

This was the case as early as 1893 (shortly after the founding of the PPS), when she urged the Zurich Congress of the Second International not to

---

* Many SPD leaders opposed Bernstein not because they objected to his reformism but because they feared that his arguments undermined the rationale for the SPD's existence as an independent organization. This concern with maintaining the organizational strength of the party, however, placed them in opposition to Luxemburg's call to endorse the mass strike, since in their view it risked having the party lose support among the broader electorate.

† This was not the case during the early years of the SDKPiL, from 1900 to 1902, when Cezaryna Wojnarowska played a leading role in the organization. Luxemburg was sidelined over a political dispute until 1903, when she and Leo Jogiches assumed complete control of the party.

recognize the PPS as its Polish affiliate—a group that was at the time much larger than her small circle of supporters, which consisted of barely a few dozen individuals. She argued that the PPS support for Polish independence—a position consistent with Marx and Engels' steadfast support for Polish self-determination—constituted "social-patriotism" and "nationalism" that had no place within Social Democracy. Years later, in 1906, when the PPS moved to the left under the impact of the Russian Revolution, expelled the putschist-nationalist tendency around Józef Piłsudski, and even agreed to put on hold the demand for Polish independence in order to work more closely with the SDKPiL, Luxemburg continued to refuse to have anything to do with them. The leading role of *her* party, in contrast to the PPS-Left and others in Poland, was emphasized throughout. It was only in 1918, when she was no longer actively involved in Polish affairs, that the SDKPiL permitted a merger with the PPS-Left.

As she put it, invoking the leader of one of the French socialist parties who was at the time widely criticized for his sectarian refusal to work with other socialist groupings,*

> How many accusations have fallen on the head of the "intransigent" Guesdists in France for rejecting the association with all the other socialist groups for decades! History proved them right by showing that the strength of the socialist party does not lie in a plurality of members cobbled together, nor in rich coffers or an abundance of party waste paper, but in the stability and clarity of its views, in the compatibility and spiritual uniformity of the ranks, in the consequences of word and deed.†

The image of Luxemburg as an inclusive figure who opposed centralism and hierarchical forms of organization, while not without merit, paints a stereotypical picture that is often inconsistent with her work in the Polish movement. The inclusion in this volume of her widely ignored writings in Polish between 1906 and 1909, none of which have previously appeared in English, provides a needed corrective to one-sided and superficial representations of her political contribution that characterize much of the English-language secondary literature on her.

Moreover, whereas her polemics with the SPD were aimed at pushing it toward the left and away from an exclusive reliance on parliamentarism, that was not the case with her work within the Polish movement—since Congress Poland at the time was a part of the Russian Empire that lacked parliamentary traditions and was under the absolutist rule of the tsar. There, she took issue

---

* The sectarianism of Jules Guesde was especially reflected in his refusal to have his party become involved in the defense of Dreyfus, on the grounds that the anti-Semitic campaign against him had "nothing to do with the working class." Luxemburg, to her credit, differed with Guesde on this, and supported the efforts of socialist leader Jean Jaurès, who played an instrumental role in Dreyfus' defense.

† See "Liquidation (Part I)" (1908), p. 344, below.

with revolutionaries who resorted to such extra-parliamentary measures as the assassination of government officials and terrorism. Her polemics on this issue constitute a large number of her writings originally composed in Polish. For instance, in 1906 she argued:

> The working population is not a regiment of soldiers who can be ordered to show up in order at a certain time at a barracks to receive their weapons. In view of this, the *best* we may accomplish in reality is to arm our own active agitators and the very small circle of workers who are closest to the party. And these arms are only to be taken as a *means of defense* for elements and isolated worker groups under attack by tsarist hooligans.*

As she put it a bit later, "And concerning that aim, I do not negate the role of violence. I simply stick, along with my party, to the standpoint that the initiative for the application of violence always proceeds from the ruling classes."†

Luxemburg's third audience was the Russian Social Democratic movement, in which she played an integral part both before and after the 1905 Revolution. In 1903, the SDKPiL entered into unity negotiations with Vladimir Lenin and Georgi Plekhanov's Russian Social Democratic Labor Party (RSDRP); Luxemburg broke off the discussion after a bitter dispute with Lenin—*not* over the question of organization (the issue that famously caused the split between Mensheviks and Bolsheviks at the congress), but over her rejection of the RSDRP program that supported the right to national self-determination by the oppressed nationalities of the tsarist empire.‡ The events of 1905 and 1906 brought them back together, as Luxemburg (for reasons that will be discussed shortly) sharply criticized the Mensheviks and worked closely (though not uncritically) with the Bolsheviks. She composed the *Mass Strike* pamphlet while in Finland in the summer of 1906 (after being imprisoned for several months because of her activity in the revolution), where she engaged in intense discussions with Lenin and other Bolsheviks. In 1907 she was a delegate at the London Congress of the RSDRP; her speeches at the conference represent some of her most important comments on the revolution as a whole.

To grasp Luxemburg's political and theoretical contributions, one must be attentive to the different audiences she addresses in the texts assembled in this volume. Doing so also places us in a position to evaluate a controversial claim made by her most eminent biographer, J. P. Nettl (whose 1966 book has recently

---

* See "In a Revolutionary Hour, What Next? [April 1905]," p. 109, below.
† See "The Mass Strike in Court," p. 284, below.
‡ For a fuller discussion of these events, and how they show that her differences with Lenin on organization, while significant, were not the *pivotal* issue in her many disputes with him, see Peter Hudis, "Luxemburg and Lenin," in *The Palgrave Handbook of Leninist Political Philosophy*, edited by Tom Rockmore and Norman Levine (London: Palgrave Macmillan, 2018), pp. 201–30.

been reprinted by Verso with a new introduction by Peter Hudis).* According to Nettl, "The full impact of the Russian revolution on Rosa Luxemburg's ideas and actions was not to become apparent for some time. Her immediate contribution to the events of the moment was important enough." However, he adds:

> unlike Lenin, she made no original contributions to the tactics or methods of revolution. Lenin swept the experience of 1905–1906 into a strongly stressed and pointed profile of future revolution in which an important place was assigned to the revolutionary peasantry. At the same time, he reiterated his organizational doctrine more firmly than ever. Trotsky produced his theory of interacting or permanent revolution. Both in their different ways looked for specific tactical or theoretical lessons, and their efforts—then still mutually hostile and incompatible—were to help make possible the October revolution of 1917. Luxemburg, however much she may have systemized both her party's programme and tactics, did not produce anything that could be adopted for use.†

Now that the full expanse of Luxemburg's writings on the revolutionary upheavals of 1905 and 1906 and her reflections on the triumph of the counterrevolution between 1907 and 1909 are finally available in English, it becomes possible to determine whether this evaluation is accurate or needs to be reconsidered. This is needed not merely for historical purposes or to set the record straight. At issue is whether Luxemburg's response to the revolution she was most directly and actively involved in, as commentator, participant, and theorist, provides an alternative to the standard Social Democratic as well as Leninist models of socialism that have dominated left-wing discourse for the past one hundred years.

LUXEMBURG'S CONCEPTION OF REVOLUTIONARY TRANSFORMATION

Luxemburg is widely renowned for her enthusiastic embrace of spontaneous mass struggles, and there is no more striking example than her response to the 1905 Russian Revolution. It is generally considered to have started with the St. Petersburg massacre of hundreds of workers calling for social reforms on January 22, 1905. As Luxemburg made clear at the time, the rising opposition to Russian authoritarian rule had a longer history, and even the new form of struggle—the mass strike—had beleaguered the Russian Empire for years before 1905. In the lead-up to the revolution, the tsar was increasingly confronted by demands from various sectors of the empire: Peasants were facing extreme deprivation post-emancipation; the nobility was heavily indebted; the military

---

* See Peter Hudis, "Introduction: Luxemburg in Our Time," in J. P. Nettl, *Rosa Luxemburg* (London and New York: Verso, 2019), pp. ix–xxiii.
† Nettl, *Rosa Luxemburg*, p. 361.

suffered defeat in the Russo-Japanese War; and the subjugated peoples of the empire, such as Poland, were increasingly making nationalist (or at least semi-autonomous) demands. These sectors of discontent were further buttressed by the emergence of an organized industrial working class in the major cities.

No one, however, anticipated the depth and breadth of the series of uprisings that swept the empire in the days, weeks, and months following "Bloody Sunday." In her writings for the German and Polish socialist press, Luxemburg has a keen eye for how the Russian masses created new forms of democratically organized grassroots committees, councils, unions, and parties to advance the revolution. The *spontaneous* actions of the working class, she held, showed that it was instinctively democratic as well as socialist in orientation.

This did not mean that she played down the role of organization. On the contrary, she held that the humus from which the revolution emerged was in part prepared by decades of careful, patient work by activists working to spread the principles of Social Democracy. Spontaneous acts are always preceded by some kind of *organization of thought*. She writes in the *Mass Strike* pamphlet:

> Social Democracy is the most enlightened, most class-conscious vanguard of the proletariat. It cannot, and must not, await in fatalist fashion, with folded arms, the onset of the "revolutionary situation"—it cannot wait for such a spontaneous popular movement to fall from the sky. On the contrary, it must, as always, anticipate the development of events and seek to *accelerate* them. It cannot do this, however, through suddenly and indiscriminately issuing a "call" for a mass strike at what might be the right or the wrong point in time, but rather, and above all, by making clear to the broadest proletarian strata the inexorable *onset* of this revolutionary period and by clarifying the internal *social moments* that lead to it and its *political consequences*.*

Just as Social Democracy cannot wait passively for the revolution, neither can it presume to lead the masses in the way a schoolmaster directs their pupils. She sharply criticizes parties that are "always to be ready to give 'marching orders' to the working class," writing:

> Social Democracy [...] is merely the advance guard of the proletariat, one part of the vast working mass, blood of its blood and bone of its bone. Social Democracy searches out and identifies the paths and slogans of a particular workers' struggle only as that struggle develops, interpreting signs for the road ahead from the struggle itself.†

She adds, "It should be borne in mind that while Social Democracy, with all its resolutions, is certainly an important factor in history, it is merely *one* factor

---

* See "The Mass Strike, the Political Parties, and the Trade Unions," p. 240, below.
† See "Critique in the Workers' Movement," p. 115, below.

among many."* Luxemburg was not one to make an absolute out of organization; as she later wrote, criticizing Karl Kautsky (who belatedly broke from the SPD and formed the centrist Independent Social Democratic Party of Germany [USPD] during World War I), "The *Swamp* continues the ideology of the official party: fetishism of organization as an end in itself."†

The main role of organization, she held, is to grasp, nurture, and develop the *class consciousness* that emerges from spontaneous struggles. But exactly *how* is such consciousness to be developed? What methods, means, and approach are needed? Writing from Warsaw (where she had arrived just before New Year 1906), Luxemburg responds to these questions in an article in the Polish-language newspaper *Czerwony Sztandar* of January 1906, discussing the overall significance of the revolution in which she is a participant:

> During the fight, as victims fall all around, as the proletariat bears down on its enemy, it *learns*, it educates itself. A victorious outcome depends on the degree of that consciousness. How, then, do members of the proletariat become conscious? They read pamphlets, appeals, and periodicals. They listen to speeches by people who give advice on various things. They must *weigh for themselves* which of these things is right, for such consideration is the basis for choosing what path to take.‡

At first sight, this seems straightforward and uncontroversial: The proletariat learns by reading, listening to speeches, becoming educated "by people who give advice on various things"—no doubt the intellectuals. But she emphasizes that the proletariat "educates itself"; it is not simply educated *by* others, like intellectuals and party leaders. She also emphasizes that its members "weigh for themselves" what is right and not right in what is conveyed to them by writers and speechmakers. They *choose* "what path to take." *Choice* is the critical word here, since liberation is impossible without self-determination—which is denied to those victimized by capitalist class relations, male domination, and imperialism. But this raises a further question: What is to ensure that the masses will choose the right path? Perhaps they will end up taking a wrong one. Indeed, history is replete with innumerable examples of this. Luxemburg responds:

> The most important precondition for raising proletarian consciousness within the struggle itself is the exercise of the freedoms of assembly and of the press. That is to say, the proletariat fights for the freedom to gather, discuss its affairs, and, through publications printed freely, learn to know its friends and foes. If the first condition

---

* See "The Mass Strike, the Political Parties, and the Trade Unions," p. 201, below.

† See "Notes on the English Revolution," p. 450, below. Luxemburg often referred to Kautsky and his allies, after 1914, as "the Swamp," over their failure to take decisive positions in favor of the proletarian seizure of power.

‡ See "Critique in the Workers' Movement," p. 65, below.

of raising the proletariat's awareness is that workers wrest from the hands of the government the freedoms of assembly, speech, and the press, then *the second is to take full advantage of those freedoms, so that the ranks of fighting workers engage freely in critical discussions.**

In a word, in order for the working class to develop the level of class consciousness needed to make a socialist revolution, *thoroughgoing democracy* is essential. She was well aware that political democracy in the modern world is a product of bourgeois society—just as Enlightenment rationalism was a product of bourgeois intellectuals. But this does not mean that democracy or rationalism is "bourgeois." These fruits of modernity are bourgeois only insofar as they are monopolized by the bourgeoisie and denied to the masses. As she put it in a series of notes on slave societies, written as part of her work at the SPD's School in Berlin around 1907, "The exclusion of slaves from mental life of course led to the rulers creating laws that benefited their own interests ... In [contrast, in] socialist society, knowledge will be the common property of everyone."† For her, the *free exchange of ideas* is the necessary condition for the proletariat to educate itself to the point of destroying capitalism and creating socialism:

> The freedom to speak and publish is one precondition to the attainment of consciousness by the proletariat; the second is that the proletariat not put any restrictions on itself, that it not say, "We can discuss this, but not that." Conscious workers the world over understand this, and they always try to give even the worst of their enemies the right to freely explain their views. They say, "Let even the enemies of the working people voice their own views, so that we may respond to them, and so the working masses can work out for themselves who is a friend and who a foe."‡

This was not merely a political imperative for Luxemburg, but a personal one as well. As she repeatedly emphasizes in her correspondence, the transformation of consciousness is not only a task for the working class; it is needed for

---

* See "Critique in the Workers' Movement," p. 66, below.

† "Slavery," in *The Complete Works of Rosa Luxemburg, Vol. I: Economic Writings 1*, edited by Peter Hudis (London and New York: Verso, 2013), p. 312.

‡ See "Critique in the Workers' Movement," p. 66, below. This notion that even "the worst of their enemies" be given "the right to freely explain their views" later became central to her critique of the Bolsheviks in her 1918 book *On the Russian Revolution*, which chastised them for closing down opposition newspapers and parties. In 1906, however, when these words were penned, virtually all Social Democrats, *including the Bolsheviks*, supported these principles. Both the Erfurt Program of 1891 (the basis of German Social Democracy) and the 1903 program of the Russian Social Democratic Labor Party affirmed "unrestricted freedom of conscience, speech, press and assembly." Luxemburg later threw these words back at Lenin and Trotsky in insisting on "the unlimited participation of the mass of the people, of unlimited democracy" in her 1918 critique of them. See *The Rosa Luxemburg Reader*, edited by Peter Hudis and Kevin B. Anderson (New York: Monthly Review Books, 2006), p. 308. A new translation of *On the Russian Revolution* will appear in the forthcoming Volume 5 of the *Complete Works*.

all those trying to understand their place in the world. The political and personal do not inhabit separate categories when it comes to fostering *self-awareness*. As she put it in a lengthy essay written in Polish in 1906,

> Self-examination—that is, *making oneself aware* at every step of the direction, logic, and basis for the class movement itself—is that store from which the working mass draws its strength, again and again, to struggle anew, and by which it understands its own hesitation and defeats as so many proofs of its strength and inevitable future victory.*

Luxemburg was attentive to the *limits* as well as the accomplishments of the revolution. Although 1905–1906 marked the first time the working class had stepped forth as the leading force in a nationwide revolution, she argued that achieving a transition to a socialist society in Russia was at the time out of the question. The most that could be hoped for in the coming years was the overthrow of the tsar and the creation of the capitalist-bourgeois preconditions for the realization of socialism—that is, a *democratic republic*. She spelled out the reasons in detail:

> No revolution has yet ended in any other way than with one class holding power, and every detail suggests that now the proletariat may become the liquidator [of the old order]. Of course, no Social Democrat fools himself that the proletariat *will remain* in power; if it remained, that would lead to the rule of its class ideas, and it would realize socialism. *Today* there is not sufficient strength [for that], since the proletariat constitutes a *minority* of [Russian] society, in the strict sense of the word. Indeed, that a minority should realize socialism is out of the question, as the very idea of socialism does not allow minority rule [...]
>
> And since the fact remains that in our society the working class is not the majority —the petty-bourgeois and the peasants are—Social Democrats will not constitute a majority in the Constituent Assembly; only democrats from the peasantry and petty bourgeoisie [will]. We may regret this, but we cannot change it.†

Luxemburg is reiterating a principle that was central to Marx: namely, that "the proletarian movement is the self-conscious, independent movement of the immense majority, in the interests of the immense majority."‡ The notion that "socialism" could be introduced by a party or grouping resting on a minority of the populace was out of the question for him. Yet Russia in the early twentieth century was a developing society in which 85 percent of the populace were peasants. While Luxemburg viewed the peasantry as an important force in battling

---

* See "In a Revolutionary Hour, What Next? [March–April 1906]," p. 139, below.
† See "The Mass Strike, The Political Party, and the Trade Unions," p. 173, below.
‡ Karl Marx, *Manifesto of the Communist Party*, in *Marx-Engels Collected Works*, Vol. 6 (New York: International Publishers, 1976), p. 495.

tsarist oppression, its natural inclination, she held, was to seek private ownership of the land—a perspective at odds with the socialization of the means of production. Since she held that socialism cannot be forcibly imposed by a minority group or party, Russia had to endure an extended period of capitalist industrialization that would ultimately create a proletarian majority.

However, the distinctive feature of the 1905 Revolution, she argued, was that the working class, and not the bourgeois liberals, played the leading role. The task of creating the capitalist-bourgeois preconditions for socialism fell to the working class. Herein lay the dual character of the Russian Revolution: It was proletarian in form, but bourgeois-democratic in content.

The notion that a bourgeois-democratic revolution, and not a socialist one, was on the agenda was not unique to Luxemburg: Virtually every Marxist thought the same. What produced bitter disputes between them was the question of *which class is to lead the bourgeois-democratic revolution.* The Mensheviks held that the liberal bourgeoisie was the leading force; the Bolsheviks as well as Luxemburg held it was the working class, since the liberals showed themselves to be far too weak and compromising to uproot tsarism. It is therefore no accident that, in the period covered by this volume, Luxemburg worked closely with Lenin and the Bolsheviks.*

This is also why Luxemburg repeatedly reflects upon Marx's experience in the 1848 Revolutions.† In 1848 the working class emerged as an independent political force for the first time; however, since it was still relatively weak and fragmented, the most that could be hoped for was a democratic republic led by the liberal bourgeoisie. Marx thereby critically supported the latter "with whips and kicks," even as he formulated the principles of a socialist revolution that could later arise once the material conditions permitted. But the world had changed since 1848; the Russian proletariat, she held, was far stronger and more mature than the proletariat in the Western Europe of Marx's time. Therefore, the task that fell to the proletariat was to *displace* the bourgeoisie from leadership of the revolution. She stated, "The Russian proletariat fights first for bourgeois freedom, for universal suffrage, the republic, the law of associations, freedom of the press, etc., but it does not fight with the illusions that filled the proletariat of 1848. It fights for [such] liberties in order to instrumentalize them as a weapon against the bourgeoisie."‡

---

* This was not to last. By 1911 Luxemburg and Lenin were involved in bitter polemics, which continued largely unabated until her death. However, this did not prevent either from deeply respecting the other, or from maintaining personal contact.

† While Luxemburg discusses the experience of the 1848 Revolutions at great length in this volume, she makes only passing reference to the 1871 Paris Commune. This may seem odd, since 1871 was on a higher level than 1848, insofar as the communards succeeded in seizing power and moved (however briefly) toward a socialistic reorganization of society. Luxemburg may have considered the 1848 Revolutions more pertinent for the contemporary Russian experience, since they, like those of 1905–1906, occurred in lands where a socialist revolution was not yet on the agenda.

‡ See "The Russian Revolution [September 25, 1906]," p. 270, below.

It may appear that her insistence that Russia endure a prolonged period of capitalist development before reaching socialism was rooted in a rigid, unilinear view of history—first feudalism, then capitalism, and ultimately socialism. But this is not the case. In fact, she criticized the Mensheviks for such determinism. For them, it was an "iron law" of history that the working class could not seize power until capitalism had exhausted its historical potential. If she adhered to a crude unilinear determinism, she would have agreed with the Mensheviks that the proletariat cannot play the leading role in the revolution. But she didn't do so, because she was attentive to the subjective aspirations and capacities of the workers who were pushing the revolution forward. It showed that they, not the liberals, were in the position to seize power and form a democratic republic. However, the workers' subjective agency could not make up for the fact that they were a minority of the populace. It was Luxemburg's attentiveness to the concrete subjective and objective conditions, not any quasi-metaphysical theory of history, that led her to argue that the form of the revolution is proletarian, while its content is bourgeois-democratic.

Revolutionary turning points have a fascinating way of creating new divisions, as well as new kinds of alliances—on both a political and personal level. One expression is the way the revolution altered Luxemburg's evaluation of some of the leading figures in Russian Marxism. Shortly before the revolution, in 1904, she issued a searing critique of Lenin's organizational concepts, accusing him of elevating "the party" above the masses in an elitist, voluntarist manner, which "seems to us to be a mechanical transposition of the organizational principles of the Blanquist* movement of conspiratorial circles to the Social Democratic movement of the working masses."† In 1906, in contrast, she rejected the Mensheviks' attack on Lenin for adhering to a Blanquist concept of organization:

> We do not agree that comrades from so-called Bolshevism in Russia have now, in a time of revolution, fallen into the Blanquist errors that Comrade Plekhanov ascribes to them. There were perhaps traces of this in the organizational plan put forward in 1902 by Comrade Lenin, but that belongs in the past, the distant past, since we live today quickly, at a dizzying pace. These errors were corrected by life itself, and it does not do to fear that they may be repeated [...] If "Bolshevik" comrades speak today of the dictatorship of the proletariat, they have never given it a Blanquist meaning. They have never fallen into the error of the People's Will, which dreams

---

* Named after the great French revolutionary Auguste Blanqui, this referred to a conspiratorial concept of revolution based on the notion that the mass of workers are not the conscious agents of their own liberation but are rather called into action by enlightened revolutionary leaders.

† See "Organizational Questions of Russian Social Democracy," in Hudis and Anderson, *Rosa Luxemburg Reader*, pp. 248–65. This will appear in a new translation in the forthcoming Volume 6 of the *Complete Works*.

about "seizing power." But they claimed that the current revolution may end in the proletariat's control of the *entire* state machine.*

This does not mean they saw eye to eye on all aspects of the revolution. Whereas Lenin argued for a "democratic dictatorship of the proletariat and the peasantry," Luxemburg held that

> the peasant movement in Russia, a convergence of various factors, interests, and strata, has no essential unity with the defined, fixed class politics of the proletariat, whose overarching goals range far beyond the most revolutionary of the passing gusts of the peasant movement [...] an alliance of the proletariat and the peasantry cannot be the basis for the work of actually achieving political revolution, for determining its objectives, or for realizing them, any more than any other conscious alliance can.†

She, like Leon Trotsky, held that the peasants were, at best, an unreliable political ally. But this did not mean that she agreed with Trotsky's theory of "permanent revolution"—namely, that the revolution could go beyond the bourgeois-democratic stage and effect a transition to socialism if the Western European proletariat came to its aid. Although she admired his work in heading the St. Petersburg Soviet in 1905, she did not take his theory of permanent revolution seriously and almost never mentions it.‡ She too, of course, held that a transition to socialism could not succeed in Russia without revolutions in the advanced capitalist lands. But, unlike Trotsky, she did not think that such subjective factors could by themselves overcome the *objective* barrier to transgressing the bourgeois-democratic phase—the fact that a minority of the populace, *even when led by a highly centralized and disciplined vanguard party*, cannot possibly push through or actualize the transition to socialism.§

---

* See "Blanquism and Social Democracy," p. 172–3, below.
† See "Lessons from the Three Dumas," p. 394, below.
‡ This is not because she wasn't thoroughly familiar with the theory. Luxemburg was a close friend and colleague of Alexander Parvus, with whom Trotsky worked very closely in developing the theory of permanent revolution in 1905; indeed, Parvus can be considered its progenitor. Yet Luxemburg never showed interest in the theory and, prior to 1918, rarely mentions Trotsky at all. After her death, in 1922, Trotsky claimed that "on the question of the so-called Permanent Revolution, Rosa took the same stand as I did" at the 1907 Congress of the RSDRP. But his theory of permanent revolution was nowhere on the agenda, and Trotsky himself did not speak on it. Nor did Luxemburg. She and Trotsky agreed that the proletariat is the leading force of the revolution, but so did Lenin—who was sharply critical of Trotsky's theory of permanent revolution. The issue on which she and Trotsky took the "same stand" at the 1907 Conference was their criticism of the Bolsheviks' overreliance on armed struggle.
§ Since Russia in 1917 was still overwhelmingly a peasant society, it logically follows from Luxemburg's reasoning that it, too, was not yet in the position to make a transition to socialism. Her skepticism, voiced in 1918, concerning the ability of Lenin and his colleagues to move the revolution in a socialist direction must have been due not only to such factors as foreign invasion,

Luxemburg upheld the need for majority support from the exploited masses in achieving *any* transition to socialism in *all* of her writings, including those pertaining to the freedom struggles in the technologically developed capitalist lands. As she put it in December 1918, in the midst of the German Revolution, "The Spartacus League will never take over governmental power except in response to the clear, unambiguous will of the great majority of the proletarian mass of all of Germany, never except by the proletariat's conscious affirmation of the views, aims, and methods of struggle of the Spartacus League."*

Nevertheless, an important question can be raised against Luxemburg's theorization of the development of the Russian Revolution: How can the working class sustain itself in power in a democratic republic after overthrowing tsarism if it represents only a minority of the populace? Given the latter, is it even possible to establish the preconditions for the realization of socialism through a democratic republic under the leadership of the proletariat?†

Luxemburg directly addresses this issue in a far-reaching analysis written in Polish in 1908, "Lessons from the Three Dumas." This remarkable essay, which can be considered one of her most important theoretical analyses of the problems facing revolutions, appears in English in this volume for the first time. It surveys the failure of the efforts to create a parliamentary counterweight to tsarism after 1905 and explores the lessons to be learned for the future, now that the counterrevolution has prevailed. She mercilessly criticizes the Mensheviks, both for holding to their mechanical conception that the liberal bourgeoisie must take the leading role in the struggle for democracy, and for failing to

---

civil war, and economic breakdown, but also to her understanding of the objective barriers facing any transition to socialism in a context in which the proletariat is a minority. As she wrote to Julian Marchlewski on September 30, 1918, "It is clear that, under such conditions, i.e., being caught in the pincers of the imperialist powers on all sides, neither socialism nor the dictatorship of the proletariat can become a reality, but at the most a caricature of both. I'm afraid that this situation is clear only for you, for me, and a few others." *The Letters of Rosa Luxemburg*, edited by Georg Adler, Peter Hudis, and Annelies Laschitza (London and New York: Verso, 2011), p. 473.

* "What Does the Spartacus League Want?," in Hudis and Anderson, *Rosa Luxemburg Reader*, pp. 349–57. A new translation of this speech will appear in the forthcoming Volume 5 of the *Complete Works*. The working class, of course, constituted the majority of Germany's populace in 1918—a quite different situation than that facing Russia at the time. The transition to socialism therefore was on the agenda as far as the Western European revolutions were concerned.

† One can argue that Luxemburg would have been on stronger ground if she had a more expansive understanding of the revolutionary potential of the peasantry. Marx argued, at the end of his life, that a revolution in Russia might be able to bypass a capitalist stage of industrialization *if* a peasant insurrection based on its indigenous communal forms obtained support from the workers of the technologically advanced countries. A worker–peasant alliance of this type, which would also involve the proletarians *within* Russia, would avoid the problem of a minoritarian revolution— and with it, the need for a bourgeois-democratic stage. This option, however, was not considered by Luxemburg or any of the Russian Marxists of her generation, who assumed (falsely, as it turns out) that the indigenous communal formations of the Russian peasantry had largely disappeared by that point. It was only with Stalin's forced industrialization drive of the 1930s that the traditional communal forms of the peasantry became completely obliterated.

acknowledge that the revolution has already suffered a massive defeat. Defeats, for her, are opportunities to learn and reorganize; as such, the high point of the most recent revolution becomes the point of departure for ensuing ones. Looking to the future, she presents the following argument:

> The working class cannot delude itself that, having overthrown absolutism and attained a dictatorship for a certain period, it will establish a socialist system. The socialist revolution can be only a result of international revolution, and the results that the proletariat in Russia will able to achieve in the current revolution will depend, to say nothing of the level of social development in Russia, on the level and form of development that class relations and proletarian operations in other capitalist countries will have achieved by that time.*

So far, so clear: This is consistent with what she argued from 1905 onward—socialist revolution is not now on the agenda for Russia, both because socialism cannot be created in one country† and because the material conditions do not yet exist to permit it. She then notes that despite this limitation, important social progress can be made by a regime controlled by the workers:

> Nevertheless, if the revolutionary proletariat in Russia were to gain political power as well, however temporarily, that would provide enormous encouragement to the international class struggle. That is why the working class in Poland and in Russia can and must strive to seize power with full consciousness. Because once workers have power, they can not only carry out the tasks of the current revolution directly—realizing political freedom across the Russian state—but also establish the eight-hour workday, upend agrarian relations, and in a word, materialize every aspect of their program, delivering the heaviest blows they can to bourgeois rule and in this way hastening its international overthrow.‡

But the question still remains: How can the workers maintain themselves in power in a democratic republic over the long haul if they constitute a minority of the populace? Her answer is that *they cannot*—and yet that the effort is still worth it:

---

* See "Lessons from the Three Dumas," p. 392, below.

† Earlier, in January 1906, Luxemburg had argued, "Capitalist rule and private property cannot be abolished in one land independently of the others." See "What Do We Want? A Commentary on the Program of the Social Democracy of the Kingdom of Poland and Lithuania," p. 26, below. This may sound counterintuitive today, since many "revolutionary" regimes came to power after 1917 that abolished private property without an international revolution. However, for Marx as for Luxemburg, "private property" does simply mean individual, personal ownership of the means of production as against collective or state ownership. "Private property" instead refers to *class* property—the ability of one class (whether through a corporation or a state) to control the means of production at the expense of the working class. Unfortunately, this basic distinction was lost from sight in the Marxist movement with the advent of Stalinism.

‡ See "Lessons from the Three Dumas," pp. 392–3, below.

The revolution's bourgeois character finds expression in the inability of the proletariat to stay in power, in the inevitable removal of the proletariat from power by a counterrevolutionary operation of the bourgeoisie, the rural landowners, the petty bourgeoisie, and the greater part of the peasantry. It may be that in the end, after the proletariat is overthrown, the republic will disappear and be followed by the long rule of a highly restrained constitutional monarchy. It may very well be. But the relations of classes in Russia are now such that the path to even a moderate monarchical constitution leads through revolutionary action and the dictatorship of a republican proletariat.

Revolution in this conception would bring the proletariat losses as well as victories. Yet by no other road can the entire international proletariat march to its final victory. We must propose the socialist revolution not as a sudden leap, finished in twenty-four hours, but as a historical period, perhaps long, of turbulent class struggle, with breaks both brief and extended.*

If nothing else, this is a remarkable expression of revolutionary realism. So much for Red Rosa with her head supposedly up in the clouds! She is fully aware that even a democratic republic under the control of the working class—which is how she as well as Marx understood "the dictatorship of the proletariat"—was bound to be forced from power in the absence of an international revolution, especially in a country where the working class constituted a minority. And yet, even though the revolution would therefore have "failed" from at least one point of view, it would have produced important social transformations that provide the intellectual sediment from which a future uprooting of capitalism could arise.

In short, Luxemburg did not think that it made sense to sacrifice democracy for the sake of staying in power, since the political form required to achieve the transition to socialism is "thoroughgoing democracy." If a nondemocratic regime stays in power, the transition to socialism becomes impossible; on the other hand, if a proletarian democracy exists even for a brief period of time, it can help inspire the transition to socialism to later arise.

One issue that makes her discussion in "Lessons from the Three Dumas" so remarkable is that it speaks to what unfolded a decade later, when tsarism was finally overthrown in the February 1917 Revolution—followed in short order by the Bolshevik seizure of power in October. Lenin and the Bolsheviks were fully aware at the time that the material conditions did not permit the immediate creation of a socialist society, even as they proclaimed the establishment of the dictatorship of the proletariat.† This is why Lenin worked so hard

---

* See "Lessons from the Three Dumas," p. 393, below.
† Many radicals have presumed, to this day, that the "dictatorship of the proletariat" is the first stage of socialism or communism. Luxemburg was far too good a student of Marx to make such a crude error. She fully understood that the dictatorship of the proletariat is a transitional

to foster proletarian revolutions in Western Europe. In this, his approach was very similar to Luxemburg's. However, two fundamental issues separated them: First, the Bolshevik regime did not take the form of a democratic republic, as seen in its suppression of political liberties—a development that Luxemburg sharply opposed in her 1918 critique of the Russian Revolution. Second, Lenin held that now that the Bolsheviks had seized power, they intended to keep it—permanently. This is far different from Luxemburg's statement in 1908 that "the inability of the proletariat to stay in power" was not the worst outcome, so long as the vision of liberation projected to the world through its creation of a democratic society based on the rule of the working class would inspire others to take up the fight against capitalism.

As it turned out, the "worst outcome" was the pretense that the "dictatorship of the proletariat" could be maintained even after the failure (by 1923) of the Western European revolutions. The only way to sustain such a claim was to drain the notion of "proletarian dictatorship" of any liberatory content by defining it in terms of an actual dictatorship over the masses—instead of as the democratic governance of society by the masses themselves.

LUXEMBURG AND OUR PRESENT PREDICAMENT

Given the materials collected in this volume, Nettl's statement that "unlike Lenin, she made no original contributions to the tactics or methods of revolution" in her reflections on the Russian Revolution is certainly open to question. Now that all of Luxemburg's writings "On Revolution" from this period are available in English, it becomes possible to re-examine her legacy with new eyes. Indeed, there are surely many new discoveries to be made as subsequent volumes of the *Complete Works* appear. We can hardly claim to have knowledge of Luxemburg's legacy without at least engaging with these texts, most of which appear in English for the first time, and doing so with an open mind—which means being willing to reconsider views that we may have held for years or even decades. Surely a thinker who placed so much emphasis on enlightenment and self-awareness as the key to human emancipation deserves no less.

What is not open to question, however, is that the perspectives for advancing the cause of socialism delineated in her writings "On Revolution" from 1906 to 1909 are the path less traveled. Many important revolutions occurred in the twentieth century, but they were led by political parties, guerrilla *focos*, or individuals who lacked the support of the majority of the oppressed. Even in the few instances where one could claim that was not the case, the revolutions did not take the form of democratic republics under the control of workers and peasants; instead, they took the form of single-party states that monopolized power

---

political phase *between* capitalism and the initial or lower phase of socialism or communism (the latter two concepts are indistinguishable in her writings, as they are in all of Marx's).

in the hands of a "revolutionary" elite. As a result, these revolutions—from Russia to China, and from Africa to Latin America—promoted a transition, not to socialism, but to new forms of class domination based on the capitalist law of value. By the early twenty-first century, the failure of these efforts to produce a viable alternative to existing society—as well as the failure of Social Democratic governments in Europe and elsewhere to pose any serious challenge to capitalist social relations and imperialism—led political pundits to proclaim that "there is no alternative to capitalism." Only in the last decade has this begun to be seriously challenged, with the emergence of a host of new anti-racist, anti-sexist, anti-capitalist, LGBTQ, and pro-environmental movements. The unanswered question that faces us today is whether this will lead to a new socialist movement that consciously seeks to navigate a very different path to a new society than taken in the past.

Luxemburg could not have anticipated these developments any more than she anticipated the rise of fascism and Stalinism that followed her death in 1919. But her body of thought, taken as a whole, does have a lot to say that provides direction for forging a renewed path to social transformation today. As she wrote in 1906,

> A truly working-class party may consider itself, and has the right to consider itself, a representative of the *interests* of working people and as their champion in the revolutionary fight; it cannot ever during the course of its activities consider itself to be identical to the people or to the revolutionary government—unless it wants to make of revolutionary government a "revolutionary" farce.*

The last one hundred years of revolutionary triumph and tragedy do not necessarily mean that Luxemburg's perspective has been "proven correct." Nor is making such claims the aim of those of us engaged in the mammoth project of issuing her *Complete Works*. Luxemburg was a product of her times, and we cannot live by the truths of a different era—any more than we can presume to make progress by blithely dismissing them. We have to account for the problems of our times, defined, on the one hand, by a century of failed and aborted revolutions, and on the other, by a capitalist system that so threatens the very existence of civilization as we have known it that the development of a viable alternative to *all* forms of capitalism, whether "free market" or statist, has literally become a matter of life and death. If discovering and engaging with the full corpus of Luxemburg's works in some way contributes to that effort, the work of producing these volumes will have been well worth it.

Peter Hudis
Sandra Rein

---

* See "Organization and Disorganization," p. 181, below.

Abbreviations

ADAV, Allgemeiner Deutscher Arbeiterverein—General German Workers' Association
FVdG, Freier Verband der deutschen Gewerkschaften—Free Association of German Trade Unions
IAA, Internationale Arbeiter-Assoziation—the International Workingmen's Association, or First International
ISB, International Socialist Bureau
KPD, Kommunistische Partei Deutschlands—Communist Party of Germany
KPRP, Komunistyczna Partia Robotnicza Polski—Communist Workers' Party of Poland (KPRP)
POF, Parti Ouvrier Français—French Workers' Party
PPS, Polska Partia Socjalistyczna—Polish Socialist Party
PPS-FR, Polska Partia Socjalistyczna-Frakcja Rewolucyjna—Polish Socialist Party–Revolutionary Faction
PPS-Left, Polska Partia Socjalistyczna-Lewica—Polish Socialist Party–Left
PPSD, Polska Partia Socjalno-Demokratyczna Galicji i Śląska—Polish Social Democratic Party of Galicia and Silesia
RGASPI, Russkii Gosudarstvennyi Arkiv Sotsialno-Politcheskoi Istorii—Russian State Archive for Social and Political History
RSDRP, Rossiyskaya Sotsial-Demokraticheskaya Rabochaya Partiya—Russian Social Democratic Labor Party
SDAP, Sozialdemokratische Arbeiterpartei—Social Democratic Workers' Party
SDKP, Socjaldemokracja Królestwa Polskiego—Social Democracy of the Kingdom of Poland
SDKPiL, Socjaldemokracja Królestwa Polskiego i Litwy—Social Democracy of the Kingdom of Poland and Lithuania
SPD, Sozialdemokratische Partei Deutschlands—Social Democratic Party of Germany
SR, Sotsialisty Revolyutsionery—Socialist Revolutionary Party
USPD, Unabhängige Sozialdemokratische Partei Deutschlands—Independent Social Democratic Party of Germany
ZRP, Związek Robotników Polskich—Union of Polish Workers

1902

Social Reform and Social Revolution*

Under the overall title *The Social Revolution*, Vorwärts publishing house has just brought out two short papers by Comrade [Karl] Kautsky, one of which deals with social reform and social revolution, while the second is titled *The Day after the Social Revolution*. Both writings are the result of lectures Kautsky gave in April of this year to the Socialist Reading Association in Amsterdam and Delft, a society consisting primarily of academics.†

That explains why the small brochures are not exactly agitation booklets in the strict sense of the word; we would at least not recommend them primarily for recruiting new members into the party. But their propagandistic value is all the greater for those socialist fighters who have gone mad over the revisionist fuss and go to and fro over the old social-revolutionary traditions of international socialism—for those who have really let themselves be persuaded that the opposition between bourgeoisie and proletariat is not increasing, but decreasing, that in every modern state there can be enough democratic institutions to enable the working class, if not *to be in* power, at least to gain power and progressively increase it, bit by bit, so that any need for social revolution would disappear.

It is impossible, within the narrow framework of an article, to even summarize slightly the historical investigations with which Kautsky introduces his evidence. Through them he justifies the difference between social reform and social revolution in a most apt way. Measures that seek to adapt the legal and political superstructure of society to changed economic conditions are reforms if they are initiated by the classes that until then had ruled society politically and economically; they are reforms, even if they are not given voluntarily, but are

---

* This article first appeared in *Leipziger Volkszeitung*, No. 152, July 5, 1902. It is translated by Manuela Kölke from Luxemburg's *Gesammelte Werke*, Vol. 6 (Berlin: Dietz Verlag, 2014), pp. 437–9. This article was not signed. We can confirm Rosa Luxemburg's authorship from Eduard Bernstein's complaint about the polemic directed against him in several pamphlets written by Karl Kautsky. Bernstein wrote: "This has also been confirmed in an article in the *Leipziger Volkszeitung*, which undoubtedly comes from a person very close to Kautsky, Comrade Rosa Luxemburg. It speaks of 'the revisionists' dithering and wavering, and it is said that Kautsky's booklet is like a breath of fresh air in the fog of revisionism." See *Protokoll des Revisionismus Verhandlungen des Parteitags der Sozialdemokratischen Partei, München vom 14. bis 20. September 1902* (Protocol of the Negotiations of the Party Congress of the Social Democratic Party, Munich of September 14 to 20, 1902) (Berlin: Buchhandlung Vorwärts, 1902), p. 124. Although this volume is devoted to Luxemburg's writings of 1906 to 1909, this and the following essay from 1902 are included here, since they were not available when we issued Volume 3 of the *Complete Works*.

† See Karl Kautsky, *Die soziale Revolution. I. Sozialreform und soziale Revolution. II. Am Tage nach der sozialen Revolution* (Berlin: Buchhandlung Vorwärts, 1902). For the original English-language edition, see Karl Kautsky, *The Social Revolution: I. Reform and Revolution; II. The Day after the Revolution*, translated by A. M. and May Wood Simons (Chicago: Charles H. Kerr & Company, 1916).

produced by pressure from the ruled classes or by the power of circumstances. Such measures, on the other hand, are products of a revolution when they are initiated by a class that has so far been economically and politically suppressed and that has now conquered political power. It must use this political power in its own interest to revolutionize the entire political and legal superstructure of society, whether more slowly or quickly, and to create new forms of social interaction.

The modern working class cannot and must not do without this social revolution if it really wants to emancipate itself. Kautsky proves in detail that capitalist development does not mitigate but sharpens class opposites, that the opposite assertion that the class opposition between bourgeoisie and proletariat is allegedly weakening comes not entirely out of thin air but is limited to certain classes of the bourgeois intelligentsia making friends with the proletarian class struggle. It is from these very classes of the bourgeois intelligentsia that all the siren songs come, which have happily caused a certain amount of confusion in the ranks of the struggling proletariat.

Let's hear these enticing songs for a moment! In all cultural states,* there is as much democracy as is necessary to facilitate peaceful, revolutionary development. Everywhere it is possible to found consumer associations that, as they spread, start their own production and thus, slowly but steadily, displace capitalist production in one area after another. Everywhere it is possible to organize unions that increasingly restrict the power of the capitalist in his factories, introducing constitutionalism into the factory instead of absolutism, and thus preparing the slow transition to the republican factory.† Almost everywhere, Social Democracy can invade municipal councils, influence public works in the interest of the workers, expand the circle of municipal tasks, and restrict private production by constantly expanding the circle of municipal production. At last, Social Democracy is penetrating into parliaments; gaining more and more influence there; imposing one social reform after another; restricting the power of the capitalists through labor protection laws; and at the same time increasingly expanding the circle of state production by working toward the nationalization of the large monopolies. Thus, by using democratic rights on the grounds already given today, capitalist society is gradually growing, without any shocks, into socialist society; the revolutionary conquest of political power by the proletariat becomes unnecessary, and striving for it is directly harmful, because it can do nothing but disrupt this slow but sure process.

---

 * *Kulturstaaten* in the original German, a term closely related to *Kulturnation*, which means "a state with a developed sense of national consciousness." *Kulturstaaten* has no direct equivalent in English.
 † That is, factories governed by the legal statutes of a democratic republic.

Kautsky's first writing[*] disproves all these disastrous illusions step by step in the most understandable, clear, striking way, and therefore we can only wish for the widest dissemination of this meritorious work among the party. It blows like a fresh wind through all the revisionist fog. Certainly, democracy is indispensable as a means of maturing the proletariat for social revolution, for the conquest of political power. But it cannot prevent this revolution; it cannot guarantee the working class' real emancipation from the shackles of wage slavery.

Democracy is for the proletariat what air and light are for the organism; without it, its powers cannot unfold. But, with the growth of one class the simultaneous growth of the opponent must not be overlooked. Democracy does not hinder the development of capital, whose organization and political and economic power increase at the same time as the power of the proletariat. Surely, the consumer associations are growing, but, at the same time, the accumulation of capital is growing even faster; surely, the trade unions are growing, but, at the same time, the concentration of capital and its organization is growing even faster, into huge monopolies. Surely, the socialist press is growing, but, at the same time, the nonparty, unprincipled press is growing, annoying, and poisoning large sections of the population; surely, wages are rising, but the mass of profits is rising even faster; surely, the number of socialist deputies in parliaments is growing, but the importance and effectiveness of these institutions is decreasing, while, at the same time, their majorities and governments are becoming increasingly dependent on the powers of high finance. Thus, in addition to the means of the power of the proletariat, the means of the power of capital are also developing, and the end of this development can be nothing other than a great struggle for the decision between the two, which will not end until the working class has become victorious.

So much about Kautsky's first writing; on another occasion we will turn to the second.

---

[*] The first part of *The Social Revolution*, entitled *Social Reform and Social Revolution*. Her analysis of the second part appears in the next article.

On the Day after the Social Revolution[*]

After discussing the first of the two short texts on social revolution published by Comrade [Karl] Kautsky eight days ago, we would now like to dedicate a few words here to the second one. It has the title *The Day after the Social Revolution*, and this title will perhaps arouse some suspicion against it. It sounds somewhat Blanquistic[†] in that it involuntarily evokes the idea that the working class is going to take political power through a violent coup. It also raises the suspicion that we have now happily reached that place where, as Marx explained thirty years ago already, he never wanted to go—devising recipes for the cookshops of the future.[‡]

In fact, there can be nothing more foolish than wanting to predict the shape of socialist society. The more complicated the social interrelationships become, the more impossible it is to prophesy their development even for years or decades, let alone for centuries or millennia. The opponents of the proletarian struggle for emancipation are immediately at hand to exploit this impossibility, in that they say: "You are therefore fighting for the socialist society, which you yourselves say you do not know what it will look like." This objection alone is nothing but a ridiculous boast that, if one were to take it seriously for a moment, would nip all social progress in the bud. Every oppressed class struggles to break the yoke that pushes them into the dust, completely unconcerned about how they will raise and stretch their limbs when the chains have been stripped from them. No one has described this "ancient state of nature" more movingly and beautifully than the great pioneers of the bourgeois classes, whose degenerate descendants now know to maunder as much about "socialist utopias" as [Friedrich] Schiller, the alleged favorite poet of the German bourgeoisie:

> When the oppress'd for justice looks in vain,
> When his sore burden may no more be borne,
> With fearless heart he makes appeal to Heaven,
> And thence brings down his everlasting rights,

---

[*] This article first appeared in *Leipziger Volkszeitung*, No. 158, July 12, 1902. It is translated by Manuela Kölke from Luxemburg's *Gesammelte Werke*, Vol. 6, pp. 440–3. It was first republished in German by Harald Koth, in *Rosa-Luxemburg-Forschungsberichte 1, Leipziger Reden und Schriften Rosa Luxemburgs* (Sachsen: Rosa-Luxemburg-Stiftung, 2007), p. 34ff. The article was not signed but was certainly written by Luxemburg.

[†] Adjective to describe followers of, and political activity modeled on, the great French revolutionary Auguste Blanqui. Luxemburg defines Blanquism in her writings as a conspiratorial concept based on the notion that the mass of workers are not the conscious agents of their own liberation but are rather called into action by enlightened revolutionary leaders.

[‡] The phrase "cookshops of the future" appears in the afterword to the second edition of *Capital*. See Karl Marx, *Capital*, Vol. 1, translated by Ben Fowkes (London: Penguin Books, 1977), p. 99.

> Which there abide, inalienably his,
> And indestructible as are the stars.
> Nature's primeval state returns again,
> Where man stands hostile to his fellow man.*

This is the simple philosophy of every oppressed class, the most powerful lever of all historical progress. [Immanuel] Kant and Schiller, [Jean-Jacques] Rousseau and Voltaire† have not lived for nothing, and they will continue as benefactors of humanity, although none of them had even the faintest idea of what the bourgeois world, of which they were pioneers, would look like a hundred or even only fifty years after their death.

Hence, the slightest shadow does not fall on the struggle for the liberation of the modern working class insofar as it refrains from painting any picture of a socialist society. On the contrary, by renouncing [the need to do so], [the modern working class] expresses greater maturity than the bourgeois class in the days when it sought to break the absolutist-feudal yoke, for that was the heyday of all kinds of utopias, including some socialist ones. It only has a reason to step out of this justified reserve if the opponents try to prove in detail that the victory of the working class will confront them with insoluble tasks, or if there are people in their own ranks who cannot help but engage in eerie prophecies that the victory of the proletariat will also be its defeat.

Showing the nothingness of these prophecies is now the task that Kautsky has set himself. Limited like this, [Kautsky's task] makes good and proper sense. Kautsky does not predict what socialist society will be but disproves what the opponents and the doubters have concluded from the presumed victory of the proletariat. However, he does not rest content with how easy it is to refute their sometimes highly foolish objections; instead, he deals in a positive way with the problems that the proletariat will face after the victory of the social revolution. But he does so—in contrast to these opponents and doubters—with that limitation that makes a scientific investigation of these problems possible in the first place. He deduces not what [a socialist society] *will* look like, but on the contrary, what it will surely *not* look like. The tasks that the proletariat will face on the day after the social revolution are surely difficult and intricate, although considering the materials available for a scientific investigation today, they are by no means unsolvable.

On the one hand, Kautsky repeatedly emphasizes that the social revolution is a long historical process in which we have been living for a long time without even being able to foresee its end. But to reduce the social revolution

---

* Friedrich Schiller, *Wilhelm Tell. Schauspiel in Fünf Aufzügen* (Leipzig: Reclam Verlag, 1967), p. 46. The above quotation appears in Act II, Scene II. See Friedrich Schiller, *William Tell*, translated by Theodore Martin (Whithorn: Anodos Books, 2019).

† Voltaire was the nom de plume of François-Marie Arouet.

to its simplest form is to assume that one day, all political power will fall to the proletariat without restriction, in one fell swoop, and that it will be guided in its exercise solely by its class interests, in the most expedient way. The former will not happen, while the latter will hardly occur. The proletariat is differentiated into different strata, especially according to its level of intellectual and economic development. But it is also very likely that alongside the proletariat, other social strata close to it will rise up as well—such as parts of the petty bourgeoisie or the small peasantry whose way of thinking does not fully coincide with the proletarian. Friction and aberrations of the most varied kinds can arise from this.

We will not always be able to do what we want, and we will not always want what we should. Of course, a scientific study must not refrain from [facing such] disturbing moments.

On the other hand, a scientific study must be based on known conditions; it cannot take as its basis a model of the conditions as they might develop in the future, for this would lead it into an unfounded, phantasmagorical abyss. And yet it is self-evident that the working class will not come to power under today's conditions. The revolution itself presupposes long and deep struggles that will already change the political and social structure of today's society. Following the conquest of political power by the proletariat, there will, therefore, be problems of which we know nothing today, and some of those we are dealing with today will have been resolved by then. Means will also emerge to solve the various problems of which we today have no idea.

Kautsky compares his method with that of the physicist, who examines the laws of gravity in a vacuum, not in moving air. Thus, Kautsky examines the situation of the victorious proletariat under conditions that will never arrive in full purity, namely under the assumption that tomorrow it will come to power in one fell swoop, and that the means at its disposal to solve its tasks are given today. He comes to results that are as different from the real course of things as the laws of gravity from the real fall of the different bodies. But despite these deviations, the laws of gravity really exist and dominate the case of every single body, which can only be understood once one has understood these laws.

First of all, we were interested in Kautsky's method; due to lack of space, we cannot go into more detail about his results.* We can also recommend these writings only tentatively to those party circles that have not yet forgotten the great goals of the proletarian struggle for emancipation over the "statesmanlike" possibilities of the day.

---

* Among the "details" in Kautsky's essay that are not touched upon by Luxemburg are the roles of private entrepreneurship, markets, and value production in socialism; of the latter Kautsky writes, "Here free production can rule without the necessity of production of commodities of value."

1906

The Russian Revolution[*]

Today's revolution in Russia is formally the last offshoot of the Great French Revolution of a hundred years ago. The entire past century has simply carried out the job that that great historical upheaval had passed on—that is, the constitution of the class rule of the modern bourgeoisie, capitalism, in all countries. In the first act of this century-long crisis, the actual revolution stirred up feudal medieval society, turning the lowest upward and the highest downward. It has shaken society, cut it up coarsely into modern classes, clarified its social and political aspirations and programs to some extent, and finally—through the Napoleonic Wars—defeated feudalism throughout Europe. In the following stages, the class division of modern bourgeois society that began with the Great Revolution is continued in and through the class struggle. In the restoration period after 1815, high finance takes over and is overthrown by the July Revolution [of 1830]. In the July Revolution, the big industrial bourgeoisie comes to power and is overthrown by the February Revolution [of 1848]. The February Revolution finally brings the broad mass of the middle and smaller bourgeoisie to power. In the form of today's Third Republic, modern bourgeois class rule reaches its most developed and final form. But now, in all these internal struggles of the bourgeoisie, a new dichotomy is forming: between all of bourgeois society and the modern working class. The formation and maturity of this new class antagonism run parallel to the *bourgeois* class struggles throughout the history of the century. The Great [French] Revolution [of 1789–93], with the first general upheaval of all elements and all internal contradictions of bourgeois society, already brings the proletariat and its social ideal—communism—to the fore. The short reign of the Montagnards,[†] which marked the height of the revolution, was the first historical appearance of the modern proletariat. Only it did not yet appear independently at that time, but was still attached to the apron strings of the petty bourgeoisie and, together with it, formed "the people," whose opposition to bourgeois society was expressed under the misleading form of the opposition of the "People's Republic" to the constitutional monarchy. In the February Revolution, in that terrible Battle of June [1848],[‡] the proletariat as a

---

[*] This undated article was written in early 1906. It is translated by Manuela Kölke from Luxemburg's *Gesammelte Werke*, Vol. 2, pp. 5–10.

[†] The Montagnards formed the radical wing of the Legislative Assembly in the Great French Revolution. From June 1793 to July 1794, this ruled in the form of the revolutionary democratic dictatorship of the Jacobin bloc.

[‡] From June 23 to 26, 1848, workers and artisans in Paris and other cities sparked an insurrection after the government tried to disband one of the major gains of the revolution, the national workshops created to ameliorate unemployment and poverty. Hundreds of barricades sprung up throughout Paris. The authorities responded with brutal repression. Minister of War Louis-Eugène Cavaignac was given dictatorial powers to crush the revolution, leading to an assault that left over

class finally separated completely from the petty bourgeoisie and realized for the first time that it was completely isolated in bourgeois society, completely dependent on itself, and in deadly hostility to this society. Only then was a modern bourgeois society formed in France, completing the work begun by the Great French Revolution.

Even though *France* was the stage for these main acts of the dramatic history of capitalist society, it was nevertheless also the histories of Germany, Austria, Italy—of all modern countries, of the whole capitalist world as well—that played themselves out in those acts. There is nothing more foolish and wrong than to regard modern revolutions as national occurrences, as events which have their full effect only within the borders of the state in question, and which exert only a more or less weak influence on the others, the "neighboring states," resulting from the "neighboring situation." Bourgeois society, capitalism, is an international, *world* form of human society. There are not as many bourgeois societies and as many capitalisms as there are modern states or nations; there is only *one* international bourgeois society, only *one* capitalism, and the apparently isolated, independent existence of the individual states behind their state barriers is only one of the contradictions of capitalism in the one and indivisible world economy. That is why all modern revolutions are actually *international* revolutions. It is also one and the same tremendous bourgeois revolution that took place in various acts throughout Europe from 1789 to 1848 and constituted modern bourgeois class rule on an *international basis*.

Apparently, the Russian Empire was an exception in this world revolution. Here medieval absolutism appeared to want to remain an indestructible part of the pre-capitalist era, despite all the storms in the rest of capitalist Europe. Today, absolutism is already crushed to the ground by the revolution in Russia as well.* What we are experiencing now are no longer struggles of the revolution against a ruling, absolutist system, but, on the contrary, struggles of the formal remnants of absolutism against modern political freedom that has already become a living fact, as well as struggles among classes and parties for the delimitation and the constitutional securing of this freedom.

Formally, as mentioned before, the Russian Revolution is the last offshoot of the period of *bourgeois* revolutions in Europe. Its next pivotal task is the creation of a modern capitalist society with open bourgeois class rule. This formal bourgeois revolution in Russia is no longer carried out by the bourgeoisie alone but by the working class—and this very fact reveals itself that even Russia, apparently rigid and closed off throughout the century, took part in the general upheaval of Europe. And the working class is no longer an appendage of the

---

10,000 dead. Thousands more were arrested and deported to Algeria. The crushing of the revolt was a critical moment in turning the tide from revolution to reaction.

* It should be kept in mind that these words were written at the beginning of 1906, at the height of the revolutionary upsurge in Russia; matters appeared far different only a few months later.

petty bourgeoisie, as in all previous revolutions, but appears as an independent class with full awareness of its specific class interests and tasks—that is, as a working class led by Social Democracy. In this respect, the current revolution in Russia is a direct continuation of the Paris battle of June 1848, where the division between the proletariat and the entirety of bourgeois society was first set into motion: a division that is now implemented by the current revolution as a pre-given fact. At the same time, in its revolutionary action the Russian proletariat draws on all the historical experience and class consciousness that the international proletariat has acquired everywhere since that first lesson in June 1848,* and also in the later parliamentary period in France and in Germany.

This makes today's Russian Revolution a contradictory phenomenon that is unparalleled in any of the revolutions that preceded it. Here, the political forms of modern bourgeois class rule are not fought for by the bourgeoisie, but by the working class and against the bourgeoisie. The working class, however—although, or rather because, it here functions for the first time as an independent class-conscious stratum—does not appear with the utopian socialist illusions with which it operated in association with the petty bourgeoisie in the earlier bourgeois revolutions. The proletariat in Russia today sets itself the task not of realizing socialism, but of creating the capitalist-bourgeois preconditions for the realization of socialism. At the same time, however, bourgeois society acquires a very peculiar character by emerging from the hands of a class-conscious proletariat. Even though the working class in Russia does not set itself the task of directly realizing socialism, it even less so sets itself the task of taking on the cause of the untouchable and unclouded glory of capitalist class rule, as it emerged from the bourgeois revolutions of the last century in the West.

Rather, the proletariat in Russia simultaneously and in one action leads the struggle against both absolutism and capitalism. It only seeks the forms of bourgeois democracy, but it seeks them *for itself*, for the purposes of proletarian class struggle. It wants the *eight-hour day*, the popular militia, the republic—all demands that are associated with the bourgeois society, not the socialist one. But at the same time, these demands here hit so hard at the extreme *limit* of the rule of capital that they appear as so many transitional forms to a proletarian dictatorship. The proletariat in Russia fights for the realization of the most elementary *bourgeois* constitutional rights: the right of association and assembly, the right of coalition, freedom of the press. But it is already using these bourgeois liberties, in the storm of the revolution, to forge such a powerful economic and political class organization of the proletariat—trade unions and Social Democracy—that while the bourgeoisie, as a class formally appointed to rule during the revolution, will end up in unprecedented weakness, the formally

---

* For Luxemburg's detailed account of the events of June 1848, see "The June Days of 1848," pp. 155–67, below.

dominated (that is, the working class) will take on an unprecedented position of power.

Thus, *in its content*, today's revolution in Russia goes far beyond the revolutions of the past, and its methods can neither tie in with the old bourgeois revolutions nor with the previous—parliamentary—struggles of the modern proletariat. It has created a new method of struggle that corresponds to its proletarian character as well as to the combination of the struggle for democracy with the struggle against capital—the revolutionary mass strike. It is, therefore, a completely new type of revolution in terms of its content and methods. Formally bourgeois-democratic and proletarian-socialist in nature, both in content and methods, it is a transitional form from the bourgeois revolutions of the past to the proletarian revolutions of the future, which—it is already clear—will entail the dictatorship of the proletariat and the realization of socialism.

This is not only logical, in accordance with a specific typology, but also *historical*, as the starting point of a certain social class relation and balance of power. The society that will emerge from this peculiar revolution in Russia cannot possibly resemble that which emerged from the earlier revolutions in the West after 1848. The power, the organization, the class consciousness of the proletariat will be so highly developed in Russia after the revolution that they will exceed the framework of a "normal" bourgeois society at every turn. Together with the simultaneous weakness and despondency of a bourgeoisie already anticipating its own downfall—a bourgeoisie without any political and revolutionary past—this will result in a combination of forces in which the equilibrium of bourgeois class rule is continually upset. This will also open a new phase in the history of bourgeois society, which will go through constant storms in the face of the lack of stable equilibrium of class relations, storms that, with greater or lesser pauses, with greater or lesser vehemence, can find no other outlet than the social revolution—the dictatorship of the proletariat.

All this refers first of all to Russia. Just as the fates of Russia and Europe as a whole were decided in the French revolutions by the battles on the streets of Paris, so the fate of not only Russian society but the whole capitalist world is now being decided on the streets of St. Petersburg, Moscow, and Warsaw. The revolution in Russia and the peculiar social structure that will emerge from it cannot avoid shifting class relations in Germany and everywhere with one push. With the Russian Revolution, the almost-sixty-year period of quiet parliamentary rule of the bourgeoisie comes to a close. With the Russian Revolution, we are already entering the transition period from capitalist to socialist society. How *long* this transitional period may last is of interest only to political weather prophets. Key for the international class-conscious proletariat is only the strengthening, clarifying insight provided into the near future of this redeeming period, and into the need to grow as quickly in tenacity, clarity, and heroism in the coming storms as the Russian proletariat now expands daily and hourly before our eyes.

Armed Revolt in Moscow*

It has only recently become possible to recreate for oneself a picture of how the struggle in Moscow unfolded, on the basis not of fake reports but of those who took part in the struggle or were witnesses to it. Revolutionary organizations in Moscow have more important tasks, of course, than to write the telegrams of quasi-governmental or governmental agencies, but on the basis of reports from the history of the movement, from this flood of messages, we may attempt to give an approximation of this, today's great fact.

The action began with a call to a general strike from the Council of Worker Delegates, the Social Democratic Party, and the Committee of Socialist Revolutionaries. A call went out to begin the strike at midday on Wednesday, December 20 [1905], with a further call attempting to transform the strike into an armed conflict. The strike began with unprecedented solidarity; all the factories and workshops stopped immediately, shops were closed, and all railroads were halted, with the exception of the Nikolayevsky line. There was no talk of needing to force anyone to strike, since the entire working populace responded to the call at once. Workers went their separate ways from the meetings bearing red flags and singing revolutionary songs. The strike had full participation from the very start.

Beginning on December 21, the movement took to the streets. Rallies were held in all of the city's neighborhoods, speeches were given, and protest marches were organized. Cossacks and dragoons† fell on the demonstrators, though they only fired their rifles into the air. In the evening of that day, a throng of 22,000

---

* This article first appeared in *Czerwony Sztandar* (Red Flag), No. 35, January 3, 1906, pp. 1–2 under the title "Zbrojna rewolucja w Moskwie." Parts of it were reprinted in *SDKPiL w rewolucji 1905. Zbiór publikacji* (Warsaw: Książka i Wiedza, 1955). It is translated by Joseph Muller from the Polish original. Luxemburg had arrived in Russian-occupied Poland to take part in the revolution only a few days before this article appeared. *Czerwony Sztandar* was the main organ of Luxemburg's party, the Social Democracy of the Kingdom of Poland and Lithuania (SDKPiL). It was published, with interruptions, from 1903 to 1913, and again in 1917–18. Usually published as a monthly, from the end of 1905 until December 1906 it was published several times a week, almost as a daily newspaper. Until 1913, Leo Jogiches was de facto editor in chief—with curbs on this activity in the period of his imprisonment and seeking refuge from the authorities in 1906–1907. During the period of revolution in 1905–1906, it was the SDKPiL's most important publication, the place where all articles dealing with fundamentals and theoretical issues were first published—the cover page was usually composed of one long, continuous article. It was also Luxemburg's most important publication outlet during the period of revolution. The only article published by Luxemburg during her stay in Warsaw under her own name in the paper—which was illegally distributed within the Kingdom of Poland—was her critique of Ignacy Daszyński. This worked to her disadvantage after her arrest in March 1906, as she could no longer credibly claim to be a nonparticipating German journalist simply passing time as an observer in Warsaw.

† The Cossacks were a paramilitary organization in Russia that had sworn loyalty to the tsar and provided regiments to the Imperial Army. "Dragoons" refers to mounted infantry.

gathered at the Aquarium Theater. It was soon surrounded by the army. Some of the people rushed the doors, but soldiers drove them back, beating them with the butts of their rifles; many more broke through the fence of the theater garden and entered the courtyard of the Komissarovsky school. There, they barricaded themselves in until the following day, when they dispersed. Approximately 70 people were arrested that day, and the police processed about 10,000 [others] before releasing them. Several dozen revolvers were confiscated.

On December 23, around 500 people gathered at the Fidler building. The army surrounded the building at ten o'clock. They demanded that those assembled surrender their weapons and disperse; the protesters refused and began to shoot at the army; the army bombarded the building, and a bomb was thrown out of the building. At three o'clock in the morning, the revolutionaries surrendered; eight had been killed, thirty wounded. They arrested 120 members of the fighting company and a few members of party committees, and they confiscated a number of weapons and thirteen bombs.

That same day, December 23, saw the first barricades being built. The first barricades were set up on Strastnoi Square and Old Triumph Square. They were poor in quality; the cavalry and infantry shot through them and later easily dismantled them. That evening, there was a skirmish on Tverskoy Street [Ulica Twerska]. The company of fighters tore down electric tram wires and made a barrier to stop the Cossack and dragoon patrols, and at the same time, they hatched a plan to construct barricades out of wooden planks, barrels, crates, old pieces of iron and barbed wire, felled telegraph poles, and grating pulled up from a nearby square. Such barricades could be held for a little longer. The next day, December 23, a whole series of especially durable barricades had been erected, and the army had to take them one by one as the day went on.* In the night from December 23 to 24, the army retreated. Evidently, it turned out that they had refused to take orders. Making use of this withdrawal, the revolutionaries repaired the old barricades that had been taken by the army and built a whole line of new barricades, such that by the morning, several of the city's districts were entirely barricaded, and all access to them had been closed off. On December 24, the army began to pummel the barricades with cannon fire; when the artillery broke through one and took it over, they soon saw standing a few steps farther down the same street a new barricade that would have to be taken in turn. Barricades were rising with astonishing speed. So again, by nightfall, the army had only managed to remove barricades on two streets, Sadovaya [Sadowa] and Neglinka [Neglińska].

By December 25, a significant portion of the city was barricaded. Still more barricades had already been erected, with tremendous skill. They were supplied

---

* December 23 is the date that appears both here and above, though the narrative identifies these as different days.

through trenches and strengthened by tightly binding all the objects together with wire. Tramcars, sleighs, and wagons were pulled into heaps. Embankments of snow were also formed, and water was poured over them to harden them, and snow was carried from the courtyards and gardens in sacks or sheets. Such barricades withstood prolonged cannon fire. For days, work on the barricades did not stop. Tens of thousands of workers labored feverishly, and by December 28, the area closed off completely by the revolutionaries covered approximately seven miles.*

These barricades had a dual purpose: They prevented the movement of troops, and they were points of resistance for groups of armed revolutionaries. Their tactics, if one may judge from the reports so far, were these: Those defending a barricade first fired a salvo toward the oncoming troops; next, they dispersed into the houses, shooting from windows, over wall tops, and around fences; finally, when the barricade was eventually demolished, the combat squads began a new barricade farther down the same street, and repeated the process.

How did the troops behave? [Observers] summarized the situation as follows: A part of the army seemed to be "untrustworthy"; these regiments were then sent back to their barracks, deprived of their weapons, and divided into different sections of the barracks. Certain details emerged that the grenadiers had become seriously agitated.

Regarding the Parnowski regiment, they are said to have sent a letter to their colonel saying, "If an officer is found who dares to command to fire on our own brothers, let him understand that the first bullet will be aimed at his head." On December 20, soldiers encamped in the Kremlin barracks held a rally. At the rally, economic demands were agreed on, and a resolution was passed not to fire on the people for any reason. On December 22, a regiment of infantry came out of the Alexandrovsky [Alexandrowski] barracks with a band playing the Marseillaise.† General [Nikolai] Malakhov appeared and ordered the regiment be surrounded by Cossacks and dragoons. The soldiers named their economic demands, and the general promised to meet them, asking the soldiers to return to their barracks.

However, a part of the army that the authorities had sorted out by taking soldiers from various regiments, and that opposed the revolutionary people, became enraged beyond all measure. These soldiers truly delighted in murder and tortured those whom they managed to catch alive. They were permitted to indulge in wild, utterly senseless barbarity. For example, they fired rifle volleys down streets entirely free of barricades, wounding and killing dozens of neutral passersby, including women and children; case shot‡ was fired into homes,

---

*   Ten versts in the original. A verst is about 3,500 feet.
†   The Marseillaise was the national anthem of the French Revolution, adopted in 1795.
‡   Pieces of iron fired from a cannon.

shattering them for no reason. One of their acts of war was to destroy Sytin's printing house,* about which the telegraph agency† again distributed pure lies. In this building, a great splendid edifice with fronts on three streets, 600 fighters barricaded themselves, most of them printers. The army began to bombard the building, as a result of which the defenders withdrew and exited through the courtyard of a neighboring building. Despite this, the artillery kept firing, and soon the soldiers set fire to the building and prevented the fire company from saving it. The residents, however, as verified by a correspondent of *Russkoye Slovo* [Russian Word],‡ were saved, thanks to the fighters. The telegraph agency reported that the fighters set the house on fire and that because of them, many families living in that house lost their lives. This is how opinion is molded to the intentions of the criminals in power!

Of the heroism of the combatants, of the heroic acts of men, women, and children alike, they speak wonders.

A correspondent for *Molva* [Opinion]§ gave the number of victims, up to December 28, at 200 dead and 1,800 wounded.

And now, after twelve days of terrible fighting, "order is restored." The first outburst of armed revolution has been stopped, and the tsarist army, having received enormous reinforcements, will suppress it totally. The fight was uneven: on one side, a handful of poorly armed revolutionaries, ill-prepared, by all accounts, for armed clashes; and on the other, tsarism, all the power of tsarism, possessed of incredible strength. Yet who was the true victor? Was it tsarism, which flooded Moscow with blood, or the revolutionaries, who left hundreds of bodies on the battlefield? Tsarism overcame a handful of armed militants, yet suppression of spilled blood in Moscow does not strengthen or perform ablutions for the might of tsarism. Most of all, the government triumphed not by the aid of the army but by that of the artillery, for it feared contact between the army and the people. Soldiers exposed to the holy fervor of the combatants, to the limitless heroism of workers—men, women, and even children—could have hesitated and passed over to the people's side. The government preferred to lock them in their barracks and take away their weapons. Only by combining

---

* Sytin's printing house, founded by Ivan Dmitrievich Sytin, was the largest publisher in Russia prior to World War I. It was renowned for publishing works by such figures as Pushkin, Gogol, and Tolstoy in inexpensive editions affordable to the poorest Russians. The attack on the printing house reflected the regime's effort to deny workers and peasants access to basic literacy and knowledge.

† The government-controlled telegraph agency was at the time a major vehicle for transmitting information in the Russian Empire.

‡ *Russkoye Slovo* was originally a conservative newspaper that was taken over by Sytin and became one of the most popular publications in the empire. It should not be confused with the earlier publication of the same name, issued between 1859 and 1866. In 1918 it existed under different names—including *Novoye Slovo* and *Nasha Slova*. The paper was banned in July 1918.

§ *Molva* was a daily newspaper, published in St. Petersburg between December 1905 and January 1906.

volunteers from various units with wild beasts did it form an "army" to oppose the revolution. This was yet another reason that instead of sending soldiers to fight at close quarters, where, in view of the people, soldiers could be chipped away by the hand of the people and won over by their voice, the government preferred the distance of cannon fire, blasting away homes for no reason and murdering innocents on the streets and even in their own apartments. This savagery, in combination with the wild cruelty of drunken dragoons and Cossacks, has revolutionized even sectors of the populace who had remained passive and reactionary up to now. Witnesses attest that even vicious brutes renowned for violence against students and revolutionaries became ardent revolutionaries. The tsar lost Moscow once and for all, as it lost Petersburg* nearly a year ago.

Moscow proved that armed revolutionary struggle is possible, and the army unstable. This time, the army could be locked in its barracks, but that will be possible to repeat only so many times. All the people of Russia will hear of the heroism of revolutionary Moscow, and the echo of its struggle will ignite new flames of struggle everywhere, but this echo will also reach the troops, and then the wild mercenaries making up the army will not be divided but united.

A movement began in January that ended, after several months, in the capitulation of autocracy; a movement began in December that can only end in the overthrow of monarchy as a whole.

The tsar was victorious, for he sapped the blood of the rebellious of Moscow; the tsar was beaten, for from every drop of this blood arises a fresh avenger of crimes against the people.

---

* Known as St. Petersburg at the time; Luxemburg almost always refers to the city as Petersburg.

What Do We Want? A Commentary on the Program of the Social Democracy of the Kingdom of Poland and Lithuania*

I.

The Social Democracy of the Kingdom of Poland and Lithuania, united with Social Democracy in other capitalist lands, aspires to bring about a socialist system.† That is, Social Democracy aspires to abolish the exploitation of the working class by the owners of land, factories, workshops, and mines, and to hand over all these means of production to the collective ownership of the working people.

From the very beginning of manufacturing industry, which developed in England and France in the late eighteenth and early nineteenth centuries, and in Germany in the 1830s and 1840s, exploitation and deprivation have driven

---

* This was first published as a pamphlet by the Social Democracy of the Kingdom and Poland and Lithuania (Socjaldemokracja Królestwa Polskiego i Litwy [SDKPiL]), in January 1906 under the title *Czego chcemy? Komentarz do Programu Socjaldemokracji Królestwa Polskiego i Litwy*. It is translated by Joseph Muller from the Polish original, which was written shortly after Luxemburg arrived in Russian-occupied Poland to take part in the ongoing revolution. Its main aim is to present a series of minimum demands that could guide the revolutionary struggle.

† The SDKPiL, founded in 1900, emerged from the Social Democracy of the Kingdom of Poland (Socjaldemokracja Królestwa Polskiego), or SDK, founded in Zurich in 1893 by Leo Jogiches, Rosa Luxemburg, Julian Marchlewski, and Adolf Warski. From the start, the SDKPiL orientated itself against the program for the re-establishment of Poland (denounced by Luxemburg as "social-patriotism"), as espoused by the Polish Socialist Party (Polska Partia Socjalistyczna, or PPS). The PPS was founded as a socialist party in Paris in 1892, and the Kingdom of Poland became its predominant sphere of activity. After 1896, most of the SDK's structures that had been built up in the Kingdom of Poland were crushed by the tsarist police, such that the party de facto ceased to exist there. Around the turn of the century, a new beginning was undertaken with the SDKPiL, which succeeded in building new structures in Vilnius and, above all, in the textile workers' city of Białystok. In 1900, a de facto inner-party disempowerment of the group of exiles based around Jogiches and Luxemburg occurred, which was not reversed until 1903, when they assumed direct control of the party after sidelining Cezaryna Wojnarowska. Until the outbreak of the 1905 Revolution, the party had between 1,000 and 2,000 members. The revolution rapidly turned it into a mass party, particularly in the workers' centers of Warsaw, Łódź, Żyrardów, Częstochowa, and Białystok. SDKPiL membership rose to 30,000 in 1906 and 40,000 in 1907. After the revolution, the number of members dropped substantially. From 1911 to 1916, the party was crippled by intense inner-party conflicts. An official reconciliation between the quarreling factions was not achieved until November 1916. In December 1918, the party joined with the PPS Left to form the Communist Workers' Party of Poland (KPRP). The SDKPiL had joined the Russian Social Democratic Labor Party (RSDRP) in 1903 with the aim of forging relations between the Polish and the Russian Social Democratic movement. Conflicting positions on the right of nations to self-determination caused it to leave the RSDRP soon after. In 1906, the SDKPiL rejoined the RSDRP, but retained its organizational and ideological autonomy. The final break between the RSDRP and SDKPiL occurred in 1912.

workers to engage in struggle. In the early days of the movement, English workers wrecked factories and destroyed machinery, seeing them as the culprits of their misery. In France, in 1831, weavers in Lyon organized hunger riots, and in 1844 cottage industry weavers in the German and Czech parts of Silesia rose up too, driven to extremes by their exploitation at the hands of industry bosses. All these movements were quickly suppressed by the brutal violence of the ruling bourgeoisie. Yet these were only the first free manifestations of the suffering and defiance of the working masses. At that time, the rebelling workers did not yet understand where the source of their deprivation lay or where to look for changes for the better.

Only then did a certain idea dawn on several brilliant thinkers of the time: the idea that the only foundational remedy for the suffering of millions of workers was to do away with the private ownership of the instruments of labor and establish a socialist system. These thinkers were Robert Owen in England and Charles Fourier and [Henri de] Saint-Simon in France. The glaring contradictions between the idleness and luxury of small handfuls of rich men and the terrible destitution of the entire mass of working people, between the moral corruption spread by capitalism in moneyed circles and the intellectual debasement of the working classes, collectively filled them with disgust at the reigning social order and begged for resolution through a complete transformation of the system. All three arrived, albeit by different paths, at the conviction that the current system was blatantly based on doing injustice and harm to the working majority. The three of them also met at the crossroads of the issue of whether the source of workers' adversity was the private property of the capitalists and landowners, and whether hope for the suffering people rested, in fact, on a socialist system.

However, at the beginning of the nineteenth century, not one of these brilliant defenders of the working class was in a position to show the way to realize the socialist ideal. They turned to the most aristocratic elements of the bourgeoisie, searching out wealthy philanthropists—benefactors—in hopes they would lead great social reforms out of pity for the wretchedness of the people. But they had no luck finding such benefactors, and even if they had found them, such individual efforts would certainly have been in vain. Neither did the thought occur to any of these brilliant men that this destitute, humiliated, ignorant mass of workers would alone be appointed and would in time be ready for the task of reforming all of society. For these reasons, the great ideas of Owen, Saint-Simon, and Fourier remained aristocratic dreams—utopias—and that is why they are called *utopian socialists*.

It was not until Karl Marx and Friedrich Engels that socialist aspiration was placed on a new, strong foundation. Marx and Engels explained that the working people cannot be helped by any kind of philanthropy from bourgeois benefactors, and that *the liberation of the working class should be the doing of* *the working class itself.* This idea was conveyed to workers in every country by the *Communist Manifesto*, published in 1847, and was then further developed by Marx and Engels as well as by Ferdinand Lassalle.* Through many years of scholarly study, they found that establishing a socialist system was not only a beautiful idea and a requirement of justice but in fact a *historical necessity.*

The development of mechanized production, of great industry, had plunged ever-greater numbers of people in every country into poverty and complete dependence on capitalists. The wages of the vast majority of workers barely safeguarded them against starvation and often did not even allow them to support their families. Workers' wives and underage children were likewise forced to submit to the yoke of the capitalist. Workers' family lives were thus ruined, and their health was weakened from a young age by hard labor. Industrial crises, regularly occurring with each new cycle and triggering periods of industrial stagnation in which goods lacked a market, deprived still thousands more diligent workers of their occupation and livelihood, adding terrible uncertainty about what tomorrow might bring to the anguish the working populace already had.

Yet, on the other hand, this same development of large industry concentrated and grew the working class, day by day, into an army of people dissatisfied with the existing order of things. Competition with factories and large private holdings brought ruin to small artisans and farmers working small patches of land. On losing possession of their workshops and farm plots, these artisans and peasants flowed in ever-greater numbers to cities and industrial settlements. As a result, the proletarian masses became concentrated more and more in the industrial centers, having been deprived of all their property, and there they became convinced that they were unquestionably a majority in society, they recognized the exploitation of which they were the victims, and they saw that great power lay in connection and unity.

Meanwhile, property became ever more concentrated in the hands of the exploiters, while the amount belonging to the people shrank. As a result of industrial competition, dozens of small and medium workshops and factories were supplanted by just a few giant factories, with thousands of workers and production in the millions. Many private industries were replaced by joint-stock companies, in which each capitalist merely owned stocks, shares apportioned according to the amount of capital he had invested in the enterprise. In such a system, production took place completely without the participation of the capitalists, under the management of a paid director, yet the profits from the work of armies of laborers flowed into the pockets of the capitalists, not to any of their credit, but only because they owned the machines, the land, and the buildings. It

---

* Praise for the contributions of Lassalle, who formed the first independent workers' party in Germany, and whose accolades neared those allotted to Marx, was a common refrain among the Marxists of the Second International, including Luxemburg.

became clearer and clearer to everyone that capitalists were merely unnecessary parasites on production.

The course of industrialization presented to workers a clearer and clearer picture of the origin of all the wealth of the bourgeoisie and all the workers' own misery—namely, the fact that the means of production were held in private capitalist hands, allowing them to take advantage of workers who had nothing to sell but their own labor [power]. The prospect of taking back the factories, land, and mines from these private exploiters and handing them over for collective use by the whole working populace seemed more and more possible, as a smaller and smaller number of owners wielded larger and larger shares of control over production.

While the number of capitalists rose, the number of workers rose at an incomparably faster rate, making them the largest of society's classes.

Meanwhile, it became more and more obvious that further development of the capitalist economy, propagating crises, prostitution, militarism, and uncertain existence and widespread poverty among the masses, would by then have led to the utter corporeal and spiritual degeneration of the people, if the resistance of the proletariat had not already stayed their hand. Human society would certainly have fallen into total savagery through the continued unchecked rule of capitalism. For this reason, abolishing the capitalist system had become as urgently needed for social progress as the overthrowing of serfdom was in its time.

To bring about a revolution, one thing was needed: that the working class *understood* that abolishing capitalism was its duty, and that it joined the struggle as an organized body with unity of purpose. Such understanding and organizing have made and will make forward progress, as the capitalist economy develops and capitalist states form relations with one another.

The development of industry has now subsumed into its control all the countries of Europe, North America, and Australia, and has also invaded Asia and even the heart of Africa. It has spread poverty and unhappiness among the working class around the world, among every nationality. Capitalism is an international plague upon humanity. This is yet another reason that workers of all countries must work together, equally, against exploitation. Capitalist rule and private property cannot be abolished in one land independently of the others. Workers in all countries where the smoke rises from factory chimneys, where poverty beds down in workers' houses, must come together all at once in joint struggle if they are to realize the socialist revolution. Karl Marx and Friedrich Engels ended their *Communist Manifesto* of 1847 with this cry: "Proletarians of all countries, unite!" This is the idea that makes Social Democracy an international party. It strives to unite workers of all nationalities and countries into one army fighting for a better future for humanity.

The system of socialism will truly liberate humanity—it will end inequality between people, the exploitation of some people by others, the control of some people by others, the oppression of conquered nations by imperialist nations, the impairment of women by the rule of the male sex, and the persecution of faith, religion, or conviction. It is not necessary to lay out in full detail how the future socialist system will look, and every attempt of this kind is rooted in fantasy. Yet we may already be entirely certain in recognizing in full clarity the *main foundation* of the future system. We know it will depend on giving ownership of all means of production to society, and further, [require] that each individual producer will not be left to his own means, but instead that society as a whole will manage production along with its elected bodies. This knowledge suffices for us to conclude that the future system will know neither want, nor luxury for the lazy, nor crises, nor uncertainty about tomorrow. When the sale of workers' labor to private exploiters is abolished, the source of all today's social inequalities will disappear.

Socialism will thus realize the very social conditions for which humanity has pined for a thousand years. From time immemorial, long before Fourier, Owen, and the other socialist utopians, who appeared when capitalist production began, the socialist ideal shone through the history of human society in nascent forms. Two thousand years ago, the early Christianity of the first apostles was imbued with rhetoric about shared property and the need to equalize the fates of rich and poor. In the sixteenth century, when the bloody "German Peasants' War" was playing out—that is, when peasant serfs who refused to submit to their yoke rose up to fight—one of their main leaders, the noble Thomas Müntzer, preached a gospel of shared property.*

But this ideal could not be realized at the time; its realization would only become possible with the development of large mechanized industry. Only capitalism has made labor so efficient that, with the current production technologies, if all the adult members of society worked for just six hours a day, that would be enough to create the conditions for a life of plenty for all.† And only capitalism has created a social class that is able to achieve a great revolution—namely, today's industrial and agricultural proletariat. The hapless, desperate slaves of ancient Greece and Rome only managed to launch a few fruitless uprisings, only to die from the torment to which their vengeful masters subjected them. Medieval serfs could do nothing but rebel spontaneously and set fire to their lords' manor houses, after which they had to return, violently suppressed,

---

* The 1524–25 peasants' revolt that swept German-speaking areas of Central Europe was the largest mass insurrection in Europe until the French Revolution of 1789. Among its demands were the abolition of serfdom, restoration of communal lands, and restrictions on excessive rent and taxation. It was violently crushed.

† Just a decade before the Peasants' War in Germany, Thomas More's *Utopia* (1516) presented a vision of a society of plenty in which everyone works no more than six hours a day. Its "utopian" character lay not in its content but its inability to be actualized given the historical conditions of the time. See Thomas More, *Utopia*, introduction by China Miéville and supplement by Ursula K. Le Guin (London and New York: Verso, 2016).

to their old yokes. The modern working class is the first exploited and oppressed class in the history of humanity that is capable of freeing itself and all of humanity from the atrocity of one group of people controlling another. We are accustomed to counting the birth of Christ as the beginning of a new era in the history of humanity. Yet Christianity has done absolutely nothing to reduce the suffering of the exploited masses. A truly new era for humanity will dawn only with the socialist revolution.

It is true that, even today, self-styled reasonable people see socialism as a pipe dream, a prank played by a sick imagination. But every era has people who cannot see farther into the future than their own nose and fear everything new. When it was announced in Germany that the medieval guild laws would be abolished, all the little master craftsmen declared that abolishing the guilds would surely unmoor the world from its foundations.* And at the beginning of the nineteenth century in Bavaria, when railroads were to be built, the city council of one of the cities in Bavaria decided that travel by rail was detrimental to people's bodily and mental health and safety, so installing railroads was unthinkable. But history and progress always strode calmly forward, ignoring the ungenerous warnings and anxieties of people trembling for fear of losing their privileges.

Today, a socialist revolution is an ever more luminous goal toward which social progress advances with inexorable strength. Hastening the arrival of this moment is the task solely of the working class—it requires that the working class of all countries develop the keenest possible consciousness of in what way, and by what roads, the task can be accomplished.

II.

The proletarian class is obligated to abolish the capitalist system, or, in other words, to take factories and land back from the capitalist and landowning classes. But this task is not so easy to achieve. Clearly, if the workers of a given factory attempted to "take back" the manufacturer's property, the workers would simply be arrested by the police. They would be brought before a court, and in the end, they would be thrown into prison for violating someone else's property. Even if a larger crowd of workers in a given city arranged en masse to take back the possessions of local factory owners, the army would rush to the aid of the endangered capitalists, using bayonets and bullets to explain to workers that the property of capitalists is sacred and inviolable.

---

* Two kinds of guilds predominated during the European Middle Ages: merchant guilds, which protected the interests of traders, and craft guilds, which protected the interests of craftsmen in a given occupation or industry. These social organizations sought to regulate and control the local economies. Craft guilds began a slow decline beginning in the sixteenth century with the expansion of market economies and the separation of laborers from control over the production process; they were not formally abolished in Germany until 1860.

These scenarios show that the property of the capitalists and means of exploitation are closely guarded by the enemies of the working class—the army, the police, and the courts. But that is not all. The laws and the courts are used to condemn workers for every attempt on capitalists' property and [the former] are written by people who guard over the interests of capitalists. The taxes that provide the means of maintaining the army, the police, the courts, and the prisons are organized such that nearly all the burden for them falls on the working population, while the capitalist class escapes nearly tax free. Schools and education in general, paid for out of government coffers, serve mainly to educate the youth of affluent townspeople, while working people have almost no access to learning, and their ignorance keeps them in passive obedience to capitalists. Even in the church, supported by a tax on the working population, priests instill workers with humble submission to the exploitation of capitalists, respect for capitalists' property, and acceptance of their poverty and subjection.

In this way, all the institutions of the state—the army, the central government, the legislature, the judiciary, the taxation system, the schools, and the church—are at the service of the capitalist class as instruments for the antagonism of the working class. The entire authority of the state is an instrument of capitalist exploitation. The capitalists not only possess the instruments of production, they also hold the power of the state in the palm of their hand. So, each capitalist reigns economically over his own workers in his own factory, and the entire class of capitalists reigns politically over the entire working population in the land.

Therefore, workers cannot take back from capitalists the tools with which they labor unless they first take back political authority: the army, the legislature, and the central government. As long as all these means of exerting power over the population and doing it violence remain in the hands of the capitalists, private property and exploitation have good watchmen, and workers cannot dream of abolishing them. The first precondition for nationalizing the tools of production is therefore that the working class seize, with its own hands, all the state's power: the government, the legislature, the army, and the taxation machine.

There is one other reason that overpowering the government is necessary for a socialist revolution. Today, every owner of private capital manages production in his own factory, and every landowner oversees his estate according to his own whims. A socialist economy must consist in joining all private estates into one and organizing production completely differently, namely for all of society according to one common plan. Similarly, the current judiciary, education system, and army—all adapted so that one social class may rule over another—will be completely unsuited to socialist society and must be remade from the ground up. Great common reforms of this kind can only be carried out by a single central authority that has the power and appropriate means to issue orders. Those who enjoy the privileges of exploitation and oppression will violently resist attempts to remove those privileges. To realize a socialist revolution, the working class must have in hand the means to compel the stubborn to obedience, to make needed changes in methods of production and distribution, and to reform state institutions from the ground up. In a word, a necessary precursor to the realization of socialism is the unilateral control of the working class throughout the state for some time—what is called the dictatorship of the working class.

For this reason, the struggle to free the proletariat from the yoke of capitalism must be, first and foremost, a *political struggle*, a struggle against the entire bourgeoisie, as a class, over the governing of the state.

The bourgeoisie that now controls the countries of Western Europe came to power no differently. Before the development of industry, from the Middle Ages to the end of the eighteenth century, the bourgeoisie was nothing to the state, and the feudal nobility, which was based on exploiting peasants through serfdom, was everything. Merchants, capitalists, entrepreneurs, and wealthy craftsmen, since they did not belong to the nobility, had as little influence on government, legislation, and finance as peasants and workers had. Artisans and merchants could do nothing but bear the burden of taxation as the nobility plundered them, giving them nothing in return but contempt and humiliation. This state of things lasted until the bourgeoisie grew enough in size and strength that it felt it had the power to throw off the yoke of aristocratic government. At that point, a series of revolutions occurred in the main countries of Western Europe. In the Great French Revolution that broke out in 1789, the bourgeoisie took the Parisian people along with it and, relying on proletarian brawn, drove the nobility out of its position in government and overturned all the medieval privileges of family crests and noble blood. The revolutionary struggle lasted many long years, until the time that complete control could be had through heaps of money, and the bourgeois rule began that lasts to this day. The same order of events occurred in Germany and Austria in 1848.*

In those times, the capitalist class had none of its disgust for revolution, spilled blood, or violence. They were desperate to keep power, and death atop the barricades was the price of revolution, paid in the end by the working populace in the service of the bourgeoisie. Today, it is time for the working class to reach for power.

When the bourgeoisie seized political power from the hands of the medieval nobility, the result for the people was simply new forms of exploitation and oppression. The whip of serfdom was replaced by the lash of hunger for every "unemployed hand," and bondage under the reins of the nobility gave way to the inferno of factory labor. The working class aspires to political power, not to beget a new form of domination and oppression, but to abolish, once and for

---

* That is, during the revolutions of that year that swept through Western and Central Europe.

all, every oppression and domination. To realize socialism, the proletariat must seize state power and wield it resolutely to eradicate the current social order. But the dictatorship of the proletariat will be the last time force is used in all human history, and the first time force is used for the benefit of the vast masses of the disinherited.

In its current state, the working class is not yet ready to accomplish the great tasks that await it. The working class of all capitalist countries must first internalize the aspiration to socialism; an enormous number of people have yet to arrive at an awareness of their class interests.

To win political power, the proletariat must build strength through daily, unflagging struggle against capitalist oppression and bourgeois rule. Struggle on the factory floor is essential for raising, even temporarily, the working populace from the depths of destitution to which oppression drives them. Struggle in the political realm serves to defend the interests of the proletariat and gradually win influence over legislation as well as the politics of the state as a whole. Workers who are scattered, acting alone and in loose groups, cannot wage struggles that improve their own livelihoods, nor can they move to take power from the state. To achieve such goals, they must organize themselves into a *political party*. And one such party is *Social Democracy*. Social Democracy defends the material and spiritual interests of the working people at every step, gathers them into one fighting army, raises socialist awareness among the masses, and attempts to exert influence on the institutions of state. When Social Democracy has a majority of the working people behind it in all the largest capitalist countries, the final hour of capitalism will have struck.

III.

Socialism is an international aspiration. It connects workers from France and Poland, Germany and Spain, Russia and England, Italy and America in one great human throng, showing them their common goal: to abolish capitalism. The international nature of the workers' cause is voiced today in every great strike, in every electoral struggle, and through the mutual brotherly aid shown by workers' organizations in many lands and regions of the world.

But, in their daily struggle, workers in various states cannot form a single common political party; they must organize themselves separately in each state. The working class in each land must use political struggle to defend its interests there, attempting to gradually adapt the existing establishments of the state to its needs. Yet, in every current state, the political institutions and conditions differ. Switzerland has a democratic republic in which the adult male population votes not only for envoys to the parliament but also for ministers—that is, members of government—in a general election. In Germany, the parliament is founded on common electoral rights, but the constitution allows the monarchy to exert considerable influence on government and legislation. In Austria and Belgium, there are still no universal, equal voting rights in parliamentary elections, and thus legislation is the privilege of the nobility and the wealthy townspeople. The bourgeoisie of each state rules first and foremost through the aid of its *particular* government, its particular parliament, and its particular army. Accounting for the differences in state institutions, the working class wages a different fight in every state with *that* government and bourgeoisie, attempting to exert influence on the institutions of *that* state.

The proletariat of the Kingdom of Poland and Lithuania is a part of the proletariat of the Russian state. For decades, Polish and Russian workers have shared the yoke of despotism side by side. The tsarist government has crushed the spirit and material livelihood of both peoples, Polish and Russian. In the despotic system, which has lasted to the present day, subjects have been sorted not by their nationality but primarily by the social class to which they belong. The Polish exploiter class found the same refuge and defense for its interests under the wings of this system as the Russian exploiter class, and Russian workers felt the sting of the lash no less cruelly than Polish workers. It is true that in addition to political oppression, the Polish workers endured oppression for their nationality and persecution for speaking Polish. Yet, for hundreds of years, the tsarist government has oppressed other groups no less cruelly than Poles, violating the freedom of belief of some of its own Russian subjects, such as Duokhobors and other sectarians.*

This commonality of class injustice and oppression has created a commonality of interests for the working class of all nationalities within the Russian state. The Polish proletariat and the Russian proletariat have an equal need to overthrow the tsar and win political freedom. In political struggle, therefore, Polish workers make up one whole with Russian workers, one political class with a single political program.

The Polish people are admittedly in a different position within the Russian state, as Poles find themselves governed by a different nation. But the Polish proletariat would not cease to be an exploited and oppressed class if it had its own national government, any more than the Russian proletariat ceases to be exploited and oppressed by its own, Russian government, or indeed than the working Polish people in Galicia cease to be exploited and oppressed by an autonomous government made up of its own, Polish nobility. If French, English, or German workers have substantially better political conditions than Polish workers, it is by no means because they live under their own national governments, rather than under the rule of foreign governments, but because social development and progress long ago removed the absolutist governments of

---

* The Duokhobors, originally composed of peasants from southern Russia, form a Christian sect that abhors materialism and the incessant pursuit of material wealth and advocates pacifism. It opposed both tsarism and the policies of the Orthodox Church.

France, England, and Germany, and so workers there enjoy *political freedoms* that have yet to be won in Russia. The ruling bourgeoisie and nobility make no distinction for the purposes of exploitation between laborers who are their countrymen and laborers who are foreign. Capitalists do not recognize workers' nationalities; they examine each worker solely as the unit of labor from which they can squeeze a profit. And the governments of today's states, which are the instruments of the ruling bourgeoisie, see the working class, undifferentiated by nationality, only as material to send to war, scrape for taxes, and exploit with capital. For while the capitalist system exists, the nation-state cannot be the salvation of the proletariat. Indeed, if the Polish proletariat were not currently subordinated to the Russian government and lived in an independent Poland, the Polish state would represent the same capitalist hell that every other current state is for its working class.

That is why rebuilding the Polish state cannot be the objective of the Polish proletariat. The working class must strive not to build new bourgeois states and governments but to *raze them to the ground*, beginning by broadening political freedoms where possible in the countries where workers live. That is why the workers' cause demands not that Poland be torn away from Russia and an independent state be built, but that absolutism be abolished and political freedoms be won for the Polish and Russian working populations.

Restoring Poland is today a dream, by itself. Independent Poland was a state for the nobility. Before it was partitioned by Russia, Prussia, and Austria, Poland had not shown the first signs of modern capitalist production.* Moreover, in the Kingdom of Poland, when industry began to rise, and a class of capitalists rose with it, they were, from the very beginning, enemies to national uprisings and attempts at independence. In Russia, the Polish bourgeoisie found a profitable market for the sale of its goods, and in the tsarist government, a sturdy ally and guardian against the Polish working class. Similarly, today, the Polish gentry, having long ago abandoned every thought of a rebellion, benefits from domestic industrial development and from the care the Russian government provides to the exploiter classes. Today, the Polish bourgeoisie and gentry are mainstays of Russian rule, and there is no class in Polish society that would dream of independence for Poland, except perhaps a handful of powerless intellectuals from the petty bourgeoisie.†

Once the revolution broke out in Russia and in Poland, those who had earlier deluded workers with dreams about rebuilding Poland dared not utter a word about a national uprising. Forced to hide their patriotism, they revealed

---

* The first partition of Poland occurred in 1772; the third and last, which eliminated it as an independent state, was in 1795.

† This was hardly the case, as seen from the fact that the PPS, which supported independence for Poland, had at least as strong roots among the working class and petty bourgeoisie at the time as did the SDKPiL.

their bankruptcy. Neither the Polish nobility, bourgeoisie, nor petty bourgeoisie set out to rebuild Poland; in fact, from the very beginning, they helped the tsarists suppress the revolutionary Polish proletariat.

If the nobility long ago abandoned their desire to rebuild Poland, and the Polish bourgeoisie never had the desire, then the Polish proletariat has even less ability to achieve such a task. To win independence for Poland, the Polish working class would have to overcome not only the opposition of three imperialist superpowers, but the vast economic power of the Polish bourgeoisie, which grew out of the same soil as Russia and has become intertwined with Russia. In other words, to rebuild Poland, the working class would have to first win political control in our own land. Yet, the moment the working class takes political power, its task will be not to rebuild a Polish state but to set up a socialist system that ensures Poles, as it ensures people of all nationalities, complete freedom and equality in the circle of nations. The national oppression that the Polish populace has endured from the tsarist government cannot be a trivial matter for the working class. With its aspiration to remove all forms of oppression and hegemony, the working class must aim equally to end the oppression of nations. But this objective is not a separate national objective of the Polish proletariat. Depriving Poles of their national identity was always just one of the violations and injuries perpetrated by a despotic government that was a mortal enemy of the Russian working class no less than of the Polish working class. The conscious Russian proletariat must also strive after its own interest, together with the Polish, to abolish every instance of national oppression within the Russian state. For this reason, the struggle for freedom of national culture is not a separate objective of Polish workers but a joint class objective for Polish and Russian proletarians.

The following are the *most important* demands issued by SDKPiL.

1. *The declaration of a republic throughout the state of Russia*

For three-quarters of a century, absolutism has ruled over our land, as over all of Russia—the absolutism of the despotic tsarist government. Under this order, a single despot sitting on the throne, though half-mad, made his lawlessness the law of the land for 130 million people. Helped by his officials and his Cossacks' whips, the autocrat ruled over the possessions, freedom, and lives of the populace. He and his advisors willfully squandered taxes pilfered from the people, arbitrarily spending them on the army, bureaucrats, and priests. He willfully plunged the state into a criminal war in which hundreds of thousands of people, the flower of the male population, lost their lives in vain.* For centuries, the

---

* That is, in the Russo-Japanese War of 1904–1905.

people were entirely deprived of every political right and freedom, captives of the tsarist system.

The last of such systems, in what are now civilized countries, disappeared sixty years ago. Imperial and royal governments everywhere have been curtailed by constitutions voicing the political rights of the people. Under a real constitution, laws originate not from the monarch and his ministers but from the *parliament*—that is, the assembly of representatives chosen by the population. Furthermore, at the very least, a true constitution guarantees the population freedom of speech, of the press, and of assembly, and limits the free rein of the government too.

This political system is called constitutional monarchy; it exists currently in Germany, England, Italy, the Netherlands, Japan, and in a majority of other civilized countries.

But the most beneficial system of government for the working class is a republic, which is a system in which there is no emperor or king, and at the head stands a president, an ordinary paid official appointed for a few years. Even under a constitution, imperial or monarchical power is always the enemy of the working class. Constitutional monarchs usually have great political privileges: to approve laws passed by parliament; to be the supreme leader of the army; to appoint ministers and officials at will, as in Germany; and to saddle the country with wars on a whim. And ruling monarchs always use their powers for the good of the bourgeoisie and nobility and to the detriment of the working populace. To cap it all, these imperial and royal governments, on top of their other harm to the working class, indulge in costly excess: The people of every land must sacrifice hard-won millions, the price of their bloody labor, to prop up the monarch's estates and the packs of sponges who swarm them (the bitterest enemies of the people). That is why conscious Social Democratic workers in every land demand that royal and imperial powers be done away with and republics set up. Admittedly, working people will still be exploited and oppressed in republics. For as long as hired labor and capitalism exist, the bourgeoisie—the exploiter class—will remain in power and do its best to weigh down the proletariat. In France, where power is in the hands of a republic, workers still endure terrible poverty, and the French bourgeoisie sometimes even uses the army against striking workers to suppress their resistance. This also happens in the United States of America, as well as in Switzerland, where there is also a republican system. But in these countries, thanks to the republican system, workers are free to mount political struggle against the rule of the bourgeoisie, to denounce the bourgeoisie's behavior loudly and openly, and to organize and educate freely, without any obstacles. Because, in a republic, both the president and the ministers—that is, the whole government—are dependent on popular elections, so conscious workers have their greatest chance of exerting influence on the state's existing establishment.

The demand for a republic is shared by the working people of Poland and Russia. The working populace of Poland cannot singlehandedly achieve even the smallest freedom if there is no freedom for the whole state. The republican system cannot be established or maintained in our land unless all Russia is governed by it. That is why the common good of millions of working people both in Poland and in Russia demands that a republican form of government become law across the whole state.

2. Equal rights for all nationalities living within the Russian state, providing them the freedom to develop their culture, establish national schools, and use their mother tongue; and regional self-government—that is, autonomy for Poland

One of the oldest means of control used by the despotic governments of the Russian state was to systematically provoke hatred and conflict between the various nations under tsarist rule. By means of various special laws put into place by various bureaucrat lackeys and hacks, this government tormented every foreign nation: Poles, Lithuanians, Jews, Finns, and Ruthenians. The spiritual life and culture of nations subject to the tsar—their language, literature, and art—were condemned to extinction by means of an elaborate framework of unusual statutes. With the goal of sowing national hatred, the tsarist government even used the police to incite looting and massacres, instigating the dregs of society against Jews in Poland, Lithuania, and southern Russia, and against Armenians in the Caucasus.* By inciting fratricidal war between its subject people groups, this government-of-the-scourge attempted to turn the attention and hatred of the persecuted populace away from itself, so as to reign over the peoples of all nations with greater ease.

Social Democracy regards the current rule of some nations over others as a result of the capitalist order, just like the rule of one class over another or the exploitation of some people by others. The rule of some nations over others can only be completely and universally rooted out by uprooting capitalism and establishing a socialist system based on solidarity between all people and nations, and not on conflict and inequality between them. Within the limits of the bourgeois system, Social Democracy is already putting up a vigorous fight against national oppression. The only effective way to fight national oppression in Russia today is to remove every last vestige of the despotic government and to establish a republic with institutions that ensure every spirit a free existence and every national culture the chance to flourish. This means, first of all, removing every existing special law issued to the disadvantage of this or that nationality. Then, every nation living in the state of Russia must be provided

---

* Massacres against Armenians occurred in the Caucasian region of southern Russia, especially in Baku, Elisabethpol, Nakhichevan, and Shusha, in 1905 and 1906. It is estimated that as many as 30,000 Armenians were killed.

the opportunity to use their own language in public and private life as well as teach their youth in their language. And finally, every citizen, regardless of nationality, must be granted equal access to all professions, offices, and social statuses.

Our land constitutes a separate whole within the state of Russia, with a different cultural life, and a partly separate economic and social life, from the rest of the state. For this reason, the SDKPiL demands, in addition to general equal civil rights for people of all nationalities, *regional self-government, including autonomy for Poland*. That is, the party demands that matters of special concern in our country be handled by the population of our country, through the work of our own officials and a separate national legislature chosen by the entire adult population of our land by means of universal, equal, confidential, and direct elections. Furthermore, it demands that Polish schools, courts, and other essential institutions be introduced and that their operations be made subject to the oversight of the legislature.

Regional self-government is as essential for guaranteeing adequate freedom to develop our national culture as it is for effectively defending the class interests of the Polish proletariat. Constituting, despite differences of nationality, merely a component of the single working class of the Russian state, the Polish proletariat must above all demand common political rights and republican freedoms with Russian workers throughout the state, so that they can use them collectively in tireless class struggle against the exploitation and control of the joint bourgeoisie of Poland and Russia. On the other hand, in Polish workers' daily economic struggles, the matters that affect them directly, such as schools, courts, governmental authorities, hospitals, and the local economy (locally necessary taxes and expenditures), the Polish proletariat faces now and will face in the future, at every step, local actors from within its own native bourgeoisie, nobility, and townspeople. That is why Polish workers must have the rights and freedoms needed to defend, now and in the future, both their class interests, in unison with the interests of all the peoples of Russia, and their local progress in the struggle against their own bourgeoisie in Poland.

3. Electoral laws providing for universal, equal, direct, and confidential elections

In a republic, as in a constitutional monarchy, laws are created by a *parliament*, which is an assembly of representatives, chosen by the population, called *members of parliament*. The parliament determines the taxes and tariffs that are to be collected. Without the approval of the parliament, the government is forbidden from spending so much as a penny from the public coffers. The parliament determines the salaries of ministers as well as high- and low-level officials. The parliament decides how many recruits are to be taken into the military and how many soldiers are to be kept in permanent service in the army and in the navy. The parliament issues all laws to which the people are subject. Finally, the parliament has the right to hold to account ministers who overstep the laws and wishes of the parliament. In a constitutional monarchy, all these decisions belong not just to parliament but also to the monarch—a king, emperor, or prince—without whose approval the determinations of parliament lack the force of law. In a republic, the parliament—that is, a body of representatives chosen by the people—has much greater significance and power. But, as in a constitutional monarchy, a republic's legislative powers, without which no laws can be made, lie in the parliament.

In view of this, it is extraordinarily important for the working class, and for every other social stratum, to possess as large an influence in parliament, and as many of its own representatives, as possible. The way to gain such influence is through parliamentary elections! That is why *electoral rights* are the foundation of all political freedoms.

Social Democracy demands that access to the parliamentary elections for the entire state, as well as for the regional congress [Sejm], be *universal*, meaning that everyone from the age of twenty-one has the right to vote in the elections. Every adult carries the burden of the state: For even the very poor, there are taxes in the price of every item bought or consumed. Every healthy man must serve in the army and, if needed, sacrifice his blood and his life to the state. That is why every adult, rich or poor, should have the right to cast his vote in the elections to the parliament and the regional congress, thereby exerting influence on the order of state power. There should be no duties without rights, just as there should be no rights without duties. Because all people have duties to the state, they should also have rights in the state, and most of all the most important right—the right to vote for parliament and regional congress.

This right is owed most of all to the working class, which holds up all of society through its labor, and on whose shoulders the whole state apparatus rests. And the right to vote should not exclude *women*. The vast majority of women of common social standing work equally as hard as men and carry great social burdens. Women are the mothers and teachers of the younger generations of society. They should have the same right as men to cast a vote when it concerns the fate and existence of the whole population—that is, the women themselves in addition to their husbands and children.

The age at which one should exercise the right to vote, both in parliamentary and regional elections, is an important question for the working class. To the detriment of the working class, the ruling classes try the world over to rob the flower of youth of the right to vote, admitting to the polls only citizens who are twenty-five years old or older. Social Democracy demands that all citizens older than twenty years, without regard to differences of sex, religion, or nationality, have the right to cast a vote in elections as well as be chosen as a member of parliament.

Today, all governments consider a man to be mature and fit for the type of service that is hardest on the body—military service—at the age of twenty-one. Laws in the civil code of every country also regard every adult who has finished the twentieth year of his life as mature and capable of disposing of himself and his fortune according to his will. In reality, maturity and independence in life begin much earlier for individuals from the working class, thanks to the capitalist order, than for members of the moneyed classes. The child of the people, the proletarian, is usually forced to go to work, to stand on his own feet, at an early age. While practically still an adolescent, at an age when the sons of the bourgeoisie still spend their time at school or at play, the worker more often than not has already graduated from the school of hard knocks, as a mature adult who earns enough through his own hard work to put bread on the table for himself and often for older parents or for siblings. Hence the justice of granting every citizen who is at least twenty-one years old, especially every adult member of common social standing, the right to vote for parliament and regional congress—that is, the right to vote in matters relating to the organization of the needs of the state and the region.

Moreover, capitalist rule, poverty, and unceasing labor drive workers to an early grave. The "average life expectancy" (as scholars would say) of the working class is much shorter than that of the moneyed classes. Thus, the average worker will have the opportunity to exercise his rights fewer times than the capitalist, nobleman, or priest (the clergy on average live the longest). In light of this, the interests of the working class demand that workers start exercising their electoral rights *as early as possible*, and a delay of those rights even by several years is an injury to the working people and a privilege for its enemies —the moneyed classes.

Electoral rights for the general state parliament, as well as for the regional congress, should be equal. That is, everyone should be treated the same; whether rich or poor, upper echelon or simple folk, each person should be able to cast one vote in each election, no more and no less. But, in situations that force those in power to give the people voting rights, they try to decrease the influence of the people by ensuring the members of the bourgeoisie a greater influence than the working class. They pass laws that give those who own land or some capital or who pay taxes of a certain amount a larger voice in the elections than those who do not own anything—that is, workers. So, for example, in Belgium, there is an electoral law saying that landowners, rich capitalists, and those who have the title of, let us say, university professor cast votes for parliament that count for three votes, while votes from the simple folk only count as one.* In Austria,

---

* Upon becoming an independent state in 1831, Belgium had very restrictive electoral laws: Poll taxes and property qualifications limited voting to only 45,000 out of a population of 3 million. As a result of the February Revolution of 1848, the franchise was considerably widened, although universal male suffrage was not introduced until 1893. The 1893 law, which prevailed at the time

the ruling classes use another method to secure an advantage over workers at the polls. Here, the entire male population does not vote together; rather, each profession votes separately, creating a separate so-called electoral curia. Thus, the owners of land make up one curia, the rich industrialists and wholesalers another, the petty bourgeoisie a third, the peasants a fourth, and the vast mass of working people including urban and rural laborers a fifth. However, in the fifth curia, the proletarians are joined by all the other voters from the more privileged curiae, who vote *again*. In this way the curiae of the rich professions elect nearly the entire parliament, and the fifth curia, in which workers vote, can only elect a handful of deputies, such that the people are doomed in advance to have representatives who make up only a tiny minority in the parliament, and who have next to no influence on legislation.* This is a brazen injury and blatant injustice against the working people. If anyone deserves to be shut out of equal treatment, it is actually that class of parasites—the noblemen and capitalists—who eat off the backs of the people. Yet because Social Democracy holds to a principle of complete equality between people, the party does not demand more rights for the working class than for others, and it requires only that all people without exception have equal rights at the polling booth, such that the vote cast by the poorest has the same meaning as the vote cast by the richest.

Voting should be direct. That means that each person casts a vote simply for [the person] he would like to have as a deputy in the parliament. The ruling classes have established *indirect* elections in a few countries, such as Prussia, to the detriment of the working class.† In indirect elections, the people themselves elect not deputies to the parliament, but rather intermediaries, and only then do these intermediaries select deputies from among themselves. This is one way to

---

Luxemburg was writing, had a plural voting system in which citizens paying a certain amount of tax got two votes and those showing "special intellectual capacity" got three.

* [Footnote by Luxemburg] In the first curia [in Austria], 5,431 *large landowners* elected 85 deputies to the parliament; in the second curia, 591 *wholesalers and industrialists* elected 21 deputies; in the third curia, 493,804 voters from the *urban population* elected 118 deputies; in the fourth curia, 1,595,406 *rural* voters elected 129 deputies; in the fifth curia, a *general election*, 5,004,222 voters elected 72 deputies.

In this way, *6,022* voters from the rich nobility and bourgeoisie (the first two curiae) together chose *106* of the deputies, while more than *5 million* voters in the fifth curia, of which a *majority* are workers, chose *72* of the deputies! The first four curiae together, made up of 2,085,232 wealthy voters, chose *353* of the deputies, and the 5 million voters of the fifth curia, only *72*!

It must be said that Austrian electoral law, which the Russian tsar generally used as a model in the Bulygin project, both the original and the modification, will soon undergo a change. Under pressure from tumultuous worker demonstrations across Austria, and in view of the danger of the revolution for the tsar, the government announced an act providing for common and equal electoral rights in November 1905.

† This staple of the Prussian system found its equivalent in the US political system, in which senators were originally chosen by state representatives instead of the popular vote, and it prevails today with the Electoral College for presidential elections.

trick the people and make a counterfeit of their will. Because in indirect elections, usually only those who pay a certain amount in taxes can be chosen as intermediaries, a certain amount of wealth is a requirement, and in most cases, only members of the bourgeoisie or petty bourgeoisie are offered up for election as intermediaries. What is more, under this system of electoral law, the intermediaries must usually cast their votes for deputies in the open, exposing them to the persecution of the capitalists and the government if they vote for a Social Democrat or generally anyone from an oppositional party. For these reasons, indirect elections are a known method of preventing proletarians from electing people who would truly represent them in the parliament. And that is why Social Democracy demands, in addition to equal and universal voting rights, elections that are *direct*.

Social Democracy demands that elections be *secret*, meaning that every person should cast his vote in such a way that no one may check who voted for which party's candidate. To accomplish this, voters should drop cards with the names of the candidates they want to elect into a ballot box, each card in a closed envelope, and the elections office should open the envelopes and count the votes only after voting has ended. For a few years, a system has existed in Germany in which workers have the right to appoint a representative to the elections office in each polling place, and this representative spends the entire election process carefully watching that government officials and bourgeois party representatives do not improperly try to track who voted for whom. This is absolutely in the interests of the working class. The worker dependent on the capitalist in today's system would be perpetually exposed to the revenge of his "superiors" and to the loss of his job if they could be sure that he voted for a true defender of the people, for a Social Democrat, and not for the candidate that the "superiors" had indicated. Ballot secrecy is especially necessary for the rural workers, who find themselves in the greatest captivity to their lords and would never, in open-ballot elections, dare oppose the will of their oppressors by voting according to their own conscience—that is, for a Social Democratic candidate.

4. Municipal and communal self-government; elections to city and town councils on the basis of universal, equal, confidential, and direct electoral rights

Other than matters concerning the population of the entire state or our region specially and thus falling under the purview of the general state parliament or the regional congress, there are a number of public matters in every city and every rural community that are important only for the residents of that city or community. Such matters include the following: local taxes to the urban or communal coffers; local school upkeep; hospital maintenance; city or community lighting; upkeep of streets, roads, and bridges; water supply to the city or community; urban transport such as streetcars, coaches, and *droshkes*;* city beautification; upkeep of public squares and gardens and city theaters; public charitable institutions such as shelters, night refuges, and public orphanages; public education centers such as libraries and rural and communal reading rooms; fire brigades; and so on, and so forth. All these numerous and highly diverse matters together constitute what is called the local economy, and they all generally concern the health, life, and bodily prosperity of the whole population of a given city or rural area. The local economy affects every aspect of the most vital material and spiritual interests of the working population. For example, the working class must take care that municipal and communal taxes are extracted not from communities of the working poor, but only from rich bourgeois and wealthy rural landowners. Further, construction and maintenance of roads and streets should not only consider the parts of a city occupied by wealthy bourgeoisie, as they currently do, while the streets occupied by the working class and the urban poor are usually narrow, dark, uneven, badly cobbled, covered with filth, and filled with close air, which makes these populations the first and most frequent victims of nearly all epidemics and infectious diseases. Workers, whose hands built all cities, houses, and streets, must demand that broad and comfortable streets be built for them too, that public gardens and playgrounds for children be built on the streets on which they live, and that hygiene be made possible through potable water infrastructure and sewage systems, not just where bourgeois parasites spin their webs, but also where proletarian worker bees build their hives.

It is equally important for the working class that workers employed by the city or township, including municipal and township office workers and public service personnel—tramway workers, night watchmen, firefighters, city hospital staff, and postal workers—be guaranteed a certain minimum wage, an appropriately regulated workday, and the promise of support from the city in old age and in the case of disability or illness. The interest of the people then requires that city services, including light, gas, electricity, water, streetcars, and horsecars, not be given over into the hands of private capitalist industrialists who would make millions off urban dwellers, but rather that the proceeds from all these branches of the public economy go into the municipal and communal coffers, for the benefit of the very same population. Workers must also take care that the city and the community do not give away urban land to private profiteers who would exploit the impoverished population with excessive rental rates for dilapidated, cramped apartments. On the contrary, the city must purchase suitable plots and build, at its own expense and according to suitable plans, good and affordable housing for the working people. Further, it is of utmost importance that the working people have a sufficient number of municipal and communal

---

* A two- or four-wheeled open cart that at the time was widely used in Russia.

hospitals and schools open to them at no cost, that their intellectual needs be fulfilled through libraries and reading rooms run by the city or township, and that facilities for art—theater, music, art exhibits, and so forth—be made more accessible to all the people, even the very poorest. The working class must look after the people with the greatest need, those deprived of all life's necessities, the disabled, the aged, the orphaned, the homeless, and the unhappiest victims of today's social systems, ensuring that cities and townships provide them with good care, but without the injuries to human dignity that so often accompany bourgeois charity.

Finally, embellishments to cities and townships in the form of works of art, wells, monuments, and so forth are not unimportant to the working class, which must make sure to give objects of veneration their due and cultivate the spirit of the enlightened segment of the working people, not the spirit and traditions of a handful of rich bourgeoisie or noblemen.

Thus, there is not even one issue of local economics on which the interests of the working class do not diverge from, and even oppose, the interests of the bourgeoisie. But as long as municipal economies are manipulated according to the whims of the tsar's officials or representatives of the wealthy bourgeoisie, they will continue to be administered in the interests of the bourgeoisie and landowning minority, and not in the spirit of the working people. In defense of the interests of the working class, Social Democracy makes these demands:

(a) That the entire municipal and communal economy be subject to the decisions of the city or town council; and
(b) That city or town councils be elected by the entire adult population of the city or community without discrimination by sex, religion, or nationality, by means of universal, equal, confidential, and direct elections.

5. Popular elections to appoint officials and judges, and legal penalties for violations of the law while in these positions

The parliament and the regional congress decide the laws, and the people are bound by them. But executing these laws is the business of officials and judges. On the execution of the law and the administration of the courts rest the fates of the entire population. Even good laws may be perversely carried out, or not carried out at all. That is to say, the working class depends on the way the law is applied by officials and judges. Because every person from the working class knows from personal experience that when a simple person, a worker or peasant, has an issue in city hall or in court, he is treated completely differently than a gentleman from the bourgeoisie or the nobility. In today's courts and government offices, there are two yardsticks, two sets of scales—one for the bourgeoisie, and the other for the working class. Clerks and judges usually twist the law to serve the system of exploitation and oppression now in power, to the detriment of the working people. Such behavior was common for decades, and not only among the tsar's officials and judges. In countries with constitutions and political freedoms such as Germany, and even in republican states such as France, clerks treat working people with contempt, and judges take every opportunity to render them an injustice. This originates in the appointment of clerks and judges by the government itself. The government gives most positions to people belonging to the bourgeois class, and some to the petty bourgeoisie. In this way, because clerks are dependent on the government that pays them and are themselves a part of the exploiter class, sharing its spirit, views, and kinship, they are natural enemies of workers, and they treat working people like dirt. Only at such a time as these gentlemen know that they are not dependent on the government or the bourgeoisie but on the masses, and that just punishment awaits them for breaking the law to the disadvantage of the people, will they feel like the people's servants, and not its masters, and only then will the working people be truly able to benefit from the rights they have won. Thus, in defense of the interests of the working people, Social Democracy makes these demands:

(a) That higher clerks and judges who give direction to the application of laws in government offices and courts be chosen by the adult population in universal, equal, confidential, and direct elections; and
(b) That any person who experiences a violation of law at the hands of any clerk or judge, from the highest to the lowest, may sue before a special court.

6. Equality of all before the law

True and lasting equality between people is impossible while the capitalist system exists. For as long as all means of production and sources of wealth—land, factories, machines, and so forth—are the private property of a handful of owners, and all the people live from the sale of the labor of their hands, then the population will be divided into exploiters and exploited, rich and poor, rulers and oppressed, those benefiting from education and those deprived of the opportunity to educate themselves. Only the abolition of exploitation, hired labor, and class rule will bring about true equality in human society.

But since the working people are condemned by the current system to *social* inequality, from which only a socialist order will free them, workers may demand of today's bourgeois state at least *formal equality before the law*. If the reign of capital so impairs the working class economically, politically, and spiritually, then the law and the courts should at least be fair and equal for all. Formal inequality before the law is a vestige from the Middle Ages, from when nobility and serfdom ruled the land. In the Middle Ages, society was legally divided into various "estates"—nobility, clergy, burghers, and serfs—and every estate had different rights and courts. When someone was killed, for example, one punishment was meted out for killing a nobleman, and another for killing a peasant; the lives and rights of lords and burghers were valued much more highly, and violations of them were much more severely punished than violations of the lives and rights of peasants and serfs.

In the revolutions of the nineteenth century in Western Europe, aristocratic governments were overthrown and new bourgeois governments were set up that established political freedoms, and at the same time these formal differences before the law according to estate were abolished everywhere. In the last few centuries, the rule of Russian absolutism combined all the qualities of capitalist government—control by a class of industrial exploiters—with relics of the medieval rule of the aristocracy. Serfdom was not abolished; rather, the inequality of various estates before the law endured. Lords who belonged to the nobility were treated differently under tsarist law than peasants or workers, and this difference was ubiquitous—from participation in local government, to tax burdens, to military service, to serving prison sentences. Under the tsarists, peasants paid special taxes from which the nobility were exempt; peasants could be legally sentenced to corporal flogging by both civil and military courts, yet noblemen were protected from this fate. Even in prison, those belonging to a noble estate were given different treatment and food than "simple people." Such inequality of the law and the courts for "lords" and for working people is yet another way to oppress and disable the working classes and to impede their struggle for full freedom.

In the interests of the working people, Social Democracy demands complete equality before the law for all the state's citizens and the removal of all the privileges of social station and wealth. This means that civil and criminal law, the courts, military service obligations, and political rights should make no distinction between the nobility and the common people or the rich and the poor, but should be equal for all citizens.

7. Inviolability of persons and homes

One of the first conditions of political freedom around the world is the personal freedom of citizens—that is, the security legally ensured to every citizen against every violent act and scheme carried out by the government against their person or private domicile. In order for a person to feel that he is a truly free citizen of the state and the land, he must be sure that he can abandon himself to his work, to relaxation, to private life, or to political activity without fear that administrative or police authorities may, independent of a judge, arbitrarily arrest and imprison him for this or that reason, or burst into his private domicile and ransack every room. Under the tsar's autocratic government, one can never be sure that he will not be unexpectedly thrown into prison by some brutal military henchmen with whom he has fallen into disfavor, or that a horde of police will not raid his home in the middle of the day or night. The tsarist government has used these violations of personal freedoms and homes especially against persons of revolutionary conviction, and most often against politically militant workers and peasants, not only imprisoning them by the thousands without due process or legal precedent, but also insulting them by trampling on their personal inviolability in the wildest manner.

Social Democracy demands that the person and domicile of the citizen be inviolable by governmental authorities, as they already are in all civilized countries. Governmental authorities may violate the personal freedom of a citizen—that is, place him under arrest—only with a court order that makes the crime and the reason clear to anyone the authorities take to jail. Governmental authorities should be forbidden by law from personally targeting citizens in word or in deed under any circumstances, punishable by the severest of penalties. The representatives of power should also be legally forbidden from crossing the thresholds of citizens' private domiciles except with the formal permission of a court.

8. Freedoms of speech, the press, unions, and assembly

The most pressing need of the working class is to have the opportunity to edify and organize itself, to unite in common defense of its interests. Each individual worker is completely hopeless against the violence of exploitative capital, as well as against the political rule of the bourgeoisie as a class. Only by uniting with his brothers, in a mass, in organization, does a worker find both the strength to fight exploitation and an understanding of his interests. Moreover, only in political organization, in their own class party, do workers recognize their ultimate historical goal—to liberate humanity from the hell of capitalism—and only in their own class party do workers become organized into a force that can aspire to that goal and fight for its realization. Both the economic fight and the political fight waged every day by the working class in defense of worker interests and in pursuit of ultimate liberty demand the broadest opportunity to come together in unions and be enlightened by the spoken and the written word. The right to parliamentary elections would be an empty illusion if the law did not guarantee the broadest possible opportunity for pre-election campaigning, at people's gatherings, by distributing magazines and books, through open and free discussion of every matter affecting social life. The people must always have the opportunity to participate in political life, to criticize the actions of parliament and government both at public gatherings and in print, to voice their demands, and to unite in unions and parties for their defense. Therefore, Social Democracy demands that the people have complete and uninhibited freedom to edify themselves and each other with the help of magazines, books, attendance at public gatherings, and speeches. They must have the freedom to unite in political and trade unions and to carry through with strikes. For ages, under the rule of tsarist despotism, workers were the ones most deprived of all these rights. The capitalists and the nobility possess, and have always possessed, the power to unite in unions for the defense of their interests—that is, to exploit workers and plunder the public. Unions of industrialists, associations of landowners and wholesalers, and mining unions have always debated right in front of the tsarist police. If the owners of coal mines or the sugar industrialists united into a syndicate and hatched a conspiracy to squeeze the public by raising the price of coal or sugar, the tsarist government would not lift a finger. Similarly, newspapers and books that antagonize the working people, disseminate drivel and corruption, sow hatred for Poles, and incite people against Jews have never been shut down. But as soon as workers united in unions with the aim of bettering their lot, the military and police smelled them out and tracked them down like hardened criminals. Periodicals and pamphlets that educate workers and promote theories of socialism and political freedom have had to be printed and distributed in secret for decades, since prison, Siberia, and torture awaited the printers and distributors of such materials. Yet not only under absolutism, but even in countries with political freedoms, such as Germany, the ruling classes make every attempt to hamper workers' opportunities to organize in unions, and they try to make it more difficult to promote consciousness among workers with periodicals and books. For example, in Prussia, the entire rural proletariat is excluded from the right to form trade unions, and women are not permitted to be members of political unions. The bourgeoisie fears nothing so much as an educated and organized worker, and it uses every means available to deprive him of the sources of his strength: education and organization. That is why one of the main demands of conscious workers in every country, besides universal and equal voting rights, is full and unfettered freedom of speech, the press, unions, and assembly, for the urban populace as for rural folk, for men as for women.

9. Freedom of conscience

From the beginning, the tsarist government persecuted its "subjects" not only for every aspiration to political freedom and education but even for belief. In tsarism, the dominant religion was Orthodoxy, and all the infidels—Catholics, Uniates,* Jews, and dissenters—were impaired in one way or another. Similarly criminal in the view of the tsarist government was the refusal to acknowledge church religion or spiritual power at all—punishable by Siberian exile or torture. Social Democracy recognizes that persecution for belief or lack thereof is a barbarity incompatible with civil freedom and civilization. Oppression of

---

* "Uniates" refers to the Eastern Catholic Churches.

conscience is the worst form of oppression. Moreover, if the state persecutes any faiths, it is always to the detriment of working people and serves the benefit only of the exploiter class. By inciting some parts of the people against others and spreading hate among the people, the enemies of the working class hope to stupefy and distract workers from their fight against exploitation and oppression. That is why workers everywhere oppose religious persecution with all their might. Every adult person should have complete freedom to believe what and how he likes. Religious adherence or non-affiliation is a matter of conviction, of a person's conscience and spiritual happiness. No one has the right to peer into someone's conscience and demand that he believes a certain way and no other way. Therefore, Social Democracy demands that the laws of state ensure full *freedom of conscience*. This means that above all, every law must be abolished that was passed to the disadvantage of any particular faith or lack thereof. People of all beliefs—Orthodox, Catholics, Uniates, Jews, Protestants, dissenters, Muslims, and irreligious persons—should be treated completely equally by the state, have identical rights, and be equally eligible for every office and station.

But that is not all. Full freedom of conscience does not exist anywhere that one faith is considered the state religion—that is, if the priests and churches of one religion are supported with state money, and lessons on the religion are taught in state and city schools. The funds in the government's coffers come from taxes paid by the entire populace without exception. If government money that has come from the whole populace is used to maintain the clergy of one or two faiths, any part of the populace that professes a different religion or is entirely irreligious is coerced and wronged. If, for example, the government spends enormous sums on Orthodox priests and churches, and also some money on the Catholic Church, that is an injury to Protestants, Uniates, Jews, dissenters, and other citizens of the state, who all pay the same taxes. True equality of all faiths and complete freedom of conscience will only be possible when the government does not support any faith and does not meddle in religious affairs at all. Faith will then be *each person's private affair*. Anyone may profess any religion he wishes and may give support of his own free will to the denomination or church of his conviction. People professing a common religion will then form faith communities in the state, the members of which will support their own church peacefully and voluntarily and teach the lessons of the religion to their children as they please.

Given the multiplicity of faiths, introducing obligatory religious lessons in schools always leads to the disadvantage of some part of the population. Besides this, religious lessons divide society's youth even as they sit in their schoolhouses, placing them in separate groups according to faith, triggering isolation and hostility, and leading them to persecute each other. Therefore, for the realization of true freedom of conscience, Social Democracy demands that all matters of religion, from the financial support of priests and churches to the teaching of religion to children, be private affairs from which the state entirely abstains, neither supporting some with public finances nor oppressing others.

10. Equal rights for women

In today's society, based on private property and the control of capitalists, a woman is deprived of every political right and treated as a secondary being, the subordinate of a man. To liberate a woman from such indignities, to return her to equal rights and human dignity, a socialist system is uniquely capable—a system that abolishes the rule of private property and together with it every inequality in human society. The development of capitalism itself is preparing the ground for the liberation and granting of equal rights to women. Great industry has destroyed the worker's family and popularized the employment of women in factories, workshops, shops, offices, and public agencies. A woman of common social standing is compelled ever more often to work to support herself and, often, her family. And when the economic dependence of women disappears, so in turn will the root of injustices against women and the social disadvantages experienced by women. The cause of equal rights for women will thus advance together with the development of large industry, the development of capital, and the development of the workers' cause. The working class is the only class that has no reason to put women at a political disadvantage. Social Democracy is the only party that genuinely demands that women be freed from their current position and fights for their liberation. Social Democracy makes the following demands:

> (1) That every public, penal, and civil law issued to disadvantage a woman or constrain in any way her personal freedoms, property rights, or power to decide about her children on an equal basis with their father be abolished; and
> (2) That women be provided with every right and political freedom that men have, especially the right to elections to the parliament, the regional congress, and the city or town council.

11. Dissolution of the standing army and establishment of a people's army

The strongest pillar holding up the despotic government, as well as the reign of capitalists over the working people, is the military, the standing armed forces. The people are usually convinced that a country needs an army to defend itself against enemy attack. In reality, these enormous armies standing always at arms are needed not for defense of the country but for two purposes: to plunder foreign lands and peoples, and to keep the people of their own land in bondage to their sovereign exploiters.

The wars that today's states wage against each other are not needed by the working class, only by the capitalists. The working class gains nothing if the state wins new territory by subjugating other lands and peoples to tyrannize them and wring them dry. Only capitalists benefit from winning new markets, since there they can transport and transform into gold the bloody labor they squeeze out of workers at home. The nobility benefit from armies and wars too, because they can occupy the top military positions and live idly in them while receiving fat salaries from the state coffers. Finally, bureaucrats high and low find in war and in newly conquered lands the opportunity to line their pockets with embezzled funds, starving soldiers and tyrannizing conquered peoples as they do so.

Yet those who profit the most from weapons, armies, and wars are the manufacturers of iron, steel, rifles, and ships, as well as the various suppliers of military clothing and food products. In these ways, hundreds of millions spent every year for upkeep of the military flow from government coffers to the pockets of a handful of capitalists. These few make enormous fortunes, especially in wartime, when the government loses battleships, weapons, and cannons in battle and places orders for yet more instruments of murder.

Armies and wars bring the working people only loss. The youth of the people waste some of their most beautiful years in the regular army, spending their time not on work that would benefit them and theirs but on mindless drills, enduring cruel harassment and humiliation from brutal drillmasters and petty officers. In war the sons of the people fall by the thousands, laying down their lives or becoming crippled for life, all to make their worst enemies, the capitalists, richer. In this way, nearly the entire cost of maintaining enormous armies and waging wars falls on the backs of the people. The countless millions the government throws away on barracks, artillery, warships, officers, and so forth flow from no other source than the pockets of common folk. Taxes paid by the impoverished masses on every last morsel placed in their mouths and on every thread of clothing worn on their bodies are the source from which all current governments grow their militarism. But the greatest injury inflicted by today's militarism on the working class is that soldiers are the instruments the government uses to oppress the people of their own land! It is true that the ranks are filled by workers themselves. A soldier is a worker or peasant in uniform. And yet, the years spent in military service in a barracks, at a distance from family and friends, and the brutal discipline of the army are intentionally set up to make of the worker or farmer in uniform a cowed animal, blind and deaf to everything but the orders of his commanders. After several years of drills, the soldier forgets that he is a child of the people, stops thinking at all about his actions, and stands ready at his officers' orders to murder his own father and mother. And so the classes and governments in power have in the army a deadly weapon against conscious workers and rebellious peasants. The tsarist government responds to every uprising of desperate peasants in Russia, to every large demonstration of workers in Russia and Poland, by spilling blood. On one side, proletarians in plain clothes fight for a better existence and for freedom, and on the other, at the order of officers, proletarians in uniform turn murderous weapons against them as they would against foreign invaders. Today's armed force serves mainly to hold the working class under the yoke of capitalism, not only in Russia but in every capitalist country. This is why Social Democracy demands the *abolition of standing armies* everywhere. To defend the land against invaders, there is no need for an army of hundreds of thousands to remain always at arms, consuming millions of roubles. It is enough for the entire adult male populace to have arms and to keep their weapons always at home. A few months' education suffices to learn to operate firearms, after which each citizen may return home, resume work and family life, and hang his rifle on a peg, keeping it in readiness.

Such uniformly armed populations, or militias, exist already in Switzerland, and they have existed too among the Boers in South Africa, showing how well a uniformly armed people can defend its own land. Arming the people does not lead naturally to the waging of bloody imperialist wars and to the plundering of other lands and peoples, because the entire people would never agree to abandon their land in order to journey far away to distant parts or across the ocean to conquer foreign territory.* But, for precisely this reason, a militia is the best measure against criminal wars such as Russia's war against Japan [in 1904–1905]. What is more, arming workers and peasants with weapons to be kept securely at home is the best countermeasure against oppression and violence at the hands of capitalists. Exploiters reckon quite differently with an armed populace than with a defenseless mass. Abolishing the standing army and arming all the people is the best guarantee of peace and prosperity in every land, and the greatest boon to the hope that the people shall be liberated in the end from the yoke of capitalism.

---

* Luxemburg's example of the Boers seems highly inappropriate, given that they were "defending" not their lands but ones that they stole from native Africans. Their "people's militia" was clearly an instrument for "the plundering of other lands and peoples." Seven years later, in *The Accumulation of Capital*, Luxemburg voiced a far more critical view of the Boers: "For a long time, the Boers had lived as nomadic pastoralists, having done their best to kill off or drive out the Khoikhoi and other indigenous peoples in order to take the best pastures from them [...] The Boers considered the Black Africans to be an object whose natural and God-given purpose was to perform slave labor for them, and held that this was an indispensable foundation of their peasant economy." See *The Complete Works of Rosa Luxemburg, Vol. II: Economic Writings 2*, edited by Peter Hudis and Paul Le Blanc (London and New York: Verso, 2015), pp. 297–8.

12. Compulsory and cost-free people's schools, support for schoolchildren at the cost of the state, and cost-free higher education for the exceptionally gifted

The state should spend public funds not on the army and guns but on the youth. The education of the people is wholly neglected today. Across Russia, millions of people have lived and died without even obtaining the first basis for knowledge: reading and writing. And a large number of these illiterate people (that is, people who cannot read and write) live in our land, in Poland. The people's lack of education is useful to the tsarist government and the capitalist class, so they deliberately maintain the people's ignorance. When the working population, both the urban workers and the rural folk, are educated, when they gain access to newspapers, books, and learning, they will refuse to humbly carry a class of drunkards on their backs.

This is why the tsarist government established so few schools for the people and provided such lousy education in those schools; it is why the government allowed capitalists to fit the yoke of factory and farm labor around the necks of the young children of the proletariat, at just the age when it is most appropriate to be taught their first lessons.

And the yearning of the people for knowledge and education is all the greater for it. Talents and abilities by the thousands die away and are lost because the people's young boys and girls are made to hold trowels and needles rather than books, regardless of their desire to learn. Meanwhile, children belonging to affluent social strata, even if unintelligent and lazy, spend half their lives sitting in classrooms and lecture halls kept up on the people's bloody dime, and society never reaps any benefit from it. The ruling class has scooped up for itself not only material riches and delights but spiritual riches and delights, condemning millions of people to life in intellectual darkness and poverty.

Social Democracy demands, in defense of the working class, that learning and study be *for everyone*. A state that is supported by the work of the people is obliged to establish schools in sufficient quantity with a sufficient quantity of well-paid teachers, such that all parents have the opportunity to send their children to school for free and are required by law to do so.

But it is not enough that people's schools should be obligatory and free for all. The working people, thanks to the exploitation of capitalists, are not in a position to provide their children with the necessary textbooks and notebooks— nay, in most cases working parents cannot even support their children during their schooling, which is another reason the children of workers and farmers start working at ages as young as twelve or even ten. In the current circumstances, people's schools, even if there were enough of them and they were free, would remain forbidden fruit for tens of thousands of working youth. Teachers in people's schools around the world have long argued that when the children of impoverished people arrive at school without even a bite to eat and nearly fainting from hunger during their lessons, they are in no proper state to receive instruction. So, to give the children of the working people the opportunity to make good use of cost-free schooling, the state is further obliged to provide them, at the cost of society, all the necessities for study—textbooks, notebooks, and also clothing and sustenance while school is in session. Such a system is already in place in dozens of communities in France, where Social Democrats have a majority on city councils. Social Democracy demands the same for our whole state. Since capitalist society supports itself entirely through the exploitation of the working people, it has an obligation at least to return a small sliver of the blood, sweat, and tears wrenched away from the people to the people's youth, providing them at an early age with vital instruction and a morsel of bread, lest they starve on the schoolhouse bench.

There is more. People's schools are equipped to provide only the most general foundations of an education. For as long as the capitalist system exists, workers' families will never be in a position to provide for the individual cost of higher education for their children, even if they display the most remarkable abilities. Social Democracy therefore demands that in addition to cost-free and obligatory people's schools, the state should, in the interests of the working class and of society in general, ensure students of people's schools who display extraordinary talents or abilities the opportunity to benefit from higher learning at no cost to them at a university, academy, or specialized school.

13. Abolition of tariffs and indirect taxes and the simultaneous establishment of one progressive tax on income, property, and inheritances

To fund public schools, pay officials, and maintain the state in general, revenue is necessary. The current capitalist and military state in particular costs an enormous amount of money. The yearly expenditures of states such as Germany and France reach into the billions. The tsarist government, as the most expensive government and the one that most plunders the populace and wastes its resources, has recently spent more than 2 billion roubles per year. These huge sums are paid to the state in capitalist countries not by the richest and most affluent but mainly by the poorest. The main source of government revenue in Russia, as in every other state today, is *indirect taxes*—that is, tariffs and charges on consumer goods: excises on liquor and tobacco; taxes on matches, lamp oil, and sugar; tariffs on wool, cotton, iron, leather, and in general on all foreign products. Taxes and tariffs for all these goods are paid into the government coffers by wholesalers at the border across which international goods move, and by manufacturers as soon as products are made.

For example, no package of cigarettes or matches can go from the factory to the shop for sale without an excise band, which is a label applied to indicate that the manufacturer already paid the excise to the government. But wholesalers and manufacturers do not pay these taxes from their own pockets; they merely cover the cost until they can recover it from the consuming public as part of the price of every item sold. When someone buys a packet of tobacco or matches in a shop, he pays not only the local price of the tobacco or matches, but also the government excise added to that packet. In this way, the government collects taxes from the people for everything the people consume, not directly, but by way of wholesalers and manufacturers (which is why they are called indirect or consumer taxes or tariffs).

Indirect taxes are paid by everyone, because everyone must buy certain objects necessary for food, clothing, and housing. No one can evade the payment of indirect taxes, because even the poorest of the poor must occasionally buy a bit of tea, sugar, coffee, lamp oil, matches, linens, and clothing, however simple.

One way or another, the people pay some tariff or tax on every morsel they place in their mouths and on every shred of clothing and every bit of furnishing in even the most destitute of homes. Indirect taxes are therefore taxes that force even the poorest beggar to hand over to the government a part of his miserable possessions.

But that is not all. Indirect taxes have the effect of falling hardest on the poorest, and lightest on the richest. The poor and the rich pay the same price for a box of matches, a pound of sugar, and a dekagram of coffee. The prices of goods and the taxes hidden in them are identical for all. But for the poor, the two cents by which the tax increases the cost of a pound of sugar constitute a considerable burden, whereas for the rich they are a trifle, an amount of no consequence. The urban worker spends his entire wages, aside from rent, on food and clothing, and of this amount, a fourth or more frequently goes to these indirect taxes. The rich man, however, who often has a hundred or a thousand times as much income as the peasant or worker, even if he lives lavishly, cannot eat and drink with his family a hundred or a thousand times as much bread, sugar, beer, and tea as the impoverished family. On the contrary, the richer the person, the lesser is the role played in his finances by expenditures on food and clothing. Thus, when the farming or working family pays consumer taxes, suppose they are a quarter or more of all earnings, while for the family of the rich capitalist, these taxes are not even 1 percent of income. So, in relation to the resources of each person, the poorer someone is, the larger the share of his income taken away by indirect taxes, and the richer he is, the smaller the share.

Now, if one compares the living expenses of a single rich manufacturer's family to those of a worker's family, it turns out that the capitalist's family spends considerably more on sugar, lamp oil, meat, liquor, wine, cigars, and various luxuries, and so pays more indirect taxes than the worker's family. However, if one takes the whole population altogether, the rich and prosperous make up only a small handful of the population, while there are tens of millions of poor working people. So, aside from luxury goods that only the rich can afford, their expenditures taken together are a small slice of what is brought in yearly, if one considers also the expenditures of all the families of working and farming people. Shops, factories, and warehouses stay open not on the luxury goods of a few rich people but on the modest spending of a great number of common people. Furthermore, the government coffers stay full not from the taxes paid by the small number of rich bourgeois, but from what is collected penny by penny in taxes from the millions-strong masses.

Indirect taxes are therefore a special means of squeezing every last drop of juice out of the working population to support the government, the army, officials, and so forth. And these taxes constitute the chief financial pillar of the state. What the moneyed classes of Russia and all other states pay today in the form of taxes on income, land, and capital pales in comparison to the revenue from consumer taxes paid by the working people. Because of this, the full weight of supporting the state falls today on the shoulders of the weakest, the working class. The capitalist class not only forces workers to make it richer through their work, giving them only the most meager pay in return, but it even snatches away a part of this pay in taxes, burdening workers with the maintenance of the state machine.

Social Democracy demands that the burden of maintaining the capitalist state be borne not by the poorest, but by affluent people, and primarily the capitalists. The government should not snatch out of the mouths of urban and rural workers the morsel that remained after capital exploited them. That is why Social Democracy demands that all *tariffs, excises, and consumer taxes be completely abolished*, so that all the goods needed to live become cheaper and the working populace may have a moment's respite from misery and want. However, to support the state and government, a single progressive tax should be levied on income, property, and inheritances. A progressive tax is one that begins only at middle income levels and increases together with the amount of property, income, or inheritance, so that the richest pay the most. If, for example, a person who has a yearly income of 1,000 roubles pays an income tax of 1 percent, then a person with an income of 10,000 roubles—already a life of luxury—should not pay 1 percent, but at least 5 percent. Someone with an income of 50,000 should pay 10 percent, and someone who has a yearly income of 100,000 should pay a 25 percent tax, and so on. Property and inheritance should be taxed progressively in the same way, so that the tax increases in proportion to a person's wealth and resources. If the capitalist lords and great landowners were required thus to support the government and the army out of their own pockets, they would immediately lose their appetite for throwing away hundreds of millions every year on guns, ships, court clerks, and flocks of bureaucrats to tyrannize the people.

14. Protective labor laws

Beside political laws giving the working class the possibility to fight freely and openly for their liberation, workers need special laws protecting their livelihoods and health from the avarice of capitalists. The rule of capital knows no bounds for exploitation, no consideration, no mercy for hired laborers. In their drive to exploit, manufacturers and landowners are prepared to ruin the working population through superhuman labor requirements and lethal working conditions, sparing neither men nor women, neither adults nor children. Wherever capital reigns with no restrictions, the working population soon begins to suffer injuries and show harm to its health. Working people are plagued by the highest death rates, workers fall ill from various diseases most often, and workers have the highest rates of unfitness for military service due to weakness of body. Capitalist exploitation is thus not simply a source of unending suffering and impairment for the working class, but a direct threat for the society of the people, destroying its foundations, ruining the bodies of whole generations, and wiping out whole family lines like the worst of epidemics.

In the interests of the exploited people, and in the name of all future societies, Social Democracy demands *thorough protections for the working people in legislation passed by the state*. The demand is for protective legislation especially for *laborers*, not only factories. That is, the charge of the state should extend not only to the proletariat of factories, as with the law passed for appearances by the tsarist government, but also to victims of exploitation in artisans' workshops, mines, shops, the cottage industry, and the countless proletarians on *farms*, who are currently entirely left to the brutal exploitative devices of landowning capitalists.

To rescue the livelihood and health of these millions of urban and farming proletarians, Social Democracy demands that all factories, workshops, mines, and manor houses be required by law to comply with the following regulations for all adult workers of both sexes:

(a) An eight-hour workday with a ban on night shifts when they are not absolutely essential, and with breaks for breakfast and lunch, as well as uninterrupted Sunday rest periods of at least thirty-five hours

Shortening the workday to eight hours not only does not decrease production, but after a short time significantly increases the productivity of workers, as the experience everywhere abroad has shown. A well-rested worker, fresh, healthy, and inventive besides, with time to read and think outside his job, works much faster and better than one who spends his whole life only in hard labor and has no chance to get a good night's rest. This is why the eight-hour workday generally does not bring about a loss in profits for capitalists, when all is said and done.

If governments and capitalists object to the establishment of an eight-hour workday on these grounds, they do so not from fear that it would lead to a reduction in their profits, but mainly because a universal eight-hour workday would mean the corporeal, spiritual, and social resurrection of the working class. The eight-hour workday, along with proper nightly and weekly rest periods, would not only save the working populace from a range of occupational illnesses, consumption (the "illness of the proletarian"), untimely death, and the countless ill-fated accidents that more often than not occur because of the weariness and numbness of the overworked laborers. The eight-hour workday would also be the surest means to prevent worker drunkenness, as was found in the Australian colonies, where taverns campaigned determinedly against the establishment of the eight-hour workday in factories. The worker with enough time to read after work, enlighten himself, and have a home life with his wife and children does not frequent drinking dens. Once drunkenness goes away, thanks to a shorter workday, so do accidents from scuffles between workers, knife fights, and other misdeeds, and morality and clarity grow. Simultaneously, the eight-hour workday will surely prompt increased material and spiritual needs and demands in the working class, as workers with the time to lead private and social lives may not settle for poor housing and clothing and may also feel the need to have certain amenities and brighten up their lives in the ways other cultured people find essential. By lifting workers' standards of living in this way, the eight-hour workday also leads to the elevation of the general wage level, which must always respond to the standards of living of the working populace. Because the eight-hour workday provides the possibility of building proper trade organizations and putting up a fight, it also opens a way for workers to force capitalists to offer wages that at least match their standard of living. In part, especially in the period just after it is established, the eight-hour workday reduces unemployment, giving jobs to a number of workers, especially in occupations where work is done by hand rather than machines, such as handicrafts and farming. Moreover, the eight-hour workday compels manufacturers to schedule work evenly over the entire year, doing away with the murderous seasonal work of many industries that requires workers to toil day and night, only to then go entire months without work. Yet the most important result of the eight-hour workday for the proletariat is that workers gain the time, strength, and energy to organize and mount a class struggle for their ultimate liberation. The current reign of capitalism is chiefly dependent on the ignorance and docility of millions of workers, who, with no time but to eke out a living under the yoke of capital, and certainly none to ponder the wrong being done to them, trudge patiently through life like dutiful oxen. The eight-hour workday gives the great majority of workers the time to read and develop greater awareness and to mount a broader political struggle; it transforms worker oxen into human citizens. And having become thinking, enlightened people, workers will not want to remain in captivity to capital and will understand that theirs is the task of putting an end to the current horrendous social relations. For this very reason, the ruling class wants nothing to do with the eight-hour workday, sensing that it will be the first nail in the coffin of their power. And for this very reason, all true friends of the working people have made loud calls for the eight-hour workday for forty years.

> *(b) Mandatory leave for women for two weeks before and four weeks after confinement without loss of pay and with guaranteed medical aid, and a complete ban on the employment of women in the most dangerous occupations, such as in tobacco and match factories*

Not satisfied with harnessing to its yoke the vast adult male populace, capitalism reaches with its factories, workshops, warehouses, and manor houses into the home and turns mothers out to work. Bourgeois society makes the duplicitous claim that a woman is the keeper of the hearth and home—that the vocation of a woman is to be a wife and mother. Meanwhile, exploitative capitalists cut the pay of men so much that they force millions of women from the proletariat to leave their hearth and home and spend all their days from dawn to dusk at the service of capital. This causes workers' family lives to utterly fall apart. Workingmen have no home to rest in comfort and quiet, and workers' children have no one to look after them. And in turn, the wife and mother of the people finds her strength and health ruined through hard labor. When superhuman work is required to make a living, especially when a woman is required to work while pregnant, nearly up until confinement itself, and then go back to work only a few days after giving birth, not only is her bodily strength ruined, but also the health of her offspring is exposed to grave risk. A child that emerges into the world from the womb of an exhausted, debilitated victim of capital is often weak and unready for life. Furthermore, in some lines of work, such as tobacco manufacturing, children consume lethal poison on drinking the milk of their laborer-mothers. Hence the terrible infant mortality rate experienced by working-class families, which mercilessly wipes out thousands of proletarians just entering the world, even before they have a chance to experience the bliss of a worker's lot in today's society.

To defend working women from the cruel exploitation of capitalists, to save entire generations, Social Democracy demands, in addition to the general eight-hour workday, that entrepreneurs be ordered by law to release pregnant women from work for two weeks before and four weeks after confinement. This will spare working women's bodies, at least during the time they most need rest, and infants newly born to the proletariat will not be separated from their mother's breast and care for at least the first few weeks of their lives.

Moreover, as is entirely natural, the cost of supporting a worker during confinement should be provided in part by the industrialist—the person who makes a fortune off the worker to spend on luxuries for his own wife and children—and in part by the state, through a special workers' insurance (more on that below). But that is not all. In certain lines of work, the ones most dangerous, especially for the children of working women, the employment of women should be entirely forbidden, unless specialists find ways of removing these harmful effects. The health of thousands of the mothers and children of the people is more important than the pocket lining of capitalists greedy for the cheap labor of women.

> *(c) A ban on the employment of children younger than fourteen years of age in factories, workshops, cottage industries, commerce, and farming, as well as a limit of six hours of work per day for adolescents of both sexes until the age of sixteen*

Requiring all the children of the working populace to attend school would remain a meaningless utterance if Social Democracy did not simultaneously demand that the employment of youths up to the age of fourteen be forbidden by law. In order to give children of the working class the opportunity to benefit from learning at the age they are most suited to it, and in order to save the proletariat, at least in the youngest years, from the disastrous health effects of work in factories and on farms, it is necessary to wrest the youth of the people back from the voracious maw of merciless capital with the help of a legal prohibition.

Members of the rich bourgeoisie defend their own children vigorously from all labor, surround them with comforts, even luxuries, and carefully look after their health, making use of a whole flock of hired persons—wet nurses, nannies, maids, governesses, and caretakers—to raise their future heirs. Yet the capitalists sentence the youth of the proletariat to hard work, meager food, and separation from the care of their parents, who are themselves beaten down in the captivity of their labor.

Moreover, children and young adults are susceptible to the most damaging effects of working to make a living. Proletarians of a young age are frequently affected for life, absorbing germs that lead to illness and early death. And in addition to all this, protecting the youth of the proletariat from having to make a living through hard labor and from leaving behind their parents' home in search of work, as well as limiting the work hours of adolescents, lifts workers' family lives from the devastation wrought by the capitalist order.

> *(d) Legal regulations with the goal of protecting the health and life of workers in factories, workshops, mines, farms, and cottage industries (workplace hygiene)*

Entrepreneurs see the proletarians they hire as working machines from which they may wring as much profit as they are able. When they employ workers, capitalists have only one goal in mind: that each worker work as much as possible and cost as little as possible. Conserving capital—that is the greatest concern of entrepreneurs. So, they often build manufacturing floors and workshops that are cramped, with low ceilings and no ventilation, where workers do not have enough air to breathe, and where they must inhale smoke, dust, soot, and an amalgam of poisonous gases. In addition, to save capital, machines often stand without protective guards in such cramped conditions that workers may barely move around them and are in constant danger of catching on a transmission or wheel.

Saving capital is also the reason entrepreneurs do not build any baths for workers and provide no other suitable space to change and clean up after work. Economy further convinces capitalists not to build factories at all, handing out work to be done at home, such as weaving: The worker toils with the whole family in their miserable hovel, eating and sleeping in the same unhealthy, dust-covered chamber. Finally, in the interest of preserving sacred capital, land magnates assign serfs to live in hovels worse than a pigsty, where men, women, and children sleep together in cramped filth and fetor.

As a result of such conservations of capital, working men and women are exposed to a variety of occupational diseases beyond the general ruination of their health through hard labor and poor food. Every type of work today warps and ruins the body of the worker in a different way. Yet science has already found a series of means and devices to make industrial labor less harmful. Often for a modest cost, devices can be set up in factories and workshops that remove some of the jeopardy to the health and livelihood of workers. And it is only through the miserliness and inhuman ruthlessness of capitalists that these measures have not been taken. In view of this, Social Democracy demands that the state require entrepreneurs to follow appropriate regulations, according to the recommendations of trustworthy physicians and engineers, to be implemented during the construction and outfitting of factories and workshops, and that they provide room to be designated as living quarters for workers in sectors where housing is provided, such as in agriculture. In the same way that the police check the fire safety of newly constructed houses and factories, it is their duty to check that the millions of men and women employed by capital are safe from illness and untimely death.

(e) Obligatory insurance of all workers in industry, commerce, domestic service, and farming against illness, unfortunate accidents, and infirmity, as well as in old age

Today the worker who falls sick or loses a limb as a result of a so-called unfortunate accident at work is usually left completely unable to provide food for himself and his family. The lot of workers who live to grow old is no less dreadful. To continue exploiting, the capitalist always needs fresh proletarian meat. When the worker grows old in service to capital and the entrepreneur sees that the proletarian's advanced years diminish his strength, that he begins to fall slightly below the margin of profitability, he throws him out of the gates with no mercy. Where the aged worker is supposed to earn a living for himself and his family when capital no longer wishes to employ him—about this no one in society takes an interest. Neither does anyone trouble themselves over where the worker who has been bedridden by an illness for several weeks or months is supposed to find support. Capitalists themselves do not and will never, of their own free will and at their own cost, decide to rescue from poverty workers who have worn out their health and strength or lost a part of their body and become crippled in their service. Capital knows no human reason in its dealings with workers, seeing in each only what a spider sees in a fly—a victim to suck dry. Having sucked the young and healthy juice out of the worker, the entrepreneur tosses him by the wayside, a worn-out wreck. One result is that older workers, who are most exposed to the revenge of capital, are often the most inclined to acquiesce to the tyranny of entrepreneurs and ready to endure the greatest humiliation rather than resist, and so they often hold the workers' struggle back. In order to protect infirm and aged workers from the choice between hopeless poverty and humiliation, Social Democracy demands that here, too, appropriate laws be made to defend workers. The obligation of the state is to *force* capitalists to do at least something for workers who are ill, injured, or advanced in years. Social Democracy demands that mandatory insurance be established for those employed in industry, shops, domestic service, and farming, both men and women, so that every working man or woman who falls ill receives a certain amount in aid to cover the cost of living and medical assistance. Working women must be provided with a similar level of support and medical aid during their confinement. In the case of mutilation that partly or wholly deprives a worker of the opportunity to earn a living—that is, making him an "invalid"—he should be assured a stable yearly pension. Similarly, in the event of the death of a worker through an "unfortunate accident" at work, a pension should be paid to the widow and young children according to their number. Finally, in old age, after the age of sixty, *all* working men and women should receive an annuity, or pension, that ensures them a reasonable chance to live without deprivation together with their family. This insurance should be administered by independent officials under the watch of workers, and the cost of the insurance should be borne half by the capitalists—each for his own workers—and half by the government from the state coffers. If the state coffers have enough money for cannons and rifles to murder protesting workers, if there is money to grace with opulence the manor houses and packs of courtiers tyrannizing the working populace, then there should be means enough to guard millions of honest, hardworking people who have fallen ill or reached a venerable age from the hunger and destitution that fall on their heads, not through any fault of theirs, but because of blatant exploitation by capitalists.

(f) Factory inspections with the participation and oversight of workers

The best protective laws will not help anything unless someone makes sure that the capitalists carry them out. To trick the working class, the tsarist government has already passed various factory laws, as if to protect workers. But the majority of these laws have remained only on paper, as the capitalists began to mock them as soon as they knew that nothing would happen to them if they did not comply with the factory laws. The tsarist government has even appointed factory inspectors to verify compliance with the protective laws, for which they receive a salary paid out of the people's pockets, yet these inspectors are the tsar's agents. Unaffected by the fortunes of workers and on good terms with the capitalists, they are just like the rest of the tsarist bureaucracy. Manufacturers also have various ways of hiding the truth from inspectors, and inspectors are usually willing to turn a blind eye to capitalists' offenses, whether for bribe money, wine, cigars, or simply out of unconcern for workers. In recent years, rather than monitoring workers' health and safety, factory inspectors in Russia have played the role of police officers more and more, making sure that workers humbly endure exploitation rather than go on strike. In order that capitalists really are monitored and compelled to abide rigorously by the protective laws, factory inspections must be carried out and watched over by people who truly and genuinely care about the fate of workers, who are friends to workers and not the servants of capitalists. And where are such people to be found except among the working class? Here and everywhere, workers may not rely on anyone but themselves for help. If workers themselves select from their midst the most trusted, open-minded comrades, and these come together with technical and medical inspectors from the administration to make sure the protective laws are obeyed, and they lead the inspection tours of industrial and agricultural facilities, then capitalists will be unable to get away with their tricks and excuses. Then and only then, for the first time, will protective worker legislation cease to be an illusion on paper for pulling the wool over workers, eyes and become an effective means to shield them from the worst influences of today's capitalist economy.

These are the demands that Social Democracy puts forward in the interests of the innumerable working masses across our land. Fulfilling them is essential for even modest improvements to the standards of living of working people, for greater opportunities for their education and organization, and for their tireless struggle in a free and open arena after full liberation. The ultimate goals that light the way of the working class, in Poland, in Russia, and abroad, is to abolish entirely the exploitation and oppression of some people by others, the rule of some by others, and the privileging of rich over poor, men over women, and ruling nations over defeated nations; to end war; and to establish universal peace, equality, and brotherhood among peoples. Only when these goals are achieved will Social Democracy lay down its arms here and around the world, and only then will the struggle of the working class be finished, because only then will the division of human society into warring classes end and what is called class society disappear.

The path to this end must be cleared by conscious workers themselves, fighting step by step for political rights and protective legislation. The program of Social Democracy shows workers which way to go and what to demand so that they arrive at the real goal—winning political power over the state, setting up a dictatorship of the proletariat, and realizing socialism.

Polish workers! Seize the banner of your own class party with an iron fist. The program of Social Democracy has led you to battle and will lead you to victory.

Critique in the Workers' Movement*

Bourgeois revolutions, like those of the eighteenth century, storm swiftly from success to success, their dramatic effects outdo each other, men and things seem to be set in sparkling brilliants, ecstasy is the everyday spirit, but they are short-lived, soon they have attained their zenith, and a long crapulent depression seizes society before it learns soberly to assimilate the results of its storm-and-stress period. On the other hand, proletarian revolutions, like those in the nineteenth century, criticize themselves constantly, interrupt themselves continually in their own course, come back to the apparently accomplished in order to begin afresh, deride with unmerciful thoroughness the inadequacies, weakness, and paltriness of their first attempts, seem to throw down their adversary only in order that he may draw new strength from the earth and rise again, more gigantic, before them, and recoil again and again from the indefinite prodigiousness of their own aims, until a situation has been created which makes all turning back impossible, and the conditions themselves cry out: "Hic Rhodus, hic salta!"†

These words were written by Karl Marx fifty years ago, and today they sound as if they were written for our time.

Proletarian revolutions differ from bourgeois revolutions, first of all, in that they contain working people fighting for their own cause. In this fight they must depend on their own strength, making use of every misstep for future struggle, always learning, always pondering whether the path they are marching down is good, and whether the means they are using will lead to their goal. The working people, which has such an important task to fulfill, does not have the time or opportunity for careful, precise observation of matters for years in advance of the struggle. The greater part of the people will turn out to battle only when the hour is struck, and only *during the fight* will they make clear to themselves, through the help of the part of the proletariat whom Social Democracy has already made conscious, the nature of their adversary as well as of their goals.

During the fight, as victims fall all around, as the proletariat bears down on its enemy, it *learns*, it educates itself. A victorious outcome depends on the degree of that consciousness.

---

* This article first appeared in *Czerwony Sztandar*, No. 39, January 9, 1906, pp. 1–2 under the title "Krytyka w rucha robotniczym." It is translated from the Polish original by Joseph Muller.

† See Karl Marx, *Eighteenth Brumaire of Louis Bonaparte*, in *Marx-Engels Collected Works*, Vol. 11 (New York: International Publishers, 1979), pp. 106–7. *Hic Rhodus, hic salta!*—literally, "Here is Rhodes, jump here!"—is a reference to a boastful athlete in Aesop's fables. Hegel cites this in the *Philosophy of Right* in arguing that "as a work of philosophy, it must be poles apart from an attempt to construct a state as it ought to be." See G. W. F. Hegel, *Philosophy of Right*, translated by T. M. Knox (London: Oxford University Press, 1967), p. 11.

How, then, do members of the proletariat become conscious? They read pamphlets, appeals, and periodicals. They listen to speeches by people who give advice on various things. They must *weigh for themselves* which of these things is right, for such consideration is the basis for choosing what path to take. Thus, the most important precondition for raising proletarian consciousness within the struggle itself is the exercise of the freedoms of assembly and of the press. That is to say, the proletariat fights for the freedom to gather, discuss its affairs, and through freely printed publications learn to know its friends and foes. If the first condition of raising the proletariat's awareness is that workers wrest from the hands of the government the freedoms of assembly, speech, and the press, then *the second is to take full advantage of those freedoms, so that the ranks of fighting workers engage freely in critical discussions*. The freedom to speak and publish is one precondition to the attainment of consciousness by the proletariat; the second is that the proletariat not put any restrictions on itself, that it not say, "We can discuss this, but not that." Conscious workers the world over understand this, and they always try to give even the worst of their enemies the right to freely explain their views. They say, "Let even the enemies of the working people voice their own views, so that we may respond to them, and so the working masses can work out for themselves who is a friend and who a foe."

The conscious part of the proletariat, Social Democracy, is, with respect to these matters, a guardian of the freedom to speak, discuss, and critique. Only in such crossfire may workers clarify the issues to themselves and develop their opinions. In the current struggle, when such heavy matters weigh on the shoulders of the proletariat of Russia and Poland, discussion is needed all the more, and critique is all the more essential. Social Democracy also labors to demonstrate by examples and models, always and everywhere, its benefit to workers.

The PPS* acts quite differently.

Reports by the hundreds from workers' associations inform us that at gatherings where members of the PPS make up a majority, the voices of members of other parties are absolutely silenced, and where they are instead a minority, they try to shut down discussion by shouting and fighting.

We are not sentimentalists. We would not utter a word in reprobation if strong passions once in a while led to a brawl, or even if the tumultuous character of discussion affected its peaceful unfolding. When fighting about matters the proletarian considers sacred, he becomes passionate, and not having a mind like a machine, he allows his blood to get the better of prudence. But one or two accidents are not what are at stake here; it is the *system*. The stacks of reports on this matter are not the only proof; the very tactics of the PPS attest to this. Since it came into being, the PPS has shut its eyes, with the obtuseness of a fool and the

---

* The Polish Socialist Party (Polska Partia Socjalistyczna); see p. 23, above.

idiocy of a clown, to the very existence of differences of platforms among Polish socialists, differences that go to the very root problems of our movement. To the PPS, Social Democracy, the first party with a political program that applied scientific socialism to Polish conditions, as recognized by the most eminent representatives of the International, was a pack of troublemakers, schemers, bearers of "dilemmas."*

This was not, however, due only to their lack of a sense of absurdity or their complete ignorance. Within their recalcitrant, bullheaded self-humiliation lay a certain "tactical" intuition.

The PPS went to great lengths never to expose themselves to a discussion with their adversaries before the working masses, making every effort to avoid it, so that the masses would not hear any criticism of their program. Indeed, because such critique only led to factitiousness, it was lost time. Workers who were members of the PPS were not allowed to bring the publications of other parties into the organization. They were supposed to believe what the PPS said, just as devout Catholics are supposed to believe what the Church teaches.

Just as churches expect their "little sheep" to believe in the shepherd's words and not talk back, so the PPS instills in the masses certain ideas, as articles of belief, using every means in its power to prevent members of the party from encountering the arguments of adversaries, denouncing every difference of opinion in the ranks of their party as disorganization and factitiousness, and attempting to form not a cadre of conscious, critically thinking workers, but a church of believers. They made fanatics of their supporters, enveloping their minds with a cloud of beliefs so dense that no light could shine in. Their work was not to raise workers' consciousness, but to distort their minds.

We, on the other hand, attempt to provide the publications of the PPS to our organization, because for us it is about the self-reliant building up of proletarian consciousness.

Today, since Social Democrats make speeches at hundreds of rallies, since the PPS cannot herd its members into secret circles to shelter them from criticism, and since the criticism, likewise, cannot be hidden or kept away from its members, the party attempts either to disallow free discussion or to convince the masses that it is harmful. At a long line of rallies, this is what we have heard from PPS speakers: "Comrades, now is not the time for discussions, nor the time for quarreling, because the battle is upon us."

We say in response, "Precisely because the battle is upon us, we must discuss it so that its character becomes clear to us."

If anything will bring an end to the political division of the proletariat, it will be discussion, it will be critique.

---

* The PPS considered itself a part of the Social Democratic movement and fought very hard to be recognized by the Second International as its leading representative in Poland.

If the PPS believed it could save its arguments from defeat, it should eagerly volunteer to expose its judgments to the light of critique.

But the PPS knows how weak its position is and will use every chance to escape criticism.

What can be done?

Let us show the masses at every opportunity the necessity for critique and discussion. Let us be an example through our behavior toward our adversaries; let us show, as we have shown up to now, that our words accord with our deeds, and that even in circles of PPS supporters, there is growing discontent for its harmful and immoral activities intended to disallow discussion. In cases where PPS supporters are the majority and, abusing this coincidence, prevent discussion, leave that place, workers, whether peacefully or through firm protest.

When a small group of them attempt to prevent discussion by shouting speakers down, peacefully or firmly point out to the crowd the baseness of such conduct, and compel the offenders to leave the place.

Absolute freedom of critique and discussion lies at the heart of the interests of the workers' movement, and it must be pursued *at all costs* if, to use the rallying cry of the International, "the liberation of the workers is to be the creation of the workers themselves."*

---

* The famous phrase is taken from the "Provisional Rules" of the First International, penned by Marx: "That the emancipation of the working classes must be conquered by the working classes themselves." See *Marx-Engels Collected Works*, Vol. 20 (New York: International Publishers, 1985), p. 14.

The Historical Services of the Polish Bourgeoisie and Mr. Świętochowski*

Kurjerek Warszawski [The Warsaw Courier]† placed a short article about the bourgeoisie in its New Year edition. The hack they ordered to hold his nose and write a defense of this good class cooked up one miserable concept—that "attorneys with no clients" and similar such more or less declassed pariahs could be equated with the bourgeoisie, and that because there are many cultured types in the bosom of this so-called intelligentsia, therefore, the bourgeoisie is not riffraff. The part after that is terrific. The German bourgeoisie, the French bourgeoisie, and the others are totally worthless, but the Polish bourgeoisie is something else entirely, because—take a guess, dear reader!—the Polish bourgeoisie has "much gentle blood." For minds fed on *Kurjerek Warszawski*, we must hit on arguments they find accessible; therefore, we will not enjoy ourselves with a disquisition but rather take our response from the field of animal husbandry. Cynology, for example—the science of dog breeding—has come to the conclusion that canine crossbreeding only occasionally leads to good results. More often, the offspring of such canine misalliances compound the defects of both breeds and none of the good points. The greyhound has its merits, as does the bulldog; the descendant of the greyhound bitch and the bulldog is a hideous being called a mutt, and the breeder will turn the monster out of the kennel to the four winds. So, as *Kurjerek Warszawski* has made mutts of the Polish bourgeoisie, let them have done with it.

Yes, but, several days later, we got the "serious" paper of the bourgeois intelligentsia, *Nowa Gazeta* [The New Gazette].‡ For several weeks, the chatter in the cafés has been that this will be a "newspaper you can call European." We took up the first issue with great curiosity, and by chance our gaze fell on a verse repeating word for word what we had read in that other journalistic trash heap: "Again, our bourgeoisie is not all that similar to the European bourgeoisie." To hell with this! We search for the byline. Oh, it's Mr. [Aleksander] Świętochowski!§ Read

---

  * This article first appeared in *Czerwony Sztandar*, No. 39, January 9, 1906, pp. 2–3, under the title "Historyczne zasługi burżuazji polskiej i p. Świętochowski." It is translated from the Polish original by Joseph Muller.

  † *Kurier Warszawski*, to which Luxemburg refers condescendingly in the diminutive form *Kurjerek*, was a daily newspaper that was founded in 1868 and continued publication until the German invasion of Poland in 1939.

  ‡ *Nowa Gazeta* was a Polish liberal daily newspaper, published in Warsaw from 1906 to 1908. It was created out of its predecessor, a newspaper for business and economics titled *Gazeta Handlowa* (Trade Newspaper), published from 1864 to 1905. *Nowa Gazeta*'s editor in chief was Stanisław Kempner.

  § Świętochowski was an important Polish journalist as well as a leading positivist philosopher. In 1904 he founded the Progressive Democratic Party (Związek Postępowo-Demokratyczny),

on, read on! With luck, we will find out how the Polish bourgeoisie is better than the European one:

> We must remember that, as a part of the only great cultural nation on earth now in captivity, the Polish bourgeoisie carries within her the smoldering embers of protest, that its historical traditions yet live within her, and that to this day she fights for the basic rights of man and nation. After 1848, when the working proletariat declared war on capitalism, the bourgeoisie of the whole world lost none of its wealth and privileges, but only changed the date of its fortune; at that time, Poland had already endured half a century of martyrdom and was beginning the second half, and up to that moment, the country was relegated to a class of political pariahs. Up to that moment, Poland had incessantly fought, suffered, endured great sacrifices, died tens of thousands of deaths in prisons and in exile, and withstood such torments that a gale of her groans might have encircled the earth. This is not, therefore, the German or French bourgeoisie, protected by rights and infringements, that Marx and other bourgeois-tamers had in mind, but that same untiring force whom Marx, Engels, [Paul] Lafargue, and [Frederick] Lessner honored with common recognition.

The Polish bourgeoisie carries the "embers of protest," "historical traditions live within her," "she fought"; the Polish bourgeoisie "died tens of thousands of deaths in prisons and in exile." Does Mr. Świętochowski laugh in the face of the readers of this "European daily," or have platitudes roosted so long in his head that he does not know what he is driveling about? Where, when, and how has the Polish bourgeoisie fought? Where and when did they die by the tens of thousands? No national uprisings have seen Polish bourgeois among the fighting ranks. This bourgeoisie not only did not sympathize with the uprising but, as a class, it sympathized entirely consciously with the enemy, cleaved to tsarism, and would have allowed itself to be chained if only the links had been gold-plated. This debased, rotten bourgeoisie dared to insult those who rebelled, denouncing their outbreak of heroic desperation as "insanity," saying they had "doomed the land." And, after that, came a period in which *Nowiny* [The News], *Przegląd Tygodniowy* [The Weekly Review], and *Prawda* [Truth]* promoted the

---

which opposed socialism while advocating liberal social reforms. The Progressive Union fought for autonomy for the Kingdom of Poland with a parliament in Warsaw, without demanding the overthrow of tsarism. This was one of Luxemburg's fundamental critiques of the progressive camp, leading her, after the 1905 Revolution, to argue that National Democrats and Progressive Democrats were essentially steering the same course against the revolution. The latter's major organ was *Prawda*. This should not be confused with the Russian-language *Pravda*, the paper co-published by Trotsky from 1909 in Vienna. Over time, numerous factions moved away from the Progressive Party, and it remained largely restricted to intellectual circles.

* Świętochowski edited *Nowiny* from 1878–79 and often submitted pieces on positivism and contemporary politics to *Przegląd Tygodniowy*. From 1881 to 1902 he edited *Prawda*.

catchphrase "organic work," which in essence came down to a brutal "Let's get rich, gentlemen." No, this Polish bourgeoisie today has no right to rob the laurels of martyrdom from the true combatants, those descendants of gentry who died honorably, who atoned in blood for the faults of their fathers. Draping the merits of the gentry on the bourgeoisie in this way is pointless. The Polish bourgeoisie never fought for the independence of Poland nor for freedom of another kind. Growing fat on easily gotten gains, the class debased itself beyond all measure before tsarism, shedding every semblance of human dignity. Blow after blow struck the land, a terrible reaction followed, the bourgeoisie bowed down at the feet of the tsar, not only holding its tongue like a coward but boasting of its doglike subservience.

Mr. Świętochowski speaks of sacrifice. Who suffered casualties in 1864?* The Polish working people! Tens of thousands of victims died in prisons and in exile, but these victims were from the working people, never the bourgeoisie. There were some among these tens of thousands who came from bourgeois circles, young socialist men and women, the children of manufacturers, merchants, and bankers; these suffered torture and exile in the name of the proletarian cause. And does Mr. Świętochowski know why there were so many champions of the cause of socialism in these circles in Poland and Russia? Because, in the atmosphere of depravity and degradation that had control of the Russian bourgeoisie, and even more the Polish bourgeoisie, those with a pure heart, with a noble spirit, cannot withstand it, for these young heroes see around themselves, among the bourgeoisie, moral depravity, an intellectual void, and brutal, derisive selfishness. So now we ask, Mr. Świętochowski, who abused these first defenders of socialism among us, who defamed them, who denied them honor and faith? Who fought against them armed with the poison of libel and slander? As a matter of fact, a Polish editorialist was found who took this disgraceful role on himself, and his name ... Mr. Aleksander Świętochowski.

The barbs Mr. Świętochowski aimed against Polish socialists for a quarter of a century were shameful, because he fought with lies. At least his old lies were cleverly put. Now this master of platitudes does not know what to do, because the sentence "Marx, Engels, and Lafargue honored the Polish bourgeoisie with common recognition" could only be written by someone who had disposed of not only his shame but also his mind.

Nevertheless, the part the Polish bourgeoisie played is so shameful that even this high priest of platitudes cannot do it justice and ends his article with this blubber:

---

* A reference to the brutal repression meted out following the defeat of the 1863 Polish national uprising.

Unfortunately, the bourgeoisie did not understand and did not perform her role. Aside from the progressive-democratic alliance, which actually only recruited her partially, she did not make any important or energetic movements in this direction. Rather than step out to fight for freedom under her own flag, she allowed herself to be shooed and chased off the field, protesting only with tender sighs, obliging whispers, and safe comments and applause.

Quite the picture, this! The class that fights without ceasing, endures great suffering, and bears great sacrifice in the decisive moment, when open battle has begun, has no role to play and can be chased off the field! They who fight without ceasing are not suddenly surprised by the course of history; they do not let their flag fall. The defender of the Polish bourgeoisie had only these platitudes at his disposal; he became entangled in them, the platitudes ate their way to the middle, and the whole beautiful encomium came to naught.

One might well ask whether we show too much honor to this gentleman, with the space we devote to his article. In response, we say that Mr. Świętochowski is of no consequence. Rather, it is the role he plays that is so remarkably characteristic of the system of political relations in which we find ourselves. After a painful labor, a bourgeois party took shape among us that might have wanted to put forth a progressive-democratic front, yet they expected this front to protect a man who, deep down, had never been anything other than a representative of foul Manchester liberalism,* a form of liberalism that long ago lost all credit in the West. Insignificant on its own, this fact bears witness to how dim are the powers, how dull the views of this group that pretentiously named itself the "Progressive Democratic" Party. And if this group represents the least reactionary part of Poland's bourgeoisie, so much the worse for the bourgeoisie.

In the above-mentioned article, Mr. Świętochowski cites [Eduard] Bernstein, who famously suggested that German Social Democracy reach an agreement with the liberal-democratic far left.

German comrades at the time responded that Bernstein, who, after many years of exile, had stopped following German conditions closely, overestimated the elements, and that there was no one with whom to unite. We are in a similar position. For our comrades in Russia, the question could have arisen of whether, and how much, they should depend on anti-government political action from the bourgeois far left. Here in Poland, this question had no chance to arise, for we are faced only with counterrevolutionary factions full of advocates of compromise and "national democratic"† Black

---

* In reference to a nineteenth-century liberalism that advocated free trade as a means to social harmony and acquisition of wealth. It is especially associated with the work of Richard Cobden.

† A reference to the conservative and nationalist National Democratic Party (Narodowa Demokracja), co-founded by Roman Dmowski in 1897, whose base of support was mainly the

Hundreds,* or else with that other mockery of a party, "Progressive Democracy," whose foremost defenders say the party "was not able to join the struggle for freedom."

Indeed, the Polish bourgeoisie differs from the bourgeoisie of the West and that of the East. It differs primarily in that it has no traditions, no political aspirations aside from reactionary ones, in that it has declined and hardened into nasty money-grubbing. We Social Democrats may lament this to a certain degree, for, as a result, we must take on ourselves the tasks that rightly ought to be the work of a radical bourgeois party. We may regret it, but we cannot change the fact.

It remains to us to fight with redoubled energy against the violence of a brutal tsar and the depravity of our local bourgeoisie.

---

urban middle class. It did not support the 1905 Revolution, advocating instead an autonomous Poland "cleansed" of Russian and German ethnic and linguistic influences. From 1900 onward, it distanced itself from the "conciliation camp" which, in the name of Realpolitik, aimed at achieving a compromise with Russia. With Dmowski's rise as the dominant personality of National Democracy after the turn of the century, there was an emphatic turn toward nationalism, particularly in the Kingdom of Poland. It rejected Poland's tradition of rebellion, which it viewed as political romanticism. It called for concession of territory to Russia in the east so that Poles would constitute the majority of his envisioned Polish nation. After World War I, National Democracy became an important political force, with Dmowski becoming the foremost domestic opponent of Piłsudski. After Piłsudski's coup in 1926, Dmowski and National Democracy were forced onto the political defensive. In promoting an idea of Poland that was as ethnically homogeneous as possible, Dmowski regarded Piłsudski's idea of a federation of eastern territories (including Belarus and Ukraine) as foolhardy and dangerous. The anti-Semitic strains in his conceptions that were obvious from the start became more explicit as time passed. After Hitler took power, he argued that Germany's "solution" to the "Jewish question" would have it become a more cohesive nation-state.

* "Black Hundreds" were an ultra-nationalist, counterrevolutionary, and anti Semitic movement that emerged in Russia in response to the 1905 Revolution. They also targeted Ukrainians and other movements in the empire that demanded national self-determination. Though financed and supported by the tsarist government, the movement had deep roots among sections of the bourgeoisie as well as the declassed lumpenproletariat. Luxemburg here connects the National Democratic Party—which Świętochowski never joined but worked with at times—with the far more heinous Black Hundreds.

The Year of the Revolution[*]

January 22 marks the end of the first year of the [1905] Great Revolution in the tsarist empire, a break in human history that can be compared to the Great French Revolution one hundred years ago.

When a telegram arrived one year ago with word that 200,000 workers had stopped working in the tsar's capital on the Neva [River] and set off on foot for the Winter Palace, demanding political freedom and an eight-hour workday, the news struck the hearts and minds of the people around the world like a thunderbolt. All humankind looked on this phenomenon, this miracle, with bated breath. They saw themselves in an amazing spectacle, a great, unending march of proletarians, a mighty pilgrimage of working people, the mass marching one step after another, with utter resolve, toward their position before the all-powerful tsar, face to face, to cry: *Freedom or death!*

A wonder surpassing all comprehension! For hundreds of years, tsarism was a vast graveyard in which millions of people were born, lived, and went to their graves in captivity, in chains, yet in gloomy silence. The silence of the grave hung over this vast prison of millions, broken only by the crack of the whip and the groans of the exhausted people, the moans of the misery of workers and peasants. The cause of freedom seemed hopeless. Isolated, self-sacrificing outbreaks of protest, especially the heroic People's Will uprisings, appeared to let in bright rays of light, yet these soon faded, letting the hopeless darkness of captivity grow still more terrible.

There in that silent grave, where millions humbly bore the iron manacles and heavy yoke of despotism, all at once the sea of human heads seethed, and all the working mass lifted itself as one. Vowing to go and win liberty or death, the mass goes up from there, and it makes war, and it marches on, unswerving, stumbling over its own slain, and slowly it forces its way into the trenches, and it overthrows the old bastion of despotism, and it overtakes line after line. Soon, on the highest rampart, it will obtain the red flag of freedom.

A miracle of miracles happened that twenty-second of January one year ago, for people who had eyes but did not see, had ears but did not hear.[†]

Only at the moment of the march in Petersburg on January 22 did the healing word become flesh,[‡] the red word of Social Democracy, which had knelled the death of tsarism for many years, heralding the spring like an early skylark. On January 22, it happened as the poet wrote in days of yore, "And when the west wind warms the land / What will become of tyranny's dam?" The

---

[*] This article first appeared in *Czerwony Sztandar*, No. 47, January 28, 1906, pp. 1–2, under the title "Rok rewolucji." It is translated from the Polish original by Joseph Muller.
[†] The passage is a paraphrase from Jeremiah 5:21 in the Hebrew Bible.
[‡] The expression is from John 1:14 in the Christian New Testament.

west wind was the breath of the proletarian idea of a workers' struggle for liberation, for socialism. Having spread to all the corners of the earth and breathed new life into millions of exploited workers everywhere, it found its way through the West to tsarism's enormous, frigid burial ground, and it began to blow and blow through the innumerable exploited working masses until a spark sprang up in their minds and a flame of protest in their hearts, until they rose up and went out to break the eternal ice dam of tyranny.

January 22 showed the world at once whence freedom for Russia would come, emerging from an enormous march of workers. Russian peasants had revolted, desperately, before that, and had fallen silent, smothered under tsarism's iron heel. The Russian gentry began a rebellion, having had their fill of an economy of bureaucrats, thieves, and Cossacks, only to retreat when, in December 1904, the bureaucrats, thieves, and Cossacks menacingly forbade protests, banned rural rallies, prohibited banquets, and ordered silence.

In that very moment, when all grew silent, and the scourge reigned more omnipotently than ever before, the working people rose, unarmed, and took a position of humility to *ask* for freedom. But such strength lies within the working class today, so mightily beats its heart, that the workers' plea for freedom sounded the death knell of tsarist government, and tsarism poured forth murderous divisions against the unarmed proletarian pilgrimage, and blood was spilled to fill an ocean.

January 22 marked the start of a new era in the history of tsarism, and a new era in the history of all modern societies. The first revolution of modern times had begun, started by the conscious working class, led forth under the banner of Social Democracy. Today the proletariat of the tsarist state, barbarism's oldest stronghold, leads the march of humanity. Today sparks of revolution from Russia and Poland fall on the thatch of the capitalist West, and already parts have caught fire, the red flames licking hungrily. In Vienna and Prague, in Leipzig and Dresden, the working masses stream into the streets demanding new political freedoms and bathing the streets of Germany in blood. Barricades have already gone up in Hamburg.* The grumbling of thunder is distant still in many places in Europe, the noiseless lightning shooting across the horizon. But the storm approaches steadily, blown in by a gale from the east. January 22, having awoken the proletariat of all Russia, *awoke the proletarians of all lands to a new conviction of their freedom, to new demands on power.* For decades, since the year 1848, the thunder of revolution was not heard in Europe. The bourgeoisie abandoned the struggle, having achieved power for themselves, and the ranks of the proletariat had not yet been deepened. After the bloody suppression of the worker uprising of the Paris Commune in 1871, revolutionary

---

* Barricades in Hamburg were erected in early December 1905, shortly after Luxemburg had given a speech there challenging the trade unions to support the mass strike.

struggles died down, the "peace" so blissful to the world's rulers ensued, the authorities and their blind and ungenerous subjects began to think generally that the revolutionary times were irrevocably in the past, that the kingdom of capital would tyrannize them for all the ages.

Until their January thunderbolt awoke them from blindness. As the harbinger of a series of future socialist revolutions of the proletariat around the world, day broke one year ago on January 22 in tsarism's northern capital.

The spontaneous uprising of the working class in Petersburg gave the movement a rallying cry throughout the entire state. Let us cast an eye back over the course of the revolution in the last year.

A massacre took place in the capital on the twenty-second, and by the twenty-fifth and twenty-sixth, hundreds of thousands of workers in the main cities across Russia, Poland, Lithuania, Livonia, and the Caucasus put down their work in a gesture of solidarity with their murdered brothers in Petersburg. All at once, the new powerful weapon of this first workers' revolution was spontaneously discovered—*the mass strike*. It was the first time in the history of tsarism and the history of the proletariat around the world that a mass of workers this gigantic, spread over such a large area, had stood up at a single command to fight for a common purpose.

And that command was given voice not by a brilliant leader, not by a new Napoleon, but only by the spirit of brotherhood and solidarity living in each worker: the very instinct of those pushed down by exploitation and class oppression was their infallible and all-powerful commander. The proletariat of Poland led the way.

They leaped up to strike in Warsaw, Łódź, Częstochowa, Dąbrowa,* Białystok, and Vilnius. The strike swept through the land, a demonstration to the tsarist government that it did not wipe out its enemies in the Petersburg massacre, for they number not in the thousands but the millions. In that first mass strike the entire working class under tsarism arose to action and to struggle, united as one army, led by one spirit, yearning after one goal. Political freedom and the eight-hour workday became, several days after the Petersburg outbreak, the slogan of workers across the state.

The youth stood up for battle together with workers. Together factories, schools, and universities took part in the strike movement—an unforeseen phenomenon that swept across the land. Tsarist education was dying.

The first mass workers' strike ended, but the revolution immediately took on a new form. In the place of one general strike, a series of countless strikes broke out in every line of work. The workers in every shop began to fight separately against their exploiters. Workers began eagerly to seek redress for the thousand wrongs done to them, borne previously with humility. The general

---

* Now Dąbrowa Górnicza.

fight for material improvements to living standards and the eight-hour workday spread rapidly in industrial regions. All spring was consumed by this fight, in which separate neighborhoods demonstrated heroism not seen before. Dąbrowa fought over food and maintained a strike continuously for six weeks.

May 1 arrived, the first workers' holiday in the era of the revolution. Again, the Polish proletariat was in the lead. Warsaw amazed everyone with its march under the banner of Social Democracy. The party of the working class appeared to the world as a power of the first order, at the head of an enormous mass. The march in May ended in the butchering of unarmed people on Jerozolimska Avenue, providing a rallying cry for vengeance, for renewed struggle across the land.* In June, Łódź gave a response to Warsaw's May holiday and outstripped Warsaw in its heroism. The mass strike led to clashes in the streets. The *first barricades* of the revolution rose on the streets of Łódź, and valiant fighters of the proletariat fell on them by the dozens. After Łódź, Białystok and Częstochowa provided more examples of workers' bravery. Riga shone with valor, and Kiev and Odessa emerged as centers of heroic struggle.

The phase of uninterrupted strikes died down for a moment in the middle of the year. The revolutionary storm was holding its breath. And then, suddenly, a new, unexpected outbreak—in the south, on the Black Sea, like a specter from a fairy tale, rose the battleship of rebellion, the *Potemkin*, an ironclad with a rebellious crew and the flag of revolution flying on its mast. This was a harbinger of outbreaks to come—in the navy, in the tsar's army. Hardly had the *Potemkin* rebellion been put down when the first signs of peasant uprising appeared. Outside the city, the countryside rose up to fight. The revolution spread, growing like an avalanche. And worker blood flowed in rivers. Marcin Kasprzak died the death of heroes, for freedom and for socialism, a death that stunned the world and fanned the flames of revolution.†

The tsar, with his cabal of criminals, attempted to deceive and incapacitate the revolution with stratagems. [Alexander] Bułygin's plotters began a scheme, a disgraceful travesty providing for the so-called right to elect representatives to the farcical tsarist "Duma."‡ The tsar believed he could still trick the working

---

* For Luxemburg's report of the May 1, 1905, massacre on Jerozolimskie Avenue in Warsaw, see "Two Camps," in *The Complete Works of Rosa Luxemburg, Vol. III: Political Writings 1*, edited by Peter Hudis, Axel Fair-Schultz, and William A. Pelz (London and New York: Verso, 2019), p. 137.

† Marcin Kasprzak was one of Luxemburg's closest comrades from the time they were teenagers. For her discussion of Kasprzak's arrest and execution, see "A Victim of the White Terror," in *Complete Works*, Vol. 3, pp. 198–204.

‡ The Bułygin Constitution was named after Alexander Bułygin, who became minister of the interior in late January 1905 in the aftermath of Bloody Sunday. In response to the threat posed by the revolution, in February 1905 he proposed a constitution that would provide a veneer of parliamentarism while leaving real power in the hands of the tsar and his administration. It went into effect in August 1905 as the so-called Bułygin Constitution. This provided for a merely advisory Duma (or parliament) in which workers, women, servicemen, and students had virtually no

people, not appreciating their political maturity. The response to Bułygin's designs was a new outburst of struggle: a mass rail workers' strike. And after that, a mass workers' strike. The Bułygin plan lay in ruins. A dying tsarism* published the October 30 proclamation, promising freedom. Before the tsar allowed it, a wave of freedom swept and crashed across the state, workers taking it by storm—public assemblies, free press, and unions sprouted up miraculously everywhere. The tsar responded with mass murder, pogroms against Jews, and crimes by the Black Hundreds. But the revolution, in response, made valiant strides forward: Echoes of the *Potemkin* were heard in naval uprisings in Kronstadt, Vladivostok, and Sevastopol. After the navy, the army rebelled in Petersburg, Moscow, Kiev, and Odessa. Martial law in Poland and a massacre in the Caucasus elicited an echo from Petersburg, a fraternal mass strike.

A peasant war engulfed the middle and south of Russia like a conflagration. Livonia lay entirely within the flames of revolution.

The tsar attempted new atrocities, arrests, and bans. The response was an outbreak of a new, as-yet-unknown revolutionary struggle—the mass strike of postal and telegraph workers. Immediately thereafter, a mass workers' strike and the first great armed uprising took place in Moscow.

Thus, on the next January 22, day broke over a terrible pool of red blood, over a vast battlefield of fallen heroes, over destitution, hunger, and the immeasurable efforts of the proletariat—yet also over the ruins of tsarism.

Petersburg began the year of revolution with a march of supplicants outfitted in Christlike agony and led by worker-priests. Moscow began the year in an armed uprising organized by the proletariat with the slogan and guidance of Social Democracy. Herein lies the meaning of the achievement of the revolution of the past year.

January 22 of last year showed immediately that the working class is the determining force that will fell absolutism. The entire subsequent year confirmed that hypothesis. An army of fighters spread and multiplied, the rural folk came onto the stage, the intelligentsia arose in Russia, there came bureaucrats, there came the navy, there came the army. But the industrial proletariat became the center, the kernel, and the director of this whole force. And in addition to broadening the struggle and commanding it, the proletariat grew continually during this time in political maturity, consciousness, and organization. The struggle not only broadened, but deepened too. What began from spontaneous,

---

representation. Peasants were permitted to vote, though they received far less representation than landowners. Luxemburg and other figures in the revolutionary left (such as the Bolsheviks) refused to participate in elections to the Duma, while others (such as a section of the Mensheviks and the Socialist Revolutionary Party [SR]) obtained seats in it.

* This is not meant literally but refers to the tsar's increasingly precarious political situation, which forced him to temporarily endorse the reforms presented by Bułygin. The tsar fired him in October 1905 when he came under pressure from more conservative forces opposed to making concessions to the revolutionaries.

chaotic outbreaks of protest and pleas for freedom has become today a disciplined forming of ranks, ready for every sacrifice, clear-eyed about their goal, and led by their own class party. Social Democracy, once a movement of sects spread across the land, has in one year become a vast people's movement. The political and economic organization of the proletariat has matured and grown dramatically.

And in that political maturity, that militant energy, that indomitable will of the revolutionary proletariat, lies the guarantee of future victories and final triumph for the revolution.

This was a year of revolution the likes of which history has not seen—without pause, without rest. A day did not pass without fighting, without sacrifice. All year long, the revolution marched from victory to victory. For every momentary reversal of its rise caused, after a time, a new, still more powerful outbreak. The revolution marched tirelessly forward, multiplying its regiments, accumulating arms, broadening its field of operation, growing in bravery and spirit. Absolutism only marched from crime to crime, from storm to storm, bankruptcy to bankruptcy. Today we stand on the brink of the last phase of revolution, the phase of armed struggle. The revolution is gathering its breath, so as to break out more powerfully, to lash out and bring its enemy at long last down to the earth.

In the current moment, the proletariat is making preparations with great concentration and iron force of will for the final phase of armed conflict with tsarism. Looking with contempt on proletarian efforts around the comedy of elections to the illegal Duma, the bourgeoisie still believes, for the moment, that the revolution is abating, that the bayonet and the machine gun will determine control of the situation, that the fighting people, driven to exhaustion, will let their rifles drop.

Rifles! They are to crush a revolution that has become a historical necessity, a verdict of time! Blind parasites on revolution forget that if the rifles ruling omnipotently on January 22, 1905, could not hamper the first outbreak of revolution, then today, shattered in pieces, they will not manage to bring down an intensified, raging revolution.

Exhaustion! Let these men who, from the safety of their hideaways, dare declaim on the fatigue of the fighting worker cast their gaze upon that abyss of ancient misery, of indignity, and of hopelessness in which the working people eked out their lives, upon that hell from which they emerged on January 22 to fight. And let them understand that this people can no longer look back, can no longer return to their yoke any more than a stream, having run through a mountain crevasse from a glacier and fallen down into the valley, can return to its source.

Their exhaustion comes not from revolution but from deprivation and disgrace, from the yoke of exploitation and oppression that followed the working people onto the streets on January 22, 1905, the day they began the revolution. That day, weary from ancient oppression, the proletarians of Petersburg cried out, "We shall not return to the yoke. Better death than bondage!"

And today, after a year of heroic struggle, the proletariat of Poland and Russia, of the entire state, repeats their resolute vow to fight indomitably to the very end, to the very day of triumph!

Before January 22 arrives a third time, the bastion of despotism shall have sunk in that sea of blood into which, one year ago, on the first day of the revolution, it strove to plunge both liberty and the struggle of the people.

"Through Fiery Smoke, in a Haze of Brothers' Blood ..."*

In every region of the tsarist state where revolution has roiled for a year, there is no corner in which the bourgeoisie has been gearing up to seize the fruits of the workers' bloody struggle as shamelessly as here in our midst. All around us, a terrible revolutionary drama plays out, the working people are locked in a mortal battle against a dying absolutism, murders and rapes have become their daily bread, and the counterrevolution wildly musters its final superhuman strength to stifle the fighting proletariat and drown it in blood. And among these struggles, these birth pangs of revolution, these death spasms of absolutism, our homegrown bourgeois stuffed shirts positively trip over themselves in their haste to make ready for the elections to the tsar's "Duma."

The advocates of compromise and the National Democrats hurry to take advantage of martial law, with its ready bayonets and whips, in order to conduct the election "peacefully," in accordance with the "clarification" given to them by [Georgi] Skalon.† Free from repercussions, they rob the Polish working class of its right to vote and at the same time gag its mouth with a Cossack fist.

As if that were not enough, the entire millions-strong urban and rural working populace has been prevented from influencing the outcome of the elections. If the elections reach their conclusion, only representatives of the compromise advocates and National Democratic reactionaries will make it to the "Duma"—only despicable scumbags from Poland's bourgeoisie and gentry. Hence the need to make further use of the cover of Skalon and his Cossacks by laying out now, in advance, program planks and policies for future representatives of Poland in the tsar's "Duma." Indeed, it is precisely under the cover of martial law that some "citizens" are visiting so-called election rallies to elaborate a program to be used by national envoys to the Duma. *Polish Circle, national solidarity, national politics, Polish autonomy*—these are their catchphrases.

"Polish Circle"! Do you know what that means, workers? That means that all the people picked to serve as envoys from our country in the Petersburg "Duma," whoever they are, are somehow supposed to stay together, create one circle, isolate themselves from all the Russian state envoys in the "Duma," and represent not Polish factory owners, Polish landowners, or the Polish petty bourgeoisie, but the "Polish nation." Those who actually represent Poland's exploiters

---

    * This article was first published in *Czerwony Sztandar*, No. 49, February 21, 1906, p. 1, under the title "Z dymem pożarów, z kurzem krwi bratniej ..." It is translated from the Polish original by Joseph Muller.

    † Skalon was govenor-general of Warsaw and implemented martial law during the 1905 Revolution. He was widely known for his brutality.

and who ride as parasites on the back of the revolution are somehow meant to act on behalf of the entire nation, on behalf of millions of Polish workers and farmhands. This Polish "circle" of profiteers is meant to represent the exploited Polish people, its interests, and the injustices it has suffered and to say at each step: "We are Poland, we are the Polish nation, the Polish people want what we want!"

"National solidarity—national politics"! Do you know what that means, workers? That means that yesterday, the advocates of compromise and the National Democrats (in other words, the fat bourgeoisie and the gentry), along with the landowners and the petty bourgeoisie, snarled at each other like dogs over a bone and dragged each other through the mud, but today they cry, "It's time to stop quarreling among ourselves. Let's extend an open hand, let's join together better in 'solidarity' in order to strip the people of their rights and political influence and share among ourselves, in 'solidarity,' the parliamentary mandates of the tsar's 'Duma,' won with the blood of Polish workers."

"National politics"! This one means that the solid "circle" of Polish exploiters in the Petersburg "Duma" is going to use every opportunity to convince the Russian people and the entire world, "There is no class conflict here in Poland, there are no exploited and oppressed workers or peasants, we are all one Polish 'nation,' and this entire 'nation' wants what we, the Polish exploiters, want." In other words, "national politics" means that those who represent Polish exploitation will use every opportunity to defend and differentiate the "Polish nation" from having anything in common with the revolutionary "nation," with the exploited Russian "nation"—that is, with the Russian proletariat, with the small-farm Russian peasants, and with the Russian revolutionary intelligentsia. To do so, they will join the Russian exploiters, manufacturers, landowners, and reactionary gentry at every step along the way, and in the name of the "Polish nation." They will endeavor, together with them in "solidarity," to rob the Polish and the Russian working populace blind.

Such are the "Polish Circle," "national solidarity," and "national politics" to which the compromise advocates and National Democrats now subscribe. There are already two such "Polish Circles," one in the German Parliament in Berlin and one in the Austrian Parliament in Vienna. In both, one can find both landowners and commoners who talk endlessly in the name of the Polish "nation." They vote for taxes and tariffs on bread and meat to starve the Polish populace, for expansions to the army and the fleet to impoverish and suppress the Polish masses, and for extraordinary laws affecting Polish farmworkers. And now our venerated "citizens" want to establish a third such "circle" of Polish shame in Petersburg.

Finally, "Polish autonomy"! Workers, do you know what Polish autonomy means coming from the lips of these gentlemen? It is not the autonomy of liberty or of cultural spirit that we want for the country. It is something else entirely. It is what exists already—a bourgeois and National Democratic autonomy—and they have already realized a piece of this "autonomy." The tsarist government has brought about a terrible unemployment crisis through a criminal war and political misrule. Polish factory owners, on their own initiative and as a result of their own "national" politics, have added factory closings and threats of closings to this situation, so as to inflict misery onto Polish workers to further erode and dishearten them. And that is just a taste of bourgeois "autonomy"!

The tsarist government has established martial law and robbed working people of the right to vote or have influence in the elections. Even in this situation of martial law, however, election rallies are open to *all*—anyone has the right to enter and speak at any election rally. But this "freedom of assembly" that the law of Skalon allows is too generous, in the opinion of our "citizens"; not even the martial law of Skalon is enough for them. So they corrected it themselves. Just as the autonomous Polish Sejm in Galicia* levies domestic taxes on peasants and workers in addition to state taxes, so our very own lords of compromise and National Democrats have themselves levied on Polish workers a domestic "tax" for the tsarist martial law. They are even organizing *ticketed election rallies, in secret*, so as to withhold the vote from the very proletariat that, with its own lifeblood, secured them this ability to assemble, this right to vote, and these very elections. To physical rapaciousness the Cossacks have added moral rapaciousness—violations of the conscience and of the freedom of belief. And in addition to Polish exploitation and disgrace in the tsarist Duma, a future "national politics" emerges, thriving under the dual protection of tsarist murders and independent "national Polish" modifications to the enforcement of martial law.

"Through fiery smoke, in a haze of brothers' blood," the Polish bourgeois voice floats up to the tsar's "Duma." To "last cries" extracted by firing squads, the loyal troop of Polish class rule "falls in for the drill …"†

And yet, if the shamelessness of the National Democrat and compromised "citizenry" has no limits, the patience of Polish workers does. And if the ancient iron "circle" of Russian absolutism is finally cracking under the blows of the proletarian fist, then in order to crush the rising "circle" of Polish "national" exploitation and "national" disgrace, workers need only muster the scorn to stomp it to pieces with their boots.

---

* The Polish Sejm (or parliament) in Galicia (at the time part of the Austro-Hungarian Empire) was a unicameral legislature that could make autonomous decisions in certain specified areas of governing.

† Here, Luxemburg ironically modifies the lyrics of a Polish song that became popular during the revolutions and conflicts of the 1840s.

Workers! Show these gentlemen the extent of their overreach in exercising "autonomous government." Break up these shameful election rallies where parasites sap the revolution, deny you the right to speak, represent the "Polish nation" behind closed doors, and leave the revolutionary people out in the cold. The honor of the revolution requires it.

The Program of "National" Trickery*

The nationalist lords are preparing for the Cossack elections in earnest: They have already used the rallying cry of "national solidarity" to mask their suspect delivery of Duma mandates to nationalists; they have already agreed to form a "circle" of Polish exploiters in the tsar's Duma; and now National Democracy† has even announced, in the form of an electoral appeal, a detailed program outlining the policies that this disgraceful Polish "circle" will pursue when they arrive in the tsar's Duma.

If there are any workers who are still unfamiliar with the typical character of National Democracy, perhaps the program recently announced will open their eyes.

National Democracy is a "national" party, and that is why it demands "autonomy" for Poland yet does not also require a republic. Thus, in reality, it wants the Russian tsar's throne to stay in place even along with political freedom. Because its program demands a "swearing in of the constitution by the monarchy," as a "national" party, it stands in defense of the Russian tsar and against the Russian and Polish working people who demand a republic for the entire state and who alone can actually defend the autonomy of Poland.

National Democracy is furthermore a "democratic" party, and that is why it fills its program with hollow promises to workers, rural folk, and small artisans.

To landless peasants and small farmers, the nationalists promise to create small peasant settlements through the parceling out and colonization of land. But this is well known in most other countries as just a means of salvation for none other than the bankrupt gentry themselves.

Members of the landed gentry who face decline want to rid themselves of bad land or mismanaged farms, so the parceling banks buy their land and create new peasant settlements. The landed gentlemen get capital in hand, and the peasants live from hand to mouth on their tiny new allotments. That is, so long as they are not expelled from the land again by large landowner rivalries, tax requirements, crop failures, or military service obligations and thus reduced to beggary again.

These days only the most dim-witted sorts of rural folk in these other countries are taken in by such parceling scams.

The nationalists promise to save small artisans and dealers with the help of credit (that is, banks), professional education, and the establishment of cooperative companies. But every artisan and small trader knows that his current ruin is

---

* This article first appeared in *Czerwony Sztandar*, No. 50, February 27, 1906, pp. 1–2, under the title "Programme 'narodowego' szalbierstwa." It is translated from the Polish original by Joseph Muller.
† That is, the National Democratic Party.

due to the competition of large capital and large factories, and that against such competition, bank loans and specialist education will help him about as much as incense helps the dead. In other countries, these means of saving the crafts and small trades also turned out to be a sham long ago.

Finally, the nationalists promise to bring about an earthly paradise with the help of trade unions, national employment agency offices, "appropriate laws" for the protection of work, universal insurance, professional education, and higher participation of workers in the life of cultural associations of "every sort." That is a pocket full of promises. But trade unions in the spirit of National Democracy are not tools for fighting for the liberation of workers, only tools for reconciling workers to exploitation and subjugation, much like the railroad union that, revolvers in hand, tried to suppress a common strike together with the tsar's hooligans.

For the most part, official employment agency offices are, as has been shown in other countries, institutions for delivering strike breakers to capitalists and for keeping labor struggles contained. Everywhere abroad, workers who have their wits about them fight these official offices with all their strength. They organize their own employment offices or demand districts under the control of labor unions. As for "appropriate laws" for the protection of work, the "national" program is careful not to specify what that could possibly mean. Finally, the part about participation in "cultural associations" is obviously a promise that workers can take joy in the knowledge that the National Democrats will pick a few workers and make them members of their "national" associations, such as the Polish "Falcons," singing groups, skating groups, and the like.

Such is the hodgepodge of measly deceptions—deceptions that have been scorned and ridiculed by knowing people for decades wherever in the world there is political freedom and open party struggle—with which the National Democratic headmen are trying to string along the Polish worker, the small farmer, and the small artisan!

As if that were not enough. The nationalists' program is even more telling in what it leaves unsaid than in what it says. In its program, National Democracy pretends, as a "democratic" party, to be a caregiver to workers, peasants, and small artisans; yet the program contains not one word about expelling from our midst the *militarism* that presents as great a prospect of ruin for the peasant and the artisan as it does for the worker; nor one word about abolishing the *tariffs and indirect taxes* that put a strain on the most basic livelihoods of all urban and rural people and suck the very breath from their lungs; nor one word about *the eight-hour workday* that, for the working class, is the cornerstone of bodily and spiritual regeneration.

And there is nothing strange about this. Indeed, how can National Democracy demand the abolition of the current military system when the factory-owning lords who belong to National Democracy have need of mercenaries to quell "rebellious" workers, and when the gentle landowner-citizens of National Democracy are terrified that, without the protection of mercenaries, they might be given a bloody christening by "plebeians" like the one given to the gentle barons of Livonia?*

How can National Democracy demand the abolition of tariffs and indirect taxes that so overwhelm working people when the capitalists and landowners so dear to its heart would then feel a tax burden pulling on their purse strings?

How, indeed, can this party demand an eight-hour workday for workers, when this could strain the "national industry," or, in other words, temporarily, marginally deplete the profits of the factory lords?

It cannot! Not only is National Democracy a party that is working to support and immortalize capitalist exploitation, and not only is it loath to cause harm to even the least powerful Polish exploiters, it also includes items especially for them in its program. And by selling the workers, peasants, and small traders on pies in the sky and vague twaddle, it gains a very clear and a very immediate means of aiding the class of exploiters. To the landed gentry, the party promises to fight to lower land taxes—no doubt by offloading them onto peasants—and to remove differential railroad tariffs that help Russian grain flow more easily into the country and thereby reduce its price. National Democracy promises, that is, to enrich the gentry *by trying to make grain more expensive—making bread more expensive!* Meanwhile, it attends to our country's industrialists by making "authorized demands for deductions and state aid"; that is, it promises that the "national" envoys in the tsar's Duma will make it their highest priority to beg for concessions and aid from the tsar's safe for Polish factory owners and merchants. National Democracy declares that, as a "national" party, it will aspire to separate all our affairs from those of the Muscovites. This means that it will do so in everything that smacks of Russian Revolution, workers, and progress, but "national" pride does not in the least prevent the party from begging the government in Petersburg for roubles "from Moscow" for Polish capitalists—roubles that must then be beaten out of Russian peasants with a cudgel or bought with the blood of Russian workers.

Such is the "democratic" and "national" program of the future envoys to the tsar's Duma. Comrades! Ask those unwitting workers in Dąbrowa and Warsaw, those duped peasants—poor country folk—what they have managed to do so far under the banner of National Democracy. Ask them if they know they are marching to the drum of a party that does not want an eight-hour workday, does not want to deal with looters or eliminate the fatal requirement to serve in the army, does not want to abolish tariffs and taxes on means of subsistence,

---

* Luxemburg is referring to the revolutionary uprising that swept parts of Livonia (a part of Lithuania) in early and mid-December 1905. For her analysis of the uprising, see "The Revolution in Russia [December 19, 1905]" and "The Revolution in Russia [December 21, 1905]" in *Complete Works*, Vol. 3, pp. 465 and 485.

does not want to overthrow the tsar's throne, and, after all that, wants to make bread more expensive, lower taxes for the landed gentry, and secure giveaways from the state treasury to Polish factory owners! Ask them if they know they are marching to the drum of a party that, in announcing its program, voices publicly, in front of the whole world, that it is a party that deceives working people for the benefit of the Polish exploiter class and the Russian tsar!

Boycotting the Tsar's Duma[*]

The longer the battle is waged over elections to the Duma, the more important it becomes for Social Democracy to apply, with the utmost resolve, tactics that are appropriate to this situation. For various external reasons, such tactics have been dubbed "boycotts." This name, however, is inaccurate, because it does not get to the heart of the matter and may lead its own supporters astray to some degree. On the question of whether to take the position of an enemy in relation to the Duma and the elections, our conscious proletariat has no hint of hesitation or misunderstanding. "Down with the Duma and the elections!" has become a popular rallying cry known to hundreds of thousands of workers.

But the question of *how* to turn that rallying cry into action, how to develop it into a complete set of tactics, into a whole sequence of political acts—that question is not so easy, and one can only become conscious of it in the course of events themselves.

At first glance, one might conclude that if the workers only ignore the elections and turn their backs on this despicable farce, everything needed for such a boycott to succeed will already be achieved.

Some people are ready to think that what the bourgeois parties do, whether they organize election rallies, what they say about the rallies, and how they campaign—that all this is none of our concern. And many people are even ready to believe that the tactic of boycotting the elections obligates workers to boycott bourgeois election rallies too—that is, obligates them to not attend the rallies, to remain at a distance in silent disdain of their bourgeois puppet shows.

But such tactics would mean only that the working class does not itself take part in the elections, thereby leaving them unharmed, without interference. That would be a politics of abstention—that is, a politics of standing on the sidelines, a politics of removing oneself from the fight, not a politics for the fight. By its nature, such a position can be neither the politics of the proletariat nor the tactics of revolution. Abstaining from the elections, like every kind of "passive resistance," is a way of fighting that is indigenous to the bourgeoisie and characteristic of parties that are weak or that talk back and forth, sometimes surrendering to the violence of the government and sometimes calling the revolutionary populace to mass action. An election boycott of this nature, encapsulated in sitting alone at home, may appeal to a party of political nothingness like our country's so-called Progressive Democracy. For the revolutionary proletariat, the fundamental question is not "Should the workers take part in the elections?" but something quite different: "What action should be taken

---

[*] This article first appeared in *Czerwony Sztandar*, No. 51, March 2, 1906, pp. 1–2, under the title "Bojkot dumy carskiej." It is translated from the Polish original by Joseph Muller.

such that the elections and the formation of the Duma do not take place, or if they do take place formally, such that their significance is completely invalidated in advance?" Because the cause of the revolution and the proletariat demands that the tsar's Duma does not take effect, workers must not only remove themselves from the elections but simultaneously do everything they can to bring the entire effort of the elections and the Duma to naught. Because, for our goal to be achieved, it would not be enough if the entire enormous proletarian population was to abstain from registering to vote. In fact, National Democracy and the compromisers have only managed, despite having the full support of the police and the Cossacks, to register a laughably small number of primary voters, which has already exposed the elections to general ridicule. Yet this alone is not enough. Social Democracy is a party of class struggle, and every act, every moment of revolution, is for us simultaneously an act and a stage in the fundamental struggle of the proletariat against the bourgeoisie. Similarly, for us, the tactic of boycotting the Duma and the elections is not only a form of direct battle with the tsarist government but, at the same time and to the same degree, a moment of struggle with the bourgeois political parties.

Despite full-scale protests by the revolutionary proletariat, and despite the imposition of martial law, our bourgeois parties, National Democracy and the compromisers, organize election rallies and attempt to carry the elections off. Given this, it is now of utmost importance that the working masses appear for battle and steadily wage the political fight against bourgeois supporters of the tsar. Closed rallies that exclude the revolutionary populace are important for National Democracy because they give the elections to the tsar Duma the character of an act of the whole "nation," the whole "society"! The party also uses these rallies to unfurl a general political program, a program with which we will have to contend at every stage of the revolution and after its end. By excluding the conscious working masses from their rallies, they try to lend their program the appearance of "national" politics.

Because of this, workers have an absolute duty to show up en masse at all election rallies organized by bourgeois parties, with these considerations in mind:

(1) The duty of Social Democracy is always to raise awareness of the broadest possible ties between people. It is an error to think in advance that the entire public that National Democracy wants to come to their rallies is "bourgeois" or utterly duped or corrupted politically. On the contrary, one must differentiate the handful of swindlers—themselves members of National Depravity—who serve as "benefactors," organizing and waxing poetic at the rallies, from the broader public to whom they give orders. This public includes many people from the petty bourgeoisie, artisans, journeymen, and so forth, who are not able as of yet to distinguish the parties and political programs, people whose eyes still need to be opened. They still have not heard clear explanations of the

positions, interests, and objectives of working people, and in service of this goal Social Democracy must claim a voice for itself at the rallies.

(2) In attending and publicizing its stance at election rallies, the conscious proletariat should lift the mask away from the "national" politics of the bourgeois parties, distinguish its own revolutionary politics from theirs, and so bring class protest and class struggle right into the place where the future chicanery of "national" politics is being kept and made ready. It is not enough for workers to profess their program and stance at their factory rallies and in their socialist publications. The proletariat cannot and should not wage class struggle, as the saying goes, on their home turf, *outside* bourgeois society. Whenever and wherever the bourgeoisie attempts to advance its politics at the proletariat's expense and in the name of society on behalf of exploiters and revolution parasites, the proletariat must show up. Doing so also clearly possesses a meaning of greater importance. When the working people advance and Social Democracy takes part in the rallies, they force the bourgeois parties to more expressly describe their policies and drop the vague bamboozling platitudes—that is, to step out before the vast working masses and the general populace with their actual positions, as political parties full of exploiters of various shades. When the conscious proletariat engages in direct confrontation and verbal sparring at rallies, this contributes, in short, as it always does, to the steady clarification and exacerbation of party relations, and thereby to the political enhancement of the proletariat itself.

(3) Finally, the immediate goal is for the working populace to negate any moral or political purchase the elections had, through their mass participation and protest at the election rallies—to declare loudly and demonstrate in front of the whole world that the vast majority of people will not accept these elections.

These are the reasons that workers should show up en masse at each and every election rally, announce that they stand for an effective boycott of the Duma and the elections, demand entry and a chance to speak, and use their presence and their voices to clearly lay out their position.

Of course, National Democracy forbids entry to workers at their election rallies. The party holds the rallies at secure gathering places and checks tickets at doors guarded by armed hooligans. This raises the question: What should workers do?

Clearly, the way the election rallies were set up, in addition to the three considerations outlined above, makes it imperative that the workers go to the rallies and gain entry to them at all costs. Because more than anything else, this has to do with *freedom of assembly and speech*—freedoms that National Democracy blatantly desires to take away from the same revolutionary class that earned them, with the express aim of preventing the working class from protesting and speaking out against the elections. National Democracy, which went as far as to limit tsarist law so that it could quickly push its electoral legislation through the

Duma, is already developing an abnormal politics, no longer consisting of viewpoints and convictions, but only naked *acts of counterrevolution*, not a hair better than or different from the action the [Pyotr] Durnovo–[Count Sergei] Witte government* took to suspend† martial law. For that reason, the exigencies of revolution directly obligate workers to take on the *serious responsibility* of bringing the fight to such violent tactics right down the line. The situation presents our proletariat with a choice: Either we gain entry to the rallies by storm in order to seize the freedom of speech for the working class and discredit the elections, or we prevent and disperse what are, based on how they have been organized so far, affairs of great violence serving the interests of the counterrevolution. In either case, taking action will result in a victory for the revolutionary cause. On the one hand, if the workers can force the bourgeois parties to open the election rallies to the proletarian masses, then the voice of revolution will thunder out over them and expose the "nation" headed to the tsar's Duma as a miserable band of privileged reactionaries. If, on the other hand, the Polish bourgeoisie prefers to provoke a series of violent scuffles and splatter itself with working-class blood in defense of the elections to the tsar's last hope, the Duma—if it prefers, indeed, to call up the tsar's Cossacks and police to the defense of its rallies—then the goal will still be met. Electoral action taken under these conditions, bathed in blood, watched over down the barrel of a rifle, will be seen immediately as an abomination throughout the civilized world. The elections will be remembered not even as a satire of political liberation but as a brazen act of bloody counterrevolution. And by then, the future "envoys" will appear not as chosen representatives of the "nation" but as messengers sent by Skalon's police.

The greatest reward for using these tactics will be what has always been the defining vision of our movement: deeper class consciousness and political development among the proletarian ranks, not only through leaflets and speeches in our own labor circles but through direct political struggle, face to face with our enemies in the bourgeoisie and the government.

---

* Durnovo was appointed minister of the interior following the tsar's dismissal of Bułygin in October 1905; Witte became prime minister on November 5, 1905. Witte initially advocated a series of reforms to save the tsarist regime but was fired on April 22, 1906, when the tsar imposed much more repressive measures.

† Witte sought to *suspend* some of the articles of martial law only because he wished to keep the governor-general of Warsaw, Georgi Skalon, from imposing a level of violence and repression that would scare away some pro-government Russian moderates. However, it is possible Luxemburg meant to refer to the initial act to *impose* martial law.

Under the Workings of Revolution*

The latest general strike has ended, the first collective uprising of the heroic working people of Moscow and other Russian cities has been put down, and the tsar's barbarians have bathed the land from Livonia to the Caucasus in blood and fire. The revolution is on pause, a foreboding silence prevails, and the vicious reaction of the government, laying waste to all Russia with the torch and the sword, is the only force that would seem able to prompt a new, even greater revolutionary movement.

Yet only from blindness and folly could one think that such a foreboding silence—of the kind that precedes the storm, the tempest of revolution—means that nothing is happening that could be compared to the revolution, that could be put in the same category as the great October moments. Absent a general strike, absent the clash of weapons, a different revolution—not less important, in fact of utmost importance—is taking place in the very heart of society. In the short time between the October general strike and the present moment, a profound overturning has altered the mutual relations between social classes. Currents have been revealed that in ordinary times murmur in the shadows of society, hidden from the normal eye. Political classes have lined up for battle with unusual speed and show of force. Social classes have demonstrated their distinct characters, revealing the potential for reaction or revolution slumbering within. And elements that could, until recently, appear to belong to progress, opposition, defense of the people, battle for Poland, radicalism, or patriotism have stepped out suddenly and dramatically as allies of the tsar, as sworn enemies of Poland, of the people, of freedom, and of the revolution.

The revolution tore the mask off the face of bourgeois society and shredded the platitudes disguising the naked truth. It forced the Polish bourgeoisie to openly expose—like an erupting volcano hurling its contents from the depths of its crater—not only the capitalist tendencies that chain it to the Russian state but also its alliance with the Russian tsar. Whoever thought that Polish nationalism meant treating the tsar as an enemy, after all was said and done, should look now at National Democracy. Look what has become of its cry for "Poland from sea to sea," which so recently struck such fear into the hearts of the country's compromisers and Galician Stańczyk-ites.† Whoever thought that today's Polish bourgeoisie was the most explosive power in the tsar's state, ready at the first hint of war to bring the fire of revolution, should look at the relations between

---

* This article first appeared in *Czerwony Sztandar*, No. 52, March 8, 1906, pp. 1–2, under the title "Pod działaniem rewolucji." It is translated from the Polish original by Joseph Muller.

† "Stańczyk-ites" was a nickname for the Polish Conservative Party in Galicia, a right-wing organization that existed from 1869 until 1918. The name derived from a pamphlet putatively co-written by a J. Stańczyk in the fifteenth century.

the Duma and the bourgeoisie and gentry. Look at how the "patriotic" petty bourgeoisie cannot wait to follow National Democracy into the "foreign" tsar's parliament. Look at how the peasants are "deliberating"—read daydreaming—about adding the one-headed eagle of the Polish gentry to the two-headed eagle of the Russian tsar on the official emblems of their villages and towns.

In the first days of November, after the tsar declared a constitution, Polish society could still seem to be a single, common, "national" bloc. The "national" processions, voices of the press, and public bourgeois gatherings were supposed to create the illusion that the whole of society was joining together in solidarity with the revolutionary working class—the class that secured the constitutional proclamation in the first place—and that the whole of society was truly ready to fight not only to obtain the freedoms that had been promised but also to achieve state autonomy. But when the revolutionary working class showed that it took the battle seriously, the tsar of national "unity" suddenly splintered. Through martial law and rapacious government measures, the bourgeois camp launched a heated, fierce battle against the revolutionaries that has lasted to this day.

In our country the battle is fought primarily over the commercial-industrial crisis, the lessening or blocking of the flow of new profits into the pockets of the bourgeoisie. The bourgeois parties and their journalists have piled the blame for widespread poverty entirely on the revolutionary workers and general strikes; in fact, they blame each new individual strike as the cause of the whole crisis. Their struggle against revolution has uncovered a deeper bourgeois hatred of workers than in any other country in the world at this moment. At the time of the Russo-Japanese War, there was also a mounting commercial-industrial crisis, but in that conflict the bourgeoisie did not lunge with such ferocity. The bourgeoisie made no move at all against the tsarist government, the government that had perpetrated the crisis and orchestrated such misery in front of the whole world. And now, Polish nationalists throw themselves on the revolutionary working class, with National Democracy at the head, together with the entire "patriotic," "national" bourgeoisie, in open alliance with the tsarist government, under the care of the tsar's bayonets. Polish nationalists attack the very same class that earned them the freedom to slander and disparage the revolution in the press without preventive censorship—the very same class that earned them the right to hold election rallies, rallies at which they use ticketed entry to allow in the self-proclaimed enemies of the revolution and bar entry to enemies of the tsar, under the threat of revolvers and government-issued bayonets.

Furthermore, the nationalists pine after seats in the "foreign" parliament, as they call the tsar's Duma, despite the martial law in effect. In fact, they do not even protest martial law, despite explicit wishes to that effect being expressed countless times by the working class at the general factory strike of January 22 and at thousands of factory rallies protesting the Duma. The nationalists ignore the lion's share of voters, who made their disgust clear when they turned their backs on the electoral registers and on the entire election-day farce. And this is to say nothing of the tsar's bayonets keeping careful watch over "national duties," over "national interests," over our "citizen patriots" in their elections offices and at their election rallies. This all would have seemed impossible to quite a few people just a few months ago, and now it is a fact!

Is it not telling that in Russia even the extremely reactionary Party of October 30,* also made up of religiously pugnacious hooligans, blames the tsarist government for the chaos, the misery, and the commercial-industrial crisis? Is it not telling that even this party has told the tsar there can be no talk of returning to normal relations while the promises of freedom go unfulfilled, while the entire "national" press piles the blame for poverty and turmoil on revolutionaries!?

Consider that while weapons were once smuggled into Poland for the fight against Russia, today National Democracy understands "national traditions" in such a way that it arms its "military organizations" with revolvers so that they can oppose the enemies of the tsar and prop up the tsar's police. Such is the extent of the unpunished slaughter committed against Social Democratic workers by National Democrats. When *Gazeta Polska* [The Polish Gazette]† and *Polska Praca* [Polish Labor] declare that no government help is needed, that the "national" elements themselves can crush us, realize how outrageous such a declaration is. It is an admission of a kind unheard of even among Russian hooligans, that our "national" sphere has already matured to the point of replacing the Cossacks who guard Skalon—that these men are as expert in serving the tsar as the Russian Imperial Guard.

It is clear that what would have taken decades of history to develop in other times—everything that until now has only germinated, staying below ground—has matured with incredible speed under the workings of revolution, pushing up to the surface, and has revealed society to be split into two hostile, intransigent camps. An abyss has opened: on one side, the bourgeoisie, the gentry, the reactionary petty bourgeoisie, and the peasantry, who have taken their stand in serried ranks guarding the tsar, and on the other, the revolutionary working class, which uses each new outbreak of conflict to gather and attract new tiers of working people to itself.

Between the one and the other rim of the abyss there stands no bridge, no means of crossing. In this landscape, the party that calls itself Progressive

---

* The Octobrists were a Russian political party that advocated a constitutional monarchy. They were named in deference to the Manifesto of the Tsar of October 30, 1905, which promised to grant civil freedoms, extend the franchise of those entitled to vote for the Duma, and provide legislative power to the legislative body. However, these turned out to be empty promises.

† *Gazeta Polska* was a daily newspaper, published legally in Warsaw from 1826 to 1907. After the defeat of the November Uprising in 1830, it was published as *Gazeta Codzienna* (Daily Paper) from 1831 to 1861. For a long period, it was the most important organ of the liberal-bourgeois political spectrum, although over time it took increasingly conservative positions. In 1906 it was taken over as a National Democratic publication, under the editorship of Roman Dmowski.

Democracy, which wanted to be both "national" and "progressive," standing in favor of fighting for freedom but against "extremism" in the fight for freedom, revealed itself as a party of political nothingness. This party did not even make it through a week of "heroic resistance" to the elections, running off to the polls in the company of National Democrats, compromisers, and tsarist scourges.

Revolution does nothing by halves. It brings everything to ultimate consequences. It builds up every contradiction to extremes. Those who take the smallest deviation from the goals of revolution are driven to the camp of the reaction, as we saw with the "open list" of Mr. [Ignacy] Daszyński, and as we will yet see across the entire PPS. That is, unless the PPS, which is vacillating between a revolution across Russia and a renewal of Poland—dancing back and forth between socialism and nationalism—takes a consistent and unequivocal stance in the more far-reaching course of revolution, on the ground of statewide class battle, on the ground of the common, statewide, equal interests of the working class.

Revolution is like a magical force that brings hidden things out into the light. Within the conditions of our lives, it sets up an inexorable dilemma:

Either the camp of Social Democracy, or the camp of the reaction!

The Tactics of Revolution*

When considering how to educate Social Democracy about the electoral activities of the bourgeoisie in this country,† one comes up against the general issue of proletarian tactics for the present season. The course and the result of the revolutionary struggle largely depend on *how consciously* the working class wages the war and on how thoroughly it realizes the nature, conditions, and purpose of its tactics. That is to say, it is important that the front ranks that lead the fight become fully aware of *the difference in the tactics of the proletariat between times of peace and times of revolution*. Ignorance of this difference may explain why one hears certain statements repeated in some Social Democratic circles, such as in one part of our sister party in Russia.‡ Such statements include the claim that to hamper bourgeois parties as they prepare for and try to realize the elections to the tsar's Duma is to adopt "non–Social Democratic" tactics—that such tactics are a kind of "terror" that the working masses do not understand. If this were the case, it would constitute the sole reason the working masses still do not sufficiently understand what revolution is and how it places certain obligations on the fighting proletariat.

The tactics of Social Democracy are always revolutionary, both in their essence and in their significance. This arises from the final goal, the very program of Social Democracy, which illuminates the path for every step of the fight. The goal is a complete social coup—the complete toppling of the present capitalist system and the establishment of an entirely new order, a socialist one. And this is the path to the working-class seizure of political power—that is, the path to the dictatorship of the proletariat. With this in mind, the typical popular gathering in Germany, at which workers calmly hear speakers out over a pint of beer to make themselves conscious of the goals and program of Social Democracy, is an act no less revolutionary than the last collective uprising in Moscow. The tactics of Social Democracy, which is to say the forms their daily struggle takes, are always revolutionary in nature in that they consciously aspire to realize the party program, since the *program* of Social Democracy is itself revolutionary.

Nevertheless, with respect to their *form*, proletarian ways of fighting must be and are different in times of revolution and in times of peace. Naturally, this difference does not consist in there being "beatings and blood flowing in the streets" during revolution, while times of peace see markedly more "civilized forms" of class struggle, as the bourgeoisie and the police think. The difference lies much deeper.

---

* This article first appeared in *Czerwony Sztandar*, No. 56, March 23, 1906, pp. 1–3, under the title "Taktyka rewolucji." It is translated from the Polish original by Joseph Muller.
† That is, in Poland.
‡ A reference to RSDRP, divided at the time between Mensheviks and Bolsheviks.

Both in peacetime and in periods of revolutionary upheaval, the essence of Social Democratic tactics is constituted in the class struggle of the proletariat. But in peacetime, this struggle takes place within the framework of political rule by the bourgeoisie. In each case, a country's existing laws determine limits and forms for worker struggle. Thus, for example, in Germany, when the working class agitates and puts up a political fight, it must stay within the bounds of the existing laws governing elections, assembly, and the press; in its economic struggle, it must hold to the existing laws governing coalitions such as unions; and so forth. It must do so even though all the laws, regulations, and restrictions that impose certain restraints and forms on the working class from above and throw up walls around its activity are the work of bourgeois parliaments, the fruits of legislation efforts in which the bourgeoisie has a majority, and the effects of laws enforced, without exception, so as to maintain the political dominance of the bourgeoisie. To return to the example of Germany, Social Democracy is admittedly fighting tirelessly to expand electoral laws, union laws, and so on for the benefit of the proletariat, in addition to making use of already-existing political rights, but again, it does not put up this opposition to the political control of the bourgeoisie through means that are not basically in line with laws already in existence.

In this way, "bourgeois legality"—that is, law that keeps watch over bourgeois power—forms a sort of iron cage in which the class struggle of the proletariat must take place. This is why the result of struggle in times of peace mainly consists in accumulating consciousness and organizing the proletariat; struggle in peacetime can only very seldom attain positive results on the order of new gains and political rights. German Social Democracy, for example, managed to gather more than 3 million adult men to its banner, but none of this force is in a position to move on protective legislation or coalition legislation, since the parliament and government are currently, as ever, in the hands of the bourgeoisie. Under the tsar, before the revolution, the "legal" cage around proletarian struggle was the omnipotent reign of "the tsar's law"—that is, the lash.

Times of revolution rend the cage of "legality" open like pent-up steam splitting its kettle, letting class struggle break out into the open, naked and unencumbered. Of course, economically and socially, the bourgeoisie still reigns during the revolution, as before, since the means of production remain in its hands and all public life still revolves around it. Politically and legally, however, the rule of the governmental authority up to that moment— absolutism—is destroyed, and the struggle of the proletariat can manifest its full might. The revolution may look like a clash between the ruling powers' brute physical force and the rebelling people. In reality, while the physical power of the revolutionary proletariat is itself only a result and expression of its *political consciousness*, this consciousness and political power emerge during revolution without having been warped by, tied down to, and overpowered by the "laws" of bourgeois society. The class power of the proletariat clashes with the power of the authorities and the ruling classes, and the interests of the proletariat with the interests of the oppressors. The clash is simple and direct, free of walls and limits of "legality" to block it. In revolution, in the face-to-face battle of class interests, is formed what Lassalle called the essence of constitutions—that is, the *actual relations of class forces*.* Based on this, the actual ground the proletariat manages to conquer in today's revolutionary battlefields will form the basis of the constitution written later, the laws that will later specify the position and conditions of the working class, perhaps for decades. The greater the political force the proletariat manifests and musters now, during the revolutionary upheaval, the greater will be its share of the law, and the more beneficial its position, under the subsequent peaceful reign of the bourgeoisie after the revolution.

That is why now, in times of revolution, the guiding light of our tactics should be for the true proletariat to take complete control, for the proletariat to strive after its intended form of political "dictatorship," not, indeed, to enact a socialist coup, but to realize the goals of the revolution. The entire revolutionary movement marches toward this guiding light. In the preliminary phase of the revolution, the rallying cry of workers in Russia was for the government to *call* a constitutional assembly. Today, no conscious proletarian believes it either possible or desirable for the rotting corpse of absolutism to call a Constituent Assembly. The revolutionary people must itself achieve the final victory by expelling the remains of the government's carcass. Only then can it produce a summons to a meeting of representatives of the people, announce a republic throughout the land, including autonomy for Poland, and establish the eight-hour workday.

But this revolutionary "dictatorship"—that is, victory of the proletariat—cannot be picked from a tree at the desired hour or caught falling from the sky. It can only occur as the end result of the proletariat's gradual, continual march toward power. The only road to this end is for the will and interests of the conscious proletariat to be realized boldly, step by step—for *power* to be won for the proletariat in every domain, at all costs.

Let us take two examples that show the difference in tactics between times of peace and times of revolution. In Germany, workers are leading an unceasing and tireless fight for the improvement of working conditions, and in the course of this fight and for its advancement they have created powerful trade organizations that today already number more than a million. In their economic struggle, however, they are severely hindered by the existing German law on coalitions,

---

* See Ferdinand Lassalle, "Über Werfassungswesen: zwei Votráge und ein offenes Sendschreiben" (On Constitutional Systems: Two Lectures and an Open Letter) (November 1862), in *Ausgewählte Reden und Schriften* (Berlin: Dietz-Verlag, 1991). For an English version of parts of one of these speeches of Lassalle, see "On the Essence of Constitutions," in *Fourth International*, Vol. 3, No. 1 (January 1942), pp. 25–31.

which, for example, denies agricultural workers and rail and postal employees the right to organize themselves. Besides this, as a matter of fact, the government hinders opposition and trade organization even for industrial workers in government plants, as do the police and the courts in private factories at every opportunity, as do the high and mighty kings of capital in the other large businesses, and, finally, as do the "cartels"—that is, the great unions of industrial capitalists. All these powers work together to ensure the factory owner preserves his rights as "master of the house" in his factory. German workers arm themselves against such forces only by making diligent use of existing union laws and by campaigning for expansions to their rights at rallies on election day and in Parliament.

Nowhere in their fight, however, do they try to break or sidestep these laws. For example, they make no bold, sweeping attempt to create agricultural or state labor unions, which are forbidden by law. Such an action would be both impossible and pointless in the Germany of today. Impossible because, in times of peace, such an action would be unlikely to so artificially trigger the fighting energy and resolve that could spur the proletarian masses to take what belongs to them by storm, disregarding the potential sacrifices and dangers of battle. Pointless because, without the momentum gained through militant action by the *entire* proletariat—a momentum only created by revolution itself—isolated branches of the proletariat who attempted to break free of the laws of the current bourgeois state would only be able to make gains for a very short time, at most, and would soon be forcibly suppressed.

For workers in Russia and Poland, the tactics required by the revolutionary situation are completely different. Here the power of the proletariat's trade organizations and its achievements in the fight against capital depend not on formal "laws" but on the actual power and consciousness of the working class. In its current fight to improve working conditions under tsarism, the proletariat does not and should not know any boundaries other than the limits of actual possibility. Where possible, workers should also aspire, in their struggle over the workplace, to break the capitalist's all-powerful grip on the factory and attain an agreement in which *workers* are the "master of the house"—not, admittedly, with respect to economic power, since the ownership of capital and the ability to profit stay in the hands of the capitalist, but at least with respect to legislating the working conditions and internal organization patterns of the factory. The guiding vision of the current labor struggle must be for labor organizations to gain the highest degree of freedom and influence within the factory that can be achieved by wage-earning victims of capitalist exploitation, and crucial for such attainment is that the proletariat exert sufficiently strong pressure by means of every manifestation of the consciousness and the will of the working masses.

The same principle applies to the political battlefield. In times of peace such as the present—in Germany, for example—existing legal and political relations prevent the conscious proletariat from expressing its will and defending its interests. Even though Social Democracy is the most powerful party in Germany, the allied bourgeois parties together constitute a parliamentary majority, which they use to pass law after law intended to clean out and enslave the working class. The only ways German Social Democracy fights this oppression are peaceful protest and organization and electoral opposition, in the hope of winning over a majority of the entire working populace to the party's goals; indeed, in the current situation no other plan of action is feasible. Under the tsar, the current goal of our activities must be not only to raise the consciousness of the broadest possible swath of the proletariat, but also for the proletariat to achieve real influence over social relations—for the proletariat to forcibly achieve the actual ability to rule over society. Whereas in peacetime the proletariat must patiently endure the tyranny of the bourgeois parties, limiting itself to the role of publicly criticizing their politics, in times of revolution, it can and certainly should try to thwart the bourgeois reaction when it tries to bring down its iron heel. The proletariat can and should try to *block* the actions of bourgeois groups hostile to it. One such necessary action, especially here in our country, is to stifle National Democracy's actions and electoral attempts in the Duma through the decisive application of force by the conscious working masses.

The fighting proletariat obviously cannot have any illusions about the stability of its rule over society. After the current revolution ends, after society returns to "normal" conditions, the bourgeoisie, reigning over both the factory floor and the country, will surely waste no time in sweeping up and tossing out the majority of the current revolutionary struggle's achievements. But the proletariat can make a crucial difference now by launching the most forceful attacks on current social relations, such that it revolutionizes as much as possible the conditions in the factories and society as a whole. The more Social Democracy is able to drive the revolutionary tide toward the political dictatorship of the proletariat, the less the bourgeoisie will be able to reverse its achievements the day after the revolution. The proletariat's aspiration to have its wishes realized wholesale—for them to be "forced on society," as National Democracy complains—is the quickest way for the working masses to achieve class consciousness and maturity, which are the most valuable and permanent accomplishments of revolution and a guarantee of further progress for socialism in times of peace. Our proletariat has already made a great effort to master these tactics, particularly in revolutionary times, in the period from the end of October to the beginning of last November in the Dąbrowa basin,* where Social Democracy was for a time the

---

* This is a reference to the strike of miners in the region, in which tens of thousands remained in the pits and took them over in a sit-down strike beginning in early November 1905. See Luxemburg's report in "The Murderous Cads of the 'Constitutional State'" (*Complete Works*, Vol. 3, p. 283): "Here, in the Dąbrowa Region, Social Democracy has constituted a kind of 'provisional government.' Countless representatives from all classes of citizens come to the office, opened

force controlling and regulating social relations in accordance with the interests of the proletariat.

The same main goal should continually guide proletarian action throughout the entire country and the entire state. Revolutionary times are not restricted to moments in which bloody battles against the military are fought in the street; they also include every moment and every seemingly peaceful day in the current revolutionary period. That is why Social Democracy should, with iron determination, hold to its tactics of revolution, always mindful that revolution is not a time to *debate* the opposition but to block it and strike it down with conscious action by the proletarian masses. It is a time for the proletariat to implement its will *by force*.

---

in all haste, to request permission to hold meetings, to inquire about directives and news, and to receive the latest proclamations. The working class is ceaselessly putting on huge meetings."

In a Revolutionary Hour, What Next? [April 1905]*

Today's revolution presents Social Democracy with problems that no Social Democratic party has ever faced before. Today's modern states developed large-scale labor movements only after their feudal absolutist governments fell. In England, France, Germany, and Austria, the bourgeoisie sought to ensure unfettered capitalist development, so it was the class that openly declared war on absolutism, triggered a political revolution, and won parliamentary, constitutional, or even, as in France, republican forms of government.

Of course, it was not the bourgeoisie but the working people who poured into the streets in Western Europe. Working people died on the barricades in the French Revolution, and working people died in Vienna and in Berlin in 1848. They sacrificed their blood battling royal armies, purchasing the political freedoms with which the bourgeoisie would build their current power.

Yet, overall, the working people were merely instruments in the hands of the bourgeoisie, which stood at the head of each revolutionary movement. They were the cannon fodder with which the capitalist class paved its path to power. Even then, French and German workers did not separate themselves from the bourgeoisie and the petty bourgeoisie as a separate class and party. They did not understand their separate worker interests and their natural opposition to the interests of the bourgeoisie. They rose up to resist the absolutist government around the banner of the capitalist class, on the heels of the petty bourgeoisie, with no knowledge of what their struggle would gain them.

Struggle between the proletariat and the bourgeoisie began only much later. As a result, Social Democracy in France and Germany always shared constitutional ground with the bourgeoisie and always had at its disposal parliamentary elections and freedoms of the press, speech, assembly, and association. Social Democrats there did not have the problem, as we under the tsar have, of how to obtain such basic political rights in the first place. They did not have to pose such questions as *what to do in a moment of revolution such as the present, how to usher in victory, and how to lead the working masses?*

---

* In 1905 and 1906, Luxemburg published three related pieces in Polish under the same title—"Z doby rewolucyjnej. Co dalej?" (In a Revolutionary Hour, What Next?). The first was published in the April 1905 issue of *Czerwony Sztandar*, No. 25, pp. 1–4. The second was written as a Supplement to the May 1905 issue of *Czerwony Sztandar*, No. 26, in the form of a pamphlet published in Kraków. The third, and much longer version, was written while in prison in March–April 1906, where Luxemburg revised and added new material to these earlier texts. This third and final version was published a few months later as a pamphlet in Warsaw. Since the pieces are integrally related, we publish all three here in their order of composition. They are translated by Joseph Muller from the Polish original.

All these questions remain for us to answer today, and if none of our sister parties in other lands can provide answers, we must find them ourselves.

There are socialists who think the most important issue over which to rack one's brain is obviously the matter of *arming the working masses*. According to these politicians, everything will go like clockwork, and victory over absolutism is certain as long as supplies of dynamite, bombs, and revolvers do not run out. For example, *Robotnik* [The Worker], the organ of the Polish Socialist Party (PPS),* declares in issue No. 59, "We already possess revolutionary *strength*, so now let us obtain revolutionary *means*, form combat organizations, and build up weapons and battle supplies, and we shall win political freedom." This view forms a core assumption of parties such as the PPS and the Socialist Revolutionary Party (SR) in Russia—parties that artificially attach themselves onto the class struggle of the proletariat, seeing the whole movement as nothing but a mass of bodies that may prove useful in a pitched battle. Members of the bourgeoisie, for whom the political power of a popular mass movement is completely incomprehensible, also see only brute physical force when they look on any sociopolitical struggle. For example, ask the average manufacturer or landowner why he thinks restoring Poland is impossible at present, and he will doubtless reply, "Why, it is very simple, sir. Where shall we find a force to resist the enormous military might of the imperial state?" This same shallow, crude view of political struggle is brought to the revolutionary movement by the species of socialists characterized by social-patriots in Poland and by terrorists in Russia. At first, for decades, they did not believe in the potential, the force, or the effectiveness of the class movement of the Russian proletariat at all. And, when that movement and force became real, comprehensible, and undeniable even to the tsar's henchmen, these "socialists" cried, "Quick, now let us only put bombs and dynamite in the hands of the masses, and the day shall be ours!"

To seize on the bare mechanical problem of weaponry when faced with a revolution like the present anti-tsarist revolution, one must have no spiritual connection at all with the class movement of the proletariat. If the number of weapons and soldiers determined the defeat or victory of the cause, then the fall of the uprising of our gentry would be a matter of great mystery. Because by all accounts, the [November] Uprising of 1830 had at its disposal significant forces of regularly trained, well-armed Polish troops, and the "leaders" of the uprising

---

* *Robotnik* was a Polish socialist newspaper and the organ of the PPS. It was founded in 1894 and published irregularly. Józef Piłsudski was one of its first editors. After the PPS split in 1906, two different papers were published under this name. In the editorial team attached to the PPS-Left, Henryk Walecki played a lead role. After 1919, the publication continued legally in Warsaw as a PPS organ in the form of a daily paper, until September 1939. During and after World War II, various papers were published at various periods under this name, to draw on the tradition of the independence movement. From 1944 to 1948, the paper was a PPS organ in the People's Republic of Poland.

eventually left the country accompanied by considerable military forces that had never seen battle.*

The proposal put forth is that a handful of socialist helmsmen will "arm" the masses—a handful, because the number of active socialist *agitators* is now and, under these conditions, will remain very small in comparison to the million-strong mass needed in a revolutionary force. The proposal is a live transplant of ideas from the world of secret associations and conspiracies into the world of proletarian class struggle. More or less in the manner of terrorists following a plan hatched in a "clandestine" meeting in a dimly lit basement, arming the half dozen members of their "combat organization" for "deployment" on attack missions,† this group now plans to set an "operation" in motion to "equip" every last member of the people. In the minds of these politicians, preparing the working masses for revolution is the same as preparing a handful of terrorists for an attack, only *on a grand scale*. They do not understand that the entire *essence*, the character, the very meaning of the mass revolutionary fight is completely different from the fight of the vigilante terrorist.

The class struggle of the proletariat is and must be, in all of its forms, and also in revolutionary clashes, an autonomous movement of all the people.

A socialist party may not play the role of caregiver of the working class by obtaining, on its own initiative, through its own means, and, as it were, behind the back of the working masses, weapons for them, importing dynamite and revolvers from abroad with money taken by force, or building bombs in resistance houses, and then placing those weapons in the hands of the people, any more than it may give a small boy a wooden sword and toy helmet and send him into battle. To provide arms to individual people, after all, one must only have money and discretion. But the arming of the masses in the moment of revolution is and may only ever be *a result and a manifestation of the strength and political maturity of the masses themselves*. In plain terms, this means that the masses may only, and should only, arm *themselves*, and *in the course of their struggle*, by their own resolve, their own desire to obtain arms, not by way of *buying* cheap weapons in stores, as one buys a shotgun for hunting, but by *seizing them through the power of their movement*, through partial victories over the government. Scenarios for such mass arms acquisition, as opposed to conspiratorial means, may already be foreseen. Examples include the capture by storm of private and, more importantly, government stores of weapons, and the

---

* The Polish national uprising began on November 29, 1830, when junior officers from the army and military academy rose up in response to the effort of the Russian government to use them to suppress the revolution that had broken out in Paris in July of the previous year. It soon became a mass national uprising as barricades went up in Warsaw and other cities. It was brutally crushed by an invasion of the Russian army.

† Luxemburg is explicitly referring to the "Combat Organization" of the SR, which carried out armed attacks and assassinations on government officials.

disarming of isolated troops. Such a list of scenarios, however, can only serve as an *example*, to better clarify one perspective on the issue of arming the masses. To teach workers solemnly that they must bring revolvers, shotguns, axes, and stakes into the streets when the revolution breaks out, or to teach them now how to build barricades in the streets—that would be absurd. Even in wars between militarized states, nearly no battle takes place in the way it is worked out on paper in advance by generals' staffs, since the course of the battle and the way it is waged are impinged by a host of circumstances that no one may anticipate. A brilliant leader like Napoleon creates a plan in wartime, on the eve of battle, according to the moment's needs, and invents entirely new tactics and strategies for waging war.

In people's revolutions, the brilliant leader is not a "party committee" or a circle that pompously calls itself a "combat organization," but a vast host ready to spill its blood. In spite of these "socialists," in spite of their conviction that the working masses must be drilled for armed conflict according to their orders, like a battalion of soldiers, the masses always find on their own—create for themselves—the means of physical struggle that are most appropriate in a given moment of revolution. This is why every modern revolution to date in Western Europe had its own separate methods and battle tactics to counter the regime in power. This is also why a revolution against the tsar, taking place under conditions completely different from the bourgeois revolutions of France and Germany, must generate its methods of struggle in the streets and arm itself as the conflict unfolds. "Calculating" such methods in advance and "preparing" the masses for armed clashes with the government would be like teaching someone to swim by seating them in front of a chalkboard and explaining the principles of swimming through diagrams.

Are we then to sit with folded hands and simply wait for a new outbreak of revolution on the streets, tossing our concern for the lives of thousands of workers to the wind and consoling ourselves with the thought that "it will work out somehow," as more than one comrade has said? Far from it! Social Democracy is not at liberty to wait with hands folded for the events to come. Quite the opposite! We have so much work before us that our hands will scarcely manage. Among other tasks, one of our objectives is to arm certain comrades as we are able. We must only make sure that no pocket of the working masses deludes itself about the scale and the *meaning* of the weapons that party resources may obtain. There can be no talk from socialists about arming the *masses* as such. A moment's simple reflection must convince every healthy mind that no socialist party under current conditions would have enough power and resources to arm the hundreds of thousands, no, millions of people that all Russia contains. The clandestine, restricted means by which socialists may today obtain and import weapons forbid the acquisition of massive stores such as would be required to arm all the people. Furthermore, even if we imagine for a moment that such enormous weapons stores are possible, arming the working masses with them remains a pipe dream. The working population is not a regiment of soldiers that can be ordered to show up in order at a certain time at a barracks to receive their weapons. In view of this, the *best* we may accomplish in reality is to arm our own active agitators and the very small circle of workers who are closest to the party. And these arms are only to be taken as a *means of defense* for elements and isolated worker groups under attack by tsarist hooligans. To defend ourselves and put up a resistance to the rapacious reach of the regime, we have a responsibility—we must do all in our power. To persuade workers that any and every socialist party is in a position to arm the working masses to the last man, and that that party will arm them with weapons sufficient to *attack* the military forces and fight with the army in a pitched battle, is to *deceive the working masses*.

And such promises are dangerous in the extreme. Today, when at long last the proletarian mass is engaging in political struggle against despotism, all our hope of victory depends on entire classes, hundreds of thousands, nay, millions of workers, to understand that they must lead the struggle forward themselves, to the very end. Absolutism shall collapse only when the innumerable people of Poland and all Russia understand clearly that they must enter into open struggle with the government and that they may win victory only by their own strength, through their own mass struggle. This is why those who drum up false hopes in the working masses, saying they are not to expect that all the means of victory will come from them, but that someone else, some "party committee," some "war organization" will come along and hand them weapons for the fight against absolutism on a silver platter, *render a great injustice to the working class*.

But, most importantly, distracting and bamboozling workers with weapons diverts their attention from their most important objective. It is essential that the working people understand that in reality they do not have to concern themselves with being defeated in conventional open battle with the army, as if in a war, by the tsarist government, with its more powerful weapons. To expect victory against the government by this means is to be fooled by a chimera. Against such powerful weapons of war as today's military states wield, against such numerous forces, artillery so ready for the attack, and such refined instruments of murder as today's cannon and case-shot guns, the people of the street must be prepared for terrible defeat should they ever enter into regular open battle with the army. Moreover, it will not be through military victories in decisive battles against the tsarist army that the working masses shall win victory and political freedom in the revolution.

Our victory and the overthrow of despotism will be possible only when the *number* of fighters expands so greatly as to change the scale of the revolution, and the number of recruits obediently murdering us at the tsar's orders decreases. Therefore, two things are necessary:

- To unite ourselves with the revolutionary struggle of rural workers; and
- To win over to the revolutionary cause as substantial a part of the army as possible.

Agitation in the countryside and agitation in the barracks are fitting Social Democratic responses to calls to arm the populace and prepare them for general combat against absolutism. And these methods to which Social Democracy points are not artificially tacked on to the class struggle of the proletariat like the calls to "arm" the masses, in which a few dozen fops from the bourgeois intelligentsia must eventually produce several thousand roubles so that a few other fops can travel abroad, import dynamite and revolvers, and surreptitiously manufacture bombs.

Agitation in the countryside and agitation among soldiers are not clever tricks conceived in desperation to resuscitate the revolutionary cause. On the contrary, they flow from the class struggle itself and are a natural part of the objectives to which Social Democracy had to come sooner or later as the labor movement grew.

Rural workers make up a part of the very same exploited and oppressed proletariat as the urban proletariat. They are a part of the working class, and they are as much victims of private property and the capitalist system as are factory laborers, artisans, and miners. The tsarist government persecutes the farming proletariat as much as the industrial proletariat. Thus, by nature, rural workers have the exact same class, economic, and political interests as urban workers. Under the tsar, the rural proletariat has as vital a need to see the tsar's downfall and hope for a socialist system as the urban proletariat. Therefore, the natural place for agricultural laborers is at the side of industrial workers, in a shared working-class party, in the ranks of Social Democracy.

If we are only now returning our broad activism to the proletariat working on farms, it is not that we only now remember them and their adversity, or that we want to use them only as a tool to make our victory over absolutism easier. No! It is simply a result of differing positions, that the urban, industrial worker begins to understand his class needs and fight against exploitation and oppression more quickly and easily than the rural people, scattered across the land. In every country, the urban proletariat gives the workers' struggle a beginning. Only when the workers' struggle has already reached a large scale in cities does the conscious industrial proletariat begin to set an example for its rural brothers and draw them into the fight.

Our land is no different. Today the workers' struggle, especially the incidents in Petersburg, the mass strike, the sounding of revolution in Poland and in Russia, have reverberated in echoes across vast stretches of countryside, reaching even those social strata that suffer utter destitution, atrocious indignities, and oppression. So now we must use all our strength to bring the light of socialism and the political struggle to rural workers, those white slaves of agrarian capital, and to small-farm peasants, those captives of their small properties, those destitute "landowners." [Our task is] not to win over from them a thousand new broad shoulders and burly hands to the service of our political revolution. No, it is to win a thousand new proletarian minds to the gospel of socialism, and to kindle in a thousand breasts the fire of protest and the yearning for freedom. We must make use of commotion in the countryside, sounding there *the rallying cry of class struggle*, rather than conceal political demands behind duplicitous, cowardly patriotic platitudes, as the PPS does in its appeals to farmworkers to shape their demands. We must win over our rural brothers to the worker movement *for good*, presenting to them an accurate account of every aspect of their proletarian or partly proletarian life, making clear to them all their interests, including their shared interest with the working people of all Russia—the felling of absolutism.

In this way, the achievement of new, powerful forces to help our political revolution will be only a natural result of the expansion of our labor movement into new classes of the proletariat. These forces will be both a means to overthrow despotism and a step forward toward the realization of socialism.

Agitation among soldiers also has its own influence on the class goals of Poland's labor movement. For this reason, the position of Social Democracy is completely different from the position of the social-patriotic PPS. The leaders of the PPS strive with all their might to separate the Polish workers' movement from the Russian one; they strive to persuade Polish workers that they have completely different needs and aims than the working people of Russia. Yet our land is *occupied by Russian soldiers*. What can the PPS say to them? Will they call on them to restore Poland? Obviously, that would be a waste of breath. Or perhaps the PPS may call on them to unite with Polish workers to fight to improve the lot of the working class? But the PPS always insists on the distinctions it draws between Polish and Russian workers. For the PPS, Russian soldiers are *only* soldiers, only enemies and servants of a government that has a higher claim to their humanity, to their sense of justice and their respect for matters beyond them.

For us, for Social Democracy, the Russian soldier is not an enemy, only an armed and dangerous beast whom we wish to tame. For us, the Russian soldier is primarily a blind instrument of absolutism, a proletarian, a worker, a part of the Russian working class, and as such our brother, a member of the *one and the same working class* to which, according to our view, both Polish and Russian proletarians belong. Therefore, the matter of our worker struggle is also their concern. By enlightening the Russian worker who occupies our land, we call on him not to sympathize with a foreign cause but to understand his own class interests and to fight together with us for common liberation, first from the yoke of absolutism, and then from the chains of the capitalist system.

Therefore, while our campaign in the army will be adapted for the current moment of revolution, it must have the character of a general labor, socialist, and class campaign. In the course of our campaign, we naturally make use of the stir of perceptions and impressions that call to mind, even for soldiers, the slaughter carried out on the tsar's orders in recent months. And the natural result of the consciousness that we raise among even a part of the army will be that when the people rise up to fight for freedom, at the order to murder us, some of the soldiers will come over to our side, and the rest will hesitate. The confusion that arises in the army will be enough to sap its strength and discipline and give moral credence to the people putting up a vigorous fight. And we must count on such confusion, on the *hesitation* of the army, far more than its defeat at the ends of murderous weapons.

This is how our prospects for victory over the tsarist government in the current revolution are linked to our general work of building the class consciousness of all social strata of the working people. By avoiding the artificial leaps and haphazard experiments to which Poland's social-patriots and Russia's terrorists must cling, we march ever closer to the victory of the revolution. Social Democracy in the present moment remains faithful to its purpose: to raise the consciousness of the proletariat and organize the working people for class struggle. The current struggle to overthrow absolutism is only one moment in the class struggle, and our victory in this revolution will be only one of the fruits of our labor: "arming" the working masses, urban and rural, with outfits and uniforms, with the most terrible weaponry in our power to give, *an understanding of their needs, whether class-determined, economic, or political.*

We are in a transitional moment, a moment of anticipation. In the heart of every conscious worker throbs impatience, a longing to see the revolution's final triumph. In such an atmosphere, the desire arises for some kind of physical, visible revolutionary action, and as a result, many are intoxicated with carrying out attacks, setting off bombs, or simply acquiring weapons and being armed.

These feelings and attitudes are understandable. Yet uproar and commotion, though it seems revolutionary, must be *resisted with the utmost resolve.* Comrades who fall into a state of uncritical intoxication with the roar and rumble demonstrate that they do not think at the level of the objectives of *Social Democracy*, that they do not grasp the full depth and gravity of the class struggle at whose head we have been appointed to stand.

There are two distinct ways to hasten the revolution and disrupt the regime. The regime is disrupted by its current war with Japan, it is disrupted by the *honghuzi* in Manchuria,* it is disrupted by famine and crop failure, and it is disrupted

---

* The *honghuzi*, or "red beards," was a derogatory term first applied to the indigenous peoples living in the Amur region of northeastern Manchuria, and later to Chinese in the region who resisted Russian colonial penetration. Although they tended to consist of loosely organized

by loss of credit in European markets. These are all factors *independent of the will and activity of the masses*. And at base these factors are not different in kind from clandestine operations to detonate bombs or kill or maim police officers of all ranks, even if the perpetrators call themselves socialists and represent themselves as operating "in the name of" the working masses.

The other way to paralyze the regime is the one enacted by the masses themselves, characterized not by chance occurrence but mass political consciousness: general and partial strikes, blockades on industry, commerce, and transport, military rebellions, railroad shutdowns through strike action, rural labor protests, mass resistance to troop mobilization, and so on and so forth.

Triggers of chaos and confusion of the first class—bombs and assaults—feel to the government, when all is said and done, like mosquito bites. For every police officer blown away in Russia, there are a hundred thousand waiting to take his place, and for every police captain, there are at least 25,000 candidates at the ready. The confusion set off by a bomb only seems to put the regime in grave danger to those who are unable to imagine or see anything but a manifestation of the moment, those who assess a political incident in terms of the horror-stricken faces of "the public" and its effect on our lily-livered, birdbrained bourgeoisie.

The second method—disrupting the regime through mass demonstrations—is singly dangerous to absolutism because it not only disrupts the ruling government but also *organizes* the political force that will bring down absolutism and set up a new order. Social Democracy is dedicated precisely to this way of hastening revolution and to this way only.

On the surface, it seems a boring, inadequate prescription. Indeed, "Agitate, organize!" has already long been our rallying call. Are we not capable of something better, something more effective, now in this moment of revolution?

Whoever poses such a question utterly fails to understand the limitless potential and revolutionary effect of Social Democratic agitation.

It is agitation and not setting off bombs or maiming policemen that truly endangers the tsarist government.

Because such agitation:

- Prepares for an outbreak of *mass strike*, a direct blow to the whole state apparatus and a harbinger of revolution in the streets;
- Spreads revolutionary turmoil *into the provinces, across the countryside*, so that it catches and grows in every domain of struggle where the physical resources of the government are not great enough to contain the blaze;
- Undermines *military discipline*, thereby hampering the government's power to inflict physical violence; and finally,

---

groups of bandits, during the Russo-Japanese War many of them formed military detachments allied with the Japanese.

- Recruits the greatest possible number of people to open struggle with the government, building a force that, as we have seen time and again in Western European revolutions, erects barricades, brandishes weapons, and defeats and disarms parts of the army here and there, winning them over bit by bit and gaining their support.

It is true that the final say in the fight against absolutism will be *physical power*. But such a physical power cannot be fabricated by a handful of berserk people heaving explosives. Such a physical power will be attained by the masses themselves as they put the revolution into action. And for just such a power do we Social Democrats prepare by carrying political and class consciousness to factories in the city, to thatched huts in the countryside, and into army barracks—rousing political life, protest, and resistance in every layer of the working people, issuing hundreds of thousands of proclamations, organizing centers of conscious workers everywhere, calling on the masses at every turn to mount opposition to the government, and making use of every available moment to trigger clashes between the people and the government.

It is true—"Agitate, organize!" is an old cry. It is as old as the class struggle of the proletariat, and it will last as long as the capitalist system itself. But every phase of struggle—every moment in history—fills our campaign with new life, new content, and new strength and imparts to it a new form. Today the essence and purpose of our campaign is to call the working people to rise up in the name of their class and political interests. Only in this way, in the very course of mass conflicts between the people and the regime, will arise, together with political consciousness, that physical power that is great enough to overcome the legions of bayonets and cannon arrayed in defense of absolutism.

In a Revolutionary Hour, What Next? [May 1905]*

The revolution in our country, a part of the larger workers' revolution against the tsar, has lasted for three months, from its beginnings in the outbreak of a general strike on January 28 to its high point in the protest strike of May 1–4 [1905]. In this short time, the revolutionary cause has grown stronger and taken shape remarkably quickly, the working class has become more powerful and conscious, and the influence of Social Democracy has expanded like never before. Yet this first phase of the revolution has raised a series of important questions to which Social Democracy, as the party of the conscious fighting proletariat, must soon find clear and compelling answers.

This is entirely natural. The working class of each country *learns* how to fight only once the fight has begun. Only a party like the PPS can claim to have a plan in their pockets, self-importantly seeing themselves as workers and socialists when in fact they are strangers to the spirit of class struggle. Only a party like that presumes always to be ready to give "marching orders" to the working class. Social Democracy, however, is merely the advance guard of the proletariat, one part of the vast working mass, blood of its blood and bone of its bone. Social Democracy searches out and identifies the paths and slogans of a particular workers' struggle only as that struggle develops, interpreting signs for the road ahead from the struggle itself.

Two main questions arise in connection with the two moments of revolution we witnessed—the strikes that began and ended the period.

The general strike in January broke out at word of the worker uprising and massacre in St. Petersburg, as a manifestation of political opposition directed squarely at the despotic system, and soon ramified into a great number of isolated economic strikes. The initial uniform rallying cry—overthrow absolutism and call a constitutional assembly to declare a republic—gave way to many diverse, small demands for every trade. The revolutionary wave broke apart into a web of feeble trickles, disappearing after a few weeks as if soaked up by the sand.

This should make every thinking comrade wonder: Was the transition to economic strikes not a temporary collapse in revolutionary energy, even a *step back*? Are not economic strikes now a pointless scuffle with capital, a vain loss of strength? And if so, in the future, should one not *prevent* the common strike

---

* This is the second piece by Luxemburg published in Polish under the title "Z doby rewolucyjnej. Co dalej?" (In a Revolutionary Hour, What Next?). It was written as a supplement to the May 1905 issue of *Czerwony Sztandar*, No. 26, in the form of a pamphlet published in Kraków. It is translated by Joseph Muller from the Polish original.

from thus foundering, by stopping it swiftly and firmly, except where it maintains its full power of a political demonstration?

In the first days of May, by contrast, revolution broke out energetically in strikes and demonstrations that remained purely political. But because of that, they flowed with unstoppable force into clashes with the tsar's army and ended in a massacre of the unarmed crowd, and working people clenched their fists with powerless rage. Thus, the wave of revolution struck this time on some sort of dead center that deflected it like a stone wall. What is to be done in such a case? How can the cause be driven forward from such a dead center? This is the question that arises and demands a solution.

For the foreseeable future, the revolutionary cause will likely flow down one of these two paths—the movement will splinter into economic strikes or crash weakly against a solid bank of bayonets. How should Social Democracy then behave?

In response to both these possibilities, as on all issues of the labor struggle, Social Democracy's response remains unchanged: Make people aware, raise their consciousness of the very essence and meaning of the struggle, its broad goals, and its demands on the present moment.

I.

The current revolution in our country, as across the tsarist state, has a twofold nature. In its direct goals, it is a *bourgeois* revolution. It is about establishing, within the Russian state, freedom, a republic, and a parliamentary system that, through the dominance of capital and hired labor, is nothing but a progressive form of the bourgeois state, a form of class rule by the bourgeoisie over the proletariat.

But the bourgeois revolution in Russia and Poland is not the work of the bourgeoisie, as in Germany and France in days gone by, but the working class, and a class already highly conscious of its labor interests at that—a working class that seeks political freedoms not so that the bourgeoisie may benefit, but just the opposite, so that the working class may resolve its class struggle with the bourgeoisie and thereby hasten the victory of socialism. That is why the current revolution is simultaneously a *workers'* revolution. That is also why, in this revolution, the battle against absolutism goes hand in hand—must go hand in hand—with the battle against capital, with exploitation. And why economic strikes are in fact quite nearly inseparable in this revolution from political strikes.

Naturally, the bourgeois classes do not like the sound of that. Our dear old capitalists were indeed eager and ready to sweep up civil freedoms and rights that did not cost them anything and for which the proletariat sacrificed everything. But don't you dare lay a hand on their purse strings! For the good of capital, in the spirit of exploitation, so-called National Democracy also instructs workers to "be tactful in issuing demands." In the public notice newly issued in the Dąbrowa basin "National Workers' Committee," workers are advised to "demand not more than the factory owner can give without exposing the industry to ruin." On the other hand, it is beyond question that the tsarist government eagerly awaits economic strikes in the current revolutionary hour. The deluded government believes that if proletarians direct their energy to fighting exploitation, they will turn their knife away from its heart, while scaring off the bourgeoisie and curing any bourgeois sympathies for the freedom movement.

Social Democracy must not rely on the outward demonstrations and ferocity of the bourgeoisie or on the profiteering and hopes of absolutism; it must analyze the economic strikes from an independent position, which is to say the position of workers' interests.

First of all, it would be an error contrary to the spirit of Social Democracy to evaluate the economic battle in the same way in every set of conditions. A normal strike in a single factory or trade that has been called solely out of a desire to improve work conditions has a completely different meaning from a general strike fever that suddenly erupts and sweeps through the whole working class as workers leap to battle readiness, infecting one trade after another and careening around the whole country like a summer storm. A strike storm like that has already fallen on the working class in our country once, though at incomparably lower and weaker levels, in the second half of the 1880s. It created the birth of the mass labor movement in our country, out of which emerged the first Social Democratic organization in the [Polish-Lithuanian] Commonwealth, the "Union of Polish Workers" (ZRP).* The same pattern occurred several times in capitalist countries in the West—in Germany, France, and Switzerland—where, for example, a general strike fever broke out in the middle of the 1860s, right after the establishment of the International Workingmen's Association (IAA), during the beginning of its active operation.

This kind of proletarian mass uprising against capital is always a manifestation of a turning point in the life of the working class, a watershed in its relations with bourgeois society. It is always a time of sudden awakening of classes of laborers to *class consciousness*.

And the current economic strikes here in February and March have the same character.

The entire, enormous mass of industrial workers—which in large part had already made efforts to improve their positions within certain isolated lines of

---

* Julian Marchlewski and Jan Leder founded the ZRP in 1889, around the same time that Luxemburg fled Poland for Switzerland. By 1890 it had locals in Żyrardów, Łódź, Zgierz, Dąbrowa Górnicza, and Sosnowiec. In 1893 it merged with the remnants of the second Proletariat Party to form the Social Democracy of the Kingdom of Poland, which was led by Luxemburg and Leo Jogiches. The SDKP, never a large organization, dissolved in 1900.

production, workshops, and factories—broke all at once, as if moved by one great push toward vigorous resistance against exploitation. All the many material and spiritual injuries to workers—inhuman exploitation, meager pay, overwork, unremitting detriments to health, sophisticated systems of punishment, manhandling and insults to workers' humanity from capitalists and foremen—this entire web of devastating and disgraceful labor conditions ensnaring workers, this comprehensive hell that makes up the daily lot of the proletarian under the yoke of capital, was uncovered, was dragged out suddenly from the shadows of the social underworld, where millions of workers live, work, and suffer like cretins, into the air, into the light of day.

At once, the entire industrial proletarian mass felt the sharp pain of all the injuries it usually carries, even patiently, in a state of passive indifference—the *collective, class* injuries that reproduce themselves with awful, terrifying uniformity in trade after trade, factory after factory, workshop after workshop. And precisely through this compilation of all sorts of isolated worker injuries—a bitter drip almost imperceptible in daily life—the struggle became and was a truly *class-based* movement that rapidly etched feelings of class consciousness deeply and clearly into the proletarian mass.

For a party that is truly a workers' party, like Social Democracy—a party in which workers are not a means to a political end but a class whose elevation and liberation are the only ultimate goals—no improvement in the daily lot of the proletariat is too small or insignificant. If the general movement of economic strikes in our country, an outgrowth of the political common strike, had no other effect than to give workers in a wide variety of trades and factories shorter working hours and modest pay raises and to abolish some of the most blatant and shameful abuses—then strikes would already have constituted an invaluable tool with which Social Democracy could lift the material existence of the proletariat from that abyss of misery into which unbridled capitalist exploitation had pushed it.

But that was not all. The movement and its effects stimulated, and still stimulate, efforts to build a broad sense of the harm done to the working populace as well as of the political *strength* of workers, a strength that lies in solid, united *struggle*. The general movement also called forth—from the camp of capital, from the industrialist circles, their helpers, and their foremen, from the bourgeois intelligentsia, and from the capitalist press—a level of respect for workers previously unknown, mixed with fear and hatred, as a class, as a new social and moral force with which they had up to now been merely acquainted. Industrialists are ready as never before to reach agreements with workers on strike, and not because they fear "bombings" or feel threatened by "war-intelligence committees," as adolescent socialists may imagine, wanting to make the struggle into an easy process of sending anonymous postcards containing "verdicts" and "threats." It is because of the power and consciousness *as a class* that our industrial proletariat demonstrated in front of the whole world through a long, heroic mass struggle for improvements to its lot, for its trampled humanity, for a little light and air in the stifling black hole of capitalist exploitation.

But that is not all. The economic movement not only strengthened class consciousness among the proletariat of industrial manufacturing, which has long made up the revolutionary heart of our working class but has also reached completely new sectors of that class.

The general strike that was started on January 27 by the working masses suddenly split with unrestrained force into two currents. It progressed upward, into spheres thoroughly petty-bourgeois in their way of living and thinking, such as office workers, railroad employees, photographers, insurance agents, pharmacists, bank employees, and sales assistants. And the strike movement flowed downward into rural spheres, sweeping through agrarian laborers. In this way the strike flowed from the largest concentrations of the industrial proletariat of large cities and manufacturing centers to the circles of society that are closest to the working class in terms of their economic position, nearly surrounding the working class, but that nevertheless have never developed bonds with the industrial proletariat through struggle. The strike flowed further into strata that had never before taken up the slogan of fighting exploitation, that had not been aware of such exploitation, had known nothing of the conflict between their interests and those of the "employers," and had never considered that they belong, in fact, to the proletariat. The industrial proletariat seized upon these classes as its own for the first time and tore them away from the social surroundings to which they had been tied.

This infectious strike movement thus marks the proletariat's rapid separation from bourgeois society, its emergence as a social class, at the top from the urban petty bourgeoisie and at the bottom from the peasant masses. Agrarian strikes began separating the rural proletariat, the seasonal farm laborers striving exuberantly for their fortune, from the landowning farmers—who were entirely unmoved, and who National Democracy keeps on the string of the "Polish school" and the "Polish community." At the same time, the wave of strikes poured over from large urban centers down into the provinces, where it instilled the fight against capital in all the great sectors of the industrial proletariat that had never before felt the difference of their interests, or where, as in the Dąbrowa basin, the path that had been partly cleared by earlier class struggle had long been overgrown by weeds and grass.

The series of strikes that have happened and still happen in the fires of revolution is therefore nothing other than the birth of an entirely new incarnation of the Polish working class. Thanks to the related economic strikes, the course of the political revolution is causing bourgeois society to splinter, to split into two hostile classes, the bourgeoisie and the proletariat. From the beginning, we Social Democrats have been merely *abstract* representatives of the regional class struggle. A small segment of the entire giant working masses first played a significant part in the struggle, and a still-narrower segment did so consciously, in the name of Social Democracy. Despite this, Social Democracy had a legitimate right to speak in the name of the entire working class because it was and is by nature nothing but an expression of the interests and needs of all working people, and because, acting in this role, it has counted and can count unwaveringly on the steady awakening of the working masses.

Even now, in the course of the revolution, this awakening takes the form of sudden leaps forward. The working class, class antagonism, and class struggle are becoming realities in our country. The *idea* of Social Democracy is becoming flesh, and the small troop of pioneers is growing into a vast army.

This emergence of the working masses from bourgeois society, as a fighting, conscious class of the exploited, constitutes the most valuable point and the real meaning of the fever of economic strikes that started at the end of January, and it also yields hints about what Social Democracy is to do.

Everywhere that the veneer of bourgeois society begins to crack under the pressure of waves of revolutionary strikes, there must Social Democracy immediately bring down the pickax of agitation with all its strength, so as to widen, deepen, and *establish* the crevice—that is, to render the class antithesis as *conscious* as possible and to strengthen its *organization* with the sturdiest aid available.

Two means to this end present themselves. On the one hand is the possibility of unifying all efforts by gathering and grouping economic demands around the demand for the *eight-hour workday*, letting that become the central axis of all economic struggle. From the very first moments in January, here as in St. Petersburg, Social Democracy called for the eight-hour workday as a fundamental economic demand, parallel and in addition to its political demands. The call must then be consciously and systematically connected to every economic strike in the country and set up prominently at each. Placed on this central axis, dispersed strikes merge into one *class* movement that fuses organically with the political struggle, lending it the unique, conscious character of a fight of labor and of socialism. Admittedly, the eight-hour workday is not quite a socialist reform; it is only an economic reform based in a bourgeois economy. But this reform, understood as a general and enforceable right, is radical enough that it constitutes a challenge thrown at the feet of capitalist property itself, of exploitation itself. And at the same time, as an *international* slogan, it specifically ties the aspirations of our political revolution here to the class struggle of the entire international proletariat.

On the other hand, economic strikes in the current phase directly make the ground more fertile for *political and socialist* agitation, for generally raising the class consciousness of workers and organizing them.'

This means one should not suppress or stem the economic struggle, as the social-patriotic PPS does, for example, in all its mindlessness (see its attempt to prevent the strike in the Dąbrowa basin). Much as the PPS announced that the January strike had happened "on its command," it demonstrated that it has no idea what is truly happening in the heart of the proletariat or what class meaning the whole strike movement possessed. Social Democracy's task in the current revolution is not to suppress or stem but to deepen and unify the economic struggle into one harmonious politically aspirational whole. For casual activists who are "also socialist"—that is, really just petty-bourgeois caricatures of the workers' party—the revolutionary aspect of the current struggle only entails political scuffles with the government. Meanwhile, massive clashes between the proletariat and capital are [viewed by them as] more of a hindrance, a prize they do not know what to do with and that they want to get rid of as soon as possible. They take part in economic strikes only with a sour face, so as not to lose entirely their connection with the masses and their influence on them.

For Social Democracy, as the party of class struggle, the revolutionary nature of the current age lies not only in fighting absolutism but, just as importantly, in massive clashes with capital. On the one hand, the economic movement should be used to show workers, especially among those in the spheres and regions newly won over to the movement, that absolutism is the most central barrier in their fight with capital, and that overthrowing it is the proletariat's most pressing need as a class. And on the other hand, the inverse is also true: In the fight against absolutism, the working masses should constantly and fully be made conscious of their antagonism with capitalist exploitation and the bourgeoisie. Only in this way, by constantly joining and counterbalancing these sides of the current revolution, may Social Democracy fulfill the double objective flowing from them.

For the current revolution has from the point of view of the working class—this is worth repeating—a *double meaning*. One is the overthrow of absolutism—a goal purely political, tangible, and designed for a given *moment* of struggle. The other is the organization of the working class into a class-conscious party to openly oppose the bourgeoisie on the day after the overthrow of absolutism—a goal fundamental and permanent, arising from our demands as a socialist party. To separate these two demands and tell workers, "Now focus all your energies only on winning political power, and set the fight with the bourgeoisie aside for tomorrow because it is a waste of strength and it scares off circles sympathetic to us from participating in our fight with the government"—this may be something that nationalists of various shades can say to workers, seeing workers as tools for the realization of their political goals. For Social Democracy, by contrast, the political freedoms for which we fight are merely the tools for the class struggle of the proletariat. And for this reason, in the current revolution, here as in Russia, as in every country at every moment, Social Democracy's final goals—its socialist goals—are inextricably bound up in daily goals; the political struggle, in the economic struggle; and the struggle against absolutism, in the struggle against the bourgeoisie.

II.

Another issue presented by the revolution can be solved with the same perspective: What should be done about these clashes with the army such as happened on May Day, and about the mood such clashes trigger in the masses?

The May Day demonstrations of Social Democracy were entirely peaceful. The working masses poured into the streets not to fight a battle with absolutism, but only to lay out their demands. Social Democracy neither aroused nor intoxicated the populace with noise about "arming themselves," nor did it provoke the police or the army with terroristic pranks. And for that reason, the more blame for the brutal mass murder on May Day* falls exclusively and entirely on absolutism's hooligans, the clearer becomes the atrocity of their crime, and the more powerfully it evokes a double mood in the working masses: a feeling of desperate powerlessness and a need to take immediate, active revenge.

Social Democracy is obligated to provide an outlet for this mood, but it can manage such a task only in a manner that accords with the very essence of Social Democratic agitation: by raising political consciousness within the mood of spontaneity.

Without an immediate sense of conflict, workers are prone to think that their powerlessness against the government, as demonstrated in the mass demonstration, can be attributed solely to their lack of *arms*, to their lack of the *physical means* to fight. After the May demonstrations, a thoughtless politician rivaled the PPS in feeding every kind of disastrous delusion to the proletariat when he cried out, "We already have the *power*, now let us only capture the *means*, the arms for battle, and victory will be ours." The task of Social Democracy, however, is not to feed but to dispel the delusions of the masses, nourishing them not with illusions but with real awareness of the situation.

Even a cursory glance reveals both Social Democratic demonstrations—the May Day celebration and the common strike on May 4 honoring the fallen victims of government violence—as expressions of the enormous power of the working class. If we intended, like the social-patriots, to impress the bourgeois intelligentsia with an external display of our strength, we could settle for the fact that a workers' demonstration this strong with respect to its numbers, this mature with respect to the consciousness of its slogans, and this disciplined in its behavior as a crowd has not occurred for as long as the socialist movement has existed in Poland. Still, it is a fact that in no other country does the history of

---

* For Luxemburg's description of the violent attacks by the authorities on the May Day marches in Łódź, Warsaw, and elsewhere, see *Complete Works*, Vol. 3, pp. 176–7.

the worker movement provide an example of such absolute and utter obedience with which Warsaw, a city of a million inhabitants, listened to the "command," in the words of the government newspaper, of Social Democracy with respect to general unemployment on May 4.

However, because Social Democracy, as the workers' party, cares not about *appearances* but about the *essence* of proletarian strength, its objective now is actually to show the working masses how inadequate its powers were for taking aim at the powers of absolutism. As a demonstration, a 22,000-strong march in Warsaw is a brilliant result of Social Democratic agitation. But, as an expression of revolutionary consciousness and a wartime army of the proletariat, it is but a small part of the several-hundred-thousand-strong working masses of Warsaw, and scarcely a handful in comparison to the entire urban and rural working populace of our country. From the very beginning, the leading tone of Social Democratic agitation was to explain to workers that only when *all the people*, when the innumerable, vast masses of the industrial and agrarian proletariat, as well as the large segment of the proletariat standing in defense of the tsar (that is, soldiers), rise up to battle both here and in Russia, victory will be ours. We must constantly renew our efforts to bring this to the attention of workers, especially where temporary, local success causes them to overestimate their power and think prematurely that physical weapons are all that is necessary to settle the fight to the advantage of the people. We must guide people who feel powerlessness before the tsar's mercenaries into an awareness that the revolution lacks not "means" but "forces," not rifles but proletarians who have become conscious.

The revolution, as a workers' revolution, is by nature a mass movement, and only as a *mass* struggle will it defeat absolutism. Today even the nationalist PPS says this, calling loudly in its May appeal, "The government is not afraid of a small armed band, and we will not defeat the tsarist government with terror alone. Our strength lies in mass demonstrations, our future in mass struggle." But understanding and recognizing the influence of the masses as a factor in the political revolution is not an art and was not invented by socialists. One cannot accomplish much in the political fight without the millions of work-worn hands of the people, and this is no secret to the bourgeois parties; the capitalists know it, the reactionaries know it, and the petty bourgeoisie knows it. This is precisely why demagogues try to latch on to the working masses.

The politics of a truly socialist party do not center on crying out, "Our future is mass struggle," but on whether the *program* of the party is adapted to the interests of the working class, and whether *its entire tactics, its entire modus operandi* is calculated for action, for the conscious action of the working masses.

Social Democratic struggle is mass struggle. But the struggle is always unfolding, and the *notion of the mass* is always unfolding, must unfold, alongside it. A 20,000-strong crowd thronging around the banner of Social Democracy is already a sign of a serious mass movement, in comparison to still-recent times when barely a few hundred took part actively and consciously in the struggle, and after that only a few thousand. But in the current phase of revolutionary struggle, the notion of the *mass* that is recruited to stand for action and square off against absolutism must develop very rapidly and must still reach hundreds of thousands, even millions. And in the process, it must cross the borders of separate urban centers and spread through the *entire country*. So, the parallel task for us, in relation to the powerlessness of workers facing government violence in their isolated locales, is to show continually that only by *broadening one's own terrain* of struggle across the entire province, across the entire country, can we gradually ensure the revolution's advantage over absolutism and final victory.

The question posed by the May demonstration is thus nothing other than *the essential question of the revolution*. We see immediately that there is a contradiction: The revolutionary cause seems to be headed down a dead-end street. The current struggle, as a mass struggle, needs mass appearances, and thus, apart from the common strike, it needs the masses to gather physically and voice their aspirations openly as a crowd. The revolution needs mass demonstrations and protests, mass rallies and marches. But demonstrations and marches lead, as we saw in May, to the slaughter of the unarmed crowd. So what should be done? Give up this means of fighting because of the slaughter that we may expect at mass demonstrations? Yet that would be the same as giving up further advances in the movement, giving up the revolution itself! Should we look for a way out by making bombs and issuing "verdicts of revenge" on those of the tsar's instruments that particularly stand out for their brutality? Yet even bombs thrown "by the dozens" and "verdicts" sent by loudmouthed "committees" to government units can only serve to drown out and quench the thirst of revolutionary individuals who, feeling the need for constant uproar and noise, take the people's revolution for a series of brawls, asking only that blood flow and thunder roll. Only provocateurs or the voluntary allies of absolutism of the ilk of "National Democrats" like *Słowo Polskie* [The Polish Word] could hurl insults at Social Democracy for not "arming" the working masses with bombs when it called them to the May protest. We would have to be a pack of fools, lacking any feeling of responsibility for the people, to delude workers that a bomb could be the appropriate tool in the struggle *of the masses*—against rifles effective at a distance of 500 or 1,000 meters, or against artillery, against cannon using case shot.

How, then, to get out of this situation? How can the revolutionary mass respond to the massacres with which the government attempts to suppress mass demonstrations?

The way out of the situation—the only answer—is this: Organize yet more frequent peaceful demonstrations throughout the country, and steadily increase the size of demonstrations.

The secret to power and certain victory for the worker revolution lies in the fact that no government on earth can last forever in a battle against a conscious and revolutionary mass of people, if the battle continually spreads and grows in scale. Brutal violence and massacres only give the government a temporary, *superficial* advantage over the masses. In reality, every such clash between the people and the government is a *step forward* for the revolutionary cause, because mass slaughter can only be an exceptional, rarely used tactic. The more crowds of workers turn out to demonstrate, the more places workers occupy. The greater the mass taking to the streets grows, and the more it spreads, the more powerless the government becomes against these demonstrations. As peaceful demonstrations by the people become a daily, common occurrence in the country, massacres become less and less possible, because they show their ineffectiveness as a means of scaring off workers, and they only cause the people to adopt a more agitated, revolutionary frame of mind and the army to hesitate and murmur more frequently. Thus, the only effective measure against massacres and military assaults on crowds of demonstrators is to show the government that such politics have the *opposite effect* from what they want—that massacres do not scare off the masses, they only inflame and incite them to demonstrate even more.

Naturally, workers going to demonstrations should arm themselves as well as they are able. The masses must respond to the attacks of the government's hooligans as well as their strength allows, in self-defense. Yet our first duty to our conscience is to explain this to the masses:

(1) In the current phase of the revolution, our goal is not to fight an armed battle with the army, but only to demonstrate *peacefully*, since that is the best means of achieving more recruits for the revolution both among the populace and among the troops; thus, right now arms should only serve for self-defense in the face of the army's attacks.

(2) No "committee" can equip the people, even just to defend themselves; that can only be achieved in other ways, such as through continual intensification of demonstrations. This is because the ever-expanding demonstrations of the masses both *decrease the chances of attack* from the army and *increase the chances that the masses will defend and arm themselves* during the clashes with the army.

Peaceful demonstrations must therefore obtain, at all costs, general acceptance in all cities and locales throughout the country where workers are gathered en masse—that is the most immediate goal, the task of the revolutionary movement. Emerging of its own accord as the only possible answer out of the politics of the robber barons in government, this task also constitutes the natural next phase of the road of further revolutionary development.

The death knell will toll for absolutism when the million-strong proletarian mass rises up to engage it and the part of the army following it in mortal battle, in the city and the country, across the land. But the available means of gathering all these innumerable masses to the struggle is nothing other than the constant, visible anti-government demonstration of the part of the working class that is already aware of the need to fight against absolutism. The most powerful means of recruiting working people to the struggle and of raising the awareness of still-indifferent strata of workers is peaceful demonstration by the revolutionary part of the proletariat. Through the natural broadening, strengthening, and popularization of protest, an army of conscious proletarians will rise up, and the moment will come when the revolution will bring itself to the still-distant final phase: open street battles between the people and an unnerved, hesitating army.

Thus, such demonstrations as the May protest are, despite the ostensible victory of the murderous government and the ostensible powerlessness of the murdered workers, a truly powerful and inevitable *step forward* toward the final victory of the proletariat over absolutism.

The way forward is full of awful sacrifices; it is strewn with the corpses of fighting proletarians. But it is unique and—from the point of view of *mass revolution*—normal. Mass revolution developed and found victory the same way in Paris, Vienna, and Berlin in 1848. And this was the way our current worker movement in Poland and Russia developed. There are some politicians who think they are socialists and speak at length about a "mass movement," who imagine that, with the help of small circles self-named "conspiratorial committees" or "war committees," they may spare the masses the need to make sacrifices, may use tricks to weasel out of the sacrifice of mass revolution, speaking *for the masses* and conducting their affairs "in the name of the masses." They again show only that they are thoroughly mistaken, even ignorant, about how the people's revolution has developed up to now and how it has reached its current dimensions.

There was a time when even a simple, modest economic strike was impossible under the tsar. Workers who only participated in simple struggles to raise their pay by pennies paid for it with enormous sacrifices, imprisonment, captivity in Siberia, and mass exile to the places of their birth—which was comparable to being sentenced to death by starvation. Yet to give up strikes was an impossibility. In the face of ever more frequent, ever more powerful strikes, workers fearless in the face of sacrifice achieved the real possibility of economic struggle, absolutism felt the powerlessness of its brutal persecutions, and economic strikes gained general acceptance. There was a time, only a few years ago, when the thought of open meetings of workers, of socialists, would have been madness. Yet despite its bloody cost, the workers' movement used this very method of improvising ever larger and ever more frequent gatherings to gain the ability to publicly discuss worker causes in Rostov-on-Don, in the Dąbrowa basin, and in other places. The mass strike, as a means of political struggle, appeared on the stage only at the end of January, and already on May 1 and May 4 workers showed that the mass strike has become commonly accepted in our country, has become a normal occurrence. The issue of mass demonstration follows the same road. The victorious revolution itself is headed down the very same road, accompanied by and making use of demonstrations, growing more and more in power and breadth.

When the revolutionary tension manages thus to reach its apex, as in early May, and provokes an exceptional level of action, the conscious class struggle of the proletariat cannot and need not deviate from its general and fundamental tactics, which suffice for every moment and phase of the struggle. In response to the proletariat's impatience and desire to act, the PPS points to all manner of false, temporary means of satisfaction, speaking of the "masses" and throwing "bombs of vengeance" to all corners. Yet Social Democracy may only provide an outlet by calling the proletariat to further *mass* demonstrations, demonstrations that grow *ever more massive*.

The revolutionary proletariat, as a class, is naturally seized by the highest forms of idealism, and does not fear the sacrifice inherent in the struggle; it regrets only losses in vain, and hates only the feeling of being powerless. Here is where Social Democracy may give aid and strength to the masses—not by putting a dozen rifles or a half dozen bombs in their hands, but by giving them a clear understanding of one fundamental law of the workers' movement: *that the only way out of all the difficulties of the mass struggle, at every point of its development, is to expand the reach of mass action and increase the numbers of people taking part in them.*

Imagine that the response to the massacre during the May demonstration of 20,000 Warsaw workers is a 40,000-strong demonstration in Warsaw next time, and that, at word of the Warsaw massacre, an even greater crowd of workers rises up to protest all around Warsaw, in Łódź, in the Dąbrowa basin, in Częstochowa, and in Białystok. Uncertainty will certainly spread through the army, in proportion to the increase in the numbers of demonstrators, and the government will hesitate before using the army against them. To the same degree, the massacre of the unarmed crowd by hooligans will be transformed into the struggle between an army and a crowd that is arming itself then and there, a struggle that cannot end any other way than *in the victory of the revolution*.

To reveal to the proletarian mass the power of its own movement, and thereby to increase its massiveness and power—that, now, always, and everywhere, is the central meaning and the great riddle of Social Democratic agitation and guidance, which, rather than "assisting" the masses in history, calls them into the arena of class struggle, not to *incite* them, but to *make them conscious*, a simple yet great task, much as the historical movement of the proletariat toward its class liberation is simple yet great.

Flowing from this broad understanding of the task, Social Democratic agitation must and will give the working masses the full depth of political consciousness, even in such exceptional circumstances as the current ones.

In such moments as May Day, one of the illusions the fighting part of the proletariat has about its own strength is also undoubtedly the illusion that "society" has sympathy for the workers' revolution. The impression that the May demonstration and subsequent massacre made throughout the city, like the undisturbed course of the mass strike in Warsaw on May 4, may very well create among worker circles the illusion of compassion, *politically*, from bourgeois circles. The social-patriots, faithful to their nationalist position, naturally feed these disastrous illusions among workers, writing in *Naprzód* [Forward],* for example:

> It must be stressed that the behavior of *all of society* (I say *all*, yet probably the "somber" elements belonging especially to the inner circles of "political" parties, due to higher, political considerations, will grumble at the unrest): *all spheres*, shopkeepers, traders, intelligentsia, industry, and bourgeois circles—all look on this movement favorably and sympathetically. Yesterday and today (May 1 and 2) were, in a manner of speaking, two *warring worlds*: one, the *society*, the other, the army and the authorities.

The responsibility of Social Democracy, as a class party, is the exact opposite: to immediately caution workers not to take the surface of things as their essence, point to the shameful fact of the complete passivity of "society" and its base subservience to the rule of criminals, point out the vile hatred that the bourgeois press displays toward the revolutionary conduct of the proletariat, and explain to workers that these "sober elements"—that is, the reactionary bourgeoisie—are not *exceptions* but the respectable representatives of our bourgeois society. In a word, in the current circumstances, the task of Social Democracy is to *separate* the working mass, as a class that is aware of its political difference, not dedicating even an iota to fleeting appearances or ostensible needs of the current moment, from *its own* fixed objective of organizing the proletariat for

---

* This was the central organ of the Social Democratic Party of Galicia and Silesia (Polska Partia Socjal-Demokratyczna Galicji i Śląska), or PPSD. Published as a weekly paper from 1895 and as a daily from 1900, it saw itself as the mouthpiece of the PPS, and criticized the Social Democracy of the Kingdom and Poland and Lithuania (SDKPiL) openly and frankly, even during the 1905 Revolution. The PPSD was originally a regional section of the Austrian Social Democratic Party. Founded in Lviv in 1892, the party, after separating from Ukrainian sections in 1897, described itself as "Polish." From 1899 on, the party just called itself the PPSD, without the appendages of Galicia and Silesia. Their preeminent leader was Ignacy Daszyński, deputy in the Imperial Council in Vienna from 1897 to 1918. Daszyński rejected the political and ideological outlook of the SDKPiL under Luxemburg and Jogiches, and, like Piłsudski, argued for a separation of the Kingdom of Poland from Russia. In 1906, after the split inside the PPS, PPSD sympathies were to the left of the Piłsudski camp. In April 1919, the PPSD merged into the PPS. Daszyński was the party leader of the PPS from 1921 to 1928, and again from 1931 to 1934. Before World War I, the party had around 15,000 members, a number that by 1919, shortly before the merger with the PPS, had grown to over 30,000.

the class struggle against the bourgeoisie, and to explain that the "two worlds" into which revolution tore our country do not consist of the Russian government on one side and Polish "society" on the other, but the fighting Polish proletariat alongside the Russian proletariat on one side, and against them the Polish bourgeois classes together with the tsarist government.

Social Democracy connects the most immediate goal of political struggle with steady class agitation in economic strikes, in common strikes, and in moments of mass protest—that is, in every expression and moment of struggle. Only in this way does it manage, in the terms of the *Communist Manifesto*, to raise common proletarian interests and the broader class movement in the midst of separate proletarian groups. Only thus does it raise, in the face of the separate temporary objectives of struggle, its ultimate goal: socialist liberation from the rule of capitalist society.

In a Revolutionary Hour, What Next? [March–April 1906]*

The mass strike of industrial, rail, and postal workers that started at the end of December [1904] has come to an end. The counterrevolution of the government and the bourgeoisie, the press run by Russian hooligans, and the press of the Polish National Democrats exult that the general strike, in particular the railroad workers' strike, did not "succeed" this time, that the rallies were poorly attended, that the spirit and military frame of mind during this strike were markedly weaker than previously. The reaction has joyfully concluded that the influence of "instigators" is waning and that the people, sapped of energy and emptied of strength, are beginning to disobey their ringleaders. The bourgeoisie, and especially the Polish bourgeois intelligentsia, play the role of spectator in the revolution, looking on the fight from their hiding place, through a gap in the bulwark, waiting until, soon enough, the struggle ends, and the bloody sacrifices of the proletariat can be enjoyed "in peace." This bourgeois intelligentsia, always ready to humble itself before the imposing might of the bayonet, is already beginning to doubt again whether the revolution will meet with victory. Those who have no spiritual connection with the proletarian mass, who understand neither the historical necessity of this revolution thundering across the land for more than a year, nor its internal logic, nor the guarantee of victory, rush to conclusions about the entire revolution whenever there is the slightest fluctuation in the scales between the people and the counterrevolution. These people are now ready to believe again in the power of absolutism and are losing faith in the strength of the proletariat, because a marauding soldier with a bayonet occasionally marches through the street with the step of a victor, because murder and injustice have become the order of the day, because the press is gagged, personal freedoms are insulted, unions forbidden, and public gatherings suspended—in a word, the entire "constitution" seems to have been destroyed.

Yet let us look deeper. At first glance, to shortsighted and essentially unthinking people, it may seem on the surface that the reaction emerged victorious from the most recent scuffle. Indeed, the mass strike was put to an end, and meanwhile martial law is still in effect, [Pyotr] Durnovo and his rapacious policies remain in place, and absolutism insists on the law of the scourge, without acknowledging the rights of rail unions or those of postal or telegraph

---

* This is the third piece written by Luxemburg under the title of "Z doby rewolucyjnej. Co dalej?" (In a Revolutionary Hour, What Next?). It was written while she was in prison in March–April 1906 after being arrested for revolutionary agitation in Russian-occupied Poland. Issued as a pamphlet in Warsaw by Czerwony Sztandar Press in June 1906, it incorporates material found in the first and second iterations of "Co dalej?" It is translated by Joseph Muller from the Polish original.

workers. The mass strike *appears* not to have reached its mark. Could it be that this powerful weapon was blunted this time, that the mass strike, to which we owe the main achievements of the revolution up to now, has ceased to have an effect?

Whoever thinks so will show only that he has been completely blind to recent revolutionary events and the role of the mass strike in those events. The mass strike is and will remain a powerful weapon of worker struggle, yet it is only that, a *weapon*, whose use and effectiveness always depend on the environment, the given conditions, and the moment of struggle. From the outbreak of the workers' revolution in January of last year up to now, we have thrice seen a mass strike that sent giant waves throughout the state, not counting the local strikes that broke out here and there in various cities and regions nearly without ceasing. Three times a strike broke across Russia and Poland, an expression of direct struggle with the tsar, and every time it had a different source, different circumstances, and a different meaning and role in the general course of the revolution.

I.

The wave of strikes that first hit Petersburg on January 22 [1905] seared that massacre forever into the memory of the unarmed Petersburg proletariat, which had succeeded in marching, 2,000 strong, to the palace of the tsar to beg for political freedom and an eight-hour workday. When the proletariat heard of this peaceful uprising of brothers in Petersburg and of the murder brought down on them by the tsar, they leaped into action, lining up to fight in every industrial region and city of the state: Poland, the Caucasus, Livonia, the South, middle Russia, and Siberia.* Workers leaped up almost exuberantly at the news from the tsarist capital; the mass strike broke out on its own, the socialist parties barely keeping up to utter the word "strike," to give expression to the militant energy of the working masses hurrying to show their solidarity with the proletariat of Petersburg. Such was the very essence and meaning of that first outbreak of the mass strike. It was the first expression of common political action, common class aspirations of the workers of Petersburg, Moscow, Kiev, Odessa, Warsaw, Łódź, Częstochowa, Dąbrowa, Riga, the Caucasus, Tomsk, and Tobolsk—the entire state. Before that, the workers of each city and each province fought against capital and tsar alone. They were joined by a common idea, identical interests, and identical aims. In the mass strike of January and February, the commonality of the proletariat's aims throughout the state became flesh for the first time, showing itself in action, in common, united struggle under a single rallying cry.

---

* Note that Luxemburg does not mention Ukraine, even though it was a major arena of strikes and struggles. She consistently treats Ukraine as an integral part of Russia and dismisses demands for its national independence or autonomy as utopian.

This same strike, as a protest against the Petersburg massacre and an expression of brotherhood with the Petersburg proletariat, forms through itself its content and meaning, because it was the first political expression of the whole proletariat of the state at once, the first act of common freedom and struggle. This mass strike was the political birth of the proletariat of Russia, Poland, Lithuania, Livonia, the Caucasus, and Siberia as a single class, and the inauguration of its common class struggle with capital and the tsar.

As could be expected, the *results* of the first mass strike were immeasurable. The strike did not overthrow absolutism yet, but it heaved and tossed the very social ground from which the class struggle of the proletariat is growing. As the fertilized earth begins, after the overflow of the river in spring, to bloom luxuriously and issue a rich crop, so the class consciousness of the proletariat, its consciousness of social wrongs, having been awoken all at once through the powerful mass strike, formed and broke out in innumerable partial, local, and trade strikes. Awoken by the very act of struggle across a whole class, the proletariat of the entire state began to shake off its shackles, fought to improve its daily lot, and spoke up about its countless injuries. The activities of this first mass strike lasted all spring and summer, forming a rallying point for untiring struggle, for the struggle of workers against the rule of capital in every region, in every place, in every factory—the struggle to concentrate the variety and diversity of local demands around one common axis, the call for political freedom and an eight-hour workday.

The circumstances in which the second mass strike broke out, at the end of October, were quite different. The struggle of the proletariat throughout Russia and Poland, having begun with the outcry over the Petersburg massacre and lasting almost half a year, forced absolutism to make its first capitulation. When the tsarist government saw that spilling its own blood could do nothing whatsoever to stifle the workers' revolution, it began to attempt to quell the revolution by stratagem, tricking the working proletariat with the *appearance* of political freedom. The government worked out that well-known scheme, [Alexander Bułygin's] "Duma," which, under cover of constitutional government, was in fact meant to strengthen only the omnipotent scourge propping up the swaying throne of the tsar, with the help of the reactionary bourgeoisie and gentry. Under the guise of political freedom, the Bułygin project was to deprive the working people of every political right.

This ruse of absolutism put the cause of freedom in great danger for a time. Both the reactionary bourgeoisie of Poland and the liberal gentry of Russia were ready at once to admit the broken, bloodied, tsarist right wing into the fold and to deceive the working class together. If the proletariat had peacefully permitted the comedy of the Bułygin "Duma" to be staged, and the comedy of "Duma" legislation to begin, involving a handful of tsarist stooges from the bourgeoisie and gentry, deprived of all legislative power, then the revolution would have subsided for perhaps a long period, and the tsar's goal of deception would have been achieved. The great mass of the urban and rural folk, having gained little to no consciousness, unable to differentiate real political freedom from masked despotism, would have taken the fraudulent comedy of absolutism as a significant change, as a true victory of the will of the people, and would have been lulled to sleep for some time, sinking again into passivity. The mass strike at the end of October put an end to the intentions of the tsarist government, thwarted the Bułygin project, the elections, the "Duma," and the tsar's whole wicked comedy. This time, abandoning their work en masse, the conscious part of the working class openly declared that none of absolutism's ruses could trick them, and they demanded not that absolutism be protected but that its rule be completely invalidated. With this strike, the conscious layer of the proletariat opened the eyes of a wide world of people to the outrageous intentions of tsarism, warning them of its dangers, and called them to immediate struggle. The effect of the strike was instantaneous: The tsar's proclamation of October 30,* promising that this time there would be true political freedom, buried the Bułygin project and opened a new phase of revolution.

Between the October mass strike and the one in January, there appear to be enormous differences in all respects. The outbreak of the January strike was largely spontaneous. Workers abandoned their work everywhere at news of the Petersburg massacre, led by a healthy class instinct. The October strike, however, was an entirely deliberate political action meant specifically to target the affront of the Bułygin "Duma" project. The rallying cry of the January strike came from the massacre of unarmed workers marching to the tsar with a plea for freedom, while the cry of the October strike came out of class-conscious Muscovite rail workers fighting under the banner of Social Democracy, and after them railroad workers throughout the state. In fact, enormous progress in the cause of labor and the revolution was made manifest in the very conditions of the outbreak of the second general strike. And for its part, the October strike advanced the cause of the revolution mightily.

The tsar's proclamation of October 30 was meant to head off the revolutionary storm with a solemn promise of true political freedoms—only it turned out that there was no longer any way to head it off simply with the appearance of freedom, given the political maturity of the proletariat. And that same political maturity of the worker has also meant that the tsar's promise, which absolutism never seriously considered implementing, was instantly fulfilled by the people, through their own revolutionary omnipotence. The next thing the tsarist satraps knew, as soon as November began, political freedom had become flesh. A press free from the bonds of censorship, a people free to assemble,

---

* Officially known as "The Manifesto on the Improvement of the State Order," it was issued by Tsar Nicholas II. The October 30, 1905, manifesto was the precursor to the first Russian Constitution of 1906.

to speak, to protest, to form unions—all this the working masses won, seized for themselves by storm, in the course of a few days. True freedom reigned in Petersburg and Moscow and Warsaw—across the entire state. But the first and most important use for the political freedom of the proletariat everywhere is open, vigorous class organization. Under the influence of Social Democracy, the working class, and with it the officials and petty bourgeoisie, threw themselves into the creation of unions. The idea, unknown in any former revolution, of permanent organization for class struggle, and in particular the class struggle of the proletariat, became the spirit of this workers' revolution. After the first strike in January, following the example of the industrial proletariat, the intelligentsia, the bureaucracy, artists, and circles of the petty bourgeoisie, as well as the rural folk, felt for the first time their class conflict with the exploiter class. They began for the first time to use the weapon of the *strike* as a way to improve their lot. Much the same, after the second general strike and the winning of true freedoms, all these spheres followed the example of the industrial proletariat and used, for the first time, the weapon of *organization*, throwing themselves into the creation of unions. The most important step in this general course of the revolution was the self-organization of postal and telegraph workers. But for that very reason, the general peak in organizing prompted a new attempt by the dying tsarist government. To forcibly block the enormous drive to organize, to block the free press and gatherings connected with organizing—that is what the tsar attempted to do with the assault on the union of postal and telegraph workers. And the postal and telegraph workers' response to that assault was a heroic general strike admired by all the world, which was brought to an end by a third and final general strike of industrial and rail workers.

The environment of the strike this time was quite different from the two earlier times. The first general strike in January was significant because it was generally possible, because it was the first united class action of the proletariat of the entire state, and because it built the class consciousness of workers under tsarism and united them for further struggle.

In this way, the revolution as a whole should be viewed as a result, as a prize, of that first strike, which was nothing but a candid expression of struggle addressed to tsarism from the working class. The second strike, in October, was a response to the deceptive ruses of absolutism and removed every possibility of keeping tsarism under constitutional protection. The result, the spoils of this strike, consisted of the October 30 declaration and the actual freedoms of the press, assembly, unions, and speech that were realized immediately after the declaration.

Finally, the third strike concerned the defense of these real freedoms, which the working class took by storm and which absolutism wished to reverse and erase. The object of struggle is no longer to throw off this or that design of absolutism. Tsarism abandoned all its deceptions at the moment their pointlessness became clear, when the Bułygin farce met its fate and the declaration of October 30 was made; stepping out from behind the mask, tsarism set out to abolish by force the political freedoms that were already taking root and growing stronger. At the moment when political freedom has come into the possession of the working masses—or, at the least, when their most elementary principles have become flesh and blood—and when, soon thereafter, the tsarist government has openly attempted to reverse those freedoms through violence, the struggle must attend to the very *existence* of the tsarist government. That is to say, the revolutionary struggle must reach toward its true goal, its final end. Not in the sense that the matter will be settled in the near future. On the contrary, the struggle may and will probably continue for some time. Yet it is reaching an end, a hard turn in relations with the tsarist government, its closest enemy. In the first phase of the revolution, the revolutionary army of the proletariat was merely gathering itself and forming ranks. In the second, the army seized actual political freedoms and invalidated actual powers held by absolutism. And now, the task is to clear the last of the obstacles the tsarist government set in the path: the reign of violence that blocks the further growth of political freedom.

One must only reflect on these stages, on this gradual development of revolution, to understand that a single general strike at a single time could not have decided the matter. The strike in January was able to fully achieve its objective, since it related to making the first united class action of the proletariat. It could meet its goal in October, when it was about the expression of protest and contempt for the comedy of tsarism, when it was enough to show that the working people are well acquainted with the deceit and fraud of the government, to force fraud and deceit to withdraw from the stage, broken, in rags, thrown out like a sharper whose fake cards have been found out.

Now, the government turns not to stratagem but to force in its attempts to reverse the political freedom that it was compelled to grant. There are no longer any misunderstandings or tricks. The revolution and the counterrevolution face off openly, the attempt to gain political freedom having served as a challenge to open, final struggle. Indeed, in the end, the cause can only be won by exerting physical force, by responding to violence with violence, by countering the assaults of the government with calls for a general uprising and street opposition. The general strike has operated, and will always operate, as the most perfect expression of the will and consciousness of the front ranks of the revolutionary proletariat, and as a means of building that consciousness and will in the as-yet-unconscious circles of the people. Therefore, the general strike remains essential. It remains the most important weapon of the revolutionary working class, for which the expression and raising of consciousness is the center and foundation of class struggle. In this sense, no strike is in vain—every one carries enormous effects. But in the current phase, since tsarism is no longer able either to pass over or deceive the will of the working people and wants simply to break the proletariat through violence—in the current phase, as a supplement to the general strike, the proletariat comes out onto the battlefield prepared, out of necessity, for armed uprisings and fighting in the streets.

Our last general strike was impacted by just such a situation, giving it a certain character of hesitation and apparent doubt. If the masses were somewhat reluctant to strike, if the socialist rallies did not evoke the enthusiasm and passion of previous phases of struggle, that is the unconscious expression of the infallible instincts of the proletarian mass, which senses from the situation that a general strike is not enough to call up and form ranks for open battle in the streets against a violent, murderous regime. In fact, if the general strike did not "succeed," it is not because the masses have had too many strikes and struggles. Quite the opposite, they feel a need for something more, for stronger forms of struggle, because a general strike does not match their feelings and instincts. In other words, the course of the last strike is proof not that the revolutionary cause is moving backward and weakening, but just the opposite, that it is moving forward and deepening—not that socialist ringleaders are beginning to lose influence over the masses, but that the masses, as in every pivotal moment of struggle, are driving those same ringleaders spontaneously to firmer actions, and that we have moved into a new phase of revolution that opens before us a field of new struggles far greater than heretofore. And, just as before, when separate sections of the proletariat outstripped the entire army in battle, showing in their partially spontaneous outbursts the methods and forms that the struggle of the whole proletariat must consciously adopt, this time too, Moscow, with its street revolution, and no less the Urals, Bakhmut, Rostov-on-Don, and Livonia, have already provided a rallying cry and lighted the path to a new phase of armed struggle. The "nonsuccess" of the last general strike, in which the blind tsarist hooligans and reactionary bourgeois took such pleasure, is itself a triumph of the development of the revolutionary cause and a harbinger of a nearing series of violent and final clashes with tsarism.

II.

From the very beginning of the struggle with tsarism, Social Democracy has stated clearly that the overthrow of absolutism and the realization of political freedom will only be possible through a general, common uprising of the politically conscious working people throughout the state. Social Democracy has also made clear, from the beginning of the revolution, that such a common uprising of the working class cannot be realized unless the most conscious circles take gradual and successive actions toward conflict. Social Democracy explained that every partial and local uprising and struggle of workers, even where put down immediately, moves the revolutionary cause forward a step. For first, at the sound of struggle, they spread revolutionary consciousness and vitality to pockets of the people still unaware and passive, thereby preparing all proletarians to be united and organized in revolution; second, they disorganize the powers of absolutism, thereby weakening its resistance; and third, they win over parts of the military by bringing them together with militant parts of the population and create some of the conditions for workers to arm themselves en masse in the very act of struggle. Social Democracy thus made it clear that all the difficulties and problems of the revolution will be resolved not when advisory socialist parties find some more effective means or miraculous device, but only as the mass struggle of the proletariat develops logically and inexorably. The task of those guiding Social Democracy is therefore only to raise awareness among the proletarian masses of their own class movement and to gather and consolidate into a permanent class organization the foremost layers, to whom the course of the revolution and Social Democratic campaigning have given understanding.

An open revolution has swept across our state for a full year, and its entire route up to now has proven every word that Social Democracy has uttered. Little by little, the embers of revolutionary struggle have slowly shifted from place to place, until the fighting proletariat united them across the domain of tsarism into one fighting force guiding every step of the opposition in Poland, in Petersburg, in Moscow, and in central and southern Russia, and compelling the revolutionaries of every city, province, or capital to turn their attention to the state as a whole. Before, each separate demonstration in Poland, Petersburg, Moscow, Odessa, and the Caucasus had a separate meaning as one more blow to or breach in the bastion of absolutism. Now, the revolutionary activities of rail and postal workers, especially, have united so many people in the revolution across the state that separate uprisings in isolated cities or even whole regions, even if valiant, lead clearly not to victory but rather to the demise of the revolution.

And yet, a general uprising leading to open battle on the streets remained necessary. Even if anticipated and promoted by Social Democracy from the start, it was still there—not as an artificial, "rabble-rousing" invention imposed on the masses, but as an effect, the logical consequence of the very course of the current revolution. This necessity arose of its own accord from the circumstances and developments of the revolutionary struggle, from the exhaustion of the tsar's store of tricks, and from heightening awareness and growing strength on the part of the revolution. And this necessity still hung over the last general strike, producing unclear feelings of expectation, uncertainty, and hesitation that projected certain qualities of demise onto a strike that was at its base a new progression, a new and concrete step forward along the path of development of the revolutionary cause.

In this way, the course of the struggle, in developing according to every rule of genuine mass struggle, met with a phase in which the very victories and advances of the revolution, which were a condition and safeguard of its future victory, created the appearance, during the transitional phase, of vacillation and powerlessness. The mass workers' revolution is built not on the strength of the "orders" of a handful of sham "leaders" but on the law of historical development. It differs from the dazzling, splendid revolutions of the bourgeoisie precisely in that it is full of apparent vacillations, apparent defeats, and even apparent steps back. "Bourgeois revolutions," writes Karl Marx in his *Eighteenth Brumaire of Louis Bonaparte*,

> storm swiftly from success to success, their dramatic effects outdo each other, men and things seem to be set in sparkling brilliants, ecstasy is the everyday spirit, but they are short-lived, soon they have attained their zenith, and a long crapulent depression seizes society before it learns soberly to assimilate the results of its storm-and-stress period. On the other hand, proletarian revolutions, like those in the nineteenth century, criticize themselves constantly, interrupt themselves continually in their own course, come back to the apparently accomplished in order to begin it afresh, deride with unmerciful thoroughness the inadequacies, weakness and paltriness of their first attempts, seem to throw down their adversary only in order that he may draw new strength from the earth and rise again, more gigantic, before them, and recoil again and again from the indefinite prodigiousness of their own aims, until a situation has been created which makes all turning back impossible, and the conditions themselves cry out: "Hic Rhodus, hic salta!"*

Self-examination—that is, *making oneself aware* at every step of the direction, logic, and basis for the class movement itself—is that store from which the working mass draws its strength, again and again, to struggle anew, and by which it understands its own hesitation and defeats as so many proofs of its strength and inevitable future victory.

In the current moment, the distant goals of revolution appear again in difficulties not yet resolved. On one hand, at first glance, the entirely peaceful general strike appears, as an instrument of struggle, to be depleted and worn out. On the other hand, the time still seems entirely unready for uprisings and armed clashes. Behold the heroic uprising of the Muscovite proletariat, suppressed in a river of blood, brought externally to defeat. Behold the marauding soldiers, ready as ever to murder at the command of their criminal rulers. And behold the great mass of people, as yet unarmed, with defenseless breasts bared against the lethal hail of bullets.

Yet such was the scene only as it appeared on the surface. In truth, the course and development of the revolution, which drove us toward the necessity of an uprising with pitched battles, had already created the conditions for

---

* Karl Marx, *Eighteenth Brumaire of Louis Bonaparte*, in *Marx-Engels Collected Works*, Vol. 11 (New York: International Publishers, 1979), pp. 106–7.

certain victory. That is to say, the revolution's course and development is clear from the very beginning, invariably and unswervingly, in two arcs: The power of the government grows ever smaller, and the opportunity of the worker's revolution blossoms and increases equally unceasingly.

In the first phase of revolution, the industrial proletariat entered the struggle alone. In Russia, the indigenous progressive and democratic intelligentsia gave moral support to the proletariat, while the liberal gentry spinelessly echoed it. Here in Poland, that did not happen. The urban worker alone, forsaken by everyone, entered unaccompanied into battle against absolutism and all of bourgeois society. No sooner had the first wave of strikes broken out than the foundations of this unified reaction began to slip away, as the popular masses broke out of their social passivity and joined with the factory proletariat. Gradually, office workers joined together, railroad workers joined together, then postal and telegraph workers formed unions, as did the navy, one military garrison after another began to join, and finally a blaze of peasant uprisings swept the Russian countryside, reaching the Caucasus, and a general rebellion broke out in Manchuria. And so, armies of fighters grew and still grow by the day, injustices and injuries, collected over the centuries, break out in yet new forms, and the field of revolution broadens without end. In such an arena, every position newly won remains a conquest that nothing can remove.

The railroad workers' strike and the postal workers' strike came to nothing because they did not achieve their direct goal: the recognition of unions by the government. But the discontentment of these white slaves of the railroad and the postal service, once awakened, cannot be thwarted by the ending of the strike, nor can their actual connectedness and union throughout the state—they remain as lasting possessions of the revolution, a constant ferment for further struggles. The navy rebellion in Sevastopol and Kronstadt and the unrest among various military units in Moscow, Kiev, and Odessa could be put down. But the upheaval in the navy and the land army did not disappear as a result. On the contrary, the more rapaciously and ruthlessly it is suppressed, the more vigorously it spreads, such that every military outbreak repulsed up to the present is a dependable guarantee of ever more frequent, powerful outbreaks thereafter. Even a peasant uprising, though it be bloodily suppressed in this or that region, cannot then come to an end unless as part of the whole revolution, since once awoken from its lethargy and directed into a movement, the rural folk does not return to a state of passivity, as long as the workers' revolution all around constantly throws new firebrands on the granaries full of injuries and pain collected through the centuries.

In this way, the revolutionary army grows constantly as it marches forward, like an avalanche, and its growth is permanent, only profiting, admitting no loss of scale. And together with the revolution's growth and the diversity of its ranks, the forms of its offensives—its fighting methods—proliferate and grow ever more varied. Recent months have seen, apart from the industrial strike, the rail and postal strikes. These structural disruptions gave revolutionary activity direct significance in international affairs, politics, and finance. Apart from the peaceful strikes in cities, apart from the revolution of "paid hands," there is a peasant war of pitchforks and flails, and apart from the workers' strike and the peasant revolt, a rebellion of tanks and a sea war.

As for the resources of the counterrevolution, they ebb with every passing day, and irrevocably. Pogroms of Jews, absolutism's most important mode of attack in the first phase of the revolution, are now a worn-out, unwieldy weapon. Their only lasting effect has been to embarrass tsarism abroad. In Poland and Russia, meanwhile, it has already become impossible to order pogroms wherever there exist conscious revolutionary ranks of workers. They may no longer make sport of Jews in Poland, Moscow, Riga, or any other important revolutionary center. They only still manage in the godforsaken backwaters of southern Russia, in the Beskidy*—that is, wherever the revolutionary movement is weak or absent. In a word, pogroms are now possible only where they are not needed, and impossible where they might serve to oppose the revolution.

Another army, or method, of absolutism—the display put on by the Black Hundreds—has been ruined and depleted, since behind the patriotic mask claiming folk origins, the whole world has recognized the despicable features of this social scum. By causing the army of the revolutionary proletariat to meet with a "patriotic" procession led by the clergy, absolutism intended to provoke the appearance of a contest of conviction between two different segments of the same people. By stoking a fratricidal war between members of the same people, absolutism hoped no longer to be the target of the struggle. But tsarism's profiteering collapsed in the thin societal framework into which it wished to deviously entice the revolution. The true character of the social scum pretending to be loyal folk emerged in a whirlwind of crime, anarchy, arson, boozing, and thieving, pursued in such an orgy that every absolutist command was bungled, and the group was utterly disgraced in the eyes of the true people as well as of the bourgeoisie. The strategy of pitting hooligans against the workers and the revolutionary intelligentsia was put to the test first and most provocatively in Moscow. Today, Moscow is also the first city in which the greatest militant uprising and most powerful armed conflict between the people and the army to date lighted the path to further struggle and to the triumph of the proletariat across the tsarist state.

Today, the tsarist government can only wage open war by drawing on its last resources: bayonets and artillery. But the troops who remain obedient to

---

* A series of mountain ranges in the Carpathians, reaching from what is now western Ukraine to the Czech Republic along the border of Poland and Slovakia. Western Ukraine remains one of the least economically developed regions in Europe to this day. Prior to World War II, as much as one-third of the populace in much of this area was Jewish.

absolutism dwindle by the day as well, and they dwindle especially quickly during scuffles with the revolutionary proletariat. For as much as the valor and discipline of the army grow after every victory over a foreign enemy in conventional warfare, so does each victory over an "internal enemy," over one's own people in a revolution, turn, doomed by a law of nature, into a disaster for the counterrevolution. The soldier who is beaten and overcome in the street by the people succumbs to fury against the people, and pride and caste brutality arise within him. Yet the soldier who "defeated" his own brothers in factory jumpers and stained himself with the people's blood turns his bitterness and frustration against his commanders, against those who used him as an instrument of evil. This is not a premeditated strategy of Social Democracy, counting on the impossibility of arming the entire working mass; rather, it is merely a historical symptom of the dual social quality embedded in bourgeois militarism, artificially turning a part of the proletariat into a tool with which to suppress the entire proletariat. The best and surest path to overcome the army in the revolution is to win it over gradually to the cause of the revolution, and the most powerful revolutionary school for the army is conflict with the revolutionary masses. Social Democratic agitation among soldiers only raises consciousness, formulating and organizing the results of that revolutionary ferment with which the workers' struggle—as well as absolutism's determination to use soldiers to quell the revolution—floods the military ranks. Revolutionary Moscow was inundated in rivers of blood. Yet, from the very beginning of the struggle in Moscow, one entire unit of the army, of the *infantry*, had to be removed from the fight, shut in the barracks, and watched, because it was "unstable." The most stable pillar of the government up to now, the *Cossacks*, also refused to serve in Moscow. Even some in the local *artillery* likewise removed themselves from the struggle against the people. In a word, the local Moscow garrison showed itself unfit to put down workers. Only by bringing in artillery and dragoons from other faraway regions, from Petersburg and the Warsaw Military District, could the government suppress the uprising. But in this way Moscow proved that only by moving its military forces from place to place can the government still use them against the revolution. So, during a *simultaneous* outbreak of armed uprisings at all the main points, it will become powerless. Further, because the units of the army still obedient to absolutism are moved to the main hotbeds of the revolution, the still-untouched ranks of the army receive their first schooling. Without a doubt, the struggle in Moscow has shaken and undermined the discipline, obedience, and fidelity of all the new army units faithful to absolutism until now. In each of its armed victories over the proletariat, the government thereby paid for victory with the loss of new regiments that passed over to passive hesitation or active revolution. The suppression of Moscow was a temporary and local failure of the revolution, but a prevention of the irreversible, total, final defeat of absolutism. The only means of maintaining the faithfulness or, at the very least, internal order and discipline of the tsar's army would be not to use it in struggle against the people, not to mix it into the perilous fray of the revolution. But the army and the use of the army are now absolutism's last hope of salvation. Tsarism has thus been put in check by the revolution, backed into a corner with no way out. Currently, the government is preparing, with all its remaining power, to ruthlessly drown every revolutionary uprising in blood after the pattern of Moscow, and it will continue to suppress them for some time. So, with each of its victories over the people, it will lose new ranks of soldiers and expand the ranks of the revolution, inexorably bringing itself closer and closer to its great and final loss.

So, the cause of the revolutionary proletariat must progress in the current, new phase of its development, and achieve victory by that same path and those same methods that brought victories up to now, opening new stages of power and strength. Not by any artificial stratagem, not by any miraculous invention, but only by the further normal and unflagging pursuit of a broader mass movement, and by organizing and raising the awareness of the sons of the proletariat who make up the tsarist military, will the revolutionary struggle march toward its ultimate triumph. In this way, through gradual, initially isolated, local, dispersed strikes, the way was prepared for the rise of common, unified, peaceful strike action across the entire state, and in this way, through isolated street battles breaking out here and there, the sparks of revolution will spread, flames will leap up, and one great blaze will unite them, a general and simultaneous uprising stretching across the vast expanse of tsarism. And much as every isolated strike seemed to fail, thereby broadening and unifying common strike action, so every isolated armed uprising of the proletariat will be put down, so as to organize and hasten the final common, triumphant uprising.

III.

The flat, bourgeois view of revolution—as a physical clash of two material forces —searches for provisions and guarantees of victory primarily in the quantity and quality of weapons. Revolvers, bombs, dynamite—these are the determining agents of struggle according to the bourgeoisie and the bourgeois-minded "friends" of the revolution. Bourgeois minds, as adherents to a coarse materialism, are not in a state to understand that even in capitalist wars, it is not weapons and physical stores that determine the outcome, but sociopolitical progress. The defeat of Russia in the [1904–1905] war with Japan was not a triumph of Japanese torpedoes, but rather of a young capitalist society over a decomposing absolutist corpse. Similarly, much as the defeat of tsarism at Sevastopol in the Crimean War half a century ago was a bankruptcy not of armadas or fortifications but of Russian serfdom,* so the defeat of the Prussians at Jena in 1807 in the war with Napoleon was a victory of the French Revolution and the renewed bourgeoisie of France over a decaying Prussian feudalism.† If the fates of epochal wars are decided not by bare physicality of arms but by the historical necessity of social development, which itself produces ideal arms, a superior strategy, and, most of all, a fighting spirit that ensures victory, then the fates of revolution are solely and entirely the work of that development. In all the revolutions of bourgeois society, the people were, are, and will remain poorly armed, and regular troops have and will always have a physical advantage over them. This is indeed the basis of the institution of the standing army and the reason the people are defenseless in capitalist countries, and also why one of the most immediate demands of Social Democracy in every country is to arm the people by creating a militia. Yet, despite this, revolutions up to now have always ended in victory for the people and the capitulation of old, outdated social and political forms. The fates of the current workers' revolution are not decided by how many firearms the fighting workers have at their disposal, but only by the fact that the fall of absolutism has become a historical necessity with respect to the powerful course of the class struggle of the proletariat, sprouting up as it does from the soil of capitalism cultivated by tsarism itself. At a time when the spineless bourgeoisie and intelligentsia of Poland have begun, under the pressure of absolutism's "successful" murders in Moscow and its shutdown of strike action, to doubt the victory of the revolution again, and to turn their gaze in admiration toward bayonets and machine guns, and when international capitalism hastens to increase the circulation of Russian bills on the market to pay tribute and cast a vote of confidence, temporarily and superficially, for the advantage of the counterrevolution in Moscow, the victory of the revolution is no longer subject to doubt. This for the simple reason that today it has already become, and becomes with every passing day, a fact. From the bourgeois point of view, overthrowing absolutism and gaining political freedom only come back down to earth after elections to the "Duma" are carried out on the basis of a miserable electoral travesty. Political freedom only becomes flesh when knights pulled out of a sack seat themselves in newly carved legislative seats in the tsarist "Duma" hall. And this kind of freedom is certainly already coming into being with each new day of continued struggle.

Absolutism as a form of government has truly ceased to exist; it has been destroyed. For the reactionary bourgeoisie, for whom governmental authority is

---

* The Crimean War between Russia, on one side, and England, France, and Turkey, on the other, lasted from 1853 to 1856 and ended in Russia's defeat.

† The Battle of Jena between France and Prussia was actually fought on October 14, 1806. It was a momentous defeat for Prussia, which lost over half its territory when its result was formalized in the Treaty of Tilsit in 1807. In the years following the defeat, Prussia moved to modernize its society and army.

embodied in the scourge, the cabal of [Count Sergei] Witte and [Pyotr] Durnovo still has full rein because it still has the power to carry out rape and murder. Yet the essence of the most common, even the most reactionary, government is not violent acts but the fulfillment of certain normal functions in a capitalist society. The current government is not able to fulfill any of these functions. It cannot ensure the capitalist class the usual opportunity to enrich itself by exploiting workers' labor, since the revolution unleashed such class-economic struggle, strikes, and demands from the proletariat that the process of capitalist exploitation lost its momentum and direction, having been interrupted and shaken at every turn. Neither can today's government ensure the landed gentry further safe and peaceful enrichment through exploitation of farm laborers, since the revolution has triggered a peasant war that the tsarist government is no longer able to stamp out. Further, the government cannot guarantee the continued functioning of public education in every bourgeois community, since the revolution has closed government schools everywhere. The government cannot maintain even the most essential elements of economic and social life in a modern state, transportation and communication, since the revolution took control over movement on railroads, as well as the postal service, telegraph offices, and streetcars. At every stage, the revolution has knocked the functions of government out of the hands of the tsarist cabal, which already lacked the shape of a government, having become an organization of violence that directed all its power to stopping the revolution. Counterrevolution has now become absolutism's sole function. True government, the regulation of the conditions of economics, classes, politics, and the public sphere, has passed to the revolution. Only inside the thick skulls of the tsar's "statesmen," of the caliber of Durnovo, can dreams appear about scooping back up all the governmental functions that have been lost, by means of piecemeal constitutional amendments, or by a greater or lesser degree of bloodshed. For the rule of the revolution over all spheres of public life, which the bourgeoisie see as "chaos" and "anarchy," is nothing but an expression that society and its class relations have indeed already outgrown the grip of absolutism. The tsarist government has remained in existence all these centuries through the unconsciousness and political immaturity of millions of working people who did not understand the antagonism between their interests and those of the ruling classes, and who did not sense the need for class struggle and the political freedom essential for waging that struggle. Today, enormous masses of workers throughout the state understand their class interests and wage war en masse every day on the bourgeoisie, making absolutism less and less possible. The class struggle of the proletariat has already given it a shock, sending a tidal wave through its frame that carried away its essence and functionality for society. For indeed, what the bourgeoisie calls the "chaos" and "anarchy" of the revolution is a direct manifestation of the maturity of the proletarian class struggle, which has grown remarkably in the fire of the revolution itself. Thus, for just this reason, no force or power can turn back the state of things. Neither piecemeal half measures, nor shoddy amendments, nor even rape and murder can return the function of governing to absolutism, which has been irretrievably surpassed by the social relations the revolution has forged.

It suffices to become conscious of the foundations and essence of the course of the revolution up to now, as well as its victories, to understand why its future fate is assured, as well as what must be done.

In the current moment, the revolution is enduring one of those ostensible pauses in which the monumental works accomplished—the triumphs, the victories—seem to grow dim or disappear from sight, and the onlookers to the revolutionary struggle begin to believe it may be crushed altogether by rows of bayonets, or that the fatigue of the combatants may exhaust the revolution itself. Both these fates surely have had their day in history. Nonetheless, those who, merely on that basis, anticipate the same fate for the current revolution at every momentary break merely establish the degree to which they misunderstand the simple fact that every revolution is subject to the iron laws of historical logic and that its fate, its defeat, and its victories are by no means a product of chance, but rather always a necessary result of the given political and social conditions.

It is entirely possible for a revolution to be exhausted or to be put down at a certain point of development through the use of violent force, but only under certain precisely defined conditions. That is to say, up to now, these fates were normal manifestations of modern bourgeois revolutions, in which the bourgeoisie was indeed the guiding force of the movement. But even the bourgeoisie was forced everywhere to call up to battle the petty bourgeoisie and proletarian masses, without which no revolution could come about, and draw them into the fray. A share of the working masses (that is, the proletariat) has always driven bourgeois revolutions toward much more sweeping and radical slogans and demands than suited the plans and interests of the bourgeois at the helm, or for that matter the given level of social development. Thus the typical manifestation of these revolutions was fatigue and a sudden decline of energy exactly at the moment when the struggle seemed to be at the height of its strength and momentum, for just then, the bourgeois classes and parties leading the movement sensed that the momentum of the revolution was lifting it too high, and all of society instinctively predicted that the revolutionary wave would inevitably and swiftly recede to a more appropriate course or, sometimes, even farther back. Such pauses from fatigue and depression were simultaneously harbingers of bloody calamities assuredly awaiting the revolution. When the militant hunger of the working class and the radicalism of its demands surpassed the intentions and demands of the bourgeoisie, tensions escalated inevitably to violent clashes with soldiers. In essence, the failure of the revolution was in these cases the failure of demands that went too far and were historically impossible to realize, a failure of the class that presented them. The victory of the bayonets was a means, appropriate to bourgeois movements, of turning the revolutionary fervor back within the bounds of historical possibility.

Such was the case in the Great French Revolution, which, having been started in 1789 by the moderate, liberal bourgeoisie with the motto of constitutional monarchy, even with severely curtailed electoral rights, was advanced by the petty bourgeoisie and proletariat of Paris for three years until a republic with a socialist hue was formed. The rule of the extreme party of the "Directorate" in 1794 was the very highest point to which the Parisian people managed to push the revolution, and the Terror carried out by the revolutionary government of the time, known as the Convention, which sent hundreds of moderate and reactionary burghers to the guillotine, was a desperate attempt by the people to hold on to power. Yet one hundred years ago, the Great Revolution was itself only the dawn of the general bourgeois system; and of all the conditions of socialist organizing, a democratic republic had not even been established in France at the time. The defeat and fall of the radical party of the "Directorate," the suppression of the proletariat, and the downfall of the entire revolution were likewise inevitable.

So it was, too, in the revolution of 1848. Begun by the liberal bourgeoisie in France merely with the slogan of electoral law reform, it moved on immediately after gaining support from the proletariat to the slogan of a people's republic, and soon further still, until the poorly understood slogan of socialist revolution emerged, in the spirit of the half-utopian, half-conspiratorial theory of socialism of the time, of Louis Blanc and Auguste Blanqui.

In the infamous June slaughter of 1848, the bourgeois classes drenched the revolution in the blood of the Parisian proletariat in order to prove to the working class that a socialist uprising in those times, when a great range of bourgeois and petty-bourgeois strata were themselves clutching after political control of the state, was a cause both premature and impossible to realize. Finally, so it was with the famous Paris Commune in 1871, that two-month period of absolute rule of the proletariat over the capital of France that was condemned in advance to failure and terrible revenge at the hands of the bourgeoisie, since this time, too, political control was given into the hands of the proletariat not as a natural result of social relations that were ready for the dictatorship of the proletariat but as accidental winnings, as a result of the choice of the cowardly French bourgeoisie to abandon the city of Paris, along with the charge of governing during the war with Prussia.

From these very examples, the logical conclusion is that fatigue among the revolutionary ranks, or suppression of the entire movement by force, while possible and inevitable in certain moments of past bourgeois revolutions, is not possible today. Today's revolution in tsarism is the first whose spirit is made up of the conscious working class. The fighting proletariat is led today not by bourgeois classes and parties but by Social Democracy. For this reason, its avant-garde has an awareness of its class interests, its objectives, and also the social conditions needed for their realization. Precisely because of this, the proletariat is not setting itself utopian or unreachable goals, like the immediate realization of socialism: The only possible and historically necessary goal is to establish a democratic republic and an eight-hour workday. On the surface, a republic may seem far removed from current conditions in the tsarist state, and the leap from yesterday's rule by savage absolutism to the highly democratic form of bourgeois polity that is a republic may seem great. Yet however far, however great, the mere appearance of such a possibility or likelihood is nothing, and historical possibility is everything. The goal set before the working class of Poland and Russia is entirely possible. That is, it is possible from the point of view of the state's social development, since it agrees with the class rule of the bourgeoisie, still unavoidable now after the revolution; and it also corresponds to the advanced stage of political development of the working class, and to class relations, in the same mature revolution.

On the other hand, the working class is the final class produced by bourgeois society to emerge with revolutionary goals. That a class more radical still could push the proletariat beyond the goals it consciously set forth—this is out of the question. The only social stratum lower than the proletariat, the class of social parasites deprived of property, such as prostitutes, professional thieves, and those eking out every kind of haphazard existence in the shadows, represents not a revolutionary but rather a counterrevolutionary factor.* They stand in the position of the Black Hundreds in their support for absolutism.

Of course, the working class itself may be lifted by the rush of revolution so far that it must push its own goals further, demanding not only a democratic republic but also significant concessions from the capitalist classes in the direction of socialist reform, which would in the end prompt a sharp clash between the proletariat and all other social classes. Yet such a turn in the revolution is in general only possible when the working class has already achieved complete victory, so much so that it must proceed by establishing a republic and holding the reins of state power in its hands for some time.

But for as long as that has not occurred, while the proletariat still does not rule over Russia and Poland and only fights for its most immediate revolutionary goals, it cannot be suppressed by rows of bayonets or halted by fatigue.

Fighters will meet with *isolated defeats*, and the bayonets will sometimes triumph; these things are not only possible but inevitable, since the whole development of the current revolution—in which the fighting proletariat joins ranks, increases consciousness, and grows—will come about only in the school of mass struggle itself, by way of isolated clashes with the still-superior strength of

---

* Referred to in Marxist nomenclature as the lumpenproletariat.

the reaction. After all, the revolution *as a whole*, advancing by way of the same path, has been unstoppable, and the apparent breaks in its progress are not, as in bourgeois movements, a sign of internal crisis or of the imminent reversal of the revolutionary wave, but only a sign that the revolution is gathering itself in preparation for sudden new leaps forward. After the first apparent pause, when the movement seemed to weaken at the end of a spring season of feverish mass strikes, mutiny broke out suddenly on the *Potemkin*. This was a sign that the revolution had reached a new field of operation, the tsarist navy. After the second pause, when the entire struggle seemed to waver as the elections to the Bułygin "Duma" approached, there was another outbreak of the general rail strike. This represented a sudden broadening of the revolutionary terrain. In the same way, the current "pause" is surely a harbinger of a new series of birth pangs, a sign of the revolution's generative activity. The objective of the role played by the conscious guardian of the proletariat, Social Democracy, remains, here as always, simply to tirelessly provide the elements, to accumulate the "flammable material" of revolution that constantly ignites in new sparks and forms of struggle. And the element or material that invigorates the revolution is none other than *political consciousness and class organization among the urban and rural proletariat, in both the factory and the barracks.*

The beginning phase of open armed struggle places on Social Democracy the responsibility of arming the front ranks of fighters insofar as it is able, working out a plan and provisions for fighting in the streets, and, most importantly, learning from the experience of the armed uprising in Moscow. Yet not in the *technical* preparations for an armed uprising, however important, even indispensable, they may be—such preparations do not ensure victory for the people in open conflict with troops. When all is said and done, the deciding factor will not be whether a small minority of the working class is organized into combat squads, turning the revolutionary struggle into their special task, but rather the broad mass of the proletariat. The proletariat's battle readiness, the proletariat's organized, disciplined movements, and the proletariat's heroism are what can safeguard final victory in a street revolution. Truly, only the kind of bohemian revolutionary who suspects a conspiracy at every turn could think of organizing the entire proletarian mass into combat squads. The working masses can only be organized on the grounds of constant, daily engagement in class, economic, and political struggle. Social Democratic labor unions, Social Democratic societies, strenuous agitation around them in city and country, the creation of martial unions in barracks—these are the central, basic tasks to prepare for future success in battle on the street. For by organizing and raising the consciousness of the working masses on the matter of their main class objectives, as well as the special objectives of the current moment, it becomes possible, first, to permanently fix the fruits of the class struggle, once extracted from absolutism, and so to safeguard the revolution against a return of the reaction to power;

second, to prepare for the current revolution, that "explosive material" which is the political maturity of the proletariat, which itself, assembled fully, will usher in new outbreaks, new forms of struggle, and new sudden advances at many different points; and third, to create in the masses that militant mindset and that readiness for victory at all costs which simultaneously render armed conflicts eventually inevitable and guide the movements of the masses in such conflicts.

In apparent "pauses" such as the current one, there is a decline not only in the belief in the power of the proletariat among bourgeois parasites on the revolution, but also in the belief of the working class in its own strength, for the horizons of revolution become constricted, and ways ahead are not discernible. The best, the only, way to energize the revolution and inspire belief in it among the fighting ranks is to raise again their awareness of the revolution's historical necessity, logical development, and record of victories. As Lassalle said, the most revolutionary action is and will always remain "stating openly that which is."*

---

* See Ferdinand Lassalle, "Über Verfassungswesen: zwei Vorträge und ein offenes Sendschreiben" (On Constitutional Systems: Two Lectures and an Open Letter) (1862), in *Ausgewählte Reden und Schriften* (Berlin: Dietz-Verlag, 1991), p. 127. For an English version of parts of one of these speeches of Lassalle, see "On the Essence of Constitutions," in *Fourth International*, Vol. 3, No. 1 (January 1942), pp. 25–31. The irony is that despite these words, Lassalle engaged in secret discussions with German chancellor Otto von Bismarck in 1864, in which he disparaged efforts to create a democratic republic and expressed his preference for an "enlightened" monarchy. Although Lassalle's correspondence with Bismarck did not become known until after Luxemburg's death, Marx's antipathy toward Lassalle was widely known—even if it did not make a major dent in his popularity among most German Social Democrats.

Traitors of Poland*

The Duma talks and talks and talks. The Cadets† apparently think that they can talk freedom into being. Around the Duma stands the old government, tricked out from head to toe in bayonets, and within the Duma building itself, the tsar's armed guards surround the envoys, yet the Duma still thinks of itself as a real power, a real parliament. Consider how the prisoners in the Tenth Annex of the Warsaw Citadel‡ are permitted by the guards to assemble, talk among themselves, elect chairs, and hold discussions—in a word, play at parliament. This caricature of a representative council differs not all that much from the real Duma. The Cadets want a fight with the government, but a peaceful fight, not a revolutionary one, and they have already found the perfect way to achieve freedom peacefully: through the Duma and the press. The moment the Cadets open their mouths to speak, the government ministers hear the desires of the nation emanating from their lips and immediately know what to do. The Duma and the liberal press know what to do, too: Let the tsar appoint a cabinet (that is, a government) that will please the Duma; let that government appoint new police, governors, and officials; and let that government govern liberally. Then everything will peacefully resolve itself. Such are the political tactics of the Cadets.

One is reminded of the purely facetious answer Polish folk give when asked how to catch a sparrow—sprinkle salt on its tail. So then, how do you knock power out of the hands of a criminal government? The Cadets reply that the government already knows what Russia wants, so it needs no help using its power for the good of the state. By this reasoning, if the government has so far done nothing but murder and pillage Russia, that was only because it did not yet know what to do, because there was no Duma to tell it that it should begin to fashion a noose to fit its own neck.

The Duma runs the risk of clashing with the government. The masses have joined their fates to the Duma's, expecting to receive "freedom and land" in return. The tsarist government wants to give them neither freedom nor land. But a sharp clash with the Duma would pose a danger to the government, as long as the Russian masses stand behind the Duma. Thus, the tsarist government is

---

* This article first appeared in *Czerwony Sztandar*, No. 70, May 21, 1906, p. 1, under the title "Zdrajcy Polski." It is translated from the Polish original by Joseph Muller.

† The Constitutional Democratic Party, known colloquially as "the Cadets," was a liberal party committed at first to a constitutional monarchy and later to a republic. Members mainly included progressive landowners, representatives from the bourgeoisie, and members of the intelligentsia. During the 1905 Revolution, it became the most important political force on the bourgeois political spectrum in Russia. The Cadets were represented in all Dumas from 1906 to 1917.

‡ The Tenth Annex was a section of the Citadel in Warsaw that was notorious for its brutal conditions. Many revolutionaries and radicals were incarcerated—and died—there after its construction in the 1830s.

still equivocating, looking for a way out, waiting until the garrulous Duma has reassured the masses with its "peaceful" tactics—until such garrulousness has lost its novelty, and the masses have stopped taking interest in the Duma. For its part, the Cadet Duma also fears a sharp clash because the end result of such conflict would have to be a new revolutionary uprising greater in size and scope than all previous uprisings. The Cadet Duma fears revolution, so it avoids scuffles and ponders how best to sprinkle salt on the sparrow's tail.

Still, there is a revolutionary peasant-worker faction in the Duma that may, by pushing for its own agrarian and labor demands, cause a sharp clash with the tsarist government and then an outbreak of revolution.* The Cadets would not have a majority in the Duma without this faction,† so they try, for now, to agree with and appease it through formal concessions and promises. If the Cadets manage to politically demoralize the peasant-worker group, then the Duma will cease to have any revolutionary importance at all. In the interests of revolution, in the interests not of "outtalking" the government but of actually knocking power out of its hands, we have to sharpen the conflicts between the Duma and the tsar, sharpen the conflicts within the Duma itself, push the Duma's most revolutionary group forward, and through it push the Cadets ever closer to a sharp clash with the government. Such is the business of Social Democracy. At every step, the party should be exposing how the Cadets long to obscure their true position and pretend that they are in a parliament, when in reality they remain, together with all of Russia, in another of the tsar's prisons.

The Cadets skirt the question of overthrowing the tsar like a cat winds around hot soup, to borrow a German expression, and in much the same way as our Polish Circle of national disgrace jumps back, as if burned, from the question of achieving autonomy for Poland.‡ The nationalists—who constantly attacked the revolution with everything they had (thereby supporting tsarism), who presented the revolutionary activities of Social Democracy as an antinationalist activism, and who promised the nation that they would secure autonomy through the Duma and not through revolution—now themselves do not know what to do with their countrywide electoral "victory."

The National Democratic papers already complain that the Cadets betray Poland. As a matter of fact, the Cadets promised us autonomy, and now they somehow do not want it, despite their promises and despite the insistence of

---

    * At the time, the Mensheviks had eighteen representatives in the First Duma, while the Trudoviks—a split from the Socialist Revolutionary Party (SR) that had boycotted the elections for it—had 136 (out of a grand total of 566 seats). The Bolsheviks also boycotted the elections for the Duma. The Mensheviks and Trudoviks comprised the "peasant-worker faction" cited here. Alexander Kerensky, who later led the Provisional Government following the February 1917 Russian Revolution, was later elected as a Trudovik to the Fourth Duma.

    † At the time the Cadets had 179 seats in the Duma, more than any party but considerably short of a majority.

    ‡ A reference to the Polish National Democratic Party.

our nationalists in the Polish Circle for such autonomy in their own subservient response to the tsar's address. We do not doubt, either, that the Cadets betray Poland, or that they would betray it if the Duma contained, in the place of National Democrats, the so-called Progressive Democrats themselves.* The Cadets doubtless support autonomy for our country, but they betray it against their will, just as they betray the entire revolution. The Cadets have not only refrained from uttering a single word about autonomy, they have also declined to put forth a single political demand of their own—such as, for example, calling for direct, universal, equal elections with secret ballots—precisely because they fear conflict with the government, and they fear revolution, albeit not as much as the nationalists. The Cadets betray Poland against their will, precisely because they want a peaceful way to make amends between the tsarist government and the cause of freedom, because they want to keep tsarism and only curtail it somewhat, because they really just want to negotiate with it, *and in negotiations with tsarism there can be no room for Polish autonomy*, much as there is no room—cannot be any room—for the full and actual democratization of the state.

This truth by itself is so obvious that it can even be found leaping from the pen of nationalists, despite their best efforts. In National Democracy's party organ, *Dzwon Polski* [The Polish Bell],† they respond to the betrayal of the Cadets by writing thus:

> The four-point [right to] vote is, as we all know, a catchphrase used by extreme factions consisting mainly of urban worker elements. After the revolution waned, perhaps temporarily, when it was dealt sharp blows during the armed uprising in Moscow, the Russians concluded that revolutionary tension had relaxed, and therefore that one could take the extreme parties less into account.
>
> And since these parties *would actually support the issue of the autonomy of the kingdom more eagerly*, one may conclude that as they weaken, our cause may too fall by the wayside, the more so since Russian peasants take no interest in this cause and gladly pass over it in pursuit of land, the lack of which they doubtless feel above all else.

Revolutionary Russian peasants surely do not want Poland to be oppressed, but for a nationalist—a chauvinist—the pleasure of suspecting them of chauvinism is too great to pass up. Although it avoids clichés about Russian peasants, *Dzwoń*

---

* The group founded by Aleksander Świętochowski in 1905 as the Progressive Democratic Party. For Luxemburg's critique of it, see "The Historical Services of the Polish Bourgeoisie and Mr. Świętochowski," pp. 69–73 above.

† *Dzwon Polski* was a National Democratic daily newspaper, published under this title in Warsaw from March 20 to April 2, 1906, and again from April 5 to November 30, 1906. The main newspaper of National Democracy was *Goniec* (The Herald), published from 1903 to 1918 with short interruptions; in 1906 it was issued under the names *Dwzon Polski* and *Praca Polska*.

Polski illuminates correctly enough the betrayal of the Cadets with respect to the cause of autonomy as the revolution waxed and waned. *Dzwoń Polski* itself writes, "The extreme parties would more strongly support the issue of autonomy of the kingdom," adding furthermore that "as they weaken, our cause may too fall by the wayside." As a matter of fact, we would add, this cause is likely to disappear completely from the order of the day together with the revolution.

But who was for the "weakening" of these parties? Who spouted claims that revolutionary Social Democracy promotes "disasters" and "anarchy" and so on? Who fought the revolution, and who hated it and hates it with all their heart?

National Democracy! The Polish Circle!

Now, the nationalists themselves, in a fit of honesty, without meaning to, have argued that the cause of autonomy is connected to the cause of the triumph of "extreme factions," the triumph of revolution. National Democracy and our entire bourgeoisie have fought, and still fight, against the revolution, and because of that alone, according to the witness of *Dzwon Polski* itself, they have undermined, and still undermine, the autonomy of Poland.

The greatest national enemies of Poland are its own nationalists.

The June Days of 1848: A Page from the History of the Workers' Struggle for Bread and Freedom*

I.

In February 1848, workers in Paris revolted for the third time, demanding a republic and complete equality and political freedom for working people. The first revolution in France, known as the Great Revolution, had taken place much earlier, starting in 1789 and lasting until 1796. Almost without pause for seven years, rebellion had churned up the land, and the blood of the people of France had flowed in the streets. In this revolution, the medieval sovereignty of the serf lords and the clergy—that is, feudalism—was completely destroyed. The nobility's last king, Louis XVI, was sentenced to die as a traitor to his country, and a republic took control of France. But not for long did working people enjoy the fruits of their struggle. The place of the gentry was taken over by an industrial and financial bourgeoisie, which, terrified of the power of the working class, prevented the working class from exercising its political rights and established the monarchy anew in 1804 through the government of Napoleon I. So passed another decade. Working people lived in misery as before, and before long, Napoleon was succeeded on the throne of France by kings from the old dynasty. The aristocracy and the clergy went back to their tyrannical ways, and it seemed that all the Great Revolution had achieved had come to naught—only the capitalists were enriched by and benefited from freedom.

---

* This has been translated from two originals, as an article in *Przegląd Robotniczy*, No. 6 (1905), pp. 51–66, and as a pamphlet printed in Warsaw by Wydawnictwo Socjaldemokracji Królestwa Polskiego i Litwy (the publishing house of Luxemburg's party, the SDKPiL) in June 1906. They are identical, except that the 1906 version omits two paragraphs at the end and adds a new three-page ending. The original article in *Przegląd Robotniczy* was entitled "Dni czerwcowe. Kartka z historii walki robotnikow francuskich" (June Days: A Page Out of the History of the French Workers' Struggle); the pamphlet version, which appears here, was entitled *Dni czerwcowe w roku 1848. Kartka z historii walki robotników o chleb i wolność*. Luxemburg wrote to Leo Jogiches on July 7, 1905: "Without intending to I have written a little pamphlet. I actually wanted to write an article for *Czerwony Sztandar*, but while reading through the material it turned into a little pamphlet. I haven't wasted any time on it, as I wrote it *in the digestion hour* from 2 till 4 [p.m.], when I normally lie on the sofa and read the feuilletons, in the space of five days. As it happens, this whole, distant field really refreshed me … I don't know if the pamphlet is good, but at least it supplies people with a little material and knowledge beyond these few *sajesshennych* [trivial] agitational tenets." See Rosa Luxemburg, *Gesammelte Briefe*, Vol. 2 (Berlin: Dietz Verlag, 1999), p. 149. It is translated from the Polish original by Joseph Muller. *Przegląd Robotniczy* (Workers' Review) was a newspaper of the SDKPiL, principally used to popularize its positions. It was published in Zurich from 1900–1901 and in Kraków from 1904–1905. Its editors included Jogiches, Adolf Warski, Julian Marchlewski, and, later, Władysław Feinstein (aka Zdzisław Leder).

Workers in Paris revolted for the second time in April 1830. Streams of working-class blood again flowed over the Parisian cobbles, but this time the bourgeoisie tricked the proletariat and, using the proletarian victory solely for their own ends, placed a new king on the throne that suited their taste. In turn, he gave up the government not to the aristocracy and gentry, as before, but to the rich class of capitalists.

For many years after, working people were impoverished and held back. They were deprived completely of political rights, including the right of parliamentary elections and the right to form unions. What is more, the industry that was quickly developing under the control of the bourgeoisie weakened working people even further, pushing them into utter destitution.

So it was that the tireless Parisian workers rose for the third time, in February 1848, now with the desperate resolution to spill their blood for others' benefit no longer, and instead to improve their own lot.

This time, after a few days of fighting soldiers on the streets of Paris, the workers won so resoundingly that a republic could immediately be declared. But, wise from the experiences of previous revolutions, the workers no longer wanted to settle for the declaration of a republic. "We already know bourgeois governments," they said to themselves. "Now we want a republic of our own. We want bread and jobs for everyone, and we want to abolish exploitation and inequality between people." The bourgeoisie, or, more appropriately, its temporary government, the one that was appointed just after the victory of the revolution, promised, out of fear of the workers, to do everything they demanded, so as to gain time. For as long as the workers were deceived by various means, the bourgeois government worked in haste and in secret to arm the military and all "citizens"—that is, the moneyed bourgeoisie. The workers waited in vain for three months, impatient and desperate from hunger and unemployment. When they decided to overthrow the bourgeois government by force in June, the government had already prepared a response to the laborers' cry for bread and work: bullets and bayonets. Thereafter, the streets of Paris witnessed the famed June slaughter, which lasted without stopping for almost four days, and whose terrible memory to this day dominates the hearts of French workers, still stirring the grandchildren and great-grandchildren of those who fought in that time to hate the yoke of capitalists with a mortal passion and to struggle heroically for the liberation of laborers.

II.

On June 22, Parisian workers tried for the last time to march peacefully to exert pressure on the bourgeoisie. A tremendous march of 117,000 laborers progressed through the streets of Paris toward the building where the government of the republic sat. A delegation of several workers, led by a worker named Pujol (pronounced "pyoozhool"), entered to speak with the government. The following conversation between the bourgeois minister and the worker then took place.

"Citizen," began Pujol. "Before the February revolution—"

"Please," the minister interrupted right away. "I think you're starting off with a bit too lengthy a speech."

"Citizen!" continued the worker undeterred. "Respect the freedom of speech of the people's delegates. I will speak as I deem necessary, or I will not speak at all."

"So speak, but please be aware that I have very little time," replied the minister.

Pujol said, "Citizen, your time belongs not to you but to the people for whom you are a minister."

To that the minister made a menacing gesture. "Citizen Pujol, you and I have already known each other a long time, and we will keep an eye on each other."

"As you please," the worker answered. "But know that on the day when I devoted myself to the cause of liberating the people, I vowed that I would let no threats intimidate me. Save your energy, citizen, for I do not fear your malice."

The minister, seeing that he would not contain Pujol, turned to the other members of the delegation with irritation. "I cannot recognize a participant in the uprising of May 15 as a representative of the people. You, others, speak. Present your complaints to me."

Pujol spread his arms to shield his companions. "No one here will speak but me!"

The other workers also said in chorus, "No, no! He will speak for us. Listen to him!"

The minister, humiliated by the solidarity and resolute bearing of the workers he had wanted to patronize, took a step back and shouted with frustration, "So, what, are you the slaves of this man?"

"Careful, citizen," Pujol thundered. "Do not mock the people's delegates!"

"Do you know," cried the minister, "that you are speaking to a member of the government?"

"Obviously," replied Pujol. "And it is because you are a member of the government, citizen, that you owe me respect."

"I—you?" shouted the amazed minister.

"Just so, citizen. You are a member of the government, and I am a delegate of the people. If you do not want to listen, then we will leave this place."

"So, speak already," answered the minister, biting his lip.

With patience and dignity, the people's delegate again began the speech that had been interrupted. "Citizen, before the February revolution, working people endured intolerable exploitation by capital. To liberate themselves from the yoke of the capitalists, the people erected barricades, handing in their weapons only when a democratic and social republic was declared that would save the people from bondage once and for all. Today the workers see that they were deplorably deceived. I tell you this to say that workers are determined to sacrifice anything, even their own lives, to defend their rights."

"I understand you," replied the minister. "Right, well, now listen to what I have to say. If the workers do not do as they are told and take themselves to the provinces, then we will use force to make them. Understand? Force!"

To this the worker said, "I see, force. Right. That tells us what we wanted to know."

"And what did you want to know?" asked the minister.

"We wanted to confirm that the acting government never sincerely considered improvements to the miserable conditions of workers. And now, we bid you farewell, citizen."

With these words, the delegation of workers left the government building and returned to their comrades, who were waiting on Saint-Sulpice Square. As soon as the crowd realized that all hope in governmental goodwill had vanished, a single shout grew into a roar from the chests of hundreds of thousands: "Death or freedom!" With chants of "Work and bread!" the workers dispersed, agreeing to reconvene the next morning at six o'clock. At dawn the next day, June 23, a Friday, every Parisian worker with breath in his lungs was on his feet. The streets hummed with activity. During the night and into the early morning hours, barricades had grown as if from out of the ground. Hundreds of trees had been cut down from streets, squares, and gardens; iron rails had been torn out from in front of government buildings to be used later for defense; and cobblestones had been torn up from the streets. House after house, apartments had been entered and every object had been taken that could be used for defense or the construction of barricades. Planks, trees, stones, carts, and various pieces of furniture were built into sturdy barricades that rose, like fortified embankments, high above the ground, up to the first and second stories of the buildings on either side. Whatever could be used was quickly taken from stores of weapons and iron. Women, working in their houses, poured bullets from lead they had melted down from roof gutters and metal windowsill sheeting. With the barricade-building experience of three revolutions, Parisian workers could erect such mighty fortresses for street warfare everywhere at once, almost in the blink of an eye. By acting swiftly, they crippled the operations of the military. By the time the army acted, the people had already installed themselves behind entrenchments, and soldiers were blocked from freely moving through the city.

As in earlier revolutions, the main network of barricades was erected not in the new, grand neighborhoods, with wide streets and rich houses, but in the old city, in the suburbs of Faubourg Saint-Antoine, Montmartre, and La Villette. Barricades were also built in Paris' poor district, where narrow, winding streets abounded, where there was little vulnerability to attacks by cavalry or artillery, where barricades could be erected easily, and where help for the struggling laborers could be counted on in every house, whether out of sympathy or plain fear. Here, too, on the morning of June 23, barricades rose with lightning speed in twos and threes across every street, block after block. This way, if workers were forced to abandon one, they could quickly move back behind the second, and soldiers could progress only with difficulty, winning ground by storm only in fits and spurts. The taking of a single barricade often took hours, and sometimes an entire day. Workers even occupied all the rooms of the buildings surrounding each barricade so they could join the fighting from positions in windows and on roofs, striking the attacking soldiers from above with stones, boiling water, and bullets.

All morning, the workers' neighborhoods buzzed with noise. Like a hive of bees, the people prepared for mortal battle. All the while, the bourgeois government looked on in feigned inactivity. It was the hellish plan of the current minister of war, [Louis-Eugène] Cavaignac (pronounced "kavenyack"), to let the "lowlifes," as the bourgeoisie called workers, "become unruly," and then to crush them all at once in a terrible sea of blood. And this criminal plan was indeed carried out. But the lords had thought it would go quickly, and that did not happen as planned. The workers sold their lives dearly, defending themselves with such lion's courage and such despairing, dogged determination that the bourgeoisie of France and of countries the world over still gnash their teeth to this day with rage at the memory of their audacious resistance.

The clock had struck half past noon when the first shots rang out and the battle began. These first shots were aimed at one of the strongest barricades, the one erected at the Porte Saint-Denis. The construction of this barricade had been directed by the very same Pujol who, the previous day, had for the last time appealed on behalf of the proletariat to the conscience of the bourgeoisie's minister. A peal of drums suddenly broke out, and a unit of the citizen guard—that is what the bourgeoisie called the militia they had armed against workers—approached the barricade. The "citizens" were greeted from the barricade with a volley of bullets. To help them, another whole battalion was rushed in. But shots began to fall densely from nearby homes, from windows, roofs, and cafés. Many "citizens" dropped dead, and others began to waver. Then, the workers rushed out of their hiding places and the melee at close quarters began. The citizen guard rallied themselves more densely, however, and launched a fierce attack. On the barricade, on top of an overturned cart, one workingman took a stand to raise a red flag. With a single rifle shot, he was killed by one of the "citizens." Soon a young woman jumped onto the barricade, her face glowing with heroism, and raised the flag back up. For a moment, even the citizen guard was struck speechless at the sight. But then, remembering how murderously they hated the "rebellious" proletariat, the "citizens" took aim at the breast of the brave worker, and the standard-bearing woman fell, slain. Not a moment had passed, however, before someone else jumped up and, holding the fallen comrade with the flag in one arm, hurled stones with the other hand at the hateful defenders of capital. In the end, the barricade could only be taken with an assault by professional soldiers under the command of General [Christophe Léon Louis Juchault de] Lamoricière.

While this was happening at the Porte Saint-Denis, another scene recorded by historians took place in the area near the Pantheon, on the left bank of the Seine. Here, a certain bourgeois, a man who was kindhearted and well intentioned but did not understand that, this time, the struggle of the workers for bread and work was an inevitable, terrible drama, took it upon himself to mediate between the government and the workers and began to implore both the workers and the soldiers to cease fighting. Such thickheaded intermediaries often show up offering advice, though no one asks them to, wherever others are fighting for life and death. That was just how this man appeared, achieving a short pause in the fighting, long enough for a short exchange to take place. Speaking for the government and the army, this Minister [François] Arago, standing in front of the barricade but shielded by a high wall of paving stones, chastised the workers and warned them that the barricade would be stormed.

To this the workers replied, "Citizen, do not try to reproach us. You sound like a kind person, but you've never personally felt what hunger and poverty are."

The minister tried promises of help and hope from the government.

"Enough of your hollow promises!" the workers called back. "We want action!"

"We have done everything we can for you," the minister called.

"That's not true. Your lot have done nothing for us. We are dying of starvation!" the workers cried.

"If you are going to insult me, our business is finished," said the minister, turning his horse around. A moment later, a volley of cannonballs was launched on the stone wall, and a deadly struggle ensued.

The battle was soon raging throughout the city. Heavy artillery usually overwhelmed the workers, and cannon were in fact the main reason for the eventual defeat of the June uprising. At several points, however, the workers enjoyed temporary victories. After taking that first barricade at the Porte Saint-Denis, General Lamoricière could only advance his army a small distance farther down the street. Each barricade had another behind it, and the soldiers soon grew weary. The troops even began to feel defeated, and their commander in chief, Cavaignac, the minister of war, had to hurry to the scene to help them. But it was not easy fighting for the minister either. First of all, in the Temple suburb, he launched seven futile attacks on one barricade. His attempt to circumvent it and attack it from the rear was also in vain, because there were barricades on all the side streets that cut off access at the narrowest point. Cannons were fired on the barricades, shattering stonework to pieces but doing no harm to workers sheltered behind them. In the end, after four hours of fighting, the minister was himself forced to call on other army units for help. It was only with the aid of an entire fresh regiment that they succeeded in capturing this single barricade! The workers defended themselves unwaveringly, maintaining so much control over the general situation as evening fell on the first day of battle that they could even build new barricades and move themselves ever farther from the suburbs toward the city hall, causing the sitting government to feel nearly already besieged by workers. A significant number of generals and officers had also been injured. The workers, viewing common soldiers as merely passive instruments of violence, usually took aim at commanders rather than foot soldiers. After midnight, the troops finally suspended their cannon fire, and the workers took advantage of the pause to tirelessly repair damaged barricades and erect new ones.

On the second day, June 24, the streets of Paris were still covered in barricades, 414 in all, each neighborhood having made them in a different way, suited to local conditions, according to the plan it had devised. In order to carry gunpowder and bullets from one point to the next, the people devised a thousand ruses: Feigned funeral processions carried weapons in caskets, little boys carried charges to fighters in milk tins and loaves of bread, and women feigned pregnancy so they could carry supplies of powder and bullets under their dresses. Thus, on the morning of the twenty-fourth, when Paris looked yet more menacing than the day before, the bourgeoisie were overcome with a frenzy of fear and hatred of workers. It was decided to field the entire armed force and spare no cost in suppressing the uprisings.

The battle began anew on the second day with unheard-of fierceness. Wherever the army won victories, they threw themselves on the defeated workers with animal cruelty and murdered them without mercy. Yet the workers, exhausted from two days of mortal battle, unending work building barricades, and hunger—the majority had not eaten a single bite of bread in half a day or even an entire day—fought on without resting. Nowhere, at any point, did anyone voluntarily surrender. The amazement and fury of the bourgeois government and generals grew with each passing moment. The lords had thought that to beat the "street scum" would be a piece of cake for their gangs of armed hooligans. They still had no idea of the mad courage and strength invigorating the struggle and resistance of people who are driven by hunger and by sacred belief in their principles and ideals. The Paris uprising of June 1848 was in general the first uprising solely of the working class in defense of its own class interests. The entire bourgeois world, to say nothing of France, looked on those terrible days and saw, for the first time, the power of the proletariat when it aspires to be free from the yoke of capital.

It is true that, in the end, the workers were defeated despite their heroism. But on the morning of June 25—on the *third day of battle!*—the outcome was still undecided. The government had to call in troops and "citizen guards" from the provinces for help. "Citizens" everywhere donned uniforms, took up rifles, and hurried in from all directions with the noble aim of defending soldiers by murdering workers who asked for bread and jobs.

In the end, in the face of such a total offensive, and under the unceasing hail of case shot, the workers were broken and began to move back. Or, rather, it would be more accurate to say the army simply began to march forward over the dead and injured, because nowhere did *living* workers retreat. On the very last barricades, the workers were killed to a man. Not even when there was no longer any hope of victory did the workers surrender or lose their spirits. On the *fourth day of fighting*, the morning of June 26, the workers went to the barricades to die. Heroically faithful to the oath of "Death or liberty!" they had taken before the uprising, they went now to the barricades and to death, leading their families with them. Surrounded by their wives and children, the destitute, wounded, sweating, starving proletarians stood atop their last barricades, crying, "If we cannot provide bread for our families, let us die together with them!" Proletarian women threw themselves into this last day of the battle for bread and work, baring their breasts against the soldiers' bayonets and crying, "Since you have murdered our husbands and brothers, also murder us!"

The heroism of this fight to the end was matched by the workers who put up a defense in the Faubourg Saint-Antoine. Even on the fourth day of fighting, they had the spirit to post an enormous proclamation on the wall that read, "To arms! We want a democratic and a social republic. We want the rule of the people. Let everyone rise to the defense of such a republic! We are determined to fight and die. To battle, brothers! Let no one remain deaf to our call. If we will not be victorious, let us all perish under the rubble of the Faubourg Saint-Antoine. Consider your wives and children, and hasten to us!"

Worker delegates from that neighborhood returned for the last time to the government to appeal for actions to alleviate the misery of the workers. By this time, the relentless bourgeoisie only wanted blood. Grimly, with faces downcast, the workers' representatives turned to go back to their friends in the neighborhood. They found their way, with difficulty, through the giant barricade blocking entry into the neighborhood and gave the answer of the government to the people gathered around in factory-floor jumpers. An enormous, terrible shout of "No concessions! No hope!" rose to the heavens from the devastated crowd, to be replaced a moment later by the cry, "And so we go to die!"

The attack on the barricades and the heroic defense of the workers in the Faubourg Saint-Antoine lasted from ten o'clock in the morning to seven in the evening. Human history knows no cases of greater heroism than that with which these simple workers fought, together with their wives and children, against terrible military violence. In the end, however, the case shot used against the workers proved overwhelming. At seven o'clock in the evening, the relentless gunfire fell silent. The battle was over.

The battle was over, but the massacre had only begun. Now the "victors"—the bourgeois and their generals—lunged forward onto the defeated laborers, onto the last heroes standing, to quench their thirst for revenge in a sea of workers' blood. The pen shudders to describe the butchery that the frenzied "citizenry" made of the working populace. Captured workers were killed by the thousands, and hundreds were thrown into the basement of the city hall, where they stood ankle-deep in reeking street runoff sewage mixed with their own blood, crammed in so densely that they suffocated. When there was no more room in the basement, the captives were led out in groups, lined up in front of a wall, and shot. Those killed were not even given burials but were simply thrown into the river. Day and night, the gunshots continued—workers were simply murdered on the streets, in apartments, wherever they were found.

The number of victims in this terrible slaughter has never been precisely counted. Criminal members of the bourgeoisie and the historians they paid have attempted to hide the disgrace of their crime behind cowardly lies. But the truth has managed to come out, revealing that there were *12,000* people killed, of whom only about 3,000 were killed on the barricades. The rest—three times as many—were murdered after the end of the battle, when the workers were no longer defending themselves, when the last resistance of the fighters "for bread and work" had been broken.

III.

When the June Days were over, the French bourgeoisie sent up a cry of wild triumph. Workers defeated! Slave rebellion crushed! The reign of capital secured for the ages! After such a terrible defeat in a sea of blood, surely the proletariat would think twice before rebelling against poverty and exploitation! The capitalist lords of France were delirious with joy.

But history would tell a different tale. It is true that the defeat of the June uprising stifled the workers' movement in France for one or two decades. The flower of the Parisian proletariat was mowed down, murdered. Its chief socialist ringleaders were slaughtered, thrown in prison, or exiled.

Yet this defeat not only did not stifle the idea of socialism—the idea of liberation—among French workers. In fact, it gave it new power. Before, French workers had still believed that it was enough to drive out the king or emperor and declare a republic, and that exploitation, inequality, poverty, and unemployment could be eliminated straight away, either at the goodwill of the reigning bourgeoisie or under pressure from workers. They did not understand that if the bourgeoisie is generally in charge of the government, whether as part of a monarchy or a republic—as long as factories, workshops, mines, and land are the private property of capitalists, and millions of people live only by selling their capacity to work—then exploitation, deprivation, and unemployment cannot be eliminated. They did not understand that liberation from the yoke of capital cannot be achieved through one street battle, even a supremely heroic one. It can only be achieved through a long, daily struggle that involves both the workplace and the political sphere, one that elevates, increases the consciousness of, and organizes the entire proletarian population, thereby preparing them for the final social revolution and the victory of the working class in all countries.

After the June massacre, French workers understood that not even gaining political freedoms and creating their own republic would bring them liberation. They realized such a feat could only be accomplished through continuous, open class struggle, and that republican freedoms and rights are necessary for just such a struggle, since the working class must openly build awareness and organize into a Social Democratic party. The idea of socialism—the idea of liberation—also began to develop quickly among workers because of the memorable "June Days," as they came to be called. Scarcely twenty-three years had passed from these bloody days when French workers rose again and, for close to three months, even ruled over the capital city of France—in the famous *Paris Commune* of 1871. Yet it was not only in Paris that the bourgeoisie could not destroy socialism with their June massacre. In the year 1848, the battle for freedom from capital was fought by the proletariat of the city of Paris. In the provinces of France, the oppressed and downtrodden people mustered the courage to break machines and hold hunger protests, as others had in Lyon in 1831.* Today the socialist worker movement in all of France, in all cities, and even in many rural areas, has made colossal advances. Today, not only Paris but nearly all working France fights the bourgeoisie every day.

In the year 1848, French workers were the only ones who attempted to win their freedom.† In many other countries—Germany, Austria, Italy, and the Netherlands—there was still no worker movement, only isolated elements that understood workers' interests and were trying to enlighten the masses. Meanwhile, in all these countries, the bourgeoisie itself had only just won freedom, having snatched it, using the bloody hands of workers, from the control of the nobility and absolutism. Today, the worker movement is growing across Europe, in America, and even in East Asia, especially Japan and Russia. Today in Poland, under the flag of socialism, working people are breaking the last bonds of the despotic government in outbreaks of revolution in the streets.

---

* The first of the so-called Canut Revolts, in which Lyonnais silk workers rose up and seized control of the town after factory owners refused to meet their demands for a living wage.

† Luxemburg does not mention contemporaneous attempts to win freedom elsewhere that took the form of national liberation movements—such as the Hungarian Revolution of 1848, which pushed the Austrian Empire to the point of collapse. The empire was saved only through the Russian invasion of Hungary that destroyed the revolution.

Today, we see blossoming, just as luxuriantly, the harvest of the idea of socialism that the French bourgeoisie wanted to permanently erase in the June Days of 1848. The heroic uprising of Parisian workers contributed enormously to this recent flowering of socialism. The echo of the battle and the massacre awakened the consciences and intentions of unaware workers the world over. The Parisian proletariat's sacred tradition of heroism and sacrifice has stayed alive through the decades, reminding workers in country after country that the ruling bourgeoisie is a mortal enemy with whom they must fight tirelessly. If the *Communist Manifesto* of Marx and Engels, published in 1849, and the academic theory therein, explained to workers of the whole world where their captivity comes from and how socialism can prevail, then the Parisian worker in the June Days showed his brothers around the world how heroically one must fight and die for the idea of liberating the working millions.

Before the June uprising of 1848 met its end in defeat, it powerfully advanced the cause of final proletarian liberation. Similarly, today each uprising, each battle waged by Polish and Russian workers, through its end, in the ostensible victory of the mercenaries, ushers closer the ultimate victory of the people.

Only duplicitous enemies of the proletariat could lament "blood spilt in vain" and shed crocodile tears for the blinding of struggling workers. In truth, not one drop of worker blood shed for the cause of victory was wasted.

Every sacrifice strengthens the foundation on which our future victory will stand.*

༻

The above was written in the year 1905. A year has passed, one short year, and the Polish and Russian proletariat, looking back, surveys a whole series of momentous clashes, defeats, and victories.

Under attack by the revolutionary proletariat, the tsarist government has had to relinquish absolutism, has had to retreat step by step. The tsar capitulated in October, granting "people's representation." He is attempting to trick the people with his Duma, presenting a caricature of a constitution in place of one. Yet trickery will not work; the people are still fighting for their rights.

The memory of the June Days in Paris has a double meaning for us today. In 1848, the bourgeoisie exploited the revolutionary movement for its own exclusive benefit. Similarly, our bourgeoisie would happily stoke its oven's flames with the hands of workers if it meant the dinner roast would be done sooner.

We have been witnesses to our bourgeoisie's degradation. In October, we saw our bourgeoisie shrink in hellish fear at the general strike. We witnessed how the bourgeoisie, after the victory of the workers, had nothing but flattery for the victors for a short while after October 30, and we witnessed how

---

* The 1905 version of the essay published in *Przegląd Robotniczy* ended at this point. What follows is the new ending added when it was published as a pamphlet in 1906.

soon after this it began to sing another tune. As long as the aim was to wring political concessions out of the tsar, as long as workers fought for freedom, the bourgeoisie was ready—not to fight alongside them, since it did not and does not want to fight—but to applaud the workers who went to their deaths. If, however, the workers began to require even modest improvements to their standard of living, if there began a period of economic strikes, then the bourgeoisie played the victim and turned up for battle, not against the tsar, but against the workers. What also quickly held sway here was a reaction of the most shameful kind: The "national democratic" Black Hundreds infested the entire bourgeoisie and provided the banner under which the Polish ruling class now fights the revolution.

It happened similarly in Russia. Only there, the fight between workers and capitalists could not take so extreme a form as here, so reactionary elements did not gain the upper hand, and the shots were called by the cleverest of all reactionary diehards: liberal bourgeois fraudsters.

In the tsarist Duma, too, the representatives of the bourgeoisie have given a loud and clear defense of their class interests. Much as the representatives of the French bourgeoisie in 1848 were especially concerned with making sure the workers failed to achieve their socialist aims, the representatives of the Russian and Polish bourgeoisies in the Duma think only of how to put an end to the revolution, having already haggled over what spoils they could take for themselves.

This bourgeoisie still needs us. It still has not consolidated its rule or reached an agreement with the tsarist government, and it knows full well that without the fists of workers, it cannot compete in its wrestling match with the government.

Yet despite this, the sheer reactivity of the bourgeoisie and its fear of revolution are manifest at every step. If the bourgeoisie were to reach an agreement with the government tomorrow—if only the bourgeoisie managed to grasp power—it would turn against the people, just as it did in 1848.

Let history, therefore, be the teacher of the working class. From the bloody lesson of the June Days in Paris, let it become clear to every worker that the working class must not trust bourgeois politicians when faced with the threat of terrible calamities and must refrain from handing in its arms until the interests of the working class are securely guaranteed, until a people's *republic* is won that will ensure workers lasting benefits.

The misfortune of the workers of Paris was that they trusted the good-natured, highly eloquent, and ingenious representatives of the bourgeoisie. Four short months after workers knocked Louis Philippe off the throne in February, the same people that the workers put in power were giving the order to General Cavaignac to brutalize the workers.

The workers of Paris committed an error for which they atoned in blood. Let this example keep us from entrusting the fates of the proletariat to the hands of those who, because of their class position, cannot be supporters of the people.

Parisian workers believed in 1848 that the bourgeoisie, without relinquishing its capitalist interests, could begin reforms that would protect workers from the catastrophes of involuntary unemployment; they demanded the "right to a job" be realized. Now, we know that as long as capitalism exists, the working people cannot benefit from the fruits of their labor. We know that the proletariat can only improve its lot by securing concessions step by step, and also that today the proletariat does not demand that the bourgeoisie guarantee a "right to a job," but fights for limits on exploitation and for freedom in the battle with capital. The eight-hour workday, the right to health and safety at work, the freedom to associate and strike—these are our demands, made on behalf of the class interests of the proletariat.

The realization of these demands will form a foundation for further advances—for the realization of socialism.

Blanquism and Social Democracy*

Comrade [Georgi] Plekhanov has published an extensive article in *Kurier*[†] [The Warsaw Courier] under the title "Where Is the Right?" in which he accuses those he calls "Bolsheviks" of "Blanquism."

It is not our place to defend the Russian comrades against whom Comrade Plekhanov sends forth the products of his erudition and dialectics; these same will surely make that attempt. Nevertheless, the question itself raises many matters that may be of interest to our readers too, so we shall devote some space to them.

To describe "Blanquism," Comrade Plekhanov quotes a passage from [Friedrich] Engels about [Auguste] Blanqui (pronounced "blan-key"), a French revolutionary from the fourth decade of the last century who gave his name to the whole school of thought:

> Blanqui, Engels says,[‡] was a "man of deeds" in his activities, a man who believed that a small, well-organized minority striving to trigger an uprising in a favorable moment could inspire the masses with initial success and in this way bring about a revolution. That Blanqui looks on every revolution as a coup (*coup de main*) of a narrow revolutionary minority leads itself to the necessity of dictatorship in the event of success—the dictatorship is understood to be not of the entire revolutionary class, of the proletariat, but of the small number of people who started the uprising and organized themselves in advance under the dictatorial control of one or several leaders.

Friedrich Engels, the collaborator of Karl Marx, is without doubt a great authority, yet we may continue to argue whether this characterization of Blanqui is entirely sufficient. Because in 1848, Blanqui must not necessarily have imagined that his club constituted a "tiny minority"; quite to the contrary, in a time of tremendous revolutionary movement, he surely was fully confident that his call would reach the *entire* people, if not of all France, then of Paris, to fight against the insidious and dishonorable politics of the bourgeois ministry, which wanted to "rob the people of their winnings." Yet the heart of the issue

---

* This article first appeared in *Czerwony Sztandar*, No. 82, June 23, 1906, pp. 1–2, under the title "Blankizm i socjaldemokraja." It is reprinted in Rosa Luxemburg, *Wybór pism*, Vol. 2 (Warsaw: Książka i Wiedza, 1959), pp. 484–91 and *Archiwum ruchu robotniczego* (Warsaw: Archiwum ruchu robotniczego, 1977), pp. 172–6. It is translated by Joseph Muller from the Polish original.

† *Kurier Warzawski* was a Polish daily newspaper, published in Warsaw between 1821 and 1939. The paper was published legally, even during the period of tsarist rule. It had a conservative political orientation.

‡ [Footnote by Luxemburg] We do not have close to hand the work of Engels from which this passage comes, so we translated not from the original, but from the Russian translation of Comrade Plekhanov.

is not this, but that Comrade Plekhanov attempts to establish that the characterization of Blanqui given by Engels can be so precisely applied to the so-called Bolsheviks (whom Comrade Plekhanov calls a minority today, without any explanation, because at the Unification Convention they turned out to be in the minority).* His exact words are these: "This entire characterization may be applied *in whole*† to our current minority." He justifies this claim in the following way: "The relationship of Blanquists to the people was utopian in the sense that they did not understand the revolutionary significance of the autonomy of the masses. In their plans only the plotters would take action, and the masses would only support them, being carried along by a well-organized minority." And thus, Comrade Plekhanov argues that it was into this "original sin of Blanquism" that the Russian "Bolshevik" comrades fell (we prefer to stay with this common term, "Bolshevik").‡ In our opinion, Comrade Plekhanov did not prove his charge. For in comparison to the People's Will, who were verifiable Blanquists, nothing is proven, and the malicious comment that the hero and leader of the People's Will,§ [Andrei] Zhelyabov,¶ had a more watchful political instinct than the leader of the "Bolsheviks," [Vladimir] Lenin, is in too poor taste to merit consideration. Yet, as we have said already, it is not our place to cross words in defense of the "Bolsheviks" and Comrade Lenin, for they have not yet permitted themselves to be trodden upon. We are concerned here with the heart of the issue. And so, the question arises: Is Blanquism in general possible in today's revolution in Russia? And, if it were possible, would it have the power to exert any influence whatsoever?

We believe it suffices to pose this question to any person acquainted with even a bit of the current revolution, anyone who encountered it directly, to receive a reply in the negative. The basis of the entire difference between the conditions of the year 1848 in France and those of the current era in the Russian state is that the relations between the "*organized minority*"—that is, the party of the proletariat—and the masses are fundamentally different. In 1848, the revolutionaries, to the degree they were socialists, made a desperate effort to instill

---

* This refers to the Fourth Congress of the Russian Social Democratic Labor Party (RSDRP), held in Sweden in April 1906. Although the congress aimed to unify the Menshevik and Bolshevik wings of the party, the Bolsheviks found themselves in the minority when the Mensheviks allied with the Jewish Bund. The two wings therefore continued to act independently of one another.

† [Footnote by Luxemburg] Our emphasis.

‡ Common insofar as "Bolshevik" means majority—the position they attained at the Second Congress of the RSDRP in 1903.

§ The People's Will (Narodnaya Volya) was formed in 1879 by Russian Populists from the Land and Liberty Party (Zemlya i Volya) who were disenchanted with the failure of efforts at social reform and advocated the use of terror to bring down the regime. Plekhanov was himself a Populist at the time and also split from Land and Will in 1879, but did so in order to form a more moderate group, Black Reparations.

¶ Zhelyabov was a founding member of the People's Will and planned the successful assassination of Tsar Alexander II in 1881, for which he was arrested and executed.

socialist ideas in the masses, to drag them away from supporting the empty liberalism of the bourgeoisie. Their socialism itself was indistinct, utopian, and petty-bourgeois. Today in Russia, things present themselves differently: neither Poland's Progressive Democracy nor the company of Cadets, neither the tsarist constitutionalists in Russia nor any ethnically "progressive" bourgeois party in other parts of the state, could win over the vast working masses. *Today, these same masses cling to the banner of socialism*; at the moment the revolution broke out, they rose at their own impulse, even exuberantly, under the crimson flag. The best evidence of this is our party itself.* We have no intention of concealing our history—in 1903 we were only a handful, a complete party only in the strict sense of the word, a group of organized comrades numbering at most in the hundreds.† During the demonstrations, a small army of workers joined us, and today our party numbers in the tens of thousands. What explains this difference? Do we simply have many brilliant leaders in our party? Or perhaps such is the level of our excellence in plotting conspiracies? Far from it. None of our leaders, which is to say none of those whom the party entrusts to be responsible for operations, will be willing to expose themselves to ridicule by imagining a comparison between themselves and that lion of revolution, the great Blanqui, and few of our activists match those plotters among Blanqui's followers in terms of personal charm or organizational ability. So how may our success and the Blanquists' failures be interpreted? Simply by the statement that that "mass" is different. The host of workers who today rise up to battle the tsar, these are people for whom life itself is to be a socialist, people who first tasted hatred for the existing order in their mothers' milk, people who were taught to think in socialist terms by necessity itself.

That is the difference. They were not caused by leaders or ideas; they were created by socioeconomic conditions, conditions under which *class struggle between the proletariat and the bourgeoisie cannot fail to exist.*

And this: Because the mass is different, because the proletariat is different, there can be no talk of conspiratorial tactics, of the tactics of Blanquism. Blanqui and his heroic comrades exerted superhuman efforts to direct the masses to greater class struggle; they did not succeed, because they were dealing with workers who had not yet gotten rid of the childlike traits that kept them bogged down in petty-bourgeois notions.

---

* A reference to the Social Democracy of the Kingdom of Poland and Lithuania (SDKPiL), formed in 1900 after what remained of the SDKP and the Union of Workers in Lithuania (led by Feliks Dzierżyński, who later headed the Cheka, the secret police, after the Bolshevik Revolution of 1917). Although Luxemburg did not play a central role in the SDPKiL during its first few years, by 1903 she had become its undisputed leader.

† Even this may be overstating matters; in 1903 the SDKPiL was a small organization with no more than a few hundred active members; in her correspondence with Leo Jogiches, Luxemburg often quipped about having "a party with seven and a half members." The SDKPiL grew rapidly in 1905 and 1906, however, approaching a membership of 50,000.

We Social Democrats now have a far simpler and easier task: To us it remains only to work to direct the class struggle that has been set ablaze of inexorable necessity. The Blanquists forced themselves to pull the masses along, but we Social Democrats are today almost pushed forward by these masses. The difference is great, as great as that between the labor of the rower who pushes a boat with great force against the current, and the labor of the rower who guides a boat carried along by a swift current; the first may not be strong enough and may not reach his goal, while the second must only heed that the boat does not deviate from the current, strike rocks beneath the water, or run aground.

Let Comrade Plekhanov calm himself, too, with respect to the "autonomy of the revolutionary masses." This autonomy exists, nothing will hold it back, and every lesson on the subject from pedants (we apologize for using this expression, for lack of a better one)* may only serve to arouse a smile from those who labor among and together with these masses.

We do not agree that comrades from so-called Bolshevism in Russia have now, in a time of revolution, fallen into the Blanquist errors that Comrade Plekhanov ascribes to them. There were perhaps traces of this in the organizational plan put forward in 1902 by Comrade Lenin, but that belongs in the past, the distant past, since we live today quickly, at a dizzying pace.† These errors were corrected by life itself, and it does not do to fear that they may be repeated. Moreover, it is not Blanquism that is dreadful, for the current conditions do not support Blanquism. Yet there is a danger that Comrade Plekhanov and his adherents from the "minority,"‡ who remain in such great fear of Blanquism, falling into the other extreme, may determine to run the boat aground. We find this other extreme when comrades are unduly fearful of remaining in the minority, when they look too much to *the masses outside the proletariat*. Hence their looking to the Duma, their erroneous calls in the "directives" of the Central Committee to support the Cadets, and their challenge to demand that "the bureaucratic ministry be done away with," along with other similar tactical errors.§ The boat will not run aground; there is no sign of this, the swift current of the swollen river will soon carry the vessel of the proletariat forward; yet it would be a pity if we were to lose even a moment to these mistakes.

---

* The word Luxemburg apologizes for is an informal term, *belfer*, from Yiddish, meaning literally a teacher's assistant in a Hebrew school.

† For Luxemburg's 1904 criticism of Lenin's organizational concepts, composed at the time of his *What Is to Be Done?* and *One Step Forward, Two Steps Back*, see "Organizational Questions of Russian Social Democracy," which will appear in the forthcoming Volume 6 of the *Complete Works*. It is also available in *The Rosa Luxemburg Reader*, edited by Peter Hudis and Kevin B. Anderson (New York: Monthly Review Books, 2006), pp. 248–65.

‡ That is, the Mensheviks.

§ This is one of many indications that during and following the 1905 Revolution, Luxemburg was consistently far more critical of the Mensheviks than the Bolsheviks.

Finally, the meaning of the term "dictatorship of the proletariat" is taken differently from before. Friedrich Engels rightly emphasizes that Blanquists did not conceive of a dictatorship of "the whole revolutionary class, but of a dictatorship of a small number of people who will launch the uprising, and so on." The current state of affairs is entirely different. No organization of conspirators "launches an uprising," nor can such an organization ponder its own dictatorship. Even the People's Will long since gave up this dream, as did its heirs, the ostensible "revolutionary socialists" of Russia.* If "Bolshevik" comrades speak today of the dictatorship of the proletariat, they have never given it a Blanquist meaning. They have never fallen into the error of the People's Will, which dreams about "seizing power." But they claimed that the current revolution may end in the proletariat's control of the *entire* state machine. The proletariat, as the most revolutionary actor, may play the role of liquidator of the old order, may "seize power" in order to prevent a counterrevolution, in order to prevent the naturally reactionary bourgeoisie from bogging down the revolution. No revolution has yet ended in any other way than with one class holding power, and every detail suggests that now the proletariat may become the liquidator [of the old order]. Of course, no Social Democrat fools himself that the proletariat *will remain* in power; if it remained, that would lead to the rule of its class ideas, and it would realize socialism. *Today*, there is not sufficient strength [for that], since the proletariat constitutes a *minority* of society, in the strict sense of the word. Indeed, that a minority should realize socialism is out of the question, as the very idea of socialism does not allow minority rule. That is to say, on the day after the proletariat triumphs over the tsar, it will be deprived by the majority of the power it has won. More precisely, after the overthrow of the tsar, power will pass into the hands of the most revolutionary part of society—the proletariat—because this proletariat occupies every post, and it will stand guard until power passes into hands that are legally appointed to hold it—that is, into the hands of a new government, which may only act to appoint a Constituent Assembly and a legislative body chosen by the entire populace. And since the fact remains that in our society the working class is not the majority—the petty bourgeoisie and the peasants are—Social Democrats will not constitute a majority in the Constituent Assembly; only democrats from the peasantry and petty bourgeoisie [will]. We may regret this, but we cannot change it.

Thus, in general terms, the matter presents itself in the way the "Bolsheviks" interpret it, and this interpretation is also held by all Social Democratic organizations and parties in the tsarist state outside Russia proper. Where "Blanquism" can be found here is hard to say.

Seemingly to justify his claim, Comrade Plekhanov must try to catch Comrade Lenin and his supporters out. Yet once we conceive of tripping

---

* That is, the Socialist Revolutionary Party (SR).

someone up in this way, we may also discover that "Blanquists" were very recently "Mensheviks"—having begun with Comrade [Alexander] Parvus,* they ended with Comrade Plekhanov. This will just be our pointless academic plaything. The tone of Comrade Plekhanov is very annoyed and grating, and that's bad: "Jupiter is angry, therefore Jupiter is wrong."†

It is long since time to stop this pedantic search for who is a "Blanquist" and who an "orthodox Marxist." Today the question is whether *the current moment* demands the tactics that Comrade Plekhanov and the "Menshevik" comrades behind him recommend—that is, tactics counting on possible cooperation with the Duma and with elements outside the Duma that are represented by it, or tactics followed by us, as "Bolshevik" comrades—that is, tactics based on the principle that the center of gravity lies outside the Duma, in the active operations of the revolutionary masses. Up to now, our "Menshevik" comrades have managed to convince no one of the pertinence of their views, and placing labels on their opponents with the inscription "Blanquists" accomplishes nothing.

---

* The pen name of Israel Lazarevich Gelfand. Parvus had co-authored with Leon Trotsky their famous theory of "permanent revolution" a year earlier. At the time, Parvus and Trotsky were closer to the Mensheviks than the Bolsheviks.

† This proverb, *Iuppiter iratus ergo nefas* in Latin, has often appeared in Russian literature—including in Anton Chekhov's 1896 play *The Seagulls*.

Why Does the Revolution Not Break Out?*

The Cadets, and all of so-called society with them—that is, the revolution's bourgeois onlookers and bystanders—stand amazed and frustrated. The Duma has been dispersed, and a silence reigns over all the land—or at least that surface appearance of silence such as reigned before.† The tsar muzzled the Cadets as they were about to speak, and this time no revolutionary blaze flared up, no storm of people's struggle of the kind these men had used to scare the government broke out, no mass strikes began, no barricades rose, no battle cries rose up or pleas of the fallen avengers of the trampled Duma.

What does this mean? Has the fighting spirit of the proletariat died out? Has the proletariat's sense of honor grown dull? Has the revolution, with whose ghost the liberal orators in the Duma threatened the tsar so many times, forgotten about its responsibility to avenge the violence done to the Duma?

About this, the liberal-bourgeois men in the Duma, together with all the rest of the bourgeoisie, were sorely mistaken. They believed that as soon as they closed their mouths, which they used so tirelessly in the Duma, the earth would leave its foundations, the world would turn upside down, and the revolution would break out and would not stop until the Duma should be restored its sacred right to talk.‡ They hoped and planned to link the workers' revolution to the fates of their miserable, stunted Duma. They imagined that the street revolution and the streams of proletarian blood would only be a temporary means to intimidate the government and force it to reopen the Duma.

The current silence of the working people is a soundless but powerful blow to the conceit of these men, a crystal-clear expression of what the revolutionary people thinks about the worth and meaning of the Duma—happy tidings of the political maturity of the proletariat.

Yes, of course! The dissolution of the Duma reopens a phase of people's rebellion in the streets. Yet that revolution intends neither to be a servant of the miserable Cadet Duma, nor to play the role of bashing the men of the liberal bourgeoisie, nor to set itself the goal of opening the Duma again! The revolution that approaches, come what may, will not be a demonstration in support of the caricature of people's representation that the tsar has thrown out, as the bourgeoisie calculated. Rather, it will only be a further sequence in the great class

---

* This article first appeared in *Czerwony Sztandar*, No. 95, July 27, 1906, pp. 1–2, under the title "Czemu rewolucja nie wybucha?" It is translated from the Polish original by Joseph Muller.

† On July 8, 1906, the tsar dissolved the First Duma in order to head off any efforts at land reform or electoral reform. Witte had been replaced as prime minister a few months earlier by the more conservative Pyotr Stołypin.

‡ Shortly after the dissolution of the Duma, several dozen leaders of the Cadets decamped to Finland (then part of the Russian Empire) and issued the Vyborg Appeal, which called for civil disobedience in response to the tsar's actions. It fell on deaf ears.

struggle that began on January 22 of last year, the struggle of the working people for their own political program. In an earlier moment, the working people looked on the tragicomic scene of the Duma and heard the metallic thunder of bourgeois elocution. Now that tsarism has lowered the curtain, the people disperse. They shrug their shoulders derisively, not as if to make light of their blood, or to cry to raise the curtain again on the clownish spectacle therein, so as to resume listening to the babble of the Duma. No, they leave to retreat from a season of buffoonery ironically observed, taking up their own serious revolutionary labors again. And, in this case, the greatness of the assignment demands not haste, not a rash outbreak, but deep thought, methodical planning, and conscious action.

Consciousness above all! The more widely swaths of people grow in maturity through self-education in the political science of the history of the ignominious Duma, the more intentional and *effective* their further revolutionary efforts will become.

This study is twofold.

First of all, why did the Duma amount to nothing, then and now, despite its liberal majority, beautiful speeches, and even the good intentions of its members? Why did it end up being kicked out the door like a dog?

It is because these liberal-bourgeois men forgot the great lesson of [Ferdinand] Lassalle about *real and paper constitutions*. They deluded themselves and the people that we have a constitution, holding up a piece of paper from the tsar that said they could go into the Taurid Palace* and talk. They forgot that a true constitution is not a law written down, but *real powers—material means of power and strength*. The whole administration, all departments, remained in the hands of the tsarist henchmen; courts stayed in the hands of absolutism; command of the army, cannons, rifles, and fleets stayed in the hands of absolutism; finances, government coffers, taxes, and banks stayed in the hands of absolutism; police, national guard, and prisons remained in the hands of absolutism. In a word, all *actual*, material state power remained in the hands of the tsarist government, at the service of the reaction, at the service of absolutism. And yet the liberal bourgeoisie could still think that, by sheer force of lips in motion, they would be able to defeat, restrict, and eradicate absolutism!

The end of the Duma sham showed what that written "constitution" was worth, and if Cadet ministers are incurable in their political blindness, then the working class should state, with so much more clarity and distinctness: We are no longer trying merely to achieve on paper the right to elect representatives who will have on paper the right to talk about a constitution; we are concerned with real winnings, a true constitution in the sense Lassalle gave; we want to

---

* The largest and most impressive palace of the tsar, in St. Petersburg.

obtain tactical state power—administration, judiciary, legislation, finance, army, and police—by wresting it from absolutism's grip.

And this is the origin, by a precise logical connection, of another lesson.

The Cadet ministers, together with all the liberal bourgeoisie, want to turn matters upside down and remove the absolutist government through parliament and with laws passed by parliamentary procedure. The revolutionary people must now understand that this great historical turn may only come about in the opposite order. Absolutism must be overthrown first, and only then may normal parliamentary legislation begin. For no parliament on earth has achieved a political revolution on its own. A parliament may only pass laws when political and class relations have come to a certain equilibrium—to the "normal" relations that create bourgeois society. A political revolution may only be achieved through the direct struggle of the working masses; liberation of the working people—not only socialist, but also political—may only be the work of the working people themselves.

In simple terms, first, the street revolution must finish its work and obtain and strengthen actual freedoms from the ruins of tsarism by means of a revolutionary government and Constituent Assembly, and only later, when a new "constitution" becomes fact, will there be a time and place for this or that parliament. At that time, gentlemen of liberalism, we will invite you to take part in your beloved "Duma" and talk to your heart's content, until such time as a new socialist revolution occurs.

The Cadet "Duma" was a feint on the part of absolutism and liberalism, a surprise meant to deceive the revolution. For a moment, the mangy cur of petty-bourgeois liberalism ran to the left of the proletarian revolution. But soon it disappeared, to be replaced slowly and haughtily by a monarchical beast, which rose up to do terrible deeds.

The people's revolution has time, because it is and will remain not a modest interlude in the farcical, abandoned Duma (as the bourgeoisie hoped), but a great, historic tragedy, in which the Duma, together with the then-obsolete role of liberalism, was but a passing lull.

Organization and Disorganization*

In the current decisive moment, when the revolution is on the cusp of a new period marked by open mortal battles with absolutism, it is nevertheless important, even essential, for the organizations of the conscious proletariat to think through every step they make. Spontaneity should play a much more subordinate role, and planning and thinking a much more dominant one, than in previous phases of mass struggle. As the short career of bourgeois liberalism ends and the focus of political life returns completely to the revolutionary activities of the proletariat, the proletariat's guardians—socialist political parties—must shoulder double the responsibility and redouble their commitment to subject every detail of their tactics to rigorous self-criticism.

Therefore, as has been the case many times since the beginning of the revolution, there is a need to critically assess tactics of war recently used against the government—tactics that essentially have nothing in common with the methods of revolutionary and class conflict or the goal of consciousness pursued in such conflict. Self-criticism is all the more urgent for us because, unfortunately, a certain part of our organization, without deep thought or deliberation, has adopted the tactics of the Polish Socialist Party (PPS), in particular that party's petty-bourgeois-anarchist "revolutionary" [posture], dangerously exposing the current consistent, uniform tactics of Social Democracy to complete destruction, and risking the descent of our party from the path of revolution into the wilderness of political adventurism.

By this is meant the methodical robbing of liquor stores and train ticket offices. A truly working-class party with healthy instincts would take as sufficient warning the admiration and awe that such heroics inspire among the bourgeois philistine rabble. It is a fact established long ago, one that we can now take as a nearly infallible touchstone, that the bourgeoisie of all countries, and especially our politically wild and supremely bourgeois classes, is more impressed by a given method of struggle and sees it as more revolutionary, the more it is based on purely external "revolutionism"—that is, on uproar and physical excess—and the less it is based on the spiritual work of raising the awareness of the people, of revolutionizing them. "Revolutionism" is comprehensible to the bourgeoisie only insofar as it resembles the methods of anarchism. The "smokeless" gunpowder of real class activism and struggle, on the other hand, does not inspire the bourgeoisie to either belief or comprehension until it finally explodes in a visible, physical street battle.

---

* This article first appeared in *Czerwony Sztandar*, No. 99, August 18, 1906, pp. 1–2, under the title "Organizacja i dezorganizacja." It is translated from the Polish original by Joseph Muller.

The standing ovation the bourgeois rabble gave to the "daring" and "plucky" attacks on liquor stores and passenger trains should be a warning to practitioners of this method that they have probably strayed from the real work and goals of the workers' revolution.

As a matter of fact, what are the goals of stunts like this, and what effects do they have? First of all, the gawkers of bourgeois revolutions are impressed when the "party" is enriched with substantial monetary resources and absolutism is impoverished in equal measure. But only in the eyes of a native son of the fat cult of Lord Capital does the power of either the revolutionary party or absolutism rest on the possession of financial capital. Of course, to the extent that absolutism, as a system of government, loses financial credit along with political credit, economic ruin is one of the forces dragging it closer to the grave. Yet striving after the financial ruin of absolutism, after its impoverishment, is not a method or objective of the conscious revolutionary proletariat. The workers' revolution *takes advantage of* the financial ruin of tsarism, much as it has taken advantage of war, as a revolutionary ferment to ease the emergence of political consciousness and class struggle among working people. But the revolution cannot itself use impoverishment of government as a means of struggle, much as it cannot itself support or kindle a capitalist war, notwithstanding the revolutionary effects of such a war.

Money and material resources are indeed indispensable in the revolutionary fight. But in a real mass movement, they are a touchstone of power only insofar as they are a natural result of its influence on the working masses as well as on circles of the petty bourgeoisie or bourgeoisie that are sympathetic to the revolution. The strength of the revolution lies in this power of moral influence on consciousness and mass movement, not indeed in accumulated money, which, not being an outflow of mass movement, does not advance the revolutionary cause by so much as a hair. Rather, accumulated money is often a burden and—in the current conditions of struggle—even a factor in disorganization within the party itself.

We should not delude ourselves even for a moment with the word "confiscation," in the way it is often used to describe the taking of cash tills from liquor stores and train stations by revolutionary parties. The confiscation of the wealth and property illegitimately held by the horde in power is the full right and the responsibility of *revolutionary government acting in the name of the people, before the public eye, under the control of the people.* Currently, because the power to govern remains in the hands of the tsar's band of thieves, and revolutionary organizations are condemned to work underground—because neither a public power appointed by the people nor any public control exists, and because the finances are not yet controlled by the people, but only by a party that by nature has only a handful of individuals standing at the helm—there can be no talk of "confiscating" the tsar's resources, and no party in the current situation can proclaim itself the holder of the rights and duties of that victorious people. The fact that revolutionary parties are making a turn, or trying to make a turn, toward seizing wealth as the business and goal of revolution changes nothing about the state of affairs.* A truly working-class party may consider itself, and has the right to consider itself, a representative of the *interests* of working people and as their champion in the revolutionary fight; in the course of its activities, it cannot ever consider itself to be identical to the people or to the revolutionary government—unless it wants to make of revolutionary government a "revolutionary" farce.

We have intentionally closely examined the goals and precise meaning of the so-called revolutionary "confiscations" in order to show that they are, in and of themselves, entirely misleading. The harm they cause is far from imaginary—it exposes to serious jeopardy the task of *organizing soldiers*. It is an incontrovertible and unavoidable fact that the robbery of liquor stores and ticket windows is connected to the killing of soldiers; the government now appoints soldiers to guard passenger trains, exposing them to the fire of revolutionaries. So, for all the consciousness-raising and revolutionizing effects of clashes with the military in mass political demonstrations, peasant movements, workers' rallies, fights to free prisoners, and so forth—for all the effects of encounters with soldiers that arise from direct political struggle—when handfuls of armed revolutionaries kill soldiers in the course of seizing this or that government cashbox, the soldiers find it incomprehensible to the same degree, and to the same degree are they embittered and demoralized. And to this the governmental authorities add enormous efforts to disparage and sully the revolution in the eyes of soldiers. They systematically lead them to believe that socialists are hooligans who fish in troubled waters and aim to kill soldiers for dirty material gains. In view of the terrible difficulties of raising the awareness of the military in general— the things that make it harder to have access to the hearts and minds of our brothers in uniform—it is necessary to rigorously avoid any misunderstanding, any ambiguity in the workings of the proletariat. Mass revolutionary struggle, as well as the unavoidable sacrifices it entails, must in the end have the effect of revolutionizing soldiers, and isolated attacks on cashboxes by a few armed scouts, in the course of which they kill soldiers, can only have a demoralizing, anti-revolutionary effect.

Furthermore, in the current moment, as the revolution enters its final phase, the attitude of the military will play a much more important and decisive role than before. Political control through revolution shall remain, and must remain, in the hands of the conscious urban proletariat, but the determination of the future victory of mass struggle lies today in the hands of the rural folk *and the military.*

---

* This criticism is especially directed against the Bolsheviks, who tended to increasingly rely upon bank robberies to finance their organization in Russia.

Considering this, every thoughtless step taken in the vein of outward revolutionary posturing is a crime in comparison to the essential activities of the revolution.

Let every sincere friend and servant of the revolution remember that today, *one soldier won over to the revolution is more valuable than 10,000 roubles* "confiscated" through armed conflict with soldiers, and that the objective of the revolutionary workers' movement is not *disorganization of the government*, but *organization*—that is, to raise revolutionary consciousness *among the masses* and to call them to battle.

The Nationalists Declare Revolutionaries Outlaws[*]

The current revolution will not only have the effect of toppling the edifice of the tsarist autocracy. In Poland, it will also have the effect of tearing down and shredding to pieces the various illusions that prove especially harmful to the class struggle of the proletariat. One of these illusions, to which a number of revolutionary workers fighting under the banner of the PPS have succumbed, is the independence of Poland. Social Democracy, since it was established in our country, has shown that the development of capitalism and of bourgeois society makes the program of Polish state independence into a utopian dream. When the revolution broke out, it immediately confirmed that Social Democracy was correct in its assessment. The PPS and National Democracy, the two parties that wrote the aspiration for independence into their programs before the current revolution began, renounced the aspiration for independence, replacing it with the aspiration for a federation. This was one result that was very important for the development of political consciousness among our working classes.

The second illusion that splinters more and more under the brunt of the revolution is the revolutionary status of separatism, of Polish nationalism. Social Democracy has always shown workers that beneath separatism—that is, beneath the aspirations of some elements of the petty bourgeoisie and the intelligentsia to separate from Russia—lies only reactivity against efforts to overthrow Russian absolutism. Meanwhile, in contrast, the PPS looks on Polish nationalism and sees revolutionary potential, such revolutionary potential that, shortly before January 22, 1905—that is, before the outbreak of the current revolution—it decided to join National Democracy at the Paris convention that was to map out a plan for revolution within tsarism. In general, the illusion prevailed that all but a very few members of Polish bourgeois society are revolutionary. To PPS members, this illusion served and still serves as one of the main factual proofs, or rather the only factual proof, that the attainment of an individual Constituent Assembly in Warsaw is desirable. Polish society, says the PPS, is overall more revolutionary than Russian society; therefore, a Constituent Assembly in Warsaw will also be more revolutionary. That is, a constitution will be more democratic in our country than in Russia.

The revolution, as it develops and matures, tears down more and more of this illusion, too. Under the revolution's powerful influence, all bourgeois parties are forced to show their true faces ever more clearly, to come out more clearly

---

[*] This article first appeared in *Czerwony Sztandar*, No. 102, August 30, 1906, pp. 1–2, under the title "Narodowcy ogłaszają rewolucjonistów za wyjętych z pod prawa." It is translated from the Polish original by Joseph Muller.

either in favor of the revolution or against it—that is, in favor of the reaction. In the present moment, a bourgeois party that does not want to take a stand clearly on one side or the other, that wants to be both against the revolution and against the reaction, becomes a political zero. Our so-called Progressive Democracy is just such a party. Nevertheless, the course of the revolution has forced all the other bourgeois parties, with National Democracy at the head, not only to renounce opposition to the tsar but to take a clear stance openly opposing the revolution, thus aiding the tsarist government.

Workers know this from the prominent events of last year. But every worker who chooses to fight for freedom should understand with utmost clarity not only the intentions of the government reaction but also those of the Polish reaction, the roads the reaction plans to march down in our very own society. These plans and intentions have already been given away somewhat by the reactionary press, revelations with which all working people should familiarize themselves.

What are the bourgeois parties in Poland plotting? What are their plans?

One answer to that question comes from Mr. Roman Dmowski, chief of National Democracy. Another can be found in *Słowo* [The Word], the party organ of these "realists," these erstwhile compromisers and possessors of great amounts of agricultural land.* *Słowo* was the first publication to appeal publicly for all "national" parties to join forces against the revolution.

In its appeal, *Słowo* conflates violent crime, a product of tsarism's slow death, with revolution, lumping them together under the label of "anarchy." It claims that the tsarist government does not have the power to crush the revolution, and, further, that only National Democracy is capable of suppressing the revolution. All that is needed, therefore, according to *Słowo*, is for the tsarist government to trust society and its organization (National Democracy), and the revolution will be crushed.

National Democracy expressed its agreement, of course, through the words of Mr. Dmowski, to the proposal to entrust to him the role of hangman of the revolution. And the entire bourgeois press, with the entirely meaningless exception of Progressive Democracy, immediately seized on this call to fight the revolution, agreeing to report for battle under the flag of National Democracy.

Thus does the reaction focus on the work of aiding tsarism, which it holds to be incapable of rooting out the *kramoly* [insurrections] on its own. But, in assuming the role of chief hangman of the revolution in Poland and commandant of the Black Hundreds bloc of the pan-Polish reaction, National Democracy

---

* *Słowo* was a conservative Polish daily newspaper, published from 1882 to 1919. This legally published paper was the most important organ of the conciliators, whose Realpolitik was based on efforts to achieve reconciliation with tsarist rule.

has issued certain conditions to all our national parties of disgrace. And one of these conditions is simply to outlaw socialists.

This is what National Democracy has proclaimed through its mouthpiece, Mr. Dmowski, in *Dzwon Polski* [The Polish Bell]:

> Socialism is an *absolute* enemy. Not an enemy of this or that faction, but an *enemy of society*.
>
> Accordingly, we hold socialist organizations to be, to a certain extent, outside of society, an element against which it falls not to a specific part of society but to society itself to fight.
>
> To us they are, to a certain extent, *hostile intruders*.

[Otto von] Bismarck also considered Germany's socialists to be "outside society," making them out as "hostile intruders," and outlawed them. And all the HKT-ists,* applauding his "national" ratiocinations, agreed to outlaw socialists and to pursue and fight them as hostile foreigners. Despite this, German Social Democracy became the largest, most important party for the German people. The government of Mr. Stołypin, promising to reform the constitution, also declared the socialists to be outlaws. As we can see, all nationalists—whether they be Bismarck and the Prussian HKT-ists, the enemy-of-Polishness Stołypin, National Democracy, or some other camp of Polish asininity—share a family resemblance, as if they were brothers. And just as Prussian nationalists did not kill German Social Democracy, so [Pyotr] Stołypin and Dmowski will not spell the end of the Social Democracy of Russia and Poland.

Still, Polish workers should take note that the entirety of the so-called national press seized, with utmost pleasure, on the condition that National Democracy imposed on them. It was as if from the heart of the press that Mr. Dmowski spoke when he said, "Socialists are not members of society, and they should be treated as hostile intruders."

This is what has emerged out of the fight against invasion that National Democracy announced such a short time ago. They have declared a holy war on another external enemy—the revolution.

There is also a second condition. Mr. Dmowski wants his "society" of goons to refrain from interfering in the battle between the socialists and the government, and only to contend with the socialists when they are fighting "with

---

* The Eastern Marches Society (Ostmarkenverein) was a German nationalist organization in Prussia's eastern territories that Polish speakers came to call *hakatyści*, or HKT-ists, from an acronym based on the organization's founders' surnames, Ferdinand von Hansemann, Hermann Kennemann, and Heinrich von Tidemann-Seeheim. Writers from the society regularly referred to Poles as "non-white" and posited a racist dichotomy between "white Germans" and "black Poles" and called for the ethnic cleansing of the latter. Many of its members later become supporters of the Nazis.

society itself"—that is, when workers are fighting for the eight-hour workday, for better pay, or for a little more bread for their hungry children. It is supposed to be a great difference, and a comfort, that when socialists are killed at the hands of Sokół hooligans,* it is not because they are fighting the government, but rather because, for example, they lead strikes among farmhands in the countryside, as in Czemierniki. Yet this second condition is actually very logical. National Democratic marauders are happy to strip workers of the fruits of their revolutionary struggles, preventing them, for example, from entering election rallies. They are happy to take advantage, for their own ends, of the freedom of the press that was won on the battlefield of revolution, even though the revolutionaries themselves do not have press freedom. They are happy, despite the fact that Mr. Dmowski and company gained a press free of preventive censorship because of the bloody victories of revolutionaries, to declare them hostile intruders in society. But to so blatantly loot of the fruits of others' labor, and, on top of that, to declare those aggrieved to be hostile intruders and outlaws— only National Democracy's hooligans are capable of that. *Słowo*, a newspaper of respectable squires, betrays gentlemanly manners, if nothing else, in knowing nothing at all of such simple, knavish politics. The paper does not want to differentiate between the two seemingly separate struggles—one against the government and one against the exploitation of "society" and the shaming of the nation. It wants to stop plundering the fruits of others' struggles entirely, much preferring to begin openly defending both the government and the immense systems of exploitation [now in place]. And that is why the paper is calling to destroy *every* manifestation of revolution, whether directed against the tsarist government or against capitalist exploitation.

This is nothing, according to Mr. Dmowski. He argues that National Democracy opposes the Russian Revolution too, so all the reactionary camps have agreed to completely eliminate socialists. Indeed, nationalist hit squads are already quite practiced at helping the Cossacks murder revolutionaries.

But besides this, all these calls in the press for hooligans to communicate and synchronize their oppression of the revolution have yet one more crucial piece of political significance for Polish workers. They show why these bourgeois-reactionary parties require a "self-contained" national operation in an autonomous Poland—that is, why they demand a federation and what they expect from it. We will return to this topic later.

For now, Polish workers should harbor no illusions as they monitor the situation, understanding that the National Democratic reaction is even now shaping the public opinion of the bourgeoisie for such a fight against the revolutionary proletariat; all murders heretofore perpetrated by scoundrels who call themselves nationalists will pale in comparison.

---

* A reference to members of the nationalist "Sokół" (Falcon) gymnastics association.

When National Democracy declares that socialists—that is, thousands, tens of thousands of workers—are hostile intruders, are people who do not belong to society, what it is doing is this:

National Democracy is justifying in advance the mass murders that it plans to carry out on the revolutionary Polish people.

The Practice of Revolution*

The Social Democracy of Poland† is the only party that has not been caught unawares or thrown off balance by the current revolution. Only its political program has remained secure and unrefuted by the course of the revolution. As a matter of fact, thus far, no claims of any party have been so substantially validated—no more excellent witness has been borne to the legitimacy of a party's ideas—than those of Social Democracy. As for the other parties in Poland, ranging from the compromisers and the National Democrats to the PPS, the contrast could not be stronger. Their political programs all hang in tatters, having been shot through and through as the current revolution against the tsar broke out and gained momentum. The revolution has been especially merciless to the PPS, which, after twelve years of stubborn struggle on behalf of a program of state independence for Poland, lost its twelve-year-old banner as soon as revolution broke out. The PPS turned out to be completely without a political program, having replaced it with a call for a Constituent Assembly in Warsaw. Eventually, it did come up with an entirely new program—the creation of a federation including the Kingdom of Poland and Russia within shared state boundaries. In other words, it transformed itself into an entirely new party that has nothing in common with the old PPS except its name.

In this way, the revolution has confirmed one of the ideas of the Social Democratic platform: that the struggle for the state independence of Poland has no grounds, and that therefore the Russian partition of Poland must win its freedom together with Russia, within state borders shared with Russia. Since it emerged on the scene twelve years ago with a call to fight for a democratic constitution and autonomy, Social Democracy has based its program on the grounds of capitalist development in Russia. Independently of anyone's conscious will, this capitalist development links our country and Russia together into one capitalist state, renders the program of independence for capitalist Poland utopian, and lays the ground for the Polish proletariat to struggle jointly with the Russian proletariat for shared freedom.

However, we need no longer exclusively invoke the Polish-Russian experiential practice of capitalist life or the interests of the proletarian class struggle in Poland and Russia. The current revolution already offers its own experience, too—a more telling experience, at that, than the ordinary, mundane, silent track of capitalist development. The revolution has already lasted a year and a half,

---

* This article first appeared in *Czerwony Sztandar*, No. 104, September 5, 1906, p. 1, under the title "Praktyka rewolucji." It is translated from the Polish original by Joseph Muller.

† That is, the Social Democracy of the Kingdom of Poland and Lithuania (SDKPiL). Luxemburg never associates the PPS with Social Democracy, even though it did so and the Second International at times recognized it as its affiliate.

and since events unfold and mature much faster during revolution than during times of normal societal life, currents and phenomena have come to light over the last year and a half that can and do reveal the clear outlines of various political aspirations. In the light of these indications gleaned from the practice of revolution, one can assess the worth of the new political program of the PPS—a call for a federation—and its new rallying cry—a Constituent Assembly in Warsaw.

The practice of revolution is something to which every socialist worker should pay close attention. What has this practice shown over the last year and a half?

First, what has emerged clearly and compellingly is that Russian society is more revolutionary than Polish society. It has turned out that in our country, other than socialist parties, nearly everything is reactionary—counterrevolutionary. This became especially clear to anyone who followed the state Duma before and after its dissolution.

Here, as in Russia, socialists boycotted the Duma. And see what happened. Russia sent progressive, democratic, and revolutionary envoys to the Duma; Poland, along with the now partly separated lands of old Poland (Lithuania and Ruthenia), sent reactionary Polish envoys to the Duma. Cadets predominated in the Duma, showing that progressive democrats make up the majority of bourgeois Russian society—more progressive, more democratic, and bolder, that is, than our Progressive Democracy, which furthermore has absolutely no political influence of any consequence in Polish society. Next to the Cadets in the Duma were the "Trudoviks"—that is, the representatives of the revolutionary Russian peasantry. The Duma's Social Democratic fraction* we will omit here because it was elected after the Duma was constituted, and at the moment what concerns us is to show the difference between bourgeois societies in Poland and Russia. And as for the nature of the Polish Circle in the Duma, no one need explain that to worker-socialists. They know full well that the Polish Circle earned high praise in *Novoye Vremya* [The New Times]† and in every Russian government and reactionary sphere in which, with hatred and foaming at the mouth, the Duma was called "revolutionary."

In our boycott of the Duma, we argued that the body would be ruffian, Cossack, and reactionary. We held this view because we took into consideration on election day the effects of electoral laws and government repression. Under such electoral laws and under such repressive electoral measures, any country, even in normal times, would elect an extremely reactionary parliament. And it appears we were right, judging from relations in our country; our country

---

* Composed of the Mensheviks. The Bolsheviks boycotted the First Duma.

† *Novoye Vremya* was a newspaper published in St. Petersburg from 1868 to 1917, and from 1869 as a daily. From 1905, it became an organ of the Black Hundreds. It was banned after the October Revolution.

filled its Duma seats with hooligans—National Democrats. Yet we underestimated the revolutionary nature of relations within bourgeois Russian society. Revolution is indeed such a powerful force that it cannot be held back, not even by the shackles of the worst electoral statutes and resulting repressive measures; it squeezes through every gap, breaks every bond, and emerges again. So it was in Russia. If revolutionary conditions on par with Russia's had predominated in bourgeois society here, too—among the gentry, the bourgeoisie, the petty bourgeoisie, the peasantry, and the intelligentsia—then bourgeois Polish society would have filled the Duma not with nationalist hooligans but, to the great astonishment of Russia and the entire civilized world, with elements at least as progressive and revolutionary as the Cadets and the Trudoviks, even during the socialist boycott.

Up to now, then, the practice of revolution has shown first of all that Poland is not, to put it mildly, more revolutionary than Russia, and that actually the situation is precisely the opposite. The PPS still says that our country's proletariat should aspire to a federation and a Constituent Assembly in Warsaw because Poland is a more progressive country than Russia. Clearly, the revolution has invalidated this new PPS program, just as it invalidated the program they announced twelve years ago.

What is more, up to this point the practice of revolution has *entrapped* the reactionary Polish parties into striving *for a federation* of Poland and Russia. We saw the National Democratic Polish Circle submit a solemn declaration demanding a return to the Polish Kingdom system enacted in the year 1814 by the Congress of Vienna—that is, the federal system joining Russia and Poland.*

During debates in the Duma on peasant issues, we saw the Polish Circle come out energetically against those who wished to force on us a plan for peasant ownership of large and medium agricultural properties, but not because the Polish peasant entirely lacks the aspirations of Russian peasants to "land and liberty"—that argument would be completely correct. The Polish Circle gave disagreements on *politics* and principle as its reasons for opposing the plan, explaining that the task of establishing *agricultural as well as many other* relations in our country should be settled *solely* by representatives of Poland, independently of representatives of Russia. At every step, the Polish Circle has advocated the principle that all matters of our internal system and of the life of

---

* The Congress of Vienna, convened shortly after Napoleon's defeat in Russia, eliminated the quasi-independent Duchy of Warsaw that existed from 1807 to 1814, which essentially had been a French protectorate. The Congress of Vienna awarded Russia most of the Duchy of Warsaw as a "Kingdom of Poland"; for this reason, it was often referred to as Congress Poland. Prussia and Austria obtained other areas that had once been part of Poland. It is for this reason that Luxemburg named her party "the Social Democracy of the *Kingdom* of Poland and Lithuania," to make it clear that it represented Russian-occupied Poland and not the Polish national entity as such. This fit with her overall opposition to the reconstruction of an independent Polish state.

our society should be settled *independently* by the envoys of Poland, in the "legislative" Polish Sejm, free from interference by Russian envoys.

And every worker-socialist knows why our nationalists care so much about "independence." Because they are opponents of the revolution, which in their view goes "too far"; because they want to isolate Poland from the Russian Revolution; because they are opposed to the rule of democracy. They know perfectly well that if it falls to Poland to work out its internal relations autonomously, then they, the reactionaries, will be able to control the process. They know perfectly well that a Constituent Assembly in Warsaw, or their "legislative" Sejm governing our internal relations independently of the Russian Revolution, will strike a blow to that revolution, crush the uniform struggle of the unified proletariat of Poland and Russia, sap the revolutionary momentum, and advance the reaction.

The experience so far yielded by the practice of revolution thus tells us that the desires for a federation and for a Constituent Assembly in Warsaw are *reactionary* aspirations aimed at isolating our land from the Russia-wide revolution and blunting the influence of the revolution among us by distancing our revolutionary proletarian struggle from Russia.

This is the tried and true revolutionary experience to date that every worker-socialist must know and understand.

This experience shows clearly, first of all, that only a unified, concentrated revolution can ensure the triumph of democracy, not a revolution disconnected and torn apart into separate constituent assemblies. Even in a Duma where control was not in the hands of socialist or revolutionary elements, but where the fight against tsarism was organized and focused by a liberal bourgeoisie—even there, our National Democrats were forced to attack not the revolution but the government alone, whereas here, in our country, they attack the revolution exclusively and engage in no struggle with the government of any kind.

Second, this experience shows clearly that if our country's autonomy were to be forged not in the fires of a united, centralized revolution, under the roof of the revolutionary struggle of the working people of all Russia, not in a statewide Constituent Assembly but in that of Warsaw, it would be the autonomy of the National Democrats and not the autonomy of the revolutionary Polish people. It would be the triumph of the reaction, not the triumph of the revolution.

The Mass Strike, the Political Party, and the Trade Unions*

I.

Almost all previous texts and declarations of international socialism on the question of the mass strike date from the time *before* the [1905] Russian Revolution—that is, before the first historical experiment with this means of struggle on the largest scale. This explains why they are for the most part obsolete. Their conception is based on the same standpoint as that taken by Friedrich Engels, as in his 1873 critique of Bakuninist pseudo-revolutionizing in Spain:†

> In the Bakuninist program a general strike is the lever employed by which the social revolution is started. One fine morning all the workers in all the industries of a country, or even of the whole world, stop work, thus forcing the propertied classes either humbly to submit within four weeks at the most, or to attack the workers, who would then have the right to defend themselves and use this opportunity to pull down the entire old society. The idea is far from new; this horse was since 1848 hard ridden by French, and later Belgian socialists; it is originally, however, an English breed. During the rapid and vigorous growth of Chartism among the English workers following the crisis of 1837, the "holy month," a strike on a national scale, was advocated as early as 1839 (see Engels, *The Condition of the Working*

---

* This text was first published as a pamphlet in 1906 as *Massenstreik, Partei, und Gewerkschaften* (Hamburg: Verlag von Erdmann Dubber). Shortly after her release from prison on July 8, 1906, Luxemburg traveled to Kuokkala, Finland, where she engaged in extensive discussions with Lenin and his fellow Bolsheviks, including Grigori Zinoviev, Lev Kamenev, and Alexander Bogdanov, on the significance of the 1905 Revolution; as Zinoviev later put it, she was "the first Marxist who was able to evaluate the Russian Revolution correctly and as a whole"; see J. P. Nettl, *Rosa Luxemburg* (London and New York: Verso, 2019), p. 357. It was during this period in Finland that she composed the *Mass Strike* pamphlet, which had been commissioned by the Executive Committee of the Social Democratic Organization of the Federal State of Hamburg, and by the Executive Committees of the Social Democratic Associations of Altona, Ottensen, and Wandsbek. This original edition is based on the printed manuscript dating from 1906. The first edition from 1906 incorporated changes to the text; additions are reproduced here in footnotes, and deletions are indicated by square brackets. It is translated by Nicholas Gray.

† This refers to the followers of Mikhail Bakunin, a leading figure in nineteenth-century anarcho-communism. Engels issued his critique of the Spanish anarchists in "The Bakuninists at Work: An Account of the Spanish Revolt in the Summer of 1873," in *Der Volkstaat*, Nos. 105, 106, and 107, published October 31, November 2 and 5, 1873; see *Marx Engels Collected Works*, Vol. 23 (New York: International Publishers, 1988), pp. 581–98. A series of revolts broke out in southern Spain between July and September 1873, organized by the Intransigents as well as Bakunin's followers, against the left-republican government of Francisco Pi i Margall, which had initiated a series of radical reforms. This seriously weakened the power of the republicans, who were overthrown by a military dictatorship in early 1874 that quickly re-established the monarchy.

Class in England)* and this had such a strong appeal that in July 1842 the industrial workers in northern England tried to put it into practice. Great importance was also attached to the general strike at the Geneva Congress of the Alliance [of Socialist Democracy]† held on September 1, 1873,‡ although it was universally admitted that this required a well-formed organization of the working class and plentiful funds. And there's the rub. On the one hand, the governments, especially if encouraged by political abstention, will never allow the organization or the funds of the workers to reach such a level; on the other hand, political events and oppressive acts by the ruling classes will lead to the liberation of the workers long before the proletariat is able to set up such an ideal organization and this colossal reserve fund. But if it had them, there would be no need to use the roundabout way of a general strike to achieve its goal.

Here, we have the line of argument that was definitive for the position taken up by international Social Democracy in relation to the mass strike in the following decades. It is completely tailored to the anarchist theory of the general strike—i.e., to the theory that upholds the general strike, as opposed to the daily political struggle of the working class as a means of inducing social revolution— and it exhausts itself in the following dilemma: Either the proletariat as a whole does not yet possess powerful organizations and funds, in which case it cannot accomplish a general strike, or it is already sufficiently powerfully organized, in which case it no longer needs the general strike. This line of reasoning is indeed so simple and, at first sight, so incontrovertible that for a quarter of a century it gave excellent service to the modern workers' movement as a logical weapon against anarchist chimeras§ and as a tool for introducing the idea of political struggle to the widest circles within the working class. The great advances of the workers' movement in all modern countries over the last twenty-five years

---

* See *Marx-Engels Collected Works*, Vol. 4 (New York: International Publishers, 1975), p. 520. The Chartists were one of the largest and most militant working-class organizations in British history. The "holy month" refers to August 1839, when the Chartists called for a general strike to bring down capitalism. They revived the call in 1842. Although a general strike spread throughout England in August of that year, it failed to secure even its minimal aims. Engels argued in *The Condition of the Working Class in England*, "If [the general strike] had been from the beginning an intentional, determined workingmen's insurrection, it would surely have carried its point: but these crowds who had been driven into the streets by their masters, against their own will, and with no definite purpose, could do nothing." For a recent reconsideration of the Chartists, see David Black and Chris Ford, *1839: The Chartist Insurrection* (London: Unkant Publishers, 2012).

† The Alliance of Socialist Democracy was a secret society within the International Workingmen's Association (IAA, or the First International) founded by Bakunin and a number of his followers on October 28, 1868. For Marx and Engels' detailed criticism of the grouping, see "The Alliance of Socialist Democracy and the International Working Men's Association," in *Marx-Engels Collected Works*, Vol. 23 (New York: International Publishers, 1988), pp. 454–580.

‡ In September 1873, competing congresses of Marx's IAA and Bakunin's Alliance of Socialist Democracy were held in Geneva.

§ *Hirngespinste*—pipe dreams or fantasies.

represent the most compelling evidence in favor of the tactic of political struggle that Marx and Engels upheld against Bakuninism, and German Social Democracy—in the power it wields today, and in its status as vanguard of the entire international workers' movement—is not least the direct product of the consistent and emphatic application of this tactic.

The Russian Revolution has now caused the above argumentation to be subjected to a thorough reassessment. This revolution has, for the first time in the history of class struggles, brought about a superb realization of the idea of the mass strike and—as will be expanded upon below—even of the general strike, thus inaugurating a new epoch in the development of the workers' movement. Admittedly, it can neither be concluded from this that the tactic of political struggle that Marx and Engels recommended was false, nor that the latter's critique of anarchism was incorrect. On the contrary, it is the very same thought processes, the same method that underlay the Marxian-Engelsian tactic and the praxis of German Social Democracy until this point, and that has now engendered completely new moments [*Momente*] and new conditions of the class struggle. Not only does the Russian Revolution—this same revolution that constitutes the first historical experiment on the model of the mass strike—imply no vindication of anarchism, but, on the contrary, it practically signifies *a historical liquidation of anarchism*. The forlorn existence to which this school of thought was condemned by the powerful development of Social Democracy in Germany in recent decades may be explained, to a certain extent, by the exclusive predominance and long duration of the parliamentary period.* A tendency that is tailored to "launching the offensive" and to "direct action," and that is "revolutionary" in the barest pitchfork sense, might nevertheless undergo a merely temporary atrophy during the lull of the parliamentary routine, only to come back to life and reveal its inner potency with the return of a period of direct, open struggle, or in a revolution on the streets. Russia seemed particularly predisposed to becoming the field of experimentation for the heroic deeds of anarchism. A country in which the proletariat had no political rights at all and was extremely weakly organized, in which there was a colorful confusion of various popular social classes with very variegated and mutually entangled interests, scant education of the masses of the population, and extreme brutality in the use of force on the part of the prevailing regime—all these factors seemed predestined to propel anarchism suddenly to power, even if such power would only be short-lived. And, after all, Russia was the historical birthplace of anarchism. Yet Bakunin's fatherland was to become the burial place of his doctrine. It is not merely that the anarchists did not and do not stand at the head of the mass strike movement, nor that the entire political leadership of the revolutionary

---

* Anarchism had been in decline in Germany since at least 1895, when its adherents were expelled from the German Social Democratic Party. However, the anarchist movement was growing at the time in other parts of Europe.

action and also of the mass strike lay in the hands of the very Social Democratic organizations that the anarchists so bitterly opposed and condemned as being a "bourgeois party," or else partly in the hands of socialist organizations that were more or less influenced by Social Democracy and that were gravitating toward it, such as the terrorist party of the "Socialist Revolutionaries."* No, the anarchists do not exist as a serious political tendency at all within the Russian Revolution. Only in a small Lithuanian town, in Białystok, where conditions are particularly difficult—with a polychromatic mix of workers of different nationalities, a predominantly fragmented small-scale industry, a downtrodden proletariat—is there, among the seven or eight different revolutionary groups, also a handful of adolescent "anarchists" that do their utmost to contribute† to the confusion and disorientation of the workforce; and latterly, a handful of this species has also made itself felt in Moscow and perhaps in two or three other towns.‡ But, apart from these few "revolutionary" groups, what is the actual role of anarchism in the Russian Revolution? It has become the flagship for common thieves and looters; in each period of depression, when revolution is temporarily on the defensive, a turbid wave of theft and looting swells; of these innumerable acts of robbery that are carried out against private persons, a large proportion are committed under the name of "anarcho-communism." In the Russian Revolution, anarchism is not the theory of the proletariat in its struggle, but rather the ideological figurehead of the counterrevolutionary lumpenproletariat that swarms like a school of sharks in the wake of the battleship of the revolution. And it is likely that this marks the end of the historical trajectory of anarchism.

On the other hand, the mass strike has been made a reality in Russia not as a means of bypassing the political struggle of the working class (especially parliamentarianism) and suddenly jumping into the social revolution through a theatrical coup, but as a means of creating the very conditions in which the proletariat can engage in daily political struggle—and in parliamentarianism in particular—in the first place. In Russia, the working population, led by the proletariat, engages in revolutionary struggle—with mass strikes figuring as the most important weapon—to achieve precisely those political rights and conditions whose necessity and significance within the struggle for the emancipation of the working class were first established by Marx and Engels (the latter having opposed anarchism within the International by forcefully championing the struggle for such rights and conditions). Thus the historical dialectic—the bedrock upon which the entire Marxian theory of socialism rests—has had the

---

* The Russian Socialist Revolutionary Party (SR), based on the peasantry, emerged in 1902 from the remains of the Populist movement (Narodniks). They defended (and often propagated) individual acts of terror in order to eliminate tsarist autocracy and establish a democratic republic.

† The 1906 first edition has "compound" instead of "contribute to."

‡ This greatly understates the influence of the anarchists in Russian left politics of the time. For a more modern and more accurate account, see Paul Avrich, *The Russian Anarchists* (Chico: AK Press, 2005).

result that anarchism, which was inseparably linked with the idea of the mass strike, now finds itself in a relation of antagonism vis-à-vis the praxis of the mass strike, whereas conversely the mass strike, which was once opposed, given that it represented the antithesis to the political engagement of the proletariat, manifests itself today as the most powerful weapon in the political struggle for political rights. If, then, the Russian Revolution renders necessary a thoroughgoing revision of the old standpoint of Marxism with regard to the mass strike, it is once again merely Marxism itself whose general methods and considerations emerge victorious in a new form. Moor's beloved shall die by no other hand than Moor's.*

II.

The first revision with regard to the question of the mass strike that results from the events in Russia pertains to the general *conception* of the problem. To date, both the keen advocates of an "experiment with the mass strike" in Germany (the [Eduard] Bernsteins and [Kurt] Eisners of this world) and the strict opponents of such an attempt (represented in the labor union camp by [Theodor] Bömelburg,† for example) fundamentally occupy the same ground, basing themselves on a common conception that is in fact the anarchist one. The apparent polar opposites do not merely mutually exclude each other—rather, as always, they also condition and simultaneously complement each other. That is to say that for the anarchist mode of thinking, speculation is directly concerned with the "great crash," the social revolution, merely as an external and inessential characteristic. What is essential for this conception is the entire abstract, unhistorical consideration of the mass strike and in general of all conditions of the proletarian struggle. For the anarchist, only two things exist as material presuppositions for his "revolutionary" speculations: first, the blue sky,‡ and secondly, goodwill and the courage to rescue humanity from the contemporary capitalist vale of tears. Sixty years ago, blue-sky reasoning yielded the result that the mass strike is the shortest, the most secure, and the easiest means of performing the leap into the beyond, into the better society. Recently, the same blue-sky

---

* Luxemburg quotes here from Schiller's *The Robbers*; see Friedrich Schiller, *Complete Works*, Vol. 2 (New York: Collier, 1902), p. 274. "The Moor" was Marx's nickname.

† The Fifth Congress of the Social Democratic Free Trade Unions, held May 22 to 27, 1905, in Cologne, strongly rejected the use of the mass strike and even prohibited (by a vote of 200 to 17) any discussion of it. Bömelburg headed the General Commission that issued these rulings. See John A. Moses, *Trade Unionism in Germany from Bismarck to Hitler, 1869–1933, Volume I: 1869–1918* (London: George Prior, 1985), p. 152: "Bömelburg's ideas on the mass strike were identical to those being expressed in circles about May Day. Both meant incurring unnecessary risks to union organization."

‡ *Die blaue Luft*—"the blue sky," evoking the emptiness of the skies. Luxemburg presumably intends irony here in the suggestion of "blue-sky thinking," "in which there are no (material) constraints upon creative thinking."

speculation would have it that labor union struggle is the only "direct action of the masses" and thus the only revolutionary struggle—this, as is well known, is the newest quirk of the French and Italian "syndicalists." What has always been fatal for anarchism in this connection is not merely that the methods of struggle improvised in blue-sky thinking constitute a reckoning without one's host (i.e., pure utopias), but that—precisely because they fail to reckon in any way with grim, contemptible reality—they most often go, within this grim reality, from being revolutionary speculations to unwitting accomplices to reaction.

Yet today, the same ground—corresponding to this abstract, unhistorical perspective—is occupied by those who would imminently call a mass strike in Germany on a given day in the calendar by means of an executive resolution, as well as by those who, like the participants in the Cologne Trades Union Congress, would eliminate the problem of the mass strike from the world through a ban on "agitation." Both tendencies proceed on the basis of the pure anarchist conception according to which the mass strike is a mere technical means of struggle that can be "resolved upon" or, alternatively, "banned" at will, in a discretionary fashion—a kind of pocket knife that can be kept ready, folded in one's pocket, "in case of emergency," or alternatively flipped open and deployed, if so decided. It is true that precisely the opponents of the mass strike can claim credit for taking into account the historical grounds and the material conditions for the current situation in Germany, in contrast with the "revolutionary romantics," who float in the air and simply refuse to reckon with hard reality and its possibilities and impossibilities. "Facts and figures, figures and facts!" call the former, like Mr. Gradgrind in Dickens' *Hard Times*.* What the labor union opponents of the mass strike understand by "historical grounds" and "material condition" are two elements [*Momente*]: on the one hand, the weakness of the proletariat, and on the other, the strength of Prussian militarism. The deficient workers' organizations and the insufficient level of funds held by these, together with the imposing Prussian bayonets—these are the "facts and figures" upon which these labor union leaders base their practical policies in any given situation. Admittedly, labor union funds and Prussian bayonets are undoubtedly very material and also very historical phenomena, yet the conception based upon them is no historical materialism in Marx's sense, but rather a police-oriented materialism in Puttkamer's sense.† The representatives of the capitalist police state also reckon very much, or even exclusively, with the actual power of the organized proletariat and the material power of the bayonet

---

* Mr. Gradgrind was the harsh superintendent of the school board in Charles Dickens' novel, often invoked in reference to cold characters who care only about facts and figures.

† Robert von Puttkamer was Prussian minister of the interior from 1881 to 1888. He further extended the Bismarckian police state by enforcing the Antisocialist Laws and forcibly suppressing strikes in the 1870s and 1880s. He openly invited the police to take unlawful measures against the workers' movement.

respectively, and from the comparative example of these two series of figures, the following reassuring conclusion is always drawn: the revolutionary workers' movement is generated by individual agitators and rabble-rousers, *ergo* with prisons and bayonets we have sufficient means at our disposal to subdue this disagreeable "temporary phenomenon."

The class-conscious German workforce has long since grasped the humoristic quality of the police theory that the entire modern workers' movement is an artificial, arbitrary product of a handful of unscrupulous "agitators and rabble-rousers."

Precisely such a conception is given expression, however, when several dutiful comrades join together to form a column of volunteer night watchmen in order to warn the German workforce of the dangerous agitation of a few "revolutionary romanticists" and their "propaganda in favor of the mass strike"; and, likewise, when, on the other hand, a lachrymose campaign of indignation is staged by those who believe themselves to have been deceived by some "confidential" arrangements supposedly made by the party executive with the General Commission of German Trade Unions concerning the eruption of the mass strike.* If it depended upon the rousing "propaganda" of the revolutionary romanticists or the confidential public resolutions of the party leaderships, we would not have had a single serious mass strike in Russia to date. As I already pointed out in March 1905 in *Sächsische Arbeiterzeitung* [The Workers' Newspaper of Saxony], in no country in the world did "agitation" for, or even discussion of, a mass strike come less into question than in Russia.† And, considering the individual instances of resolutions taken, and agreements entered into, by the Russian party executive, whereby a mass strike was to be proclaimed as an act of volition (such as the most recent attempt, in August of this year, after the dissolution of the Duma),‡ it can be seen that such attempts have almost completely failed. If the Russian Revolution teaches us anything, it is above all that the mass strike is not artificially "fabricated," "resolved upon" out of the blue, "propagated"—rather, it is a historical phenomenon arising with a historical necessity out of the existing social relations at a certain moment in time.

---

* In a secret consultation between the Executive Committee of the Social Democratic Party of Germany and the General Commission of German Trade Unions that took place on February 16, 1906, the party executive had made a concession to the union leaders to the effect that they would not agitate for a political mass strike without the latter's consent—instead, they would act to hinder it if possible. In the event that such a mass strike was nevertheless to break out, the labor unions would be under no compulsion to participate in it.

† See Rosa Luxemburg, "A Test Based on a Sample," in *Complete Works*, Vol. 3, pp. 108–11.

‡ The First Imperial Duma was first convened on April 27, 1906. Under pressure from the revolutionary movement, the Duma was forced to present projects for the solution of the agrarian question. The tsarist government subsequently dissolved the Duma on July 8, 1906, due to having (according to the authorities) "exceeded its constitutional powers."

Thus the problem of the mass strike cannot be grasped through abstract speculations over its possibility or impossibility, or over its utility or harmfulness; instead, it can only be broached through investigation into those moments and social relations out of which the mass strike has arisen in the current phase of the class struggle—or, in other words, not through the *subjective judgment* of the mass strike from the standpoint of what is desirable, but rather through the *objective inquiry* into the sources of the mass strike from the standpoint of what is historically necessary.

In the free air of abstract logical analysis, both the absolute impossibility and inevitable defeat of the mass strike and its complete viability and certain victory can be demonstrated equally forcefully. Therefore, the value of the proof is the same in both cases—i.e., nil. It also follows that the fear of the "propagation" of the mass strike, which has even led to the formal excommunication of those accused of this crime, is in particular the product of a comical misidentification. It is just as impossible to "propagate" the mass strike as an abstract means of struggle as it is to propagate "revolution." "Revolution" and "mass strike" are concepts that themselves merely signify an external form of class struggle: They only have a sense and content in connection with very determinate political situations.

If someone were to undertake to make the mass strike in general, as a form of proletarian action, the object of veritable agitation, and to go peddling this "idea" in order to gradually win the working class over to it, such activity would be as pointless, fruitless, and unsavory as that undertaken by someone attempting to make the idea of revolution or the struggle on the barricades the object of particular agitation. The mass strike has now become the focal point of a vivid interest on the part of the German and international working class because it represents a new form of struggle and signifies as such the assured symptom of a profound internal reversal in class relations and in the conditions of the class struggle. It is a measure of the healthy revolutionary instinct and vibrant intelligence of the German proletarian masses that they are turning their attention to this new problem with such keen interest—notwithstanding the obstinate resistance of their labor union leaders. Yet this interest, this fine intellectual thirst and revolutionary zeal on the part of the workers, cannot be satisfied by treatises that engage in abstract mental gymnastics on the possibility or impossibility of the mass strike; on the contrary, this can only be achieved by making clear to them the development of the Russian Revolution, the international significance of this revolution, the intensification of class antagonisms in Western Europe, the further political perspectives of the class struggle in Germany, and the role and tasks of the masses in the coming struggles. Only in this form will the discussion of the mass strike lead to the broadening of the intellectual horizons of the proletariat, the sharpening of its class consciousness, the deepening of its mode of thinking, and the hardening of its drive [*Tatkraft*].

From this standpoint, however, the disciplinary proceedings initiated by the opponents of "revolutionary romanticism" against those who do not abide by the precise wording of the Jena Resolution are manifested in all their ludicrousness.* The "practical politicians" settled upon this resolution because it binds the mass strike principally to the question of the fate of universal suffrage, from which they believe they can conclude two things: firstly, that the mass strike retains a purely defensive character; and secondly, that the mass strike itself is subordinate to parliamentarianism—that it is transformed into a mere appendage of parliamentarianism. However, the true core of the Jena Resolution in this connection lies in the fact that in the current situation in Germany, an attack by ruling reactionary forces on the right to vote in elections to the Reichstag would in all likelihood usher in a period of tempestuous political struggles in which the mass strike would be used for the first time as a means of struggle in Germany. Yet to seek to restrict and to artificially delimit the social bearing and the historical scope of the mass strike as a phenomenon and as a problem of the class struggle through the wording of a party convention resolution is an undertaking as myopic as the Cologne Trades Union Congress ban on discussion of the mass strike. In the Jena party convention resolution, German Social Democracy has officially registered the profound turnaround that has occurred in the international conditions of proletarian class struggle through the Russian Revolution, and evinced its capacity for revolutionary development and its adaptability to the new exigencies of the coming phase of class struggles. Therein lies the significance of the Jena Resolution. As for the practical application of the mass strike in Germany: History will be the arbiter, just as it was the arbiter in Russia—and here it should be borne in mind that while Social Democracy, with all its resolutions, is certainly an important factor in history, it is merely *one* factor among many.

III.

The mass strike, as it mostly figures in the contemporary discussion in Germany, is an individual phenomenon that is conceived of in very clear and simple terms, and sharply delineated. It is exclusively the political mass strike that is the object of discussion. What is imagined here is a one-off, immense walkout by the industrial proletariat, a mass strike whose cause is political and of the greatest import, and that is undertaken specifically on the basis of a timely mutual agreement between the executive bodies of the party and labor unions. The strike is to

---

* A rather vague resolution that was submitted by August Bebel was adopted at the Jena Congress of the Social Democratic Party of Germany, held September 17–23, 1905, which referred to the use of the mass strike as one of the most effective means of working-class struggle, but it essentially restricted the use of the political mass strike to the defense of the right to vote in elections to the Reichstag and the right of association.

be carried out in the most orderly fashion and in the spirit of discipline, and likewise broken off with impeccable order when the word is given at the opportune moment by the party and union leaderships, with all matters such as the provision of support, the costs and sacrifices to be incurred—in a word, the entire material balance sheet of the mass strike—being precisely specified in advance.

Now, if this theoretical schema is compared with the mass strike in reality, such as it has occurred in Russia over the last five years, it must be concluded that the notion of mass strike around which the German discussion revolves corresponds to hardly any of the mass strikes that have actually happened, and furthermore that the mass strikes in Russia exhibit such a multiplicity of the most diverse varieties that it is totally impossible to speak of "the" mass strike—i.e., of an abstract, schematic mass strike. It is not merely that all of the elements of the mass strike and its character have varied according to the different cities and localities of the empire, but that, above all, its general character has altered several times during the course of the revolution. Mass strikes have undergone a determinate history in Russia, and they continue to do so. Therefore, whoever refers to the mass strike in Russia must retain sight above all of its history.

What we might refer to as the current official period of the Russian Revolution is dated—justifiably so—from the uprising of the Petersburg proletariat on January 22, 1905, when 200,000 workers marched to the tsar's Winter Palace, culminating in a dreadful bloodbath. As is well known, the bloody massacre in Petersburg was the signal for the outbreak of the first huge wave of mass strikes that rolled across the whole of Russia within a few days, carrying the revolution's call to arms from Petersburg to all corners of the empire and to the broadest strata of the proletariat. The Petersburg uprising of January 22 was, however, also merely the most extreme moment of a mass strike that had taken hold of the proletariat in the capital city of the tsars in January 1905. Now, the mass strike in January in Petersburg undoubtedly followed its course under the immediate impression of the enormous general strike that had broken out shortly before, in December 1904, in Baku and in the Caucasus, and that had kept the whole of Russia on tenterhooks for a while.[*] However, the December events in Baku were in turn nothing other than a final, powerful offshoot of the tremendous mass strikes that shook all of southern Russia like an intermittent earthquake throughout 1903 and 1904—a strike whose own prologue was the mass strike in Batumi (in the Caucasus) in March 1902.[†] This first mass strike movement, which extends, in the ongoing chain of events,

---

[*] Luxemburg first reported on the strikes in Baku, which began on December 26, 1905, in the January 1905 issue of *Czerwony Sztandar* (Red Flag). See "The Uprising of the Petersburg Proletariat," in *Complete Works*, Vol. 3, p. 41.

[†] Batumi, on the southwest coast of Georgia, became a center of Social Democratic organizing in the early 1900s. In March 1902, a mass strike broke out at the Rothschild oil refinery in Batumi. Joseph Stalin, who had begun working in the refinery a year earlier, was one of its organizers.

into the current revolutionary eruptions, is ultimately only separated from the great general strike of the Petersburg textile workers of 1896 and 1897* by four or five years; indeed, while this latter movement appears on the face of it to be separated from the current revolution by a few years of apparent stagnation and stiff reaction, anyone who is acquainted with the internal political development of the Russian proletariat toward its current level of class consciousness and with its revolutionary energy will begin the history of the current period of mass struggles with the general strikes in Petersburg. These latter strikes are important in relation to the problem of the mass strike in the first instance because they already contain, in germ form, all of the principal moments of the later mass strikes.

The Petersburg general strike of 1896 initially manifested as a purely economic partial wage struggle. Its causes were the intolerable working conditions of the spinners and weavers of Petersburg: thirteen-, fourteen-, and fifteen-hour working days, miserable piecework rates, and a whole array† of despicable chicaneries on the part of the entrepreneurs. The textile workers had nevertheless long endured this situation, until an ostensibly trivial circumstance proved to be the last straw. This occurred in May 1896, when the coronation of the current tsar, Nicholas II, finally took place, having been postponed for two years out of fear of the revolutionaries; this gave the Petersburg entrepreneurs the occasion to demonstrate their patriotic fervor by imposing three days' compulsory leave on their workers—but curiously enough, they had no intention of paying wages for this period. Incensed at this, the textile workers began to mobilize. After a consultation between approximately 300 highly enlightened workers in the Ekaterinhof Garden,‡ a strike was resolved upon and the following demands formulated: (1) payment of wages for the coronation days; (2) a 10.5-hour working day; (3) an increase in piecework rates. This occurred on May 24. A week later, *every single* weaving and spinning mill was at a standstill, and 40,000 workers were on general strike. Today, such an event might seem trivial when compared to the enormous mass strikes of the revolution. During the political freeze of the Russia *of that time*, a general strike was unprecedented—it was itself a whole micro-revolution. There began, of course, the most brutal persecution; 1,000 workers were arrested and deported to their homelands, and the general strike was suppressed.

---

* In May 1896, about 40,000 textile workers went on strike in St. Petersburg under the leadership of the (Marxist) League of Struggle for the Emancipation of the Working Class. They demanded a shorter workday and payment for the days of work lost during the holidays celebrating the coronation of Tsar Nicholas II. To prevent the strike from expanding into a general strike, the workers' demands were partly granted, and after three weeks the strike ended.

† *Musterkarte* in the original—pattern-cards used in the textile industry. Luxemburg is using metaphor and illusion here, since many of the strikes were in the textile industry.

‡ First edition: "300 of the most enlightened workers." Ekaterinhof Garden is in southwest St. Petersburg; at the time it housed gardens, a library, and an amusement park.

Here, all the basic features of the later mass strike can already be seen. The most immediate cause for the movement was a completely incidental, subordinate one, and its outbreak was elementary; however, the fruits of Social Democratic agitation over several years showed themselves as the movement materialized, and as the general strike took its course, Social Democratic agitators stood at the head of the movement, giving it direction and using it for the purposes of active revolutionary agitation. Furthermore, the strike was outwardly a mere economic struggle over wages, but the position taken by the government and the Social Democratic agitation turned it into a political phenomenon of the first order. Ultimately, the strike was suppressed, and the workers suffered a "defeat." Yet the Petersburg textile workers repeated the general strike as early as January of the following year, 1897, this time achieving an outstanding success: the introduction of legislation limiting the working day to 11.5 hours throughout Russia. A far more important result, however, consisted in the fact that since that first general strike of 1896, which was undertaken without any trace of organization or strike funds, there began in Russia proper an intensive labor union struggle that soon spread from Petersburg to the rest of the country, opening up entirely new prospects for Social Democratic agitation and organization; it was this struggle that, in the apparent peace of the graveyard of the subsequent period, prepared the proletarian revolution through the unseen work of the mole.

The outbreak of the strike in the Caucasus in March 1902 was likewise an ostensibly incidental one: it was induced by purely economic, partial factors, even if these were completely different from those of 1896. The strike's eruption was bound up with the crisis in heavy industry and trade that in the case of Russia formed the prelude to the Japanese War; together, this crisis and war had constituted the most powerful factor in the incipient revolutionary ferment.* The crisis generated massive unemployment, which fed agitation in the proletarian mass; for this reason, the government began a policy of forced transportation of "superfluous hands" to their respective homelands in order to subdue the working class. It was just such a measure—affecting approximately 400 petroleum workers—that elicited a mass protest in Batumi; this in turn led to demonstrations, arrests, a massacre, and ultimately to a political process in which the purely economic, partial affair was suddenly transformed into a political and revolutionary event. The strike in Batumi that had been crushed without yielding any results at all resonated in a series of revolutionary mass demonstrations of the workers in Nizhny Novgorod, Saratov, and other cities, and thus constituted a powerful advance for the general wave of the revolutionary movement.

---

* From January 1904 to September 1905, Japan had waged an imperialist war against Russia for hegemony in the Far East. The heavy defeat inflicted on the Russian troops in 1905 weakened tsarism and intensified the revolutionary crisis in Russia.

The first genuinely revolutionary reverberation followed in November 1902 in the guise of a general strike in Rostov-on-Don. This movement was triggered by wage differentials in the workshops of the Vladicaucasus* Railroad. The administration intended to lower wages, at which the Don Committee of Social Democracy issued a call for a strike with the following demands: a nine-hour day, increased wages, the elimination of penalties, the dismissal of unpopular engineers, etc. There were walkouts at all railroad workshops. All other professions immediately followed suit, and suddenly an unprecedented situation prevailed in Rostov-on-Don: All industrial workplaces were at a standstill, while huge meetings of 15,000 to 20,000 workers were held each day in the open air, sometimes surrounded by a cordon of Cossacks; here, for the first time, popular Social Democratic speakers appeared publicly, rousing speeches on socialism and political freedom were delivered and received with immense enthusiasm, and tens of thousands of copies of revolutionary appeals were distributed. In the midst of rigidly absolutist Russia, the proletariat of Rostov-on-Don conquered the right to assembly and to freedom of speech for the first time, taking these rights by storm. Here, too, events did not proceed without a massacre. Within a few days, the issue of wage differentials in the Vladicaucasus Railroad workshops had grown into a political general strike and a revolutionary battle on the streets. An echo followed immediately: another general strike at the Tikhoretsk station on the same railroad. Here, too, there was a massacre, and subsequently a trial—as an episode, Tikhoretsk, too, has woven itself into the indissoluble chain of revolutionary moments.

The spring of 1903 gave the answer to the defeated strikes in Rostov-on-Don and Tikhoretsk: the whole of southern Russia stood in flames in May, June, and July. Baku, Tbilisi,† Batumi, Kropyvnytskyi,‡ Odessa, Kiev, Nikolaev,§ and Jekaterinoslaw¶ were literally on general strike. But here, too, the movement did not arise according to a preconceived plan issuing from a central command; rather, it coalesced from various individual points, at each of which the movement had different causes and took different forms. Events commenced in Baku, where several partial wage struggles in individual factories and branches finally converged, resulting in a general strike. In Tbilisi, the strike was initiated by 2,000 commercial employees, who had a working day lasting from 6 a.m. to 11 p.m.; at 8 p.m. on July 4, they all left their shops and went on a demonstration through the city, calling on the proprietors of the shops to close their premises. Victory was total: The commercial employees gained a working day

---

* This refers to the railroad that ran through the city of Vladikavkaz in North Ossetia, an important center of industry and a transportation hub at the time. North Ossetia borders Georgia to the north and Chechnya to the west.
† Tiflis in Luxemburg's time.
‡ Jelisawetgrad in Luxemburg's time; formerly known as Zinovievsk, Kirovo, Kirovograd.
§ Mykolaiv in Ukrainian.
¶ Dnipropetrovsk in Ukrainian.

lasting from 8 a.m. to 8 p.m., and they were immediately joined by all the factories, workshops, and offices. Newspapers did not appear, and streetcars could only run under the protection of the military. In Kropyvnytskyi the strike began in all factories, with purely economic demands. These were mostly met, and on July 14 the strike ended. Two weeks later, however, it erupted again; this time it was the bakers who issued the rallying cry, and they were followed by the stonemasons, carpenters, dyers, mill workers, and finally by all factory workers once again. In Odessa, the movement began with a wage struggle in which the "legal" workers' union that had been established by government agents according to the program of the famous gendarme Zubatóv became embroiled.* The historical dialectic once again took the opportunity to play one of its sweetly mischievous tricks: The economic struggles of the earlier period—including the great general strike of 1896 in Petersburg—had enticed Russian Social Democracy into adopting an exaggerated "economism,"† through which it had prepared the ground within the working class for Zubatóv's demagogic machinations. After a while, however, the great revolutionary current turned around the little boat with the false flag and forced it to sail at the very head of the revolutionary proletarian flotilla. It was the Zubatóvian unions that gave the signal for the great general strike in Odessa in the spring of 1904 and the general strike in Petersburg in January 1905. The workers in Odessa, who had been nurtured by the illusion of sincere worker-friendliness on the part of the government and by its benevolence toward purely economic struggles, suddenly decided to put this goodwill to the test and forced the Zubatóvian "workers' union" to call a strike over the most modest demands in a particular factory. The entrepreneur responded by simply throwing them out onto the street, and when they requested the protection guaranteed them by the patronage of their union leader, the good gentleman vanished, leaving the workers in a state of wild ferment. The Social Democrats immediately took the lead, and the strike movement spread to other factories. On July 1, 2,500 railroad workers went on strike, followed on July 4 by the dockworkers, who demanded a wage increase of eighty kopeks to two roubles and a shortening of the working day by half an hour. On July 6, the seamen joined the movement. On July 13, a walkout by streetcar staff began. At this point, an assembly of all those on strike—some 7,000 to 8,000 men—was held; they formed a column that marched from one factory to the next and swelled like an avalanche, such that the crowd numbered 40,000 to 50,000 by the time it reached the port in order to bring all work

---

* The colonel of the gendarmerie, Sergei Zubatov, established a system of surveillance to monitor revolutionary organizations as head of the Okhrana, or secret police. Between 1901 and 1903, the tsarist government sought to divert the workers from revolutionary struggle by creating legal workers' organizations controlled by the police.

† Advocates of economism, which became a major force in the 1890s, promoted labor union forms of struggle while opposing the political struggle of the proletariat. They were Lenin's main target of criticism in his famous pamphlet *What Is to Be Done?*

there to a standstill. Soon the general strike prevailed throughout the city. In Kiev, the industrial stoppage began on July 21 in the railroad workshops. Here, too, miserable working conditions constituted the immediate cause, and wage demands were issued. On the next day, the foundries followed suit. Then, on July 23, an incident occurred that gave the signal for the general strike: Two of the railroad workers' delegates were arrested during the night; the strikers immediately demanded that they be released, and when this demand was not met, they decided not to let trains leave the city. At the station, all the strikers, together with their wives and children, staged a sit-in on the railroad tracks, forming a sea of human heads. They were threatened with rifles. The strikers bared their chests and shouted, "Fire!" A volley of rifle fire rained down on the defenseless crowd sitting on the tracks, and thirty to forty corpses, some of them women and children, were left lying on the ground. When the news spread, the whole of Kiev rose up and joined the strike. The corpses of those murdered were lifted up by the crowd and carried through the city in a mass procession. Assemblies, speeches, arrests, isolated battles on the street—Kiev was in the midst of a revolution. The movement soon came to an end; in the process, the printers had won a shortening of their working day by one hour and a one-rouble increase in wages, however; in a yeast factory, the eight-hour day was introduced; the railroad workshops were closed down by order of the ministry; in other branches, partial strikes over specific demands continued. In Nikolaev, the news from Odessa, Baku, Batumi, and Tbilisi had an immediate effect, and the general strike erupted in spite of the resistance of the Social Democratic Committee, which aimed to delay the outbreak of the movement until the time when the military was to have left the city on a maneuver. The masses were not to be held back; the initiative was taken in one factory, the strikers went from one workshop to another, and the resistance of the military merely poured oil onto the fire. Soon mass demonstrations were formed and revolutionary songs intoned, and these columns swept along all workers, employees, streetcar personnel, men and women. All workplaces were at a complete standstill. In Jekaterinoslaw, the strike was initiated by the bakers on August 5, followed by the workers of the railroad workshops on August 7, and then by all remaining factories; on August 8, streetcars stopped running and newspapers didn't appear. So it was that the magnificent general strike arose in southern Russia in the summer of 1903. A multiplicity of little channels of partial economic struggles and minor "incidental" occurrences rapidly flowed into a mighty sea, transforming the whole south of the tsarist empire into a bizarre, revolutionary workers' republic for several weeks. "Fraternal embraces, cries of delight and enthusiasm, songs of freedom, gleeful laughter, good humor and elation—all this was to be seen and heard in the crowd of many thousands that surged through the city from morning until evening. Spirits were high; one could almost believe that a new, better life was beginning on earth. A profound and simultaneously idyllic, moving image"—thus wrote the correspondent of the liberal *Osvobozhdenie* [Liberation], the journal of Mr. Pyotr Struve.*

The beginning of 1904 brought with it war and, for a while, a lull in the mass strike movement. First, a turbid wave of "patriotic" demonstrations organized by the police swept over the country. "Liberal" bourgeois society was, for the time being, smashed to the ground by official tsarist chauvinism. But Social Democracy soon took charge of the arena once more; the police-orchestrated demonstrations of the lumpenproletariat were opposed by revolutionary workers' demonstrations. Finally, the ignominious defeats of the tsarist army aroused liberal society from its stupor; there began an era of liberal and democratic congresses, banquets, speeches, addresses, and manifestos. Temporarily crushed and distracted by the humiliation of the war, absolutism allowed these gentlemen a free hand, and soon they began to fancy that they heard the sound of liberal violins in the heavens.† Over a period of six months, bourgeois liberalism occupied center stage, and the proletariat retreated into the shadows. As for absolutism, only after a long depression did it get back on its feet: The camarilla gathered its forces, and with a single powerful stamp of the Cossack's boot, the entire liberal movement was sent scampering for cover. Their banquets, speeches, and congresses were summarily proscribed as an "impudent presumption," and liberalism suddenly found itself up against the wall. But, precisely at the point where liberalism reached the end of the line, the action of the proletariat began. In December 1904, the great general strike broke out in Baku against the background of unemployment: The working class had returned to the battlefield. When speech was prohibited and silenced, action resumed. In the midst of the general strike in Baku, Social Democracy prevailed for a few weeks as the absolute master of the situation, and the unique events in December in the Caucasus would have created a sensation, had they not been so rapidly surpassed by the surging wave of the revolution that they themselves had whipped up. The fantastic, sketchy news of the general strike in Baku had not yet reached all parts of the tsarist empire by the time the mass strike broke out in Petersburg in January 1905.

As is well known, the trigger for this strike was also a trivial one. Two workers were dismissed from the Putilov Works on account of their membership in the legal Zubatóvian union. These disciplinary measures provoked a solidarity strike by all 12,000 workers at the factory. The strike spurred the Social Democrats to initiate a vigorous agitation in favor of the extension of

---

* The journal *Osvobozhdenie* was published as an illegal organ with a liberal orientation in Stuttgart from 1902 to 1905 under the editorship of Struve. He began his career a decade earlier as a leading theoretician of the "Legal Marxists," which argued that the development of capitalism in Russia was both inevitable and beneficial. Struve broke from Marxism in 1901, at the time of the founding of *Osvobozhdenie*.

† *Sie sehen bereits den Himmel voller liberaler Geigen*—literally, "They began to see a sky replete with liberal violins."

the demands, which they were able to impose as the following: an eight-hour working day, the right of association, freedom of speech and of the press, etc. The ferment among the Putilov workers rapidly spread to the rest of the proletariat, and within a few days 140,000 workers were out on strike. Jointly held assemblies and stormy discussions led to the drafting of a proletarian charter of bourgeois freedoms, among which the eight-hour working day featured most prominently; it was with this charter that 200,000 workers, led by a priest, Father [Georgi] Gapon, marched to the [Winter] Palace of the Tsars.* The conflict over the two dismissed Putilov workers had transformed itself into the prologue of the most tremendous revolution of modern times.

The events that immediately followed are well known: The bloodbath in Petersburg prompted enormous mass strikes and general strikes in January and February across all industrial centers and cities in Russia, Poland, Lithuania, the Baltic provinces, the Caucasus, Siberia—from north to south, east to west. It is only on closer inspection that it becomes evident that mass strikes were now occurring in different forms than in the preceding period. This time, it was everywhere Social Democratic organizations that took the lead with calls to action; in all cases, there were emphatic declarations that revolutionary solidarity with the proletariat of Petersburg represented the grounds for, and purpose of, the general strike; across the board there were simultaneously demonstrations, speeches, battles with the military. Yet, in this case, too, there could be no suggestion of a preconceived plan, or of organized action, since the calls to action issued by the parties were scarcely able to keep step with the spontaneous uprisings of the masses; the leaders hardly had the time to formulate slogans for the proletarian masses, which were storming ahead. Furthermore, the earlier mass and general strikes arose out of individual wage struggles as these coalesced, and as they rapidly became political rallies in the general atmosphere of the revolutionary situation and under the effects of Social Democratic agitation; the economic factors and labor union fragmentation formed the starting point, whereas comprehensive class action and political leadership emerged as the final result. Now, the movement is in the opposite direction. The January and February general strikes erupted in advance as unitary revolutionary action under the leadership of Social Democracy; yet this action soon disintegrated into an endless series of local, partial, economic strikes in individual localities, cities, branches, and factories. Throughout the entire spring of 1905 and right up to the height of summer, an unremitting economic struggle of almost the entire proletariat against capital was fermenting throughout the immense empire. This was a struggle that reached upward to grip all petty-bourgeois and

---

* Acting on instructions of the police and under police protection, Gapon had established workers' organizations in Petersburg between 1903 and 1904, in order to keep the workers at a distance from the Social Democratic movement. Gapon was the convener of the Petersburg demonstration of January 22, 1905.

liberal professions (commercial employees, bank officials, technicians, actors, the artistic professions), and that also spread so far downward as to sweep along domestic servants, the subaltern officialdom of the police, even penetrating the stratum of the lumpenproletariat, at the same time as it flowed out of the cities into the countryside and even pounded at the iron gates of the army barracks.

This is an enormously colorful picture of a general confrontation between labor and capital, one that reflects the full diversity of the social structure and of the political consciousness of each stratum and each corner of society: Visible here is the broad spectrum ranging from the veritable labor union struggle of a reliable heavy-industrial elite troop of the proletariat to the amorphous outbreak of protest among a crowd of rural proletarians and the first dull stirrings of an agitated military garrison; from the well-mannered, elegant revolt by those in cuffs and stiff collars in the offices of a banking house to the [confused] timid-brazen grumbling of an awkward assembly of discontented policemen in a smoke-filled, gloomy, dingy police barracks.

According to the theory propounded by devotees of "orderly and well-disciplined" struggles that follow a plan and a scheme—i.e., according to those in particular who, far removed from events, always claim to know better "how it ought to have been done"—the disintegration of the great political general strike action of January 1905 into countless economic struggles was probably "a great error" that had "paralyzed" that action, transforming it into a mere "flash in the pan." Social Democracy in Russia—which, though a participant in the revolution, does not "make" the latter, and indeed has to learn the laws of the revolution from the latter's own progression—was at first also somewhat disconcerted for a while when the first storm tide of the general strike seemed to have ebbed without yielding any results. Yet history, which committed these "great errors," thus executed—untroubled by the reasoning of its unbidden schoolmasters—a gigantic task of the revolution, one that was as ineluctable as it was unpredictable in its consequences.

The sudden general insurrection of the proletariat in January under the tremendous impetus of the Petersburg events was outwardly a political act—the revolutionary declaration of war on absolutism. Yet inwardly, this first universal, direct class action had a retroactive effect that was all the more powerful in that in millions upon millions of people, it aroused class sentiment and class consciousness for the first time, as if through an electric shock. And this awakening of class sentiment immediately expressed itself in the fact that, all of a sudden, the masses of proletarians, who numbered millions, became acutely conscious of the intolerability of the social and economic existence that they had endured for decades under the bondage of capitalism. There thus began a spontaneous, generalized shaking off of, and straining against, these fetters. All the thousand-fold sufferings of the modern proletariat remind it of old, bloody wounds. Here the struggle is for the eight-hour day, there it is against piecework; in one place brutal foremen are "escorted out" in a sack on a handcart, elsewhere infamous disciplinary systems are resisted; everywhere the struggle is for better wages, and here and there it is for the abolition of the putting-out system of labor.* Backward, degraded occupations in cities, small provincial towns that had been gradually declining in an idyllic sleep until that point, the village with its legacy of serfdom—all of these, having been aroused by the lightning flash in January, suddenly began to focus on their rights and attempted feverishly to make up for all omissions of the past. In reality, then, the economic struggle was not so much a disintegration, a fragmentation of the action; rather, it represented a changing of fronts, a sudden and natural reversal of the first universal battle against absolutism into a universal reckoning with capital that, in accordance with its character, took on the *form* of individual fragmented wage struggles. It was not that the political action of the class was fractured by the disintegration of the general strike into economic strikes, but rather the reverse: Once the content of political action that was possible within the given situation and at the given stage of the revolution had been exhausted, it disintegrated into, or rather switched into, economic action.

Indeed, what more could the general strike in January have achieved? Only an utterly unthinking approach would have reckoned with the elimination of absolutism in one fell swoop, through a single general strike that "perseveres to the end," as per the anarchist schema. In Russia absolutism must be overthrown by the proletariat. But in order to accomplish this, the proletariat requires a high level of political schooling, class consciousness, and organization. These it cannot acquire from pamphlets and leaflets, but only from the living political school, from struggle and in struggle, in the progressive course of the revolution. Furthermore, absolutism cannot be overthrown at will at any given moment in time; if the reverse were true, then it would merely be a question of a sufficient "effort" and "perseverance." The demise of absolutism is merely an external expression of the internal social and class development of Russian society. Before absolutism can be toppled, and in order for this to occur, the future, bourgeois Russia—its modern separation into classes—must be generated and formed within absolutism itself. This includes the delimitation of the various social strata and interests vis-à-vis each other, the formation not only of a proletarian revolutionary party, but equally of liberal, radical, petty-bourgeois, conservative, and reactionary parties, too; it likewise implies self-reflection, self-knowledge, and class consciousness on the part not merely of the popular strata, but also of the bourgeois strata. Yet nor can the latter educate themselves and achieve maturity other than in struggle, within the process of revolution itself, through the living school of events, in the clash with the proletariat and in their own internal conflict and interminable mutual

---

* A production system in which employers assign rural producers to do work in their homes.

friction. This division into classes, this class maturity within bourgeois society, and the action of these classes in the struggle against absolutism are, on the one hand, undermined and impeded—but, on the other hand, fomented and accelerated—by the peculiar, leading role of the proletariat and by its class action. The various undercurrents of the social process of the revolution run counter to each other and inhibit each other, thus intensifying the internal contradictions of the revolution; yet, as a result, they merely accelerate and increase exponentially its violent eruptions.

Thus, the problem that is ostensibly so simple and naked, and purely mechanical—the overthrow of absolutism—requires the completion of a lengthy process, the total turning over of the soil of society: the lowest stratum must be brought to the top, the upper stratum to the bottom; the apparent "order" must be transformed into chaos, and the apparent "anarchic" chaos into a new order. Now, in this process of the social reconfiguration of old Russia, it was not only the January lightning bolt of the first general strike that played an indispensable role; the subsequent great thunderstorm of spring and summer—i.e., the economic strike—did so to an even greater extent. The bitter universal confrontation between wage labor and capital contributed in equal measure to the separating out of the various popular strata as well as of the bourgeois strata, to the class consciousness of the revolutionary proletariat and to that of the liberal and conservative bourgeoisie. And just as urban wage struggles played a role in the formation of the strongly monarchist industrialists' party in Moscow,* so the flames of the immense rural uprising in Livonia led to the rapid liquidation of the renowned aristocratic-agrarian zemstvo liberalism.†

At the same time, however, the period of economic struggles in spring and summer 1905 gave the urban proletariat the opportunity, in the form of active Social Democratic agitation and direction, to retrospectively internalize all of the lessons of the January prologue, and to gain clarity as to the further tasks of the revolution. In connection with this, there was another result of a lasting social character: *a universal raising of the living standards of the proletariat*—economically, socially, and intellectually. The strikes of spring 1905 were, almost without exception, successful. As a sample from the enormous factual material (that for the most part is too voluminous to afford an overview), a few details can be adduced here in relation to several of the most important strikes led by Polish and Lithuanian Social Democrats in Warsaw alone. After a strike lasting four to five weeks (from January 25/26) in the largest factories of the *metal industry* of

---

* The Trade and Industry Party was a counterrevolutionary party representing large-scale capital in the central industrial region. It was founded following the publication of the October Manifesto of 1905 and disintegrated at the end of 1906.

† The zemstvos were a system of rural assemblies in tsarist Russia, formed in 1864 and given limited powers to deal with economic and cultural issues. They tended to be dominated by the landed gentry. Zemstvo liberalism refers to efforts to reform the tsarist system through constitutional means, based on the zemstvo system.

Warsaw (Lilpop, Rau & Loewenstein, Ltd.; Rudzki & Co.; Borman, Schwede & Co.; Handtke, Gerlach & Pulst; Geisler Bros.; Eberherd, Wolski & Co.; Konrad & Jarmuszkiewicz, Ltd.; Weber & Daehn; Gwizdzinski & Co.; Wolanowski Wire Works; Gostynski & Co., Ltd.; Brun & Son; Fraget; Norblin; Werner; Buch; Kenneberg Bros.; Labor; Dittmar Lamp Factory; Serkowski; Weszyzki—twenty-two factories in all), the workers won a nine-hour day, a 25 percent wage increase and various minor concessions. In the largest workshops of the *timber industry* of Warsaw (Karmanski; Damiecki; Gromel; Szerbinski; Treuerowski; Horn; Bevensee; Tworkowski; Daab & Martens—twelve workshops in all), the strikers had won the nine-hour day by February 23; they did not settle for this, however, and insisted upon an eight-hour day, which they also achieved, together with an increase in wages, after a further week of strike action. The entire *bricklaying branch* began a strike for the eight-hour day (in accordance with the goals set by the Social Democrats) on February 27, and won the nine-hour day, an increase in wages for all categories of workers, regular weekly payments of wages, etc., etc., on March 11. The *painters, wainwrights,** *saddlers,* and *smiths* all won the eight-hour day without any decrease in their wages. The telephone exchanges went on strike for ten days and won the eight-hour day and a wage increase of between 10 and 15 percent. After a nine-week strike, the large *linen mill* Hielle & Dietrich, with 10,000 workers, achieved a one-hour reduction in working time and a wage increase of between 5 and 10 percent. And infinite variations upon the same result could be observed in all of the other industrial branches in Warsaw, Łódź, and Sosnowiec.

In Russia proper, the *eight-hour day* was conquered in December 1904 by some categories of oil workers in Baku; in May 1905 by the sugar workers of the Kiev district; in January 1905 in all of the printing works of the city of Samara (where an increase in piecework rates and the abolition of sanctions were simultaneously pushed through); in February in the factory manufacturing medical instruments for the military, in a cabinet-makers' factory, and in the cartridge factory in Petersburg; also in February, an eight-hour shift was introduced in the mines of Vladivostok; in March in the state-owned mechanical workshop for government documents; in April in the smithies of the city of Babruysk; in May by the employees of the Tbilisi municipal electric railroad; also in May, the eight-and-a-half-hour day was introduced in the enormous Morozov cotton weaving mill (night shifts were also eliminated and wages were increased by about 8 percent); in June, the eight-hour day was introduced in some of the oil mills of Petersburg and Moscow; in July, the eight-and-a-half-hour day was established in the smithies of the Petersburg harbor; in November, the eight hour day was achieved in all the private printing works in the city of Orel (time wage rates were simultaneously raised by 20 percent and piecework rates by

---

* *Stellmacher*—wagon-makers; cartwrights; wheelwrights.

100 percent, and a conciliation board was established on which workers and employers were equally represented).

The *nine-hour day* was introduced in all railroad workshops (in February), in numerous of the state-owned military and naval workshops, in most factories in the city of Berdiansk, in all printing works in Poltava and Minsk; the nine-and-a-half-hour day was established in the shipyard, the mechanical workshop and foundry of the city of Nikolaev, and in June it was introduced in many restaurants and cafés in Warsaw after a general strike by waiters (along with a wage increase of between 20 and 40 percent and two weeks' annual leave).

The *ten-hour day* was established in almost all factories in the cities of Łódź, Sosnowiec, Riga, Kaunas,* Tallinn,† Tatu,‡ Minsk, and Kharkiv; in the bakeries of Odessa; in the craft workshops of Chişinău;§ in some hat factories in Petersburg; in the match factories of Kaunas (along with a 10 percent wage increase); in all state naval workshops; and for all longshoremen in the various ports.

In general, wage increases occurred on a lesser scale when compared to the reduction in working time; they were nevertheless significant. Thus, in Warsaw a universal wage increase of 15 percent was established by the municipal factories commission in mid-March 1905; in Ivanovo,¶ the center of the textile industry, wages were increased by between 7 and 15 percent; in Kaunas, the wage increase affected 73 percent of the entire workforce. A fixed *minimum wage* was introduced in a portion of the bakeries in Odessa, in the New Admiralty Shipyard on the Neva, etc.

Admittedly, these concessions were in many cases soon revoked; however, this merely provoked renewed, even more bitter retaliatory struggles, and thus, from its own dynamic, the strike period of spring 1905 became the prologue to an endless series of ever-expanding and interweaving economic struggles that continue to this day. During the periods of ostensible standstill in the revolution, when telegrams bear no sensational news from the Russian battleground to the outside world, and when disappointed Western European readers put down their morning newspapers with the remark that "nothing has happened" in Russia, in reality the great underground work of the mole for the revolution is carried out day by day, hour by hour in the depths of the entire empire. With its rapidly abbreviated methods, the incessant, intensive economic struggle accomplishes the transition of capitalism from the stage of primitive accumulation and of patriarchal, predatory exploitation to a stage that is highly modern and civilized. Today, the situation with regard to actual working time in Russian industry has left behind not only Russian legislation—i.e., the eleven-and-a-half-hour

---

* Kowno in Luxemburg's time.
† Reval in Luxemburg's time.
‡ Dorpat in Luxemburg's time.
§ Kishinev in Luxemburg's time.
¶ Iwanowo-Wosnessensk in Luxemburg's time.

working day stipulated by law—but also the actual conditions obtaining in Germany. The ten-hour day prevails today in most branches of Russian large-scale industry, whereas such a goal is considered unattainable in social legislation in Germany. What is more, the very "industrial constitutionalism" that is so yearned for and so fancied in Germany, and for the sake of which the adherents of opportunistic tactics would keep any sharper breeze from the stagnant waters of the hallowed parliamentarianism, is being born in Russia precisely in the midst of the revolutionary storm—it is being born *of* the revolution, together with political "constitutionalism"! What has in actual fact occurred is not merely a universal raising of living standards—or rather of the cultural level—of the working class. The material standard of living finds no place in the revolution as an enduring level of well-being. Replete with contradictions and contrasts, the revolution simultaneously brings surprising economic victories and the most brutal acts of vengeance on the part of capitalism: today the eight-hour day, tomorrow mass lockouts and naked starvation for hundreds of thousands. The most valuable dimension—since it is an enduring one—of this acutely revolutionary ebb and flow is its *intellectual legacy*: the surging intellectual and cultural growth of the proletariat, which provides an inviolable guarantee of its irresistible further progress in both the economic and the political struggle. This is not all, however. The very relation of the worker to the entrepreneur is being turned upside down; since the general strike in January and the following strikes in 1905, the principle of capitalist "dominion" has been de facto abolished. In the largest factories in all of the most important industrial centers, the organizing device of workers' committees—with which the entrepreneur deals exclusively, and which decide over all conflicts—has taken form as if spontaneously. And finally, a further dimension is the following: The apparently chaotic strikes and the "disorganized" revolutionary action after the January general strike have become the point of departure for a febrile *organizational work*. Looking on from a distance, Dame History laughingly cocks a snook at the faceless bureaucrats grimly keeping watch at the gates to the fortune of the labor unions. In Germany, it is considered that fixed organizations are to be fortified in advance like an impregnable citadel as the absolute precondition for a potential attempt at a potential mass strike; yet in Russia, precisely the reverse obtains: these very organizations are being born out of the mass strike itself! And while the guardians of the German labor unions fear most that these organizations would be smashed to smithereens like precious porcelain in the revolutionary turbulence, the Russian Revolution presents us with an image that is diametrically opposed: Rising out of the whirlwind and the cyclone, out of the flames and the incandescence of the mass strike and the street battles, like Venus from the foam, are labor unions—fresh, young, powerful, and buoyant.

At this point, what is once again merely a small example—but one that is typical for the whole empire—can be provided. At the second congress of Russian labor unions, which took place at the end of February 1906 in Petersburg, the representative of the Petersburg labor unions said the following in his report on the development of labor union organizations in the capital city of the tsars:

> January 22, 1905—the day on which Gapon's union was flushed away, formed a turning point. Workers from the rank and file have learned from their experience of events to appreciate the significance of organization, and that only they themselves can create these organizations. The first labor union in Petersburg—that of the printers—was formed in direct connection with the January movement. The commission that had been selected to draw up the collective bargaining agreement drafted the statutes, and on June 19 the labor union began its existence. At around the same time, the labor union of clerks and accountants was established. Alongside these organizations, which existed virtually openly (i.e., legally), semi-legal and illegal labor unions emerged between January and October 1905. Examples of semi-legal unions were the assistant pharmacists' union and the commercial employees' union. Most notable among the illegal unions was the association of watchmakers, whose first secret meeting was held on April 24. All attempts to convene an open general assembly were foiled by persistent obstruction by the police and the entrepreneurs in the person of the Chamber of Crafts. These setbacks have not prevented the union from existing, however. It held secret general assemblies on June 9 and August 14, in addition to various meetings of the executive committee. The tailors' and seamstresses' union was founded at an assembly held in the forest and attended by seventy tailors in the spring of 1905. After the question of the foundation of the union had been discussed, a commission was elected to draw up the statutes. None of the attempts by the commission to achieve a legal existence for the union have met with success. Its activity is limited to agitation and the recruitment of members in the individual workshops. A similar fate was allotted to the shoemakers' union. In July a secret assembly was convened at nighttime in a forest outside the city. More than one hundred shoemakers gathered; a presentation was given on the significance of labor unions, on their history in Western Europe and their tasks in Russia. It was then decided to found a labor union; a twelve-member commission was elected to draw up the statutes and convene a shoemakers' general assembly. The statutes were drafted, but attempts to have them printed and to convene a general assembly were initially unsuccessful.

Such were the first, difficult beginnings. Then came the October Days, the second general strike, the tsar's manifesto of October 30,* and the brief "constitutional

---

* Confronted by the political general strike in Russia, the tsarist government found itself obliged to make constitutional concessions. In the manifesto of October 30, 1905, civil liberties were guaranteed, the franchise was extended for elections to the Duma, and the latter was given legislative powers.

period."* The workers cast themselves with great zeal into the swell of political freedom, immediately taking the opportunity to set about the work of organization. Alongside the political assemblies, debates, and launches of political associations that occurred on a daily basis, there was an immediate drive to expand labor unions. In October and November, *forty* new labor unions were formed in Petersburg. A "central bureau"—i.e., a labor union combine—was established forthwith, various labor union newspapers began to appear, as did, from November onward, a central organ, *Nyi Soyuz* [The Labor Union]. By and large, that which was reported above in relation to Petersburg also applies to Moscow, Odessa, Kiev, Nikolaev, Saratov, Voronezh, Samara, and Nizhny Novgorod, to all larger cities in Russia, and, to an even greater degree, to Poland. The labor unions in individual towns and cities sought to establish contact with each other, and conferences were held. The end of the "constitutional period" and the return to reaction in December 1905 also put a temporary stop to the open, broad activity of the labor unions, but failed to extinguish their flame. They continue to operate as clandestine organizations and simultaneously engage quite openly in wage struggles. A condition has formed in which a peculiar combination of legality and illegality characterizes labor union life in accordance with the contradictory revolutionary situation. In the midst of struggle, however, the work of organization was carried on and extended with an extreme thoroughness, even painstakingly. The Social Democratic labor unions of Poland and Lithuania, for example, which were represented at the last party convention (in June 1906)† by five delegates from a paying membership of 10,000, are equipped with regular statutes, printed membership cards, adhesive labels, etc. And the same bakers and shoemakers, metalworkers and printers from Warsaw and Łódź that defended the barricades in June 1905, and that stood ready to engage in street fighting upon receiving the watchword from Petersburg in December—these same workers find the time and the devotion to engage in thorough and attentive discussion of their labor union statutes between one mass strike and the next, between prison and lockout, and while under siege. Indeed, on more than one occasion, these barricade militants of yesterday and today have, during assemblies, ruthlessly given their leaders a piece of their mind and threatened to withdraw from the party because the wretched labor union membership cards had not been printed in time—even though this had to be undertaken by clandestine printing presses under relentless police persecution. This zeal and this earnestness remain undiminished to this hour. In the first two weeks of July 1906, for example, fifteen new labor unions were formed in Jekaterinoslaw, six in Kostroma, several in Kiev, Poltava, Smolensk, Cherkasy, and Khmelnytskyi,‡

---

* This refers to the period from the beginning of 1906.
† The Fifth Party Convention of the Social Democracy of the Kingdom of Poland and Lithuania was held illegally in Zakopane in June 1906.
‡ Proskurov in Luxemburg's time.

right down to the smallest provincial backwaters. In the session of July 4, 1906, of the Moscow labor union combine,* it was decided upon receipt of reports from individual labor union delegates

> that the labor unions should discipline their members and restrain them from street rioting because the time is not considered opportune for a mass strike. In the face of possible provocations on the part of the government, they should ensure that the masses do not stream out onto the streets.

Finally, the combine resolved that when a given labor union is on strike, the other labor unions are to refrain from participating in any movements over wages. Most economic struggles were now led by the labor unions.†

Thus the great economic struggle issuing from the January general strike—a struggle that continues to this day—has formed a broad background to the revolution, a background that has given rise again and again to actions by the proletariat that have continuously had an effect upon, and been affected by, political agitation and the external events of the revolution; on occasion, these actions by the proletariat have manifested as singular explosions here and there, whereas at other times they have taken the form of universal, large-scale movements. This, then, was the backdrop to the following successive eruptions: On May 1, 1905, there was an unprecedented absolute general strike in Warsaw to celebrate May Day, and an utterly peaceful mass demonstration that ended in a bloody encounter between the defenseless crowd and soldiers. In June, a mass march in Łódź was dispersed by bands of soldiers, leading to a demonstration by 100,000 workers at the funeral of some of the victims of this clash; here, there

---

* *Gewerkschaftskartells*—labor union cartel or trade union council.

† [Footnote by Luxemburg] The first two weeks of June 1906 alone, the following wage struggles were waged: the printers in Petersburg, Moscow, Odessa, Minsk, Vilna [Vilnius], Saratov, Mogilev, and Tambov fought for the eight-hour day and for Sunday rest; there was a general strike by seafarers in Odessa, Nikolaev, Kerch, Crimea, the Caucasus, on the Volga fleet, in Kronstadt, Warsaw, and Płock for the recognition of the labor union and for the release of the workers' delegates that had been arrested; there were wage struggles by the longshoremen in Saratov, Nikolaev, Tsaritsyn [Volgograd], Arkhangelsk, Nizhny Novgorod, and Rybinsk. There were strikes by bakers in Kiev, Arkhangelsk, Białystok, Vilna [Vilnius], Odessa, Kharkiv, Brest-Litovsk [Brest], Radom, and Tiflis [Tbilisi], and by agricultural workers in the districts of Verkhnodniprovsk, Borisov [Barysaw], and Simferopol, in the governorates of Podolsk, Tula, Kursk, in the districts of Kozlov [Michurinsk], Lypovets, in Finland, in the governorate of Kiev, and in the district of Yelisavetgrad [Kropyvnytskyi]. During this period, there were strikes in *almost all branches of industry* simultaneously in a number of cities, among them Saratov, Arkhangelsk, Kerch, and Kremenchuk. In Bakhmut, there was a general strike by the colliers of the entire district. In other cities, the wages movement took hold of *all* branches of industry *successively* within the above-mentioned two-week period—this was the case in Kiev, Petersburg, Warsaw, Moscow, and the entire rayon of Ivanovo-Voznesensk. The aim of the strikes in all cases was the reduction of the working day, the establishment of Sunday rest, and the satisfaction of wage demands. *The majority of strikes ended in victory.* It is emphasized in local reports that these strikes encompassed strata of the working class that had not previously participated in a wages movement.

was a renewed encounter with the army, ultimately provoking a general strike that segued into the first struggle on the barricades on June 23, 24, and 25. Also in June, the first great revolt by the sailors of the Black Sea Fleet was triggered in the harbor of Odessa by a minor incident on board the battleship *Potemkin*;* this mutiny immediately provoked reactions in Odessa and Nikolaev in the form of enormous mass strikes. Further echoes were to follow: the mass strike and sailors' revolts in Kronstadt,† Liepāja,‡ and Vladivostok.§

In the month of October came Petersburg's great experiment with the introduction of the eight-hour day. The council of workers' delegates resolved to push through the eight-hour day via the revolutionary route. This was to occur as follows: On the appointed day, all workers in Petersburg were to declare to their employers that they were not willing to work longer than eight hours per day, and were to vacate their workplaces at the corresponding hour. This idea stimulated vigorous agitation, and it was enthusiastically received and carried out by the proletariat, which did not recoil from the greatest sacrifices. Thus, the eight-hour day entailed an enormous loss of wages for the textile workers, who had previously worked an eleven-hour day on piecework rates; this they were willing to accept, however. *Within one week, the eight-hour day prevailed in all the factories and workshops of Petersburg*, and the joy of the workforce knew no bounds. Soon, however, the initially dumbfounded entrepreneurs prepared to mount resistance: Factory closures were threatened across the board. A portion of the workers relented and engaged in negotiations, achieving the ten-hour day in some cases, the nine-hour day in others. Nevertheless, the resolve of the elite of the proletariat of Petersburg—the workers of the large state-owned metalworks—remained unshaken, and a lockout ensued, leaving 45,000 to 50,000 workers out on the street. Through this turn of events, the movement for the eight-hour day flowed into the general mass strike of December, which was to a great extent undermined by the great lockout.

In the meantime, however, there came about a second colossal, general mass strike in the entire tsarist empire as a response to Bulygin's Duma project;¶ this

---

* On June 27, 1905, a sailors' mutiny erupted on the Russian battleship *Potemkin*; this represented the first revolutionary mass action within the tsarist armed forces.

† On November 8 and 9, 1905, there was a revolt by sailors and soldiers in Kronstadt. The uprising was crushed, and 1,500 sailors and several hundred soldiers were sentenced to death by a military tribunal. A solidarity strike by the workers of Petersburg rescued those convicted from the firing squad.

‡ On July 15, 1905, a sailors' mutiny erupted in Liepāja. Since it was unorganized and received no support, it suffered defeat.

§ November 12 and 13, 1905, a sailors' revolt broke out in Vladivostok; it was crushed by the tsar's military command.

¶ On August 19, 1905, the tsarist government had issued a law drafted by the Interior Minister, Alexander Bulygin, for elections to an Imperial Duma. According to the law, the Duma was intended merely as an advisory organ, and elections were to be carried out following the estates principle and in accordance with a property census that had been stipulated.

time, the rallying call was issued by the railroad workers. This second major revolutionary action by the proletariat already bore an essentially different character from that of the first one in January. The element of political consciousness now played a much larger role. Here too, the initial reason for the outbreak of the mass strike was admittedly a subordinate and ostensibly incidental one—namely, the conflict of the railroad workers with management over the pension fund. Yet the subsequent general uprising by the industrial proletariat was sustained by clear political thinking. The prologue of the January strike was a rogation procession to the tsar to ask for political freedom; the slogan of the October strike was "Down with the constitutional farce of tsarism!" And thanks to the immediate success of the general strike, and the tsar's manifesto of October 30, the movement did not recede back in on itself, as was the case in January, so as to be able to resume the incipient economic class struggle; instead it flowed outward into the ardent exercise of freshly conquered political freedom. Demonstrations, assemblies, a young press, public discussions, all culminating in bloody massacres, followed in turn by new mass strikes and demonstrations—such was the turbulent scenario afforded by the November and December days. In November, the first demonstrative mass strike was staged in response to an appeal by the Social Democrats as a protest rally against the bloody deeds and the imposition of the state of siege in Livonia and Poland. The ferment that followed the brief constitutional dream and the cruel awakening finally led in December to the outbreak of the third general mass strike throughout the entire tsarist empire. On this occasion, the strike took a completely different course from those taken by the previous ones, and it also had a completely different outcome. Political action did not switch to economic action, as in January; nor did it win the rapid victory that had been achieved in October. The tsarist camarilla no longer pursued its experiments with real political freedom, and the entire range of revolutionary action thus came up against the rigid wall of the material* power of absolutism for the first time. Through the logical internal development of the events as they proceeded, the mass strike this time turned into an open uprising, an armed struggle on the barricades and in the streets in Moscow. Marking the high point of the upward trend in political action and the mass strike movement, the December days in Moscow concluded the first work-intensive year of the revolution.

At the same time, the Moscow events provide a sample image, on the micro level, of the logical development and the future of the revolutionary movement as a whole: They do so through their inevitable conclusion in a general, open uprising that for its part can only come about through the schooling of a series of preparatory, partial revolts that as such are provisionally concluded through partial, external "defeats" and might accordingly appear as "premature" if each is regarded individually.

---

* The 1906 first edition has "physical" in place of "material."

The year 1906 brought the elections to the Duma and the Duma episode. Guided by a powerful revolutionary instinct and a clear appraisal of the situation, the proletariat boycotted the entire tsarist constitutional farce, and, for a few months, liberalism came to the fore on the political stage once more. It seems that the situation of 1904 has returned: A period of talking replaces action, and the proletariat retreats into the shadows for a period, in order to devote itself all the more assiduously to the labor union struggle and the work of organization. The mass strikes fall silent, while rattling rockets of liberal rhetoric are fired off on a daily basis. Finally, the iron curtain suddenly comes clattering down, the actors are driven apart, and nothing remains of the liberal rockets but smoke and vapor. An attempt by the Central Committee of the Russian Social Democrats to call a fourth mass strike throughout Russia as a demonstration for the Duma and for the reopening of the period of liberal speechmaking falls flat. The role of the political mass strike alone is exhausted, and yet the time is not ripe for a transition of the mass strike into a general popular uprising and street battle. The liberal episode is over, but the proletarian one has not yet recommenced. The stage remains temporarily empty.

IV.

In the foregoing, we have attempted to sketch the history of the mass strike in Russia in a few scarce strokes. A fleeting glance at this history already reveals a picture that in none of its features resembles that usually formed by the discussion of the mass strike in Germany. Instead of the rigid and hollow schema of a barren political "action" prudently executed according to plan upon the resolution of the highest authorities, we see a piece of living life, of flesh and blood, that can by no means be excised from the greater frame of the revolution, and that is bound through a thousand veins to the entire organic whole of the revolution.

The mass strike, as it manifests in the Russian Revolution, is a phenomenon so mutable that it mirrors within itself all phases of the political and economic struggle, and all stages and moments of the revolution. Its applicability, its effectiveness, and the elements of its emergence are all continually altering. It suddenly opens up new, broad perspectives for the revolution, just when the latter appeared to have gotten stuck at a choke point, and yet it fails at the very point where it is reckoned to be utterly reliable. Sometimes it flows like a broad swell, surging over the entire empire; at other times it divides into a gigantic network of narrow streams; sometimes it bubbles forth from under the ground like a fresh spring; at other times it seeps away into the ground, petering out entirely. Political and economic strikes, mass strikes and partial strikes, demonstration strikes and militant strikes,* general strikes in individual branches

---

* *Kampfstreiks*—strikes as a form of struggle.

and general strikes in individual cities, peaceful wage struggles and street battles and struggles on the barricades—all these phenomena crisscross each other, run parallel to each other, intersect with each other, flow into each other; this is a perpetually moving, fluctuating sea of manifestations. And the law of motion of these phenomena becomes evident: It lies neither in the mass strike itself, nor in the latter's technical peculiarities, but rather in the political and social relation of forces within the revolution. The mass strike is merely the form taken by revolutionary struggle, and each shift in the relation between the forces in struggle, each alteration in the development of the party and the division into classes, each displacement in the position taken by the counterrevolution—all these immediately influence strike action in a thousand invisible and scarcely verifiable ways. All the while, however, strike action itself barely stops for even an instant. It merely alters its forms, its dimensions, its effect. It is the living pulse of the revolution and simultaneously its most powerful driver. In a word, the mass strike, as it presents itself to us in the Russian Revolution, is not an ingenious means that has been devised for the purpose of achieving a more powerful effect of proletarian struggle; it is rather *the mode of motion of the proletarian mass, the form of manifestation of proletarian struggle within the revolution.*

Several general aspects can thus be derived for the evaluation of the problem of the mass strike:

(1) It is completely perverse to conceive of the mass strike as an act, an individual action. The mass strike is rather the designation, the collective concept for a whole period of class struggle spanning several years or even decades. Of all the countless mass strikes of all different kinds that have occurred in Russia over the last four years, the schema of the mass strike as a purely political, brief individual action that is induced and executed according to a deliberate plan merely fits one variety, and a subordinate one at that: the strike as mere demonstration. In Russia over the entire course of the five-year period, there have only been a handful of demonstration strikes, and it should be noted that these have usually been restricted to individual cities. These strikes were the following: the annual May Day general strike in Warsaw and Łódź (in Russia proper, May Day has not yet been celebrated as a nonworking day to any significant extent); the mass strike in Warsaw on September 11, 1905, that was called as a mourning ceremony in honor of the executed Marcin Kasprzak; the mass strike of November 1905 in Petersburg that was called as a protest rally against the imposition of a state of siege in Poland and Livonia; the mass strikes of January 22, 1906, in Warsaw, Łódź, Częstochowa, and the coal basin of Dąbrowa,* and, to a lesser extent, in some Russian cities, as a commemoration of the first anniversary of the bloodbath in Petersburg; the general strike of July 1906 in Tbilisi, *called* as a rally in solidarity with the soldiers condemned by military tribunal

---

* Now Dąbrowa Górnicza.

in connection with the uprisings within the armed forces; and finally, the mass strike called for the same reason in September of the same year during the hearings of the court-martial in Reval. All other large-scale and partial mass strikes and general strikes were not demonstration strikes, but militant strikes; as such, they mostly occurred spontaneously, and in all cases their causes were specific, local, and incidental—they arose without a deliberate plan, and grew with elemental power into great movements. These movements did not subsequently engage in an "orderly retreat"; instead they either transformed themselves into economic struggle or into street battles, or they collapsed of themselves.

Within this general picture, the purely political demonstrations play an utterly subordinate role—they are single tiny dots in an enormous expanse. If this picture is regarded from a temporal point of view, the following characteristic can be observed: Demonstration strikes, which differ from militant strikes in that they exhibit the greatest degree of party discipline, conscious leadership, and political thought, and which thus ought—according to the usual schema— to manifest as the highest and most mature form of the mass strike, play in truth the biggest role in the *beginnings* of the movement. Hence, for example, the absolute cessation of work on May 1, 1905, in Warsaw represented an event of great bearing, as it was the first time that such a resolution by the Social Democrats was executed so astonishingly. Likewise, the sympathy strike in November of the same year in Petersburg made a great impression as the first experiment with conscious, planned mass action in Russia. Equally, the "trial mass strike" by Hamburg comrades on January 17, 1906,* would come to play a salient role in the history of the future German mass strike as the first, fresh assay with this controversial weapon—an assay that was extremely successful and that spoke so convincingly of the fighting mood and appetite for struggle of the workforce in Hamburg. And, just as surely will the period of mass strikes in Germany, once it has begun in earnest, lead of itself to a truly universal cessation of work on May 1. May Day might naturally come to be celebrated as the first great demonstration in the era of mass struggles. In this sense the "lame horse," as May Day was described at the labor unions' congress in Cologne,† has a great future, and an important role in the proletarian class struggle in Germany, ahead of it. And yet, the significance of such demonstrations rapidly declines with the development of earnest revolutionary struggles. Precisely those moments that objectively make it possible for demonstration strikes to take place according to a preconceived plan when parties give the word—i.e., the growth in the political

---

* In Hamburg, 80,000 workers had stopped work in the afternoon of January 17, 1906, in order to take part in assemblies and street demonstrations in protest against the restriction of suffrage for elections to the Hamburg State Parliament.

† At the Fifth Congress of the Trade Unions of Germany, held from May 22 to 27, 1905, in Cologne, the discussion of May Day as a day of struggle for the working class had been broken off. The congress proceeded with the agenda without allowing a vote on the motions that had been proposed.

consciousness and education of the proletariat—render this type of mass strike impossible; the proletariat in Russia today—to be more precise, the most capable vanguard of the masses—will hear nothing of demonstration strikes; the workers are in no mood for playing games, and will now consider nothing other than struggle in earnest, with all its consequences. And if the demonstrative element still played a great role—not in a form that was intentional, but rather in one that was instinctive, spontaneous—in the first great mass strike in January 1905, conversely the attempt of the Central Committee of the Russian Social Democratic Party to call a mass strike in August as a rally in favor of the dissolved Duma failed due to the positive disinclination of the educated proletariat to engage in tame half actions and mere demonstrations.

(2) If, as opposed to the demonstrative strike (a merely subordinate type), we consider instead the militant strike, such as the latter represents the actual bearer of proletarian action in Russia today, it is clear, furthermore, that the economic and the political moments within this latter type of strike are inseparable from one another. Here, too, reality deviates far from the theoretical schema, and the pedantic conception according to which the purely political strike is logically derived from the labor union general strike as the most mature and highest stage, but is simultaneously clearly demarcated from the latter, has been thoroughly refuted by the experience of the Russian Revolution. This is not merely manifested historically, by the fact that the mass strikes, from the first great wage struggle of the Petersburg textile workers in 1896 to 1897 right up to the last great mass strike in December 1905, have passed over quite indiscernibly from economic into political strikes, so that it is virtually impossible to draw a boundary between the two. It is also the case that each individual instance of these great mass strikes repeats on a micro level, so to speak, the universal history of Russian mass strikes and begins with a purely economic, or in any case partial, labor union struggle, only then to traverse the successive stages that culminate in the political rally. The great cyclone of mass strikes in southern Russia in 1902 to 1903 had its origins, as we have seen, in the following: in a conflict that flared up in Baku as a consequence of the persecution of the unemployed; in wage differentials in the railroad workshops in Rostov-on-Don; in a struggle by commercial employees for the reduction of working time in Tbilisi; and in a wage struggle in a single small factory in Odessa. The mass strike of January 1905 developed out of the internal conflict in the Putilov Works; the October strike proceeded from the struggle of railroad workers over pension funds; and, finally, the December strike ensued from the struggle of postal and telegraph employees over the right of association. The progress of the movement as a whole does not express itself in the fact that the initial, economic stage no longer obtains, but rather in the velocity with which the stages culminating in the political rally are traversed, and in the extremity of the position attained by the mass strike.

However, the movement as a whole does not only proceed in a direction leading from economic to political struggle—it also traces the opposite route. Having attained a political zenith, each of the great political mass actions switches into a whole medley of economic strikes. And this applies not only to every single one of the great mass strikes, but also to the revolution as a whole. It is not merely that the economic struggle fails to recede with the propagation, clarification, and strengthening of the political struggle; in fact, for its part, the former spreads, becomes increasingly organized and fortified, in step with the political struggle. There is a completely reciprocal interaction between political and economic struggle.

Each fresh iteration and new victory of political struggle transforms itself into a powerful impetus for economic struggle by broadening the latter's external scope at the same time as it boosts the internal drive of the workers to improve their situation and augments their militancy. After each frothing wave of political action, a fecund deposit remains, from which new stems of economic struggle immediately shoot up by the thousand. And vice versa. The unremitting economic state of war between workers and capital ensures that the former's energy for the struggle is maintained at a high level during any political pauses—it forms the ever-replenished reservoir of proletarian class energy, so to speak, from which the political struggle continually draws its power anew. Simultaneously, this state of war leads the proletariat, in its subversive economic underground activity, to individual acute conflicts that occur first in one place and then in another; it is these conflicts, in turn, that cause the unexpected eruption of large-scale political confrontations.

In a word, economic struggle is that which permits a transmission from one political conjuncture to the next, and political struggle is the periodic fertilization of the soil for economic struggle. Cause and effect here continually change places, and thus the economic moment and the political one in the period of the mass strike are far from cleaving apart neatly, let alone standing in a relation of mutual exclusion, as the pedantic schema would have it; on the contrary, they merely form two interwoven sides of proletarian class struggle in Russia. And *their unity* is precisely the mass strike. When fantasist theory performs an artificial logical dissection of the mass strike in order to arrive at "the pure political strike," such an operation, like all others of its kind, fails to identify the phenomenon in its living essence, and instead merely kills it off.

(3) Finally, the processes in Russia demonstrate to us that the mass strike is inseparable from the revolution. The history of Russian mass strikes is the history of the Russian Revolution. Now, when the proponents of our German opportunism hear mention of "revolution," they immediately think of bloodshed, street battles, gunpowder, and shot, and their logical reasoning runs as follows: The mass strike leads inevitably to revolution, ergo we cannot engage in the mass strike. Indeed, we can observe in Russia that virtually every mass

strike results in an encounter with the armed guardians of the tsarist order; in this respect, so-called political strikes are no different from the larger of the economic struggles. Yet revolution is something other, something more than bloodletting. In contrast to the conception formed from the perspective of the police, which views the revolution exclusively in terms of street disturbances and rioting—i.e., in terms of "disorder"—the conception of scientific socialism identifies in the revolution above all a profound internal transformation in social relations between classes. And from this standpoint, there obtains a further interconnection between revolution and the mass strike in Russia that is utterly different from the one established by the trivial observation that the mass strike usually ends in bloodshed.

We have seen above the internal mechanism of the Russian mass strike, a mechanism based upon the continuous reciprocal interaction between political and economic struggle. Yet precisely this reciprocal interaction is conditioned by the revolutionary period. It is only in the sultry air of the revolutionary period that every partial, minor conflict between labor and capital has the potential to develop into the catalyst for a general explosion. In Germany, the most ferocious and brutal clashes between workers and entrepreneurs occur on an annual or even a daily basis without the struggle in question spreading beyond the confines of the respective individual branch, city, or even factory. Disciplinary measures such as those meted out against organized workers in Petersburg, unemployment similar to that in Baku, wages conflicts like those in Odessa, struggles over the right of association like those in Moscow—occurrences such as these are the order of the day in Germany. In the latter context, however, not a single of these instances turns into a collective action by the class. And even when they do grow into individual mass strikes with an unmistakably political complexion, still they fail to unleash a general storm. A striking example is provided by the general strike by the Dutch railroad workers,* which, despite enjoying the warmest sympathy, bled to death amid the utter motionlessness of the proletariat in that country.

And, conversely, it is only in the revolutionary period—when the social foundations and the walls of class society have been loosened and are constantly being displaced—that each political class action by the proletariat has the potential to wrench entire, previously unaffected strata of the working class out of their torpor; this naturally manifests in a stormy economic struggle. The worker who has been roused by the electric shock of a political action initially engages with his immediate situation and mounts resistance against his relation of economic slavery; the stormy gesture of political struggle suddenly causes him to feel with

---

* The general strike by Dutch railroad workers began on April 6, 1903. It was called in opposition to a bill proposed by the government that made provisions for lengthy prison sentences for strikers. On April 10, 1903, the labor union defense committee resolved to break off the strike after the bill had been passed by parliament.

unforeseen intensity the weight and the pressure of his economic fetters. And while, for example, the most ferocious political struggle in Germany, such as the electoral campaign or the parliamentary struggle over customs tariffs, scarcely exerts a perceptible and direct influence on the course and intensity of the wage struggles being conducted in the country at the same time, each political action by the proletariat in Russia immediately expresses itself in the broadening and deepening of the planes on which economic struggle occurs.

It is thus revolution that generates in the first place the social conditions in which the process is made possible whereby the economic struggle immediately turns into political struggle and vice versa, a process that finds expression in the mass strike. And, if the vulgar schema perceives the interconnection between mass strike and revolution only in the bloody street encounters that mark the end of mass strikes, a somewhat deeper look into the Russian events reveals a *diametrically opposed* interconnection: In reality, it is not the mass strike that produces the revolution, but the revolution that produces the mass strike.

(4) In order to gain insight into the question of conscious leadership of the mass strike and the taking of the initiative in this regard, it suffices to summarize the foregoing. If the mass strike does not imply a single act, but rather a whole period of class struggle, and if this period is identical to a period of revolution, then it is evident that the mass strike cannot be conjured up out of sheer volition, even if the resolution to call the strike issues from the highest authority within the most powerful Social Democratic party. As long as Social Democracy is not in a position to stage and call off revolutions at its own discretion, the greatest enthusiasm and impatience on the part of the Social Democratic troops will not be sufficient to summon into life an actual period of mass strikes as a living, powerful popular movement. It is perhaps possible to stage a one-off, brief demonstration, such as the Swedish mass strike,* the recent Austrian mass strikes,† or the Hamburg mass strike of January 17. Yet the difference between these demonstrations and a real period of revolutionary mass strikes is as great as that between the famous demonstrations by the fleet in foreign ports during periods of tension in diplomatic relations and an actual naval war.‡ A mass

---

* In Sweden, a political mass strike was conducted from May 15 to 17, 1902, based on a resolution passed by the Social Democratic Party; the strike was intended to reinforce the demand for a reform of the electoral law. The strike, in which approximately 116,000 workers participated, was broken off without result after both chambers of the Riksdag (the Swedish parliament) had passed a resolution calling on the government to propose a new electoral bill by 1904.

† In Austria-Hungary between October and December 1905, mass strikes and mass demonstrations were staged in favor of universal suffrage after a resolution by the Social Democratic Party of Austria.

‡ In the summer of 1898, during the Spanish-American War, a German naval fleet appeared off Manila in order to press the claim of German naval and colonial power to as many Spanish colonial possessions in the Pacific and Far East as could be gained. On March 31, 1905, Wilhelm II landed in the Moroccan port city of Tangiers in order to forestall French hegemony in Morocco and thus to bring about a situation that favored Germany.

strike born purely of discipline and enthusiasm will at best play a role as an episode, a mere symptom of the fighting mood of the workforce, only for conditions to return back to the normal, everyday routine thereafter. Of course, mass strikes do not fall from the sky during the revolution either. They must be brought about by workers one way or another. The decision and the resolve of the workforce also play a role here, and although it naturally falls to the organized and most enlightened, Social Democratic core of the proletariat to take the initiative and subsequently to lead such strikes, this initiative and this leadership enjoy a certain leeway only in relation to individual actions or strikes when the revolutionary period has already commenced, and mostly within the boundaries of a single city, at that. Thus, as we have seen, Social Democratic parties have on various occasions directly issued the call for mass strikes: in Baku, Warsaw, Łódź, and Petersburg, for example. Similar initiatives are far less successful when applied to general movements of the proletariat as a whole. Furthermore, very determinate restrictions obtain with regard to any initiative to launch a mass strike and to assume conscious leadership of such a movement. Precisely during the revolution, it is extremely difficult for any leading organ of the proletarian movement to anticipate and to determine which cause and which moments can—and *cannot*—lead to explosions. Here, too, initiative and leadership consist not in commanding out of sheer volition, but in adapting as skillfully as possible to the situation and developing the keenest sense for the disposition of the masses. As we have seen, the element of spontaneity has played a great role in all Russian mass strikes without exception, whether as a driving or inhibiting factor. This does not stem from the fact that Social Democracy is still young or weak in Russia, but rather from the circumstance that, as is the case with every individual act within the struggle, so many inestimable moments—economic, political, and social; general and local; material and psychic—are effective, that no single act can be determined or handled as if it were an exercise in arithmetic. Even though the proletariat, with the Social Democratic Party in the vanguard, plays a leading role in the revolution, the latter is no maneuver on open terrain, but rather a struggle in the midst of the incessant cracking, crumbling, and shifting of all the foundations of society. In short, the element of spontaneity plays such a predominant role in the mass strike in Russia not because the Russian proletariat is "unschooled," but because revolutions heed no schoolmaster.

On the other hand, we see in Russia that the same revolution that renders it so difficult for the Social Democratic Party to take command over the mass strike—mischievously knocking the conductor's baton out of the hand of the Social Democratic Party one moment and thrusting it back into its hand the next—nevertheless also resolves by itself all those difficulties of the mass strike that are deemed in the German discussion to be the main concerns of "leadership": the questions of "provisioning" and "financing" the strike, and that of the "sacrifices" to be made. Of course, the revolution by no means resolves these problems in the way that they are settled *on paper* during a hushed, confidential colloquy between the leaderships of the highest authorities of the workers' movement. The "settling" of all these questions consists in the revolution bringing the popular masses onto the stage in such enormous numbers that any attempt to calculate and regulate the costs incurred by their movement—in the same way that the costs of civil proceedings are determined in advance, for example—would represent an utterly hopeless endeavor. It is blindingly obvious that the leading organizations in Russia have also made every effort to support the direct victims of struggle. Thus, for example, the courageous victims of the colossal lockout in Petersburg that ensued from the campaign for an eight-hour working day were supported over a period of several weeks. Yet all such measures are a mere drop in the ocean compared to the enormous balance sheet of the revolution. At the point at which a real period of mass strikes begins in earnest, all "cost assessments" are transformed into an enterprise that consists in draining the ocean with a drinking glass. For this ocean is one of terrible privations and suffering—it is the price paid by the proletarian masses in order to achieve any revolution. And the solution that a revolutionary period provides to this seemingly insurmountable difficulty consists in the enormous surge in mass idealism that such a period unleashes, such that the masses become impervious to the most acute hardships. Neither revolution nor mass strike would be feasible with the psychology of the labor unionist—i.e., with the mindset of the man who will only participate in a cessation of work on May Day on condition that he is given prior assurances that he will receive a precisely determined level of support in the event that disciplinary action is taken against him. In the storm of the revolutionary period, however, the proletarian is transformed from the provident family man who anxiously enlists support into a "revolutionary romanticist" for whom material well-being—and even the highest good, namely life itself—possesses less value when compared with the ideals of struggle.

Yet if leadership of the mass strike—both in the sense of exercising command over its origin, and in that of computing its costs and providing finances to cover these—is a matter that pertains to the revolutionary period itself, direction of the mass strike in a completely different sense falls instead to Social Democracy and its leading organs. Rather than racking their brains over the technical side of mass strikes, over their mechanism, Social Democrats are called upon to assume *political* leadership, even in the midst of the revolutionary period. To formulate the slogans of the struggle and to orient it, to configure the *tactics* of political struggle such that in every phase and at every moment within the conflict, the existing proletarian power that has already been unleashed and activated can be realized and can find expression in the combative stance of the party, and such that the tactics of the Social Democrats, in terms of their resolution and acuteness, never fall *beneath* the level demanded by the actual balance of forces, but rather forge ahead of this relation—this forms the most important task of "leadership" in the period of mass strikes. And, to a certain extent, such leadership turns of itself into technical direction. A Social Democratic tactic that is consistent, resolute, and progressive elicits feelings of security, self-confidence, and combativeness in the masses; by contrast, a wavering, feeble tactic—a tactic based on an underestimation of the proletariat—has a debilitating and disconcerting effect on the masses. In the former case, mass strikes erupt "of themselves" and always at an "opportune" moment; in the latter case, direct calls by the leadership for a mass strike occasionally fall flat. And the Russian Revolution provides eloquent examples of both instances.

V.

The question that now arises is that of the extent to which the lessons that can be drawn from Russian mass strikes are applicable to Germany. Completely different social and political relations obtain in Germany and Russia, and likewise there is a wide divergence between the history and status of the respective workers' movements in the two countries. At first sight, it might appear that the internal laws of mass strikes in Russia as registered above are merely the product of specifically Russian relations that do not hold in the case of the German proletariat. There exists the tightest of internal connections between the political and economic struggles in the Russian Revolution; their unity is given expression in the period of mass strikes. But is this not simply a consequence of Russian absolutism? In a state in which all forms and expressions of the workers' movement are prohibited, where the simplest strike is a political crime, every economic struggle must logically turn into a political one.

Moreover, if the converse is true—namely, that the very first outbreak of political revolution entailed a universal settling of accounts between the Russian working class and the entrepreneurial class—this is, in turn, the simple consequence of the circumstance that the Russian worker had the lowest standard of living up to that point and had never engaged in any kind of regular economic struggle over the improvement of his condition. To a certain extent, the proletariat in Russia had first to work its way out of the harshest of conditions, and it is no wonder that it took to the task with youthful audacity as soon as the revolution had introduced the first breath of fresh air into the asphyxiating atmosphere of absolutism. And finally, the stormy revolutionary course of the Russian mass strikes, as well as their predominantly spontaneous, elemental character, can be explained, on the one hand, as following from the political backwardness of Russia and the necessity of first overthrowing Oriental despotism,* and on the

---

* It was common among European Marxists of the time (including Russian ones) to refer to tsarist absolutism as a form of "Oriental despotism," in part due to the alleged influence of the Mongol invasion and occupation of large parts of southern Russia from the thirteenth century onward.

other, as a consequence of the lack of organization and schooling of the Russian proletariat. In a country in which the working class has at its disposal thirty years of experience in political life, a 3-million-strong Social Democratic Party, and an elite troop consisting of 1.25 million unionized workers, political struggle and mass strikes cannot possibly have the stormy and elemental character that they do in a semi-barbarian state taking the first leap out of the medieval era and into the modern, bourgeois order. Such is the generally accepted conception among those who would infer the degree of maturity of the social relations of a given country from the wording of its drafted legislation.

Let us examine these questions in sequence. First of all, in terms of historical dating, it is perverse to claim that economic struggle in Russia only began with the outbreak of the revolution. In actual fact, strikes and wage struggles had increasingly been the order of the day in Russia proper since the beginning of the 1890s, and in Russian Poland* even since the end of the 1880s; these movements ultimately achieved de facto civil rights. Although brutal police repression often ensued from such struggles, the latter were nonetheless a daily phenomenon. In Warsaw and Łódź, for example, a significant general strike fund was already in existence in 1891, and the enthusiasm for labor unions in these years even generated the "economic" illusions that would be so rampant a few years later in Petersburg and the rest of Russia.†

Likewise, there is much exaggeration in the notion that proletarians throughout the tsarist empire had without exception the living standards of

---

* Russian Poland (Congress Poland) refers to the Kingdom of Poland, a state established in 1815 by the Vienna Conference. Existing until 1915, the Kingdom of Poland was connected by personal union with Russia and subjected to tsarist rule.

† [Footnote by Luxemburg] Comrade [Henriette] Roland-Holst thus commits a factual error when she states the following in the prologue to the Russian edition of her book on the mass strike: "The proletariat (in Russia—R.L.) had become acquainted with the mass strike virtually since the emergence of large-scale industry for the simple reason that partial strikes had proven impossible under the political repression of absolutism" (*Neue Zeit*, 1906, No. 33). The reverse was in fact true. Thus the rapporteur of the Saint Petersburg Labor Union Combine made the following declaration at the beginning of his report to the Second Conference of Russian Labor Unions in February 1906: "In view of the composition of this conference, I do not need to emphasize that our labor union movement has its origins neither in the 'liberal' period of Prince Svyatopolk-Mirsky (in 1904—R.L.), nor in the events of January 22, as is asserted by some; the labor union movement has far deeper roots, and is inseparably bound up with the entire past history of our workers' movement. Our labor unions are merely new organizational forms for the purpose of directing the economic struggle that the Russian proletariat has waged for decades. Without going too far back in history, it can be said that the economic struggle of the workers of Saint Petersburg has taken on more or less organized forms since the memorable strike of 1896–97. Favorably combined with the leadership of the political struggle, the leadership of this struggle becomes the affair of the Social Democratic organization formerly known as the Saint Petersburg League of Struggle for the Emancipation of the Working Class, which transformed itself into the Saint Petersburg Committee of the Russian Social Democratic Workers' Party after its conference in March 1898. A complex system of factory, district, and suburban organizations was created; these represented innumerable threads that connected the headquarters to the masses of workers, allowing it to react to all of the needs of the working class by producing leaflets. This established the possibility of supporting and leading strikes.

paupers before the revolution. The stratum of workers in large-scale industry in the urban centers that was most actively and ardently engaged in the economic as well as the political struggle had a material standard of living that was scarcely beneath that of the corresponding layer of the German proletariat, and, in some occupations, the same level of wages was to be found in Russia as in Germany—with wages in Russia in some instances even outstripping those of workers in corresponding industries in Germany. Similarly, there was scarcely a significant difference between the two countries with regard to working time in large-scale industrial enterprises. Thus, notions of a supposed material and cultural helotry on the part of the Russian working class are pure fiction. Given a little reflection, the mere fact of the revolution itself—and the prominent role played by the proletariat within it—ought to suffice to dispel such conceptions. With paupers, no revolutions of such political maturity and lucidity are to be made, and the industrial worker at the forefront of the struggle in Petersburg, Warsaw, Moscow, or Odessa is far closer to his Western European counterpart in cultural and intellectual terms than is reckoned by those who regard bourgeois parliamentarianism and standard labor union practice as the only—and indispensable—cultural schooling for the proletariat. The modern large-scale capitalist development of Russia and the intellectual influence exerted over a decade and a half by Social Democracy—during which time it has galvanized and directed economic struggle—have both had a significant cultural effect on the proletariat, even without the external guarantees provided by the bourgeois legal order.

The contrast becomes even less marked if we look a little more closely at the actual standard of living of the *German* working class. In Russia, the great political mass strikes have from the first instant roused the broadest strata of the proletariat and hurled them into febrile economic struggle. In Germany, on the other hand, are there not entire dark zones within the topography of the working class—areas until now scarcely penetrated by the warming light of the labor unions—entire, broad strata of workers that have until now made no attempt at all, or only unsuccessful attempts, to raise themselves up out of social helotry by means of ordinary wage struggles? Take, for example, the destitution of *the miners*. Even within the peaceful, leisurely working routine in Germany, amid the cool atmosphere of its parliamentary monotony—just as in other countries, even in that labor union El Dorado, England—the wage struggle of the miners manifests as virtually nothing other than tremendous eruptions, as mass strikes of a typical, elemental character. This simply demonstrates that the antagonism between capital and labor here is too acute and too enormous for it to allow itself to be dissipated through peaceful, scheduled, partial labor union struggles. However, this destitution of the miners, in all its volatility, which forms a most vehement cyclone even in "normal" times, ought to erupt immediately and inevitably into a tremendous economic and social struggle in

Germany with every large-scale political mass action on the part of the working class, with every larger jolt that disturbs the momentary equilibrium of everyday social life. Consider further the misery of the *textile workers*. In this case, too, the bitter outbreaks of the wage struggle that sweeps through Vogtland every few years—outbreaks that for the most part end without result—offer only a faint intimation of the vehemence with which the large, agglomerated mass of the helots of cartelized textile capital ought to explode during a political convulsion, during a powerful and audacious mass action on the part of the German proletariat. Take the further examples of the destitution of *the workers of the putting-out system*, *the assembly workers*, or *the electricity workers*—all these are akin to the eye of the storm, in which it is all the more certain that tremendous economic struggles will erupt with every political turbulence in Germany; the less frequently the proletariat in these branches takes up the struggle in quiet times, the more unsuccessfully it struggles each time, and the more brutally it is compelled by capital to return to the yoke of slavery, gnashing its teeth all the while.

Now, however, entire broad categories of the proletariat come into consideration that, in the "normal" course of events, remain altogether excluded from any possibility of engaging in a calm economic struggle to improve their situation, and that are barred from any exercise of the right of association. The example par excellence to be cited here is that of the abject poverty of the *railroad* and *postal employees*. For these state employees, Russian conditions obtain in the heart of the parliamentary constitutional state of Germany—i.e., Russian conditions like these prevailed *prior to* the revolution, during the untarnished splendor of absolutism. The Russian railroader already towered above his German counterpart with regard to his economic and social freedom of movement during the great strike of October 1905. The Russian railroad workers and postal employees conquered the right of association de facto by storm, and although lawsuits and disciplinary action hailed down upon them, nothing could take their internal solidarity from them. It would be an entirely false psychological prognosis, however, to assume, as is done by German reactionaries, that the slavish obedience of the German railroad workers and postal employees will last forever, that it is a rock that cannot be eroded. If the German union leaders have also become so accustomed to the prevailing conditions that they can survey with gratification the successes of labor union struggle in Germany, undisturbed by this ignominy that is almost without precedent in Europe, the latent, pent-up resentment among the uniformed state slaves will inevitably seek to vent itself in the context of a general uprising of industrial workers. And when the industrial vanguard of the proletariat attempts to seize further political rights or to defend the old ones through mass strikes, the great contingents of railroad workers and postal employees will, as a natural necessity, be compelled to focus on their own particular ignominy and to finally rise up in order to emancipate themselves from the extra portion of Russian absolutism that was specifically established for them in Germany. The pedantic conception, which aims to expedite large-scale popular movements according to a schema or formula, regards the conquest of the right of association for railroad workers as the necessary *precondition* that would first "permit any thought" of a mass strike in Germany. The actual and natural course of events can only be the reverse: It is only a powerful, spontaneous mass strike action that can engender the right of association for German railroad workers and postal employees. And those tasks that are insoluble under the prevailing conditions in Germany will suddenly discover their feasibility and their solution under the influence of, and pressure from, a general political mass action on the part of the proletariat.

Finally, consider the largest and most important case: the misery of *agricultural workers*. If British[*] labor unions are exclusively tailored to industrial workers, this is a phenomenon that can be understood in terms of the specific character of the British national economy and the reduced role of agriculture in economic life as a whole. In Germany, a labor union organization—no matter how brilliantly developed—that merely encompasses industrial workers and that is thus inaccessible to the entire great army of agricultural workers will only ever give a faint, partial picture of the situation of the proletariat as a whole. In turn, it would be a calamitous illusion to believe that rural conditions are immutable and fixed, that neither the tireless work of enlightenment undertaken by Social Democracy nor even the entire internal class politics in Germany serve to continually undermine the external passivity of the agricultural worker, and that the rural proletariat would not also rise up during any given large-scale general class action taken for whatever purpose by the German industrial proletariat. Such an uprising can naturally only manifest initially as a turbulent general economic struggle, as tremendous mass strikes by rural workers.

Thus, the image of the alleged economic superiority of the German proletariat over its Russian counterpart is altered very significantly if we shift our focus from the index of unionized branches of industry and crafts to those large groupings of the proletariat that stand entirely outside the union struggle or whose particular economic situation cannot be forcibly made to fit inside the narrow framework of the everyday guerrilla warfare waged by the labor unions. In so doing, we see one enormous sphere after another in which the intensification of antagonisms has reached its outer limits, with explosive material galore ready to be detonated and a series of vast regions that contain a great deal of "Russian absolutism" in its most naked form, and in which, in economic terms, the most elementary settling of accounts with capital is yet to be undertaken.

All these unsettled accounts would inevitably be presented to the ruling system within the context of a general political mass action by the proletariat.

---

[*] *Englischen* in the original.

Of course, an artificially arranged one-off demonstration by the urban proletariat, a mass strike action executed merely through discipline and following the conductor's baton wielded by the party executive, might leave the broader strata of the population cold and indifferent. Only a real, powerful, and ruthless action of struggle by the industrial proletariat—an action born of a revolutionary situation—would be guaranteed to cause a reaction among deeper-lying strata and to draw along into a turbulent general economic struggle precisely all those who in normal, peaceful times stand beyond the daily union struggle.

Yet if we return to the organized vanguard of the German industrial proletariat while on the other hand retaining a focus on the goals of the economic struggle as striven for today by the Russian workforce, we find that the latter are endeavors that the oldest of the German labor unions would have no reason at all to view with condescension, much as one might regard the worn-out shoes of childhood. Thus, the most important universal demand of Russian strikes since January 22, 1905—the eight-hour day—certainly does not represent a standpoint that the German proletariat has already surpassed; on the contrary, it constitutes in most cases a beautiful, yet distant, ideal. The same is true of the struggle with the "landlord's standpoint," the struggle for the introduction of workers' committees in all factories, for the abolition of piecework, for the abolition of the putting-out system of labor in handicrafts, for the full implementation of the day of rest on Sunday, and for the recognition of the right of association. To be sure, on closer inspection all of the objects of the economic struggle of the Russian proletariat in the current revolution are also highly relevant for the German proletariat, touching as they do nothing but sore points in terms of the worker's existence.

From this it follows, above all, that the purely political mass strike—the preferred mode of operation—is also in the case of Germany nothing but a lifeless theoretical schema. If it is true that mass strikes—in the form of a resolute political struggle by the urban workforce—will ensue by natural means from a powerful revolutionary ferment, they will equally naturally flip over into an entire period of elementary economic struggles, just as they did in Russia. The fears of the labor union leaders—that the struggle over economic interests could be simply sidelined and smothered during a period of turbulent political struggles, of mass strikes—are founded upon a schoolchild's notion of the course of things, a conception that hovers in midair. On the contrary, in Germany as well, the revolutionary period would transform the character of labor union struggle and reinforce it to such an extent that today's guerrilla war by the labor unions will be child's play in comparison. And on the other hand, the political struggle would also constantly gain fresh impulses and new forces from this elemental economic mass strike cyclone. The reciprocal interaction between economic and political struggle that forms the internal driving force of today's mass strikes in Russia and simultaneously constitutes the regulating mechanism, so to speak, of the revolutionary action of the proletariat—such an interaction would ensue equally naturally from those in Germany, too.

VI.

In this connection, the question of organization also assumes an essentially different aspect in its relation to the problem of the mass strike in Germany.

The position taken by some labor union leaders with regard to this question usually amounts to no more than the following: "We are not yet strong enough to risk such a hazardous trial of strength as a mass strike." Now, this point of view is untenable, insofar as it is an insoluble task to determine by means of a calmly considered arithmetic calculation when the proletariat would be "strong enough" for any given struggle. Thirty years ago, the German labor unions had 50,000 members. This was evidently a number that, according to the yardstick outlined above, ruled out any consideration of a mass strike. Fifteen years later, the unions were four times as strong, and had a combined membership of 237,000. If, however, today's union leaders had been asked at the time whether the organization of the proletariat was then sufficiently mature for a mass strike, they would surely have responded that this was not the case by a long shot, and that the unionized workforce would first have to number millions. Today, there are more than a million organized labor union members, but the views of their leaders are unchanged, and apparently could remain so ad infinitum. The tacit assumption here is that the entire working class in Germany, down to the last man and the last woman, must first be affiliated to labor unions before these can be deemed "strong enough" to risk a mass action—an action that would in any case probably turn out to be "superfluous," according to the old formula. This theory is completely utopian, however, for the simple reason that it exhibits an internal contradiction and is beset by vicious circularity. Before the workers can engage in any direct class struggle, they must all be organized. Yet the relations, the conditions, of capitalist development and of the bourgeois state entail that in the "normal" course of things, without turbulent class struggles, determinate strata—and in fact these form the majority, the most important, the most downtrodden strata of the proletariat, the strata most oppressed by capital and the state—cannot be organized at all. We see, even in Britain, that all that has been achieved by a whole century of relentless labor union work without any "disturbances"—disregarding for a moment the period of the Chartist movement—without any "revolutionary romantic" deviations or distractions, is the organization of a *minority* of the better-situated strata of the proletariat.

On the other hand, the labor unions, like all organizations of struggle of the proletariat, cannot maintain themselves in any other way than through struggle —and, more precisely, not only through struggle in the sense of *The Battle of*

Frogs and Mice* in the stagnant waters of the bourgeois-parliamentary period, but also in the sense of the turbulent, revolutionary periods of mass struggle. The rigid, mechanical-bureaucratic conception will only recognize struggle as the product of organization that has attained a certain level of strength. On the contrary, however, the living, dialectical development gives rise to organization as a product of struggle. We have already witnessed a superb example of this phenomenon in Russia, where a proletariat that was barely organized—if at all—created a comprehensive network of incipient organizations within a year and a half of turbulent revolutionary struggle. Another example of this type is provided by the German labor unions' own history. In 1878, labor union members numbered 50,000. According to the theory of today's labor union leaders, such organization was, as noted above, far from being "strong enough" to engage in an intense political struggle. Yet, as weak as they might have been at the time, German labor unions *did* take up the struggle—namely, the struggle against the Antisocialist Law—and not only proved themselves "strong enough" to emerge victorious from this struggle, but also saw their strength increase by a factor of five as a result: Their combined membership following the repeal of the Antisocialist Law in 1891 mounted to 277,659. It is true that the method with which the unions prevailed in the struggle against the Antisocialist Law did not correspond to the ideal of a peaceful, beelike, uninterrupted expansion; first, they were reduced to ruins in struggle, only to soar up out of the next wave and be reborn. Yet this is precisely the specific method of growth corresponding to proletarian class organizations: to test themselves in struggle, and to emerge from the struggle having reproduced themselves within it.

On closer inspection of German relations and the situation of the various strata of workers, it is evident that the coming period of turbulent political mass struggles will not entail the dreaded impending demise of German unions; on the contrary, it will afford new, unforeseen perspectives of a rapid, spasmodic expansion of its sphere of power. Yet the question has another side to it. Any plan to undertake mass strikes as serious political class action with organized workers alone is generally an utterly hopeless one. If the mass strike is to be successful, or rather, if mass strikes are to be successful, they have to become *popular movements*—i.e., they have to draw the broadest strata of the proletariat into the struggle. Already in the parliamentary form, the power of the proletarian class struggle does not depend upon the small organized core, but upon the broad surrounding periphery of the revolutionary-minded proletariat. If the Social Democratic Party were to attempt to contest an electoral campaign with only its few hundred thousand organized members, it would condemn itself to oblivion. And if Social Democracy tends toward the recruitment, as

---

* *Batrachomyomachia*, or *The Battle of Frogs and Mice*, is an ancient parody of the *Iliad*; its authorship has not been conclusively established. Marx often used the phrase to refer to the endless feuds between radical sects, especially of those in exile.

far as is possible, of almost the entire great reserve army of its electors into its party organizations, after thirty years of experience of Social Democracy, the mass of voters has not increased through the growth of the party organization; instead, the reverse is true: the fresh strata of the workforce won over through each electoral campaign form the fertile soil in which the seed of organization can be subsequently sown. Here, too, it is not merely the case that the organization provides troops for the struggle: On the contrary, the struggle also supplies new recruits for the organization, and does so to an even greater extent. The same tendency that can be identified in parliamentary struggle evidently applies to a far higher degree to direct political mass action. While it is true that the Social Democratic Party constitutes, as the organized core of the working class, the leading vanguard of the entire working population, and that it is precisely from this organization that the political clarity, the strength, and the unity of the workers' movement, all flow, the class movement of the proletariat should never be conceived of as one of an organized minority. Each truly large-scale class struggle must be based on the support and involvement of the broadest masses, and any strategy for the class struggle that did not reckon with such involvement, that were merely tailored to neatly executed marches by the small contingent of the proletariat that is quartered in barracks, would be condemned in advance to being a dismal fiasco.

Mass strikes or political mass struggles cannot be sustained alone by those who are organized, nor can they be quantified on the basis of veritable leadership emanating from a party headquarters. However, what is decisive here—as in Russia—is neither "discipline," nor "schooling," nor indeed the most meticulous prior calculation of the requisite levels of support and financing, but rather class action that is truly revolutionary and resolute, namely action that would be capable of winning over and sweeping along the broadest strata of the disorganized, but—given their mood and situation—revolutionary, proletarian masses.

The overestimation and false evaluation of the role of the organization within the class struggle of the proletariat is usually complemented by the underestimation of the disorganized proletarian mass and its political maturity. It is only in a revolutionary period, in the tempest of large-scale, rousing class struggles, that the entire educational effect of rapid capitalist development and of Social Democratic influences upon the broadest strata of the population first reveals itself; by contrast, charts detailing membership of organizations and even election statistics in quiet times merely yield a faint idea of this effect.

We have seen in Russia over the last two years that a large-scale, general action by the proletariat can arise out of the most minor partial conflict between the workers and the entrepreneurial class, out of the slightest local brutality on the part of the organs of government. Everyone regards this as natural, because in Russia there is "the revolution." Yet what does this mean? It signifies that class sentiment, class instinct, is alive to the highest degree among the

Russian proletariat, such that the latter experiences each partial issue concerning any given small group of workers as a general matter, as a class issue, and thus the whole proletariat reacts in lightning fashion to the dispute. Whereas in Germany, France, Italy, or Holland, even the most intense labor union conflicts do not elicit a general action by the working class, the slightest affair in Russia raises an entire storm. As paradoxical as it might sound, however, this implies nothing other than that class instinct is currently infinitely stronger among the young, unschooled, dimly enlightened, and even more feebly organized Russian proletariat than is the case among the organized, schooled, and enlightened workforce in Germany or any other Western European country. And this is no particular virtue of the "young, unspent East" in contrast with the "lazy West": It is rather a simple result of immediate revolutionary mass action. In the case of the German enlightened worker, the class consciousness that has been implanted within him by Social Democracy is a *theoretical, latent* one: In the period of the rule of bourgeois parliamentarianism, it cannot as a rule be activated as direct mass action; in this case, class consciousness consists in the ideal aggregate of the 400 parallel actions in the various electoral districts, the many partial economic struggles, and the like. In the revolution, where the mass itself appears in the political arena, class consciousness becomes *practical* and *active*. Thus, a single year of revolution gave the very "schooling" to the Russian proletariat that thirty years of parliamentary and labor union struggle could not give by artificial means to the German proletariat. Admittedly, this vibrant, active class sentiment of the proletariat in Russia will also significantly fade, or rather be transformed into a concealed, latent one after the conclusion of the period of revolution and the establishment of a bourgeois-parliamentary constitutional state. Yet the reverse is equally certain: In a period of powerful political actions in Germany, a vibrant and effective revolutionary class sentiment will grip the broadest and deepest strata of the proletariat, and will do so all the more rapidly and forcefully, the more extensively the Social Democratic organizations have performed their educational task up to that point. This educational work and the agitational and revolutionizing effect of contemporary German politics as a whole will express themselves in the circumstance that all those cohorts that, in an apparent state of political stultification, currently remain insensitive to all attempts at organization by the Social Democrats and by the labor unions will, in an earnest revolutionary period, suddenly obey the flag of Social Democracy. Six months of a revolutionary period will accomplish the work of schooling these currently disorganized masses that a decade of popular assemblies and distribution of leaflets would not have been able to achieve. And when relations in Germany have attained the degree of maturity for such a period, the most disorganized and backward strata today will naturally form the most radical and tumultuous element in the struggle, as opposed to being merely dragged along by it. If it should come to mass strikes in Germany, it is virtually certain that it will not be the best organized—the printers, for example—but rather the worst organized or those that are completely disorganized—the miners, the textile workers, perhaps even agricultural laborers—who will develop the greatest capacity for action.

In this way, we reach the same conclusions with regard to the actual tasks of *leadership* and the role of Social Democracy vis-à-vis mass strikes in Germany that we drew previously in our analysis of the processes in Russia. That is, if we abandon the pedantic schema of a demonstrative mass strike of the organized minority, a mobilization artificially contrived by order of the party and the labor unions, and turn our attention instead to the vivid image of a real popular movement that has emerged with elemental force from the extreme intensification of class antagonisms and the political situation, it is evident that the task of Social Democracy consists not in the technical preparation and direction of the mass strike, but first and foremost in the *political leadership* of the whole movement.

Social Democracy is the most enlightened, most class-conscious vanguard of the proletariat. It cannot, and must not, await in fatalist fashion, with folded arms, the onset of the "revolutionary situation"—it cannot wait for such a spontaneous popular movement to fall from the sky. On the contrary, it must, as always, anticipate the development of events and seek to *accelerate* them. It cannot do this, however, through suddenly and indiscriminately issuing a "call" for a mass strike at what might be the right or the wrong point in time, but rather, and above all, by making clear to the broadest proletarian strata the inexorable *onset* of this revolutionary period and by clarifying the internal *social moments* that lead to it and its *political consequences*. If the broadest strata of the proletariat are to be won over for a political mass action on the part of Social Democracy, and if, conversely, Social Democracy is to seize and retain effective leadership during a mass movement and to gain control over the entire movement *in the political sense*, then it must be capable of implanting its *tactics* and *goals* within the German proletariat with the utmost clarity, coherence, and resolution in the period of the coming struggles.

VII.

We have seen that, in Russia, the mass strike did not represent the artificial product of a deliberate tactic on the part of Social Democracy, but rather a natural historical phenomenon on the basis of the current revolution. But what are the factors that have engendered this new phenomenal form of the revolution in Russia?

The Russian Revolution has as its next pending task the elimination of absolutism and the establishment of a modern bourgeois-parliamentary constitutional state. In terms of form, this is precisely the same task that confronted the March [1848] Revolution in Germany and the Great Revolution in France at the conclusion of the eighteenth century. Yet the relations, the historical milieu within which these formally analogous revolutions occurred, are fundamentally different from those of Russia today. The decisive factor here is the circumstance that the entire cycle of capitalist development has run its course between those bourgeois revolutions in the West and today's bourgeois revolution in the East. For this development has not only gripped the Western European countries, but also absolutist Russia. In Russia, large-scale industry, with all its consequences—modern class divisions, acute social disparities, modern urban life, and the modern proletariat—has become the predominant form of production (i.e., the decisive form with regard to social development). This has given rise to the peculiar, contradictory historical situation, however, that the revolution that is bourgeois in view of its formal tasks will be executed primarily by a modern, class-conscious proletariat and in an international milieu that is marked by the expiry of bourgeois democracy. Now, the bourgeoisie is no longer the leading, revolutionary element as it was in the previous revolutions in the West, when the proletarian mass, dissipated within the petty bourgeoisie, served the bourgeoisie as a reserve army; today, the reverse is true: The class-conscious proletariat is the leading, driving element, whereas the large-scale bourgeois strata are partly directly counterrevolutionary, partly moderately liberal, and, alongside the urban petty-bourgeois intelligentsia, only the rural petty bourgeoisie is resolutely oppositional or even revolutionary minded. However, the Russian proletariat, whose leading role in the bourgeois revolution is determined in this way, itself enters the struggle free from all illusions in bourgeois democracy, having instead a strongly developed consciousness of its own specific class interests within the acutely intensified antagonism between capital and labor. This contradictory relation finds expression in the following circumstances: that in this formally bourgeois revolution, bourgeois society's antagonism toward absolutism is subordinated to the proletariat's antagonism toward bourgeois society; that the struggle of the proletariat is directed with equal force against absolutism and against capitalist exploitation simultaneously; and that the program of revolutionary struggles is oriented equally emphatically toward political freedom and the conquest of the eight-hour day, together with the attainment by the proletariat of a material existence that is worthy of human beings. This ambivalent character of the Russian Revolution manifests itself in the intimate connection and reciprocal interaction between the economic and the political struggle with which we have become acquainted through the processes in Russia, and that find their corresponding expression precisely in the mass strike.

In the earlier bourgeois revolutions—given, on the one hand, that it was the bourgeois parties that provided political schooling and leadership for the revolutionary mass, and, on the other, that it was a question of openly overthrowing the old regime—the brief battle on the barricades was the appropriate form of revolutionary struggle. In today's context, where the working class must enlighten itself in the course of the revolutionary struggle, it must marshal its forces and direct itself, and where revolution is, for its part, directed as much against capitalist exploitation as it is against the *ancien régime*, the mass strike manifests itself as the natural means of recruiting, revolutionizing, and organizing the broadest proletarian strata through action itself, just as it is simultaneously a means of undermining and overthrowing the *ancien régime* and curbing capitalist exploitation. The urban industrial proletariat is now the soul of the revolution in Russia. Yet in order to carry out any direct political action as a mass, the proletariat must first gather itself up into a mass, and for this purpose it must above all leave the factories and workshops, the mines and smelters, it must overcome the atomization and fragmentation to which it is condemned in the individual workshops under the daily yoke of capital. The mass strike is thus the first natural, impulsive form of every great revolutionary action taken by the proletariat, and it also follows that mass strikes must become all the more powerful and decisive; the more industry becomes the predominant form of social economy, the more salient the role of the proletariat in the revolution and the more developed the antagonism between labor and capital. The earlier principal form of bourgeois revolutions—the battle on the barricades, the open confrontation with the armed power of the state—is in today's revolution merely a culminating point, merely one moment within the entire process of proletarian mass struggle.

And, thus, the civilization and mitigation of class struggles prophetically forecast by the opportunists of German Social Democracy—the [Eduard] Bernsteins, the [Eduard] Davids, et al.—have been attained in this new form of revolution. The latter of course anticipated, in the spirit of petty-bourgeois democratic illusions, that the yearned-for mitigation and civilization of class struggle would consist in class struggle being limited to parliamentary struggle and revolution on the streets simply being eliminated. History has found the solution in a somewhat more profound and refined manner—namely, in the rise of the revolutionary mass strike, which of course by no means replaces the naked, brutal struggle on the streets or renders it superfluous. The revolutionary mass strike, instead, reduces the latter struggle to being a mere moment of the long political period of struggle and simultaneously connects an enormous work of civilization—in the most precise sense of the word—with the period of revolution: This work consists in the material and intellectual elevation of the entire working class through the "civilization" of the barbaric forms of capitalist exploitation.

The mass strike thus reveals itself not as a specifically Russian product emerging from absolutism, but instead as a universal form of proletarian class struggle resulting from the contemporary stage of capitalist development and class relations. From this standpoint, the three bourgeois revolutions—the Great

French Revolution [of 1789], the German March Revolution, and the current Russian Revolution—form a sequence of continuous development in which are reflected the fortunes and the end of the capitalist century. In the Great French Revolution, the still entirely undeveloped internal contradictions within bourgeois society gave room for a long period of tremendous struggles, a period in which all those antagonisms that only burgeon and mature in the heat of the revolution could run riot, unhindered and unconstrained, in a spirit of reckless radicalism. Half a century later, the revolution of the German bourgeoisie that erupted at a halfway point along the path of capitalist development would indeed be suppressed halfway through by the antagonism between the respective interests of, and by the balance of forces between, capital and labor, then to be suffocated by a bourgeois-feudal compromise and reduced to a brief, pathetic episode, silenced in mid-speech. Another half century later, today's Russian Revolution comes at a point in the path of history where the high point of capitalist society has already been passed, where the bourgeois revolution can no longer be smothered by the antagonism between the bourgeoisie and the proletariat, and where, on the contrary, this antagonism is developed into a new, lengthy period of tremendous social struggles, in which the settling of old accounts with absolutism appears a trivial matter in comparison with the many new accounts opened by the revolution itself. The current revolution thus simultaneously realizes in the particular case of absolutist Russia the universal results of international capitalist development, and manifests itself not so much as a last, trailing instance of the bourgeois revolutions of the West, but rather as a precursor to the new series of proletarian revolutions in the West. Precisely because its bourgeois revolution has been so inexcusably delayed, the most backward country is now in a position to indicate the paths and methods of further class struggle to the proletariat of Germany and of the most advanced capitalist countries.

Accordingly, it is manifestly completely misguided, from this perspective, too, to regard the Russian Revolution from afar as a fine spectacle, as something specifically "Russian," and at most to applaud the heroism of those in struggle—i.e., to laud the external accessories of the struggle. It is much more important that German workers learn to regard the Russian Revolution as *their own affair*, not merely in the spirit of international class solidarity with the Russian proletariat, but above all as *a chapter of their own social and political history*. Those labor union leaders and parliamentarians who consider the German proletariat to be "too weak" and German relations to be "not yet ripe" for revolutionary mass struggles have evidently no idea of the fact that the measure of the ripeness of class relations in Germany and of the power of the proletariat lies not in the membership statistics of German labor unions or in electoral statistics, but rather in the processes occurring in the Russian Revolution. Just as the maturity of French class antagonisms under the July monarchy and the [1848] June

Days uprising in Paris* were reflected in the March Revolution in Germany, in the latter's course and its fiasco, so the ripeness of German class antagonisms is reflected today in the processes and potency of the Russian Revolution. And while the bureaucrats of the German workers' movement rummage in the drawers of their branch offices for evidence of their strength and maturity, they fail to see that what they are looking for lies right before their eyes in a great historical revelation, since the Russian Revolution is, when apprehended historically, a reflection of the potency and maturity of the international workers' movement, thus first and foremost of the German workers' movement.

It would therefore be an all too feeble, grotesquely insignificant result of the Russian Revolution if the German proletariat were merely to draw from it the conclusion, as do Comrades [Karl] Frohme, [Adolph von] Elm, and others, that the external form of the struggle—i.e., the mass strike—is merely to be borrowed from the Russian Revolution and emasculated, so that it becomes no more than a piece of artillery held in reserve in case the franchise in elections to the Reichstag is removed, and thus no more than a passive means within a parliamentary defensive campaign. If the right to vote in elections to the Reichstag is stripped away from us, then we will defend ourselves. Such a resolution is absolutely self-evident. But, for such a resolution, it is not necessary to adopt the heroic pose of a [Georges] Danton, as done, for example, by Comrade Elm in Jena,† since the defense of the modest measure of parliamentary rights already acquired is hardly a Promethean innovation that could only occur on the basis of the encouragement provided by the dreadful hecatombs of the Russian Revolution; on the contrary, it is the simplest, primary duty of any opposition party. Yet the merely defensive campaign must never exhaust the politics of the proletariat in a period of revolution. And if, on the one hand, it is difficult to predict with any certainty whether the elimination of universal suffrage in Germany will occur within a situation that will necessarily elicit an immediate mass strike action, it is completely certain, on the other hand, that as soon as we have entered the period of turbulent mass actions in Germany, Social Democracy can by no means afford to restrict its tactics to the merely defensive parliamentary campaign. Social Democracy does not have it within its power to determine in advance the cause and the moment that will induce the outbreak of mass strikes in Germany, since it does not have it within its power to bring about historical situations through party convention resolutions. What it can

---

* *Die Pariser Junischlacht*—literally, "the June battle in Paris."

† At the conference of the Social Democratic Party of Germany from September 17 to 23, 1905, Adolph von Elm had declared that the proletariat would defend itself in the case that it were deprived of its right to vote in elections to the Reichstag by the ruling class, and that it would "put its life on the line in the trenches for freedom." See *Protokoll über die Verhandlungen des Parteitages der Sozialdemokratischen Partei Deutschlands. Abgehalten zu Jena vom 17. Bis 23. September 17–23, 1905* (Protocol of the Negotiations of the Party Congress of the Social Democratic Party of Germany, held in Jena September 17–23, 1905) (Berlin: Buchhandlung Vorwärts, 1905), p. 332.

and must do, however, is clarify the political guidelines of these struggles once they have emerged, and formulate such guidelines within decisive and coherent tactics. Historical events are not kept in check by issuing directives to them, but rather by developing in advance an awareness of their probable, predictable consequences, and by adjusting one's own mode of action accordingly.

The immediate threat for the German workers' movement—the political danger against which the latter has braced itself for a number of years—is a coup d'état by the forces of reaction; such a coup d'état will undoubtedly aim to wrest the most important political right, namely the right to vote in elections to the Reichstag, from the broadest strata of the laboring popular masses. Despite the immense bearing that such an eventuality would have, it is, as has already been asserted above, impossible to predict with any certitude whether an open popular movement would immediately erupt in the form of mass strikes, since the innumerable circumstances and moments that codetermine the situation during such a mass movement are unknown to us. Yet, taking into consideration, on the one hand, the current extreme aggravation of relations in Germany, and, on the other, the manifold international feedback effects of the Russian Revolution and, furthermore, of the future renewed Russia, it becomes clear that the upheaval in German politics that would ensue from the elimination of the franchise in elections to the Reichstag could not possibly be restricted to the struggle for the right to vote. Instead, such a coup d'état would, within a shorter or a longer time frame, give rise with elemental force to a great universal political reckoning with the forces of reaction by the insurgent popular masses thus spurred to action. This would be a reckoning on account of bread profiteering, the artificial raising of meat prices, impoverishment through boundless militarism and naval adventurism, corruption within colonial policy, the national disgrace of the Königsberg trial,* the standstill in social reforms, the deprivation of rights suffered by railroad workers, postal workers, and agricultural workers, the cheating and deriding of the miners, the sentence passed in Löbtau† and the system of class justice as a whole, the brutal system of lockouts—in short, a reckoning on account of twenty years of oppression by the ruling coalition between East Elbian Junkers and the cartels of large-scale capital.

Once the stone has started rolling, however, it can no longer be stopped— whether Social Democracy wills it or not. The opponents of the mass strike are

---

* Between July 12 and 15, 1904, nine German Social Democrats were put on trial in Königsberg, now Kaliningrad, on charges of smuggling illegal writings opposing tsarism into Russia. It was Karl Liebknecht, a defense counsel in the trial, who exposed the cooperation between the Prussian and tsarist authorities.

† In February 1899 in the district of Löbtau, nine construction workers were sentenced to a combined total of sixty-one years' custody in houses of correction or imprisonment for having protested against the fact that work was being carried out beyond the stipulated working time on a neighboring building site. Violence had broken out after the site manager had fired blanks from a revolver.

wont to deny that the lessons and examples of the Russian Revolution can serve as criteria in the case of Germany, above all because in Russia the immense leap from an Oriental despotism to a modern, bourgeois constitutional order had first to be taken. The formal distance between the old and the new political order is supposed to serve as sufficient grounds for explaining the vehemence and violence of the revolution in Russia. In Germany—so the argument goes— we have long had the most necessary forms and guarantees of a constitutional state, for which reason social antagonisms cannot rage here with such elemental force. Those who speculate in this way overlook the fact that for these very reasons, once open political struggles have erupted in Germany, the historically conditioned goal will be completely different from that of Russia today. Precisely owing to the fact that the bourgeois constitutional order has existed in Germany for a long time, that it has thus had time to exhaust itself completely and is in the process of extinguishing itself, and that bourgeois democracy and liberalism have had the time to become extinct—precisely for these reasons, there can be no more talk of a *bourgeois* revolution in Germany. And therefore, in a period of open political popular struggles in Germany, it can only be a question of the *dictatorship of the proletariat* as the final historically necessary goal. However, the distance between this task and today's conditions in Germany is even more immense than that between the bourgeois constitutional order and Oriental despotism, which implies that this task cannot be accomplished at one stroke, but must likewise be carried out during a lengthy period of gigantic social struggles.

Yet is there not a glaring contradiction in the perspectives registered here? On the one hand, it is argued that in an eventual future period of political mass action, above all the most backward strata of the German proletariat—agricultural workers, railroad workers, postal slaves—will first have to conquer the right of association, and that the worst excesses of exploitation will first have to be overcome; on the other hand, however, it is asserted that the task of such a period is none other than the political conquest of power by the proletariat! On the one hand, we have economic, labor union struggles over immediate interests, for the material elevation of the working class, and on the other, nothing less than the ultimate goal of Social Democracy! To be sure, these are blatant contradictions; yet they are not contradictions in our reasoning, but rather in capitalist development itself. The latter does not proceed in a neat, straight line, but rather in a sharply zigzagging or lightning-like trajectory. Just as the various capitalist countries represent the most varied stages of development, so too do the various strata of the same working class within each country. History does not wait patiently, however, until the backward countries and strata have caught up with the most advanced ones, such that the organic whole can move forward symmetrically, like a rigid column. Instead, history causes explosions in the foremost, most exposed points as soon as relations here are ripe for this, and then, in the turbulence of the revolutionary period, leeway is made up within a matter of days and months, disparities are compensated for, and, in one jolt, social progress as a whole shifts into double-quick step.

Just as in the Russian Revolution the various points along the spectrum of development and the entire range of interests of the various strata of workers have united in the Social Democratic program of revolution and the innumerable partial struggles have coalesced in the great common class action of the proletariat, so too will a similar process occur in Germany when relations are ripe enough for this to transpire. And as soon as this is the case, it will be the task of Social Democracy to orient its tactics not toward the most backward phases of development, but rather toward the most advanced ones.

VIII.

The most significant exigency of the period of great struggles that lie in store for the German working class—a period that is coming sooner or later—will be to develop, alongside utter resoluteness and coherence of tactics, the greatest capacity for action, and thus the greatest degree of unity of the leading, Social Democratic part of the proletarian mass. Yet the first feeble attempts to prepare a larger mass action have already immediately exposed an important deficiency in this regard: The complete separation and autonomization of both organizations of the workers' movement, i.e., the Social Democratic Party and the labor unions.

It is evident from closer consideration of the mass strikes in Russia, as well as from relations in Germany itself, that any larger mass action—if it is not to be merely restricted to a one-off demonstration and is instead intended to become a real action of struggle—cannot be conceived of as a so-called political mass strike. In Germany, the labor unions would be just as involved in such an action as the Social Democratic Party. Not for the reason imagined by the labor union leaders—namely, that the Social Democratic Party, given its much lower level of organization numerically, would be reliant upon the cooperation of the 1.25 million labor unionists, "without whom it would not be able to accomplish anything," but rather owing to a much more profound circumstance: Each direct mass action or period of open class struggles would be simultaneously a political *and* an economic one. Any great political struggles or mass strikes occurring in Germany, for whatever reason and at any given point in time, will simultaneously inaugurate an era of tremendous labor union struggles in Germany, in which events will not pause to inquire whether or not labor union leaders have given their blessing.* If the latter stand aside or even attempt to oppose the movement, all that they will achieve by such behavior will be to be swept aside

---

* First edition: "their agreement."

by the tide of events, with both the economic and the political struggles of the masses being fought out without them.

Indeed. The separation between the political and the economic struggle, and the autonomization of each, is nothing other than an artificial—if historically conditioned—product of the parliamentary period. On the one hand, the economic struggle is fragmented here, in the tranquil, "normal" course of bourgeois society, and dissipated into a multiplicity of individual struggles in each enterprise and in each branch of production. On the other hand, the political struggle is not waged by the mass itself through direct action, but rather—in accordance with the forms of the bourgeois state—via the representative route, through pressure exerted upon the legislative assemblies. As soon as a period of revolutionary struggles has commenced—i.e., as soon as the masses enter the arena—both the fragmentation of the economic struggle and the indirect, parliamentary form of political struggle fall to the wayside; in a revolutionary mass action, political and economic struggle are one, and the artificial barrier between labor union and Social Democratic Party as two separate, completely independent forms of the workers' movement is simply swept away. Yet what is given expression in conspicuous fashion in the revolutionary mass movement also holds for the parliamentary period as the true underlying circumstance. There are not two different class struggles of the working class—i.e., an economic and a political one—but only *one* class struggle that is simultaneously oriented toward the restriction of capitalist exploitation within bourgeois society, on the one hand, and the abolition of exploitation and of bourgeois society itself, on the other.

If these two sides of the class struggle also become separated from each other on technical grounds during the parliamentary period, they nonetheless do not represent two forms of action running in parallel; rather, they merely constitute two phases, two stages of the struggle of the working class for emancipation. The labor union struggle encompasses the current interests of the workers' movement, and the Social Democratic struggle the latter's future interests. According to the *Communist Manifesto*, communists represent the common interests of the entire proletariat vis-à-vis the various group interests (national and local interests) of proletarians, and stand for the interest of the movement as a whole in the various stages of development of the class struggle—i.e., the end goals of the liberation of the proletariat.* Labor unions represent the group interests of the workers' movement and a stage of its development. Social Democracy represents the working class and the interests of its liberation as a whole. The relation of labor unions to Social Democracy is, accordingly, that of a part to the whole, and if the theory of the "equal rights" of labor unions vis-à-vis Social Democracy

---

* See Karl Marx and Friedrich Engels, *Manifesto of the Communist Party*, in *Marx-Engels Collected Works*, Vol. 6 (New York: International Publishers, 1976), p. 518.

finds so much resonance among labor union leaders, this has its basis in a thoroughgoing misapprehension of the very essence of labor unions and of their role within the universal struggle for the liberation of the working class.

This theory of the "equal rights" of labor unions vis-à-vis Social Democracy is hence no mere theoretical misunderstanding, no mere mistake—instead it is the expression of the well-known tendency of the opportunistic wing of Social Democracy, which actually aims to reduce the political struggle of the working class to the momentary struggle and to transform the Social Democratic Party from a revolutionary, proletarian party into a petty-bourgeois, reformist one.[*] If Social Democracy were to accept the theory of the "equal entitlement" of labor unions, it would thereby indirectly and tacitly accept the very transformation so long striven for by the representatives of the opportunistic tendency.

Such a shift in relations within the workers' movement is more impossible in Germany than in any other country. The theoretical relation whereby labor unions are merely a part of Social Democracy finds its classical illustration precisely in Germany in the facts, in living praxis; this circumstance expresses itself in three ways. Firstly, German labor unions are directly a product of Social

---

[*] [Footnote by Luxemburg] Given that the presence of such a tendency within the Social Democratic Party of Germany is usually denied, the candor with which the opportunistic faction recently formulated its actual goals and aspirations is to be welcomed. At a party assembly held in Mainz on September 10 of this year, the following resolution from Dr. David was adopted:

> Considering that the Social Democratic Party understands the concept of "revolution" not in the sense of a violent overthrow, but in the peaceful sense of development—i.e., the gradual implementation of a new economic principle—the public assembly of the Social Democratic Party in Mainz rejects any "revolutionary romanticism."
>
> The assembly regards the conquest of political power as nothing other than the conquest of the majority of the people for the ideas and demands of Social Democracy; a conquest that cannot occur by violent means, but only through the revolutionizing of minds by means of intellectual propaganda and practical efforts at reform in all areas of political, economic and social life.
>
> In the conviction that Social Democracy thrives to a much-greater extent through legal means rather than through illegal ones and subversion, the assembly rejects "*direct mass action*" as a tactical principle and adheres to the principle of *parliamentary action for reform*—i.e., its desire is that the party remains earnest in its efforts *to achieve our goals gradually via legislation and organic development.*
>
> The fundamental presupposition of this reformist method of struggle is of course that the *possibility of the involvement of the propertyless popular mass in legislation* in the empire and in the individual states will not be reduced, but rather expanded, until *full equal rights* have been attained. On these grounds, the assembly considers it to be an indisputable right of the workforce, when all other means have failed, to refuse to work for a shorter or a longer period in defense of its legal rights when these come under attack, and in order to attain new rights.
>
> However, since the political mass strike can only be successfully conducted on behalf of the workforce when such a strike *remains on a strictly legal track*, and when the strikers for their part provide no justifiable grounds for intervention by the armed forces, the assembly considers that the only necessary and effective preparation for the use of this means of struggle is the further expansion of political, labor union, and cooperative organization. For only in this way can the preconditions be established among the broad masses that guarantee that a mass strike can be successfully prosecuted: goal-oriented discipline and appropriate economic backing.

Democracy: It was the latter that engendered the first beginnings of the labor union movement in Germany and reared this movement, just as it is Social Democracy that provides to this day this movement's leaders and the most active supporters of its organization. Secondly, the German labor unions are also a product of Social Democracy in the sense that the Social Democratic doctrine forms the soul of labor union praxis—labor unions owe their superiority over all bourgeois and confessional unions to the thought of class struggle; their practical success and their power are a result of the circumstance that their praxis is illuminated by the theory of scientific socialism and is raised above the lowlands of narrow-minded empiricism. The strength of the "practical politics" of German labor unions lies in their insight into the more profound social and economic interconnections of the capitalist order; however, they owe such insight to nothing other than the theory of scientific socialism on which their praxis is based. In this sense, the quest for the emancipation of labor unions from Social Democratic theory, for another labor union theory as opposed to the Social Democratic one, implies,* from the standpoint of labor unions themselves,† nothing other than a suicide attempt. The dissociation of labor union praxis from the theory of scientific socialism would entail for German labor unions the immediate loss of their entire superiority over all kinds of bourgeois labor union and a plunge from their previous heights to the level of a disoriented floundering and a pure, flat empiricism.

Thirdly, labor unions are ultimately also directly—in terms of their *numerical* strength—a product of the Social Democratic movement and of Social Democratic agitation, although the union leaders have gradually lost awareness of this fact.‡ From the proud heights of their membership of 1.25 million, some labor union leaders are wont to look down somewhat triumphantly [and with a certain measure of schadenfreude] upon the pitiful membership of the Social Democratic Party, which numbers not even half a million, and to remind Social Democrats of the time, around ten or twelve years ago, when many in the ranks of the latter still thought pessimistically about the perspectives for the development of labor unions. They fail to notice that there is to a certain extent *a direct, causal interconnection* between these two facts—namely, the high figure for labor union membership and the low figure for those organized within the Social Democratic Party. Thousands upon thousands of workers do not join party organizations, precisely *because* they join labor unions. According to theory, all workers would have to be doubly organized: They would have to go

---

* First edition: "is."
† Inserted in first edition: "and of their future."
‡ Inserted in first edition: "It is true that in some districts, labor union agitation preceded—and continues to precede—Social Democratic agitation, and that everywhere labor union work paves the way for party work. In terms of their *effect*, party and labor unions work hand in hand. Yet when the picture of the overall class struggle in Germany is surveyed and its deeper-lying interconnections are taken into account, the relation undergoes a considerable shift."

to* two kinds of assembly, pay contributions twice, read two kinds of workers' press,† etc. Yet this requires a high degree of intelligence, the kind of idealism that, out of a sense of duty toward the workers' movement, does not shy away from daily sacrifices in terms of time and money, and ultimately also the kind of passionate interest in the pure, internal‡ life of the party that can only be satisfied by membership in the party organization. All these criteria are fulfilled in the case of the most enlightened and intelligent minority of the Social Democratic working class in the cities, where the life of the party is rich in content and attractive, and where the standard of living of workers is higher. By contrast, this dual organizational relationship is harder to establish in the case of the broader strata of the urban mass of workers and in the provinces, in the smaller and smallest backwaters, where local political life lacks independence and forms a mere reflection of the processes in the metropolis, where the life of the party is consequently an impoverished and monotonous one, and, finally, where the economic standard of living of the worker is mostly a miserable one.

For the worker from the masses who is disposed toward Social Democracy, the question resolves itself insofar as he joins his labor union. This is because he cannot satisfy the immediate interests of his economic struggle other than through joining a professional organization—this circumstance being determined by the nature of this struggle itself. The contribution that he pays, which often represents a significant sacrifice in terms of his standard of living, brings him an immediate, visible benefit. Yet he is able to act according to his Social Democratic disposition without belonging to a specific party organization, insofar as he votes in parliamentary elections, attends Social Democratic popular assemblies, follows the reports of Social Democratic speeches in the various representative bodies, and reads the party press—compare, for example, the respective figures for Social Democratic voters and the readership of *Vorwärts*§ [Forward] with the number of organized party members in Berlin. And the crucial factor here is the following: The average worker from the masses with a disposition toward Social Democracy, who as a simple man has no understanding of the complicated and subtle¶ two-souls theory of the labor union leaders, in fact feels *Social Democratically* organized in the labor union too. Although the headquarters of the union confederations bear no official party sign, the workingman from the masses in every city and every town sees that the most active leaders at the head of his labor union are also

---

* First edition has "visit" in place of "go to."
† First edition: "worker's newspapers."
‡ First edition has "actual" in place of "pure, internal."
§ Founded in 1876, *Vorwärts* was the main daily newspaper of the SPD. In October 1905 Luxemburg became the leading political editor of *Vorwärts*, with responsibility for the column "The Revolution in Russia." *Vorwärts* was also the SPD's publication house, which issued numerous books and pamphlets.
¶ Inserted in first edition: "so-called."

the colleagues that he knows as comrades, as Social Democrats from public life, whether these are Social Democratic deputies in the Reichstag, the federal state parliaments, or the municipal councils, Social Democratic spokespersons, members of electoral committees, party editors, party secretaries, or simply as speakers and agitators. Furthermore, in the agitational work carried out by his labor union, he mostly hears the thoughts about capitalist exploitation, about class relations, that are familiar to him—and that he has learned to appreciate and understand—from Social Democratic agitation; indeed, most speakers, and certainly the most popular ones, in the labor union assemblies (those speakers who are the only ones to "bring the place to life," and who make the otherwise poorly attended and drowsy union assemblies attractive) are of course well-known Social Democrats.

The effect of all these factors is to give the average class-conscious worker the feeling that by being organized in a labor union, he also has an affiliation to his workers' party and is a part of the Social Democratic organization. *And therein lies the actual appeal of German labor unions.* It is not due to the semblance of neutrality, but thanks to their real Social Democratic essence that the labor union confederations have been able to attain their current strength. Indeed, nobody in Germany is deceived today by any such semblance of neutrality. Such a semblance has simply been rendered impossible* by the very coexistence of the various unions—Catholic ones, Hirsch-Duncker ones,† etc.—that are commonly adduced in attempts to justify the necessity of this alleged‡ "neutrality." When the German worker, who can freely choose to affiliate himself to a Christian, Catholic, Protestant, or liberal labor union, elects to join the "free labor union" instead or even switches affiliation from the former to the latter, he only does so because he grasps the labor union confederations as explicit organizations of the modern class struggle, as Social Democratic labor unions (in Germany these are one and the same thing). In short, the semblance of "neutrality" that exists for§ labor union leaders does not obtain for the mass of those organized in labor unions. And this is the good fortune of the labor union confederations.¶ If this semblance of "neutrality," this estrangement and dissociation of labor unions from Social Democracy were ever to become true, and in particular if it became a reality in the eyes of the proletarian masses, the labor unions would immediately lose their entire advantage vis-à-vis the competing bourgeois confederations, and with it their appeal and their animating fire. This has been conclusively proven by facts that are generally known. This is to say

---

* First edition: "justified."

† These were unions organized by Max Hirsch and Franz Gustav Duncker of the liberal-leaning Progressive Party, beginning in 1868, that claimed a harmony of interests between workers and employees, and opposed strikes.

‡ First edition: "political."

§ Inserted in first edition: "some."

¶ First edition: "labor union movement."

that the semblance of the party-political "neutrality" of labor unions could be of outstanding service as a means of attracting affiliates in a country in which Social Democracy itself enjoys no credit among the masses, where the odium attaching to it damages a workers' organization in the eyes of the masses rather than being beneficial,* where, in a word, labor unions must first recruit their troops from completely unenlightened, bourgeois-minded masses.

Throughout the entire previous century, the paragon of such a country was *England*—indeed, to a great extent, it remains so to this day. In Germany, however, there is an altogether-different configuration of party relations. In a country in which the Social Democratic Party is the most powerful party, in which the latter's appeal is manifested by an army of over 3 million proletarians, it is ridiculous to speak of the dissuasive effect of the odium attaching to Social Democracy, and to claim that it is necessary for an organization based on the workers' struggle to simulate† political neutrality. It would be sufficient merely to compare the figures for Social Democratic voters with those for labor union organizations in Germany in order to explain to any child that German labor unions do not recruit their troops from the unenlightened, bourgeois-minded masses, as is the case in England, but from the masses of proletarians who have already been roused by Social Democracy and won over to the thought of class struggle—i.e., from the masses of Social Democratic voters. With a good measure of indignation—which is in fact a mere prop for the "neutrality theory"—labor‡ union leaders reject the idea that labor unions can be regarded as recruiting schools for Social Democracy. Indeed, such a presumption—as impertinent as it might seem to union leaders, while in reality being so flattering—is [unfortunately] a mere fancy in Germany, because relations are diametrically§ opposed: It is Social Democracy that forms the recruiting school for the labor unions. While the organizing work carried out by labor unions is still mostly cumbersome and arduous—such that for the labor union leaders, the impression is aroused and nourished that it is they who have dug the first furrows and planted the first seed in this new proletarian land—not only has the soil in actual fact¶ already been cultivated by the Social Democratic plough, but the labor union seed itself, and ultimately the sower, must also be tinged a Social Democratic "red," in order for the crop to flourish. Yet, if we compare in this manner the statistics measuring the strength of labor unions not with those registering the membership of Social Democratic organizations, but with those quantifying the Social Democratic mass of voters—which is the only correct method—then we come to a conclusion that significantly deviates from the triumphant image of superiority

---

* First edition: "useful."
† First edition: "maintain."
‡ Inserted in first edition: "some."
§ First edition: "mostly."
¶ First edition: "by and large, with the exception of some districts and instances."

harbored by labor union leaders.* For it transpires that the "free labor unions" in actual fact still represent only a minority of the class-conscious body of workers in Germany, and that, with their million-strong† organized membership, they have not [even] managed to tap half of the mass of workers thrust in their direction‡ [and won over to the class struggle] by Social Democracy.

The most important conclusion to be drawn from the facts adduced above is that the total *unity* of the labor union and Social Democratic wings of the workers' movement—a unity that is absolutely necessary for the coming mass struggles in Germany—*is in fact at hand*; more precisely, this unity is embodied in the broad mass that simultaneously forms the basis of Social Democracy and of labor unions, and in whose consciousness both sides of the movement are fused into an intellectual unity. Given these factual circumstances, the supposed opposition between Social Democracy and labor unions shrinks to an opposition between Social Democracy and the upper stratum§ of labor union officials, which is simultaneously an opposition within labor unions between one¶ section of labor union leaders and the unionized proletarian mass. The strong growth of the labor union movement in Germany over the course of the last fifteen years, particularly in the period of the economic boom between 1895 and 1900, has by itself entailed a high degree of autonomization of labor unions, a specialization of their methods of struggle and of their leadership, and ultimately the emergence of a regular labor union bureaucracy. All of these phenomena are a completely explicable and natural historical product of the growth of the labor unions over fifteen years, a product of the economic prosperity and political lull in Germany. They represent a historically necessary evil—this is especially the case with regard to the labor union bureaucracy.** However, the dialectic of development also implies that when a certain level of organization has been attained and when relations have reached a certain degree of maturity, these necessary means for the promotion of the growth of labor unions turn into their opposite, into obstacles to further growth.

In the case of labor union officials, the specialization of their professional occupation as labor union leaders and the naturally narrow horizon associated with fragmented economic struggles in a period of calm lead all too easily to bureaucratism and to a narrow-mindedness in their outlook. Yet both afflictions express themselves in a whole series of tendencies that could prove fatal for the labor union movement itself. Most prominent among such tendencies is that

---

    * First edition has "from the commonly held notion in this regard" in place of "from the triumphant image of superiority harbored by labor union leaders."
    † First edition: "1.25 million-strong."
    ‡ First edition: "aroused."
    § First edition: "a certain section."
    ¶ First edition: "this."
    ** First edition: "Even if they are inseparable from certain adverse developments, they undoubtedly represent a historically necessary evil."

of overestimating organization, which is gradually transformed from a means to an end into an end in itself, into the highest good to which the interests of struggle are [repeatedly] subordinated.* These tendencies also explain the need for calm that is openly conceded by labor union leaders who shrink from any greater risk, from supposed perils that could allegedly threaten the existence of labor unions, and from the uncertainty associated with larger mass actions; they also account for the overestimation of the labor union mode of struggle itself and of its prospects and successes. Constantly absorbed by low-intensity economic warfare, labor union leaders themselves—whose task is to render plausible the great value of each slightest economic gain, each increase in wages or reduction in working time—gradually end up losing their grasp of the deeper interconnections and their overview of the situation as a whole. This is the only explanation for the circumstance that† German labor union leaders refer, for example, with such immense gratification to the gains of the past fifteen years, to the wage increases worth millions of marks, instead of placing emphasis on the other side of the coin—i.e., on the enormous downward pressure upon the proletarian living standard through bread profiteering, through fiscal and customs policy as a whole, through the land profiteering that has driven residential rents up so exorbitantly; in a word, on all the objective tendencies of bourgeois politics that render the gains of fifteen years of labor union struggles illusory once again.‡ Thus the labor union *half*-truth, which highlights only the positive aspects of daily struggle, is pruned from the *whole* Social Democratic truth, which, while stressing the work of the present and its absolute necessity, lays the main emphasis on the *critique* and the restrictions of this work. And ultimately, the concealment of the objective restrictions that bourgeois society places upon labor union struggle turns into a direct animosity toward any theoretical critique that alludes to these restrictions in connection with the final goals of the workers' movement. Absolute base flattery and boundless optimism become the duty of any "friend of the labor union movement." Yet, given that the Social Democratic standpoint consists precisely in combating uncritical labor union optimism as much as uncritical parliamentary optimism, ultimately forces are joined against Social Democratic theory itself: Labor union officials search gropingly for a "new theory"§ [that would correspond to *their* needs and *their* outlook], i.e., for a theory that contrasts with the Social Democratic doctrine by opening up completely unrestricted prospects of an economic ascent on the terrain of the capitalist order. Such a theory has in fact been in existence for some time, for this is the theory put forward by Professor [Werner] *Sombart*¶

---

* First edition: "are to be subordinated."
† Inserted in first edition: "some."
‡ First edition: "offset" in place of "render … illusory once again."
§ First edition: "new labor union theory."
¶ Although Sombart originally identified himself with Marxism, he adopted views consistent

with the explicit intention of driving a wedge between labor unions and Social Democracy in Germany and of luring labor unions over to bourgeois terrain.

Most intimately connected with this theoretical turnaround on the part of a section of labor union leaders is a reversal in the relation of the leader to the masses—a reversal also in keeping with Sombart's theory. Collegial agitation undertaken for no payment and out of pure idealism by local commissions of comrades themselves is replaced by the businesslike and bureaucratically regulated management by the labor union official, the latter being mostly drafted in from the outside. Through the concentration of the strings of the movement in his hands, the capacity to make judgments in labor union matters becomes his own professional specialization. Comrades from the rank and file are thus degraded to the status of a mass incapable of making judgments, whose duty is mainly to exhibit the virtue of "discipline"—i.e., passive obedience. In comparison with Social Democracy, where—contrary to the tendentious fable of "Bebel's dictatorship"*—the greatest democratism indeed prevails through electoral processes and collegial management, and where the party executive is in actual fact merely an administrating organ, the relation of authority over the subordinate masses is present to a much greater degree in labor unions.† A further ramification of this relation is precisely‡ the line of argument that disparages any critique of the prospects and possibilities of labor union praxis and alleges that any such criticism represents a threat to the pious labor union sentiment of the masses.

---

with the revisionist wing of German Social Democracy. In 1888 he became part (with Max Weber) of the Social Policy Association (Verein für Sozialpolitik), which advocated reform through existing state institutions. In 1895 he published the first work appreciative of Marx's *Capital* by an academic economist, but by World War I he had moved much further to the right, advocating a statist "socialism" from above that ascribes duties but not rights.

* August Bebel, who helped found and led the SPD for many years, was often attacked by his adversaries, especially on the right, for ruling the SPD in a dictatorial manner. While Luxemburg had her differences with Bebel, she consistently defended him from this charge. See especially her "Geknickte Hoffnung" (Deceived Hopes) in *Neue Zeit*, Vol. 1, No. 2 (1903/1904), pp. 33–9.

† First edition: "Intimately connected with these theoretical tendencies is a reversal in the relation of the leader to the masses. Collegial management through local commissions—as deficient as these may be—are replaced by the businesslike management of the labor union official. The capacity to take the initiative and to make judgments becomes, so to speak, professionally specialized within the figure of the latter, whereas it is incumbent upon the masses to exhibit the more passive virtue of discipline. These shadow sides of officialdom undoubtedly hold significant dangers for the party, dangers that can very easily arise from the latest innovation—the appointment of local party secretaries—if the Social Democratic masses are not careful to ensure that these secretaries remain purely executive organs and are not regarded as those invested with the competence for the taking of initiatives and the management of local party life. However, there are more narrow limits to bureaucratism within Social Democracy than within the life of the labor union due to the nature of the object, due to the character of political struggle itself. In the case of the labor union, it is precisely the technical specialization of wage struggles, for example the negotiation of complicated collective agreements and the like, that brings about a situation in which it is frequently asserted that the unionized masses have no 'overview over industrial life as a whole,' and that they thus lack the capacity to make judgments."

‡ First edition: "This conception is particularly expressed in."

This line of argument is based on the view that the working masses can only be won over to, and maintained in such a positive disposition toward, organization if they retain a blind, puerile belief in salvation through labor union struggle. There is a sharp contrast with Social Democracy in this regard: The latter bases its influence precisely on the insight of the masses into the contradictions of the prevailing order and into the entire complicated nature of the development of these contradictions. In other words, Social Democracy grounds its influence on the critical disposition of the masses toward all the moments and stages of their own class struggle. By contrast, the influence and power of labor unions rests—according to the labor union theory referred to above—upon the lack of discrimination and judgment of the masses. "The people's faith must be maintained": It is according to this maxim that some labor union officials brand any criticism of the inadequacies of the labor union movement as an assault on this movement itself. And ultimately a result of this specialization and bureaucratism on the part of labor union officials is also the substantial autonomization and "neutrality" of labor unions vis-à-vis Social Democracy. As labor union organization has grown, its external independence has ensued as a natural condition, as a relation accruing from the technical division of labor between the political and the labor union form of struggle. For its part, the "neutrality" of German labor unions emerged as a product of both reactionary legislation governing associations[†] and the Prussian-German police state. With the passage of time, the nature of both relations has altered. Out of the police-enforced condition of political "neutrality" of labor unions, a theory has been retrospectively fabricated that asserts their voluntary neutrality as a necessity allegedly grounded in the nature of labor union struggle itself. And the technical independence of labor unions that is alleged to rest on the practical division of labor within the unitary Social Democratic class struggle is transformed into the independence[‡] of labor unions from Social Democracy, from its point of view, and from its leadership—it is transformed into the so-called "equal rights" of labor unions vis-à-vis Social Democracy.

Yet this semblance of the independence[§] and equal entitlement[¶] of labor unions vis-à-vis Social Democracy is principally incarnated in labor union officials and is nourished by the administrative apparatus of labor unions. Outwardly, through the separate existence of an entire staff of labor union officials, a completely independent headquarters, an extensive professional press, and finally

---

[*] First edition: "among."
[†] With its antidemocratic character, the legislation governing associations was above all directed against the political associations of the working class and restricted the right of association. Since labor unions were also deemed to be political associations in Prussia, they were under constant threat of dissolution.
[‡] First edition: "detachment."
[§] First edition: "detachment."
[¶] First edition: "equality."

the labor union congresses, the semblance is generated of an outright parallelism with the administrative apparatus of Social Democracy, the party executive, the party press, and party conventions. This illusion of "equal entitlement"[*] held by Social Democracy and the labor unions has also led, among other things, to the monstrous phenomenon whereby the agendas of conferences of the Social Democratic Party of Germany and those of labor union congresses are clearly partially analogous, and yet diverging, and even diametrically opposed resolutions are passed in each case. A dichotomy has been constructed out of the[†] division of labor between the party convention, which represents the universal interests and tasks of the workers' movement, and labor union conferences, which deal with the much narrower area of the special questions and interests of day-to-day workplace struggle: the dichotomy between a supposed labor union worldview and a Social Democratic Weltanschauung with regard to *the same* universal questions and interests of the workers' movement. Once this abnormal state of affairs has been generated, there is a natural tendency for it to expand and become intensified. Once the deplorable practice of setting parallel agendas for labor union congresses and party conventions has been initiated, the very existence of labor union congresses constitutes a natural incentive to an ever-greater demarcation and distancing from Social Democracy at these latter events. In order to document for the benefit of themselves and others their own "independence," and so as not to demonstrate their own redundancy or subservience by simply repeating the statements issued by party conventions, labor union congresses (which are principally congresses of officials, as is well known) must instinctively seek to emphasize that which sets them apart from party conventions, that which is specific to labor unions. Likewise, the very existence of a parallel, independent central leadership of labor unions leads this leadership, on a psychological level, to make tangible its independence vis-à-vis the Social Democratic leadership at every turn, and to approach each and every contact with the party above all from the standpoint of "limits of competence."

Thus, the peculiar condition has arisen according to which the very same labor union movement that below, at the level of the broad proletarian masses, is completely at one with Social Democracy, above, within its administrative superstructure, rushes to distance itself from Social Democracy and to set itself up as an independent, second great power vis-à-vis the latter. The German workers' movement thus acquires the peculiar form of a double pyramid, the base and body of which consist of a massif, while its two peaks are set wide apart.

From the above exposition it is clear that there is only one way to achieve, in a natural and successful manner, the compact unity of the German workers'

---

[*] *Gleichberechtigung*—literally, "equal rights."
[†] Inserted in first edition: "natural."

movement that is as absolutely necessary with regard to the coming political class struggles as it is indispensable for the interests of the further development of labor unions. Nothing would be more perverse or hopeless than to attempt to bring about the desired unity via sporadic or periodical negotiations between the leadership of the Social Democratic Party of Germany and the labor union headquarters over individual questions of the workers' movement. For as we have seen, in both forms of the workers' movement it is precisely the uppermost levels of the respective organizations that incarnate the separation and autonomization of these forms within themselves and that are* bearers [and sustainers] of the illusion of the "equal entitlement" and parallel existence of Social Democracy and labor unions. To attempt to achieve the unity of both by establishing a connection between the party executive and the labor union General Commission is tantamount to building a bridge where the chasm is widest and the passage most fraught. If this type of relation between party and labor unions—i.e., a negotiation between great powers over each individual matter—were to become systematized, this would entail nothing other than the canonization of the very relation that is to be eliminated as an anomaly, namely the federative relation between, on the one hand, the proletarian class movement as a whole and, on the other, a partial manifestation of this movement. The diplomatic-federative relation between the respective governing bodies of the Social Democratic Party and the labor unions can lead only to an ever-greater estrangement and to a cooling of relations, and cannot be anything other than the source of ever-new friction. And this lies in the nature of the matter. This is to say that the very form of this relation entails that the great question of the harmonious unification of the economic and political dimensions of the proletarian struggle for emancipation is transformed into the trivial question of a "cordial, neighborly" relation between the respective "authorities" on Lindenstraße and on Engel-Ufer,† and the major concerns of the workers' movement are eclipsed by petty considerations of status and other such sensibilities. The first test of the method of diplomacy between the respective executives—the negotiations of the Social Democratic Party executive with the General Commission of German Trade Unions over the question of mass strikes—has already provided sufficient evidence of the hopelessness of this procedure. Reassurances that such diplomatic relations are being maintained may well, from the point of view of mutual etiquette, have a soothing and uplifting effect—according to a recent declaration by the General Commission, both it and the party executive have already, in individual cases, requested and undertaken a series of consultations with the other respective body. Nevertheless, the

---

* Inserted in first edition: "thus themselves."
† The Executive Committee of the Social Democratic Party of Germany had its offices on Lindenstraße in Berlin, while the General Commission of German Trade Unions had its headquarters on Engel-Ufer, also in Berlin.

German workers' movement—which, given the serious times that are coming, must gain a somewhat deeper grasp of all of the problems relating to its struggle—has every reason to push this Chinese Mandarin bureaucracy to one side and to seek the solution to its task where relations ensure that such a solution is, of itself, given. The guarantee of the real unity of the workers' movement is not to be found up above, at the uppermost level of the leaderships of the respective organizations and the federative alliance between them, but down below, in the organized proletarian mass. In the consciousness of the 1 million labor union members, party and labor union are actually *one*—that is to say, they are the different forms of the *Social Democratic* struggle for the emancipation of the proletariat. And hence also derives—in and of itself—the necessity of adapting the mutual relation between Social Democracy and labor unions to the consciousness of the proletarian mass—i.e., the necessity of *re-affiliating labor unions to Social Democracy*—in order to eliminate [the estrangement and] the friction that have arisen between these two forms.[*] This merely expresses the synthesis of the actual development, which had led from the original incorporation of labor unions within Social Democracy to their separation from the latter, only then to pave the way for the coming period of great proletarian mass struggles through a period of strong growth on the part of both labor unions and the Social Democratic Party of Germany; this latter progression in turn has rendered the reunification of Social Democracy and labor unions a necessity in the interests of both.

Here, of course, it is not a matter of the dissolution of the entire[†] labor union structure within the party; rather, it is a question of establishing the natural relation between the leadership of the Social Democratic Party of Germany and the labor unions—between party conventions and labor union congresses—that corresponds to the actual relation between the workers' movement as a whole and its partial manifestation in the form of labor unions. Such a change will inevitably elicit fierce opposition from a section of labor union officials.[‡] Nevertheless, it is high time that the Social Democratic masses of workers learned to give expression to their capacity to make judgments and take action, and thereby to demonstrate their maturity and readiness for those times of great struggles and great tasks in which they, the masses, are to play the role of active chorus and the respective leaderships are merely to act as spokespersons,[§] as interpreters of the will of the masses.

The labor union movement is not that which is reflected in the completely explicable, but erroneous illusions of a few dozen[¶] labor union leaders; instead

---

[*] Inserted in first edition: "or between Social Democracy and a section of the labor unions."
[†] First edition: "current."
[‡] First edition: "labor union leaders."
[§] Inserted in first edition: "that is."
[¶] First edition: "a minority of."

it is that which is alive in the consciousness of the great mass of proletarians who have been won over to the class struggle. In this consciousness, the labor union movement is a component of Social Democracy. "But let it dare to seem the thing it is!"*

---

* "But let her dare to seem the thing she is!" is a phrase from a play by Friedrich Schiller. See his *Mary Stuart: A Tragedy*, translated by Joseph Mellish (London: Cotta, 1801), p. 50.

Party Congress of the Social Democratic Party of Germany in Mannheim [September 23–29, 1906]

I. SPEECH ON THE QUESTION OF THE MASS STRIKE*

[Karl] Legien's speech follows that classic, typical pattern that sets the attitude that certain trade union leaders have recently adopted toward Social Democracy and the most important party issues. First, for an entire hour, he sharply criticized the Jena Resolution† and demonstrated the impossibility and perishability of the idea of a mass strike, warned us against it, and finally, of course, there was the heartrending and soothing reassurance that we are all one heart and one soul! So, we don't need to have any disputes at all; we can unite on a resolution. And this unity is produced in the most curious of ways: by declaring the Cologne Resolution,‡ which already makes the mere discussion of the mass strike pernicious, identical to the resolution of Jena. When I heard that Legien had tabled this motion, I said to myself that it takes a good deal of courage and audacity to assume that we would agree to the motion. And I was not a little surprised to hear that the party executive sympathized. ("Hear! Hear!" "Quite right!")

A few words about Legien's criticism of the Jena decision! His appeal to tradition is characteristic: We all grew up with the idea that the general strike, which he easily identifies with the mass strike, was general nonsense. Yes, we would be nice Social Democrats if we didn't know how to emancipate ourselves from ideas one has as a small child. We are a party of historical development so that we can learn from history. ("Quite right!") If today, in the face of the great Russian Revolution, which will be the teacher of the revolutionary movements

---

* This speech was first published in *Protokoll über die Verhandlungen des Parteitags der Sozialdemokratischen Partei Deutschlands, Mannheim vom 23. bis 29. September 1906* (Protocol of the Negotiations of the Party Congress of the Social Democratic Party of Germany, held in Mannheim, September 23–9, 1906) (Berlin: Buchhandlung Vorwärts, 1906), pp. 260–2. It is translated by Manuela Kölke from Luxemburg's *Gesammelte Werke*, Vol. 2, pp. 171–3. The phrases in parentheses are the recorded responses of the audience.

† In response to growing divisions with the SPD over attitudes toward the mass strike, the party established a "Fifteenth Commission" at its Jena Congress of September 1905 in order to look into the disagreements on this issue between different SPD newspapers, in particular *Vorwärts* and *Leipziger Volkszeitung*. The commission rejected calls from right-wing figures that the discussion of the mass strike be shelved because it allegedly (as claimed by the rightists) represented a mere "squabble among the literati." For Luxemburg's extended defense of the Jena Resolution, see "Remarks at the Jena Congress on Relations between the Party and the Trade Unions, with Reference to the 1905 Revolution in Russia" [September 1905], in *Complete Works*, Vol. 3, pp. 205–11.

‡ The Fifth Congress of the Social Democratic Free Trade Unions, held May 22 to 27, 1905, in Cologne, strongly rejected the use of the mass strike and even prohibited any discussion of it.

of the proletariat for decades to come, one studies the problem of the mass strike mainly in relation to the events in Italy and France, one finds substantiation for what Legien has proved with his appeal to tradition—that one knows to forget nothing but learn nothing. (Restlessness. Agreement.) Indeed, you know how to learn nothing from the Russian Revolution. (Legien: "Quite right!") Otherwise, you would not have the courage to claim that the mass strike movement was the greatest danger to the existence of the trade unions. You obviously have no idea that the huge Russian trade union movement is a child of the revolution. ("Quite right!" and dissent.) The Russian proletariat has entered the revolution without the trace of an organization, and today the whole country is suffused with strong organizational structures. It is precisely the old ossified English view that trade unions can only thrive if they develop calmly. The Russian Revolution has shown that in many cases the most powerful proletarian organizations can be born and thrive out of struggle. [Eduard] David, on the other hand, criticized the idea of the mass strike from his special legal point of view in Mainz.* He presented the machine guns to us as a bugaboo. He also has no idea what is going on in Russia (laughter); he forgets that the machine guns are operated by living people, by soldiers—and that they do not lose their effectiveness when the time is right. They remain just as deadly; they are only turned about and set up against the ruling regime. (Loud applause.) Legien's last argument was such that it proves that he honestly remained in some respects entirely rooted in the concepts of childhood. (Laughter.) He said we had committed a careless act by adopting the Jena Resolution; we had betrayed our plans to the enemy. Since when have great historical movements, great popular movements, been carried out by secret agreements in closed rooms? ("Very good!") This is a childish idea of a general strike if one believes that one's fate depends on what the General Commission decides, even with the party executive in a silent chamber.† (Lively agreement and laughter.)

I wanted to say a few words about [August] Bebel's speech, but I'm not sure I understood it correctly, because I was sitting on the left side, and today he always spoke to the right. (Great amusement.) But I did discover a striking contradiction. He once said: "Everything remains, of course, in the hands of the Jena Resolution. If we were to be deprived of universal suffrage, then we would, of course, have to defend it by all means, even if we should fall by the wayside." I remembered the words, they refreshed my heart, but then, in the end, came what could and should happen in Germany if we were brought into a war with

---

* For David's comments criticizing the mass strike at the assembly in Mainz on September 10, 1906, see p. 249 above.

† On February 16, 1906, the executive of the General Commission of Social Democratic Trade Unions declared in an internal statement not available to the public that the mass strike should never be propagated without its consent and that it would take active measures to prevent one from ever happening.

Russia by an intervention of Prussia. I am not sure whether I understood Bebel correctly there, and I would think it would be good if he would prevent all misinterpretations of the final words of his speech. As far as I could understand him, the meaning was that if we are brought before a war, there is nothing we can do about it. Our friends in France would be very embarrassed if Bebel's speech could be interpreted in this way, because there our brave and courageous comrades declared, by [Édouard] Vaillant: If it came to war with Russia, then they would veto it. Our friends have coined the saying "Plutôt l'insurrection que la guerre"—"Better a popular uprising than war." That was the robust language of the French proletariat, and I hope the German too will find the courage to say: "It must not be allowed to happen against our will." (Loud applause.) Bebel said: "Do you think the mass strike could be realized by the party executive? No, the party leadership must be pushed by the masses." Now, if the Party Executive Committee does not consider its role differently, it should and will be pushed, and I ask you, in this sense, to reject the agreements of the Executive Committee with the General Commission made behind our backs and to approve Kautsky's motion.* (Loud applause.)

II. SPEECH ON THE RELATION BETWEEN PARTY AND TRADE UNIONS[†]

Party comrades! I do not think there will be anyone among us who does not agree with the basic idea of the resolution of the party executive.[‡] Hopefully, we are all in agreement that central organization is the most suitable form for the modern trade union struggle and that anarchism in Germany today, as in the entire capitalist world, must at most be regarded as a consequence of the intellectual aberrations and decadence of the workers. In spite of all this, however, I would regard the adoption of the resolution tabled by the party executive as a major error. ("Quite right!") Most of all, I cannot, with my limited subservient

---

* Karl Kautsky and thirty-two others demanded in a motion that the resolution of the party executive on the question of the political mass strike should include, among other things, an unequivocal statement that every Social Democrat should adhere to the decisions of the party congresses and that Social Democracy was the highest and most comprehensive form of the proletarian class struggle. Kautsky withdrew this most vital aspect of the motion after reformists raised objections.

† This is the second speech delivered by Luxemburg to the congress. It was first published in *Protokoll über die Verhandlungen des Parteitags der Sozialdemokratischen Partei Deutschlands, Mannheim vom 23. bis 29. September 1906* (Protocol of the Negotiations of the Party Congress of the Social Democratic Party of Germany, held in Mannheim September 23–9, 1906) (Berlin: Buchhandlung Vorwärts, 1906), pp. 315–16. It is translated by Manuela Kölke from Luxemburg's *Gesammelte Werke*, Vol. 2, pp. 174–6.

‡ The resolution of the party executive demanded fighting the anarcho-syndicalist efforts in the local trade union organizations and to exclude the anarcho-syndicalists from the Social Democratic Party. Although Luxemburg uses the term "anarcho-socialist" in the text, she means anarcho-syndicalism; very few anarchists of the time used the former term.

mind (amusement), see how the position of the representatives of the central associations on this resolution can be reconciled with their position on the previous resolution by Kautsky. Although it seemed the most obvious thing in the world for every Social Democrat to act as a Social Democrat also within the union and to respect the decisions of party congresses, there was a violent reluctance to do so, because it would give the impression to the outside world that the unions were completely in the grip of Social Democracy. Here, however, there is complete agreement that Social Democracy should take sharp action in favor of a particular form of trade union organization. I fear that, in such a dual position, the relationship between the trade unions and Social Democracy will be similar to that of that well-known peasant marriage contract in which the woman told the man: "If we agree on a question, let your will be done; if we disagree, let it be done according to my will." (Amusement.) Furthermore, I find it irresponsible if the party is to be used here as a kind of rod of discipline against a certain group of trade unionists, meaning that we will only succeed in yoking ourselves to quarrel and strife. There is no doubt that there are a great many good comrades among the local organizations, and it would be irresponsible for us to bring quarrel into our ranks, simply in order to directly serve the trade unions on this issue. We respect the view that the localists* should not push the dispute in the trade union organizations so far that, in the process, they thoroughly hamstring the trade union organization, but in the name of so much vaunted equality, one must at least demand the same of the party as well. If, as the party executive proposes, we directly exclude the anarcho-socialists from the party, we are setting a sad example of how we can find energy and determination to demarcate our party on the left but still leave the gates wide open to the right.† ("Quite right!")

[Adolph von] Elm has cited here as an example of anarchist nonsense that in *Die Einigkeit* [Unity],‡ or in a conference of a local organization, it is stated that the general strike is to be regarded as the only means of real revolutionary class struggle. Now, of course, this is nonsense and nothing else. But, ladies and gentlemen, it is just as far removed from Social Democratic tactics and from our principles as when David declares that the legal, parliamentary means are the only means of Social Democracy. ("Quite right!") We are told that the localists, the anarcho-socialists, are undermining the Social Democratic principles at every turn through their agitation. But exactly the same undermining of Social Democratic principles took place when one of the central associations, like

---

* That is, those associated with anarcho-syndicalist positions.

† The SPD had in fact expelled the anarchists as early as 1895 but refrained from expelling Bernstein and other revisionists—much to Luxemburg's displeasure.

‡ *Die Einigkeit* was the organ of the anarcho-syndicalist Free Association of German Trade Unions (FVdG), published since 1897.

[August] Bringmann* at your conference in February,† declared itself against the principle of class struggle. (Dissent.) Anarchism in our ranks is nothing more than a reaction to the left in reaction to the riots of the right. ("Quite true!") If you want to fight anarchism, you should remain true to our tried and tested principle: Nobody is excluded here because of their views. We want to render those people harmless and undermine the whole anarcho-socialist movement by taking the front against opportunism, because it is the real father of the anarchist improbities. If we have not excluded anyone from the extreme right, we certainly have no right to exclude the extreme left. (Loud applause and dissent.)

---

* Bringmann had expressed his view a year earlier in his book *Geschichte Der Deutschen Zimmerer-Bewegung* (History of the German Carpenters' Movement) (Stuttgart: Dietz Verlag, 1905).
† The conference of representatives of the central authority's executive boards was held in Berlin from February 19 to 23, 1906.

The Russian Revolution [September 25, 1906]*

Comrade Luxemburg remarked in the introduction, with regard to her illness, that it had taught her something about the Russian Revolution; if it were believed to be dead, it will rise again. ("Bravo!")†

Today I believed I was sick, but I was told to come here and say a few words about the revolution. I will do so as far as I have the strength to do so. At the end of his speech, the previous speaker called me a martyr and a victim of the Russian Revolution. I must begin my speech with a protest against this. Anyone who does not look at the Russian Revolution from afar, who has worked for it themselves, will not say that they are a victim and a martyr. I can assure you without any exaggeration and in all honesty that the months I spent in Russia were the happiest of my life. I feel deeply saddened that I had to leave Russia and return to Germany.‡ You get a completely wrong picture of the revolution from bourgeois telegraph agencies' sensationalist telegrams. Such reports paint a great sea of blood for those outside Russia, an unheard-of suffering of the people, without the slightest ray of light. This is the view of the decadent bourgeoisie, but not of the proletarian class. For centuries, the Russian people suffered, but the terrible sufferings during the revolution, they are only slight in comparison with the terrible sufferings that the Russian people had to endure *before* the revolution, under the quiet domination they had to accept. ("Quite right!") For centuries, Russia lived under the yoke of absolutism, but did anyone ask how many thousands died of scurvy, or of hunger? Did anyone ask about the thousands of proletarians that fell on the battlefield of labor without even drawing the attention of the statistician? How many children have degenerated or have not reached the first year of life due to lack of food in Russian villages? They will understand that against these innumerable victims, the present sacrifices and sufferings are minimal.

But now the other side of the coin. Whereas in the past, the Russian people lived without any prospect of escape from their terrible suffering, now they know what they are dying for, what they are suffering for, what they are fighting for. Everyone knows that at least for their children, their grandchildren, they are working for the liberation of the people. The Russian people have simply

---

* This article was first published in *Leipziger Volkszeitung*, No. 226, September 29, 1906. It was originally delivered as a speech on September 25, 1906, in Mannheim at a People's Assembly. It is translated by Manuela Kölke from Luxemburg's *Gesammelte Werke*, Vol. 2, pp. 177–81.

† This sentence is a prefatory remark made by the reporter of Luxemburg's speech, briefly paraphrasing her introduction.

‡ She was arrested on March 4, 1906, and released from prison (on bail) on June 28, 1906, on the basis of her state of health.

moved terribly slowly. They have lagged half a century behind the other nations of Europe in their development and are now fighting as the last stragglers for their liberation through revolution. History knows what it is doing, and even if it has kept us waiting, here it gives us a very different gift than the other nations ahead of us. For us, this revolution is a very different phenomenon than the March Revolution in Germany [of 1848] and the Great French Revolution [of 1789]. It is true that in Russia we are fighting for the same bourgeois liberties—a parliament, the right of association, freedom of the press, etc.—for which we fought in Germany back in 1848 and in France half a century earlier, but today it is not the aspiring bourgeoisie that leads this movement, but the proletariat which has taken the leading role in the struggle. The Russian proletariat does not indulge in the illusions of the proletariat of 1848; it knows quite well that the introduction of the rule of socialism overnight is an impossibility; it knows that nothing other than a bourgeois constitutional state can come into being. But we would not be worthy of the name of Social Democrats, we would not be worthy of being disciples of Marx and Engels, if we stuck to the mere form and did not distinguish that under one and the same form there can be different social and historical contents. It is precisely from the fact that our constitutional state is formed by the callused hand of the proletariat that it will receive a firm imprint that benefits the proletariat more than the bourgeoisie. The Russian proletariat fights first for bourgeois freedom, for universal suffrage, the republic, the law of associations, freedom of the press, etc., but it does not fight with the illusions that filled the proletariat of 1848. It fights for [such] liberties in order to instrumentalize them as a weapon against the bourgeoisie.

For anyone who has an insight into Russian conditions, it is clear that Russian liberalism has already shrunk to a dwarf, just as the proletariat swells increasingly like an avalanche, gathering its strength. But it is also clear that, on the basis of this phenomenon, the rule of law in Russia will be something quite different from that of today's Germany. The Russian Revolution can never give rise to the monstrosity [*Spottgeburt*] of liberalism as it has in Germany. It is an incorrect view to look at the Russian Revolution only from the standpoint of the so-called legal order and eagerly await the existence of a parliament in its own right.

You are all familiar with the history of the first Duma. Liberalism already felt liberated from the terrible dream of the revolution when the destruction of the Duma took place.* Yet the dissolution of the Duma was not a sign of the power of absolutism, but of the powerlessness of Russian liberalism. The dissolution of the Duma showed that the Russian bourgeoisie was completely finished. Every further attempt will show that it lacks the strength to fight against absolutism.

---

* The First Duma was dissolved by the tsar on July 8, 1906, after its representatives pressed for more radical changes than his government was willing to contemplate.

When the message came to leave the Duma to heaven,* its representatives knew nothing better than to flee to Finland and fabricate there a paper protest for the dustbin of world history.†

The Russian proletariat, despite the low stage it is at, has shown itself to be far more mature than the Russian bourgeoisie. It has understood from the outset that parliamentarism is powerless as long as absolutism is at the helm, as long as it is not crushed by the aspirations of the revolutionary class. Today we are faced with the question of the revolutionary proletariat seizing power. Liberalism has already played itself out, as the Duma has shown. The task of the proletariat is not an easy one; it is a struggle for death and life between the aspiring Russian people and Russian absolutism. In this struggle, the fate of the future Russian freedom shall be decided. Apparently, there are also some timid comrades who say that the revolution could be suffocated in a sea of blood by the present brutality of the rulers. Anyone who has been there knows that this cannot be true. Nothing is more erroneous than to assume that Russian freedom could be violently withheld. Here, too, the teachings of Marx and Engels hold true: that every social order is a historical necessity, that it must be born, just like the fruit of the mother's womb, no matter what it takes. The struggle that still awaits us is the most difficult phase of the whole revolution. Just imagine the mass strike as a repetitive action taken in all directions; it was a continuous series of developments in the revolutionary movement that has carried the proletariat higher and higher. It is the proper development toward inner maturity and knowledge that has brought us to the present point of revolution. This awareness consists in the realization that it is not enough to carry out mass strikes to overthrow absolutism, but that sooner or later the question of a popular uprising against the bearer of the absolutist regime will also have to be considered in order to bring the revolution to a proper end.

The whole course of this revolution proves just how different it is from all other earlier revolutions—they were all brief street battles of a few hours or days. Nowadays, when the destiny is in the hands of the people, a revolution is a long and difficult process; it is only through a long series of mass strikes that the mighty army has been able to gather for the final decisive blow. Those who grasp the course of the revolution in their innermost being will by no means give in to any pessimism. One has to admire the heroism of the Russian proletariat. Not only do I not wish to dispute this view, but I also wish to point out that tribute and admiration of heroism is paid too much to the individuals who are at the

---

* Luxemburg is here paraphrasing the phrase from Shakespeare's *Hamlet* about leaving Cordelia to heaven.

† In protest against the dissolution of the First Duma, the representatives of the Constitutional Democratic Party (Cadets) met with other deputies of the Duma in Viborg, Finland, on July 22, 1906. In an appeal to the people, they called for passive resistance, in particular by refusing tax payments and military service.

forefront of the struggle and far too little to the great masses, who make enormous sacrifices. I would like to point out to you that it is much more important to make it clear from Russian events that the development of a revolutionary power does not depend on the number of organized Social Democrats alone. Only the hour of the struggle will reveal the enormous idealism of the people. The Russian events indicate that, in line with the general situation in Germany, we should also prepare ourselves for such struggles in which the masses will turn the tables.

The political mass strike is at the center of the negotiations of the party congress; it is proof that class consciousness is taking on deeper and deeper roots in the proletariat. By its very nature, it senses that sooner or later the proletariat must be prepared to defend and extend its vested political rights through the mass strike. The Russian Revolution is a great teacher to the German proletariat. There is no doubt that the Russian Revolution is to have the greatest possible impact abroad. The Russian constitutional state will also bring about a shift in the political conditions in Germany. The Russian proletariat must then serve as a model for us, and not only with regard to parliamentarism. By this I am referring to the determination and audacity to set up and carry out political tasks to the highest level required by the historical situation. If we are to gain anything from the Russian Revolution, it is not with pessimism but the greatest optimism that we await the future, with the greatest boldness in calling out with tenfold force: In spite of everything, we will prevail! (Applause for minutes.)

General Strike and German Social Democracy*

The question and fate of the general strike reveal the influence of Russian events on German Social Democracy in the most vivid terms.† The conscious section of the German proletariat had an extremely negative—we could even say derisive—attitude toward this issue until relatively recently. Ignatz Auer's slogan "General strike—general nonsense" had become a catchphrase in Germany. This hostile and belittling attitude toward the idea of the general strike was seen as a specifically Marxist characteristic of German labor movement tactics, in contrast to "romantic" tactics; characteristic German sobriety and thoroughness, in contrast to French and Italian ease and insouciance. Indeed, the contrast between the German proletariat's conception of the general strike, and French, Italian, and Spanish conceptions of the same issue, was traced back for a long time to fundamental differences in outlook between Social Democratic and anarchistic Weltanschauungen. Until today, the strictest rejection of the general strike idea was identical to defending the necessity of a broad-based and thorough organization of the worker masses, as the nonnegotiable condition for successful class struggle. This has also been seen as identical to the necessity of the working classes' daily struggle for political rights, and the necessity of using parliamentary forms of political life in the interest of the proletariat. These convictions were undoubtedly the core meaning of the general strike resolutions that German Social Democracy's representatives defended at international socialist congresses, from the Zurich Congress in 1893 to Amsterdam in 1904.

Yet just as delegates met for the most recent international congress in Amsterdam, the first thunderclaps of the gathering storm rang out in Russia, the thunder that is called upon to turn around the tactics of the fighting international proletariat. And the first and most surprising consequence of this storm was to enable the general strike to appear in an utterly new light.

To the conscious German proletariat's great honor, we recognize that despite its opposing the general strike most vehemently in an earlier period, it was also the first to react to the Russian liberation movement's ostentatious lessons, and to position itself with fiery enthusiasm behind the idea that it had ridiculed previously, for more than a quarter of a century. The German working masses

---

* This introduction to the Russian edition of Luxemburg's *The Mass Strike, the Political Party, and the Trade Unions* (see above, pp. 193–261) was written in October 1906 and published in Russian as *Wseobschtschaja sabastowka i nemezkaja sozial-demokratija. S predislowijem awtora k russkomuisdaniju Perewod* (Kiev: W. S. Majera, 1906). It is translated by Henry Holland from Luxemburg's *Gesammelte Werke*, Vol. 6 (Berlin: Dietz Verlag, 2004), pp. 915–22.

† In the Russian text of this preface, Luxemburg mainly uses the term "general strike." Within German Social Democracy, however, "mass strike" was more widely used.

demonstrated such flexibility in thought, and such revolutionary sensitivity and political maturity, that they have again raised themselves a step above many of their leaders.

And how true that is. While Social Democratic organizations, in all parts of Germany and from spring 1905 onward, inundated speakers—connected to the movement in Russia through their own organizations or through other channels—with demands to report about the mass strike and the experiences of the proletariat in Russia, and while public speeches on this subject, conducted with revolutionary spirit, unleashed tremendous enthusiasm among the worker masses they addressed, trade union leaders at the Trades Union Congress in April* 1905 in Cologne declared the idea of the mass strike in Germany to be not only non-realizable, but even dangerous. These same leaders even adopted the resolution proposed by [Theodor] Bömelburg, chair of the Central Union of Masons, which *banned* propaganda† supporting this method of struggle!

Concurrently, the mass strike became a political football among the ranks of Social Democracy, generating a sustained and acutely heated discussion between both wings of the party: the revolutionary and the opportunistic wings. Henriette Roland-Holst's pamphlet‡ became the object of impassioned attacks—which ignored the pamphlet's utterly moderate form—led by *Vorwärts* [Forward], German Social Democracy's central organ, during a period in which this paper was still in the hands of those who supported opportunistic tactics. The mass strike discussion, which had erupted between Karl Kautsky and *Vorwärts*' former editorial board, assumed an acrimonious form that grew out of long-simmering dissatisfaction with the central organ's political direction. This provided the final prompt for the debates about the tactics of the *Vorwärts* editors§ at the Social Democratic Party conference in Jena in 1905.

As we know, events in Russia influenced the Jena party conference to an uncommon [degree]. By the end of proceedings, the leftist, revolutionary wing had recorded a decisive victory, which expressed itself in both the ardent adoption of the resolution supporting the concept of mass strike,¶ and the "subversion"

---

* The conference was actually held from May 22 to 27, 1905.

† This word had a different meaning in 1906 than today: It meant material that supports the arguments of a particular political group or party, rather than mendacious material that distorts facts to fit a particular political agenda.

‡ See Henriette Roland-Holst, *Generalstreik und Sozialdemokratie Mit einem Vorwort von Karl Kautsky* (General Strike and Social Democracy, with a Foreword by Karl Kautsky) (Dresden: Kaden, 1905).

§ Since the death of Wilhelm Liebknecht, Kurt Eisner, *Vorwärts*' new editor in chief, had steered the paper into what Luxemburg regarded as the opportunists' sphere of influence. It sided with the political mass strike's opponents in 1905, a position that unleashed huge outrage among the majority of Social Democrats. The controversy played a major role in the SPD party conference at Jena in 1905. At the request of August Bebel, Eisner was forced out as editor (along with five other co-editors) and replaced by Luxemburg on November 1, 1905.

¶ The resolution passed at the SPD's party conference at Jena, held between September 17

of the central organ's editorial board, from which six representatives of "moderate" tactics resigned. With a newly composed editorial board, *Vorwärts* began to illuminate events in Russia and the question of the mass strike in an entirely different spirit than previously.*

But that was precisely what deeply upset the party's opportunistic circles, and which sparked a systematic witch hunt against *Vorwärts*. This witch hunt's most vociferous expression was the public press statement by three party members of parliament from the greater Hamburg and Kiel region: [Karl] Frohme, [Adolph von] Elm, and [Friedrich] Lesche.† They warned the party that the dangerous "revolutionary romanticism," which *Vorwärts*' new editors were supposedly preaching in articles and at public meetings, was threatening Germany with every catastrophe that the revolution brings with it.

In connection with these attacks, the question arose as to the correct or false *exegesis* of the Jena Resolution. Social Democracy's opportunistic circles argued that the Jena party conference had supported the use of the mass strike in Germany exclusively in case a situation were to come about in which the government would attempt to deprive the working class of its universal and equal right to vote for the Reichstag. Or for a situation in which Social Democracy would decide to fight at all costs for entry into the Prussian, Saxonian, or any of the other reactionary, regional parliaments [*Landtage*] in which working class participation is blocked by means of a tiered, unjust voting law.

---

and 23, 1905, described the comprehensive application of the mass strike as one of the working class' most effective means of struggle. However, it restricted its application to cover only the defense of the right to vote for the Reichstag, and the defense of the right of assembly.

* Alongside Luxemburg, the new staff of the paper was composed of Hans Block, Georg Davidson, Wilhelm Düwell, Arthur Stadthagen, Karl Wermuth, Heinrich Cunow, Heinrich Ströbel, and Fritz Kunert. "Dear Róza," wrote Karl Kautsky on a visiting card on October 28, 1905, "Well, tomorrow the interregnum's over, and you as staff member are solemnly invited, i.e., officially, to take part in the new editorial team. First duty: *You must report tomorrow, Sunday, on the dot of ten in the morn[ing] for the editorial meeting,* which will clear up everything else. An article is expected from you by Tuesday, sort out everything else with the Menshinstvo [the Mensheviks]. Long live the revolution, in every nook and cranny! Yours, K.K." See Rosa Luxemburg, *Gesammelte Briefe* (Berlin: Dietz Verlag, 1999), p. 225.

† This refers to an article by Adolph von Elm, Karl Frohme, and Friedrich Lesche on November 23, 1905, in the *Hamburger Echo*, No. 275. These authors saw themselves acting according to the view of the majority in the SPD, and according to the spirit of the Jena Resolution on the mass strike. They describe the new current in the party, which includes revolutionary Social Democrats like Luxemburg, as belonging to a "revolutionary romanticism that is downright ruinous for the party." Further, they claim the leftists have attempted to interpret the Jena mass strike resolution as if "the party was already so fixed on the political mass strike, that one could organize it now already, in all seriousness, today or tomorrow. And that anyone who doesn't join in with their revolutionary romanticism is suspected of being a 'wet defeatist,' a revisionist, a 'denier of the revolutionary spirit' of the party, or an 'I'm a socialist too'; and [that these leftists'] attempt to incapacitate [this sort of skeptic], in his activity in the workers' movement." The authors imply in this same article that this new political current, and Luxemburg above all, denigrates trade union work as a "labor of Sisyphus." Moreover, they argue that this current belittles parliamentary work.

The October Days in Russia crashed into the middle of these debates.* Russia's massive influence showed itself immediately in the Austrian proletariat's tumultuous movement to demand universal and equal suffrage.† Demonstrations and mass strikes in Vienna, Prague, and Graz influenced German workers in turn, particularly in Austria's neighbor, Saxony,‡ roughly a decade after the reactionary upheaval that had locked the working class out of Saxony's regional parliament. Concurrent to this, the bourgeoisie in the "Free Hanseatic Republic of Hamburg"§ dared to rob the workers of the right to participate in the elections to the city's law-making body. Finally, in Prussia, the ferment among the working masses threw open the question of whether it was not time to try out the new powerful weapon in the battle for political rights. The upcoming anniversary of the events in Petersburg on January 22¶ seemed to be the most favorable moment to launch the [new] movement, if it was going to take place at all. The German government, anxious about the general ferment and events in Russia, readied itself for its part in the proceedings, in order to face up to January 22, 1906, and the demonstrations that were expected on this day, by using "extraordinary measures" and "armed force" that had been prepared in advance.

Under these circumstances, German Social Democracy's executive considered it necessary to deal seriously with the question of what attitude should be adopted this time in Germany to the mass strike: Should the call for new kinds of mass actions be voiced or not? Unfortunately, these discussions led the party executive to chance upon the pretty hapless idea of holding a secret conference with the General Commission of Trade Unions. As is usual in such cases, the facts and the fruits of this conference soon became widely known, partly in corrupted forms. The organ of the so-called local trade unions, which are at loggerheads with the centralized trade unions, but which are mainly, or rather almost exclusively, financed by committed Social Democrats, rushed to tell the world about the "treachery" of which German Social Democracy's

---

* At the end of October 1905, political mass strikes took place in all of Russia's industrial centers, with demands that included bringing down autocracy, boycotting the Bułygin Duma, convening the Constituent Assembly, and establishing a democratic republic.

† Large strikes and street demonstrations took place in October and November 1905 in the Austro-Hungarian Empire demanding universal suffrage. This movement spread to Moravia, Galicia, Carniola (parts of which are in present-day Slovenia), Tyrol, and other areas. Social Democratic slogans, including "Let's speak Russian!" and "Long live the general strike!" were taken up. The disturbances also expanded into the army and the navy. In February 1906, the government promised to put a voting law reform before Parliament. A new voting law with a variety of restrictions was finally proclaimed in January 1907.

‡ Under Social Democratic leadership in Saxony, demands were raised for a new, democratic voting law, with political agitation focused particularly on Chemnitz, Dresden, and Leipzig. Violent clashes between police and demonstrators took place in Dresden.

§ These are Luxemburg's own quotation marks, conveying her skepticism as to how "free" the "Republic of Hamburg" really was at this point in history.

¶ The one-year anniversary of "Bloody Sunday," which initiated the 1905 Revolution.

party executive was apparently guilty. Together with the leaders of the General Commission of Trade Unions, the executive had apparently renounced the idea of the mass strike at this secret conference.[*]

This "revelation" naturally caused a big row, and the party executive considered it necessary, in order to avoid misunderstandings and false interpretations, to start publishing the minutes of its "confidential" consultations with the General Commission of Trade Unions. But precisely this led to a brusque collision between party representatives and trade union representatives. The latter insisted—without the least deference to the major commotion among party members and the extremely embarrassing position of the party executive—that party representatives keep the "secret." In defiance of the trade union protests, the party executive then decided to publish not only the results of their consultation with the unions, but also the minutes of a no less "confidential" consultation of all trade union leaders that had addressed the mass strike and relations between the trade unions and Social Democracy in general.

What this set of minutes "revealed" to the party was of course not the "treachery" of their party executive, but the trade union leaders' most violent campaign against Social Democracy. A battle against the "lefties,"[†] against the "revolutionary romantics," against the "literati," against the supporters of the mass strike, whereby the strongest blow was reserved for the author of these lines, whose head has been heaped with guilt: That was the battle cry of this "confidential" consultation, in which several hundred trade union tribal chiefs took part. In this context, the trade unions also reviewed their relationship with the party itself. The wish was articulated that a "new theory" of trade unionism be created, independent from the theory of class struggle and from Marxism.

It is understandable that the publication of these minutes ignited the liveliest debates about the relations among political and economic organizations of the proletarian struggle.

The battle of opinions about the mass strike in Germany and its chances caught fire again in other arenas in January of last year. As became clear, the party executive had in fact decided against the calling of a mass strike during its consultation with the trade union leaders—though of course not in general, but rather for this concrete situation—that is, for the coming months. What [the executive] actually agreed was that if the mass strike were to break out nonetheless, its leadership should fall wholly and exclusively to the Social Democratic Party executive, and that the trade unions should stay completely on the sidelines. However, material support for the victims of the strike should be borne by both Social Democracy and the unions. As we know, in reality, neither the mass

---

[*] This secret meeting of the party executive with the General Commission of Trade Unions took place in Berlin on February 19, 1906. A conference of delegates from the commission's central executives followed, between February 19 and 23, 1906.

[†] The term used by Luxemburg is *Linken*, a pejorative in the eyes of her opponents.

strike nor mass demonstrations followed in Germany. Hamburg was the only location in which workers conducted a half-day mass strike,* in connection with a whole series of people's assemblies† that were thoroughly successful, and that generated large-scale fervor among the whole worker population of Hamburg.

But what is peculiar is that as soon as the party executive's decision about the mass strikes and demonstrations—which the spring was expected to bring—was made public, a huge commotion broke out among the ranks of the arch-opportunists about the party's "shameful backwardness." All those figures who, a year previous, had countered the lessons and examples of the liberation movement in Russia in an extremely skeptical manner, now entered the fray angrily against the party executive, because it didn't "produce" a mass strike in Prussia aimed at reforming the regional state parliament's voting laws. The editorial board of *Vorwärts*, together with Kautsky and the left wing [of the party] as a whole, were now given cause to demonstrate the unscrupulousness of the hopes that a mass strike would break out in Germany in order to fight for a [new] Prussian voting law. Henriette Roland-Holst made efforts in the *Neue Zeit* [New Times], to explain why the spring ferment had not brought any results, by linking it to the Russian revolutionary wave's temporary abatement, which had also caused a waning of revolutionary mood of the masses in Western Europe. It appeared that the antagonists were swapping roles. In truth, however, only the object of discussion had changed. Instead of the question of *for* or *against*, [combatants] now posed the question of *how* to understand the mass strike. As a demonstrable weapon of an orderly action by the organized proletarian center, or as a historical expression of the revolutionary mass struggle? Today, almost none of the politicians of the workers' movement in Germany take a stance against the mass strike in general. But every political current fills the idea of the mass strike with different concrete contents.

So, bit by bit, the problem of the mass strike is edging toward the center of intellectual life and of German Social Democracy's own intellectual interest, and it's highly likely that it will occupy this position for a long time. The mass strike functions as a crossroads and as a focus for all contentious questions of the German workers' movement. Questions about parliamentarism and the immediate role of the masses; about the proletariat's political and economic struggle; about the significance and role played by organization; about the foreseeability and spontaneity of the workers' movement; about a peaceful tactic and about clashes with the ruling classes' armed power; about gradually "growing up into"

---

* On January 17, 1906, 80,000 workers staged a walkout in Hamburg in order to protest against new restrictions on the right to vote for the city parliament, or *Bürgerschaft* as it is still called. This was the first political mass strike in Germany and was accompanied by clashes between workers and police.

† *Volksversammlungen* is translated here as "people's assemblies," and not "people's councils," to distinguish these gatherings from the *Räte* or *Volksräte* that Luxemburg discusses at other points in her work, which are translated here as "councils" or "people's councils" respectively.

a Social Democratic order, and revolutionary "leaps" in the development of the class struggle, and finally—last but not least*—the way people interact with the mass strike problem in Germany today reflect various ways of behaving toward and interacting with the proletarian struggle in Russia. These include the belief in its future victory—and/or the disbelief in the same—the Western European proletariat's feeling of most intimate connectedness with this struggle, or the cavalier feeling of superiority held by the "civilized" workers' movement regarding the desperate [Russian] attempts to wrest control of the first legal preconditions for a de jure existence. To sum up, the question of the mass strike has become a symbol for a whole Weltanschauung within the German workers' movement.

That's why the debates about this question are not without interest to the fighting, conscious Russian proletariat. There is also no doubt that a particular aspect of these debates has a special significance for the workers' party [the RSDRP] in Russia. The Russian Social Democrats are known for their position (in opposition to Polish Social Democracy) that unions should neither be created nor stand under the Social Democratic Party flag, but rather take the ground of political "neutrality." In arguing this, the Russian comrades cite the example of German Social Democracy—as do many other comrades—concerning the tremendous development of their "neutral" unions. They completely lose sight of the fact that the "neutrality" of the German unions is neither an ideal nor a deliberate tactical aim of Social Democracy, but rather something forced upon them by reactionary police terror during the period of the Antisocialist Laws.† This Russian position also fails to see that the German unions are not the child of a revolutionary epoch, but rather the child of political and social conditions during the thirty-year period of bourgeois parliamentarism. These two circumstances alone must actually suffice to prevent Russian Social Democrats from slavishly imitating the German movement, and to lead them to the commitment that it would most befit Russia's proletariat to demonstrate to their Western European brothers, by their example, how to apply Social Democratic principles in a self-determined manner in an entirely new revolutionary situation. This would befit them more than assiduously modifying their own strides forward to fit into the worn-out shoes of the German movement, which has grown up exclusively in the context of the undisturbed parliamentary rule of the bourgeoisie.

In their boundless trust in the "historical process" and its benign intentions toward Social Democracy, the Russian comrades really do arrive at results that in Germany would be absolutely unthinkable—and incomprehensible for every

---

* Luxemburg uses the English expression here.

† The Antisocialist Laws in Germany, in effect from 1878 to 1890, banned dozens of socialist periodicals and book publishers. They did not, however, ban the SPD directly, and the party made rapid gains in membership and parliamentary representation after its suspension.

Social Democrat. [Onlookers] observed a characteristic example of such thinking at the Kiev Assembly in May of this year, at which [the participants] founded the Union of Printing Workers. A Social Democratic speaker argued against including a clause in this union's founding charter stating that the union's aim was to defend the workers' *class* interests. This speaker explained that the term *class* interests would give the union "party livery." The proletariat's struggle, [he argued,] is already a class struggle in itself, and its Social Democratic character is conditioned by the nature of the proletarian movement. This selfless admirer of the historical process particularly invoked the experience of the German workers' movement, which supposedly had drawn together the "lethargic mass" of the working class—and that in a country with millions of Social Democratic voters!

Thinking about these voters, the Russian comrades should look primarily at the current frictions between the unions and Social Democracy in Germany. When they look more closely at the abnormal division that has arisen in the ranks of the German workers' movement because of the "neutrality" of the unions—the artificial distancing of the unions from Social Democracy, and the massive difficulties that this cleavage causes during any attempts at larger, mass action of the German proletariat—then [the Russian comrades] can taste the fruits they will harvest in the future in Russia in the wake of the artificial creation of "neutral" unions without "party livery." The Russian comrades can already start to imagine their own future Rexhäuser,* eager to protect the Book Printers' Association from the "terror of the Monsieur Social Democrats"; or their own set of Leimpeters, who ridicule the workers' global May Day holiday as a "dead fairy tale"; or their own set of Bringmen† who want to create a "new theory" of unions, independent of the theory of class struggle.

When the revolutionary flood waves have died down and the unsightly, rocklike contours of "normal" class rule by the bourgeois classes have reemerged, then the "historical process," which attempts to deliver ripe fruits to Social Democracy in Russia, will also stop. Social Democracy will, resultantly, only have acquired that amount of power and influence that it understands must be won for itself during the revolutionary epoch—through influencing the workers' struggle consciously and openly.

---

* Ludwig Rexhäuser was editor of the *Correspondent für Deutschlands Buchdrucker und Schriftgiesser*, the organ of the Union of German Book Printers (Verbandes der Deutschen Buchdrucker).

† Johann Leimpeter was a Social Democratic trade union leader. August Bringmann was a reformist socialist who argued for a trade union movement that "transcends" class struggle in his *Geschichte der Deutschen Zimmerer-Bewegung* (History of the German Carpenters' Movement) (Stuttgart: Dietz Verlag, 1905). Luxemburg mocks the latter by giving his surname in English in the text as "Bringmen."

The Mass Strike in Court*

Presiding Judge: I now grant the accused the word. But I request that she *express herself briefly*.

Defense [Attorney Kurt Rosenfeld]: I must request that the *accused's freedom of speech is not restricted*.

Presiding Judge: I merely wanted to avoid repetitions.

Rosa Luxemburg: President of the court: I usually take care not to repeat myself. Now that my defense has outlined the judicial aspects, I merely want to make some remarks about the general position of my party regarding the question of the mass strike and the use of violence. But first a word about the last argument made by the honorable state attorney. I must say that I was literally astonished about the imprudence with which an official representative of the law is able to dump the blame for proceedings such as the Hamburg riots[†] onto a 3-million-member party, which is what Social Democracy is.

The presiding judge interrupts the accused, to upbraid her for using the word *imprudence*, and to warn her against using other statements of this kind, which do not serve the issue at hand in the slightest.

Rosa Luxemburg: But I believe I must draw attention to the—shall we say recklessness—with which the state attorney wants to make us responsible for the Hamburg riots, in contradiction of an explicit court judgment [on the issue]. Because this verbal offering is also characteristic of the improvidence with which he attempts to project onto me the intention of incitement to violent acts during my Jena party conference speech.

Above all, my passionate tone incriminates me. Well, tone is a matter of individual temperament. But it's obvious that one can speak in a very passionate way while representing a strictly scientific position, just as one can speak very

---

* First published in *Vorwärts*, No. 25, December 13, 1906, Luxemburg made these remarks at her trial the previous day at the regional court [*Landgericht*] in Weimar. It is translated by Henry Holland from Luxemburg's *Gesammelte Werke*, Vol. 6, pp. 923–7. She was charged with "incitement to violent acts" following a speech about the political mass strike at the Jena party conference in 1905. The regional court sentenced her to two months' imprisonment in the Berlin Women's Prison on Barnimstraße from June 12 to August 12, 1906. She actually served her sentence a year later, in June and July 1907, since from January 1906 she participated in the revolution in Poland and was imprisoned there from March to early July 1906. A report about the whole trial was published under this headline in the second supplement of *Vorwärts* of December 13, in which her defense speech was reported much more comprehensively and differently than in the *Leipziger Volkszeitung*, which was taken as the source for the comments as reproduced in the *Gesammelte Werke*, Vol. 2, pp. 188–9. The *Hamburger Echo* of December 14, 1906 (No. 291), published a similarly comprehensive report. Her comments first appeared in book form in *Die Russische Revolution von 1905–1907*, edited by Leo Stern (Berlin: Spiegel der Deutschen Presse, 1961).

† For Luxemburg's description of the mass protests in Hamburg in January 1906, termed "riots" by the authorities, see p. 76 above.

quietly while representing a very crude, unscientific, and incendiary position. Regarding my position on the mass strike question, my perspective is precisely that [no one and no single thing] can artificially produce or provoke either a revolution or a large, serious mass strike.

As the honorable state attorney has referred to my Mannheim speech, I allow myself to read several excerpts from a text I have written to clarify my position—namely, from the pamphlet about the mass strike written specifically for the Mannheim party conference. There I say, on page 33 for example:

> In order to gain insight into the question of conscious leadership of the mass strike and the taking of the initiative in this regard, it suffices to summarize the foregoing. If the mass strike does not imply a single act, but rather a whole period of class struggle, and if this period is identical with a period of revolution, then it is evident that the mass strike cannot be conjured up out of sheer volition, even if the resolution to call the strike issues from the highest authority within the most powerful Social Democratic party. As long as Social Democracy is not in a position to stage and call off revolutions at its own discretion, the greatest enthusiasm and impatience on the part of the Social Democratic troops will not be sufficient to summon into life an actual period of mass strikes as a living, powerful popular movement.

And finally, on page 50:

> And if, on the one hand, it is difficult to predict with any certainty whether the elimination of universal suffrage in Germany will occur within a situation that will necessarily elicit an immediate mass strike action, it is completely certain, on the other hand, that as soon as we have entered the period of turbulent mass actions in Germany, Social Democracy can by no means afford to restrict its tactics to the merely defensive parliamentary campaign. Social Democracy does not have it within its power to determine in advance the cause and the moment that will induce the outbreak of mass strikes in Germany, since it does not have it within its power to bring about historical situations through party convention resolutions. What it can and must do, however, is clarify the political guidelines of these struggles once they have emerged, and formulate such guidelines within decisive and coherent tactics. Historical events are not kept in check by issuing directives to them, but rather by developing in advance an awareness of their probable, predictable consequences, and by adjusting one's own mode of action accordingly.*

That is my position concerning the mass strike, and from it you can see how far removed it is from the notions of the honorable state attorney.

---

* See above, pp. 227 and 244.

The fact that I so often referred to the Russian Revolution during my speech is perceived as particularly incriminating. But the Russian Revolution does happen to be the first large historical experiment that uses the mass strike as the method of struggle, and every serious social researcher—including even bourgeois scholars—who wants to study and evaluate the problem of the mass strike must also turn to the Russian Revolution without fail, to draw their own conclusion from it.

But now for another important consideration. What was the nature of the audience in the auditorium, which I allegedly incited to violent acts? I was not even speaking at a people's assembly, but rather at a Social Democratic Party conference; that means I was speaking in front of an assembly of men who represent the elite of the enlightened component of Germany's working class. And now I would argue that it is a truly colossal underestimation of the political maturity and intelligence of the Social Democratic agitators, if one believes that [anyone] could incite them so easily to violent acts by a passionate speech. This claim contains a truly colossal underestimation of the enlightening and ennobling intellectual influence that forty years of Social Democratic education has had on the German working class. And as I have said, I could have delivered exactly the same explanations not at the party conference but at any Social Democratic people's assembly chosen at random, without our workers having had the slightest thoughts about violent deeds. Indeed, hasn't the German proletariat proven sufficiently in recent decades how politically mature it really is, and how very capable it is of keeping a tight rein on its passions, in the face of all possible goading? Because, truth be told, there are sufficient provocations, day in, day out, in the form of deeds rather than words. *Do you really believe that a mass of the people—who have not been goaded into violent deeds by the Antisocialist Laws,** by the draft bill that sanctioned the suppression of Social Democracy [the so-called *Umsturzvorlage*],† by the Draft Bill on Forced Labor Prisons, by the Import Duty Causing Starvation [the so-called *Hungertarif*],‡

---

* The "Law against Social Democratic Activities That Endanger the Common Good" was passed by the Reichstag by 221 votes to 149, and came into force concurrent to its proclamation on October 21, 1878.

† On December 6, 1894, the government brought the "Draft Bill Relating to Changes and Extensions to the Criminal Law Code, the Military Criminal Law Code, and the Press Law" before the Reichstag. This *Umsturzvorlage* (literally, "draft concerning agitation or overthrow" of the existing political order) was intended to provide official approval for the politics of suppressing Social Democracy. In light of the mass protests that followed, and particularly the energetic Social Democratic resistance, the Reichstag rejected the draft bill at its second reading on May 11, 1895.

‡ A large Social Democratic protest movement against an increase on import duties on grain and meat began as early as February–March 1901, after details of a draft law on import duty were made public. According to these, the government planned enormous increases on duties on both agricultural products. These would have brought about a major worsening of living conditions for the majority of the population. On December 5, 1901, the SPD's Reichstag faction handed

or by the current Draft Anti-Trade Union Bill*—would *let themselves be stirred up by a few words about the revolution?* I am astonished that the state attorney does not press charges against the creators of all these laws and drafts instead of accusing me, because these are the *deeds* that are truly suited to stirring the propertyless masses to the highest degree, and these same deeds certainly *would* lead to violent acts if—yes, if it wasn't for the deep and clarifying influence of Social Democracy.

The state attorney says that I deny absolutely the revolutionary character of my Jena speech. That is an absolute error. I *did* speak in a revolutionary manner and I always speak in a revolutionary manner, just as the whole of our Social Democratic agitation has a revolutionary character. But not in the sense of the strange conceptions of the state attorney, who traces the causes of the Hamburg riots back to Social Democracy's revolutionary impact, but rather in the sense that we aim for a complete and thorough upheaval of the existing social order. And concerning that aim, I do not negate the role of violence. I simply stick, along with my party, to the standpoint that the initiative for the application of violence always proceeds from the ruling classes, the standpoint that our mentor *Friedrich Engels* articulated more precisely in 1892 in *Neue Zeit* [New Times]. Engels wrote:

> How often have the bourgeois requested of us that *we should forego the use of revolutionary methods under any circumstances and remain within legal boundaries*, now that the emergency laws† have been rescinded and the everyday law is back in place for everyone, including socialists! *We unfortunately are not in a position to do the bourgeois lords this favor.* Which does not, however, alter the fact that it is not us who are "breaking the state of lawfulness" at present. On the contrary, they are working in such an exemplary manner for us that we would be fools to hinder them, *as long as things proceed thus*. The more pressing question is whether it is in fact the bourgeoisie and the government who are violating laws and the state of law, in order to

---

over a petition with around 3.5 million signatures against the planned increase on import duties. On December 11, 1901, Paul Singer justified German Social Democracy's rejection of the draft bill to increase grain import duties, as presented by the *Bundesrat* (literally, "Federal Council," the legislative body representing the various German regions). Further, he exposed the draft bill as having been authored by the largest landowners. The SPD then went on to fight the draft bill in the Reichstag between October 16 and December 14, 1902. Despite this, both the new import duty law and the specified import duty were passed on December 14, 1902, with a total of 202 votes to 100, and came into force on March 1, 1906.

* "Draft Anti-Trade Union Bill" refers to a law concerning trade and professional associations brought before the Reichstag by the government on November 12, 1906, through which professional associations could acquire legal standing. The aim of the law was to curb the trade unions' ability to act. The dissolution of the Reichstag on December 13, 1906, had the effect of rescinding the draft law.

† That is, the Antisocialist Laws.

squash us by violence? We shall see. The current maxim remains: "Please be so kind as to shoot first, my lords of the bourgeoisie!"*

Do not worry, they *will* shoot first. One fine morning, the German bourgeoisie and their government will be tired of observing the spring tide of socialism, which flows over everything, with their arms crossed; they will find refuge in lawlessness and in the violent deed. What good will it do? Violence may be able to suppress a small sect on a fenced-in area of land; but the power still needs to be invented that is capable of extinguishing a party of over 2 or 3 million people, which is spread over a whole, large empire. The momentary, counterrevolutionary excess of power may be able to forestall socialism's triumph by a couple of years, but only so as to make it more complete and more concluding in the end.

This is our position. And now, to conclude, I request you to pronounce me innocent. Not because I am scared of any possible prison sentence. As every Social Democrat agrees, it is our lot to put up with the prison sentences for our convictions dictated to us by the ruling justice system. To quote [Otto von] Bismarck's cod Latin: "Nescio, quod mihi magis farcimentum," or, in German: "I don't know what I give less of a damn about." But I plead innocent, because a conviction would be an injustice, and would cause offense in Social Democratic circles.

---

* Friedrich Engels, "Der Sozialismus in Deutschland" (Socialism in Germany), *Die Neue Zeit*, Vol. 1, No. 19 (1891–92), p. 580.

1907

The Lockout of Textile Workers in Łódź*

Since the counterrevolution won the upper hand, capitalist entrepreneurs throughout the Russian Empire have been eager to reverse the economic improvements they had to concede to the workers. In the central Russian industrial area, such as Petersburg, the workers were not able to resist such attacks, and no great economic struggles took place. In Russian Poland, the opposite was the case. Using the same tenacious perseverance and revolutionary vigor with which the factory proletarians led the political struggle, they defended their interests in the economic sphere, and, especially in Łódź, the past two years have been a time of uninterrupted struggles. It is almost self-evident that the workers did not always maneuver skillfully, that many mistakes were made. It happened that the work was stopped before any demands were formulated; often enough, the demands were unclear and confused. How could it be otherwise if the economic organizations are only at an early stage, if the workers cannot hold public meetings and if they have no press at their disposal? It is rather to be admired that, under these conditions, the struggle did not degenerate into raw destructive rage. We stress: *Not one case of destruction of the machines, etc., has occurred during this time in Łódź or anywhere else in Poland*, while such incidents did occur in all other countries in similar situations. This is undoubtedly the merit of the Social Democratic Party,† whose moral influence is strong enough to keep the workers from excesses in order to prevent heavy riots in the turmoil of struggle.

Toward the end of last year, the capital magnates of the Polish Manchester‡ struck a decisive blow: They prepared a general lockout of the workers in the textile factories. The situation seemed favorable to them. The economy in the Russian textile industry is depressed, the sales volume is low. This is a direct consequence of the credit blockage and the famine in Russia. Łódź works only

---

* This article appeared anonymously in *Vorwärts* (Berlin), No. 13, January 16, 1907. Luxemburg's authorship was confirmed in the Luxemburg bibliography compiled by Feliks Tych in 1962. Luxemburg had followed the events in Łódź with great interest and commitment since the beginning of her political activity. See especially "Der Sozialismus in Polen" (Socialism in Poland), in *Gesammelte Werke*, Vol. [X], p. 82ff.; and "A Giant Demonstration in Łódź," "Strike-Revolution in Łódź," and "The Street Battle in Łódź," in *Complete Works*, Vol. 3, pp. 146–7, 175–7, 178–81. This article is translated by Manuela Kölke from Luxemburg's *Gesammelte Werke*, Vol. 7.1, pp. 86–9.

† Luxemburg is referring to the party she led at the time, the Social Democracy of the Kingdom of Poland and Lithuania (SDKPiL).

‡ As one study notes, "In 1825, Tsar Aleksander I visited the then small town of only 1,004 inhabitants to encourage industrial development. This led to the city's golden age in the late nineteenth century and the first decade of the twentieth. Łódz became a mixed city of Poles, Germans, Jews, Russians and also Czechs. As a flourishing center of industry, the city became popularly known as 'the Polish Manchester' or 'the Promised Land.'" See Joanna B. Michlic, "Łódź in the Post-communist Era: In Search of a New Identity" (Cambridge, UK: Center for European Studies Programme, on Eastern and Central Europe, 2008), Working Paper Series, No. 65.

for the Russian market; the starving farmer cannot buy any goods, the merchant is careful not to fill his stock, especially since he cannot access any credit. Under such circumstances, the closure of the large factories does not represent too great a loss for the capitalists. It should be borne in mind that these capital magnates do indeed have enormous means at their disposal. Fabulous profits have been made in Łódź in just two human generations; although the factory facilities have been expanded at dizzying speed, their debts have been written, and its [the city's] cotton kings are not dependent on credit; on the contrary, [Karl] Scheibler, [Izrael] Poznański, and [Juliusz] Heinzel have immense cash capital at their disposal, and dominate the banks.* Under such circumstances, the closure of factories for weeks, even months, is a loss that can be borne. Yes, it is possibly even good business: There are still dozens of smaller factories in Łódź, especially weaving mills, that are annoying competitors for the giant companies. If the big factories are now closed down, these competitors are paralyzed because they cannot get any yarn; but they cannot withstand such stagnation in production, because they are all working on credit and can only exist with uninterrupted turnover. The lockout could therefore have the desired outcome—for the Scheiblers, Poznańskis, and their associates—that the resistance of the workers would be broken and the small competitors, who have not yet been destroyed by the economic depression of the revolutionary period, would be given the death blow. A trust of the cotton magnates to plunder the consumers is the next goal.

So, the lockout was arranged by the main industry stakeholders, who waited for a "decent" opportunity.

This was offered by the factory of Poznański. This is very clear to anybody closely following goings-on in Łódź, because gentlemen like Poznański are the personification of the dirtiest greed for profit and lack of scruples in all of Poland. Just forty years ago, the founder of the company, the father of the present millionaires, was a shabby little Jewish haggler[†] on his way to wealth. The father and sons more than once saw the insides of the penitentiary. There is, for example, one incident of such kind: Poznański is building a weaving mill with its own gasworks. But as the town's gas pipeline touches his property, the gentleman drills into the pipe of the town's pipeline and steals the town's gas for years. There are concealed lawsuits for the distribution of false money, lawsuits for the theft of samples, etc., etc. As employers, these gentlemen are the filthiest

---

* Scheibler, Poznański, and Heinzel were the founders of Poland's textile industry at the end of the nineteenth century and became fabulously wealthy at the expense of their workers, who were grossly underpaid. Poznański was a Polish Jew, as was obvious by his first name, Izrael.

† The original German, *schäbiges Schacherjüdlein*, is a troubling turn of phrase that was common at the time and blatantly anti-Semitic. Luxemburg, who was herself Jewish and spoke out vociferously against anti-Semitism on numerous occasions, was not averse to sometimes using such phrases herself.

social group in the whole of Łódź, and that means something. Of course, the employees of the company are mostly worthy servants of their masters. Among them there are people who have a whole set of criminal charges on their tally, because even decent technicians and master craftsmen do not hold out for that long with such entrepreneurs, but flee from their position abruptly, and usually in dispute—whereby the bosses often find themselves slapped in the face. What a miracle, then, that in the factory of Poznański the relationship between workers, on the one hand, and administration and craftsmen, on the other, was and is the worst imaginable, and that since the outbreak of the revolutionary movement the conflicts there have not stopped. Such a conflict occurred again in November [1906]. One of the engineers felt insulted and the factory management imposed the following conditions on the workers: They should humbly ask the offended person for forgiveness, eighty-nine workers were to be removed, from now on the factory management should be allowed to dismiss workers at will without notice, and finally, the workers should commit themselves to "work regularly and under no circumstances disturb the operation." The workers rejected this request because the condition of dismissal without notice was unacceptable. This would mean that the workers would submit to all forms of despotism, that they would undertake to accept without resistance any reduction in wages, any deterioration of working conditions. Moreover, the last condition would mean that the workers would commit themselves to renounce demonstrations and political strikes "in order not to disturb the operation."

As a result, the lockout occurred at Poznański, and a number of other factories, Scheibler, Heinzel, [Juliusz] Kunitzer, [Alfred] Biedermann, Steinert, etc., terminated their workers in such a way that they threatened to block the factories if the workers of Poznański did not get back to work.

But the situation is this: More than 20,000 people work in the large factories involved in the conspiracy; if the small factories can be brought to a standstill by blocking their access to yarn, another 10,000 to 15,000 workers go without their daily bread. If the workers took up the fight nevertheless, it is because everything is at stake for them. Through the wage struggles to date, the workers have achieved wage increases of 25 to 33 percent; their situation has therefore improved somewhat, but it must be taken into consideration that food prices have also risen consistently. So, it is above all a question of defending what has been achieved. But it is also necessary—and the workers immediately grasped this with real instinct—to defend the social achievements of the revolution. The workers of Łódź have achieved the following: that the businessmen are no longer allowed to treat them like slaves with no will of their own, and that they negotiate with them on equal terms; if the entrepreneurs now enforce their will, if they break through the resistance of the workers, then the old conditions return, then the factories of Łódź become anew an unbearable hell for the workers, then the old slavery is introduced once again. And faced with this, the workers simply resist; this is why they fearlessly took up the desperate struggle.*

Fortunately, the factory owners were unable to reach full agreement. There are "outsiders" among them. A number of large companies—Geyer, Rosenblatt, Silberstein, etc.—preferred to stay out of the game. They now receive numerous orders; they have secure sales for their goods, and in addition, the shortage of yarn of the small enterprises is at least partly prevented. In the last few days, the above-mentioned companies that did not lock workers out have hired new ones and are working day and night. As a result, a few thousand of the locked-out workers are again employed. The organizations have set up the matter in such a way that the workers in these factories take turns working only three days a week.

So, the situation at the moment is that: *The workers have a chance to stop the attack*. It is important to support several thousand men for some time. *Help is urgently needed*. If the workers of Europe are engaged in international solidarity, then victory in Łódź is certain.†

---

* The lockout of the textile workers of the Poznański Corporate Groups began on December 7, 1906. Workers were threatened that on December 29, all factories of the textile industry in Łódź would carry out a lockout unless the previously locked-out workers unconditionally surrendered themselves to the employers and agreed that "as a punishment" every fifth worker would be laid off. The general lockout lasted from December 29, 1906, to April 19, 1907. As many as 80,000 to 100,000 people lost their jobs, remaining without bread, and poverty increased daily. For more on these events, see Luxemburg's "A Giant Struggle in Łódź," in *Complete Works*, Vol. 3, pp. 146–7.

† See "The Epic of Łódź," below, pp. 369–73.

The May Day Celebrations*

May Day celebrations are a living historical part of the international proletarian class struggle, and because of this, they accurately reflect the last twenty years of all phases, all moments of this struggle. Viewed from a distance, it is always the same monotonous repetition of identical speeches and articles, identical demands and resolutions. That is also why those whose gaze only clings to the rigid surface of things and who do not feel the imperceptible inner becoming of the circumstances believe that the May Day celebration has lost its meaning through the repetition, that it has almost become "an empty demonstration." But under this seemingly identical form of appearance, the May Day celebrations conceal the changing pulse of the proletarian struggle, which shares a life with the workers' movement and therefore changes with it, reflecting in its own ideas, in its mood, in its tension the changing situations of the class struggle.

May Day has gone through three great phases in its history. In the first years, when it had to initiate its course, it was greeted by proletariats of all countries with tense expectations and high spirits. The working class added a new weapon to its armament, and the first attempts to use this weapon bolstered the sense of strength and the joy of fighting for the millions of exploited and oppressed. On the other hand, the bourgeoisie of all countries met the new demonstration of class struggle with the greatest fear and deepest hatred. The thought of the international socialist demonstration appeared to them as the reborn specter of the old, much-hated International,† the bold attempt at a simultaneous, worldwide labor celebration as the death knell of all capitalist glory. Hence the frantic preparations in the initial years to confront the dangers of May Day with brutal police and military force. And as the vanguard of this weapon-studded convoy of the frightened bourgeoisie, the "free republic" of France threw itself into battle, joined only afterward by tsarist absolutism. The first proletarian blood for the cause of the May celebration flowed in 1891 in Fourmies;‡ in 1892, there was a bloody May battle in Russian Poland, in Łódź.§

But, soon, the ruling classes calmed down and recognized the purely demonstrative character of the May Day celebrations. On the other hand, a long period

---

* This article was first published in *Die Gleichheit* (Stuttgart), Vol. 17, 1907, No. 9, p. 71. It is translated by Manuela Kölke from Luxemburg's *Gesammelte Werke*, Vol. 2, pp. 201–4.

† A reference to the International Workingmen's Association (IAA), also known as the First International.

‡ On May 1, 1891, a workers' demonstration took place in the northern French town of Fourmies, during which the police shot at the demonstrators.

§ This refers to the Łódź Rebellion of May 1892, when 30,000 workers spontaneously walked out of their jobs—to the great surprise of many at the time, including the Polish socialists. Although initially caused by demands for higher wages, ethnic discrimination against Polish workers in job appointments also appears to have been a factor. The general strike was bloodily suppressed by tsarist authorities.

of predominantly parliamentary struggle and quiet expansion of political and trade union organization was to follow in the wake of the workers' movement. The first year of May Day celebrations saw the end of the Antisocialist Laws in Germany; and the proletariat seized access to the parliaments in Belgium* in 1893 and Austria† in 1896. Everywhere, the 1890s brought a period of diligent trade union work and unstoppable growth in the parliamentary representation of the working class. In the face of the struggle to achieve worker representation in the parliaments, as well as positive steps taken to develop workers' parties in many countries, the demonstrations of the working masses themselves, as well as the idea of the international community of the proletariat, were overshadowed. The May Day celebrations are gradually becoming a peaceful popular festival, which bourgeois society observes with a certain peace of mind.

In recent years, there has been a noticeable shift in the situation of the workers' movement. A sharp wind is blowing over the battlefield again. In the east, there is the great Russian Revolution; in Germany, a culmination and intensification of the economic and political struggle: a comprehensive lockout action against industrial workers and a union of all bourgeois parties for the parliamentary lockout of the working class. In France, there is a brutal campaign by the "radical" government against the unions and a series of bitter wage struggles. Alarmed by the powerful growth of proletarian organizations in the last fifteen years and agitated by the Russian Revolution, international capitalism becomes nervous, wild, and aggressive.

And this also marks the beginning of a new phase for May Day. From the outset, May Day was a direct demonstration of the *masses*—its only direct political action so far apart from the elections. Now, it fills itself with new content, with a new spirit—to the extent that the intensification of the class struggle increasingly pushes the role of the proletarian masses back into the foreground. The more the reaction—which reveals the naked tyranny of the bourgeoisie in the economic as well as in the political sphere, contesting every whisper of a move to support proletarian interests—the closer we get to the time when the masses themselves take the reins, where they have to defend the interests of their class liberation, in their own person. To counter the inevitable arrival, sooner or later, of such times, to be equipped for these times in full consciousness of one's own duty and power—that is currently the task of the proletariat.

---

* In April 1893, for the first time in the history of Belgium's workers' movement, a political general strike for universal suffrage took place, involving some 250,000 workers. As a result of this strike, Belgian electoral law had to be substantially extended.

† Due to the strikes and demonstrations of the Austrian working class for universal suffrage, the Austrian government was forced to make concessions. In 1896 a reform of the electoral law was enacted, based on a bill presented by Prime Minister Eduard Taaffe in 1893. A fifth, general electoral class (curia) was introduced to the four existing electoral classes. Since the electoral census was no longer applicable to them, a larger circle of voters was included. For the first time, Social Democrats had the opportunity to send its representatives to Parliament.

The May Day celebrations, as a direct demonstration of the masses, represent a means to these ends. In Germany in particular, the response to the parliamentary defeat of the Social Democrats on January 25* must be an imposing and powerful celebration of May 1. The working masses must call out to the united reactionary mass of the bourgeoisie: "You want to force our representation out of your legislation—well, here we are in the flesh; you see us more determined, more united, and more ready to fight than ever!"

At the same time, that other element of the May Day celebration comes to the fore with added force—that is, the internationalism of the workers' cause. As long as the class struggle in each country has a minimum of democratic elbow room, and as long as the parliamentary working day maintains its positive standing, the workers' movement will be dominated by the specificity of each state milieu, by national fragmentation. But, as soon as the basic forces of class struggle rise to the surface from the depths of capitalist society, as soon as the struggle verges sharply on the clash of the masses with the ruling powers, the idea of the one and indivisible world proletariat comes to life with increased force. The preparations of the bourgeoisie for May Day in all countries remind the proletariat powerfully again this year that its liberation struggle is one and the same in all countries. But today, the *Russian proletariat*, the proletariat in the empire of revolution, is at the head of the workers' army of all countries. And the revolutionary struggles of this proletariat, its experiences, its problems, constitute the great historical school for our own future battles.

Thus, the first of May comes up again this year, bolstered by new, strong winds, greeted again as always by the bourgeoisie with hatred and fear, and by the working masses with determined joie de vivre. From the outset a proletarian demonstration for the eight-hour day and *for world peace*, May Day gradually transforms into a demonstration for the *proletarian revolution*. The May Day celebrations are not facing a decline, but an unexpected upswing, because they are carried and lifted up by the same storm wind that is already blowing over the surface of bourgeois society, and that will lead us into the fiercest struggles, but also to final victories.

---

* In the January 1907 federal elections for the Reichstag, the SPD won only 43 seats (of a total of 397), down from the 81 it held from 1903, even though it received more votes than any other single party. This was largely because the proportion of seats was heavily weighted in favor of the conservative rural-based parties.

For May 1, 1907*

World Labor Day, that symbol of the international solidarity of the proletariat, is approaching, and the ruling classes from all countries are eager to demonstrate the internationalism of the class struggle in a tangible way. In France, the police "rescue" operation against the unions is the means whereby Clemenceau's Radical cabinet seeks to prove to the bourgeoisie that, as the guardian of the sacred order of capitalist exploitation, it can confidently take on Constans' cabinet.† In Germany, there is a comprehensive lockout action by capital in coalition against the workforce to break the backbone of the movement, the power of the organization. In Russia, there are massive preparations by the counterrevolution for an open, decisive counterattack directed at the revolutionary masses of the people. Everywhere, we see a noticeable intensification of the class struggle, albeit to varying degrees and in different forms.

Precisely for this reason and due to a massive hiring wave, it is difficult to openly celebrate May Day in its actual form this year in a way that reflects the mood of the combative working masses, especially in Germany. Unlike the first years of May Day celebrations, the bourgeoisie no longer fears that the mere idea of May Day represents the beginning of the end of the capitalist world. But it can also no longer accept May Day celebrations as a peaceful manifestation of the socialist idea with a more or less calming sense of mind, as was almost the case in the last decade. The escalation of the economic and political class struggle, the enormous growth of proletarian organization and class consciousness in all countries, and finally, the great Russian Revolution—all this has aroused the nervousness of the bourgeois classes, their fear and hatred against the socialist proletariat. As in the early years, the May Day celebrations once again face the deepest mistrust and the most brutal provocations of the bourgeois world.

All the greater, however, is the significance of these demonstrations for the struggling working class. No, we are not moving toward a decline, but toward a powerful upswing of the idea of May Day celebrations. For by expressing the

---

* This manuscript was first published as a facsimile in *Rosa Luxemburg mit Selbstzeugnissen und Bilddokumenten* (Rosa Luxemburg with Testimonials and Images), edited by Helmut Hirsch (Hamburg: Rowohlt Verlag, 1969), p. 82. It is translated by Manuela Kölke from Luxemburg's *Gesammelte Werke*, Vol. 7.1, pp. 103–4. Luxemburg sent this contribution in a letter of April 19, 1907, to Alexandre-Marie (Bracke) Desrousseaux. See *Gesammelte Briefe*, Vol. 6, p. 146ff.; see also *Gesammelte Briefe*, Vol. 2, p. 285. Combined with statements by E. Belfort Bax, Pablo Iglesias, Paul Singer, and Arthur Groussier, the article appeared under the heading "Rénovation" on the first page in *Le Socialiste*, Paris, No. 104, April 28–May 5, 1907.

† In March 1906, Georges Clemenceau was appointed minister of interior in the cabinet of Ferdinand Sarrien and immediately imposed severe repression of the French workers' movement. He ordered the military to break a miners' strike on May 1, 1906, leading to several deaths. Jean Constans was a left-of-center politician who served as minister of interior in the cabinet of Pierre Tirard in 1890; he resisted pressure to suppress the French workers' movement.

international unity of the proletariat of all countries more vividly than ever before in these hard times, it carries forward and permeates with a fresh, strong wind the most important battle of the international proletariat today, the struggles that, sooner or later, await us everywhere. The May Day celebrations are increasingly not only becoming a demonstration for the eight-hour day and world peace. They are also turning into a demonstration of sympathy and for the victorious revolution of the proletariat—first of all the proletariat in Russia.

Speeches at the 1907 Congress of the Russian Social Democratic Labor Party*

I. SEVENTH SESSION

Comrades! The Central Committee of the German Social Democratic Party, upon learning of my intention to attend this party congress, decided to use this opportunity to ask me to pass on their brotherly greetings and that they wish you every success.

The class-conscious German proletariat, in all its millions, has been following the revolutionary struggle of its Russian brothers with the keenest sympathy, and German Social Democracy has already shown through its actions that it is ready to draw fruitful lessons from the rich store of Russian Social Democratic experience. At the start of 1905, when the first crack of revolutionary thunder was heard in St. Petersburg, after the proletarian action of January 9, the ranks of German Social Democracy started to come alive. This excitement poured into the fierce debates on tactics, and the first important result of this, and the one that our party took from the fight of the Russian proletariat, was the resolution for a general strike at the party convention in Jena.† True, this decision has still not been acted upon, and it is unlikely to be implemented in the near future. Its principled significance, however, is unquestionable. Until 1905, the view of general strikes was entirely negative in the ranks of the German Social Democrats; the idea was considered a purely anarchist slogan, and, accordingly, a reactionary, harmful utopia. But, as soon as the German proletariat saw in the general strike of the Russian proletariat a new form of struggle, not in opposition to the political struggle, but as a weapon in that struggle—not as a miraculous tool to make a sudden leap into a socialist system, but rather as a weapon of the class struggle for the winning of the most elementary freedoms from the modern class state—it hastened fundamentally to change its view of the general strike root and branch, acknowledging its possible applicability, under the right circumstances, in Germany as well. Comrades! Here, I consider it essential to draw your attention to the fact that—to the immense credit of the German

---

* These comments were delivered by Luxemburg to the seventh and twenty-second sessions of the Congress of the Russian Social Democratic Labor Party (RSDRP), held in London from May 13 to June 1, 1907. It is translated by Zachary King from *Protokoly i stenografi cheski otechety s'ezdov i konferenski Kommunistcheskoi Partii Sovetskovo Soyuza: Pyati Londskii S'esd RSDRP, Aprel'-mai 1907 goda, Protokoly* (Protocols and Stenographic Reports of the Congresses and Conferences of the Communist Party of the Soviet Union) (Moscow: Gosudarstvennoe Izdatel'stvo Politcheskoi Literatury, 1963), pp. 97–104, 383–92, 432–7.

† The resolution adopted at the Jena Congress of the Social Democratic Party of Germany from September 17 to 23, 1905, referred to the use of the mass strike as one of the most effective means of struggle of the working class. For more discussion of this, see p. 201 and pp. 263–5, above.

proletariat—it did change its orientation toward the question of the general strike, without having access to the impressions of the foreign successes that would impress even the bourgeois politicians. The resolution of the Jena party convention was approved more than a month before the first and, still today, the only major victory of the revolution, before the memorable October Days and the first constitutional reforms that they snatched from the absolute monarchy in the form of the October Manifesto.* Even in Russia, the revolutionary struggle has only delivered defeats, but the German proletariat, with its unerring class instinct, sensed that these outward defeats masked an unprecedented wave of proletarian strength, a certain guarantee of their future victory. The fact remains that the German proletariat hurried to pay tribute to the experience of the Russian Revolution before any of its outward successes, incorporating a new tactical slogan into its previous forms of struggle, which were already oriented, not only toward parliamentary means of action, but toward the unmediated intervention of the broad proletarian masses.

Further developments in Russia—the October and November Days and especially the highest point reached by the revolutionary wave in Russia [in the fall of 1905], and the December crisis in Moscow†—have been reflected in Germany in the raised spirits and the powerful animation of thought in the ranks of Social Democracy. In December and January, after the huge demonstrations in Austria for universal suffrage,‡ animated discussions began in Germany on whether the time was ripe to immediately make a decision, in one form or another, on a general strike in connection with the struggle for universal suffrage in the regional parliaments [*Landtage*] of Prussia, Saxony, and Hamburg. This question was decided in the negative: The idea of artificially bringing about a large mass movement was rejected. On January 17, 1906, however, a first attempt was made—a half-day demonstrative general strike in Hamburg that was led brilliantly and that, in its turn, invigorated the working masses in the largest center of German Social Democracy and increased the consciousness of their strength.§

From the outside, it would seem that the following year of 1906 brought only defeats to the Russian Revolution. In Germany as well, the year ended with the outward defeat of the Social Democratic Party. You know that during the election of January 25, Social Democracy lost almost half of its electoral

---

* The manifesto signed by Tsar Nicholas II at the end of October 1905 promising a constitutional monarchy. Most of its terms were never fulfilled.

† A reference to the arrest of the members of the St. Petersburg Soviet in December 1905. This was followed by a massive workers' insurrection in Moscow, which was bloodily suppressed.

‡ From October to December 1905, mass strikes broke out in various parts of the Austro-Hungarian Empire demanding universal suffrage.

§ The Social Democratic movement in Hamburg was known as one of the most radical in all of Germany. On January 17, 1906, workers there called a "trial mass strike." The Hamburg left later played an important role in the 1918 German Revolution.

districts in Germany. But even this parliamentary defeat is closely connected to the Russian Revolution. There can be no doubt, for anyone who knows the mutual position of the parties in the last election, that one of the most important moments to define the outcome of this campaign was the Russian Revolution. It is certain that the impressions of the revolutionary events in Russia, and the fear this provoked in the bourgeois classes in Germany, were some of the factors that united and brought together all the layers and parties of bourgeois society, with the exception of the center, into a single reactionary bloc under a single slogan: "Down with the class representation of the class-conscious proletariat, down with Social Democracy!" Never has [Ferdinand] Lassalle's statement about the bourgeoisie as "a single reactionary mass"* been realized so palpably as during this election. But, on the other hand, this electoral outcome has forced the German proletariat to turn its gaze all the more attentively to the revolutionary struggle of their Russian brothers. If one were to sum up the political and historical result of the last Reichstag election in a few words, then it must be said that, after January 25 and February 5, 1907, Germany remained the only modern country not to contain even a trace of bourgeois liberalism or bourgeois democracy, in the strict sense of the word: It stood definitively and irrevocably on the side of reaction in its struggle against the revolutionary proletariat. More than anything, it was precisely liberalism's betrayal that delivered us into the power of the Junker reaction in the last election, and even though the liberals have now gone into the Reichstag in greater numbers, they are nevertheless currently nothing but pitiful servants of reaction hiding behind the sign of liberalism.

And so, in connection with this, a question arose in our ranks that has occupied you, our Russian comrades, to an even greater degree. As far as I know, one of the circumstances that has played a fundamental role in defining the tactics of our Russian comrades is the view that the Russian proletariat has an absolutely unique task that represents a certain inner contradiction—namely, the task of creating at the same time the first political conditions of bourgeois society and waging class struggle with the bourgeoisie. This situation supposedly differs radically from the circumstances of our proletariat in Germany and in all of Europe.

Comrades! I think that this view can only be a purely formalist statement of the question. To a certain extent, we are also in the very same difficult situation. In Germany, this very fact has been shown most demonstratively by the last election—the proletariat had to become the only fighter and defender of the democratic forms of a bourgeois state.

---

* Lassalle often stated that in comparison to the working class, all other classes—including the petty bourgeoisie—are "only one reactionary mass." Marx sharply criticized Lassalle's conception in his *Critique of the Gotha Program* (as well as elsewhere) on the grounds that it ignores the importance of peasant struggles—a convenient omission on the part of Lassalle, since he sought an alliance between the workers' movement and the landed aristocracy (the Junkers).

Not to speak of the fact that we do not have universal suffrage in the majority of regional parliaments in Germany, that we are left to suffer from a mass of vestiges of medieval feudalism—and even those few freedoms that we do have, such as universal suffrage for Reichstag elections, the freedom to strike, freedom of association and assembly, are not secured in a serious way and are subject to constant infringements by reactionary social groups. And in all these questions, bourgeois liberalism is a completely untrustworthy ally; in all these cases, the class-conscious proletariat is the only firm stronghold of democratic development in Germany.

In this connection, the failure of the last election once again pushed the question of our relationship to bourgeois liberalism to the forefront. Voices were heard—true, very few of them—who mourned liberalism's premature death. In the same connection, in France, we were given the advice to pay attention to bourgeois liberalism's weak position and to spare what was left of it, to use it as an ally in the struggle against reaction and in defense of the common foundations of democratic development. Comrades! I can state that both these voices, lamenting the results of political development of Germany, and this advice were met by unanimous sharp rebuke among the class-conscious German proletariat. (Applause from the Bolsheviks and part of the center.) And I will gladly state that in this case, it was not just one wing, it was the entire party that declared as one: "We can regret the sad results of our historical development, but we cannot give up a single iota of our principled proletarian tactics for the sake of liberalism." The conscious proletariat of Germany came to, as it were, the opposite conclusions from the last Reichstag election: If bourgeois liberalism and bourgeois democracy turn out to be so frail and precarious that they are ready to fall into the abyss of reaction at every more energetic gesture of class struggle by the proletariat, then that is precisely what they deserve! (Applause from the Bolsheviks and part of the center.) Under the influence of the outcome of the election on January 25, it became clear to the broadest strata of the German proletariat that, in the context of liberalism's decay, it will be necessary to give up every last illusion and hope for its help in the fight against reaction and, now more than ever, depend on itself and itself alone in both the struggle for its own class interests and the struggle against reactionary attempts against democratic development. (Applause from the Bolsheviks and part of the center.) In light of this same election, a sharpening of class antagonisms with unheard-of clarity has surfaced as never before. The internal development of Germany has reached such a level of ripeness, as it turns out, such as had been inconceivable to even the greatest optimists before now. The analysis by Marx of bourgeois society's development has once again found its most obvious confirmation, more brilliant than we could have expected. But, at the same time, it has become clear to everyone that this development, this sharpening of class contradictions will, sooner or later, but inevitably, lead to a period of tumultuous political struggle here in Germany as well. And, in this connection, questions about the various forms and phases of class struggle are being discussed by us with particular interest.

This is why the German proletariat has turned its gaze to the struggle of its Russian brothers with redoubled attention, looking at them as upon its frontline fighters, like the vanguard of the international working class. From my own humble experience in the electoral campaign, I can note that, at all of the electoral meetings—and I had to appear at meetings with 2,000 to 3,000 people—voices were heard from among the workers themselves: "Tell us about the Russian Revolution!" And this didn't only express natural sympathy, stemming from the instinct of class solidarity with brothers-in-arms; it also expressed the consciousness of the fact that the interests of the Russian Revolution are its own business. The important thing that the German proletariat expects from the Russian [proletariat] is the expansion and the enrichment of proletarian tactics, the deployment of the principles of class struggle in a completely new historical situation. Indeed. Social Democratic tactics, as employed by the working class in Germany today and to which we owe our victories up until now, is oriented primarily toward parliamentary struggle, it is designed for the context of bourgeois parliamentarianism. Russian Social Democracy is the first to whom the hard but honorable lot has fallen of using the foundations of Marx's teaching, not in a time of the correct, calm parliamentary course of state life, but in a tumultuous revolutionary period. The only time when scientific socialism had to grapple with practical politics in a period of revolution was the activity of Marx himself in the Revolution of 1848. The very course of the Revolution of 1848, however, cannot at all serve as an example for the current revolution in Russia. What could be learned from it is perhaps only how not to act in a revolution. The schema of this revolution is as follows: The proletariat fights with its usual heroism, but doesn't know how to make use of its own victories; the bourgeoisie sidelines the proletariat to usurp the fruits of its struggle; finally, absolutism throws the bourgeoisie out in order to crush both the proletariat and the revolution. At that time, the class differentiation of the proletariat was in embryonic form. True, the *Communist Manifesto* already existed—that great charter of class struggle. True, Karl Marx had already participated in this revolution as a practical fighter. But precisely as a consequence of that particular historical situation, he was forced to play the role not of a socialist politician, but of an extreme bourgeois democrat, and the *Neue Rheinische Zeitung* [New Rhenish Newspaper] was not so much an organ of class struggle as the most extreme left-wing post of the revolutionary camp.* True, even the kind of bourgeois democracy for which the *Neue Rheinische Zeitung* was the intellectual expression did not particularly

---

* The masthead of the *Neue Rheinische Zeitung*, published by Marx between June 1848 and May 1849, was "Organ of the Democracy."

exist in Germany at that time. But it was precisely these politics that Karl Marx led in the first year of the revolution with iron consistency. There is no doubt that these politics consisted of the fact that Marx used all his means to support the fight of the bourgeoisie against absolutism. But what did this support consist of? Of the fact that from the beginning and until the end, he pitilessly and ruthlessly thrashed all the half measures and inconsistency, all the weakness and cowardice of bourgeois politics (Applause from the Bolsheviks and part of the center); of the fact that he supported and defended every action of the working mass without the slightest hesitation—not only action that delivered the first fleeting victory, March 18*—but also the memorable assault on the Berlin Zeughaus of June 14,† which the bourgeoisie claimed so doggedly both before and after to be a trap of reaction set up for the proletariat, and the September uprisings, and the October uprising in Vienna‡—these final attempts by the working masses to save the revolution already dying from the weakness and the betrayals of the bourgeoisie. He supported the national movements of 1848, considering them to be allies of the revolution.§ Marx's politics consisted of pushing the bourgeoisie at every moment to the limits of the revolutionary situation. Yes, Marx supported the bourgeoisie in its fight with absolutism, but he supported it with whips and kicks. Marx considered it an unforgivable mistake that the proletariat, after its first brief victory on March 18, allowed the formation of the acting bourgeois ministry of Camphausen-Hansemann.¶ But as soon as the bourgeoisie came to power, Marx demanded, from the very beginning, that it establish a revolutionary dictatorship.** He categorically declared, in the *Neue Rheinische Zeitung*,

---

* March 18, 1848, marked the beginning of the 1848 Revolutions that swept Europe. These involved a series of revolts in France and within the German Confederation, in which the working class took the lead in demanding radical improvements in living and working conditions.

† The Berlin Zeughaus, the city arsenal, was attacked by a crowd of demonstrators on June 24, 1848, in search of weapons. Although none were found, a number of the demonstrators were killed, and the government used the attack as an excuse to ban numerous revolutionary organizations.

‡ On October 6, 1848, a mass uprising erupted in Vienna against the government's use of troops to crush the national revolution in Hungary. Workers, students, and deserting soldiers built barricades and occupied much of the city, forcing Emperor Ferdinand I to flee. On October 31, the Austrian army crushed the revolt by a massive invasion.

§ This especially included Marx's support for the national independence of Poland and Hungary—a position that Luxemburg herself considered "outdated" when it came to the realities of her time.

¶ David Hansemann was a German bourgeois liberal who was appointed minister of finance by Gottfried Camphausen, a banker who served as minister of state beginning on March 29, 1848. Their efforts to strike a compromise between the monarchy and the radicals inside and outside of the National Assembly ultimately proved fruitless. Marx viewed them as spineless compromisers.

** That is, a revolutionary dictatorship *of the proletariat* that suppresses the forces of counterrevolution. Revolutionary *dictatorship* for Marx and his followers at the time represented the democratic rule by the vast majority, the working class—not the elimination of democracy by a party ruling *over* the working class. For Luxemburg's discussion of the concept, see

that the transitional period after each revolution requires the most active dictatorship.* Marx understood the powerlessness of the German "Duma"—the Frankfurt National Assembly†—all too well, but he did not perceive this as an extenuating circumstance but, to the contrary, pointed it toward the only escape from this position of powerlessness, and the way out was to fight and win real power in an open struggle against the old regime, leaning on the revolutionary mass of the people for support.

But, comrades, how did this political direction end for Marx? One year later, Marx had to abandon his position as an extreme bourgeois democrat—a position that was quite isolated and hopeless—and transition to a purely working-class politics. In the spring of 1849, Marx, along with his fellow thinkers, withdrew from the bourgeois-democratic alliance, and they decided to begin organizing workers themselves; they also wanted to participate in a planned all-German workers' congress, the idea for which came directly from the proletariat of East Prussia. But, when Marx wanted to change the direction of his politics, the revolution was already waning in its last days, and the *Neue Rheinische Zeitung* perished as one of the first victims of jubilant reaction, before Marx had managed to deploy new, purely proletarian tactics.

It is clear that you, comrades, will now have to start not where Marx began but where Marx ended his politics in 1849—with a clearly articulated, independent class politics of the proletariat. Right now, the proletariat in Russia is not in that embryonic condition that it was in Germany in 1848 and represents a cohesive and class-conscious political force. The Russian proletariat, in its current struggle, should see itself not as an isolated army, but merely as a part of the worldwide international army of the proletariat. It should not forget that its current revolutionary struggle is not an isolated skirmish—it is one of the most significant battles in the common course of the international class struggle. It is also clear, furthermore, that when in Germany, sooner or later, according to the corresponding maturity of class relations, the proletarian struggle streams out into inevitable mass conflicts with the ruling classes, at that point it will not be the experience and the example of the bourgeois revolution of 1848 that the German proletariat will have to draw on but the experience of the Russian proletariat in the current revolution. This is why, comrades, you have obligations

---

especially "The Tactics of Revolution," pp. 99–104 above, and "Lessons from the Three Dumas," pp. 375–94 below.

* See Marx, "The Crisis and the Counterrevolution," first published in *Neue Rheinische Zeitung*, No. 100, September 13, 1848: "Every provisional political set-up following a revolution calls for dictatorship, and an energetic dictatorship at that." *Marx-Engels Collected Works*, Vol. 7 (New York: International Publishers, 1977), p. 431.

† This was Germany's first freely elected parliament, established as a result of the revolution, on May 18, 1848. Its effort to create a constitutional monarchy failed, due to the vacillations and compromises of its leaders as well as the refusal of the established political elite to allow their powers to be delegated to it. It was dissolved a little more than a year after its formation.

in regard to the international proletariat. And the Russian proletariat will take the lead in this task only if, in its means of struggle, in its resoluteness, in the clear consciousness of its goal, in the scope of its tactics, it heeds the results of international developments in their entirety, if it takes heed of the degree of maturity of all of capitalist society. The Russian proletariat must show through its actions that more than half a century of capitalist development took place between 1848 and 1907 and that we, from the point of view of this development taken as a whole, do not stand at the beginning of bourgeois class rule, but instead at the beginning of its end. It must show that the Russian Revolution is not so much the last act in a series of nineteenth-century bourgeois revolutions as much as the forerunner of a new series of future proletarian revolutions, in which the conscious proletariat and its vanguard, Social Democracy, are historically predestined for the role of leader. (Applause.) The German proletariat is expecting not only victory over absolutism, not only a new supporting pillar for the liberation movement in Europe, but also the expansion and deepening of the perspectives of proletarian tactics: It wants to learn from you how to act in moments of open revolutionary struggle.

But, in order to successfully execute this task, one important condition is necessary for Russian Social Democracy, and this condition is the *unity* of the party. Not an outward, purely mechanical unity, but an inner coherence and inner strength that, naturally, should be the result of clear, committed tactics that correspond to the inner unity of the class struggle of the proletariat. As to how emphatically German Social Democracy believes that the unity of the Russian party is crucial, you can ascertain from words of the Central Committee of the German party itself, from the very same letter it gave me to pass on to you. After the brotherly greeting sent by the Central Committee to all the representatives of Russian Social Democracy, which I conveyed to you at the beginning of my speech, the letter reads:

> German Social Democracy has enthusiastically followed the struggle of its Russian brothers against absolutism as well as against the plutocracy that is endeavoring to share power with it.
>
> The victory won in the elections to the Duma, accomplished despite a reprehensible electoral system, filled us with joy. It proved the spontaneous, victorious strength of socialism that cannot be vanquished by any obstacle.
>
> As everywhere else, the bourgeoisie in Russia is also striving to make peace with the government. It wants to halt the victorious forward movement of the Russian proletariat. In Russia, too, it is endeavoring to steal the fruits of hard struggle from the people. This is why the role of leader falls to the lot of Russian Social Democracy and will remain with it in the movement to liberate the Russian people.
>
> To lead the struggle for liberation powerfully, the unity and coherence of Russian Social Democracy is a necessary condition. From the representatives of our Russian

brothers, we expect that the proceedings and decisions of their congress will lead to the fulfillment of our expectation and desire and that they will bring about the unity and coherence of Russian Social Democracy.

In this spirit we send your congress our brotherly greetings.

Central Committee of the Social Democratic Party of Germany
Berlin, April 30, 1907
W[ilhelm] Pfannkuch

II. TWENTY-SECOND SESSION

The question under discussion interests me and the representatives of the Polish delegation, not from the point of view of an internecine factional fight, [but] from the point of view of international proletarian tactics. The position of the right wing of our party* regarding the bourgeois parties is a perfectly consistent construction supported by the well-known view of the historical role of the bourgeoisie, as of the proletariat, in the current revolution. There is a definite schema at the heart of this view that is formulated precisely and clearly by one of the most deeply respected veterans and the most profound theorist of Russian Social Democracy. In his *Letters on Tactics and Tactlessness*,† Comrade [Georgi] Plekhanov says: "The creators of the *Communist Manifesto* wrote fifty-eight years ago: 'The bourgeoisie played a highly revolutionary role in history ... The bourgeoisie cannot exist without constantly revolutionizing the means of production and its organization, and, consequently, all its social relations.'"‡ And continuing on the political mission of the bourgeoisie:

> The bourgeoisie leads a constant struggle, at first against the aristocracy, then against the strata of its own class whose interests contradict the development of large industry ... In each of these cases, the bourgeoisie is forced to turn to the proletariat, ask it for help and push it onto the path of political movements. It therefore imparts its own political education to the proletariat, that is, it puts weapons against itself into the hands of the proletariat.§

There you have that view of the political role of the bourgeoisie, a view that, according to the opinion of one of the wings of our party, should define the entire tactics of the Russian proletariat in the current revolution. The bourgeoisie is a

---

* That is, the Mensheviks.
† Luxemburg is quoting from the fifth letter of Plekhanov's essay, first published in 1906 in the Menshevik journal *Kur'yer* (Courier) and reprinted as *Pis'mo pyatoe* (St. Petersburg: Glagolev, 1906). The "tactlessness" in the title refers to Lenin and the Bolsheviks.
‡ See "Manifesto of the Communist Party," in *Marx-Engels Collected Works*, Vol. 7, pp. 486–7.
§ See ibid., p. 490.

revolutionary class that engages the masses of the people in the fight with the old regime, the bourgeoisie is the natural vanguard and educator of the proletariat. And thus, in Russia today, only cruel reactionaries or hopeless Don Quixotes could "hinder the bourgeoisie" in obtaining power, and so we should tuck away our criticism of Russian liberalism until the time when the Cadets will be in power, and so we shouldn't throw any sticks into the wheels of the bourgeois revolution, and so a proletarian tactics that is capable of weakening or confusing the liberals is the greatest act of tactlessness, while any endeavor to isolate the proletariat from the liberal bourgeoisie constitutes direct aid to reaction. This is, without a doubt, an integral and consistent system of views, but it is very much in urgent need of examination, both from the perspective of historical facts and from the point of view of the very foundations of proletarian tactics.

"Fifty-eight years ago, Marx and Engels wrote in the *Communist Manifesto* ..." Unfortunately, I am not familiar with all of the writings of our esteemed theorist and creator of Russian Marxism, but I do not know of a single work of his in which it is not impressed upon Russian Social Democracy that only metaphysicians hold discussions according to the formula: Yes means yes, no means no, and anything beyond that is the devil's deceit.* Dialectical thought, on the other hand, as is typical of historical materialism, demands the consideration of phenomena not in their frozen form, but in motion. The reference to Marx and Engels' characterization of the bourgeoisie fifty-eight years ago represents, in application to current reality, an astounding example of metaphysical thought, a transformation of the living, historical view of the creators of the *Manifesto* into petrified dogma. It's enough to take a look at the physiognomy and relations of the political parties, especially at the state of liberalism in Germany, in France, in Italy, in England, to understand that the bourgeoisie long ceased to play that politico-revolutionary role it once played. Its current universal turn toward reaction, to the politics of fiscal protectionism, its reverence of militarism, its ubiquitous dealings with agrarian conservatives—all this proves that the fifty-eight years that have taken place since the time of the *Communist Manifesto* have definitely not passed for nothing. But doesn't the short history of Russian liberalism show how little this schema, drawn from the words of the *Manifesto*, applies to it? Let us remember what Russian liberalism represented even five years ago. Then, it was possible to doubt whether this "educator of the proletariat," who we are not supposed to "hinder from taking power," even existed in Russia. Before 1900, liberalism endured and calmly bore all the oppressions of absolutism, all the displays of despotism. And only after the Russian proletariat, educated through many years of Social Democracy's efforts, shaken by the [1904–1905] Japanese War, stepped out into the arena of grand strikes in the South of Russia

---

* Plekhanov used this aphorism a number of times elsewhere at the conference in his criticism of his political adversaries. See especially his "A Critique of Our Critics" (1901), in Georgi Plekhanov, *Selected Philosophical Works*, Vol. 2 (Moscow: Progress Publishers, 1976), pp. 474–595.

and appeared in mass demonstrations, only then did Russian liberalism decide to take a first timid step—the notorious epic of the Russian zemstvo congresses, professorial petitions, and lawyers' banquets. Liberalism, drunk on its own eloquence and the freedom proffered it so unexpectedly, was even ready to believe in its own strength. But how did this epic end? We all remember that remarkable moment when, in November–December 1904, the "liberal spring" came to a sudden halt and a recovered absolutism unceremoniously, all at once, put a muzzle on liberalism's mouth—having simply ordered it to be quiet. We all saw how it only took one kick, one lash from absolutism for liberalism to slide down from the heights of its imagined might and instantly fall into an abyss of desperate impotence. Liberalism could not come up with any answer at all to the strike of the Cossack's whip; it cowered, went silent, and thereby proved its total worthlessness firsthand. And, at that time in the Russian liberation movement, there was a noticeable interruption of several weeks before January 9 drove the Petersburg proletariat into the streets and showed who is really destined to be the vanguard and the "educator" in the current revolution. In place of the corpse of liberalism, a living force entered. (Applause.)

Russian liberalism reared its head a second time when pressure from the popular masses forced absolutism to convene the first Duma. The liberals felt they were in the saddle again, and again began to believe that they were the leaders of the liberation movement, and that something could be accomplished with lawyerly speeches, and that they were a force. But then, this was followed by the dissolution of the Duma, and liberalism again flew headfirst into an abyss of powerlessness and nullity. All it was in a position to do by itself in responding to the attacks of reaction was issue the notorious Vyborg Manifesto,* that classic document of "passive resistance," the passive resistance about which Marx wrote in 1848 in the *Neue Rheinische Zeitung* as representing the resistance of the calf to the butcher who wants to slaughter it.† (Applause.)

This time, liberalism thoroughly rid itself of the illusion of its strength and its leading role in the current revolution. It was precisely in the first Duma that it rid itself of the illusion that it could tear down the walls of the absolutist fortress with lawyerly and parliamentary oratory, like trumpets at Jericho, and during the dissolution of the Duma it rid itself of the illusion that the proletariat is only destined to play the role of a scarecrow for absolutism, a scarecrow kept backstage by the liberals until needed, and which they call forth to the stage with the wave of a handkerchief when it needs to scare absolutism and strengthen its own position. Liberalism should understand that the Russian proletariat is

---

* For Luxemburg's critique of this document issued by a section of the liberal Cadets, see pp. 211–12, above.

† See Marx's article "A Decree of Eichmann's" (November 18, 1848): "*Passive* resistance must have *active* resistance as its basis. *Otherwise it will resemble the vain struggle of a calf against its slaughter.*" *Marx-Engels Collected Works*, Vol. 8 (New York: International Publishers, 1977), p. 38.

not a mannequin in its hands, does not want to be cannon fodder always at the service of the bourgeoisie, but that it is a force taking its own path in this revolution and, in its actions, obedient to the laws and the logic of its own movement, independent from the liberals. Since then, liberalism has backed down quite decisively, and we are now witness to its shameful retreat in the second Duma, in the Duma of [Fyodor] Golovin* and [Pyotr] Struve, in the Duma voting for the budget and conscription, voting for the bayonets that will dissolve the Duma tomorrow. This is the bourgeoisie that we are advised to see as a revolutionary class, one that we are not supposed to "hinder" in taking power and that is called upon to educate the proletariat! It turns out that this calcified schema is completely inapplicable to today's Russia. It turns out that the revolutionary liberalism striving for power, to which we are advised to apply the tactics of the proletariat, for whose sake they are prepared to curtail the proletariat's demands, this revolutionary Russian liberalism does not exist in reality but in the imagination; it has been made up, it is a phantom. (Applause.) And this is the politics, built on a lifeless schema and imagined relations and heedless of the particular tasks of the proletariat in this revolution, that calls itself "revolutionary realism."†

But let us take a look at how this realism accords with proletarian tactics generally. The Russian proletariat is advised, in its tactics of struggle, to conform by not sapping the strength of liberalism too soon and not isolating itself from it. But if this is what is called "tactless" tactics, then I am afraid that we will have to admit that all the activity and the whole history of German Social Democracy is one continuous lack of tact, for, starting with Lassalle's agitation against the "Fortschrittlers"‡ and up to the current moment, all of Social Democracy's growth has occurred at the expense of the growth and strength of liberalism, every step forward by the German proletariat undermines the foundation under liberalism's feet. And the same phenomenon has accompanied the class movement of the proletariat in all countries. The [1871] Paris Commune will have to

---

* Golovin helped found the liberal Constitutional Democratic Party (or Cadets) and served as chairman of the Second Duma, from February 20 to June 3, 1907. The Bolsheviks and Mensheviks (as well as the Socialist Revolutionaries) participated in the Second Duma (in contrast to their boycott of the first) and entered into sharp conflict with Golovin, Struve, and other Cadets, especially over such issues as land reform (which the RSDRP, in contrast to the Cadets, fervently championed).

† Plekhanov had stated earlier at the congress: "Comrade Lieber asked Comrade Rosa Luxemburg on which chair is she sitting. Naive question! Comrade Rosa Luxemburg is not sitting on any chair. She, like Raphael's Madonna, reclines on clouds ... lost in day dreams." Lenin immediately countered, "It is a pretty bad thing to have to resort to Madonna in order to avoid analyzing the point at issue." See Raya Dunayevskaya, *Rosa Luxemburg, Women's Liberation, and Marx's Philosophy of Revolution* (Champaign-Urbana: University of Illinois Press, 1982), p. 12.

‡ A reference to the German Progressive Party (Deutsche Fortschrittspartei), founded in 1861 as the first modern political party in Germany. A liberal grouping, it opposed Bismarck and was the most important left-wing opposition party until it was eclipsed by Social Democracy.

be called tactless for its deep isolation of the French proletariat and for instilling such mortal fear in the world's bourgeoisie. The actions of the proletariat during the famous June Days* will equally deserve to be called tactless, as they irrevocably "isolated" themselves as a class from bourgeois society. Even more tactless was the open action of the proletariat in the Great French Revolution, when, in the middle of the very first revolutionary movement of the bourgeoisie, it scared the bourgeoisie with its extreme behavior and threw it into the arms of reaction, thereby preparing the ground for the epoch of the Directorate and the liquidation of the Great Revolution itself. And, finally, the greatest act of tactlessness will have to be considered, without a doubt, the historical birth of the proletariat as an independent class onto God's green earth (Applause), for it was this birth that laid the foundations for both its "isolated situation" in regard to the bourgeoisie, and the gradual decline of bourgeois liberalism. But here, doesn't the history of Russia's revolutionary development itself show how fundamentally inconceivable it is for the proletariat to avoid those "tactless actions," which are used to scare us under the threat of acting as the unintentional accomplices of reaction? The very first intervention by the Russian proletariat, which formally inaugurated the epoch of the current revolution—I mean January 22, 1905— at once sharply isolated proletarian tactics from those of the liberals, cut the revolutionary struggle in the streets off from the liberal campaign of banquets and zemstvo congresses that were stuck in a dead end. And later, every step, every demand from the proletariat continues to isolate it in the current revolution. The strike movement isolates it from the industrial bourgeoisie, the demand for an eight-hour working day isolates it from the petty bourgeoisie, the demand for a republic and a Constituent Assembly isolates it from every stripe of liberalism, and finally, the end goal—socialism—isolates it from the whole world. And thus, there are no red lines to be drawn here. The proletariat, guided by the fear of isolating itself from liberalism and cutting the ground out from under it, would have to renounce, piece by piece, its entire struggle, the entirety of proletarian tactics, its entire history in the West and, incidentally, the entire current revolution in Russia. The problem is that what are taken as the special circumstances and tasks of a particular stage in the history of the proletariat—its position vis-à-vis liberalism under the conditions of the fight with the old autocratic regime—are, in reality, the conditions that have accompanied the historical development of the proletariat from its very birth, and will to the end. These are the fundamental conditions of the proletarian struggle that result from the simple fact that the proletariat appears on the stage of history together with the bourgeoisie, grows at the expense of it and, gradually emancipating itself from the bourgeoisie through this process, approaches its ultimate

---

* That is, June 22 to 26, 1848, in Paris, when the French workers launched a major insurrection against the regime.

victory over it. It is even less possible for the proletariat to betray this strategy in Russia today. In previous revolutions, class contradictions were exposed only in the course of the revolutionary conflicts themselves. The current Russian Revolution is the first to emerge out of the fully developed and conscious class contradictions of capitalist society, and the tactics of the Russian proletariat cannot conceal this fact artificially.

The view of the conditions and forms of class struggle generally and the significance of parliamentarianism in particular are very closely tied with these radical views on the relationship to bourgeois liberalism. The other esteemed veteran of Russian Social Democracy[*] presented this side of the question in what was, in a certain sense, a classic speech at the party's Stockholm Congress.[†] This view runs through the speech like a red thread: Just let us get to the right bourgeois structure, to any kind of constitution with a parliament, elections, etc., then we will be able to lead the class struggle properly, then we will stand on the firm ground of Social Democratic tactics created through the many years of the German party's experience. And, as long as there is no parliament, we also do not have the most elementary conditions for class struggle. And that very same esteemed theorist of Russian Marxism exhaustively seeks out the tiniest "footholds" to class struggle in contemporary Russian reality—"footholds" being his favorite expression in this speech—discerning them in the most cartoonish hints at parliamentarianism and a constitution. Here, truly, the words of Schiller apply:

> Ein Mensch, der räsonniert,
> Ist wie ein Thier auf dürrer Heide,
> Im Kreis herumgeführt—
> Und ringsumher liegt schöne, grüne Weide.
>
> (A man who reasons
> Is like a beast
> That's led in circles round a barren heath—
> While all around it lies a pasture, fine and green.)[‡]

These reasoners think that there is no arena for class struggle, while actually, Social Democracy does not have the initiative or strength and cannot take advantage of all the opportunities, the broad possibilities offered up by history.

---

[*] The "other esteemed veteran" was Pavel Axelrod, a leader of the Mensheviks. At the Sixth Congress of the RSDRP in Stockholm (April 23–May 8, 1906), he expressed these views in a report on attitudes toward the Duma.

[†] The Fourth Congress of the RSDRP, held April 10–23, 1906, which the Mensheviks tended to dominate. Luxemburg's SDPKiL was readmitted to the party as a result of the Stockholm Congress.

[‡] Luxemburg is actually quoting not Schiller but a comment by Mephistopheles in Goethe's *Faust*, Part I, Faust's Study (iii).

In the heat of the current revolution in Russia, there is no possibility of leading class struggle, there are only insignificant "footholds." All the political demands of the proletariat "and even the republic itself"—notes the orator—are not really expressions of class struggle, as they do not represent anything specifically proletarian. But then, in that case—to appeal again for certification of the practice of the international labor movement—even in Germany we have not yet really led a class struggle, because, as is well known, the entire daily political struggle of German Social Democracy has been set on the demands of the so-called minimum program, consisting almost exclusively of *democratic* slogans like "universal suffrage," "the right to assembly," and so forth.* And we have asserted these demands against the entire bourgeoisie. But even the demands that are the most proletarian in form, like the demand for labor laws, do not represent, as you know, anything specifically socialist—they only articulate demands for a progressive capitalist economy. Thus, an analysis that denies the element of class struggle in the political slogans of the proletariat in the current revolution is not so much a shining example of Marxist thought as of the state of mind usually referred to by the phrase "missing the forest for the trees." Indeed, one needs a very stubborn bias for an exclusively parliamentary form of political struggle not to notice the grand sweep of class struggle in Russia today, and instead, fumbling and faltering, to seek out weak "footholds," so as not to understand that even all the political slogans of the current revolution, precisely because the bourgeoisie renounced or is renouncing them, are just as much expressions of the class struggle of the proletariat. It behooves Russian Social Democracy least of all to underestimate this situation. It is enough for it to look at itself and its recent history to understand class struggle's colossal educative significance in the current moment, even without any parliamentarianism. It is enough to remember what Russian Social Democracy was before 1905, before January 9, and what it is today. Half a year of a revolutionary and strike movement since January 1905 has transformed it from a small handful of revolutionaries, from a weak sect, into a huge mass party, and the trouble for Social Democracy lies not in the difficulty of finding "footholds" for class struggle but, to the contrary, in the difficulty of seizing and utilizing the boundless field of action that the gigantic class struggle of the revolution is opening up to it. To look for salvation and clutch desperately, like a drowning man grasping at straws, at the barest suggestion of parliamentarianism as the only guarantee of a class struggle that lies somewhere in the future, after the victory of the liberals—this means not understanding that a revolution is a productive period when society breaks up into classes. In sum, the schema to which they want to adapt the class struggle of the Russian proletariat is a crude schema that hasn't

---

* This distinction between a minimum and maximum set of demands was enshrined in the founding document of the Second International, the Erfurt Program of 1891. It was treated as an article of faith in the SPD.

been realized anywhere in Western Europe, and it is only a jagged fragment of the full variety of reality.

The truth is that real Marxism is just as distant from this one-sided overestimation of parliamentarianism as it is from the mechanical view of the revolution and the overestimation of so-called armed rebellion. This is where my Polish comrades and I depart from the views of our Bolshevik comrades. In Poland, from the very beginning of the revolution, when this question was not even on the agenda of our Russian comrades, we had to deal with attempts to impart an aspect of conspiratorial speculation and crude revolutionary adventurism to the revolutionary tactics of our proletariat. We declared from the very beginning—and I think we were successful in thoroughly consolidating this view in the ranks of the class-conscious Polish proletariat—that we consider the plan to arm the broad popular masses clandestinely to be a utopian enterprise, no less than the premeditated plan to prepare and organize a so-called armed uprising. We declared at the very beginning that the task of Social Democracy is not a technical one—it is political training for mass struggle with absolutism. Of course, we believe it is necessary to explain to the broad masses of the proletariat that their direct encounter with the armed forces of reaction and a universal popular uprising are the only conclusion to a revolutionary struggle that is capable of guaranteeing its victory and the inevitable finale of its progressive development, but that Social Democracy is not capable of designating and preparing this denouement in its technical details. (Applause. Plekhanov: "Absolutely right!")

Comrades on the left side are saying: "Absolutely right!" But I am afraid they won't agree with me in the following conclusions. Namely, I think that if Social Democracy is to avoid the mechanical view of revolution, a view according to which it will "create" revolutionary flash points and "designate" its denouement, then it will furthermore require redoubled strength and decisiveness to point the proletariat toward the broad political line of its tactics, a line that will only become clear when Social Democracy explicates even the concluding point of this line: the endeavor to take political power to carry out the tasks of the current revolution. And this is, once more, closely connected to the view of the mutual role of the liberal bourgeoisie and the proletariat in the revolutionary struggle.

I see, however, that the time for my report is running out and I will have to interrupt it in the middle of my account of the views on the relationship to the bourgeois parties. So, I will just add a few general observations *pro domo sua*[*] that, in general terms, explain our position on the constellation of controversial questions at this congress.

The comrades who defend the views I have just considered here like to refer particularly often to the fact that they, especially, represent the true Marxism in

---

[*] "On our behalf."

Russian Social Democracy, and state these propositions in the name of Marxism and the spirit of Marxism, and recommend this tactic to the Russian proletariat. Polish Social Democracy has stood on the ground of Marx's teachings from the time of its founding, and in its program, as in its tactics, considers itself a disciple of the founders of scientific socialism and particularly of German Social Democracy. So, allusions to Marxism, undeniably, have an especially important value to us. But when we see these ways of applying Marx's teachings, when we see this instability and these shaky tactics, when we see these wistful sighs for constitutional-parliamentary conditions and for the victory of liberalism, this desperate search for "footholds" for class struggle amid the grand sweep of the revolution, this casting about from one side to another in the search for artificial means to become "immersed in the masses," like workers' congresses in the search for artificial slogans to "spark the revolution" when it has momentarily subsided,* and this inability to make use of it and take the lead when it boils up again—when we see all of this, we automatically want to cry out: "Comrades, what a mess you've made of Marx's teachings, whose distinguishing features may include flexibility, it's true, but also include acuity and the deadliness of the glittering blade of Damascus steel!"

You've turned these teachings into the fussy clucking of a chicken trying to pluck out someone else's grain on the trash heap of bourgeois parliamentarianism, this teaching that represents the mighty flapping of the proletariat's aquiline wings! After all, Marxism contains two essential elements: the element of analysis and critique and the element of the active will of the working class as a factor of revolution. And anyone who embodies only analysis, only critique, doesn't represent Marxism at all, but a pitiful self-corrupting parody of this teaching.

You, comrades of the right wing, complain a lot about parochialism, intolerance, about a certain mechanicalness in the views of the so-called Bolshevik comrades. (Shouts of "That's the Mensheviks!") And we are in complete agreement with you on this matter. (Applause.)

Our Polish comrades, who are used to thinking more or less in the modes accepted in the Western European movement, are perhaps even more shocked than you by this particular callousness. But do you know, comrades, where all these unpleasant traits come from? For anybody familiar with the intraparty relations in other countries, these are very familiar traits: they are the typical spiritual guise of that tendency within socialism that has to stake out the very principle of the independent class politics of the proletariat against another, also very powerful tendency. (Applause.)

Callousness is the form that Social Democratic tactics inevitably takes, on the one hand, while, on the other hand, it takes the formlessness of jelly creeping

---

* This is a reference to Axelrod's call at the conference for the party to build a broad-based "workers' congress," in contrast to Lenin's emphasis on a party of professional revolutionaries.

out in all directions under the pressure of circumstances. (Applause from the Bolsheviks and part of the center.)

In Germany, we can afford the luxury of being *suaviter in modo, fortiter in re*—hard and unbending in substance, soft and tolerant in form—because the very principle of the independent class politics of the proletariat is such a firm and unshakeable feature for us, is supported by such a huge majority of the party, that the presence and even the activity of a handful of opportunists among us is absolutely harmless. On the contrary, the freedom of our discussions and the variety of opinions is frankly crucial, considering the enormity of the movement. And, if I am not mistaken, it was precisely certain leaders of Russian Marxism who were previously unable to forgive the fact that we in Germany were not callous *enough*, that we, for example, haven't forced Bernstein out of the ranks of the party.* But if we turn our attention from Germany to the French party, we will find that, at least several years ago, it had completely different relations. Wasn't the Guesdist party once distinguished by its very significant eccentricities of a callous nature? What, for example, did it cost our friend [Jules] Guesde—whose enemies tried so hard to manipulate him—when he announced that it essentially doesn't make a great difference to the working class whether the head of state is the republican president [Émile Loubet] or Emperor Wilhelm II? Didn't the guise of our French friends carry some of the typical traits of sectarian rigidity and intolerance, traits that they had picked up naturally over the many years of championing the class self-sufficiency of the French proletariat against blurry and "broad" socialism of all stripes?† And, despite that, we didn't waver then for a moment—Comrade Plekhanov was with us at the time—we had no doubt that the essential truth was on this side and that it was crucial to support the Guesdists with all our strength against their opponents. We look now at the one-sidedness and parochialism of the left wing of Russian Social Democracy in the same way, as the natural result of the history of the Russian party over the last few years, and we are convinced that these traits cannot be suppressed by any artificial means, and that they won't be able to even out until after the principle of the class independence and the revolutionary politics of the proletariat become sufficiently solid and triumph conclusively in the ranks of Russian Social Democracy. We therefore strive quite consciously to secure the victory of these politics—not in this specific Bolshevist form, but in the form that most closely resembles the spirit of German Social Democracy and the spirit of true Marxism. (Applause.)‡

---

* Luxemburg is referring to Georgi Plekhanov, who had argued in 1898 for Eduard Bernstein to be expelled from the Social Democratic Party of Germany.

† Guesde's notorious sectarianism was reflected in his refusal to support the campaign (led by French socialist leader Jean Jaurès) to defend Dreyfus against anti-Semitic victimization, on the grounds that supporting such "petty-bourgeois" individuals "was not the business of the workers' movement."

‡ The protocol commission of the RSDRP that produced the minutes of the conference

III. CONCLUDING REMARKS

First of all, I have to respond to certain misunderstandings that have resulted from the chance circumstance that I, for lack of time, had to interrupt my report on the fundamental views of the relationship of the proletariat to the bourgeois parties, barely at the halfway point. What was especially advantageous to my critics was the fact that I did not manage to get into more detail on the relationship of the proletariat to petty-bourgeois tendencies and, particularly, to the peasantry. How many daring conclusions were made from this fact that I only spoke about the relationship of the proletariat to the bourgeoisie, [is seen from the opinions] of [Julius] Martov. His is nothing more than the equation of the role of the proletariat with that of all other classes (besides the bourgeoisie) in the current revolution; in other words, it signifies that very same "left block" that whitewashes the class distinction of the proletariat and subjects it to the influence of the petty bourgeoisie—that same "left block" that our comrades the Bolsheviks are defending.*

In the opinion of the speaker from the Bund, the fact that my speech was only concerned with the politics of the proletariat in relation to the bourgeoisie results quite obviously [shows] that I completely negate the role of the peasantry and the "left block" and therefore stand in direct opposition to the position of our Bolshevik comrades. Finally, the other speaker from the Bund took the pitilessness of his conclusions even further, declaring that to speak about a single proletariat as a revolutionary class distinctly smells of anarchism. As you see, the conclusions are quite diverse, and they only have one thing in common—that being that they are all supposed to be equally damning to me.

As a matter of fact, I must admit I am somewhat surprised by the tizzy my critics fell into due to the fact that I mainly illustrated the mutual relationship between the proletariat and the bourgeoisie in the current revolution. Now, of course, there is no doubt that it is precisely this relationship, precisely the definition of the proletariat first and foremost in its relationship to its social antipode, the bourgeoisie, that represents the crux of the matter, that it is the main axis of proletarian politics around which its relationship to the other classes and groups crystallizes, its relationship to the petty bourgeoisie, to the peasantry and so on.

And if we come to the conclusion that the bourgeoisie in the current revolution does not play, and cannot play, the role of leader in the liberation movement; that it is, according to the very essence of its politics, counterrevolutionary;

---

inserted the following statement of Luxemburg that was not included in the text of her speech: "We acknowledge that there is a kernel of truth in the theory of our Bolshevik comrades, one that is covered by the shell of factional stratification." Given the political bias of the commission, the insertion should be read with some caution.

* Luxemburg is referring to Lenin's slogan (projected at the start of the 1905 Revolution) of "the revolutionary-democratic dictatorship of the proletariat and the peasantry."

when we, in keeping with this, declare that the proletariat must look at itself not as the auxiliary squad of bourgeois liberalism, but as the vanguard of the revolutionary movement—not defining its politics in a way contingent on other classes, but generating it exclusively from its own class problems and interests—when we say that the proletariat is not only the stable boy of the bourgeoisie, but is called to have its own politics; when we say all this, then these same people are quite certain they heard that the conscious proletariat should use any popular revolutionary movement, subjecting it to its own leadership and its own class politics. Especially concerning the revolutionary peasantry, no one could have any doubt that we have not forgotten about its existence and are by no means ignoring the question of its relationship to the proletariat. The directives to the Social Democratic faction in the Duma, suggested to the congress several days ago by our Polish comrades, including me, spoke to this question perfectly clearly and precisely.

Here, I will use the opportunity to touch on this question in at least a few words. The relationship of the right wing of our party to the question of the peasantry is defined, as it is on the question of the bourgeoisie, by well-known, ready-made, predetermined schema, where current relations are brought in underneath it. "For us, Marxists," says Comrade Plekhanov, "the working peasant, as he appears in the contemporary setting of commodity capitalism, represents nothing more than one of the varieties of the petty independent commodity producer, and it is not without reason that we count petty independent commodity producers among the petty bourgeoisie." From here it follows that the peasant, as a petty bourgeois, is a reactionary social element, and whoever considers him to be revolutionary is idealizing him and subjecting the self-sufficient politics of the proletariat to the influence of the petty bourgeoisie.

The argument cited here is, once again, a classic example of that notorious metaphysical thinking according to the formula "yes means yes, no mean no, and anything beyond that is the devil's deceit." The bourgeoisie is a revolutionary class—and anything beyond that is the devil's deceit. The peasantry is a reactionary class—and anything beyond that is the devil's deceit. Certainly, the characteristics of the peasant in bourgeois society in the quote cited is correct insofar as we are talking about so-called normal, calm periods in the existence of this society. But, even within these limits, these characteristics err in their narrowness and one-sidedness. In Germany, all the more or less numerous strata of both the rural proletariat and the petty peasantry align with Social Democracy and thereby prove that to speak of the peasantry as one coherent and homogeneous class of reactionary petty bourgeoisie is, to a certain extent, dry and lifeless schematism. And, even in this still-undifferentiated mass of the Russian peasantry that has been brought into motion by the current revolution, there are significant strata, not only of our temporary allies, but also of our future natural comrades. And it would be nothing less than sectarianism, unforgivable for the forward guard of the revolution, to renounce bringing them even now under our leadership and our influence.

But, more than anything else, mechanically transferring the schema of the peasantry as a petty-bourgeois reactionary stratum to the role of the same peasantry in a revolutionary period is clearly an error against historical dialectics. The role of the peasantry and the proletariat's position in relation to it is defined in exactly the same way as that of the bourgeoisie—not by the subjective desires and efforts of these classes, but by their objective position. The Russian bourgeoisie is, despite liberalism's verbal declarations and printed programs, an objectively reactionary class because its interests in the current social and historical setting demand the quickest possible liquidation of the revolutionary movement by means of rotten compromises with absolutism. As far as the peasantry is concerned, it is—despite all the ambiguity and inconsistency of its demands, despite the foggy nature of its efforts, venting themselves in different shades—an objectively revolutionary factor in the current revolution because, putting the question of the agrarian revolution on the agenda of the revolution in the most abrupt form, it therefore advances a question that is unresolvable within the confines of bourgeois society, that by its very nature goes beyond the scope of this society. It could very much be the case that, as soon as the waves of revolution settle, as soon as the agrarian question eventually finds one solution or another in the spirit of bourgeois private ownership, the major strata of the Russian peasantry will turn into a clearly reactionary petty-bourgeois party along the lines of the Bavarian Peasants' League.* But, as long as the revolution continues, as long as the land question has not been regulated, it remains not only a political stumbling block for absolutism, but a social sphinx for the entire Russian bourgeoisie and thus an independent catalyst of the revolution, giving it, in interaction with the proletarian movement in the cities, that broad scope that is characteristic of spontaneous popular movements. The Russian peasant movement's socialist and utopian coloration is a result of this, and by no means the fruit of artificial implantation and demagoguery on the part of Social Democracy. This has accompanied all large peasant revolts in bourgeois society. It's enough to recall the Peasants' War in Germany and the name of Thomas Müntzer.†

But, precisely because they are utopian and hopeless by [their] nature, peasant movements are completely incapable of playing an independent role and in every historical situation follow the leadership of other, more active and defined classes. In France, the cities' revolutionary bourgeoisie actively supported the peasant uprisings, the so-called jacquerie. If the management of the

---

* The Bavarian Peasants' League was an agrarian political party operating in Bavaria from 1893 to 1933. It represented farmers' interests and was often classified as a liberal political party.

† Leader of the German Peasants' War of 1525, the most significant mass upsurge in Germany prior to the nineteenth century.

Peasants' War in medieval Germany did not fall into the hands of the advanced bourgeoisie, but into the hands of the antagonistic petty aristocracy instead, it is only because the German bourgeoisie—as a consequence of Germany's historical backwardness—executed the first phase of its class emancipation only in the misshapen ideological form of a religious reformation and because, out of weakness, instead of welcoming the peasant wars, it was frightened by them and threw itself into the arms of reaction. This is just as with Russian liberals today, who, scared by both the proletarian and the peasant movements, are now throwing themselves into the arms of reaction. It is clear that politically managing the peasant movement and guiding it is, in today's Russia, the natural historical task of the conscious proletariat.

And, if it were to reject this role out of fear for the purity of its socialist program, then, once again, it would find itself at the level of a doctrinal sect instead of at the height of the natural historical leader of the whole mass of the bourgeois system's dispossessed victims, the leader it is according to the spirit of the theory of scientific socialism. Recall that place in Marx where he talks about how the proletariat is called upon to fight for all the dispossessed.

But, let us return to the question of the relationship to the bourgeoisie. I will not, of course, provide a serious answer to the objections and critique from the Bund. The entire political wisdom of the Bund, as it turns out, amounts to an extremely simple position: Without proceeding from any hard and fast principles, take advantage of the good sides of any situation. The comrades from the Bund want to use this little piece of political wisdom for guidance in their relationships both to factions within our party and to the different classes in the Russian Revolution. In relations within the party, this position, as a matter of fact, amounts to a politics that assumes the existence of two different factions ahead of time, instead of taking on the role of an independent political center. When transferred to the wide ocean of the Russian Revolution, this position leads to completely pathetic results. Here, the politics defended by the representatives of the Bund amount to the long-familiar classic slogan of German opportunists: a politics of *von Fall zu Fall*, that is, case by case, or, if you will, from collapse to collapse.* (Applause.) The Bund's distinctly defined physiognomy is important and interesting not so much for its own characteristics, but rather because, through its alliance with and support of the Mensheviks at this congress, the Bund underscores the political tendency of the Menshevik comrades.

---

* At this point in her speech, Luxemburg referred to the Bundists as *schäbiges Schacherjüdlein*, "shabby little Jewish money grubbers," an anti-Semitic slur that provoked an uproar from their members that temporarily put a halt to the proceedings. Luxemburg refused to retract her words, but after lengthy discussions it was decided not to include the phrase in the conference minutes. For more on Luxemburg's attitude toward anti-Semitism, see Kevin B. Anderson and Peter Hudis, "Rosa Luxemburg: Universalism and Particularism," in *Makers of Jewish Modernity*, edited by Jacques Picard, Jacques Revel, Michael P. Steinberg, et al. (Princeton: Princeton University Press, 2016), pp. 159–72.

Comrade Plekhanov has reproached me, saying I represent a kind of disappearing Marxism that soars above the clouds. Comrade Plekhanov, who is kind even when he does not intend to be, has really paid me a compliment this time. For a Marxist to orient himself in the course of events, it is crucial to survey relations, not by crawling along the lower depths of the daily and hourly conditions, but from a certain theoretical height, and the tower from which we should survey the course of the Russian Revolution is the international development of bourgeois class society and the level of maturity it has achieved. Comrade Plekhanov and his friends have reproached me bitterly for painting such attractive and sparkling prognoses of the current revolution, as if the Russian proletariat had nothing but limitless victories ahead. This is absolutely wrong. My critics attribute a view to me here that is completely foreign to me—supposedly, that the proletariat could and should deploy its fighting tactics, in all its breadth and decisiveness, only under the condition that its victories are assured in advance. I find, conversely, that it is a poor leader and a pitiful army that only goes into battle when victory is already in the bag. To the contrary, not only do I not mean to promise the Russian proletariat a sequence of certain victories; I think, rather, that if the working class, being faithful to its historical duty, continues to grow and execute its tactics of struggle consistent with the unfolding contradictions and the ever-broader horizons of the revolution, then it could wind up in quite complicated and difficult circumstances. Furthermore, I even think that, if the Russian working class finds itself up to the challenge of its task, that is, pushing the course of revolutionary events with its own actions to the outside limit of the possible in the objective development of social relations, then, almost ineluctably, a major temporary defeat awaits it at this far limit. But I think that the Russian proletariat must have the courage and resolve to face everything prepared for it by historical developments, that it should, if it has to, even at the cost of sacrifices, play the role of the vanguard in this revolution in relation to the global army of the proletariat, the vanguard that discloses new contradictions, new tasks, and new paths for class struggle, as the French proletariat did in the nineteenth century. I think that the Russian proletariat should not be guided in its tactics, generally, by estimations of defeat or victory, but draw its tactics exclusively from its historical tasks as a class, keeping in mind that the defeats of the proletariat, as they arise from the revolutionary sweep of its class struggle, are only local and temporary forms of the expression of its global forward movement when taken as a whole, and that these defeats are the inevitable historical steps that lead to the ultimate victory of socialism. (Applause.)

1908

Liquidation (Part I)*

Every revolution is an era of political liquidation.† On the one hand, it suddenly sets into motion all the healthy and viable paths of development; on the other hand, it suddenly sweeps away all the ideological relics and fictions that, long deprived of any real foundation, remained on the social surface in an era of immobility like mold on stagnant water. For three years the great broom of the Russian Revolution has been tirelessly sweeping out the Augean stables of Russian absolutism, and simultaneously, in the midst of this Herculean work, it has been cleansing our own native stable as it goes by. One of the results of this revolutionary labor has been the sudden liquidation of social-patriotism. Two months of revolution were enough to bring this tendency, which had been preserved for twelve years in the crypt-like atmosphere of absolutism, to bankruptcy. And three years of revolution were enough for a party well endowed with workers, rich in intelligentsia, with many writers, abundant material resources, and inexhaustible strength of energy and perseverance, to turn to rubble.‡ Four different

---

* This essay was first published under the title "Likwidacja" in *Przegląd Socjaldemokratyczny*, Vol. 4, No. 1 (March 1908), pp. 46–62. *Przegląd Socjaldemokratyczny* (Social Democratic Review) was the Social Democracy of the Kingdom of Poland and Lithuania's (SDKPiL's) theoretical organ, published as a monthly magazine from 1902 to 1904, and again from 1908 to 1910. Leo Jogiches was the de facto editor in chief; his closest staff members included, alongside Luxemburg, Julian Marchlewski and Adolf Warski. It was not possible to publish the magazine during the revolutionary years of 1905 and 1906. This essay is translated from the Polish original by Zachary King.

† *Likwidacja* has a broader connotation in Polish than its cognate in English. In Polish, its primary sense is the elimination of harm or damage (in the sense of righting a wrong and of eliminating a right)—in contrast to English's more limited use as a financial term or an informal term for killing. On the other hand, Luxemburg's argument here depends on an analogy with the economic term as a transformation of one political reality into another (the Polish for cash, *gotówka*, comes to mind, although it does not play an explicit role here). Given the eagerness of the Polish Socialist Party (PPS) to sell off its own positions for immediate gain (at least in Luxemburg's view), "liquidation" is an appropriate translation, but occasionally "destroy" or "eliminate" is used, where more appropriate.

‡ This refers to the 1906 split in the PPS, which occurred after a bitter internal dispute over the direction of the party. Opposing the increasingly adventurist and nationalist positions of PPS leader Józef Piłsudski, the PPS-Left argued for temporarily suspending the struggle for Polish independence in order to prioritize cooperation with the Russian revolutionary movement. Piłsudski and his followers, who argued instead for immediate armed insurrection to create an independent Polish state, were expelled from the PPS. The PPS-Left's outstanding leaders included Henryk Walecki and Maria Koszutska. Of the 60,000 PPS members in autumn 1906, about 45,000 were in the PPS-Left, at least at first. When the PPS-Left adopted a new program at its Tenth Party Congress at the end of 1907, it still had over 12,000 members. The decline was largely due to the ebbing of the revolutionary wave and brutal measures taken by the government to crush the revolution, which impacted all workers' parties in Poland equally. Its party program of 1907 raised three main demands: (1) abolition of the monarchy and the transformation of Russia into a democratic and republican state; (2) abolition of bureaucratic state centralism and the decentralization of state machinery; and (3) far-reaching autonomous powers for Poland, underpinned by a parliament empowered to pass laws and provide substantial rights for minorities, including for Jews and

programs in the course of three years, countless jumps and tactical turns to the right and the left, an unprecedented degree of disengagement and demoralization in a party organization that split into two factions in the aftermath,* with one faction further disintegrating into pieces while the other falls into confusion and instability in an exhausting search for some saving grace as the ground slips away constantly under their feet: This is an image whose analogy in the sphere of revolutionary activity we can only find in the bankruptcy and decay of Russian absolutism. Instead of rebuilding Poland,† the urgent question of reconstruction in the moment following the revolution became the rebuilding of the PPS itself, as *Przedświt* [Proletariat] says (No. 1, 1908).‡ But, when one faction, rebuilding a thoroughly rotten house, is breaking into pieces, the other one is simultaneously forced to publicly renounce the slogan of "reconstruction" and accept the program of Social Democracy that it had fought for so many years,§ as well as to deny the terrorist-anarchist tactics that have until recently been defended by both factions, and adopt the views that have guided Social Democracy on this point the whole time.

Thus, one of the two wings of the PPS began to openly liquidate its own past,¶ and the Polish proletariat has every reason to carefully observe the latest change of mind among the castaways of social-patriotism. If the existence of the PPS over ten years ago was, thanks to its nationalist-utopian stance, a barrier

---

Germans. Luxemburg was highly critical of the program. After the defeat of the 1905 Revolution, members of the PPS-Left committed themselves to working together organizationally with the SDKPiL as a partnership of equals. Luxemburg and Leo Jogiches rejected their overtures, even as the PPS-Left moved closer to the positions of the SDKPiL. Luxemburg questioned the genuineness of their disavowal of the PPS' past and insisted they dissolve their organization and fuse with the SDKPiL. It was not until the very end of Luxemburg's life, on December 18, 1918, that the PPS-Left merged with the SDKPiL, forming the Communist Workers' Party of Poland.

* The two being the PPS-Left and Piłsudski's "PPS Combat Organization," which after 1906 became known as the PPS Revolutionary Faction (Polska Partia Socjalistyczna-Frakcja Rewolucyjna [PPS-FR]). Piłsudski's was the smaller grouping in the 1906 split within the PPS. It held firmly to the commitment for Polish independence that dated from the PPS' early years; even after the outbreak of the 1905 Revolution, it saw no alternative other than separation from Russia. It did not focus on political and educational work, but concentrated almost exclusively on armed struggle and terrorist attacks against Russian rule. In 1909, it went back to using the name PPS, without "Frakcja Rewolucyjna" as an appendage.

† *Odbudować/odbudowanie Polski*: translated here as "rebuilding," "reconstruction," and "reconstitution" depending on context, although in all three cases, the meaning involves the recreation of some version of a pre- or post-partition Poland.

‡ *Przedświt* was the publication of the PPS-FR. Led by Piłsudski, it called for immediate armed insurrection in order to obtain the national independence of Poland, while advocating "transition of means of production and communication (land, mines, factories, railroads, etc.) to joint and social property; deliberate and conscious control of the general public working on all economic life for the common good; and the abolition of wage labor and all exploitation." Its founding congress was held March 3–11, 1907. The Revolutionary Faction rejoined the PPS in 1909.

§ A reference to the PPS-Left, which drew close to the SDKPiL during this period.

¶ That is, members of the PPS-Left, which (according to Luxemburg) were trying to distance themselves from their earlier support for nationalism.

to class struggle and the development of class consciousness among the Polish proletariat, then the liquidation of this party can and should serve as a very important and valuable political lesson, enriching the experience among the ranks of socialists, deepening consciousness, and strengthening political maturity.* After all, the more thoroughly the liquidation process of the PPS' left wing is carried out and the more clearly the internal causes leading to this tendency's bankruptcy are revealed, the greater the benefits its liquidation will provide to the cause of socialism in our country. Thoroughness in this liquidation is also in the self-interest of the reformist wing of the PPS. This branch is making a firm break with the past, renouncing the program of reconstruction in Poland and admitting that the program was utopian. And yet the recognition of the fact that Polish nationalism finally went bankrupt during the Russian Revolution is only a statement of what the whole world sees, of what cannot be denied. The mere fact of renouncing the old program does not, therefore, mean anything but resignation. A frontal change in the left wing of the PPS can only mean true progress on its part and be evidence of development if its break with the past is conscious, only if the forced recognition corresponds to the undeniable fact but also to understanding the historical context of that fact. In other words: The political value of the current position of the PPS-Left is determined above all by its position in relation to its own past. As the current PPS justifies its old position of social-patriotism to itself and others, and since it understands the reasons that now force it to abandon it—this is the first question whose careful consideration can only provide a certain basis for judging the latest program of this organization.†

Let's hear some of these justifications.

"Nowadays," writes H. Kowieński in *Myśl Socjalistyczna* [Socialist Thought], "under the influence of revolutionary events in Russia, and under the influence of experiences provided by the sociopolitical development of Poland and Western Europe over the last fifteen years that separate us from the period of our party's establishment, our position has been subject to profound change" (No. 1, p. 13).‡

---

* The judgment proved premature, since instead of "liquidating," both the PPS-Left and Piłsudski wings of the party remained in existence. After World War I, the PPS rapidly rose to become one of the most important political forces in the newly founded Republic of Poland. After Piłsudski's coup d'état in May 1926, the party distanced itself from the personality who had formerly led it.

† The suggestion is that the PPS-Left should completely renounce support for Polish self-determination in breaking from the PPS' past—a step that many in the PPS-Left were unable to accept, even as they moved closer to the SDKPiL.

‡ Marian Bielecki, who wrote under the pseudonym of M. Kowieński, was a leading figure in the PPS-Left and a major theoretician in his own right. Luxemburg is commenting on his "Hasło niepodległości dawniej a dziś" (The Demand for Independence Past and Present), in *Myśl Socjalistyczna*, No. 1 (1907), pp. 10–31. In direct opposition to Piłsudski, Bielecki argued that a social revolution was imminent in Russia and that the fate of the Polish workers was bound up

What were these "experiences"? Here's the answer:

"In order to examine the origins of the belief in the possibility of an armed uprising against Russia under the slogan of regaining independence, we need to know the data used by the Polish socialists fifteen years ago (and later) to determine the future paths of our movement" (p. 15).

These data are fourfold:

First of all, the founders of social-patriotism

> began from the assumption that a strong revolutionary movement in Russia is a thing of the distant future. The news we received from the depths of the Russian state during that period fifteen years ago fully justified this pessimism. The tsarist government successfully suppressed the revolutionary movement of the "narodowcy,"* and since the fall of this movement there have been no signs of a revolutionary wave. On the contrary, the period from the end of the 1880s was a period of ominous reaction in the ideological and cultural life of Russia. The socialist workers' movement did not yet exist ... The liberal opposition was completely taken off the stage under Alexander II. In a word, Russia generally looked like a dead country in political terms.

The second basis of social-patriotism was the view on the development of Poland itself:

"To the extent that the predictions about Russia erred with too much pessimism, the hopes for the speed of the development of the socialist movement in Poland were exaggerated." When the PPS was founded, the country began to have an "impressive mass workers' movement." The celebration of May Day took place with a loud echo in Poland, and the "huge Łódź movement in May 1892" revealed "a whole enormity of revolutionary energy lying in the working people." The conclusions are the following:

> No wonder that when the Polish socialists, who after long years of secret, underground work, at last saw a wonderful phenomenon in the mass awakening of the proletariat to the struggle, they overestimated the socialist movement's chances for

---

with that of the Russian working class. For an appreciative evaluation of Bielecki, see Eric Blanc, "The Rosa Luxemburg Myth: A Critique of Luxemburg's Politics in Poland (1893–1919)," *Historical Materialism*, Vol. 25, No. 4 (2017), pp. 3–36.

* *Narodowcy* is the Polish name for the members of the Polish nationalist National Democracy (Narodowa Demokracja) movement, which only became active in the 1880s as an explicitly nonrevolutionary party with a liberal ethno-nationalist and social Darwinist political ideology. This and the fact that the author is speaking specifically about Russia suggest that it is rather the Russian movement that is intended, the Narodniks (Populists), associated with attempts by its educated middle-class supporters to "go to the people." Later, the underground revolutionary group the People's Will (Narodnaya Volya) was violently repressed by the government after it succeeded in assassinating Tsar Alexander II. Both movements derive their names from the Russian word *narod* (*naród* in Polish), which in both languages means "people, folk."

development in Poland due to their own joyous intoxication; they thought that this movement would flood the entire country with its unstoppable stream, and then the Russian worker would wake up once and for all.

Because it "seemed" that the movement was going to "flood" [the whole country], "everyone had to understand that our movement was going to be met with a powerful counterreaction from the tsarist government and bloody repressions. The necessity of an impending and fierce fight for political freedom was self-imposed." Hence the conclusion that the need to reconstitute Poland was only one step away. For "it is understood that in the absence of a revolutionary workers' movement in Russia, the struggle for political freedom in Poland would have to take on the character of a separatist uprising."

But this conclusion was supported by a third party.

"This uprising did not seem at all impossible, as the hope was to gain a powerful ally in the West in the form of workers' revolutions in neighboring countries."

"One should be aware," writes Kowieński, "of the enormous revival in the socialist movement in Western Europe at the beginning of the last decade of the last century."

"On the first of May (in the year 1890), the entire bourgeois world fearfully expected the revolution to take place as if it were on the threshold." Even very critical minds were deluded regarding the proximity of the revolution, underlined by the fact that "it was actually Friedrich Engels" who, as early as 1893, in response to the news of the colossal growth in socialist voices in Germany, "expressed the hope that on the fiftieth anniversary of the March Revolution [of 1848] (and thus by 1898), the current political system of Prussia will have already been liquidated."

These predictions of a near revolution in the West "weighed on the minds of the Polish socialists for a long time." With these predictions it was "eagerly imagined" that the revolutionary Polish people would play the role of defending the Western revolution against the invasion from Moscow. Michał Luśnia-Krauz himself,* "our outstanding theoretician," "one of our most eminent companions," the same man who so "excellently" justified the program of reconstruction and whose position is now supported by the whole left wing of the PPS, the very same Krauz who, according to the testimony of F. Zaorski† (*Myśl Socjalistyczna*, No. 2, p. 99), was still "spinning out" his "predictions" in 1900.

---

* Michał Luśnia-Krauz was a pseudonym used by Kazimierz Kelles-Krauz, the leading theoretician of the PPS and an outstanding Marxist thinker. He died a few years before the composition of this essay, in 1905.

† F. Zaorski was the pseudonym used by Alfred Lityński, a leader of the PPS-Left and editor of *Myśl Socjalistyczna* (Socialist Thought). One of the earliest Polish ecologists, he started his career as a zoologist and hydrobiologist before joining the PPS in 1905. In 1910 he withdrew from political activity in order to pursue his work in natural science.

Fourth, the social-patriotic program was also based on a certain view of the political aspirations of the Polish classes of the bourgeoisie.

"It was believed that the movement, under the slogan of independence, initiated by the proletariat, would find a lively response in other layers of the Polish nation—at least among the peasants and middle classes." On what principle was this "believed"?

"The spiritual and political face of these layers was unclear, and it was impossible to see whether a radical-national movement in Poland was possible or not," explains Kowieński. And "the same comrade Luśnia" said, "from the depths of his convictions," that the Polish petty bourgeoisie, thanks to its insurgent traditions, was far more progressive than the Russian one. The PPS was deceived not only by Krauz, but also by another "outstanding theoretician," as the "publicists" of PPS "eagerly cited [Karl] Kautsky's brochure," who "predicted" that the majority of the Polish petty bourgeoisie and peasants would follow the slogan of independence. In fact, "it is often thought" that even our bourgeoisie "will become oppositional and separatist as a result of the policy of harassment through customs and tariffs applied by the tsarist government to our industry!"

Fifth, in order to justify the social-patriotic program, "one more factor was invoked"—the possibility of forming separatist movements among other nationalities on the borders of tsardom. "It is believed that, over time, there would be a strong tendency to break away from Russia in Lithuania and Ukraine, in the Baltic region and in the Caucasus." Admittedly, Kowieński confesses, "there were no facts to confirm these assumptions." Rather, there was complete political stagnation in the eastern borderlands.* But, as this author concludes, "there could not have been any data on the political tendencies that would emerge when the period of awakening and political struggle arrived."

This was the basis on which, according to the present PPS, the party's program was founded fifteen years ago. We have quoted the version above so extensively because it is repeated in the brochure "Contribution to the PPS Program," by H[enryk] Walecki, and other articles.† Here we have a different kind of official historiosophy for today's PPS than what we heard from the old PPS. Then, when there was the question of explaining the nationalist

---

* The claim is surely debatable: As early as 1902, the peasants of the southwest region of Georgia initiated a rebellion that led to independent Gurian Republic, which lasted until 1906. The Republic was supported by the Social Democrats. In any case, by 1917–18 efforts to break away from Russian domination in Ukraine, the Caucasus, and the Baltic region became ubiquitous.

† Henryk Walecki was the pseudonym of Maksymilian Horwitz, a founding figure of the PPS-Left and later of the Polish Communist Workers' Party. During the 1905 Revolution he was elected to the Central Committee of the PPS; after the split of 1906, he co-edited the PPS' Warsaw daily newspaper, *Kujer Codzienny*, and co-authored the program of the PPS-Left. In a book published in 1907, *W kwestyi żydowskiej* (On the Jewish Problem), he criticized Luxemburg's assimilationist position on Jews in arguing that Social Democracy include demands for Jewish national rights in its program.

leap of 1893, in blatant contradiction to the tradition of the party of the old "Proletariat,"* this regularly began with a story: When our predecessors started their activity, it seemed that the revolutionary movement would soon break out in Russia; even men like Marx and Engels believed that the People's Will, etc., [were a progressive force,] while in Poland the impressions of the defeat of the last uprising† were still fresh, etc. This story was supposed to explain why the Proletariat [Party] did not want to reconstitute Poland—of course only due to accidental, external circumstances that had intervened and after which PPS had to begin to rebuild. Today, the same anecdote, now with the views simply reversed, is used to explain the turn of the current PPS against the old PPS. When, in the year 1893, the so-called Paris program of the PPS was established, Russia was at a dead end, while in Poland it seemed that the movement would soon be flooded [with members] ... and it seemed so in Europe, too ... Engels himself predicted it, etc. This story, which returns with the same regularity as Fredro's comedy *When We Hunted for Wild Ducks*,‡ contains one main idea: to explain the old nationalist program of the PPS as a result of the historical circumstances to which the party fell victim, making a mistake in its calculations. A simple accounting mistake! And it was not at all the fault of the party—for who could have predicted that the reckless breeze of history would want to overturn all these prophecies that had been deduced so "rationally," with such a "class orientation"?

"You understand," says Kowieński, "if all these assumptions and predictions were correct, organizing a separatist uprising against Russia would be a completely rational policy for the Polish Proletariat Party." Quite a good point. As we know, if auntie had had whiskers, she'd have been an uncle. But—unfortunately!—"life has crossed these predictions out." It crossed them out so thoroughly that, as Kowieński admits, "life" did not want to take the paths "predicted" by the PPS, "neither in Russia, nor in Poland, nor in Western Europe." In Russia, the necrosis did not want to remain in that state and gave way to a revolution; in Europe, by contrast, the revolution did not want to break out; in Poland, the mass movement was not "flooded" and did not cause an independent "fierce

---

* Luxemburg is referring to the Second Proletariat Party (founded in 1888), which she joined as a teenager. It, as well as its predecessor, the First Proletariat Party (founded in Warsaw in 1882), opposed calls for the national independence of Poland. The latter was Poland's first socialist party and was also known as the Great Proletariat. Party founder Ludwik Waryński was instrumental in disseminating Marxist thought in Poland at the time. The party was crushed in 1884–85 in the course of a wave of arrests and incarcerations. The Second Proletariat Party dissolved in 1892 and was supplanted by the PPS, founded in Paris in the same year; this is the "nationalist leap" referred to above.

† A reference to the Polish national uprising of January 1863. Marx and Engels were far more impressed with the Russian Populists than the early Russian "Marxists"; the former were the first to translate and circulate his major works (especially *Capital*) in Russia.

‡ A reference to a play by Aleksander Fredro, a Polish poet, playwright, and author of numerous children's stories.

fight for political freedom," the petty bourgeoisie not only did not turn out to be nationalistic, but even the slightest scrap of a reconstruction program was rejected by National Democracy, "our bourgeoisie" did not think of enflaming passions against the "tariff and customs policy" of the tsarist regime to the point of "breaking away," and even so it bravely took the side of the tsarist regime, and in the end the border regions showed no sign of wanting to break away.

Indeed, the strange adventures of the Socialist Party and the rational program! It can happen to the most ingenious statesman that he makes a mistake in his reckoning. Even a genius like Napoleon made a mockery of it with his untimely expedition to Moscow. It may happen to the political party. "Who among you is without sin ..." say the scriptures.* And one still makes mistakes. To a certain extent, "mistakes" are not only inevitable in the development of the workers' movement—they are, of course, a historical school through which the proletariat class realizes the proper mode of its struggle. How fruitful in terms of consequences and results were the "errors" of the French proletariat in the [1848] February Revolution, in the Paris Commune! But to make mistakes in a way such that nothing but nothing at all can be "predicted," so that from every word, every thought, every conviction of the party "life" would make a ram out of a goat, so that everything, literally everything, would rise up and turn upside down—such an example, with the exception of the PPS, has not come down to us in the history of political parties from Nebuchadnezzar's times to our own.

It is a kind of "calculation," which for the authors of these erroneous reckonings themselves ought to eventually arouse a suspicion in their souls that it cannot just be a matter of chance or a mere accounting error, and that something must have failed in the very basic attitude of the whole program and its tactics. In fact, after honestly adding up its erroneous calculations, it would be appropriate for the leaders of the "left" PPS to ask themselves one more question: What did the PPS actually know, and what did it foresee in the fifteen-year period of its existence? It did not "foresee" the general political development of the government under which it operated. It did not understand the social development of its own land, the site of its activity. It did not estimate the physiognomy, interests, and politics of the bourgeois and the popular classes in its own society. Having appointed itself the advocate of the working class, it did not understand that class' views and real needs. The fate of the national question, which it had taken as the axis of its politics, was not foreseen either in its own country or in any other part of the tsarist system. Lastly, it did not evaluate the general shape of the socialist movement in the international community. These altogether make up the public statements of the current left wing of the PPS. But can one not then ask, putting aside all of the other urgent questions: On what grounds can a party, for which social and political development, class

---

* John 8:7— "Let him who is without sin cast the first stone."

physiognomy, the direction of the labor movement in Poland, Russia, and Europe were all equally closed as under the seven seals, on what grounds can such a party claim for fifteen years to be the representative and leader of the Polish proletariat?

Indeed, is not the role of the socialist party based entirely on the fact that a certain group of young people, forming the "Central Committee" or other "committees," determine to "lead" the working class? The role of the Socialist Party is based to this day on what Marx and Engels, the creators of scientific socialism, formulated in the *Communist Manifesto* in 1847, as the essence of the "Communist" Party itself, as socialists called themselves at that time:

> The Communists are distinguished from the other working-class parties by this only: (1) In the national struggles of the proletarians of the different countries, they point out and bring to the front the common interests of the entire proletariat, independently of all nationality.
>
> (2) In the various stages of development that the struggle of the working class against the bourgeoisie has to pass through, they always and everywhere represent the interests of the movement as a whole.
>
> The Communists, therefore, are on the one hand, practically, the most advanced and resolute section of the working-class parties of every country, that section which pushes forward all others; on the other hand, theoretically, they have over the great mass of the proletariat the advantage of clearly understanding the line of march, the conditions, and the ultimate general results of the proletarian movement.*

These are the real foundations of the leading role of the socialist party. Not the "decisiveness" with which this or that party, adhering to the principles of the socialist ideal, "takes on for itself" the role of the most advanced, "most energetic" part of the proletariat, already giving it the character and right to play the role of such a party. Conversely, decisiveness in the praxis of a socialist party and its leading role in "pushing" the workers' movement "forward," according to Marx and Engels, are themselves the result and consequence of the fundamental politics that characterizes the essence of socialist activity—namely, a politics that always raises the general interests of the proletariat in relation to its special local and national interests, as well as its permanent interests in relation to each individual phase of the movement. Beyond this, to be a strong, unwavering center, concentrating on the proletariat's constant struggle to its class axis, based on dispersing its separate "national" tasks, to be at the same time a worthy guard, pointing toward the great outlines of the path of class struggle amid temporary turns, zigzags, and deviations from this struggle, when the

---

* See *Manifesto of the Communist Party*, in *Marx-Engels Collected Works*, Vol. 6 (New York: International Publishers, 1977), p. 497.

wide, well-trodden road of history is lost from sight behind a hill—this is the essence of the socialist party. In the end, this fundamental mode of politics, for its part, has a very specific basis and source: It is an outflow of the theoretical advantage of socialists over the mass of the proletariat, an advantage consisting of understanding the conditions, the course, and the overall results of the proletarian struggle.

The PPS, as it now admits publicly, understood neither the conditions, nor the course, nor the overall results of the proletarian struggle in our country. It lacked what is, according to the *Communist Manifesto*, the only justification for socialists' leading role: their theoretical superiority over the mass of the proletariat. Correspondingly, PPS' politics did not and could not possess the essential features that the creators of scientific socialism require of socialist politics: Instead of being the class axis of the international interests of the proletariat, the PPS tried to make the special national (and imaginary) interest of the Polish proletariat into the axis of its class struggle; instead of pointing to a broad line of development, leading the Polish proletariat, with the proletariat of the whole state, down a single wide revolutionary path, the PPS put all its effort into tailoring the whole politics of the Polish proletariat and narrowing its horizons to a single temporary phase in Russia's apparent stagnation.

Furthermore, from the point of view of what the *Communist Manifesto* formulates as the essence of the socialist party, PPS' self-justification to the role of that party is quite unjustifiable. The recognition of the ideal of socialism and the propaganda of the general principles of socialism do not change anything in this respect. Only a completely abstract, circular, and utopian understanding of socialism can see activity aimed at the realization of socialism in explaining to workers that capital becomes ever more concentrated and that capitalist production causes inevitable crises and proletarianization. The path of social development toward the realization of socialism is not a mathematical line running through the air. Rather, in each country, it is reflected in the individual historical structure of the social and political relations of a given society. In our country, the path to the realization of socialism leads through this actual development of capitalism, through the actual realization of the political freedom that historically takes place, through the entire system of relations that led three years ago, at the outbreak of revolution in the tsarist regime, to the unification of the Polish proletariat with the Russian one in a common class struggle, to the rejection of nationalistic separatism by the Polish bourgeoisie and the Polish petty bourgeoisie, to the annihilation of separatist currents in the tsarist era—in a word, the road to the realization of socialism in our country leads through all these particular phenomena, forms, and relations, whose "completely rational politics of the Polish proletarian party" did not "predict" it, did not guess it, did not understand it, did not recognize it, did not evaluate it, and whose action to counter it was a guideline of this "policy."

Let us take a closer look at the strange "mistakes" of the PPS. According to how the current liquidators of the old program represent the sad fortunes of this party, it appears wearing the face of a somewhat embarrassed and troubled, but not guilty, pupil [żaka] whose only error was too much naive faith in the illusory promises of history. That these promises were not kept is the fault of, of course, an unbelievably tedious story, not the good-natured PPS one. "If" everything had gone the way that PPS thought … Let's see why everything didn't go as the PPS had intended.

First of all, the PPS "started from the assumption" that the political necrosis in Russia, for the foreseeable future, would remain fixed. What was the basis for this "assumption"? The "news" that came from the depths of Russia on the triumphs of reaction in suppressing the socialist movement, and the fact that Russia "in general" "created the impression" of a dead country. Purely external facts and symptoms from the surface of political life, "news" and "impressions," the evaluation of relations by "judging roughly," as by a salesman from the window of a wagon, or a courier reporter—this was the "assumption" of the main, foundational program of the PPS. But political development can never be evaluated or deciphered by "judging roughly" in any country in a similar way, since the external facts, in their chaos, contradict one another, and often contradict altogether the essence of social development, being a late reflection of its past phases, a mirror to the country's past and not its future.

In order not to get lost in the chaos of superficial "impressions," the parties of the proletariat use the key of scientific socialism, which provides the opportunity to look into the depths, into the very core of social development, and therefore provides protection from the surprise of history. This key—the research method of historical materialism, the theory of class struggle, the theory of capitalist development—applied to Russia, led to the conclusion by Friedrich Engels as early as 1874 that Russia's stagnation is only a temporary phenomenon, that the relevant "impressions" are illusory, superficial.*

True, the PPS is providing a justification, saying it only made a mistake in assessing the pace of development. Indeed, only a prophet of the Old Testament could have predicted that the revolution in the tsarist regime would break out in January 1905. And even if one could believe that the revolutionary eruption was imminent, another could nevertheless assume that it would not be imminent. Indeed, the PPS today hides in vain behind the fact that the January uprising in Petersburg was "a surprise to the whole world." The point is not whether the PPS assessed the pace and speed of social development in Russia rightly or wrongly, but rather whether it took something that was incalculable, unpredictable, and, to some extent, random as the whole basis for its program and politics: the pace

---

* See Engels, "On Social Relations in Russia," in *Marx-Engels Collected Works*, Vol. 24, pp. 39–50.

of development instead of its direction, the only constant, unchanging, and infallible basis for the party of the proletariat to function.

The second "assumption"—an "impressive mass labor movement" has begun in Poland, hence the "joyful intoxication" of the PPS, in which it thought that this movement would soon "flood the whole country" and that "a fierce struggle for freedom" was "near." Suppose that the celebration of May Day in the country in 1891 and 1892 could have induced an impression of an "impressive mass movement." But the way in which the founders of the PPS accepted this sign, their "intoxication" in response to the "great phenomenon"—as [Fridtjof] Nansen described the phenomenon of the northern lights on the glaciers below the pole,* or as St. [Giovanni] Gualbert knelt down and adored the "miraculous phenomenon ringed by rays" hovering above the remains of the last Veneti in a mental state commonly called "doe-eyed admiration"—sharply contrasts with the psychology of mature leaders in the class struggle of the proletariat.† This doe-eyed admiration and "intoxication" in response to the first signs of a mass movement reflects the typical psychology of the bourgeois intelligentsia, for whom it is a "miraculous" surprise how a socialist, with a scientific foundation and connected truly and spiritually with the proletarian class movement, can anticipate and develop expectations with the certainty and rigidity of mathematics. The other side of this "intoxication" and "admiration" is also a quick disappointment and shock for the intellectual as soon as the mass movement temporarily stops or seems to fail. Thus were Mr. [Stanisław] Kempner and company, along with the whole rabble of the bourgeoisie, so "intoxicated" by the first revolutionary displays of the proletariat in 1905 that they were ready to prostrate themselves before its power and even give a few roubles to the "revolution," only to immediately start to doubt the whole revolution and turn their backs on it after the first victory of the reaction in December of the same year. "Feast or famine," or "shouting to the heavens, dejected to death" [*Himmelhochjauchzend zu Tode betrübt*]: that old and familiar formula for the psychology of the unstable bourgeois intellectual.

For the socialists, who have been on the firm ground of class struggle and its development in Poland and Russia from the very beginning, the mass movement could not be a "miraculous surprise." It was and still is a historical necessity in every place where capitalism is active. On the other hand, the socialist, united with the theory and history of the proletariat's struggle, would not immediately develop an uncritical faith in the unbroken power, in the unlimited development

---

* Nansen, a Norwegian explorer and scientist, traversed the interior of Greenland in 1896, reaching the northernmost latitude of any European explorer of the time.

† Gualbert was a Dominican monk in eleventh-century Italy who sought out the murderer of his beloved brother; according to tradition, upon finding him, the killer fell upon his knees with arms outstretched in the form of a cross, begging for mercy. Gualbert considered it a miracle from the heavens and expressed his admiration by granting the killer mercy.

of this mass movement and its power to move mountains. For whoever knew and critically digested the history of Chartism in England, the June Days in France, or the Paris Commune, the very fact of a mass movement "awakening" in Poland would similarly never appear to be a magic rosary whose power could transform the whole history of society, its class relations, its political conditions—could let us say, shoot with words beyond the borders of the world and reach "where reason does not reach." Let us say more. The socialists, had they had any stronger tactics than "joyful intoxication," had no means of concluding from the list of the few May Day celebrations that the socialist movement in Poland was about to "flood" the whole country and become a "fierce fight for political freedom." For any mature socialist with an idea of the internal sources and foundations of the class struggle of the proletariat had to understand that for this to happen, completely specific historical circumstances were required— namely: (1) the long-term gradual development of the class struggle, an awareness of the broad [social] layers, the organization, the economic struggle of the masses, all those things that the utopian conspirator imagines can appear suddenly at the drop of a hat; and (2) a certain loosening of the iron chains of absolutism that provide the opportunity of expanding the mass struggle—a loosening that could only occur as a result of an internal watershed moment and turmoil in Russia itself, in the whole country. The fate of the mass movement in Poland was connected in advance to the fate of development in Russia. Only "politicians" could fail to understand this, politicians who, in their own country as well as in Russia, could only observe mere external facts, and who therefore rushed from the mere fact of the "awakening of the mass movement" in Poland to build a whole series of houses of cards without even trying to understand the social and economic background of this movement, that is, the specific capitalist development of Poland, the relationship of this development with Russia, etc.

The third "assumption": "It was hoped" that a revolution would break out in the West as well, soon after the first May Day celebrations. On what grounds? The PPS refers to the fact that the "entire bourgeois world" thought that "the revolution stands on the threshold," as the psychology of the social-patriotic intellectual was again the faithful reflection of the psychology of the "bourgeois world." But besides that, it also recalls one of the leaders of international socialism, Friedrich Engels. Friedrich Engels, in fact, was just as "joyfully intoxicated" as the intelligentsia of the PPS, even expressing the hope that there would be a revolution in Prussia in 1895. Indeed, why shouldn't the PPS intelligentsia get intoxicated, predict, and make mistakes, when such a measured socialist theoretician as Friedrich Engels is intoxicated, predicts, and makes mistakes? But let us take a look. Engels was indeed "intoxicated" and made predictions. As we know, this was also done by another leader of European socialism, August Bebel. They both predicted Germany's imminent revolution, and both were mistaken. In the end, was one or the other of them even slightly guided by their intoxication and predictions in the program or tactics of the party? Did they suddenly change the [political] line and trim it, or advise trimming it, to fit the politics of the German proletariat and their imminently anticipated revolution? Not at all! In 1894, when Engels made his predictions, he wrote the famous foreword to Marx's *The Class Struggles in France*, where he thoroughly revised the old "revolutionary" tactics of the barricade and showed that German Social Democracy thrives best under legal parliamentary tactics. What about Bebel? In almost the same year in which the collapse of the emergency law[*] and the first electoral victory of German Social Democracy led him to optimistic "predictions" about the imminent revolution, the German party, led by Bebel, triumphantly threw out a group of "young" intellectuals[†] who, like the founders of the PPS, were "independent" of theory and historical logic and who demanded trimming the party tactics in Germany down to the "fierce struggle for political freedom" said to be close at hand, so that the mass movement would "flood the whole country." No other socialist party in the West turned their tactics on their head either, whether the French, Italian, Dutch, much less their program, based on "intoxication" with May Day or the electoral victories, and did not deviate one step from the line already established on the basis of "understanding the conditions, the course and the overall results" of the class struggle. And here only the leaders of the PPS hurried to play the role of the intelligentsia, swarming around their secret utopias based in "moods" and "impressions."

The fourth "assumption": The "spiritual character" of the petty bourgeoisie and peasantry in Poland "was unclear," and "it was not possible to know" what politics these classes would support in the event of an open fight. Why was it "not possible to know"? The PPS, searching in "ignorance," in the naivete of justifying its own past, admits that it did not have and did not look for any key to solving this political puzzle. But this key existed: It is again nothing more than a materialist conception of history, class interests, capitalist development, and its political consequences. With this key in hand, Social Democracy had demonstrated many times since 1893 that it was "possible" to "know" quite well what the political physiognomy of the petty bourgeoisie in Poland is, just as it "was possible" to perfectly predict the revolution in Russia, the direction of the proletarian movement in Poland, in the West, etc., and so on. The social-patriotic *ignoravimus*[‡] sheds much of its childish naivete here and begins taking on rather suspicious forms of stubbornly denying the facts, when we consider that all the riddles and sphinxes that have deceived social-patriotism have long been solved and proven using Marx's theory and research method. However, the most striking is the lesson the PPS draws from its ignorance: Because it "was not possible

---

[*] That is, the Antisocialist Laws, which expired in 1888.

[†] A reference to die Junge (the Young), a quasi-anarchist tendency in the SPD that was expelled from the party in 1895.

[‡] Latin for "we do not know."

to know" the physiognomy of the petty bourgeoisie and the Polish peasantry, the PPS concluded ... that the petty bourgeoisie and the Polish peasantry were nationalists to the marrow of their bones. The same goes for the "borderlands." Since "there was no data at all" as to what political tendencies would be present there over time, the PPS naturally concluded that these would be nationalistic tendencies. The superficial assessment of facts turns here into a biased substitution of missing facts with random invention.

Finally, the fifth "assumption": It was "believed" that the Polish bourgeoisie would be passionate about reconstituting Poland. On what basis? On the basis of the "customs and tariff" policy of the Russian government toward "our" industry. But the customs and tariff policy of the tsarist government was just one of the strongest links by which the capitalist development of Poland and Russia was forged and that made our bourgeoisie the vicious enemy of all separatist tendencies and a pillar of tsarist reaction! Here, the superficial assessment of facts is transformed such that they are turned upside down for the sake of a political line chosen in advance.

Furthermore, the background of the program, which put the PPS at risk of so many deafening surprises on the part of history, is presented in the party's own interpretation in the following way: Instead of studying social development, analyzing the real interests of the class of the Polish proletariat, the PPS intelligentsia "had impressions," "had hopes," "became joyfully intoxicated," "assumed," "predicted," things "appeared" to be the case, it "eagerly imagined." In a word, it did a lot of unnecessary things and not one single thing that was crucial to the socialist party. It faithfully recreated the typical psychology of an intellectual rushing, like a gust of wind, to the right and left, or dancing like a ball on a wave, up and down, without the slightest theoretical ballast, without any rules. But all these "impressions," "hopes," "seemings," "intoxications," and "imaginings" had a very concrete trend: All of them were characterized by a tendency toward the nationalistic ideal of the reconstruction of Poland, which was supposed to be shown by both the East and the West, stagnation and revolution, class silence and spoken facts, even when they simply contradicted them: Russian absolutism, Polish socialism and Western democracy, May Day and electoral victories, Friedrich Engels and Karl Kautsky, the proletariat, the petty bourgeoisie and the bourgeoisie, customs and tariffs—"To him sang the early dawn, to him the earth, to him the sea, to him sang all the elements."* Gods and men, past and future, earth and heaven cried out with one voice that Poland must be rebuilt, and that lone voice was heard by every PPS intellectual, but, what's more, he "knew nothing," "did not predict." Such a confession of the justification of the program and tactics of the PPS is a public admission of the fact that

---

* A reference to a text from Franciszek Karpiński's *Pieśni nabożne* (Pious Songs), published in Polish in 1792, named "Pieśń poranna" (Morning Song).

in reality there was neither the trace, nor the shadow, nor the appearance of a socialist justification, that it was the purest stuff of petty-bourgeois nationalism, simply tacked on to the socialist movement and unscrupulously transforming the program of proletarian class struggle into a program of "national unity" for all classes of society, and the scientific formulation of objective historical development into a flat speculation of underground utopianism.

The surprises that history had in store for the PPS are therefore far less random and incomprehensible than the current liquidators of the old program want to understand. This is the known fate of all nationalists who consider the whole history of mankind only from the perspective of their favorite utopianism and are surprised that history, together with this utopianism, leaves them stranded in the shallows. There are also rumors from the likes of Kowieński, Walecki, and others that "if" all their "predictions" had worked out, then the PPS' program "would have been" the most rational program in the world for the Polish proletariat, worth exactly as much as the pilgrimages of our insurgent emigration after each new "debacle" with the national cause—that "if" Bonaparte had not been victorious at Berezina,* and if the villain [Jan] Skrzynecki had not conducted his evil policy,† and if the Hapsburgs had not understood their own interests well, and if Europe had not betrayed us, and if [Giuseppe] Mazzini had not betrayed us,‡ and if there had been a few other "ifs," there would have been freedom and a Polish republic today. This, even more, shows the fatal resemblance between the scolding of the imploding PPS and the wails of our old émigrés. It proves that today's castaways of social-patriotism learned just as little from their own bankruptcy as our old émigrés learned from the bankruptcy of the national cause.

Here, however, the resemblance ends. Our insurgent castaways of the national cause had nothing left but to lament their cruel fate and chance errors in their calculations. That phase of Poland's historical development only brought its reactionary side into view: the partition by Russia and the helplessness of the national ideal. To renounce the openly patriotic utopia was at the time the same thing as standing in a camp of traitors, minions of Moscow, and parasites of the "primitive accumulation" of capital in the country. At that time, the history of Poland did not leave any other choice, and every honest man and sincere

---

* The Battle of Berezina took place in late November 1812, between Napoleon's troops that were retreating from Russia and the Russian army. The French suffered enormous losses.

† Skrzynecki, a Polish general, was commander in chief of the 1830–31 Polish national uprising. After suffering a defeat at the Battle of Ostrołęka, he tried without success to have himself named dictator of Poland. His actions are widely considered to have contributed to the defeat of the uprising.

‡ Mazzini helped spearhead the Italian nationalist movement of the mid-nineteenth century. Originally a strong supporter of Polish independence, he refused to come to the defense of either the Polish national uprising of 1863 or the Paris Commune of 1871; Marx referred to him at the end of his life as a "reactionary old ass."

revolutionary was doomed to cling desperately with both hands to the national utopia, to its last semblances, its ridiculous caricature.

The situation was completely different in the 1890s. The revolutionary side of the capitalist bankruptcy of the Polish cause had already come to light: the labor movement, socialism. Thus, by attaching the old specter of national utopia to the socialist movement, the PPS soon had to lower itself to manipulation, to which the old insurgent democracy had never needed to resort, and which already went beyond the scope of "mistaken calculations." No sooner had the PPS assembled its program, as described above, than a huge strike broke out in the textile industry in Petersburg in 1896. The first harbinger of the awakening of the mass movement in Russia shone over the ice of the tsarist regime in its own capital city. But—oddly enough—this time, instead of "joyful intoxication" before this miraculous phenomenon and instead of believing that a mass movement would soon "flood" all of Russia, the gullible and enthusiastic intelligentsia of the PPS welcomed the awakening of the Russian proletariat in a completely different way—with a cold face, on which, apart from disdainful disbelief, one could make out more visibly sad annoyance than sincere joy. In 1897, the mass strike was repeated in St. Petersburg and began a series of long proletarian movements in Russia, but the PPS retained its calm thanks to the fact that Russia "gives the overall impression of a dead country." In order for the phantom of Polish nationalism to live, the Russian proletariat had to be declared dead, so when the "corpse" got up too early and started to stumble, it had to be put back in the grave—at least according to the literature of the enthusiastic and sentimental PPS. And when a few years had passed, and the first bloody mass demonstration occurred in Petersburg in March 1901—the harbinger of the revolutionary storm—here, too, the PPS persevered with astonishing stubbornness with the first "assumption" of its program, that Russia was "a generally dead country" and, with astonishing persistence and enthusiasm, warned the Polish proletariat against reaching out to the rising Russian proletariat, since the living can never walk together with the dead. In fact, Russia's "political necrosis," becoming a source of life for the PPS, was preserved so long that by a strange twist of fate, when the revolution finally began in earnest in Petersburg in January 1905, when "dead" Russia thundered so as to damage even the deafest living eardrums, the PPS solemnly declared in *Robotnik* [The Worker], No. 58, "In the present situation, our political action must necessarily become more active, and its only goal at the moment can be to bring working people to light ... on the Polish cause."

That was stability for Zosia Dobrzyński.* Or, in the words of one of the

---

* A character in the epic poem *Pan Tadeusz*, by Adam Mickiewicz. It is set in 1811–12, during the period of the Napoleonic occupation of Poland. Written after the failure of the November Uprising in 1830, first published in Paris in 1834, and viewed as the Polish national epic, this was Luxemburg's preferred work of Polish literature, and the one she most often quoted and utilized.

thinkers from *Myśl Socjalistyczna*: Such was the power of the "abstraction" of social-patriotism!

And, on the other hand, just as Russia's necrosis had to be artificially maintained until the last moment in spite of its signs of life, the life of the galvanized corpse of nationalism in Poland had to be artificially maintained in spite of its real necrosis. The PPS operated under the "assumption," it "thought," that both the proletariat and the petty bourgeoisie in Poland, as well as the peasantry and the bourgeoisie, would be keen to rebuild Poland. After all, one, two, five, ten years passed, and even the blind must have seen that the "assumptions" of the PPS were fictions. This could not have been understood or predicted if one was a nationalist utopian, but it was impossible not to see that there was no nationalist movement whatsoever, that not a single class made any motion toward rebuilding Poland, that everywhere was quiet and deaf to the national cause. After the sham of the Kościuszko commemorations in 1894,* after the reception of the tsar in Warsaw in 1897,† after the necrosis and spiritual fossilization of bourgeois Polish society in the years following, it was impossible to "think" that all classes were still burning with the desire to rebuild. The PPS, here again, went from passively nourishing to actively maintaining the fiction, from naive victim of its own "errors" to a systematic factory of mistakes, whose victims would be the Polish proletariat and the public opinion of socialists abroad. The huge nationalist movement of Polish society, which had no trace in reality, was finally created in the literature of the PPS, and while not a single mouse in the country seriously thought about reconstituting Poland, at the same time, in 1901 and 1902, the "main staff" of the PPS considered the question: "Isn't it time to lead the people to the uprising" and roll out cannons? Here the power of "abstraction" from reality and truth reaches heights not dreamt of even by [Immanuel] Kant.

And today, the castaways of social-patriotism are forced to admit this. "Life corrected the methodological error of the authors of the 1892 program," writes H. Walecki.‡ "These circumstances, together with the natural class instinct of the Polish proletariat, made the PPS, despite the external form of the Paris program, stick to class tactics and class views on the particular tasks of the movement

---

The verse epic begins with the famous sentence: "Lithuania, my fatherland! You are like health; / How much you must be valued, will only discover / The one who has lost you."

* Tadeusz Kościuszko was the leader of the 1794 national uprising in Poland. On the one-hundredth anniversary of the uprising, celebrations were held throughout Russian-, German-, and Austrian-occupied parts of Poland. Hopes that the commemorations might result in a mass uprising failed to materialize.

† During Tsar Nicholas II's visit to Warsaw in 1897, the Polish aristocracy gave him a warm welcome; leading figures such as Kelles-Krauz were to attack it, and the Polish noblemen and bourgeoisie, for selling out the struggle for Poland's independence.

‡ See Henryk Walecki, *Przyczynek do programme PPS* (Warsaw: Wydawnictwo Polskiej Partji Socjalistycznej, 1906), p. 4.

in its vibrant activity." In other words, it is a modest confession that the PPS' powerful work in the spirit of its nationalist program, which was glorified in its literature regarding Poland and Europe for almost fifteen years, actually existed only in "abstraction," on paper. In its "vibrant activity," the PPS did nothing at all to realize the program of reconstruction because it could do nothing but feed the fiction and fuel the nationalist instincts of the proletariat.

This is one side of the coin. But the PPS was at the same time a "socialist" party and, as such, it takes consolation today from the very fact of the nationalist bankruptcy. While the program of rebuilding Poland was and continuously remained a simple mystification of its activity thanks to the "corrective" hand of "life," todays liquidators of the PPS believe that by confessing this, they can at least conclude from the same fact that this activity was based on class struggle and appropriate class tactics. And yet, "every class struggle is a political struggle." It is, and must be, the class struggle of the socialist party in particular, and the double struggle of a party operating under absolutism. In order to conduct a political class struggle and class tactics, the party must above all have, of course, a political program calculated according to the specific political conditions in which it operates and fights. The program may be one or another, better or worse, but it must be something. Meanwhile, the PPS had a very detailed program for reconstituting Poland and had not neglected a single demand for electoral legislation, the tax system, the election of officials, or protective legislation for this future independent Poland. It did not, however, have a political program for the Poland existing under Russian partition in the hands of the tsarist regime. And this is what the destroyers of social-patriotism have to confess today: the "PPS has not yet had," says Walecki, "a program for Russian partition (defining its immediate political tasks). In its agitational and consciousness-raising activity, it has only been using the program of the three partitions, based on the postulates of unification and independence common to all three districts of Poland."

The present heirs of the PPS do not understand that, without having any political program calculated according to existing state conditions, the party cannot actually conduct a political struggle. But, not understanding that, they speak with childlike simplicity: "The fact that during the whole period of our activity until last year," Walecki confesses, "there were no calculations for political work in an immediately structural sense, led to our being particularly insensitive to the lack of a special program for Russian partition."*

A party that could not only exist and "act" under the knout of Russian absolutism for several years without a special program to fight this absolutism, and what's even better, did not even "particularly" feel that lack—this is an invaluable example in the history of socialism of "a completely rational policy for the

---

* Ibid., p. 11.

proletariat"! The PPS thereby publicly declares, in its own words, that not only was its practical activity in the spirit of the nationalist program a mystification, but also, and in equal measure, its political class struggle was a fiction. In any case, it was not the PPS alone who did "not particularly feel" the lack of a political program for the fight against absolutism until the outbreak of the revolution. Neither did Progressive Democracy "feel" this, nor did Mr. [Pyotr] Struve and company, nor did National Democracy. All these parties and party-ites likewise felt the urgent need for a political program only once the possibility of "immediately constructive" work [arose], that is, the work of fabricating constitutions, manifestos, elections to the Duma, awaiting the "constituent"—in other words, the possibility of baking one's own roast in the great fire of the revolution. All these bourgeois and petty-bourgeois parties and party-ites, newly born in the storm of the revolution, have left the whole work of preparing this "immediate construction"—of the political consciousness of the proletarian masses in the class struggle through propaganda and agitation in the spirit of this political program, whose realization and "direct construction" has now begun—to Social Democracy.

And if, with the outbreak of the revolution in January 1905—the revolution that threw the social-patriots on their heads like lightning from the blue—the Polish proletariat in the whole of its conscious and fighting mass, including the proletarian ranks of the PPS itself, threw itself without a moment's thought on the side of the slogans spoken by Social Democracy for the last fifteen years, a political lesson has emerged from this that is all too often ignored, not only in our own ranks, but in Russia: that the existence of an entirely class-based proletarian party, operating on a theoretical understanding of its activities, unaffected by tactical compromises, unbending in the application and defense of all its views, untouched by any mixed or half-hearted shades of socialism, [depends upon] the existence of a party that actually spreads its action and influence far beyond its own organization and is constantly weighing other factions and shades of socialism upon the whole labor movement. How many accusations have fallen on the head of the "intransigent" Guesdists in France for rejecting the association with all the other socialist groups for decades! History proved them right by showing that the strength of the socialist party does not lie in a plurality of members cobbled together, nor in rich coffers or an abundance of party wastepaper, but in the stability and clarity of its views, in the compatibility and spiritual uniformity of the ranks, in the consequences of word and deed.

And the same history of social-patriotism, from the moment of the revolution's outbreak, has shown that the influence of Social Democracy, as the only conscious center of the class struggle of the proletariat in Poland, acts on the whole of this struggle like the magnetic needle of a compass on the course of a ship.

The way in which the present PPS explains the past it is liquidating arouses the strong suspicion that even this process of transformation is only passively thrown, like a ball, by chance, under the blows of life. Whether the discussion of the program in the PPS and the justification of its latest program confirm this suspicion is something we will see in the next article.

Liquidation (Part II)*

We have seen how little the current liquidators of social-patriotism know about the history of their own tendency and its true character. A question therefore arises that is decisive for the recent reversal in the program of the PPS-Left: What actually caused this reversal, or rather, how is it reflected in the reasoning of yesterday's social-patriots, who are today's followers of the official program of Social Democracy?

The answer to this is found in the discussion of the program that preceded the Tenth Congress of the PPS-Left, as well as commentary on the congress' resolutions on the program.†

Our attitude toward Polish independence, writes [H.] Kowieński in *Myśl Socjalistyczna* [Socialist Thought] (Vol. 1, No. 1), can be summarized in the following statements:

> An independent democratic Polish republic is the political form best suited to the interests of the Polish proletariat. The unification of Poland's three partitions and its rebirth within its national [*narodowy*] borders is something desirable in the interests of democracy and progress. However, the Polish proletariat cannot achieve this goal through separatist uprisings, owing to the clear superiority of the forces of the partitioning powers over Polish forces, owing to the Polish propertied classes' renunciation of their aspirations for independence, and owing, finally, to the need to fight for political freedom in the most direct possible unity with the proletariat of the partitioning states.
>
> This has been previously recognized in relation to the two other partitions—by Austria and Prussia—but now, in view of the imminent triumph of Russian democracy over tsarism, it must also be recognized in relation to the Russian partition.
>
> Reconstituting a democratic Poland can only be a part of a more general historical revolution: the rebuilding of the European countries in a democratic and republican spirit, and the creation of a pan-European federation of free peoples, rather than retaining the countries with their current borders. Achieving this political ideal is essential for the decisive triumph of republican and democratic principles that is essential to pave the way for proletarian rule in society.
>
> Agitation for independence can therefore only be understood by us as indicating the necessity of the historical transformation of political relations in Europe, not as a call for the Polish people to rise up against invasion.

---

* This essay was published under the title "Likwidacja," in *Przegląd Socjaldemokratyczny*, Vol. 4, No. 2 (April 1908), pp. 112–31. It forms the second part of the preceding piece of the same title.

† The Tenth Congress of the PPS, dominated by the PPS-Left, was held in Cieszyn (formerly Teschen) in January 1908. The congress called for a legal struggle based on a united workers' movement and allied itself with some of the positions of the Russian Mensheviks.

The fact that this is indeed the prevailing view in the ranks of the reformed PPS, at least among its intellectual leadership, is proven by the fact that it is repeated many times over in the party's publications.

In Walecki's brochure, "A Contribution to the Program of the PPS," we read on page 7, for example: "Among the factors shaping democratic republican states, the following must play the primary role from the standpoint of the interests of the proletariat: a certain uniformity in the level of economic and social relations in a given territory and nationality." According to this, a united democratic Polish republic should stand in a network of democratic republics connected by the bonds of federation. This is the most convenient political form in which the proletariat of all three Polish partitions will be able to conduct the class struggle to its end with the greatest efficiency. In this sense, and in this form, the postulate of a three-partition republic should be included in the working program of the Kingdom [of Poland],* Galicia, Silesia, and Poznań.

The same is true for those who clearly oppose the addition of the "three-partition" postulate to the program and in accordance with which the current program of the PPS was accepted by the Tenth Congress. In *Myśl Socjalistyczna* (Vol. 2, No. 1, January–February 1908), Mar.† writes:

> The nation-state, as the most advanced lever for the development of the social economy, excluding any internal friction that hinders this development and at the same time removing the illusions of national solidarity in relation to outside factors, is undoubtedly the most convenient terrain for class struggle, and therefore the need to renew Polish statehood is obvious to the proletariat of Poland. The impossibility of realizing this postulate within the limits of capitalist development has not yet been proven incontrovertibly, and reconstituting the Polish state is something that can undoubtedly be conceived of even within the framework of the capitalist system.
>
> And yet this need can only take the form of a demand by the working class if and when, within the scope of its activity, it becomes possible for the working class to increase the probability of this slogan being fulfilled—to make it a reality.
>
> In view of the doubts about the natural "disintegration" of the partitioning states, the bankruptcy of the irredentism of the nobility and the bourgeoisie, and the complete hopelessness of the proletariat's efforts to pass the torch of rebellion to other classes, it will be possible to rebuild the Polish republic only as a consequence of a set of external factors that have not been yet been recognized today and remain outside the sphere of influence of the working class; however, such unforeseen "possibilities" beyond the reach of the proletariat cannot be included in the scope of the practical demands of current politics.

---

* The Kingdom of Poland, referring to the Russian-occupied areas of Poland.
† It appears that the article was written by Kazimierz Sosnkowski, a PPS member from 1905. He later worked with Piłsudski's Revolutionary Faction.

On the slogan of independence, as a "guiding star" whose meaning is entirely agitational and lacks practical significance (as [Kazimierz] Kelles-Krauz acknowledged in his last works), it should be noted that this postulate is not applied against any clear opponent, and by removing the character of realistic demands from the workers' program, it actually becomes its "wandering star" and opens up a wide field for socialist utopia (perhaps: nationalist?—R.L.) and noisy petty-bourgeois "socialism."

I. and K., who are in favor of preserving the slogan of the Warsaw Constitution and the federation in the program, articulate their views in the same way in *Myśl Socjalistyczna* (Vol. 1, Nos. 3–4):

In regard to the Polish proletariat, this means striving to create a united and independent Polish republic. This is in line with the general trends of development and, at the same time, would create the political terrain most conducive to the development of the class struggle of the Polish proletariat. However, until the conditions for realizing this aspiration arise, and thus until all three partitions of Poland are forced to remain in a state relationship with the partitioning powers ... the authors are ready to settle for the transformation of Russia into a "commonwealth state."

As a result, to this day there is still only one view in the heart of the PPS, from the extreme opponents of the utopia of nationalism in their ranks through their lesser and greater expressions to the open supporters: The Polish program of independence is without a doubt perfect, the best, and necessary; it would be the most suitable for capitalist development and for the class struggle of the proletariat, but—unfortunately!—it has one defect: It is not viable. Polish national independence, in the current understanding of the PPS, has become a lot like that mare which belonged to the knight Roland, and whom [Adelbert von] Chamisso praises: "The mare was exceptionally fine / Just not, unfortunately, alive."*

In any case, it is unique in the history of socialism and in the contemporary international workers' movement to have a political program that is both necessary and perfect and desirable for the proletariat, while that same proletariat does not set that goal for itself, because it is unachievable. The historical impracticability of a goal that is "necessary" for historical development is the basic view of the reformed PPS toward its former nationalist program. On the one hand, this view corresponds logically to the lack of critique and the ignorance with which the party, as we have seen, evaluates the past it is now liquidating along

---

* Luxemburg quotes Chamisso in German: "Ausnehmend schön war die Stute / Sie aber war leider tot." The poem by Adelbert von Chamisso (1781–1838), entitled "Roland ein Rosskamm," features in the volume *Gedichte: Ausgabe letzter Hand*, published 1837. Chamisso was author of *Peter Schlemihi*, about a man who sold his shadow.

with the unprecedented history of failures of its old program. Nor does the PPS try to look more deeply into the historical reasons for the bankruptcy of its program, which might convince it that bankruptcy was not a chance surprise or the result of coincidence, but emerged inevitably from the utopia of the program itself, which had nothing to do with the class interests of the Polish proletariat. It is therefore entirely logical that it continues today under the view that the slogan of "rebuilding Poland" is "the best" for the proletariat today, just as it was fifteen years ago, but, as there is no possibility of realizing it, it must be removed from the program. It is clear that the PPS-Left is here standing on essentially common ground with the "Revolutionary" Faction. The difference lies only in their views on the viability of the "best" program. If, however, the dispute is only about its viability, then we must admit that the advantage is on the side of those who believe that the "best" program is also viable, as total utopians generally have the advantage over half-hearted ones.

Almost half a century ago, in 1859, Karl Marx wrote in his preface to the *Contribution to the Critique of Political Economy*, where he first formulated the method of the materialist understanding of history*: "Humanity thus inevitably sets itself only such tasks as it is able to solve, since closer examination will always show that the problem itself arises only when the material conditions for its solution are already present or at least in the course of formation."†

These words shed a bright light on the problem of the impracticability of the "best" program and on the perfection of a "program" that is impracticable for the proletariat. Individual socialist "thinkers" can think up and consider whatever comes into their heads, or what can be figured out through abstract calculation, and call it "necessary" and "the best" for the proletariat. In order for a given aspiration, however, to become the guiding task of a broad social movement, of the historical struggle of a class—e.g., of the proletariat—it is necessary for this task to arise from the social conditions of this class, that is, from its historical development. The idea that there may exist social or political forms necessary for the development of capitalism that are necessary for the class struggle of the proletariat and at the same time devoid of any detectible chance of realization —this is an understanding of the tasks and conditions of class struggle that has just as much in common with the basic views of scientific socialism as the politics of Mr. Buchman, who, as we know, in his brilliant readings and projects, had the bad luck that "due to lack of time, it all came to a standstill, as it couldn't please Buchman's counsel." Instead of inferring from the impracticability of the reconstruction program that this "best program" had nothing to do with the

---

    * Luxemburg was not aware of earlier works of Marx on the "materialist theory of history," such as the manuscripts that came to be known as *The German Ideology*, since they were not published until after her death.

    † See *Contribution to the Critique of Political Economy*, in *Marx-Engels Collected Works*, Vol. 29 (New York: International Publishers, 1987), p. 263.

class struggle of the proletariat and that this urgent "need" is and was only an invented need, alien to the interests of the Polish proletariat and to the material development of Polish society, the reformed PPS concluded, to the contrary, only that it must renounce the "best" of programs, renounce the struggle to satisfy the urgent "need" of the proletariat. And if recognizing an impossible program as "the best" and "necessary" is a striking symptom of a purely intellectual utopianism in its understanding of the historical struggle of the proletariat, then, on the other hand, the renunciation of the struggle for a demand considered essential for the proletariat is nothing more than a symptom of pure opportunism, of a politics of "survival," of hiding under the skin of an ass, as the Jesuit Basilio commends in *The Marriage of Figaro*,* in other words, under a politics of conjuncture.

Let us see, then, why the reconstruction program is and was impossible, according to the revisionist PPS.

Kowieński, as we have seen, lists three conditions:

The Polish proletariat, he says, cannot achieve this goal through a separatist uprising (1) "due to the clear superiority of the forces of the partitioning powers over Polish forces," (2) "due to the Polish propertied classes' renunciation of their aspirations for independence," and (3) due to the need to fight for political freedom "in the most direct possible unity with the proletariat of the partitioning states." The recognition of these three hurdles to reconstruction is now necessary "in view of the imminent triumph of democracy in Russia."

Let's start at the end. The Polish proletariat would have to renounce a political goal of primary importance, a goal that is "necessary" from the point of view of its class interests, in order to maintain unity with the proletariat of the "partitioning" states! But the "unity of the proletariat" is not some kind of Mosaic commandment dictated by supernatural powers. The unity of the Polish proletariat with the proletariat of the partitioning states is itself nothing more than a historical expression and a result of the commonality of the class interests of the whole proletariat of those states, regardless of nationality. This unity can only arise from and for the fulfillment of the interests of all the units of the proletariat, and not the other way around—from the sacrifice and renunciation of the interests and tasks of any of these units. The idea that the Polish proletariat must buy out its unity with the proletarians of the portioning states by sacrificing any of its interests clearly shows how the PPS understands this unity as mechanical and purely external: not as an organic class cohesion, growing into a single foundation of social development, but rather as an artificial one. For any "alliance" of allies in the spirit of bourgeois politics is an alliance for which, due to its value, appropriate sacrifices must be made: for example, to give up separatism. This

---

* In Mozart's comic opera, Basilio, the count's music teacher, tries to hide his affections for Susanna by having her cover him with her dress.

attitude is in complete harmony with this general understanding of the tactics of the proletariat, whereby the proletariat can and should generally achieve one of its aspirations by sacrificing others that are nearer and more urgent and at hand in the given conjuncture, by sacrificing more distant and "outdated" aspirations. "Kanonen für Volksrechte"—"to give the government cannons in exchange for popular rights," as it was articulated in this drastic form ten years ago by one of the representatives of opportunism in German Social Democracy*—also defines the current PPS politics of "unity."

A second consideration: the Polish propertied classes' renunciation of their aspirations for independence! But this "renunciation"—just like the necessity for "proletarian unity"—is not a symptom in and of itself, but a result of a certain direction in the economic and social development of our country. Before the birth of the PPS, this turned the most ordinary petty-bourgeois utopia and an invented proletarian need into the "best" program. For this reason, the betrayal of the idea of independence by the propertied classes obviously cannot thereby be a reason for the proletariat to renounce it as well. Using the same analogy, we would come to the conclusion that the proletariat of all the capitalist states would have to renounce their aspirations for democracy because the propertied classes had likewise renounced them. Today in Prussia, for example, Social Democracy is the only party really fighting for the right to universal, equal, direct, and confidential suffrage in the Reichstag, and all the attempts to introduce the "torch of rebellion" to the "other classes" in opposition to the rotten three-class franchise have turned out to be quite fruitless. Should Social Democracy, in light of this, renounce the struggle for the overthrow of the Prussian franchise system? Only, perhaps, if it were to follow the opportunistic tactics of Eduard Bernstein, who loudly declared several years ago that the proletariat "on its own" is incapable of realizing the tasks of democratizing the modern state and therefore should protect bourgeois liberalism from premature death via "cautious" tactics.

And, finally, the first consideration: "the clear superiority of the forces of the partitioning powers over Polish forces," which literally turns the entire question of Poland's independence into a question of bayonets. Just as the old PPS "Masurians"† from *Przedświt* [Proletariat] thought that rebuilding Poland was only a matter of gradually smuggling "cannons" into the country against the forest of Prussian-Austrian-Russian bayonets, so the present "reformed" PPS

---

* A reference to Clara Zetkin's speech before the October 1898 Congress of the SPD, "Wider die Kompensationspolitik," reprinted in *Ausgewählte Reden und Schriften*, Vol. 1 (Berlin: Dietz, 1957), pp. 142–8. In her speech, Zetkin—a close friend and political ally of Luxemburg—sharply critiqued Wolfgang Heine, a leading revisionist, for arguing that the workers' movement should not stand in the way of allowing the state to procure new armaments so long as it granted it some social reforms.

† Masurians were an ethnic minority of Polish descent living at the time in the southern parts of East Prussia. A significant number of the leading Polish nationalists of the middle and late nineteenth century were Masurian.

has let go of this idea with a sigh, in the belief that it will not be able to get the "cannons" to win victory for the "best" of programs against the bayonets, this program that is a "vital need" of the Polish proletariat. "For the neighboring countries," writes the same Kowieński, "are holding on firmly. They are the same military monarchies that they were fifteen years ago, very strong, jealously guarding every inch of their territory. All the prophecies of an impending revolution in Germany and Austria have proven false." And the state of the triumphant bayonet will continue throughout the "present historical era" as long as "Austria and Prussia are the same military states they are today" (*Myśl Socjalistyczna*, Vol. 1, No. 1, p. 26).

Therefore now, after Russian militarism has just been devastated,* it is the dangerous militarism of Prussia and Austria, "holding on firmly," that stands in the way of Polish liberation. The shiny bayonets and copper buttons of German military uniforms impress the castaways of social-patriotism as uncritically today as they were impressed yesterday by the "Russian necrosis" guarded by bayonets. And if, in the next European or world war, Austrian and German militarism is seen by experts and serious politicians as rotten only in appearance—rather than a symptom, at the bottom, of tormenting its soldiers to an unheard-of degree, and at the top, of constant scandals in the officer corps—how can it anticipate its Sedan† if they are by chance to be "firmly" beaten? Could this renunciation of the "best" program be revised again—this renunciation founded on the "conjuncture" of the idolatrous honor of "iron" German militarism? Today, the castaways of social-patriotism see in Germany and Austria only the external social surface as they saw before the revolution in Russia; they only see that "all the prophecies of an impending revolution in Germany and Austria have proven false." And as they hurried to build a political house of cards fifteen years ago with their nationalist utopia based on "prophecies" of "an impending revolution," so today they see the "deepest disappointment" and, rolling like a ball in the opposite direction, now believe again in the unshakeable power of bayonets and the triumph of reaction "in the present historical era" of Germany and Austria. [They see this] instead of the "imminent triumph of democracy in Russia." What if its "triumph" is not "imminent"? What if, by chance, Russia sees a long phase of a seemingly triumphant reaction, while in Germany the omnipotence of the bayonets is unexpectedly shaken? No one will be able to predict the outward political "conjuncture," but, as we can see, the entire revision of the program of the current PPS is built on conjecture. What then? Will "democracy return to the land a baron, changed into Napoleonic dress"?

But social-patriotic revisionists forgot about one more fatal conclusion deriving from their belief in the decisive historical role of bayonets. The same

---

* As a result of its defeat in the 1904–1905 Russo-Japanese War.

† Sedan, France, was the site at which French Emperor Napoleon III met a humiliating defeat at the hands of the Prussian army in 1871.

German militarism is the guardian not only of the partition of Poland, but also of all the agencies of political and economic reaction in Germany. The German proletariat encounters it at every step of the way in its class struggle. If the unshakeable power of German militarism were to survive the entire "present historical era," and if it were to be a reason for the proletariat to renounce the aspirations necessary for the development of the class struggle, then a whole range of other political aspirations, or rather the entire socialist struggle, would have to follow after the example of the ideal of Polish independence into the museum of "necessary but unrealizable" demands. Due to the unshakeable power of bayonets, the German proletariat would have to renounce any thoughts of demonstrations, a national assembly, direct mass action—everything without which the future prospects of class struggle in Germany, its development, and its victories, are unthinkable. We are thus fortunate, along with the revisionists of social-patriotism, to be able to reach the exact positions from which the opportunists of German Social Democracy and especially the bureaucracy of German so-called Free Trade Unions reject any attempt to extend socialist tactics beyond the rigid framework of parliamentarianism—"due to the clear superiority of militarism" over the class of the proletariat.

As we see, the entire explanation of the change in the program of the PPS is not at all interested in any fundamental approach to the question of the class position of the proletariat. But the PPS is not the first to go down this path to abandoning the idea of rebuilding Poland and replacing it with a more modest postulate of autonomy. It is only following in the footsteps of National Democracy, which smelled the new opportunism at least four years before the PPS and, understanding what the revolution could buy them, hurried to change the weathercock of reconstruction to the flag of autonomy.

And yet, there is an important difference here as well. The openly bourgeois party, conducting a politics of conjuncture by its very nature, only gained in strength by removing its utopian ballast and, skillfully adjusting to the circumstances, began to feel solid ground under its feet, and became a factor in political life. But the party that considers itself socialist jettisoned utopia for a politics of conjuncture, for reasons of a completely outward, opportunistic character, losing all the ground under its feet.

The explanation of the current position of revised social-patriotism runs as follows: Polish socialism has long suffered from the "addiction" of resolving the Polish question in a fundamental and theoretical way. This addiction pushed it in two different directions, there was a "split of socialist thought in Poland" that meant: social-patriotism and Social Democracy. "Both of them, however," reads the opening article in the post-congress issue of *Myśl Socjalistyczna* (entitled "On the Margins of the Resolutions of the Tenth Congress"), had one thing in common: each of them, like a cornerstone, was based on a finalized, apodictically formulated theory of the formation and development of modern states. According to one of these theories, modern states must centralize first and foremost, regardless of the differences within the territories they occupy and of national distinction among their peoples; the opposing theory takes as its starting point the claim that modern states must be or become uniformly national. (Vol. II, No. 1, p. 4)

In the same issue of that organ of PPS revisionists, two other authors provide the very same explanation.

There are three types of views on the issue of independence in the socialist program. One type can be summarized in the basic thought that independence is a stage in the history of our country. Hence the conclusion that it should be included in our program. The second type of view is just a reversal of the previous one: not only that independence is not an inevitable stage of development, but development is moving in the opposite direction. Therefore, including this aspiration in the program is both utopian and reactionary. Finally, the third type of view (that of the revised PPS) is something like an intermediate between those two. It differs from the previous ones in that it makes conclusions only about the present day. More precisely, it states that under present conditions, the temptation of gaining independence would be nothing but a chimera, and therefore cannot be dictated to the proletariat by the program. (p. 28)

Having thus presented the view of the PPS, the authors add naively: "This last view is undoubtedly correct, but a proper commentary is required on what a socialist political program is and may be."

And there follows the "proper commentary," which tries to show that the whole flaw in Polish socialism has so far consisted in the addiction to fundamentally solving the question:

Both these mutually contradictory views (of the old PPS and the SDKPiL) have a common basis—namely, a common conception of the political program of the Polish proletariat: They both try to solve the Polish question in a fundamental way, they both want to establish laws that guide the formation of states and make guesses as to whether Poland will ever be independent or not, whether it must become independent, or, to the contrary, can never become independent. (ibid.)

This is truly where the original sin of Polish socialism lies!

By taking this path, one will necessarily reach a false doctrine. It doesn't matter how this doctrine looks, or whether it says in the end: *finis Poloniae* or vice versa: *Polonia resurrectura.** Both cases have to be equally false. Or does the socialist method, and science in its present state, give us the ability to determine the political future of contemporary states and peoples? (ibid., p. 29)

The theory of some "finalized, apodictically formulated theory of the formation and development of modern states," which is supposedly the "cornerstone" of both the former PPS and Social Democracy, is, quite simply, merely a finalized and apodictically formulated triviality, invented ad hoc in a cumbersome search for a "proper commentary" to the new position of the revised PPS.

The fact that the former PPS never had any intentions of creating or formulating any general "theory of the formation and development of modern states," and that it didn't err with any "theory" at all, is confirmed by the same group of *Myśl Socjalistyczna*'s current thinkers, who trot out arguments in various issues and articles of their organ that earlier led the PPS to adopt the "Paris program."† We have seen that this litany contains all possible "appearances," "hopes," "imaginings," and "predictions" vis-à-vis Russia's necrosis, the impending revolution in Western Europe, the May Day celebrations, customs and tariffs. But there is not a single word noting that "it seemed" to the PPS that generally all modern states are forming and developing in the direction of nation-states. Although it placed great hopes on the "separatist aspirations in the borderlands," on the "collapse of the Russian Empire," as conditions favorable to the plans of *Przedświt*'s strategists, these were completely independent of the practical effects that these aspirations would lead to in reality. The independent Polish republic was to emerge from the salutes of smuggled cannons like Venus from the foam of the sea, through "the release of all factors" opposed to the Muscovite invasion—including the imaginary struggles of the populations in the border regions. But, with all these predictions, they did not even "imagine" that, in the Caucasus, for example—according to the "theory of formation"—as many independent states would have to form as there are peoples living there. Nor did they predict that Germany would have to join with the German parts of Austria in a single nation-state, or that historical development was moving in the direction of "reconstituting" a nationally unified, independent "Republic of Ruthenia":‡ (let alone Lithuania)—at the cost of Galicia and southern Russia. To the contrary, the PPS' Ruthenians only wanted to secure a generous national freedom within a reconstituted Poland, and Lithuanians were promised broad autonomy, but also only under the wings of the white eagle.§ No one will find another such general "theory" in all the social-patriotic party wastepaper of the last fifteen

---

* Latin for "Poland's end or vice versa, Poland shall rise again."
† The program adopted in 1892 at the founding of the PPS, in Paris.
‡ In the modern era Ruthenia generally referred to the region south of the Carpathian Mountains, comprising much of western Ukraine and parts of eastern Hungary and Galicia.
§ That is, the Polish state—the "white eagle" being the Polish coat of arms.

years—including all the truckloads of *Przedświt*, *Robotnik* [The Worker], and all the other publications, for a very simple reason. Social-patriotism is a typical nationalist tendency, has always defended Polish independence not as a rule for the hoi polloi of peoples, but as the right of a chosen nation. Poland's special role as the forerunner of European civilization vis-à-vis Muscovite barbarity was a leading aspect of the views of social-patriotism. Just as Poland was to be the "Christ of nations" in the ideology of the former rebels, the PPS' ideology, making an accommodation to the "class" position, featured the reconstruction of Poland as a special requirement for international socialism. The official formulation of this view of the PPS was given in its famous motion at the International Socialist [Workers and Trade Union] Congress in London in 1896. It was precisely that the congress eliminated the Polish national as the general platonic formula of the "right" of all nations to "self-determination" by removing the special justification for Polish independence—this was the first official failure of social-patriotism.* As late as 1900, "our outstanding theoretician" [Michał] Luśnia-Krauz wrote, in his brochure *Niepodległość Polski w programie sojalistycznym* [Polish Independence in the Socialist Program]:

> The tradition of European reaction is to bring aid to the tsarist government; the tradition of tsarism is to assist it against the revolution; the tradition of Polish democracy is to lie down like a symbolic Rejtan† on the threshold of a Europe in the process of democratization and declare to the tsarist government: "You shall not pass." That is why European democracy has always demanded that Poland be rebuilt to act as a bulwark against tsarism; that is why Social Democracy—Marx, Engels, Liebknecht, and so many others—in taking the leadership for the further development of European civilization from the enfeebled hands of bourgeois democracy, inherited this fundamental demand from it. It still remains vital. And so, if the

---

* Kelles-Kraus (here referred to by his pseudonym Luśnia-Krauz) proposed a resolution in his capacity as representative of the PPS at the 1896 Congress that supported the independence of Poland as in the interests of the international working class. After heated discussions—including Luxemburg's sharp criticism of the proposal—the resolution was defeated in favor of one stating, "This Congress declares that it stands for the full right of all nations to self-determination and expresses its sympathy for the workers of every country now suffering under the yoke of military, national, or other absolutism. This Congress calls upon the workers of all these countries to join the ranks of the class-conscious workers of the whole world in order jointly to fight for the defeat of international capitalism and for the achievement of the aims of international Social-Democracy." The language, intended as a compromise, angered the PPS—but it was hardly a complete "failure" for advocates of national independence, since it affirmed "the full right of all nations to self-determination"—a position that Luxemburg consistently opposed. Many defenders of Polish independence (such as Lenin) cited the 1896 resolution in subsequent years in defense of their position in polemics with Luxemburg.

† Tadeusz Rejtan was a Polish nobleman who made a dramatic gesture to prevent the first partition of Poland in 1773. He laid down in a doorway to block other members of the Polish Sejm, which had capitulated to Russian demands shortly beforehand, from leaving the chamber. The event made him a hero to defenders of Polish independence.

German or Austrian governments cannot quickly suppress the revolution at home, if it is truly a threat to them, then there is no doubt that it will turn to the Russian government for help, and there is no doubt whatsoever that the latter would hurry to help, since the victory of the revolution in these neighboring countries would present too great a threat to it. Then it will fall to Poland to fulfill its traditional function; then a single moment of action will come for the socialists and the democrats who sincerely yearn for independence.

Really! Social-patriotism operated so little according to any kind of general theory of the development of all peoples toward nation-states that its clear contempt for other nationalities and national claims is rather marked, as for example for "the Mordvins, Cheremisa,* and similar *"interessante Völkerschaften,"*† as *Przedświt* wrote, for the Jews, Lithuanians, etc. Hence the clashes between the PPS and the Jewish Bund, hence the antagonism between the PPS and the Lithuanian group of social-patriots, since generally speaking two nationalisms—by which we mean Lithuanians—exclude one another by their very nature and cannot be reconciled, like two hungry rats in one trap.

On the other hand, Social Democracy has never formulated an opposing "theory" or "prophecy" to that of "Modern states must (!) centralize (!) first (!) and foremost (!), regardless of the differences within the territories they occupy and of national distinction among their peoples." Even if they put it under a hydraulic press, the author of the quoted "apodictic" nonsense would not be able to squeeze out a single sentence from the literature of Social Democracy where it justifies its position on the question of Polish independence by the idea that "modern states must centralize first and foremost." Such a general prescription applied wholesale and once and for all to all "modern states," as a means of resolving all national issues, would perhaps correspond to the intellectual level of the "socialist thinkers" of the PPS, but would be in complete contradiction to the scientific worldview of Marxism, whose first principle is not to use ready-made templates and, in each case, to examine the existing system of material relations and the direction of their development. Social Democracy likewise reached its position on the Polish question through the analysis of concrete post-partition relations in Poland, the history of Polish capitalism, the class interests and the political physiognomies of the Polish bourgeoisie, the Polish nobility, the Polish petty bourgeoisie, and the Polish proletariat—not through the use of a template as to the centralization of all modern states generally speaking. This analysis led to the conclusion that the capitalist development of Poland and Russia bound them as one economic and social organism, not owing to the power of a general

---

* The Cheremisa, now known as the Mari, are a Finno-Ugric ethnic group in northern Russia; the Mordvins are part of the Uralitic language group living in the middle Volga region.

† Luxemburg uses the German term in the original, which literally means "interesting smaller peoples."

"law" of centralization but through the effect of a whole series of specific historical, geographical [conditions], etc., etc.

How little Social Democracy has been guided by any binding template regarding the centralization of all modern states is proven, for example, by the fact that at the very same time in 1896, the same author accused of using this template by the above-mentioned PPS thinkers actually opposed the prevailing traditional internationalist policy of Social Democracy on the Eastern question in the Balkans—a position defended chiefly by [Wilhelm] Liebknecht. In a number of articles in *Sächsische Arbeiterzeitung* [The Workers' Newspaper of Saxony] that analyze the special history of Turkey's internal development in the nineteenth century, the author* comes to the opposite conclusion from that on Poland—that the decentralization of Turkey and the emergence of a number of nation-states from it was an inevitable historical development:

> Of course, the conclusion of one of the above-mentioned articles is that external politics should be no more dependent on templates than internal politics. The national struggle is not always (as it was in Turkey) a suitable form of the desire for freedom. The national question developed differently in Poland, Alsace-Lorraine, and Bohemia, for example. In all these cases we quite simply see the opposite process— namely, the capitalist assimilation of annexed countries, a situation that condemns separatist aspirations to powerlessness, and the interests of the workers' movement require that we concentrate our forces rather than waste them on national movements. In Turkey, on the other hand, things are different: The Christian countries remain with Turkey only as a result of force, they do not have a labor movement, and they do not break off from Turkey by the force of natural development but as a result of social disintegration. The desire for freedom can therefore only be expressed in the form of national struggles, and thus our position cannot be subject to any "doubt" here.†

But trivialities about some two "finalized and apodictically formulated theories of the formation and development of modern states," which seem to provide the foundation for social-patriotism on the one hand and Social Democracy on the other, are aimed at something completely specific—namely, a polemic against any theoretical solution to the Polish question in general, against any fundamental position on this question. And this is really where we find the center of gravity in social-patriotism's "revision." As early as the beginning of 1906, *Robotnik*, in announcing the second revision to the PPS program since the outbreak of the revolution—that is, the program of federation—said

---

* The author was none other than Rosa Luxemburg.
† See Rosa Luxemburg, "Die nationalen Kämpfe in der Türkei," first published in *Sächsische Arbeiterzeitung*, Nos. 234, 235, and 236, 1896. See also Luxemburg, *Gesammelte Werke*, Vol. 1, pp. 57–68.

that "during the revolution there was no time for theoretical investigation." Of course, this did not mean a lack of time owing to heightened pressure in the struggle for practical goals, because since then, as its internal decay and bankruptcy has advanced, the PPS has come even further in this direction during the revolution's stagnation—namely, it has taken up the conviction that "theoretical investigations" are completely inappropriate and harmful at all times:

> Does today's method and science of socialism provide us with the ability to determine the political future of modern states and nations? ... The hypothesis of the materialist conception of history does not yet give us, or at least has not yet given us, the key to solving these difficult puzzles. We simply do not yet have enough material for this yet. The link between economic phenomena and the independence of nations and states has not yet been captured in a more precise and specific way. (*Myśl Socjalistyczna*, Vol. 2, No. 1, p. 29)

The immature state of Marx's "hypothesis" does not prevent the same social-patriotic revisionists from simultaneously propagating, as we have seen, a completely baseless utopia about some future United States of European Republics, which will include a Republic of Poland with its own seat at the table. These "further perspectives" are clearly necessary as a "proper commentary" for those who need to be given any old nationalist scraps or at least promised, as proof, that they have "not renounced" the best of programs. But if the concern is for a basic illumination of the Polish question, for any theoretical approach to its fate or the relationship of the class struggle of the proletariat to this question, the "method and science of socialism" turns out to be insufficiently developed, and "we simply do not yet have enough material." Thus all theories "simply" become identical to "prophecies" (ibid., p. 28), to "abstraction" (p. 29), and with one more step, even a theory is nothing more than a "formula," a "doctrine," a "geometrically deductive politics" (p. 34); oh, theory is nothing more than a "utopia" (pp. 34, 36)!

> As if independence or any other similar, and even, for example, diametrically opposed centralist formula (!) based on some more general hypothesis, some doctrine about the formation of modern states—as if such an abstraction, completely independently of its scientific credibility, could serve us as a political *Endziel* [final or ultimate goal]! We state firmly that no, it should not. If that were the case, this program based on utopia would constantly threaten to distort the party tactics toward a geometric-deductive politics and would be a constant threat to the realism of proletarian politics. Utopia would still stand between party and life: it would hinder the immediacy of political observation ... This would lead the party to systematic underestimation, to counterfeiting reality, to unconscious rebellions against it, it would hinder the party's freedom of movement, etc. (ibid., p. 35)

Accordingly, no one "has succeeded" in grasping the link between economic development and the fate of the independence of "nations and states." Although every upper-class secondary school student in Germany already knows that the entire German national movement and the unification of Germany in the 1830s and 1840s were products of capitalist development that could not be reconciled with the existence of thirty-six fatherlands, each with the same number of customs barriers, monetary policies, judiciaries, administrations, measures and weights, communication systems, etc., etc. To be sure, any young man in Germany would fail his exams as early as the fourth grade if he had remained unaware that the foundation of the current German Reich lies in the so-called Zollverein and that the historical predecessor of the current Reich's parliament was the so-called Zollparlament.* The independence and national unification of Italy was only the reverse side of the bourgeois development of the Italian states and provinces in the nineteenth century, for which both the fragmentation of the territory and the backward policy of Austrian absolutism were barriers. These facts have already been "grasped" by anyone with an awareness of the history of modern Europe and its political history in the nineteenth century, with the exception of the revisionists of social-patriotism, who confidently explain that the national unification of Italy is a product of [Giuseppe] Verdi's "national opera."

To be sure, only the politically illiterate are unaware that the eighteenth-century struggle for independence in the United States was the result of England's economic policy toward its colonies, a policy aimed at preventing and artificially suppressing any autonomous industrial development by prohibiting colonies from trading with any country other than their "native" country, prohibiting the export of machines from England to America and the emigration of skilled workers, crippling the colonies with burdensome taxes, particularly on all industrial and commercial enterprises. It is also well known that the final motive for the United States' rebellion was a fact of a strongly "economic" nature—namely, the new stamp tax imposed on the colonies by the English Parliament.

To be sure, it is just as clear that the very same economic policy in England, aimed at the systematic suppression and eradication of any development of independent industry, and at the mass proletarianization of the peasants for the sake of the "primitive accumulation" of English capital—this same policy provoked

---

* The Zollverein was a customs union between German states. It was created on the initiative of Prussia in the 1830s, prior to the creation of a unified German state, to promote commercial connections between the many fragmented states and principalities. It eventually laid the economic groundwork for the political unification of Germany in 1871. The Zollparlament refers to members of the Prussian Reichstag and North German Federation, elected in February and March 1868. Though Bismarck hoped it would create a unified German nature, the latter did not come into existence until several years later.

the national movement in Ireland, which, however, lacking the same conditions of independent economic development as the United States, was defeated in an unequal fight against the giant of English capitalism.*

To be sure, even elementary textbooks on general history teach that the united uprising of the Netherlands against the Spaniards in the sixteenth century was, under the ideological cover of the struggle with Spain, actually the rebellion of the manufacturers and merchants of the ports stifled in their economic development, a rebellion of the warriors of the new capitalist system of production and the new capitalist policy of colonialism against the outdated feudal absolutism of Spain, its rusty policy of internal oppression, and its primitive method of colonial exploitation.

To be sure, almost every busboy knows and can explain the fact that in Asia, Africa, and America, entire nations and tribes have lost, and are losing, their independence on the sacrificial altar of European and American capital and that, in turn, for the countries unable to develop capital, such as Spain, their colonies eventually slipped out of their hands and fell into those of the emerging countries in the full bloom of capitalism, like the United States.

To be sure, in an article on the national struggles in Austria in *Die Neue Zeit* [The New Times] in 1898, Karl Kautsky, praised by *Myśl Socjalistyczna* as a "careful writer," identified "three roots" that gave rise to "modern nationalist movements"—namely: the desire of the capitalist bourgeoisie to control the internal market, a political democratization tied to capitalism, and a popular education equally tied to it. This is a theory that is fully in line with Poland, where the highest aspirations of capitalist development—which find themselves, as a result of special political and historical circumstances, at cross purposes with national independence—not only failed to provoke a "modern national movement" in Poland, but, on the contrary, condemned the traditions of the old *szlachta* movement to hopelessness.

Indeed, it follows from all this not only that have we "succeeded" in "grasping" the "link between economic phenomena and the independence of nations and states," but also that this link is obvious, whether we take the relevant historical facts from the present or from the recent or more distant past—that it was not, therefore, the "socialist science and method" that was immature, but rather the "thinkers" of the PPS who, while presenting such a serious face, do not have the slightest idea what they are dealing with.

But let us suppose that these things, which have long been proven and known to every educated European, remained a secret to the revised PPS, which "did not succeed in grasping" the most elementary knowledge from political history. Neither Western Europe nor other parties of the world have lost

---

* On these grounds Luxemburg consistently argued that demands for Irish national independence were "utopian" as well.

anything by this failure, and the universal course of history will not be derailed by it. Things are different, however, when we return "home" to Poland. From the very beginning, Polish socialists have found themselves working under exceptional conditions. Less fortunate than their German, French, or Italian comrades, they started their activity not within the framework of a ready-made, normal bourgeois state, where their proper task would have been to formulate the interests of the class of the proletariat, but within a society whose entire domestic and external history took place under the overwhelming influence of a single fact: the loss of national independence. In a society divided nationally into three parts and incorporated in three foreign and completely different state entities, in a society that has lived through three national uprisings, in which the national cause has been the axis of political life for almost a century, in which the national traditions have dominated everyone's minds, defined the whole political masquerade of classes and parties, created a whole different ideology, literature, art, and conventional language—in this society, every political party entering the public stage must first of all take a completely defined position on the national question. The first word of Polish socialism, the first reflex on announcing the birth of a new class party of the proletariat in the late 1870s and 1880s, was to separate itself from the national cause and its traditions, which was tantamount to isolating itself from the ideology of the ruling classes, from bourgeois society in Poland. There is, however, a deep and special relationship between Polish socialism and the national cause. The question of the existence and fate of socialism in Poland, as in all modern countries, is inseparably connected with the question and fact of capitalist development. On the other hand, this development exists in the closest connection with the political life of the country. The partition of Poland at a time when it was still almost exclusively a country with a natural economy, its incorporation into the borders of three absolutist states, the different geographical and economic conditions and different economic policies of each of these states—all this determined the fate of capitalist development in each Polish partition, which in turn negatively determined the fate of the national cause. Therefore, to learn the conditions and the paths of capitalism in Poland as the foundation of the socialist movement is the same as to examine the conditions and the fate of the Polish national cause. The fate of socialism and the fate of the national question in Poland are only two sides of the same development of modern capitalism. It is, then, obvious that, unless Polish socialists want to remain within a circular-conspiratorial point of view, from which the task of the party of the proletariat is limited to writing down the "most far-reaching demands" from the "best" foreign socialist programs and translating them into Polish, if Polish socialism is to be a meaningful transplant of the general international theory of the proletariat onto peculiar soil, then the first task of the socialists is precisely to "grasp" the link between the "economic factor and the independence" of the Polish nation, to imagine a theory that would explain the peculiar history of capitalism in Poland and the link between this history and the national cause.*

It is only in this way that Polish socialism will be in the position to answer a whole series of questions of prime importance for any political party in our country that wants society to take it seriously, and especially for a party that claims to be leading the proletarian mass movements in Poland. And it is only the study and theoretical illumination of the modern economic development of Poland that will provide an explanation of the fate of the national cause in the past—and of the fate of the uprisings—in a less simplistic way than "the power of Muscovy" and the "betrayal" of the leaders of the uprising. The investigation of the development of Polish capitalism, with the help of Marxist theory, provides the only key to understanding the political face of the classes and parties of our bourgeois society; [it is crucial for] deciphering its specific "national" language, in which "language lies to the voice, and the voice lies to thought," which at every step exposes the party of the proletariat to being caught in the thickest of mystifications.

Only in this way—that is, in relation to the direction of capitalist development in Poland—can Polish socialists fundamentally resolve the question of the mutual relationship of the Polish proletariat in the three partitions, on the one hand, and the relationship between each of the factions of the Polish working class and the proletariat of the partitioning powers, on the other. This is, in other words, as much a question of class, political, and occupational organization as it is one of tactics in the class struggle.

Finally, only such theoretical illumination of the history and tendencies of Polish capitalism has provided, and continues to provide, Polish socialists with the opportunity to take a conscious and fundamental position on the most radical phenomenon in contemporary history—on the Russian Revolution—to indicate the role and tasks of the Polish proletariat itself in relation to this revolution, not as a foreign, external "conjuncture" fallen from the sky, in which one can bargain for a bit of "democracy," but as the logical result of Poland's own economic development as one common to Russia. This worldview, operating on a theoretical basis, gave Polish Social Democracy the opportunity to predict the inevitable revolution in the tsarist regime in advance and to point this out to the Polish proletariat, directing the entire tactics of class struggle in this direction even at a time when socialism in Russia was a feeble sapling and the revolution seemed to be a mirage, to actively accelerate the onset of that revolution and prepare the proletariat for the tasks of the revolutionary era.

In brief, only this kind of theoretical basis and a fundamental solution to the national question can give Polish socialism the opportunity to create an

---

* This link was the precise subject of Luxemburg's dissertation, published as *The Industrial Development of Poland*. A new and revised translation appears in *Complete Works*, Vol. 1, pp. 1–78.

independent and fundamental class politics at every point, developing in an organic and logical connection as one stitch follows another, and to play the role of an influential factor in social life, not a parasite of historical development and a weathercock on the roof that mindlessly spins around every "conjuncture."

It thus becomes completely clear what the revised PPS' diatribe against all "theory" and all "addictions" means for the fundamental solution of the Polish question.

> From all sides we hear voices saying that there, nevertheless, is a Polish question and we must resolve it, that is to say, resolve it completely, and radically predetermine it by accepting or rejecting independence. Everything else is called small-mindedness, insincerity, eclecticism. But why? Why do we have to decide what we cannot decide? It would be a different thing if life itself presented this issue, if the political constellation of this historical era were to push for a radical solution to the Polish question, if it were a question of: to fight, or not to fight—today or in the near future. (ibid., p. 32)

Why should Polish socialists "radically predetermine" their attitude to the Russian Revolution four years ago, when on January 22, 1905, there was still no question of: "To fight or not to fight?" Why should German Social Democracy "radically predetermine" the question of the universal and equal right to vote for the Prussian Sejm "by accepting or rejecting" it, when the "political constellation" had not yet dropped the question on its plate: "To fight or not to fight?" Why should German Social Democracy "predetermine" its position on the general strike, as it did in Jena in 1905, when the "political constellation" had not yet come up with the question: "To strike or not to strike?" Why should socialists "radically predetermine" their attitude toward socialism, when neither today nor in "the near future" is it a question of "to fight or not to fight"—of seizing political power?

The conclusion of the above is clear. In view of the fundamental importance of the Polish question for socialism in our country, the PPS, rejecting all "theory" and any fundamental position on this issue, has "simply" hung in the wind with all its "socialism." Having no guiding thread in its hand to address the social history of its own country, its past, future, and present, the conditions and tasks of class struggle, the politics of such a party follows a straight path down a slanting plane to adapt to the "constellations," to chase after the political "conjuncture."

Indeed, in its general revision to the program, the PPS did not stop at rejecting "theory," but also revised the minimum program itself. In the discussion of the new program in *Myśl Socjalistyczna*, there were serious considerations from various sides of the very concept of the minimum program. And here are the conclusions they reached. One of the "thinkers" declares:

In view of all this, the program cannot be written at all in the long run, since it is completely useless, and besides, it cannot remain unchanged over a long period of time. Such a program would have to be based on the current balance of social forces and with every major change it would have to be subject to criticism and revision. (Vol. 1, No. 45, p. 117)

Two other very eloquent, or at least long-winded, "thinkers" together rewrite the minimum program that defines, in every socialist party, the class aspirations of the proletariat that are feasible within the bourgeois system, making it into "simply" a parliamentary program: "The minimum program is essentially a summary of certain legal and political devices that the socialist proletariat would like to implement through legislation" (ibid., p. 132).

And having thus reduced all the activities of the socialist proletariat today to parliamentarianism, the same thinkers add: as there is no parliament yet in our country under Russian partition, "until then, the minimum program of the usual type is still to a certain extent getting ahead of ourselves in our country" (!), and "actually, alongside such a minimum program and before it, we would need slogans for the revolution, we would need to formulate its nearest goals and fill in the blanks" (ibid., p. 133). The minimum program, first transformed here into a purely parliamentary program, is then replaced by a kind of "temporary program," to be amended and revised with each change to the "constellation." A politics previously monopolized by bourgeois liberalism alone in its deepest decline, specifically by the infamous German "National Liberals" commonly called the "Fraktion Drehscheibe"*—which roughly means the same thing as the party of the weathercock on a roof—this politics of spinning according to the wind of the "constellation" is openly raised here to the level of a principle.

And this is the discussion through which the PPS, in revising its program, reached the newest program adopted by the Tenth Congress—"for the time being," that is, until the next change in the "political constellation." We have to admit—and the commentary on the adopted resolutions in the post-convention issue shows this all too clearly—that it paid dearly for its dispute with the nationalist stance: the denial of the need for any theory that would guide the history and fate of Polish society, the rejection of any fundamental policy, the undermining of all basic concepts of the socialist agenda and its importance for the struggle of the proletariat, all while raising the most ordinary opportunism up as the only guiding principle—a very wreckage, a complete ruin, a total bankruptcy of socialist thought; this is the result of the revision to social-patriotism.

It is only in this image of the terrible sterilization and total loss of the ground under the feet of the revised PPS that one can see how much nationalism was its

---

* Literally, "the Faction of Turncoats"—an appellation often applied by German socialists of the time to liberals.

heart and soul, while proletarian socialism was only a coating for this tendency. [Nationalism's public bankruptcy] in the course of the revolution [sufficed] for the entire PPS to fall rapidly into a state of hopeless decay. And in the wing of the party that decided to openly reject nationalist aspirations, that dispute, contrary to the expectations of the superficial optimists, led not to healing and putting the ideology of this organization on firm ground, but to it staggering completely. After nationalism was abandoned, the revised PPS lost all support, and "socialism," which had been, in its social-patriotic phase, a rag clipped on mechanically to a nationalist mast, has now, after being torn off, become a pile of formless tatters.

The PPS rejects the program of reconstituting Poland. Why? Not because it is switching from a nationalist point of view to the class perspective of the proletariat, which never had anything to do with the utopia of reconstruction, but "simply" because it became apparent that "there is not enough strength" for reconstruction, because "thinking about independence in these specific conditions is a mirage, it is something that simply doesn't exist in the flesh of society, in its broadest underlying layers" (*Myśl Socjalistyczna*, Vol. 2, No. 1).

But why doesn't "thinking about independence" exist "in the flesh of society," even though it existed for almost fifteen years in the flesh of language and in the patient blotting paper of social-patriotism? Why did nationalism turn out to be a "mirage"? The PPS cannot give the slightest answer to this. All it knows is that it got a powerful, shocking slap in the face from the revolution, and this fact is enough for it. To delve more deeply into the reasons for this unpleasant surprise would be "theory," or "deductive-geometrical politics," or "abstraction," or "utopia," because the "science and method of socialism" is not yet mature enough to solve such problems.

But how then does the PPS justify its current program of autonomy? Again, "simply" because, with the current revolution, autonomy can be achieved that is without the slightest internal connection to the class position of the proletariat, but only from the external viewpoint of the conjuncture—that is, [in terms of] what "can be achieved" and [the view] that "there is not enough strength."

Today, the PPS knows only one thing about the Polish question that constitutes its entire program: that Poland cannot be rebuilt, but that something "democratic" can be achieved. So, it knows exactly as much as any slightly more intelligent waiter in Warsaw. And beyond that, it knows nothing whatsoever, neither what happened, nor what will happen, and waits for whatever God will bring it, living from day to day, ready to receive new slaps and revise things again according to the "constellation." By its very nature, such a party can exist only insofar as there is a Social Democratic Party that knows its principles, paths, and goals, leading the mass of the proletariat; it can exist as a marauder, lagging behind the proletarian army and imitating its every turn of phrase without the slightest comprehension, like a parasite and a burden on the class struggle, lowering its resilience, cohesion, and political awareness.

But the bankrupt social nationalists are, by the same token, also no more Social Democratic than was Russian absolutism following the manifesto of October 30 on constitutional government. The Social Democratic program adopted by the Tenth Congress—as shown by the whole pre-congress discussion and the official interpretation of program resolutions following the congress—is only the fruit of opportunism, of adapting itself to the conjuncture; it is a dead letter behind which there isn't a trace of the Social Democratic spirit or any kind of class socialism. And in this sense, unfortunately, all we can say about the current PPS, adorned with the new program, is this: "The mare is exceptionally fine / Just not, unfortunately, alive."*

Shaken from the nationalist point of view by the hard hand of history, unable to accept the class viewpoint of the proletariat, the revised PPS is now neither this nor that, neither fish nor fowl; it is an organization trying to hold on to the border between Social Democracy and social-patriotism, unfit to live and doomed in advance to strife and to drift between the two contradictions. The revolution that so quickly turned social-patriotism to ruins will soon blow out this last manifestation of its spirit as it repents on the ruins.

---

* Luxemburg again quotes Chamisso in German, this time with the tense changed from past to present: "Ausnehmend schön ist die Stute / Sie aber ist leider tot."

The Epic of Łódź[*]

It may have seemed at the beginning of the revolution that the bourgeoisie of Poland occasionally had an inkling of its own historical role. But, as events have developed, the bourgeoisie has stooped lower and lower, and now it stands shoulder to shoulder with blatantly reactionary forces. This course of events reaffirms the principle that the objective interests of a class and the subjective understanding of interests by the members of the class do not coincide in every moment of development.

Our Łódź, with its tragic history, provides a most extreme expression of this principle. For every student of class struggle, the history of the struggle of labor and capital in Łódź is an invaluable resource. Here is revealed in distinct and thorough detail the role of capitalists in the Russian state in general and in our land in particular, and here the evolution of the industrial bourgeoisie is outlined as plain as day. Here every twitch of the bourgeoisie has a recognizably bourgeois expression and forceful tone, showing its class colors. Yet the struggle of Łódź also has meaning for the historian of Polish culture, because in and around it are arrayed those stores of spiritual and ethical power over which the bourgeoisie has control.

Moreover, this struggle expresses the particular physiognomy of Łódźian capitalism—its sociological nature.

Łódź is a city still reminiscent of the hastily created gold mining towns of Australia and America. It is a mixture of the most diverse cultural and national elements. Germans, Russian Jews, Poles, Polonized Germans, non-Polonized Germans—all these remain unconnected by any deep threads of cultural cohabitation, and they lack any traditions of class or shared historical memory whatsoever. Hence the special uncivility, strange brutality, and unthinking, belligerent tactics favored by the Łódźian capitalists. Here, even the most elementary social bonds are lacking. While you cannot say that a capitalist society, or every class society in general, is a society in the exact meaning of that phrase—since it would have to constitute a full form of coexistence allowing the broadest-possible share of people to have psychic influence on each other and to use and produce culture together—Łódź does not have even a trace of the conditions that other industrial centers have. The industrial bourgeoisie in other countries, and in our country outside Łódź, may be tied by various psychic and social threads to a given culture, which it influences and co-opts. But Łódźian manufacturers—a mixture of highly diverse elements, various cultures, and various

---

[*] This article was first published as "Epopeja łódzka" in *Przegląd Socjaldemokratyczny*, Vol. 4, No. 2 (April 1908), pp. 159–63. It was signed "Spartacus"—an anticipation of the name Luxemburg chose for the grouping she founded following the outbreak of World War I, the Spartacus Group. It is translated by Joseph Muller from the Polish original.

nationalities—despite determining the political and social life of our country to a certain degree, possess nearly no points of commonality with Polish culture, stand completely outside of so-called society, and are connected to nothing so closely as to an urge to profit and plunder. And this unties their hands, freeing them from undue "sentimentality."

When word of the proletarian victory first spread, and Łódźian workers had a little room to breathe after their long former captivity, the manufacturers of Łódź, with unrelenting energy, gathered themselves to reverse what they saw as their losses. They set out to do so in a way that was not especially rational given the culture of the entrepreneur—that is, they did not base their efforts on so much as a recognition of the fundamental needs of capitalist production and of the more or less free struggle of labor with capital, among other things. Instead, they decided to draw yet another tsarist scourge, and not only that—they decided to enhance it and extend its dominion, if only by reverting to the earlier norms of unbridled lawlessness and exploitation. Before long, they forgot about the dreams of their recent youth, constitutional rights, the freedom of workers to associate, and many other beautiful things. Yet they remembered long workdays, dirt pay, and brutality on the factory floor. For them, the growing reaction—the temporary suppression of the revolution—was a wonderful moment to seize with feverish enthusiasm.

As one of the standard arguments invoked to justify their wolfish appetite, one hears these gentlemen say that anarchy needs to be finished off, that workers are destroying production and ruining industry, and that there is no way out of these circumstances except through an alliance with the scourge. Violent crime, in their opinion, is a product of just such revolutionary anarchy; violent crime needs to be crushed by the might of the tsar.

It is beyond question that a societal process as complex as the Russian Revolution, not to mention as lengthy, must be accompanied by manifestations of anarchy, viciousness, and ill-conceived outbreaks. No one understands this more deeply or assesses it as thoroughly as the Social Democratic vanguard of the revolutionary proletariat. And it is precisely the Social Democrats who have shown that the only possible way to eliminate anarchy is to fundamentally restructure the political system of Russia, to *overthrow the tsar*, the source of all anarchy.

Has it not repeatedly been demonstrated to the capitalist lords that criminal policies high among the spheres of power must be answered from below by manifestations of anarchy? Has not Mr. [Sergei] Witte himself, in the October 30 manifesto, asserted that the roots of all violent acts lie deep in the foundations of the tsarist system? After all this, cannot Łódźian capitalists understand the basic principle that their actions—such as using the military during strikes, turning the most influential workers over to the police, and starving workers through lockouts—produce the very same economic terror in response, produce acts of despair, because of a lack of freedom to form coalitions and a lack of strong trade unions, especially by certain individuals who are not yet conscious? Are the industrial barons of Łódź incapable of understanding that the rankest spate of violent crime in Łódź occurred *right after the establishment of court-martials, right after the quelling of the revolution*, and not at its high point? Do the industrialist lords not know that their complaints of the "mindlessness" of strikes and the "destruction" of industry through unreasonable demands lead not to the kissing of [Nikolai] Kaznakov's boot but to the abolition of rule by the scourge?! If one wishes to establish order in the ranks of the proletariat, if one wishes upheaval and instinctiveness to be replaced with sober thought, one need only give them the opportunity to organize themselves, give them the opportunity to have higher discussions of the needs of the proletariat, certainly not suppress that opportunity through brute physical force, certainly not crush even the weakest manifestations of independence in the working class, as the industrialists of Łódź have done with the help of the tsar's bayonets.

If the capitalists of Łódź do not acknowledge these obvious facts beating them in the face, how then could they seek a deeper understanding of anarchy in social life, an understanding inextricably connected, here and everywhere else, with the capitalist economy? Our capitalists shift the blame for industrial crises of the kind Łódź goes through onto anarchy in the ranks of the proletariat; their remedy for this is the familiar scourge of serfdom and the old feudal-parasitic protectionism of tsarist rule. Neither fundamental changes to the finances of the state economy, nor complete destruction of relics of the old economy, nor improvements to industry, nor proletarian trade organizations, nor a general elevation of the well-being of the impoverished peasantry and the creation thereby of highly influential consumers, nor even the overthrow of the tsar—the most significant obstacle to the realization of these reforms—will generate better conditions for the further development of industry; but the boot of Kaznakov, the cruel, mindless harassment of the proletariat, the reprehensible trampling of the downfallen will!

Recent months in Łódź have been, on one hand, an orgy of wild crimes by capitalists, and on the other, a terrible, despairing, extraordinarily heroic fight by hungry, harried working people. We have seen the revenge of capitalists and harassment by capitalists. But less now than later—*après nous le déluge!*[*] Consumed by personal hatred, the soul of the Łódźian parvenu craves revenge, craves triumph! The shockingly repulsive nature of our great industrial bourgeoisie emerges naked and plain, and to the applause of every class except the proletariat, it passionately pursues its work of revenge and its program of crime.

---

[*] An expression attributed to Madame de Pompadour, the lover of French King Louis XV, which translates as "After us, the deluge."

It is true that the capitalists are using this reprehensible war to organize themselves. But what of it? Their organizations, as long as the tsar remains, cannot have lasting political significance. Of course, they may temporarily strengthen the power of the capitalists, but with the politics they pursue, increasing the misery of workers, they also dig the graves of the political interests of these same capitalists. The great Łódź lockout started this orgy, and now every day brings us new surprises.

The city has been handed over as loot to the tsar's henchman, the bloodthirsty Kaznakov. Łódźian manufacturers pay out as much as 900,000 roubles in regular support in return for police and snoopers, and they arrange banquets in honor of their torturer-in- chief. Kaznakov tortured eighty-three workers at the Silberstein factory, executed eight innocent proletarians by firing squad without a trial, and every day, on his orders, hundreds of striking workers are tormented in the police stations around Łódź, and hundreds more exiled, condemned along with their families to death by starvation. Every day, under the protection of this man, the capitalists take away, bit by bit, even that spoonful of nourishment which the worker had managed to secure. The braver, more conscious workers are handed over to Kaznakov. Sometimes a factory is shuttered for two weeks to force the haggard, exhausted slaves of capital to return to their wheelbarrows—under worse conditions. Several dozen factories were recently closed in this manner with this goal. Even if there is a crisis, such as in a branch of the wool industry, it pales in comparison to the scale on which the capitalists carry out their criminal acts. The best proof of this is that small owners closed their factories for two weeks, owners so small that they could go bankrupt in the case of a real crisis, that they could in fact be unable to carry out further production, even if their workers agreed to work for significantly less pay. Crisis is not the root cause; immense greed and class revenge are.

That the mark may be overstepped, that Kaznakov's system is not immortal, that through it a powerful source of revolutionary movement is created and, concurrently, anarchy is fed—the factory bosses are oblivious to these things. The tragedy in Łódź continues to play itself out through the cynical glee, or the indifference, of the moneyed classes—both those who follow the ethical Mr. [Stanisław] Kempner and Mr. [Aleksander] Świętochowski, with his "making of culture," and those who follow the Pole Purishkevich-Dmowski.* But the Łódźian knights of coin are deluded if they think they can thus suppress what the confluence of relations is creating, must create. It may be that the proletariat will temporarily succumb, that it will breathe yet more heavily; but in this heavier atmosphere, suffused with injustice, explosive forces are gathering that will obliterate the devices of oppression. Łódźian factory bosses delude themselves that they are fighting against anarchy, whereas in reality they are

---

* In reference to right-wing politicians Vladimir Purishkevich and Roman Dmowski.

stoking its flames. They delude themselves that they are saving industry, when in reality they are ruining the political bases of its development. And again, what they mean by "saving industry" and "fighting anarchy" falls on the shoulders of the only consciously progressive and revolutionary force—the proletariat. The Łódźian workers, choked, trampled on, yet fighting to the bitter end, not tolerant of endless exploitation—they are the true guardians of industry, they are the true enemies of anarchy.

The epic of Łódź was and is inscribed in the history of the proletariat with strokes of blood. Bearing eloquent witness to the utter ethical bankruptcy of our bourgeois society, it reveals a depraved barbarian horde incapable of culture. It manifests the vacuous destruction both of culture and of the economic foundations of social life.

Lessons from the Three Dumas*

I.

For more than a year, we have been living through a period of steep decline in revolutionary activity. Absolutism's rule takes wilder forms than ever; society is repressed and held under a state of siege by the band of thieves in government; court-martials, gallows, and firing squads proliferate; prisons grow overcrowded; prisoners are harassed; and so on, without any reason, with no end in sight, and with no discernible depletion of the reaction's strength. Meanwhile, acts of resistance by the masses are almost nonexistent: Trade unions have been crushed; gatherings are prevented; mass demonstrations, which were our daily bread for three years, today seem a distant dream; advisory party organizations keep collapsing in ruins because of arrests and repressions, and they can barely hold on to passable connections with the people. In the Russian countryside, too, retreat has long been the order of the day, and the troops have again largely become a trim and obedient army in the palm of absolutism's hand, as before the revolution. Emboldened by the triumph of political reaction, industrial capital has gone from a defensive position to an offensive one, taking back all the urban proletariat's achievements, saddling it with oppression, and incapacitating it systematically through lockouts, while landowners have managed to take back from rural people nearly everything they had won in the first two years of revolution. Thus, on top of terrible political repression, poverty haunts the working masses. And following grimly in the footsteps of poverty and repression plods depression, welling up in a sense of powerlessness. The situation indeed looks hopeless: The reaction has managed to take back every position won during the first year of revolutionary upheaval and has strengthened its ranks, while on the side of the revolution, resistance is nowhere to be seen.

After the December [1905] uprising in Moscow, another outbreak was expected any time. After the dissolution of the Duma [in July 1906]† and the

---

* This essay, entitled "Nauki trzech Dum," was originally published in *Przegląd Socjaldemokratyczny*, Vol. 4, No. 3 (May 1908), pp. 177–94. It is translated from the Polish original by Joseph Muller.

† The first Russian Duma, or parliament, opened on April 27, 1906, and lasted seventy-three days, until July 8, when it is was dissolved by Tsar Nicholas II in an effort to maintain his hold on power. The Second Duma was in session from February 23 to June 3, 1907, and included representatives of such revolutionary parties as the Bolsheviks, Mensheviks, and Socialist Revolutionaries that had boycotted the First Duma. The dissolution of the Second Duma, referred to at the time as "the coup of June 1907," occurred after Prime Minister Pyotr Stołypin accused the Social Democrats of plotting an insurrection. After changing the electoral laws to grant greater powers to rural landowners, the tsar permitted the formation of the far more compliant Third Duma on November 7, 1907; it was dissolved on June 9, 1912.

collapse of the uprising in Sveaborg and Kronstadt [in July 1906],* hope was placed in the agrarian movements expected in the fall. Once the fall had passed, hope was again placed in the spring. After a year passed, these expectations subsided. And, well, we found ourselves again in that typical vicious cycle in which socialist activity was stuck in the long years before the revolution: The revolutionary ranks respond to the repression of absolutism with weak silence. But how can that weakness be broken and resistance called up, when it has become impossible for the revolutionary ranks to gather, take action, and direct themselves for want of these very rights and freedoms? Social Democracy thus stands again before a sphinx that rises up to the surface of society every time the creative strength of revolution sinks down into its depths and hides at the foundations: This sphinx is the immobility of the masses. Even if revolution reveals its wonders, leads legendary marches out onto the streets, as on January 22 [1905] in Petersburg, suddenly improvises powerful organizations, like the Council of Workers' Delegates, blends into one body and moves a 100,000-strong mass with one word, as in June 1905 in Łódź, rebuilds a city from its foundations, as in Moscow in December of that year, and creates people's republics under absolutism's nose in twenty-four hours, as in Baku—no one bats an eye. The greatest collective works of revolution are perceived as completely predictable and natural occurrences. Since the working class only retreats and stays still, drudgery and weakness seem to be its "natural" state, and the task of leading it from this state belongs to Social Democracy—an unsolvable task, like the stone face of a sphinx.

For many long years before the revolution, Social Democracy in both Poland and Russia supported their difficult position with a mighty pillar: their unshaken belief in the historical necessity of revolution as the outcome of capitalist development in Russia. Russian Marxists knew that economic development leads, with the iron consistency of historical dialectics, to the undermining and toppling of medieval absolutism and to the creation of a modern bourgeois system. They also knew that the proletariat, as the historical product of capitalist development, and as the most naturally revolutionary class—the most interested in political freedom—must play a leading role in such a revolutionary coup. That is why they were also armed against every doubt and skepticism leveled by various "nationalists," whose take on the matter came from a flat mechanical perspective, and who pointed out with obstinacy, for example, that according to statistical data, there were "too few" industrial workers in Russia to be able to play a prevailing political role, that the proletariat could only play such a role after the rule

---

* Both were mutinies by sailors of the Imperial Navy at a moment when the revolution was subsiding in much of the rest of the empire. The Sveaborg rebellion occurred in late July 1906 at a fortress close to Helsinki; by August 1 the uprising was crushed. The Kronstadt uprising of 1906 (not to be confused with the much more successful one of 1905) occurred around the same time as the Sveaborg rebellion but was quickly suppressed.

of the liberal bourgeoisie, and so forth. The Russian Marxists' buckler against this whole way of trying to understand things with a tape measure was their understanding of internal tendencies in the social development of Russia. From their point of view, it was a futile task to count which exact percentage of people in the official statistics had to belong to the manufacturing proletariat for it to play a decisive role in the political revolution, or to rack one's brain over "how" exactly the proletariat masses could play this role while handcuffed by a lack of political maturity that only open class struggle could produce.

History has borne great witness to Marxism throughout the territory of Russia, as it has in Poland, and in all countries, for that matter. Contrary to the calculations of "healthy minds," the revolution did break out in Russia, and it broke out as an uprising of the proletariat. But not for the first time, the sorcerer called up spirits that it was not able to control. When the revolution, foreseen, prepared, and charmed by Russian Marxists, appeared on the scene, a part of it strayed, as the Russian proverb says, among three pines. This particular revolution had to be a bourgeois revolution, because a socialist system could not yet be established in Russia. This meant that the class that prevailed in this revolution could only be the bourgeoisie, and it also had to govern. The proletariat could play only the role of stirrup, helping the bourgeoisie take the reins over the ruins of absolutism. Hence the need to adopt a policy of alliance with bourgeois liberalism, and hence the proletariat's condemnation of its own "fruitless" revolutionary riots, such as the Moscow uprising, and of the aspirations they masked related to a dictatorship of the proletariat. This was the formula with which the so-called Mensheviks in the Russian Social Democratic Party walled up the current revolution and with it the class politics of the proletariat. We will not recount here how much influence this view has had on the entire course of the revolutionary struggle and on the tactics of the Russian proletariat. Let the present atmosphere of revolutionary stagnation serve as its touchstone.

The current revolution is and must be—according to Menshevik theory—a strictly bourgeois revolution, meaning that only the bourgeoisie can march at its head and seize the reins of power. But the present phase of stagnation shows not only the weakness of the proletariat but something else—perish the thought!—the collapse and disintegration of bourgeois liberalism! In the time between the First and Second Dumas and between the Second and Third, gradual shifts took place within bourgeois parties toward the side of the counterrevolution: Progressive Democrats to Cadets, Cadets to Octobrists,* Octobrists to the right wing and the Union of the Russian Nation [the Black Hundreds]. Over the course of the last year, the Russian bourgeoisie not only has shown no desire to stand at the head of a "bourgeois revolution," but has grown to support absolutism.

---

* The name given to members of the Union of October 17, a Russian party with a national-liberal outlook, formed after the release of Sergei Witte's self-styled October Manifesto. It advocated a constitutional monarchy and was largely supported by industrialists and wealthy landowners.

Of course, according to the formula for bourgeois revolution, the current situation in Russia is not just abysmal—it is a complete dead end. The proletariat cannot and should not take a leading role or win political power, they say, because this is not a socialist revolution. Yet the bourgeoisie, rather than take up on the revolutionary side, unfurls its flag on the side of the reaction. What do social development, historical necessity, and dialectical materialism, which lead to bourgeois revolution with iron logic, say about this? The erstwhile-unshaken logic of Russian Marxism, which was active throughout the decade before the revolution, has of course been badly shaken by the last few years of revolutionary events. Now, the Menshevik steering body assures, from its office, that the "revolution has been overcome, but not defeated," yet this assurance appears quite pallid for the simple reason that it is not supported by any plausible theory about where we can expect such a new wave of revolution to appear. In fact, to the proponents of this formula, nothing remains except to lose faith in their abilities and in the social foundations of revolution. Sure enough, the bravest and frankest of them have now happily reached, in 1908, the conclusions for which the Russian Narodniks, twenty years ago, suffered such painful blows from the Marxists. They aver that the revolution is completely over, and they try to prove, with meticulous statistical analysis such as "two plus two is four," that the proletariat in Russia is "too small" to play a leading role in the revolution.* They add that according to these statistics, the destitute peasantry is "too small," the democratic townspeople are "too few," and thus in general there is "too little" of everything, and all that remains to be solved is a single riddle: by what magic the revolution of 1905, amid such a dearth of social resources, could have popped out of the ground, throwing us all for a loop. The counter-revolution has therefore achieved what surely surpasses their wildest dreams: not only have they suppressed the masses through physical violence and politically demoralized bourgeois liberalism, they have also triggered a loss of faith in the very possibility of revolution throughout most of the revolutionary bloc. The proletariat, as a class, is now obligated not only to fend off the counter-revolution's attacks on its right to progress in the *present*, but also to defend its right to *history* against those who are also obligated to express that right!

II.

The depression and pessimistic frame of mind currently so overwhelmingly dominant in the revolutionary ranks partly obscures a view of revolution far more responsive to bourgeois liberalism than to the Marxist stance of the party of the proletariat. Profound disenchantment at the long pause in revolutionary

---

* [Footnote by Luxemburg] See [Fjodor] Cherevanin, *Sowremjonnoje położenie i wozmożnoje buduszczeje* (The Current Situation and the Possible Future) (Moscow, 1908).

struggle is obviously only one side of the story; there is also conjecture that revolution can and should develop in a single unbroken line of progressive attempts and successes. The basis of such expectations is the view of revolution as a strictly political coup for which society is presumed to be internally ready and entirely ripe. Every revolution, however, is a social revolution—that is, society goes through a season of extraordinarily focused inner maturation: a season of rapid class formation, differentiation, and self-awareness. The straight course of the political coup doubles back and crosses itself through this process of class maturation, periodically stopping external revolutionary activity in order to absorb the results thereof and gather material for longer-term operations. So, in order to understand whether a revolution is experiencing a temporary lull, either long- or short-term, or is truly finished, it is necessary to understand what its *objectives* were, as historical necessities, and what *specific set of conditions* affected the carrying out of those objectives, as a result of the formation of class struggle during the revolution and under its influence.

The faction of Russian Social Democrats who operate by the formula that the current revolution is a purely bourgeois revolution do not sin through their faulty formula per se.* Rather, their error is to examine this limited, dry schematic for a solution to all the problems of the revolution, even though it is not itself an elucidation or resolution, but only the same problem differently formulated. For, truly, the fundamental question is this: How, given the historical situation, can what is entailed by the objective of bourgeois revolution be realized and shaped in Russia?

Above all, the current conception of the fall of the revolution, which so heavily weighs on minds throughout the socialist ranks, rests largely on the perception that the current victorious reign of the savage reaction echoes the repressions before the revolution. In reality, between the current system of repression and the earlier one, there happens to be one giant difference, even though, or rather precisely because, these repressions have taken on a character ten times more savage than before: The current political reaction is not just absolutism's rule, meaning some kind of government, it is something greater—it is the rule of the counterrevolution. Between the current and former seasons of reaction lies a revolutionary season, along with its effects. And only by casting a superficial glance could one see the flat, negative fact that "the revolution was beaten" as the only result. Far more important is the positive social-class import of that fact. On what did absolutism base its power over the course of the last decade? On the political passivity of all classes: The proletariat was not yet primed for active mass resistance, the peasantry was limited by its social nature to partial, sporadic movements of a chaotic and unpolitical character, and the moneyed classes—the bourgeoisie and gentry—became politically

---

* A reference to the Mensheviks.

undifferentiated from the masses of economic parasites lapping up absolutism's care for them; they became devoid of any definite political aspirations, unless one includes the hopeless and spineless "constitutional fantasies" of territorial autonomy. The revolutionary period in 1905 changed all this at its foundations: Not only did it recruit the proletariat and the peasantry to open mass struggle, but it also differentiated the moneyed classes into parties and groups, even political shades. Such parties and groups may change their character in the course of revolution; they may merge, fall out, move to the right, or blend into one "mass reaction," as they have essentially done thus far. Yet all these manifestations do not change the crucial fact that the bourgeois classes have stepped out onto the political scene and created separate parties and groups, and that their fates are, and from now on will be, their own fates, the result of their own class development, and not a mere product of absolutism's existence. The reaction we see is therefore not only a symptom of the form of government still in control but also a sign of the political order of Russia's bourgeois classes and parties; it is a result of the political cooperation of the ruling classes with absolutism. From this point of view, the stories of the three State Dumas constitute invaluable framing material as expressions of the political lives and trajectories of bourgeois parties.

From beginning to end, the year 1905 was a season of mass action by the proletariat, and from beginning to end, a season of rising revolutionary tide. From January 22, from the alarm rung by the Petersburg proletariat, to the sustained, ever-larger strikes, the uprisings in the army and the navy, the mass strike in October, all the way to the Moscow uprising in December, the revolutionary waters rose and rose and rose. In October, after wavering at the point where the battle tactic of the first period—the mass strike—had achieved its greatest effectiveness, only to immediately show its weakness after the constitutional proclamation, the revolutionary operation switched, by the power of its internal logic, to a new phase and took up new tactics—street uprisings and open battle. The suppression of the Moscow uprising, natural and inevitable for a first attempt at a new battle tactic that will only begin to reap successes for everyone after being honed through a series of local uprisings, stopped the activity of the proletariat, and with it the rising tide of revolution.

With the year 1906, a second season began, lasting to now—a time of parliamentary action and of an ever-deeper decline of revolution.

In the place of the proletariat, the First Duma led bourgeois liberalism onto the stage, and in the place of direct mass action (the mass strike and the uprising), parliamentary action. But bourgeois liberalism immediately found itself, together with the First Duma, before an issue of decisive significance. A year of revolutionary struggle had shaken the foundations of absolutism but had not demolished them. All political power, all the material means of such power—the army, the treasury, the administration, the judiciary—stayed in the hands of the absolutist bureaucracy, and the ancient dynastic throne survived as well.

Political power, in a word, remained in the hands of absolutism. In such a situation, what role could the Duma play? The role of a Constituent Assembly, eradicating absolutism and establishing political freedom? Except that would be an assembly called not by a revolutionary government but by an absolutist one, and immediately after the revolutionary people were crushed. An assembly thus deprived in advance of any influence on executive power could not be the voice that proclaims a new political order and new powers for itself. Was it supposed to be a parliament—that is, a body for ordinary, normal legislation, as they exist in constitutional states, to address the issues of the day within a framework established by a constitution? Except the foundation for a parliament's existence and operations must be a preexisting and consolidated constitutional order. That is, the executive power must submit to the legislative parliament, or at least coexist and cooperate with it, as in Germany. Furthermore, those civil freedoms without which parliamentary lawmaking cannot exist—the freedom of speech and of the press, of unions and of assembly, and so on—must be established in advance and placed on strong constitutional foundations. When the old absolutist government in Russia was in power, and the constitution sat on paper like a "donation" to the autocrat, power was in fact exerted through states of siege and court-martials, and the prelude to the opening of the first "parliamentary" session was an infernal orgy of pogroms. Unable to be either the organ of a political coup or a regular parliamentary legislature, the Duma could only serve as an earthwork behind which absolutism could repair and reinforce the batteries the revolution had damaged.

In a situation so rife with contradictions, bourgeois liberalism saw a way out by insisting on being a legislative body—without any constitutional grounds—and attempted to use that same legislative path to defeat absolutism and create a constitutional foundation for itself. This political work, comparable more or less to the attempt to build a house by starting with the roof and "working your way down" to the foundations, ended in the way that it had to end—with the dissolution of the Duma by the real power, the absolutist government. It was a clear defeat of liberal parliamentary action, much as the suppression of the Moscow uprising was a defeat of proletarian insurgent action.

Government victories over proletarian action always indirectly have the ultimate effect of weakening the government's position, demoralizing the soldiers it uses to contain mass movements, and introducing slackness to the entire state apparatus. However, the period of parliamentary action in this case also gave absolutism the time and means to recover from the fright it suffered, build its position back up, regather its resources and forces, and regain belief in itself. The suppression of the Moscow uprising was absolutism's first successful act of resistance, and dismissing the Duma was its official entry into offensive politics.

The fate of the First Duma predetermined that of the second, and yet the Second Duma was not a simple repetition of the same "comedy" but another phase on the path of development. Convinced, after the dissolution of the First Duma, that it could not establish a constitutional system and seize governmental power by parliamentary means, liberalism was forced to lower its aspirations. Instead of tempting itself with the thought of carrying out a political coup with the help of the Duma, liberalism decided to limit itself to the role of a typical legislative body; and instead of trying to match the government and "subordinate executive to legislative power" in service to the letter of the parliamentary system, it decided to avoid rather than clash with government authority and settle for the humbler role of parliamentary opposition. But the Duma, as an organ of parliamentary legislation amid a void of constitutional order, hovered in midair, just like the earlier Duma, in the role of a parliament trying to create such constitutional order. Within the chimerical nature of the parliament itself, the role of parliamentary opposition was also a delusion. For liberalism's second plan—not to overcome governmental power but to remain in opposition to it (an attempt in certain respects even more fantastical than the first)—could only meet an equally disastrous end. The dissolution of the Second Duma was not only a defeat, but a bankrupting of liberalism's parliamentary operations; having tried on roles from the boldest to the humblest one after another, it was unable to play any of them.

That was not the end of the parliamentary system in the history of the revolution. The logical result of the experiments of the First and Second Dumas, as well as the next phase of their development, had to be ... the current [Third] Duma. This time, the operation of the parliament is not just a futile means to enact a revolutionary coup, nor is it a means of powerless liberal opposition; now it serves directly as an instrument of the counterrevolution. From the First to the Third Duma, the parliamentary system thus underwent a full cycle of development. Absolutism set it up as a battery of reaction against the very same revolution for which, according to the liberal illusions of part of Russian Social Democracy, it was supposed to serve as a battering ram to shatter the walls of absolutism.

In the second half of the 1890s, when a current of economic opportunism ran through the Russian Social Democrats,* party proclamations could be seen announcing timid demands for the right to strike, form unions, and assemble, and for the freedom of speech and the press—but unaccompanied by demands for a parliamentary legislature or a republic, and thus ostensibly the rule of absolutism. History played a trick on these fantasies of "partial" socialist politics, showing the opposite monstrosity to be the possible one: a legislative parliament without the freedom of speech, of the press, of unions, of assemblies, and of coalitions, a parliament overlooking the gallows, as if in approval of the authorities' nooses and bullets.

---

* A reference to the tendency known as the Economists, which emphasized the immediate economic struggle of the working class over that of the need for political leadership.

In the Cadets' liberal imagination, as well as in the imagination of Social Democrats who look through the political prism of liberalism, this outcome is a natural result of the "coup d'état" of [Pyotr] Stołypin, who, unable to tolerate the opposition as it invariably crowed over its elections to the First and Second Dumas, resorted to changing the electoral laws so as to drive the Cadets and the left from their decisive position and create a majority convenient for and obedient to him from among the counterrevolutionary Octobrists and the moderate part of the right. In reality, the coup d'état enacted by the government after the dissolution of the Second Duma, the repeal of the electoral law, and the declaration of the electoral statute of June 16 [1907] played a minor role in this.* That the counterrevolution has already dared to carry off the proletariat's last remaining worldly spoils from 1905 is merely an important indicator of the degree to which the position of the counterrevolution gained strength during the operation of the two Dumas. The Third Duma's role as an instrument of counterrevolution—a move by the Octobrists, who made up a majority with the right, on the position of the Cadets, who in the first two Dumas made up an opposing majority with the left—is not an artificial result of a special electoral law but a natural consequence of the course of revolution and the development of relations. The coup d'état of June 16 is by itself an effect and a sign of this development.

After all, what remained for the liberalism of the Cadets to do after the experiments of the First and Second Dumas? Their role as the party of sincere parliamentary constitutionalists was entirely played out and over, as the delusional nature of parliamentary constitutionalism with respect to power that remains in the hands of absolutism had revealed itself in the grim fates of the first two Dumas.

It is a cheap thing to revile the shame and misery of the Cadets and the downfall of their liberalism in the Third Duma, or even their unsound tactics of "avoiding conflict" with the government in the Second Duma. Far more productive for the party of the proletariat, and at a further remove from the illusion of liberalism, is to become aware of the state of affairs that, by inexorable logic, had to lead to precisely these tactics and to the final total collapse of Cadet liberalism. The Cadets occupied an exclusively parliamentary position and could not take any other, since they were the party of the intelligentsia, the urban petty bourgeoisie, and the progressive gentry and had to contend with highly developed class conflict in both the city and the countryside. What says the most about the parliamentarian idiocy of the liberal bourgeoisie is its search to explain its bankruptcy in all manner of external "obstacles," such as, for example, the tactics of

---

* The statute spelled out a significant change in the electoral law and deprived most workers and peasants of the vote and provided most of the mandate to the propertied classes as a way to prevent a repeat of the Second Duma, in which many of the seats were held by parties of the revolutionary left.

the Social Democratic fraction, which, according to Mr. [Pavel] Milyukov and his friends, gave the government a pretext to dissolve the Second Duma. One group within Russian Social Democracy provides a fitting supplement to such liberal farsightedness when it blames the fall of the revolution on the industrial workers, saying they overestimated their strength and neglected beforehand to form an alliance with the liberals and take the role of their modest helper. In truth, the party of the Russian liberals enjoyed more support from the population, unprompted by anyone from its side, and stepped onto the scene with happier *outward* conditions than nearly any other parliamentary party. An exceptionally splendid *parliamentary* post was created for them because great electoral victories to the First and Second Dumas fell on their heads on the credit of future heroic acts, and they occupied the strong position of the opposing majority, thanks to the left, in both of the first two Dumas. The only sticking point in their position was that the whole parliament was brought to a standstill after the street revolution was crushed. As a result, the party that wanted to take such a parliament seriously as the basis for a political coup had to fall in the end, after its liberal frolics in the clouds were over, deep into a morass of reaction. The first result of the Cadets' experiments was that the landed gentry quickly stepped from liberalism over to the side of the reaction, under the pressure of agrarian unrest and the Cadets' agrarian projects. Their party was subsumed by the bourgeois intelligentsia and a part of the urban petty bourgeoisie.

As liberalism, after the experiences of the Cadets, lost ground to stand on, as it surely lost some belief in its own power through the experience of fighting absolutism through a parliament, as it adopted, on the basis of these experiences, the entirely correct belief that the "Duma-esque" parliamentary system exists only at the will of those in power, and as it sank from opposing absolutism down to the level of submissive bureaucratic lackey, the hour became ripe for the Octobrists to take the lead. The liberal Cadet campaign faced gradual decline until they were even with the Octobrists, and the latter stepped out with complete ease onto center stage.

In the place of the bourgeois intelligentsia and the progressive part of the gentry—who had initially sought their ideal in a parliamentary system with complete subordination of executive to legislative power, with the comportment of monarchist etiquette and the social conservatism of liberalism—appeared a party of the industrial haute bourgeoisie, an extremely counterrevolutionary party, but also one that since 1904 had understood the need to "soothe" the country and safeguard undisturbed industrial and agrarian exploitative systems with the help of a constitution of the Prussian kind. This class, whose social interests were threatened by movements of the proletariat, was ready in its heart to accept only a constitutional order that came from the government, so after that government's position was strengthened and the Cadets' campaign went bankrupt, the politics of the Octobrists in turn had to sink to complete sycophancy relative to "hard power." The Octobrists never attempted to broaden the powers of the Duma or set it on a foundation of constitutional forms of civic life within the state, as was the guiding policy of the Cadets. Instead, they saw it as both possible and singularly desirable to retain a Duma in which they would become the authoritative fraction and set electoral laws that made a numerical majority possible for them. But they had to recognize, because of their interest in resisting the proletariat's campaign and their experience of two Cadet Dumas, that the Duma could be preserved only if they abandoned all oppositional designs and gave absolute support to the government's policies. Thus, after the dissolution of the Second Duma, while Milyukov and company publicly denied affiliation with Social Democracy in order to distance themselves from the revolution and prove their readiness for a coalition with the Octobrists, [Alexander] Guchkov and company broke all ties with the opposition and ostentatiously turned away from the Cadets to prove their readiness for cooperation with the government. Under pressure from the same circumstances, then, that caused the liberalism of the Cadets to sink, the Octobrists turned to the ranks of the right—to open backers of absolutism and to partly open opponents of the Duma. And it is this Third Duma that constitutes the consolidation of Stołypinian power, the product of a coalition of the haute bourgeoisie and the landed gentry under the banner of counterrevolution. This Duma is a place where the Octobrists vote against the rules of October 30, where the Cadets, removed from all functions and entirely lacking a political orientation, thoroughly disgrace themselves with every patently aimless step, and where the tsarist minister [Vladimir] Kokovtsov announces, at long last, as if celebrating the counterrevolution outright, what liberalism failed to voice in the interests of the revolution on entering the First Duma: There is no parliament in Russia!

When our party announced before the First Duma that the Duma was, and under these conditions could only be, the fig leaf of absolutism, only a "Cossack Duma," the statement triggered outrage in the Russian part of the party. After the magnificent electoral triumphs of the opposition, and especially after the thundering speeches of the Social Democratic faction and the eloquent missiles of Cadet liberalism in the Duma, a great many supporters of the old strategy of electoral boycotts saw a need to admit the error of their ways and recognize the Duma as the real center of the revolution and of revolutionary attacks on absolutism.* But in the end, it was again demonstrated that, as Ferdinand Lassalle argued, a "constitution" is not a declaration on paper but a material relation of forces that is stronger than the ideological appearance of things. What the Duma is and may be in a given political situation becomes clear only if one examines all three Dumas as one whole, and only by thus presenting things can

---

* This is reflected in the agreement of the two factions of the RSDRP, the Bolsheviks and Mensheviks, to compete for seats in the Second Duma.

one account for the political continuity of its development and understand the logic of events hidden deep beneath the surface. Having begun as an assembly with the comportment and loftiness of the Convention, the Duma became, by the force of its internal relational logic, an ordinary counterrevolutionary club that characterized itself as "the real Russian people." Having shed its thin skin of liberal ideology, the Duma revealed its essential function as a "Cossack Duma," as the fig leaf of absolutism. What was already clear, as the conclusion emerging from the entire first year of the revolution, has now been proven and demonstrated through three years of facts. The Third Duma has shown—*and from this flows its enormous political significance*—that a parliamentary system that has not first overthrown the government, that has not achieved political power through revolution, not only cannot defeat the old power (a belief the First Duma vainly held), not only cannot hold its own against that power as an instrument of opposition (as the Second Duma tried to do), but can and must become, on the contrary, an instrument of the counterrevolution. The Third Duma is a bloody satire of both the parliamentarian illusions of the Cadets and the liberal illusions of part of Russian Social Democracy.* Inasmuch as states of consciousness of classes and parties can influence the course of events, the illusions in this case played entirely into the hands of absolutism.

III.

In the Third Duma, the course of the revolution thus returns to that Gordian knot before which it stood in December 1905, but it returns enriched by the experience of two and a half years of bourgeois class development. The first result of this development is the fate of the Cadets. As the party of the progressive intelligentsia and the petty bourgeoisie, they were crumpled by their class position between the counterrevolutionary industrial haute bourgeoisie and agrarians on one side, and the revolutionary proletariat on the other. As a party of political compromise between tsarism and democracy, they were trapped inside the figure of constitutional monarchy. And as a faction based on fear of the revolutionary masses, they were tied exclusively to parliamentary modes of operation. Further, while it was the First and Second Dumas that demonstrated the inability of the Cadets to create a constitutional-democratic monarchy, it was the Third Duma, in which the Octobrist bloc rules from the right, that showed the inability of the haute bourgeoisie to create a constitutional monarchy, even one designed, after the Prussian model, only for capitalist and agrarian class rule. The Cadets' capitulation to the Octobrists and the Octobrists' capitulation to the right are essentially capitulations of the petty bourgeoisie to great industrial capital, and of the political interests of capital to its economic-class

---

* A reference to the Mensheviks.

interests. They represent the political bankrupting, all at once, of constitutional monarchy as the goal, of parliamentary action as the means, and of bourgeois liberalism as the executor of this program. The prominence and vividness of these events have led to a state of depression that clouds our thinking, causing the distinct sensation that the revolutionary cause has become stuck in the experiments of the First, Second, and Third Dumas, with no way out. In truth, only liberalism is stuck, and the surety of future prospects for revolution lies in the hopelessness of the political results of the three Dumas. If the actions of bourgeois liberalism had been able, with the help of the Duma, to create and hold on to any form of constitutionalism, however weak—as long as it limited absolutism to some degree and ensured even a partly normal system of class relations, as required by a modern bourgeois state—then perhaps the matter of revolution and radical politics might have fallen dormant for a long time and yielded its place to slow-moving class conflicts within the halls of a parliament. But constitutionalism could not be realized, even in a weak form, even by the Octobrists, because the historical objectives of revolution were not accomplished even in the smallest, most fragmented way, and in the current situation they cannot be accomplished. Furthermore, the way to achieve these objectives through compromise is closed off, and the only possible way left is a radical coup by means of mass action taken by a dictatorship of the revolutionary proletariat rallying in the name of a democratic republic. The questions of *how*, *when*, and especially *in what forms* this mass movement may rise again from under what seems at present to be complete suppression, as well as in what circumstances such radical results may be achieved, are matters of secondary importance and personal interpretation.

For Social Democracy, as the party of the proletariat, of crucial importance is the fact that within the given political and class conditions in Russia, revolutionary action and proletarian victory have become historically inevitable, in precisely the same degree to which the abolition of absolutism is a historical necessity, namely as the inevitable result and condition of the capitalist development of Russia. This same capitalist development that made essential both the modern bourgeois system and the current "bourgeois revolution" in Russia also made the revolutionary victory and dictatorship of the proletariat, as the events of the last three years have demonstrated, essential instruments of that revolution. Some Russian Social Democrats search for the central crux of tactical problems to determine whether the current revolution is bourgeois or socialist. They commit an error, but the worst of it is not that they transfix with such rigid logic what amounts at most to a dialectical contradiction in the course of history in the current moment. Rather, it is that they remain unaware of the essential conditions and the internal logic of bourgeois revolution, that they reason on the basis of a lifeless formula thought up in someone's study, instead of living accounts of historical experience. Given this, a worthwhile exercise is to familiarize oneself with the history of that most bourgeois of revolutions, and that most bourgeois of republics—*the French*.

According to official historians and public opinion throughout bourgeois Europe, the history of the Great Revolution is divided into two epochs: the "good," about which they speak with sympathy and acknowledgment and which took place in the years 1789–91, and the "base," about which they speak with horror, having in mind mainly the year 1793. According to liberal theory, the "excesses" of 1793—Jacobinism and the madness of the "Parisian mob"—ruined the work of revolution, and the actions of that year, breaking all norms and bounds, triggered the unavoidable reaction, the epoch of the Directorate, and finally the military dictatorship of Napoleon and the empire. Understanding these events through materialism has already long allowed one to comprehend the "excesses" of Jacobinism as an entirely natural manifestation of the aspirations of working people that have awoken to their class instincts against bourgeois society but have not yet formed into a class-conscious proletariat, have not yet separated from the petty bourgeoisie and its illusions—indeed, the aspirations of a people to overcome bourgeois rule just when that rule was about to begin for good. The dictatorship of the Jacobins and their outbursts of terror were desperate attempts to remain in power by a class that social relations had condemned for more than a century to walk under the yolk of bourgeois society, rather than rule over it. But the other side of things is yet more instructive: namely the fact that this utopian dictatorship of the Parisian people, already shown to be a fiasco, a hopeless scuffle against the historical necessity of bourgeois rule, alone served as the most effective tool for strengthening that rule. Not through the reaction or the concentrated resistance it caused in bourgeois society, but through the very radicalism through which it defended the work of bourgeois revolution.

The Constitutional Assembly and the Legislative Assembly had to be followed by the Convention and the proclamation of the republic on September 22, 1792, not because constitutional monarchy was revealed to be insufficient but because the moderate liberal bourgeoisie could not secure even a constitutional monarchy against the machinations of counterrevolution that threatened it. Similarly, out of the Convention, the Committee of Public Safety and the Revolutionary Tribunal had to emerge, not because these were necessary for the realization of the hopeless social utopia of [Louis Antoine de] Saint-Just* but because what was constantly threatened most of all was the very existence of the republic. The creators and defenders of the republic, the Jacobins, soon died under its ruins, but their historical work remained, even though its shape was soon disfigured. Today, from the perspective of a century later, it is clear

---

    * As Robespierre's most trusted follower, Saint-Just used his position in the Committee of Public Safety to monopolize power by executing both rightist and leftist critics of the regime.

that only the dictatorship of the Parisian people and its ruthless revolutionary radicalism could lure out from their social stations the forces and means necessary to overthrow ancient feudal France, shake ancient feudal Europe, and defend a modern bourgeois society newly arisen out of the revolutionary storm from the intrigues of the dynasty, the schemes of the émigré nobility, the plots of the clergy, the Wars of the Vendée [of 1793–96], the betrayals of generals, the opposition of fearful members of the bourgeoisie itself, the seditions of the sixteen departments and main provincial cities, and the coalition of all the monarchs in Europe. The dictatorship of the Parisian people was fruitless and utopian in its goals. But without it, France would not have had a First Republic. And without pressure from the Parisian people, there would not have been the Second Republic of 1848. Though utopian, the ideal of a "social republic" operated as ideological swaddling clothes in which the French proletariat could bring their bourgeois republic out into the world. Although the conspiracy of [François-Noël] Babeuf, as the last gasp of fallen Jacobinism, managed to be yet more hopeless and utopian an undertaking than the dictatorship of the Convention, he played an outsize role in the events of the class struggles that followed as the story of 1793 unfolded. Ideas from Babeufism and 1793 completely dominated radical democratic thinkers and proletarians in France in the 1830s and 1840s; this was the political school and revolutionary tradition of the workers who pushed forward bold constitutional reforms for the liberal burghers in 1848, fashioning a radical political coup and the birth of a Second Republic, this time in the course of only a few days. As before, the utopia of the "social republic" was soon drowned in the blood of the victims of the June [1848] massacre, and the Second Republic fell together with its makers, the proletarian leadership of the most recent months. Yet history allowed the French proletariat into the role of executor of bourgeois revolutions a third time, making it the author of the Paris Commune of 1871 and of the current French Republic.

This Third Republic is certainly easiest to explain as a natural effect of the moral depravity and wartime ruin of the Second Empire after its war with Prussia [in 1871]. But in fact, it derives from far deeper causes—above all, the Paris Commune and the effects of a century of revolution. The republican constitution and the republican government of contemporary France, remember, were brought into the world by a National Assembly with a *monarchical majority*. The February elections of 1871 had given the monarchists the majority, and similarly, control over the politics of this virtuous Assembly, which for four years had held the political helm of France in its hands, was given to a ferocious, blood-crazed reaction that only grew worse after the Commune was crushed. The political mood of this new bourgeois France, a France of [Adolphe] Thiers and [Jules] Favre, can be compared to the classic formulation of Jules Guesde, who in his memorable 1872 pamphlet branding Versailles as crime-ridden called it a "republic without republicans."* Bourgeois France in 1871 was a republic without republicans, as it had been in 1792 and in 1848. And if, despite everything, the same reactionary, monarchist bourgeoisie managed to found a Third Republic, this time permanently, it was for two main reasons. The proletariat was feared, on the one hand, because of a belief that after a century of revolution, even this proletariat, struck down but not destroyed, could no longer be mollified except through a republican constitution. And, on the other hand, this proletariat, crushed as it was, was surely incapable of retaking the helm of the republic, having alarmed bourgeois society with its "social" delusions and coup-themed aspirations. On January 4, 1874, *Le Rappel* [The Recall] loudly shared this secret about the Third Republic: The workers quietly endure their misery because the government is called a republic—"This word works magic on the minds of workers; it's a delusion that keeps their hope alive."†

This delusion, intended to keep the class struggle of the proletariat in check and shield it from class antagonism, became the basis on which to build the new republican party of the opportunistic bourgeoisie, which inaugurated the absolute class rule of the bourgeoisie in the Third Republic, and for which [Léon] Gambetta gave a three-word program in 1874: a republic is a bourgeois-proletarian alliance. Only a few years were needed, given the circumstances, with a proletariat that was incapacitated for nearly ten years, for the republic essentially to duck out from under the illusory cover of the "social equality" ideal and expose its thoroughly prosaic soul to the light of day—a soul devoted to bourgeois dominance. Finding this very thing to be its true meaning, the republican order had definitively achieved and consolidated its raison d'être in France.

In this way, the arch-bourgeois French republic of today is, in a historical view, a product of a three-part revolutionary proletarian operation; yes, bourgeois republicanism in France today is itself the historical work of a pair of inopportune proletarian dictatorships. From this we may conclude, first, that even a typical "bourgeois revolution" needs the help of radical revolutionary action to reach and maintain modest results, and more importantly, that the logic of the mutual historical relation of proletarian class action and bourgeois liberalism contradicts the formula of a certain part of Russian Social Democracy.‡

According to their schema, in bourgeois revolutions, the bourgeoisie, in its role as advocate of capitalist development, serves as an exponent of liberalism

---

* Guesde's pamphlet *Le Livre Rouge et la Justice Rurale, documents pour servir à l'histoire d'une République sans républicains* (The Red Book and Rural Justice: Documents on the History of a Republic without Republicans) (Genève: T. Blanchard, 1871) played an important role in his conversion to Marxism and was one of the most widely read books on the Paris Commune at the time.

† *Le Rappel* was a French daily newspaper founded in 1869 with the support of Victor Hugo that strongly supported the Paris Commune. Upon the suppression of the Commune, many of its writers and editors were jailed or sent into exile.

‡ That is, of the Mensheviks.

and thereby recruits the proletariat to help it fight against the old political order. "Liberalism," along with bourgeois republicanism, is here treated as something set, defined, already given. Casting only a superficial glance at the course of the French Revolution, we can already see that reality in this case shows much more life, variety, and change over time. We can see that the French bourgeoisie, having begun from a position of quite moderate liberalism, was only pushed to extreme republicanism through the revolutionary activities of the working masses, and that it moved back toward a position of highly restrained liberalism as soon as the revolution was suppressed, until the virtually ancient pressure of the proletariat at last trained the republican bourgeoisie we see now. In the current revolution—the last of a series of bourgeois revolutions—the political development of the bourgeoisie has already run completely counter to their formula. In Poland, Lithuania, and neighboring countries, liberalism generally does not exist, but a single reactionary mass of noblemen, bourgeoisie, and petty bourgeoisie does, albeit one of many varying shades whose recognizable diversification and clear variations in emphasis are the only mark of the revolutionary period. In Russia, meanwhile, it was not bourgeois liberalism that spurred the proletariat's revolutionary drive but quite the opposite: The revolutionary uprising of the proletariat triggered what, for lack of a better word, we can call the liberalism of the bourgeoisie—the Cadets, the Octobrists, the Peaceful Regeneration group,* and so on are the creations and not the creators of the Revolution of 1905.

Without question, such proletarian revolutionary activity also operates the other way on the liberalism of the bourgeois classes, paralyzing it and casting it into the arms of the counterrevolution. But that is precisely the dialectical aspect of the revolution's course, advancing through contradictions, an aspect that we can understand and seize on as an essential factor in the political calculations of the proletariat if we remain aware that the elemental basis of bourgeois liberalism can be found in given historical conditions. Under the current social conditions, given the advanced state of class struggle, the liberalism of the bourgeoisie is nothing but a desire to end the operations of the revolutionary proletariat, to end them as early as possible and restrict their effects to the degree beneficial to the class interests of the bourgeoisie. The Cadet party, having emerged in 1904 as a response to the gigantic mass strikes, demonstrations, and rages of the working masses in the years 1902–1904, soon began to offer its services of "banquet" liberalism, such that it simultaneously advanced and held back the proletarian revolutionary movement. Yet because its offer was premature, and absolutism, still confident of its power, rejected the gesture, the liberal primrose wilted abruptly at the end of 1904. The proletariat's renewed revolutionary operations

---

* The Peaceful Regeneration group was formed by conservative noblemen following the 1905 Revolution as part of an effort to coax those advocating constitutional monarchy (such as the Cadets) to move further to the right.

in 1905 prompted a reanimation of liberalism and renewed hope. Acting on its belief that redemption for the struggles and sacrifices of workers could be found in the form of the ministerial purse, the Cadet party offered its services a second time. And because absolutism still depended more on bayonets than on Cadet ministers, bourgeois liberalism again went bankrupt, the expression of which was the Third Duma. However, to view the Russian bourgeoisie as incapable, now or ever, of a more liberal position would be quite erroneous. The political career of the bourgeoisie in Russia is by no means finished—rather, it has only just begun. As not the ringleader of the campaign but a parasite on both the revolutionary proletariat and counterrevolutionary absolutism, it can and must adjust its political physiognomy to each new situation, and to this extent, the forecasts of [Fyodor] Dan, [Fyodor] Cherevanin, and others contain a kernel of truth. Only that these forecasts have been made upside down: The reawakening of bourgeois liberalism is not a precondition for the revolution's revival, but quite the opposite—if the proletariat renews its actions and gathers strength, its success will give liberalism new life.

When the substantial political power of absolutism crumbles under the blows of mass proletarian uprisings, and liberalism is the historically inevitable form to be taken by bourgeois aspirations to steal proletarian spoils, liberalism will blossom perhaps even among Łódźian bourgeois such as the Poznanskis, the Silbersteins, and the Scheiblers.

The current revolution in Russia recapitulates both the results and goals of all the modern Western European revolutions. The forward ranks of the Polish and Russian proletariat stood ready for battle from the very first moment, harboring fewer illusions about the use of Jacobin methods of operation through a ruling "revolutionary minority" than about immediately uprooting bourgeois power and establishing "social equality," to say nothing of the miracle-working properties of the republican model of government. On the other hand, they know that the republic is only the highest political form of a mature bourgeois society. Indeed, their freedom from illusions not only does not weaken the revolutionary might of the proletariat but even enhances it. The working class in Russia does not await final salvation in a future republic but sees such a republic as an indispensable *means* of salvation. Further, the working class cannot delude itself that, having overthrown absolutism and attained a dictatorship for a certain period, it will establish a socialist system. The socialist revolution can only be a result of international revolution, and the results that the proletariat in Russia will be able to achieve in the current revolution will depend, to say nothing of the level of social development in Russia, on the level and form of development that class relations and proletarian operations in other capitalist countries will have achieved by that time. Nevertheless, if the revolutionary proletariat in Russia were to gain political power as well, however temporarily, that would provide enormous encouragement to the international class struggle.

That is why the working class in Poland and in Russia can and must strive to seize power with full consciousness. Because once workers have power, they can not only carry out the tasks of the current revolution directly—realizing political freedom across the Russian state—but also establish the eight-hour workday, upend agrarian relations, and, in a word, materialize every aspect of their program, delivering the heaviest blows they can to bourgeois rule and in this way hasten its international overthrow.

Worrying about whether the current revolution maintains an appropriately "bourgeois" character is an entirely unnecessary task for the proletariat. The revolution's bourgeois character finds expression in the inability of the proletariat to stay in power, in the inevitable removal of the proletariat from power by a counterrevolutionary operation of the bourgeoisie, the rural landowners, the petty bourgeoisie, and the greater part of the peasantry. It may be that in the end, after the proletariat is overthrown, the republic will disappear and be followed by the long rule of a highly restrained constitutional monarchy. It may very well be. But the relations of classes in Russia are now such that the path to even a moderate monarchical constitution leads through revolutionary action and the dictatorship of a republican proletariat. The historical work of the First, Second, and Third Dumas provides a demonstration of this conclusion. And this moderate constitutional monarchy that would rule Russia after the dictatorship of the proletariat rises and falls would also conceal deep within, under its reactionary political form, such mature and radicalized class relations that the normal, peaceful bourgeois rule made possible by these relations would be an edifice built on volcanic ground.

Revolution, in this conception, would bring the proletariat losses as well as victories. Yet, by no other road can the entire international proletariat march to its final victory. We must propose the socialist revolution not as a sudden leap, finished in twenty-four hours, but as a historical period, perhaps long, of turbulent class struggle, with breaks both brief and extended. It may seem that this perspective, with its multiplicity of objectives, and the proletariat's insufficient strength in the face of them, could sap the courage of the proletarian vanguard, particularly in the current period of triumphant counterrevolution and complete suppression of the masses. Not only is this impossible, but, in fact, only a strong conviction of the greatness and historical necessity of these objectives can again instill strength, courage, and confidence in the ranks of the proletariat. The entire course of the revolution to date—including the internal logic of the recent counterrevolutionary era—indicates that the rekindling of proletarian revolutionary activity and its eventual victory are historical necessities because they are the only road to realizing the objectives of the revolution. This fact suffices to give the forward ranks of the proletariat ironclad belief that this drive will come, and there will be victory. Building up this consciousness in the masses, explaining to them the historical logic of revolutions past, constitutes the maximum of what Social Democracy can do at the present and the minimum of what it ought to do.

We have focused here entirely on the proletariat, without mentioning the peasantry. This is not because the peasant movement does not exist as a distinct revolutionary movement in Poland. In Russia, it acts as a highly important revolutionary force, and the agriculture question has already become inextricably bound up in the history of the revolution to date. Indeed, whoever wishes to look ahead to find outward signs of future struggle must first take into consideration, more than the movements of the working masses in cities, the movements of the rural folk. However, because we are concerned not with external prospects but with the lodestar and direction of political revolution, Social Democracy finds only the autonomous class politics of the proletariat to be reliable. The objective of the party of the proletariat is to support the peasant movement and to guide it when possible, pulling it along whenever it can provide direction. Nevertheless, cooperation during revolutionary outbreaks still does not give rise to a unity or identity of conscious politics. The peasant movement in Russia, a convergence of various factors, interests, and strata, has no essential unity with the defined, fixed class politics of the proletariat, whose overarching goals range far beyond the most revolutionary of the passing gusts of the peasant movement. To capture these gusts in one's sails where possible, to make use of the revolutionary part of the agriculture question in the interests of the entire movement, resolving it in accordance with the social course and interests of the revolution—that is the cardinal objective of the proletariat. But an alliance of the proletariat and the peasantry cannot be the basis for the work of actually achieving political revolution, for determining its objectives, or for realizing them, any more than any other conscious alliance can. Common, uniform operation in such times may depend on the unconscious political alloying of various social strata, as happened, for example, in the Great French Revolution as well as in the first phase of the Revolution of 1848, when the proletariat with the urban petty bourgeoisie operated as one undifferentiated mass of "the people." Of course, to cooperate with the peasantry in this way would be impossible for Russia's current conscious proletariat. While relying on the revolutionary movements of other social classes, the class-conscious proletariat can and must strive only to complete its own mission, to lead a vigorous campaign for its own politics, to independently guide the enormous revolutionary army, and to take power into its own hands; for only a politically conscious, naturally revolutionary, and self-reliant class will be able, having won power, to bring about the immediate historical objective of revolution, and then to stay the course to the extreme point to which the situation of class conflict, both internationally and domestically, will bring it.

The Cancan of the Counterrevolution[*]

> Till Russia's tsar by the neck He seizes,
> Mary and Jesus!
> And Novosiltsov's life he outsqueezes,
> Mary and Jesus!
> . . . .
> Never will we be the allies of kings,
> Never will we bend our necks to power ...
>
> (*Forefathers' Eve*)[†]

I.

In the gloomy night of the raging counterrevolution, history's fantasy suddenly staged a scene in colors so bright that a scholar and historian would hardly believe his eyes, reading off a card with the description "Slavic Days" in Petersburg, Warsaw, and Prague. What happened? Some "social activist" under the dark star of General Vladimirov quietly set off on a tour of the Slavic cities, starting from Petersburg: he was in Vienna, in Prague, Kraków, Warsaw, and we do not know who or what he was sniffing for, but soon after, a trinity set off from Vienna, likewise under the dark star of the "Slavic" envoys and with the Czech arch-reactionary Mr. [Karel] Kramář at its head,[‡] and arrived directly at the tsarist capital, where it received an enthusiastic reception at the station from various national societies and clubs. The authorities, their protection strengthened, made no attempt to disturb the clamor and crowds. To the contrary, the "Slavic guests" went directly from the railroad station, having barely brushed off the dust from their journey, to pay visits to the military authorities: to State Council Chairman [Mikhail] Akimov, to Minister of Foreign Affairs [Alexander] Izvolsky, "with whom," as reported in the newspapers, "Dr. Kramář

---

[*] This essay was originally published as "Kankan kontrrewolucji," in *Przegląd Socjaldemokratyczny*, Vol. 4, No. 4 (June 1908), pp. 277–88. It is translated from the Polish original by Zachary King.

[†] Luxemburg mistakenly attributes as one quote from Mickiewicz what are actually two quotes from works by two different Polish poets. The first quatrain is taken from the third part of Adam Mickiewicz's poetic drama *Dziady* (1832), Act I, Scene I, translated into English by Charles Kraszewski as *Forefathers' Eve* (London: Glagoslav Publications, 2016), p. 113; the second quote comes from Juliusz Słowacki's play *Ksiądz Marek*, Act I, Scene I. The full quatrain reads: "Never will we be the allies of kings, / Never will we bend our necks to power, / For we are orderlies of Christ, / Servants to Mary."

[‡] Kramář was a conservative nationalist who headed the Young Czech Party in the Austro-Hungarian Empire from 1891 to 1915. He was a Russophile who wanted Austria-Hungary to ally with tsarist Russia instead of Germany. Hence Luxemburg's reference to his warm reception upon arriving for a visit to St. Petersburg.

had a long conversation"; to the mayor of Petersburg, the chairman of the Third Duma [Nikolai] Khomiakov, the Austrian embassy; three humble Slav arrivals, who hold no office besides the delegatory mandate of the pacified Czech peasantry in the Viennese Parliament, who have no qualifications besides the sudden, burning pan-Slavic love bursting in their private breasts and have no mission besides the sudden need, coming from who knows where, to unite all the Slavs to fight against some threatening danger. These three travelers, whose names, with one exception, were still unknown yesterday beyond the corridors of the Vienna State Council, have been accepted kindly everywhere. As if by the wave of a magic wand, the heavy gates of officialdom in Pyotr Stołypin's Russia swing open at their approach.

On the second day after his arrival, Mr. Kramář was "very warmly" received in the Winter Palace by Stołypin himself, with whom, as with Izvolsky, he had a long confidential conversation. On the third day, the Petersburg City Council held a noisy reception in honor of the three guests with the participation of Stołypin and all the military brass, where a toast was raised "in honor of His Most Serene Highness." It was repeated in the thunderous echo of 500 throats, and when that echo died down, Mr. Kramář's eloquent lips started thrumming about a shared Slavic culture, about the necessity of sticking together, about the necessity of reconciling Poles with Russians, about the importance of Russian state power for the Poles because "the strength of the Poles in Russia depends on the power of the Russian state." Then the same three apostles are asked to come over for a spoonful of soup by Mrs. Komarova, publisher of the anti-Polish and anti-Semitic organ *Svet* [The World], where they sit between Mr. [Alexander] Bashmakov of the *Pravitel'stvennyi Vestnik* [Government Gazette], Father Eulogius [Georgiyevsky], the patron of pogroms,* and Mr. S. N. Alexeyev, a member of the Black Hundreds from the Warsaw Russian Club.† And here, too, we hear speeches about Slavic culture, for which Russia's power is the only recourse, and Mr. Kramář and the organizers of massacres drink toasts to each other in honor of "reconciling Poles and Russians." A "Slavic Commission" has seemingly sprouted from the ground amid these banquets, speeches, and toasts, and is now suddenly preparing a project for an all-Slavic congress in Prague in order to prepare for a pan-Slav congress in Petersburg, an all-Slavic exhibition in Moscow, an all-Slavic telegraph agency in Russian with its headquarters in Petersburg, propaganda for the introduction of the Russian language in schools in the Slavic lands, etc., etc.

---

* Eulogius, bishop of Volhynia, was a reactionary Russian Orthodox priest who worked to Russify western Ukraine through highly repressive measures. He was put in charge of eliminating the Greek Catholic Church in Russian-occupied Galicia. In 1908 he was a member of the Russian Duma.

† Alexeyev was a notorious anti-Polish chauvinist who was a member of the Third Duma. The Warsaw Russian Club was a gathering place of Russian xenophobic nationalists.

In Petersburg, there is a "national" delegation for Polish "society," there are deputies from Poland in the Duma. Did they slap Mr. Kramář and his masters' friends, or did they spit on the agents of "reconciling Poles and Russians" under the auspices of "Russian state power" who were patronized by Stołypin and those swallowing up wine in honor of the Poles with Father Eulogius and Mr. Alexeyev? To the contrary! Mr. [Roman] Dmowski and company participated in the whole "Slavic action," flitted around, gabbed and cheered, took part wherever they could, and even though they were not allowed to attend the city council soirée and had to listen to the toast in honor of His Most Serene Highness from over the fence, they nevertheless then gave speeches at a meeting of the "Slavic Commission" that caused a huge sensation in all the Russian press and immediately turned "our deputies" into central figures of the whole action, to the glory of the nation.

"A deeper impression," quoting from the *Słowo Warszawskie* [The Warsaw Word],

> was made by the speech of Count Olizar in particular ("our" member of the State Council), who emphasized that, more than anything, it was necessary to eliminate the mistrust that hinders mutual understanding. This mistrust on the Russians' part arises mainly from two assumptions. The first one concerns the Poles' aspiration for independence. This assumption is unfounded. That, having lost their independence, the Poles would fight to regain it, this was understandable. Otherwise they would not have been worthy of the title of nation. But now times have changed. Poles sincerely want Russia's greatness and power because the Polish nation depends on the power of the Russian state. Poland's independence would be dangerous above all for itself with today's political conspiracies. This old wives' tale of Polish aspirations for independence must end once and for all. The second mistaken assumption is the fear of the possibility of Polonization in Lithuania and Russia. This is also unfounded [...] The Poles are sincere Slavs and unreservedly bound to the Slavic idea.

The speech of the leader of National Democracy, Mr. Dmowski, was even more wonderful and sensational. According to the exact text provided in the organ of the Polish Group in the Duma, *Głos Warszawski* [The Warsaw Voice], the chairman of the group, in a comprehensive historical account, showed that Poland, whose civilization was created in the struggle against Germanism, only temporarily went astray with the struggle against Russia, and the last expressions of this deviation were our national uprisings. Now, however, Poland is returning to its proper historical mission—the fight against the German West:

> The breakthrough in the position and historical role of Poland, which I mentioned at the beginning, is that once again its main struggle is the fight in the West against the German deluge. The eastern areas, which in the past were of major importance

to Poland (Lithuania and Rus), are no longer so important in this struggle, and the attention of the nation is focused on the West, on the native lands of Poland, to the three countries who own them. In this fight, our natural allies are the Slavic peoples who are struggling against Germanism and are threatened by it as much as we are. Their cause is our cause. That is why I find it incomprehensible to ask what conditions are required for Poles to participate in the Slavic cause. For us, I repeat, the Slavic cause is our own, unconditionally and unreservedly. Today we are warriors in the fight for the future of the Slavic region, and the cause of Slavic unity will not encounter any obstacles from our side.

There was, of course, a great sensation following this speech from the "nationalist" Dmowski. Mr. Vladimirov and Mr. Kramář must have been scratching their heads during their confidential meetings, how to stage the "Slavic" nonsense here, when "all of Slavdom" has had a hole as big as the Polish question in it for a hundred years. In 1848, when all the "Slavic" scoundrels were holding counterrevolutionary meetings in Prague,* nothing at all was said in the heart of Poland—in the Kingdom—about all the noise in "Slavdom." Since then, Polish-Russian relations have been enriched with one quashed Polish uprising and a million bloody lashes on the body of Poland from the Russian knout. At present, martial law is rattling its chains, having already surrounded the Kingdom for three years now, and the creak of the gallows, where on average five victims hang every day in Warsaw and Łódź, is still fatally unfitting as a companion to the slogan of all-Slavic love with Russia. The kindly General Vladimirov and the Czech Kramář must have schemed secretly to devise the "conditions" for the Poles and trembled in their souls for fear that the whole nonsense would end in embarrassment when the first Pole rose and, "pointing to his bloody breast," then declared: "You have no Slavic language without Poland!" At least there was a fear that the most urgent issue—the issue of Poland's autonomy—would be raised immediately. Autonomy is the program of "all of Polish society," autonomy is the focal point in the program and parliamentary policy of the strongest Polish party in the Duma, the National Democrats. But Poland has surpassed all expectations. The Dmowskis said that both Kramář and Vladimirov, as well as *Novoye Vremya* [The New Times] and the leader of the right wing in the Third Duma, are virtually "true Russian men"—to which Count [Alexei] Bobrinsky opened his mouth in admiration. Autonomy was not even mentioned in the speeches by Mr. Olizar and Mr. Dmowski. "Unconditionally and unreservedly!" The nonsense could therefore quietly go on to the end. "Prime Minister Stołypin gave the Slavic delegates permission to stop in Warsaw on their return trip and hold meetings with organizations, etc."

---

* Luxemburg is referring to the First Pan-Slav Congress, held in Prague in June 1848. Some of its participants favored national autonomy for Slavs living in the Austrian Empire; others desired an alliance with tsarist Russia.

The end of "Slavic Week" in Petersburg therefore became "Slavic Monday" in Warsaw. The "Slavic guests" arrived at the railroad station and were first received at Count Krasiński's, where the collected crème de la crème of the nation received cordial bows from Count Bobrinsky's neighbor in the Duma, then directly at Count Krasiński's table at the house of General Governor [Georgi] Skalon, for whom they were forced to wait for a quarter of an hour, as he was busy with a small Slavic action. On that day, he signed sentences to the gallows for ten Slavs in the Sokół case* and reprieves for four Slavs to forced labor for life in a land of Slavdom called Siberia. From [the meeting with] Skalon they went on to a banquet at the Resursa Obywatelska Palace issued in honor of Slavic brotherhood, where, in a huge gathering of various parties, "National Democracy and the Party for Realpolitik† had a decisive advantage," where everything was mentioned except for Polish autonomy and where, among other speeches and toasts, Professor Baranowski reminded us that the "Slavic idea" was already cultivated by [Count Aleksander] Wielopolski and [Włodzimierz] Spasowicz,‡ while Ludwik Straszewicz,§ in *Kurjer Polski* [The Polish Courier], reminded us that the true protoplast of Polish brotherhood with Slavs like Stołypin and Skalon was none other than Adam Mickiewicz, the author of *Forefathers' Eve* [*Dziady*]. Then from the Resursa Obywatelska Palace the three Slavic pilgrims went to Nowy Świat Street in a hurry to the Russian Club of Mr. Alexeyev and company, where, for lack of time, only three speeches in honor of the reconciliation of Poles and Russians were delivered under the slogan of "equality, freedom and brotherhood." The guests went to the station, and a crowd of the Polish national intelligentsia accompanied them and bid them farewell.

"The first impression of this historical fact," wrote the Petersburg correspondent of *Kurjer Warszawski* [The Warsaw Courier],

> was a bit chaotic, mainly due to the fact that both Russian society and the Russian press had no idea that the Slavic question had not only reached this stage, but that

---

* Sokół was the abbreviation of the Polish Sport Association. Founded in Lviv in 1867, it was also active in the Province of Posen from 1885, and from 1905 in the Kingdom of Poland, in both cases on an illegal basis. The association was dominated, particularly in Russian-occupied Poland before 1914, by the National Democrats, which lent the organization a paramilitary character.

† The Party for Realpolitik (Stronnictwo Polityki Realnej) was formed in 1904, and represented the interests of large landowners, higher levels of the clergy, and conservative parts of the bourgeoisie and the intelligentsia. After the 1905 Revolution, it forged close relations with the National Democrats.

‡ Wielopolski was a conservative politician in the mid-nineteenth century who was appointed president of the Council of State because of his warm relations with the tsarist regime. He opposed the Polish national uprising of 1863. Spasowicz was a famous Polish lawyer who argued that Poland should maintain close political as well as cultural ties to Russia. He was one of the lawyers involved in the trial of Russian anarchist Sergei Nechayev.

§ Ludwik Straszewicz was one of the founders of the Party for Realpolitik. In 1907 he helped found the centrist National Alliance with members of the Progressive Party.

the most necessary agent of its resolution—the Poles—had indicated their goodwill in this cause without reservations.

Mr. Koskowski is correct: The pan-Slavic action and Polish participation therein is a historical fact.

II.

Pan-Slavism has always been an ideology of reaction, as is any racial ideology by nature. Pan-Slavism first played an active political role in 1848 in mobilizing the counterrevolutionary forces of Austria. "Pan-Slavism," wrote Marx in 1849 in *Neue Rheinische Zeitung* [The New Rhenish Newspaper],*

> did not originate in Russia or Poland, but in Prague and Zagreb. Pan-Slavism means the union of all the small Slav nations and nationalities of Austria, and secondarily Turkey, for struggle against the Austrian Germans, the Magyars and, eventually, against the Turks (…) The direct aim of pan-Slavism is the creation of a Slav *state under Russian domination*, extending from the Erzgebirge and the Carpathians to the Black, Aegean, and Adriatic seas—a state that would include, besides the German, Italian, Magyar, Wallachian, Turkish, Greek, and Albanian languages, also approximately a dozen Slav languages and basic dialects. All this would be held together not by the elements which have hitherto held Austria together and ensured its development, but by the abstract quality of Slavism and the so-called Slav language, *which is at any rate common to the majority of the inhabitants.* But where does this Slavism exist except in the minds of a few ideologists, where is the "Slav language" except in the imagination of [František] Palacký, [Ljudevit] Gaj, and company, *and, to some extent, in the old Slav litany of the Russian Church, which no Slav any longer understands?* In reality, all these peoples are at the most diverse stages of civilization, ranging from the fairly highly developed (thanks to the *Germans*) modern industry and culture of Bohemia to the almost-nomadic barbarism of the Croats and Bulgarians; in reality, therefore, all these nations have most antagonistic interests (…) Thus, pan-Slav unity is either pure fantasy or—*the Russian knout*.

To sum up, Marx adds:

> In Austria apart from Poland and Italy, it is the Germans and Magyars in 1848, as during the past thousand years already, who have assumed the historical initiative. They represent the *revolution*.

---

* Unbeknownst to Luxemburg, the article that she is quoting from was written by Engels, not Marx. The article was part of a series of reports by Engels on the events leading up to the declaration of the Hungarian Republic.

The Southern Slavs, who for a thousand years have been taken in tow by the Germans and the Magyars, only rose up in 1848 to achieve their national independence in order to thereby at the same time suppress the German-Magyar revolution. They represent the *counterrevolution* (…)

The Hapsburg dynasty (…) is now prolonging the last moments of its existence (as Austrian absolutism—R.L.) through the union of the Southern Slavs in the struggle against the Germans and Magyars.*

Pan-Slavism has not only always been an ideology of reaction in general, but also of Russian imperialism in particular. Marx was wrong to think that this movement was not created in Russia. The whole theory, philosophy, literature, and journalism of pan-Slavism originated in Russia.

As early as 1842, Professor [Mikhail] Pogodin developed a program for the pan-Slavic rule of the Russian knout:

Russia is a population of 60 million people, besides those that are not yet counted, a population that grows by 1 million every year and will soon reach 100 million people. Add to this the 30 million brothers and cousins, the Slavs scattered all over Europe from Constantinople to Venice, from the Morea to the Baltic and Northern Seas, the Slavs whose veins flow with the same blood as ours, who speak our language, and who therefore sympathize with us through the laws of nature and, contrary to their geographical and political divisions, form a single moral whole together with us. Let us deduct them from Austria to Turkey and add them to ourselves, and see what will be left of those countries, and how much will come to us! The thought is breathtaking! A ninth of the settled globe, almost a ninth of its population, half of the equator, a quarter of the meridian!†

Later, [Nikolai] Danilevsky, the creator of a proper pan-Slavic catechism, set a clear goal that became the leading part of the tsar's policy of partition through the 1880s:

The goal of the aspirations of the entire Russian nation from the first dawn of its political awakening, the ideal of civilization, fame, wealth, and greatness for our ancestors, the center of Orthodoxy, the subject of conflict between us and Europe—

---

* In addition to wrongly attributing Engels' article to Marx, Luxemburg's translation of the article into Polish marks several ellipses in her citation, but nevertheless does not quote a few phrases from Engels' article and leaves their absence unmarked. These omissions, especially the first, indicate an understanding of Russia's role in the movement—a relevance that Luxemburg then accuses Marx of overlooking. For the reader's benefit, these omissions have been reinserted and highlighted in italics. See "The Magyar Struggle" in *Marx-Engels Collected Works*, Vol. 8 (New York: International Publishers, 1977), pp. 235–6.

† It is not clear which essay of Pogodin's is being quoted here by Luxemburg.

what historical importance would Constantinople have for us, a city torn away by the Turks to the detriment of the whole of Europe! What a triumph would have filled our hearts if we had again affixed the radiant cross on the dome of St. Sophia!

Orthodoxy, absolutism, and imperialism were the core of pan-Slavism from the very beginning.

But this pan-Slavism was a true ideology of reaction—that is, an honest confession of faith, a spiritual movement of a specific generation based on specific historical conditions. In Russia it was based on the same traditional "native" social system, its peasant *obshchina** economy, which was the foundation of absolutism and which the Slavophiles defended against the capitalism of the "rotten West" with their pens just as absolutism defended Russian stagnation against liberalism and the European revolution with the *katorga* and the knout.† The pan-Slavic counterrevolution of the Southern Slavs in 1848 was also an expression of the opposition of the conservative peasant lands, with their natural economy, against the march of capitalism that was pressing upon them. That is why pan-Slavism, as a true ideology with deep social roots and its own existence, which at one time attracted a whole host of great talents and outstanding figures to its service in Russia, was not a tapestry of absolutism by sordid command, but rather an inspiration to it. [Sergei] Aksakov and Pogodin, who offered "soul cleansing" perspectives on Slavo-tsarist imperialism, were forced by the still-red ink of Nikolai's censors‡ to remain silent as dangerous troublemakers. And when, in the 1870s and 1880s, pan-Slavism finally gained the position of an official worldview, its apostles [Mikhail] Katkov and [Konstantin] Pobedonostsev shook Russia, and the bureaucracy trembled before this private editor and Orthodox clerk on whom the tsarist clergy waited hand and foot. South-Slavic pan-Slavism was nothing but an unwitting ally of the counterrevolutionary mannequin. The Prague Convention in 1849 was, after all, dispersed by [Alfred] Windisch-Grätz with bayonets, and not organized by paid agents.

Today, the social foundations of pan-Slavism in both Russia and all of Slavdom are finished, together with the patriarchal peasant economy. Capitalism has buried both the Russian *obshchina*§ and national Slavic unity, having split all

---

* The *obshchina* was a traditional communal administrative form and property relation in Russia up to the time of Stalin's forced industrialization campaign of the 1930s.

† In fact, Marx also defended the *obshchina*, although on very different grounds than pan-Slavists. He viewed its communal and reciprocal form of social organization as providing a possible material condition for an alternative path to socialism in Russia that shortens or bypasses the capitalist stage of development. See his "Draft Letters to Vera Zasulich," in *Late Marx and the Russian Road: Marx and 'The Peripheries of Capitalism*, edited by Teodor Shanin (New York: Monthly Review Books, 1983), pp. 97–126.

‡ That is, the censors working for Tsar Nicholas I, who reigned from 1825 to 1855.

§ The judgment was premature; though suffering from many internal and external forces promoting its dissolution, the *obshchina* actually increased its range and influence in some parts of

Slavic nations with the wedge of modern class struggle. Russia's defeat in the [1904–1905] Japanese War, and then the outbreak of the revolution, struck the last blow to the worldly dreams of the knout.

For a long time now, there has not been a peep about the aspirations of the whole of the Slavic peoples. But if pan-Slavism, as a bona fide ideology with specific historical conditions, has given up the ghost, then it is not that it has sprung back to life today so much as there is a new interest in bringing back its ghost from the grave—the interest of the counterrevolution in Russia. Having strangled the revolutionary proletariat, having demoralized the liberal opposition, having cheated itself in the Third Duma, the counterrevolution is now suddenly trying to turn its temporary triumph into a permanent state, to strengthen and consolidate its position. Along with martial law and the gallows, the means of achieving this is the tried and true salvation of every weakened Caesarism: foreign policy. Stołypin's course has been more and more bold in putting forward an imperialist posture. The right wing, Black Hundreds, and for-hire press are expressing themselves more and more vocally in favor of war. At the same time, the zealous efforts of Russian diplomacy are achieving a number of successes thanks to the support of the Western European bourgeoisie. The alliance with England, the visits of [King] Edward [VII] and [Armand] Fallières to Russia, the Russian Cossack dictatorship in Persia, the quarrels with Turkey and provocations with China, the hasty reparation of the Tsushima navy*—all this confusion has no clear direction, but it does have a clear purpose: to divert the attention of society from internal affairs to foreign affairs, to create an atmosphere of chauvinism, of adoration for "strong power," a moral halo for absolutism. The unhappy war has become the prelude to revolution, and its end could still be a happy one ...

And the Stołypin cabal has not erred in its calculations. The only opposition whose acquisition and exploration is at all possible—the liberals—are clearly doing well, if only because foreign policy is one of the many Achilles' heels of this particular political animal. From the very beginning of the revolution, Mr. [Pyotr] Struve started to develop an organ of liberal imperialism in the Paris organ *L'Humanité*,† which was supposed to demonstrate the ability of statesmen from the Cadets to take over the ministerial portfolios. At the same time, absolutism explained that its interests lay not in the East, in Japan, where it had been misled by its servants, but in Constantinople. The current pan-Slavic improvisation is therefore just a mere episode in these counterrevolutionary measures, a

---

the Russian Empire as a result of the 1905 Revolution. This, however, was noticed by virtually none of the Marxists of the time.

    * An ironic reference to the Battle of Tsushima of May 1905, when the Russian navy was decisively defeated by the Japanese, losing over two-thirds of its ships during the battle.

    † Founded in 1904, *L'Humanité* was a daily newspaper with close ties to the French Section of the Second International (SFIO).

supplement to the pogroms that have already been worn threadbare, a refreshment of the props of the *ancien régime*.

And it must be admitted that in ingenuity, as well as self-confidence and courage, the counterrevolution has once again surpassed the significance of some revolutionary areas. In this kind of humiliation, slander, and disorder, after such moral and material ruin, after such political defiance, to stage a tribute to universal Slavic culture at the foot of the throne in Petersburg—that is a remarkable feat of courage.

But nevertheless, the organization of this farce was brash, and Stołypin and company's wildest ideas were surpassed. Reality has gone beyond dreams: The rescue operation for absolutism has been led by Polish nationalists. The whole pan-Slavic action lacked an aggressive character, it lacked sharpness. The matter was delicate. Official and obvious harassment toward foreign powers was not in the interests of its directors. No more could Mr. Stołypin intend to officially provoke the German bourgeoisie, for the Russian counterrevolution depends on it. That's why, in its appearances and in the division of roles, a certain caution and restraint was maintained so as not to get too involved. Hence the new name of "neo-pan-Slavism," hence its purely "cultural," "apolitical" character, as our naive "progressive youth" put it in its "announcement," rushing to add a splinter to the pyre arranged by the hands of absolutism for the revolutionary cause. They also lacked any kind of pretense to a sudden explosion of Slavic "culture," lacked relevance, lacked a historical lineage after the official rupture with the old pan-Slavism. Polish nationalists provided everything. Mr. Dmowski was the first to turn "neo-pan-Slavism" from a "cultural" fantasy into an aggressive, cutting policy against Germany, and the Polish press was the first to sound the alarm about the military ruckus against the "predatory attempts" of the Germans and about the fight for fields in Greater Poland. Mr. Dmowski and the "national" press provided news, a historical lineage, ideology—through the historical mission of Poland and its most recent defeats in Prussia, transferring the line of historical tradition from those who fought against Prussia's Teutonic knights to Stołypin, Skalon, and company. Russian imperialism, crawling into the world through blood, spit, and mud, somewhat hesitant and incredulous, was suddenly transformed into Poland's ennobled protector, benefactor, savior, the heir and executor of God's judgments on Polish history, it was clothed in the mantle of the Polish heroes who died at Grunwald!* While efforts in the service of "neo-pan-Slavism" were rewarded in cash, Slavic roubles with the likeness of a Romanov cheek were naturally found only in the pockets of Mr. Vladimirov and his Black Hundred companions. But Mr. Straszewicz, Mr. Dmowski, and the Polish press could have written no differently than they wrote, and continue

---

* At the Battle of Grunwald in 1410, the Polish-Lithuanian Commonwealth won a decisive victory over the Germanic Knights of the Teutonic Order.

to write, about the cause of neo-pan-Slavism if they had been paid by the line by Stołypin or if they had been given the pens of the most talented publicists of the tsarist police department.

The Slavic nonsense is just a counterrevolutionary episode in the history of the great Russian Revolution, a farce that was not intended to have any serious consequences or even to last very long. But this nonsense did not create Polish pan-Slavism. It was only an unexpected opportunity in which the stinking miasmas of reaction, which have built up in Polish society in its more than half a century of bourgeois development, broke out.

III.

There is a historical relationship between pan-Slavism and the Polish national cause, in that pan-Slavism has always been its antithesis. "The Poles," wrote Marx* in 1849,

> are the only Slav nation that is free from all pan-Slavist aspirations. They have, however, very good reasons for that: they have been oppressed mainly by their own so-called Slav brothers, and among the Poles hatred of Russians takes precedence over hatred of Germans, and with full justification. But because the liberation of Poland is inseparable from the revolution, because Pole and revolutionary have become synonymous, for Poles the sympathy of all Europe and the restoration of their nation are as certain as are for the Czechs, Croats and Russians the hatred of all Europeans and a most bloody revolutionary war of the entire West against them.†

And, conversely, all betrayals to the national cause in Poland took the form of Slavophilism. Mr. Baranowski is right: The most outstanding "Slavophile" after the Targowica traitors [*targowiczanie*]‡ was Margrave [Aleksander] Wielopolski. But Wielopolski was never a pan-Slavist "unconditionally and unreservedly." Indeed, he had very clear conditions and reservations: He called for a great autonomous and national reform in Poland at a time when, in Russia herself, no one presented absolutism with any "conditions" whatsoever. And in Poland,

---

   * This article was actually not written by Marx, but rather Engels. It was widely (and wrongly) assumed in Luxemburg's time that Marx authored the articles in the *Neue Rhenische Zeitung* on pan-Slavism and so-called "non-historic peoples" such as Czechs, Croats, and Serbians. For more on this, see Roman Rosdolsky, *Engels and the 'Nonhistoric Peoples': The National Question in the Revolution of 1848* (Glasgow: Critique, 1987).
   † See "Democratic Pan-Slavism," in *Marx-Engels Collected Works*, Vol. 8 (New York: International Publishers, 1977), p. 375.
   ‡ A reference to the Targowica Confederation of 1792, an alliance of Polish and Lithuanian noblemen who allied themselves with Russian tsarism in opposition to the Constitution of 1791, which had limited the powers and privileges of the nobility. The Targowica Confederation fought their fellow Poles in the Polish-Russian War of 1792, leading to the Second Partition of Poland in 1795. Hence their treasonous reputation.

Wielopolski was, as Mr. Dmowski says, a "maverick" [*samotnik*], and the social response to his Slavic policy, with its conditions and reservations, was the outbreak of the January Uprising [of 1863] under the slogan of national independence, unconditionally and unreservedly—an outbreak that broke Wielopolski. This was the end of the first serious attempt to "reconcile the Poles with Russia" under the aegis of Slavdom.

Only after the failure of the last of our uprisings did capitalist development create the right conditions to "reconcile" the broad mass of bourgeois Poles with tsarist Russia on the ashes and rubble of national aspirations: siphoning off the surplus value from the veins of the Polish proletariat on a mass scale under the caring wings of tsarism and reaping that surplus value in clinking gold on the "Eastern markets." But, if the transformation of mutual relations initially took place quite slowly and unnoticed, it has now been taking place at breakneck speed since the outbreak of the revolution. This kaleidoscope is perfectly reflected in the fate of individual classes and parties. The oldest national faction, the faction of the aristocracy and the nobility [*szlachta*]—the Conciliationists [*ugodowcy*]*—started with Wielopolski's program of great political reform and ended in the seventies with schnapps, beetroot, and Ludwik Górski's program of land-improvement credit. The next in the line of industrialist bourgeois factions emerged, in its turn, from the ashes of the last uprising at the beginning of the 1870s with its pretentious and noisy cultural-philosophical-ethical-progressive program of organizational work, ending in naked political abstinence—that is, the silent accumulation and consumption of surplus value under the aegis of absolutism. The petty bourgeoisie have preserved the national traditions the longest. And the youngest "faction" to represent this in society, National Democracy, which held out a full year before the revolution of the all-Polish program of "reconstruction," managed not only to change the program of national independence into Wielopolski's program, but also to stow away its own most recent program of autonomy and cross over "unconditionally and unreservedly" to the program of Russian Empire. In the "Slavic" days, the political abstinence of the Polish bourgeoisie is officially transforming into an active politics of support for the Russian counterrevolution, into public fraternity with the government that brutally rejected the proposal to give Poland the barest shadow of autonomous freedoms, and that has stifled Poland with the bloodiest repression over its entire territory. This is only a political consequence of the economic history of Poland. Being a parasite of Russian absolutism from the

---

* The Conciliationists saw themselves as practitioners of Realpolitik, and aimed at reconciliation with tsarist Russia. In 1904, the Party for Realpolitik (Stronnictwo Polityki Realnej) was founded, which principally joined together large landowners, higher levels of the clergy, and usually arch-conservative parts of the bourgeoisie and the intelligentsia. After the outbreak of the 1905 Revolution, there were increasing signs that the Conciliationists and the National Democracy camp were merging with one another.

very first moment of its existence, the Polish bourgeoisie, being additionally threatened by the revolutionary uprising of the proletariat, recognizes that rescuing autocracy is its most urgent class interest. This historical alliance between Polish capitalism and Russian absolutism, the springboard of Poland's entire post-partition history, is only fully expressed in the rescue of the Polish bourgeois classes of the tsarist regime.

For those who knew about the salient direction of Poland's social development, this turn of events is no surprise. Only nationalist utopians, like *Goniec* [The Messenger], who represent the oppositional remnants of National Democracy and are unable to keep up with the rapid evolution of the party, are capable of losing their heads at the sight of this pan-Slavic orgy and shout hoarsely about the betrayal of Mr. Dmowski, whose sin is only being the most faithful expression of the interests and the aspirations of all of property-owning Poland.

This is not even the first time that Polish society has made supporting absolutism into an open policy. The first sensational attempt in this direction was the reception of the tsar in Warsaw on September 1, 1897. The intention of the demonstration then made by Poland's lackeys for the knout was formulated openly by the deputy to the governor-general: "We hope that the time has finally come for us to become an even more important agent in the organically united wholeness of the state." And at the time, the entire press accepted the fact—the Russian press with astonishment, the reptilian press with a gnashing of the teeth—that Polish society was already at such a level of political "maturity."

But the difference between the attempt at open subservience by bourgeois Poland, which was rejected by absolutism, and today, is that during this demonstration ten years ago it was a Conciliationist faction that was leading society, and today—in the midst of the revolution that overwhelmed Russia and Poland—this role has been taken on by the National Democrats. The Party for Realpolitik rightly takes note of the fact that today's National Democracy has simply stolen its policy from the Conciliationists. It has welcomed National Democracy's "rational evolution" with an indulgent smile, "not only without the slightest reproach to anyone," but, moreover, "with the most sincere satisfaction": "For we have never been concerned," *Słowo* adds with irony, "as to who it is that provides important service to the public cause, just so long as the public cause is not harmed."

It must also be admitted to the realists that, as masters of Conciliationist politics, they have never dirtied themselves as much as their National Democratic pupils, and while one can talk about dignity in the case of the lackeys' politics, what is left of that can only be found today in the realists' press. The Conciliationists see themselves as simply forced to restrain the nationalists' enthusiasm for wallowing in the swamp of pan-Slavism, reminding them in *Słowo*, "who knows whether all this exuberant 'mutual assistance' is advisable?

Who knows whether the whole issue should not better be treated with less cheering and embracing?" The same Realpolitik faction even holds itself back publicly from excessively attacking the dignity of its own leader, Straszewicz, adding that "the opinions and arguments of Mr. L. Straszewicz, as elaborated in *Kurjer Polski*, align with the strict platform of the Party for Realpolitik only insofar as they concern Poles' participation in preliminary negotiations, which are only to narrowly elucidate and define our role and character at the all-Slavic congress." Even the Conciliationists, therefore, make some reservations, want to impose some conditions, even if only in soberly peddling their own conscience.

This, however, is precisely why today, Poland is being led not by Conciliationists but only by the National Democrats. The evolution of capitalist Poland has reached the culminating point where the greater the party's reactionary cynicism and the more it tramples on the national tradition, the greater its influence on bourgeois society, as it thereby all the more accurately expresses the material interest of this society. It was not the "realist" party, the open apostates of the national cause, but the last party of the nationalist banner that was destined to discover that Poland's historical mission is to defend the state power of tsardom. "Russia's recent defeat in the war with Japan," writes Mr. Dmowski in his most recent book, *Niemcy, Rosja i kwestja Polska* [Germany, Russia, and the Polish Question],

> along with the internal crisis in the tsarist state, have shown that the power, before which Europe has trembled for so long, was built on a much-weaker foundation than it seemed. Russia has turned out to be weaker than necessary for the interests of European equilibrium in the face of Germany's growing power, and its position on the East Asian front, in the conditions created by the last war, threatens to reduce it to a completely passive role in Europe. Today, it is not in the interests of the countries of Western Europe to weaken Russia, but to strengthen it and make it capable of opposing Germany; otherwise it (Western Europe) will be forced to become a passive tool of Berlin, a sphere of German influence, and an object of gradual German conquest. In a situation thus contrived, it is clear to Polish society that, if it is threatened with the loss of national existence in the future, this threat comes not from Russia but from Germany (…) Poland's relationship to Germany is also a source of an interest that the Polish question is starting to arouse in Europe. The threatening growth of Germany's power and the southeastern direction in German expansion point toward Poland's role as the main dam on its victory march. Our people's role today necessitates that the Polish question become one of the most important issues in Europe in the near future.

Polish nationalists are a Swiss Guard at the throne of the autocratic Russian tsar; Poland is like Rejtan, lying on the threshold of sovereign Russia and saying to the West: "You shall not pass!" Poland is the last defense of Russian absolutism and empire—never on earth has capitalism turned any relations more upside down, never has it more mercilessly humiliated now-outlived and once-pure banners.

When, in 1794, the revolutionary Parisian people were overcome, when their last leader had been sent to be executed, the half-naked whores of Paris began a mad dance of debauchery and the triumph of the counterrevolution all around the wagon of Robespierre, bound and pensive.

History will write pensively that in the wild cancan of the Russian counterrevolution, beside the gagged and blood-drenched Polish-Russian proletariat, the most debauched, whorish dance was performed by the last party of Polish nationalism.

The Black Card of the Revolution*

I pick at random from the timeline of cases and court sentences published over several days:

Warsaw, May 25. The Warsaw District military court sentenced eighteen-year-old Antoni Morski, Stanisław Ignaczak, and a worker, Fabisiak, to death by hanging for the robbery of a factory paymaster, Zalcman, in Warsaw in April of the current year, who was violently relieved of 150 silver roubles.†

Warsaw, May 31. The district military court in the citadel sentenced fourteen people to death for assaulting a postal van at the Sokołów station.

Warsaw, June 2. The governor-general of Warsaw‡ approved a death sentence issued by the Warsaw District military court against Stanisław Krawczyk for shots fired at a factory foreman and policemen.

Warsaw, June 6. Mateusz Susko, a resident of the Łukowski District who had been sentenced to death by the Warsaw military court for two murders in the Łukowski District, for the attempted murder of policemen and for membership of the Polish Socialist Party (the PPS), was hanged in the citadel at night.

Warsaw, June 8. The district military court examined the case of the murder of a captain of the Mikhailovsky gendarmes, which took place on March 4 of this year on Lubelska Street in Radom. The court sentenced the six defendants to death.

Warsaw, June 20. Ferdinand Tyszkiewicz, a participant in the attacks on a monopoly in Baczyn and the railroad station in Międzyrzecze was executed on the slopes of the citadel, as was Stanisław Olesiuk, an accomplice to the robbery of that station and a post office in Kadym.

Łódź, June 5. The military court sentenced Bolesław Strzała to death by hanging for four robberies and the killing of Jan Baranowski on January 25 of this year.

Łódź, June 6. Several brigands attacked a waiter, Chaimowicz, taking thirty-six silver roubles cash and various documents.

Łódź, June 8. The military court sentenced Karol Banaszkiewicz and Szymon Gralaka to death by hanging, accused of a series of robberies.

The same court sentenced Walenty Nowicki to death, accused of wounding a guard, Górniak, with a shot from a revolver.

---

* This article was originally published as "Czarna karta rewolucji," in *Przegląd Socjaldemokratyczny*, Vol. 4, No. 5 (July 1908), pp. 369–74. It is translated from the Polish original by Zachary King.

† In the original "silver roubles" is given as "rs." It likely refers to *rubli srebrem*, the Russian silver roubles still in use in Poland until some point in 1907.

‡ The position was held at the time by Sergei Skalon, who himself survived an assassination attempt by Polish revolutionaries in August 1906.

Łódź, June 9. The military court sentenced Lucjan Zajączkowski, Karol Banaszkiewicz, and Bolesław Warjuk to death, accused of armed robberies.

And thus, the bloody chronicle of sentences and executions goes on forever. The terrible mechanism of the military court and gallows works with automatic rigidity and perseverance. On the map that shows the red marks of counterrevolution, Poland is the bloodiest spot. And all this takes place not only amid the total indifference of Polish bourgeois society, but even with the tacit or audible applause of the bourgeoisie and petty bourgeoisie, who seek refuge from the "plague of banditry" in the arms of the [Nikolai] Kaznakovs and the [Georgi] Skalons.

Casting the stone at banditry, bourgeois society is scared of its own shadow. The capitalist order is based on the constant expropriation of small-scale property, on the ruins of the peasant and artisan economy, on the reserve army of the proletariat, on unemployment and poverty in the broad popular layers and on the blatant social contrast between the idleness of the rich and the poverty of the working class. It produces, apart from the class of the proletariat that maintains society through its labor, a proletarian layer of scoundrels who live by chance by committing crimes against private property.* Capitalism produces theft and looting with the same necessity as it produces surplus value, as by a law of nature. In times of crisis, historical ruptures in bourgeois society, the silent war on the private property of the bourgeoisie breaks out violently on the surface in the form of banditry. The very first steps of capitalism in the historical arena were marked throughout Western Europe by a widespread, rampant outbreak of banditry. Dislodged from its place, a subdued medieval society, loosened ties and social relations, the sudden ruin of millions of small estates brutally stripped of their property and livelihoods by the landed aristocracy—all this was reflected in the unprecedented spread of banditry. During Elizabeth's reign in England, bourgeois society began a bloody crusade against its own shadow, there was draconian legislation against "vagrancy," there were the most savage atrocities against the destitute, branding with a burning iron, cutting off ears, thousands of hangings per year. From England, the bloody trail passes through France, the Netherlands, Italy, everywhere through which capital the conqueror tramples in its march. Society used fire and iron to quell the rebellion against the legal order that protected the sanctity of private property, but in every great social crisis, banditry comes out of thin air as a mass phenomenon. In the Great French Revolution [of 1789–93], it was of enormous proportions in the time of the Directorate. "It is possible," wrote [Albert] Vandal in his work *L'avénement de Bonaparte* [Bonaparte's Accession to the Throne],

---

* Traditionally referred to by Marxists as the lumpenproletariat.

to travel around France from north to south and from west to east without hearing any other conversation than of the "Royalist bandits," of stagecoaches stopped, robbed couriers, and murdered patriots (...) In many villages and towns, only the day belongs to the revolution—to the officials wearing the tricolor sash, to the pompous and despotic platitudes. When night comes, the past's vengeance returns with it: Mysterious shadows appear in the village, the tree of freedom is chopped down or distorted, the Phrygian cap is taken down from the pole (...) The anonymous saber blow takes care of old bills with some local Jacobin; sometimes a whole family is attacked, the head of the family is chopped up with a saber, the women are raped, the house is set on fire and the red glow of the fire illuminates the horizon.*

It is understood that "royalism" was, for the most part, only banditry's signage. A special commission, sent to investigate this scourge in the provincial consulates, found that in some departments, travelers were obliged to secure safe passage from the robber chiefs and buy their way out of being robbed. Coachmen were warned by posters that if they did not carry at least four louis d'or,† they would be shot, something that took place many times. In another area, seventy-four communities armed themselves to defend against bandits and actually waged war on them. The same happened in France and Germany during the Revolution of 1848. Crisis, unemployment, hunger, and banditry—these are the symptoms that have accompanied every revolution. The current proliferation of banditry in the Kingdom and in parts of Russia is therefore only a new and astonishing phenomenon brought forth by the "socialists" for the same bourgeoisie to whom the normal and inseparable symptoms of rule always appear to be anomalies, at least if they are directed against it.

But one feature distinguishes the violent "anarchy" in today's revolution from all previous ones: There has always been a gap between banditry and revolution. Banditry has always been an ally of counterrevolution, not only from its core but also in its outer colors. The short days of the political reign of the proletariat in 1848 and 1871 in Paris were marked by, among other things, blank cards in court records—a complete lack of theft and robbery. It was only with the bourgeoisie's return to power that prostitution and crime returned to Paris like its inseparable shadows. Today the gulf is filled, the border is blurred, the guerrilla war of hooligans against private property has mixed with the class struggle of the workers against the social and political system, the methods of the lumpenproletariat are merging with the action of the revolutionary proletariat; on the defendants' bench in military court, in prison cells, on the gallows, there is no such distinction between today's revolutionary, who dies for the idea

---

* Albert Vandal, *L'avènement de Bonaparte* (Paris: Librairie Plon, 1902).
† A series of coins named after King Louis XIV, who first introduced them in 1640. Four louis d'or is equivalent to about fourteen US dollars today.

of liberating humanity, and the scoundrel, who fell victim to his incompetence by fishing in murky waters and who pointed the barrel of his Browning at a human breast without any hesitation, in order to get "thirty-six silver roubles."

This mixing of groups, unprecedented in the history of revolution—banditry under the flag of the revolution, the lumpenproletariat under the flag of socialism—has changed the character of the drama taking place today within the stone walls of Łódź and the casemates* of Warsaw. Not only a wide river of blood flows down the slopes of the citadel; mud is also streaming down from the places of execution where before only the pure were killed. The terrifying demoralization in the ranks of prisoners, the betrayal and the sale of conscience, becoming a common symptom, gave rise to scenes from hell in the military courts and the grave silence of the execution. Yesterday's "fighters," who point out today to the court dozens of their fighting criminal companions with icy cynicism; yesterday's traitors, thrown by the gendarmes, after being exploited by them, into the cell of those they have betrayed, to be torn apart like Jelonek: desperate attempts at suicide driven by false promises, or tortured into betrayal and regretting their failure ... And, on the other hand, the scenes of terrible parody: that of [Zofia] Owczarkówna in the role of Charlotte Corday†—a naive, simple girl who once helped Wanda Krahelska-[Filipowicz] in an unsuccessful assassination attempt on Skalon‡—and then, with the naivete of a child and without leaving anything out, giving a description of her crime to the spy who presented himself as a lawyer, leading her to the gallows. And, right next to the three young stooges who, in a suburban restaurant, ordering themselves goose, took the leftovers of their feast with them, and shot at the ceiling with Brownings instead of paying, for which they also receive three death sentences. That is why the gloomy picture of the bloody trial of the counterrevolution, with its victims today, despite the terrible number of victims and the constant streams of blood, awakens more disgust than sympathy in wide circles, more pity than reverence and more gloom than enthusiasm.

These are the results of today's insane tactics from social-patriotism—of "expropriation," "partisans," terror, practiced blindly by the PPS for several years despite Social Democracy's constant warnings. And in Russia, there is a

---

* A fortified gun emplacement or armored structure from which guns are fired.

† Corday murdered the great French revolutionary Jean-Paul Marat in July 1793.

‡ On August 18, 1906, twenty-year-old Catholic socialist Krahelska-Filipowicz, seventeen-year-old Albertine Helbertówna of the PPS Combat Organization, and twenty-year-old Owczarkówna tried to assassinate Skalon, the governor-general of Warsaw, by throwing three sticks of dynamite at his coach; two of them did not explode, and Skalon survived. It was one of the few cases in which three young women attempted to assassinate such a prominent Polish official. Krahelska-Filipowicz fled to Austria-Hungary and later became a major figure in Poland's underground resistance to the Nazis, saving scores of Jews from arrest and extermination; she was not charged in the attack and worked for many years as a labor organizer in the garment industry. Owczarkówna and Helbertówna were convicted of the attack and executed in 1908.

party with a similar petty-bourgeois character that adheres to a thick material conception of revolutionary struggle in the form of a Browning and a bomb.* But the instinct of sincere socialists and serious politicians, if not their fundamental position, warned the Russian Socialist Revolutionaries against slipping from terror tactics to the method and tactics of the lumpenproletariat. Only our brainless nationalist utopians, completely lacking the spirit of class struggle, managed to completely mix up the revolutionary tactics of the most mature and revolutionary proletariat with the practice of hooligans. Adventurism when it comes to understanding the tasks and conditions of class struggle, which resulted from the fact that the social-patriots were wading up to their heads in the rags of the "partisan" tradition, with insurgent delusions, combined with a purely mechanical understanding of the means of revolution and hence an overestimation of the technical tools of struggle [such as] financial resources and weapons. And finally, their nationalist position toward the army in Poland— [seeing it] as an alien and hostile element by nature and not as a part of the working people that should be made conscious and won over to the cause of the proletariat—led naturally to this outburst of anarchist tactics in the ranks of the PPS, which soon turned the meaningless shooting of policemen and vodka shop robberies into the main "activity" of a party that calls itself socialist. A further unavoidable result of this "activity" was the specialization of "fighting techniques," the separation of agitation from the party's spiritual focus. Their idealist notion of class struggle had to be followed by lowering the moral and intellectual level of the "fighting" ranks. Such cynicism and moral depravity soon had to arise among the people whose only "revolutionary" craft was the systematic robbery of cash registers and armed robbery, who were used to playing with human life—both their own and others'—coolly, alone, without the elevated moments of class struggle. The party robberies had to be followed by the "fighters'" own robberies, and then the reckless fanfare of exaggerated heroism—until, too often, anyone who could distinguish this sad anarchist harlequinade from the historical drama of proletarian class struggle could have predicted the moral decay toward the specter of the gallows.

Social Democracy's warnings proved to be all too severe in the fate of this party, with its practice of shameful tactics. The PPS collapsed in the Russian Revolution† because it was a nationalist party built on petty-bourgeois traditions and social reaction, not on social development and the resulting class struggle. But history had ruled that the final reason for its collapse, the sword that would bring about its inevitable fate, was the same anarchist tactic that the party itself had led in Poland with the greatest recklessness, to the shame of the

---

* That is, the Social Revolutionary Party, or SRs.

† By "collapse" Luxemburg is referring to the 1906 split in the PPS, which at the time she heralded as spelling its demise. In fact, the PPS lived on and had a larger membership in many of the ensuing years than the Social Democracy of the Kingdom of Poland and Lithuania (SDKPiL).

revolutionary cause. And it will remain a stain on the emblem of this wing of the PPS* that is now trying to break with its entire past as a party, claiming it has developed a critique and doubts about the benefits of terrorist adventures, and made this step not when the cause of the proletariat had been too damaged, but only when the party organism itself, gangrenous with the venom of anarchism, began to disintegrate into pieces.

Terrorists, just like anarchists, exhaust themselves after a time as symptoms of sterile tactics. Social-patriotic experiments in this field will inevitably end in total exhaustion. But the proletariat and the revolution will, unfortunately, continue to feel the effects of these experiments for a long time to come. A continuation of these deviations is the current gloomy drama of execution, the government of gallows throwing the funeral pall into the already-dark era of counterrevolutionary triumph. There cannot be any revolutionary struggle without victims. But every drop of blood shed by the fighters should help to sow the future, a light should stream from every gallows to illuminate the cause of the revolution, to enlighten minds, raise spirits, strengthen faith in victory. The victims who die today in the dozens on the slopes of the Citadel and in the casemates of Łódź for banditry and for terrorist attacks are victims who went to waste, blood spilled in vain. The repulsive drama of these victims of political madness is only capable of causing confusion and doubt in the popular circles that are not yet conscious.

Hence the strict obligation of the revolutionary proletariat to settle its accounts with the whole attraction to the tactics of anarchist adventurism. From the present phase of counterrevolutionary triumph, our proletariat should emerge hardened by political experience, thoroughly cleansed of anarchist tendencies. For Social Democracy, on the other hand, the task is once again to erect the border walls and ramparts partially destroyed or ruined by social-patriotism that stood between the camp of the fighting working class and the scum of bourgeois society, between the tactics of revolution and the method of the lumpenproletariat.

The future resumption of the revolutionary attack must find a "house tidied of its rubbish," and the sad victims who are dying today by the dozens at the hands of the tsarist hangman should at least find the reward that with their blood they will cleanse the revolutionary ranks of one of its most fatal political mistakes.

The black card in the history of the revolution, filled with the history of this mistake and its victims, is, once again, the historical legacy of nationalism, whose ultimate function is to be—in its conservative tendency—a counterrevolutionary saber and a pillar of Russian Empire; while, in its "revolutionary" tendency, this function is a scandal and a disgrace to the revolutionary camp.

---

* That is, the PPS-Left.

Speech about May Day as a Day of Working-Class Struggle*

At the Mannheim Party Congress,† when the question of cooperation with the trade unions was examined in all its aspects, and ways and means were sought to be able to achieve the inevitably necessary close cooperation in the interests of both branches of the workers' movement, I was among those comrades who least expected a fruitful collaboration, through close communication and a reaching of agreements, between the senior organizational heads of both branches of the workers' movement that would indeed become binding for either branch. I believe that after the first two important attempts at collaboration under this dualist system that we have now experienced, our previous fears have been fully confirmed.

These two discouraging attempts are May Day and the youth organization [of the party]. The question of May Day has rightly been debated at all German party congresses. This perfectly corresponds to the colossal significance of the situation for our workers' movement. However, only recently a whole new aspect has been thrown into consideration, one that could have calamitous consequences for the cause of May Day: the question of support. When we in the German delegation reached the decision in Stuttgart‡ that the party is also prepared to participate in supporting the May Day victims, this was only intended to accord with the purpose and spirit of the agreement that the party wishes to do everything in its power to build up the celebration of May Day in a manner that affords it as much honor as possible. In practice, the question of support very quickly proved to be a noose that may strangle the May Day celebrations if we do not resolve this issue in an appropriate way as soon as possible.

Comrade [Richard] Fischer has said that he cannot grasp the logic of advocating the idea that the solution to the question of support would reduce the impact and spread of May Day. On the contrary, he says that by taking measures to support the bravest and most courageous victims of the May Day celebrations, rather than leaving them by the wayside, we are ensuring a worthy celebration of it. I see no logic on Fischer's part. The party executive and the General Commission are completely right to declare: "We may have found a

---

* This speech was first published in *Protokoll über die Verhandlungen des Parteitages der Sozialdemokratischen Partei Deutschlands abgehalten zu Nürnberg vom 13. Bis 19. September 1908* (Protocol of the Congress of the Social Democratic Party of Germany Held at Nuremberg) (September 13–19, 1908) (Berlin: Buchhandlung Vorwärts, 1908), pp. 267–9. It is translated by Manuela Kölke from Luxemburg's *Gesammelte Werke*, Vol. 2, pp. 256–9.

† The Party Congress of German Social Democracy in Mannheim took place from September 23 to 29, 1906. For Luxemburg's comments at the Congress, see above, pp. 263–7.

‡ The International Socialist Congress in Stuttgart took place from August 18 to 24, 1907.

wrong solution to the question of support, now please give us a better one and we will adopt it, up to now we have not found a better solution." I maintain that a total resolution to the question of support—in the sense that the May Day celebrations become ever more prevalent and all the victims are effectively supported—cannot be found at all. ("Quite right!") Therein lies the noose, which will strangle May Day if we continue to engage in identifying all possible combinations in order to regulate support in such a way that all victims are properly looked after while the May Day celebrations continue to be strengthened. The previous practice of celebrating May Day, not only in Germany but in all other countries, has shown that there is only one way to prevent people from becoming victims of the May Day celebration. That does not consist of some kind of regulation of support, but rather of the most possible expansion of the May Day celebrations. Only when the number of people celebrating becomes so huge that it becomes impossible to impose disciplinary measures, only when the real power of the class-conscious, organized fighters of the working class is set against entrepreneurship with all its force, only then does [the latter] not dare to carry out disciplinary measures against us. (Dissent and agreement.)

We have experiences that confirm this at every turn. (Interjection: "Where then?") I ask you to take a look at a country where the workers are cut from exactly the same cloth as the German workers, Russian Poland. (Dissent.) This year again we had a May Day celebration in Warsaw, which is unique in the world. All the factory workers celebrated. That did not happen at the peak of the revolution, when all spirits were flying high. For a long time now, there has been a decline, a certain stagnation of the revolution, of the revolutionary movement in Russia and Russian Poland. We see a terrible economic depression, a colossal spiritual depression, and yet despite all of that, May Day was celebrated on a massive scale. And precisely for this reason, just as in the past, the disciplinary measures for the May Day celebrations have been minimal this year. Exactly the same experience has been had in Germany. I believe it was a payment office of Berlin woodworkers this year that concluded exactly the same thing in a meeting after the May Day celebrations, namely that only the greatest-possible expansion of the number of people celebrating will prevent disciplinary measures against the masses of people celebrating. That is why we would be going down a very wrong road if we really wished to overly concern ourselves with the question that has been thrown at us—of how to support those joining the celebrations. Fischer himself has involuntarily shown how hopeless it is to go down this path by saying: "You are all dissatisfied with the arrangement made so far that the local organizations want to support those affected by fines—but who else should support them? The central party treasury does not exist for that, but for political purposes."

[Fischer continues,] "We are unable to cover these colossal sacrifices. For their part, the central associations (of the trade unions) also declare that they must keep their funds available for other struggles, and who should pay for the costs of support?" In this way, it is clear that neither one nor the other can find a satisfactory solution to the question of support. The only solution, regardless of this or that support arrangement, is to promote the idea of May Day with all our might, and not in the timid, unenthusiastic spirit that the Party Executive Committee and the General Commission have displayed in the last year. ("Quite right!" and dissent.) The latter is precisely the way in which the victims of the May Day celebrations increase, for this timidity on the part of the leading authorities of the workers' movement gives the employers and their associations the courage to counter our struggles with disciplinary measures. We have all the more reason to insist with the utmost ferocity on propagating the idea of May Day with full force, without being tangled up in all sorts of minor details such as the question of support, as we will most likely face serious struggles. In Germany, not only have the May Day celebrations, it must be said in light of previous experiences, not yet shown what they can actually achieve, but they still have a promising future ahead of them. In order to advance toward this future, we now have every reason to insist with all force that the concept of celebrating May Day be propagated by us in all its purity, and with all our might. (Applause.)

1909

May 1 and the Class Struggle*

The first of May, which we are celebrating for the twentieth time this year, takes place in the midst of an apparent peace.

Once again, the bourgeois world considers the foundations of its rule to be absolutely secure. Has it not just chased away the stormy clouds of war by diplomatic miracles?† Isn't the grandiose Russian Revolution on the ground, bloodied, smashed, and oppressed under the boot of the triumphant reaction? War and revolution, these grim shadows of fate, are banished—for now. Bourgeois society sees itself again a master of its own destiny, and of the millions of people it forces to kowtow. The aspirations of the proletarians in both worlds,‡ the ideal of socialism, the foolish dream of a society created by free and equal people—how distant this seems to the honest bourgeoisie, which believes that it holds the reins of the world firmly in its hands!

But a shadow clouds this picture. This is the threatening shadow of an *economic crisis*. Hundreds of thousands, one could say millions of workers without work in America and Europe are demanding bread that capitalist society is unable to provide. This crisis, which for years has been gnawing away the social body like an invisible disease, cannot be overcome by any diplomatic *cunning*, nor by a coup de main. It follows every revolution, every modern war, like a shadow, and also lays its black veil over the celebrations of May Day. This is the watertight proof that the victory over war and revolution allegedly won by bourgeois society is only a false appearance, that security and peace of mind are nothing but a superimposed pretense.

In the night of misery born out of the crises of capitalism, ghosts arise announcing that inexorable destiny that was already looming in the early days of the capitalist era.§

---

* - This article was published first in *Le Socialisme* (Paris), No. 74, May 1, 1909. It is translated by Manuela Kölke and Olivier Surel from the republication of the French original in *Rosa Luxemburg: Le Socialisme en France. Œuvres complètes—Tome III*. Édition établie et préfacée par Jean-Numa Ducange (Marseille and Toulouse: Agone, 2013), pp. 265–7.

† In October 1908, Austria-Hungary annexed the territories of Bosnia and Herzegovina, which it had previously administered, thereby exacerbating the already-tense relations with Serbia. The German government had supported Austria-Hungary and forced Russia to recognize the annexation. This act led to the further isolation of Germany and Austria-Hungary as the Entente Powers united more closely. Italy, which had a secret agreement with Russia in October 1908 to stand up for neutrality and preservation of the status quo in the Balkans and in return had been given a free hand by Russia for the conquest of Tripoli and Cyrenaica, moved away from the Triple Alliance.

‡ It is unclear what exactly Luxemburg is referring to with "two worlds," but it could be a reference to the Old World and the New World—that is, Europe and America or, more precisely, France and the United States.

§ Luxemburg has in mind the events of January 21, 1908, when numerous meetings and demonstrations of the unemployed took place in Berlin and Magdeburg. There were clashes with the police and arrests. In Berlin, 12,000 people took part in nine events.

The class struggle, the source of the crises that tears bourgeois society apart and that will inevitably bring about its downfall, has left a trail of blood throughout the history of a whole century. This struggle was already vaguely taking shape in the great turmoil of the French Revolution [of 1789–93]. It appeared in black letters on the banners of the insurgent silk workers of Lyon, who revolted out of hunger, and who in 1834 cried out: "Live working or die fighting!"* It rekindled the red flames of the torches lit by the English Chartists in 1830 and 1840. It rose like a pillar of fire from the terrible massacre of June 1848 in Paris. It cast its purple spark on the capital of France in the movement of 1871, when the victorious bourgeois scoundrel took revenge on the heroes of the Commune with the lethal fire of the machine guns.

It is precisely this atmosphere of class struggle—a struggle that will only end with the complete collapse of the capitalist world—that dominates the worldwide celebration of May Day.

It is the gentle season of spring, nonviolent demonstrations, peaceful gatherings, joyful excursions with women and children. What a sight of deep peacefulness! What an idyll! The terror of the bourgeoisie, who trembled behind closed shutters before the demonstration of May 1, 1890, has vanished!† The first of May has come. It has passed. The world remained the same. And the next day the bourgeoisie woke up with a sigh of relief, with the contented smile of people who have escaped a natural disaster that had been forecast. Bourgeois fear has turned into arrogance, into revenge, as always. To thank the proletariat for the order and peace on May Day, the bourgeoisie let the whip of hunger and retaliation crack on their bent back.

A peaceful May 1! But could May Day be something other than that annual *memento mori*, the words "Brother, we must die"‡ whispered by the working classes of both worlds into the ears of the bourgeoisie? Gentle May 1! But could it be something other than the parade of mortal enemies, of the gravediggers of the capitalist system? Idyllic May Day—idyll of slaves!—is it anything other

---

* The silk weavers of Lyon rose in April 1834 under the leadership of secret organizations advocating the elimination of hunger and misery and the establishment of a social republic. Parisian workers followed their example. After fierce barricade fighting, the insurgents were defeated by the military.

† The International Congress of Workers, the founding congress of the Second International, which met in Paris from July 14 to 20, 1889, called for the abolition of standing armies and declared "peace as the first and indispensable condition of any workers'" emancipation. It called for international labor protection legislation, in particular the eight-hour workday, the prohibition of child labor, and measures to protect youth and women, and encouraged workers to fight for democratic rights. It decided to organize rallies in its member countries on May 1, 1890. In Germany, some 200,000 workers responded by going on strike.

‡ "Frère, il faut mourir." This expression seems to have gained autonomy in mid-nineteenth century France. Its most well-known mention is in Gustave Flaubert's *Dictionnaire des idées reçues*, in the entry entitled "Chartreux": "Chartreux: Passent leur temps à faire de la chartreuse, à creuser leur tombe et à dire: 'Frère, il faut mourir.'"

than the annual call to the numerous and ever-growing armies to remain with arms at the ready, with dry powder, to gather around the banner of the revolution? The peaceful rural delights of the exploited, of the overwrought! But is all this anything other than the repeated oath of millions of fighters not to stop the struggle as long as even one stone of the fortress of exploitation and slavery remains? *Eight-hour day—world peace—brotherhood of nations*! These are the death sentences against a society based on unlimited exploitation, theft of territories, and hatred of nations.

The goal of May Day is a resounding declaration of war, a merciless war against this society, pronounced by millions, echoing all over the globe.

In this international unity of our movement lies the guarantee that our troops will no longer be defeated in this heroic but unequal struggle; never again will they be isolated as those in June [1848] and in the Commune, or as the glorious fighters of Petersburg, Warsaw, and Moscow.

May Day is the worldwide celebration of labor, the annual commemoration of the glorious revolutionary struggles of the modern proletariat; it continues this tradition and solemnly proclaims the truth that one day the hour will come when not only isolated detachments of the proletariat from different nations, but the proletariat of all countries, will rise in common struggle to cast off the abhorrent yoke of capitalism.

Revolutionary Hangover*

I.

History has not coddled the proletariat of Russia. Under the rapacious, absolute reign of the counterrevolution, it has become impossible for the people to stage open protest, and the work of revolution has been driven underground. The last remaining "legal" means of class struggle is to send proletarian Social Democratic envoys to the state Duma. The Duma podium is the last place where Social Democrats can voice the rallying cries of class struggle with even moderate freedom. At this podium it has also become clear, however, that the particular envoys who are currently legally representing the proletariat are not up to the task. They have blundered on more than one occasion. They have often made insufficient systematic use of the Duma platform to give voice to the rallying cries of class struggle, to critique bourgeois parties for their part in the revolution and for their counterrevolutionary games, and to build up the working masses politically. This platform has even frequently become a stage where proletarian envoys dither indecisively, and this dithering has made a consistent plan of political action impossible and has often simply stood in contradiction to the demands of proletarian tactics. If one were to take these facts at face value and assess the situation on the surface, one could say that the current representation of Social Democrats in the Duma is simply a sad state of affairs. But such an axiomatic statement is easier to make than it is useful. Because what is also sad and revealing is that the imperfections of our representation in the Duma have caused a certain current to flow through the party ranks, culminating in either open or covert proposals to recall the Social Democratic delegation as the only way out of a nasty situation. The delegation has shown through its operations in the Third Duma how ineffectively it serves as the weapon of the class struggle, and thus it should be recalled.† This is how some of our Russian comrades make decisions. In posing the question of recall, they effectively equate their touching simplicity and categorical political reasoning with true revolutionary strength and spirit. Unfortunately, or perhaps fortunately, proletarian politics do not get their revolutionary quality from such oversimplified methods of reasoning. On the contrary, in this case as in all others, such politics first require analysis of the

---

    * This essay was first published as "Rewolucyjny katzenjammer," in *Przegląd Socjaldemokratyczny*, Vol. 5, No. 11 (May 1909), pp. 14–24. It appeared simultaneously in Russian translation in *Proletary*, the journal of the Petersburg and Moscow Committees of the RSDRP. It is translated from the Polish original by Joseph Muller.
    † This was the position articulated by a faction of the Bolsheviks, the Otzovists (or recallists), who argued that the RSDRP should cease to participate in any institution of the tsarist state, including the Duma. Among its leaders were Alexander Bogdanov and Anatoly Lunacharsky. Lenin sharply opposed their position, as did Luxemburg.

objective conditions of the struggle of the proletariat, exposition of the dialectical relations that contain the real source of difficulty that Social Democracy has happened upon, and an effective way to extricate oneself from the difficulty.

The question of how the Social Democratic contingent should operate in the Third Duma can be examined from two perspectives: from the point of view of the personal competencies of the representatives, including the ineffectiveness of their speeches; or from the point of view of the objective conditions that are probably making it impossible to use real proletarian tactics in the Third Duma.

Let us begin by looking at the matter from the first perspective. It must be said that the individual composition of a parliamentary delegation means something different for bourgeois parties than for the party of the conscious proletariat, as it should, given the fundamental differences in how the former and latter relate to the parliamentary system. Since the bourgeois parties base their political struggle on a desire to implement certain legal directives and occupy positions in government, they see a parliament as a focused mechanism for political change and a center of political confrontation, and thus the personal merits and faults of the delegation have enormous significance for them. As a place where every type of transaction can take place between the government and the parties—ranging from short-term machinations to industrial pacts in which they milk the economic situation in pursuit of the bright clink of coin in their hands—a bourgeois parliament is a wonderful arena for the personal talents of party leaders. Yet in such a parliament, personal qualities are also constrained by the objective limits of purely "material" circumstances, in that the power or impotence of a bourgeois party is not determined by the individual qualities of its parliamentary leaders. On the contrary, a party's general political standing throughout the country, as well as the influence or ineffectiveness it garners as a result of its class character and primary political trajectory, set the stage for the talents or ineptitudes of its parliamentary representatives.

Thus, in the Center Party, the Catholic party in Germany, the era of persecution of Catholics by [Otto von] Bismarck saw a remarkable leader in [Ludwig] Windthorst, but when the party became a mainstay of the governing reaction, Windthorst was replaced by mediocre figures such as [Julius] Bachem. Similarly, eminent figures such as [Johann] Jacoby were fixtures at the forefront of German liberalism when it was militant and oppositional, but now that it has fallen deep into the muck of "bloc" politics, a handful of complete nobodies fill the liberal seats in the German Parliament. On the other hand, in Russia, while the Cadets possess an array of [persons of] unquestionably formidable parliamentary abilities, the internal hopelessness and bankruptcy of their party make that array into something tragicomically superfluous, luridly emphasizing their pitiful state. Meanwhile, the Duma is ruled by the fervent boosters of a particularly foul type of idiocy—[Vladimir] Purishkevich.

The situation is somewhat different for the party of the proletariat. Because the proletariat sees parliamentary action merely as one of many weapons in the fight between the classes, it does not primarily direct all its efforts to achieving immediate, tangible benefits in the form of small legal gains, but instead uses every opportunity it has in the parliament to explain its class interests and demands. The Social Democratic parliamentary delegation and its operations therefore merely reflect the political consciousness of the foremost layer of the proletariat, and the excellence of that delegation should be viewed in terms of the fullness and exactness of its reflection and expression of the spirit and meaning of the proletarian class struggle throughout the country. The individual means and talents of various parliamentary actors have a much-smaller role to play in Social Democracy than in bourgeois parties.

Except for the improvised actions and behaviors of each individual, the parliamentary tactics of the Social Democratic delegation are structured in advance according to a framework of theoretical and tactical class-struggle principles, which are formed in every country by a conscious and organized representative of the proletariat—that is, a Social Democratic *party*. By reason of having been appointed, Social Democratic envoys are merely the heralds and executors of the tactics determined by the party of the proletariat as a whole, with the greatest-possible level of involvement and direction from the working masses. That is why, leaving aside the minor question of whether someone performs less or more nimbly on a given day in the parliament, the tactics of proletarian envoys cannot by nature be the business of the parliamentary circle alone, either in general or in specific cases, and must be the business of the party as a whole. German Social Democracy has pursued a set of parliamentary tactics to this level of specificity for forty years, such that they have become routine and may be carried out almost mechanically, according to traditions and opinions firmly rooted among the party ranks, by nearly any envoy.

Nevertheless, two conditions are necessary to achieve the level of predetermined tactical uniformity that would oblige Social Democratic envoys to behave in accordance with the party's wishes: Equilibrium must be achieved among both the political relations and the class relations of a state; and the principles of the party of the proletariat must be unified, firmly established, and stabilized over time. While German Social Democracy can still serve as a classic example of the presence of these two conditions, the French socialism of the era of the [Alexandre] Millerand crisis* can serve as a more or less classic example of their absence, demonstrating how an internal split in the party's organization

---

* The crisis was initiated by the decision of Millerand, a French socialist, to join the cabinet of conservative René Waldeck-Rousseau in 1899, in response to the threats to the French Republic posed by the campaign against Dreyfus. Luxemburg sharply criticized Millerand's actions in "The Socialist Crisis in France," published in 1900 and 1901. See *Rosa Luxemburg Speaks*, edited by Mary-Alice Waters (New York: Pathfinder Press, 1975), pp. 91–105.

and principles immediately becomes manifest in the unsteadiness of socialist envoys, and in their isolation and individualization from the party that is supposed to be their body. From each case can be drawn a convincing conclusion about the very essence of proletarian parliamentary action—namely, that *each socialist party possesses exactly the parliamentary delegation accorded to it* by external and internal conditions.

These two essential preconditions for consistent Social Democratic parliamentary tactics are clearly lacking in Russia. While Social Democracy's parliamentary actions in the Second Duma were buoyed up for a time by the last waves of mass revolutionary insurrection, when the waters subsided, things took a bleak turn. An unsteady political balance ensued because the counterrevolution began a state of siege, the positions of class and party forces shifted constantly, and most of all, the Third Duma took on an entirely peculiar nature as neither a legislative parliament nor indeed a weapon of revolutionary action. This has made it quite impossible to adopt any kind of common practice and has demanded, given the total lack of parliamentary traditions in Russia, that one work spontaneously and creatively to apply the principles and goals of class struggle to the specific conditions of each situation. However, if these barriers merely make it obvious that such creative work must too be the concern of the party of the proletariat, then it must be said that the party life of Social Democracy in Russia leaves much to be desired in this respect, on a number of points. First, there is no strong, cohesive organizational nucleus that could serve even somewhat adequately as a surrogate for the open, direct influence of the working masses on their representatives in the Duma; such a nucleus has been impossible under the counterrevolution's rule of white terror. Furthermore, even the elements of organization that do exist are undermined by constant, unrestrained infighting, which some people—as far as one can gather from the press—have taken to the point of openly calling for the dissolution of their own party.* Many Russian comrades are highly indignant over the "insubordination" of the Duma faction toward the party's principal authority, the Central Committee. Yet they are simultaneously utterly resigned to a number of other facts: that this highest party authority calmly refers to itself in party publications as "a small group of people managing the official authorities of the party"; that in defiance of formal party unity, as if in mockery of it, open, fierce fighting between factions, albeit not formally organized, courses through the long-term framework of the party, unmistakably aimed against the party as a whole; that the question of Duma tactics is itself made into an object of the infighting; and

---

* A reference to the Liquidationists, a tendency within the Mensheviks that argued for dismantling the RSDRP's underground apparatus and devoting itself exclusively to participating in such legal institutions as the Duma. The main voice of the Liquidationists was the journal *Nacha Zariia* (Our Charge), edited by longtime Menshevik leader Alexander Potretsov. Its position was sharply opposed by Plekhanov, Martov, and other Menshevik leaders.

that one segment of the party thinks its sacred duty is to defend and explain the behavior of the faction that drew such deserved criticism from the other segment of the party. These comrades obviously do not realize how deeply they have fallen into a none-too-original paradox. Five or six years ago, the French socialists complained without ceasing about their parliamentary envoys' systematic betrayal of party principles and their stubborn disobedience to central institutions. But their complaints were invalidated by the image of organizational and fundamental rifts in the ranks of the socialist proletariat in France. Similarly, the advice from Russian comrades that the Duma faction absolutely must be castigated immediately and thoroughly through the use of an "ultimatum"* essentially amounts to advice to let the party play the role of the widow of Poshliopkina in [Nikolai] Gogol's *The Inspector General*—that is, to whip itself.†

Special perspicacity is not needed, put simply, for one to realize that the above-outlined state of Russian Social Democracy is far from an accidental phenomenon. The organizational confusion reigning within it derives primarily from the force of counterrevolutionary pressure, hindering the movements of the proletariat and warping the normal forms and functions of its party life. Furthermore, these factional troubles are embedded to a certain extent in the common conditions of Social Democracy's development. Since the matter thus presents itself, those comrades who wish to frighten the Duma faction and force them to improve through an "ultimatum" should redirect their energies. Rather than focus on an ominous "ultimatum," they should turn to the objective conditions of Russian social life that currently prevent Social Democracy from becoming a powerful and unified organization of the working class and thereby prompting the parliamentary faction, according to the natural order of things, to come into its true role—[that of] an obedient instrument in the hands of the conscious proletariat.

II.

On the other hand, those who negatively evaluated the actions of the Duma delegation, giving rise to the idea of recalling the delegation, had a generally peculiar comprehension of the tactical goals of the proletariat with regard to the Third Duma. In resolutions drawn up in Moscow and Petersburg, supporters of a recall quite clearly expressed the view that to use the Third Duma

---

* A reference to the Ultimatists, a faction of the Bolsheviks that insisted that an ultimatum be sent to the Bolshevik representatives in the Duma demanding that they make no compromises on any issue with the government or other parties.

† In Gogol's play, Poshliopkina is the wife of a locksmith who begs a low-level government official to take measures against a governor for having forced her husband to be drafted into the army.

as a platform to agitate in the spirit and principle of class struggle would be absolutely impossible because of external conditions. They wrote, "Getting out of the present situation requires that Social Democratic envoys hand in their mandates, which will emphasize both the true character of the Duma and the revolutionary tactics of the Russian Social Democratic Labor Party." Here an issue of individuals—a question of how to evaluate the actions of a given Social Democratic delegation—is transported into the domain of an unquestionably more general and fundamental tactical matter: whether the conscious proletariat should boycott the Duma. Logically, recalling the Duma delegation would indeed come down to boycotting the Duma, at least for as long as the electoral law of June 3/16* and its repositioning of forces in the Duma remain in place. A boycott, as a simple *exodus* of Social Democratic envoys, is recommended only as a truly "revolutionary" tactic in the face of a counterrevolution ruling the Third Duma. By comparison, the authors of this newest "revolutionary" idea must acknowledge that originality is not one of its strengths, and after all is said and done, it cannot be said to have taxed their mental faculties overmuch. In fact, their newest recipe for proletarian radicalism blatantly rehashes the boycott catchphrase employed during the first Duma election, a catchphrase that kept much of its charm in the Second Duma election and was even brandished by some comrades on the eve of the Third. But the current circumstances are the freshest example of this crude, vulgar understanding of proletarian revolutionism, which boils down to an outward appearance, to a couple of short, hollow clichés, avoiding the work of investigating the relationship between the militant tactics of the proletariat and living, changeable reality.

"Boycott" by itself is an abstract catchphrase applicable in any situation; there is nothing particularly revolutionary about it, and it can even be an expression of a completely different nature. In the Revolution of 1848 in Germany, as a result of the weak, equivocal, betrayal-ridden behavior of the bourgeoisie for six months, the unavoidable end came in the form of a state coup on November 1. The [Ernst von] Pfuel cabinet was dissolved,† and the openly reactionary feudal cabinet of Count [Friedrich] Brandenburg was formed.‡ In response to absolutism's coup, the stupefied National Assembly proclaimed a boycott of the government as a way to mount "passive resistance." In opposition to this rallying call from the bourgeoisie, *Neue Rheinische Zeitung* [The New Rhenish Newspaper], then published by Karl Marx, immediately proclaimed the need for a series of direct actions in the Rhineland with the goal of supporting the

---

* According to the Old (Julian) and New (Gregorian) calendars, respectively.

† The Pfuel cabinet, in which he served as prime minister and war minister of Prussia, was dissolved in October 1848, only a few months after coming into existence. Pfuel was instrumental in violently suppressing the uprising in Poznań during the 1848 Revolution.

‡ Brandenburg was an arch-reactionary who succeeded Pfuel as prime minister in November 1848. He was directly responsible for dissolving the National Assembly.

National Assembly. They ranged from refusal to pay taxes to the creation of revolutionary committees, and the paper added, "Wherever counterrevolutionary powers attempt to hamper the formation or operation of these committees, violence must be opposed with violence of any form. *Passive resistance must have active resistance as its foundation. Otherwise it is like the resistance of a calf against the butcher.*"*

In other words, Marx thought that an instant transformation would be necessary to turn the passive resistance announced by the German bourgeoisie in response to the coup into a series of directives leading proletarians to plunge themselves into a street revolution.† But the German bourgeoisie in 1848 feared a street revolution and independent proletarian fighting even more than absolutism and the feudal party connected to it, so it laid down its arms before absolutism. Members of the bourgeoisie were determined to fixate on the catchphrase "passive resistance," since they had decided that not for all the world would they appeal to the intervention of the folk masses. Thus, Marx's November appeal remained a voice crying out in the wilderness, much as the rest of his politics during the 1848 Revolution. There were no revolutionary disturbances in response to the provocation of the counterrevolution, and the famed "passive resistance" of the German bourgeoisie ended the way "the resistance of the calf before the butcher" always ends: The liberal calf was mercilessly slaughtered by the absolutist butcher.

In fact, it is no secret even to the bourgeoisie that passive resistance must be connected to active, militant resistance to be a true weapon in political struggles. The bourgeoisie also advances in unison with the spirit of the Marxist rallying cry of 1848 whenever permitted by its class interests and levels of antagonism toward the proletariat. Another historical example of the use of passive resistance can be found in the political struggles of the Czech nationalists who boycotted the central Austrian state parliament for fifteen years. After being jolted awake by [the battles of] Magenta and Solferino,‡ Austrian absolutism decided to return to the path of "legal order" and recommended [Anton von] Schmerling's centralized constitution for the country.§ The Czech nationalists, demanding a federal system, refused to elect ministers from the Czech Sejm to

---

* See Marx's "A Decree of Eichmann's" (November 18, 1848), in *Marx-Engels Collected Works*, Vol. 8, p. 38: "*Passive* resistance must have *active* resistance as its basis. *Otherwise it will resemble the vain struggle of a calf against its slaughter.*"

† See Marx's "The Crisis in Berlin," originally published in the November 5, 1848, issue of the *Neue Rheinische Zeitung*, in *Marx-Engels Collected Works*, Vol. 8, p. 3: "The *greater right* is on the side of the *greater might*. Might is tested in *struggle*, The test of the struggle is *victory*. Each of the two powers can prove it is right only by its victory, that it is wrong only by its *defeat*."

‡ In these two battles of the Second Italian War of Independence in 1859 between the Austrians and a Franco-Sardinian alliance, the Austrians were decisively defeated.

§ In 1860, Schmerling became interior minister of the Austrian Empire and promoted a new constitution that would greatly centralize power at the expense of such national minorities as the Czechs, Croats, and Hungarians. His effort to Germanize the empire failed after a few years.

the central parliament in Vienna, insisting on this position until 1878, when they won broad concessions from the [Eduard] Taaffe cabinet.* To be sure, their reactionary ideal of federation† was not realized; in fact, the political development of Austria pushed it bit by bit into utopian obscurity. They did achieve other, unquestionably more concrete, concessions, including a new law governing elections to the national Sejm, a recognition of the Czech language as a legally binding state language, a Czech university, and so forth. Yet Czech politics of this era encompassed more than just the boycott of the parliament in Vienna. Soon after the boycott was declared, a current of wide-reaching, tumultuous agitation spread throughout the country. Unafraid to attend the movement's mass meetings under the familiar flag of nationalist, class-antagonism-blurring mystification, the Czechs tried with all their might to ground their "passive resistance" against the parliament on the active resistance of the impassioned folk masses. And the nationalist campaign did not lack support in the highest circles of society, as can be seen in the declaration of a state of siege in Bohemia in 1868; the numerous arrests and bloody clashes with the police and the army in the seventies; the later series of clashes in the 1890s, when Czechs renewed their military activities; the well-known *Omladina* trial,‡ in which members of the movement were sentenced to draconian punishments for "conspiracy"; and finally, the proclamation of martial law in Prague in 1897. In essence, Czechs could not call a revolution in the feeble and reactionary name of nationalism, even though they certainly succeeded in transforming passive resistance against the parliament into the active resistance of the nation.

In revolutionary proletarian politics, worked out in advance to closely follow the autonomous actions of the masses, a boycott of parliament can only be an episode in the course of active mass struggle. Some comrades see the boycott of the First Duma, which was proclaimed at that time by a majority of Social Democrats across the state, as a revolutionary tactic par excellence precisely because it was a boycott. They want to resurrect such tactics as soon as possible, even immediately. In their view of boycott, they have something in common

---

* Czech nationalists refused to take part in the Austrian Parliament for many years, largely because Austrian liberals as well as conservatives refused to accept them as equal partners in the empire. This changed in 1878 when Taaffe conceded some limited powers to the Czechs.

† Luxemburg viewed the demand for a federal system as "reactionary" on the grounds that it strengthened nationalist tendencies and weakened the bonds connecting the working class in the multiethnic empire. Many Austro-Marxists, on the other hand, endorsed demands for a federal structure as an alternative to the suppression of minority rights and the possible breakup of Austria-Hungary.

‡ *Omladina* was the name of a Czech journal connected to the radical wing of the nationalist movement, which included many socialists. The Austrian government used the murder in 1893 of police informer Rudolf Mrva to arrest seventy-six young activists associated with the journal, charging them with crimes ranging from public disorder to high treason and revolutionary activities. Two working-class members of *Omladina* were charged with the actual murder. Their convictions ushered in a period of intense repression.

with the fiercest opponents of boycott, those who reject it always and everywhere as a mortal sin against the sacred dogma of the parliamentary system.

In neither case does anyone pay attention to the concrete political conditions that made the boycott of the Duma a fundamental duty, even a point of honor, for the revolutionary proletariat.

The entire year 1905, from the beginning to the end, was an era of mass struggle of the proletariat and, at the same time, a rising revolutionary tide. After January 22, when workers in Petersburg gave the signal, the current of revolution grew ever broader, surging through an unbroken series of strikes and army and navy uprisings to a general strike in October, and finally to an uprising in Moscow. Responding to the steady intensification of the revolutionary fight, the internal logic of the struggle developed quickly and vigorously. The common weapon of the first period of revolution—the mass strike—brought the struggle to its zenith by November. The practical effects of this measure were exhausted in the October Days, revealing its limits, so the struggle encountered a short pause, only to shift in the next moment, through the force of internal dialectics, to a new, necessary result of mass proletarian action—open street warfare. The uprising in Moscow was, on the one hand, a critique of the first period of the revolution and, on the other, a transition in the revolution—a shift from preliminary maneuvers on the battlefield with absolutism to the battle's essential Gordian knot, revealing the revolution through its development into a final struggle for political power. The Moscow uprising was the beginning and the rallying cry of the second period of the revolution, much as the uprising of January 22 in Petersburg had been the rallying cry of the first. The revolution was set to go through a full period of further growth in breadth and depth through the experience of open street battles with the old authorities, much as it had during the strikes from January to October. The Petersburg strike had sent out waves in larger and larger circles, like growing rumbles of thunder, building into a storm of common economic conflict that gripped Russia from end to end, churned up social spheres across the country, and awakened the entire proletariat. So too the Moscow uprising should have metamorphosed into a series of gigantic uprisings exploding everywhere that, by the definitive strength of their own logic, would have matured internally and concentrated themselves into common working-class uprisings aimed at open struggle. These uprisings would have led the matter of revolution to its end—that is, they would have destroyed the old power and cleared the ground for a new political system. The Moscow uprising "should have" been a rallying cry for a series of others—to the extent the revolution was to unfurl further, advance, and keep its position in line with its goal. It is clear that the Moscow uprising by itself, in isolation, could not possibly end in victory. Yet it is also clear that the historic role the Moscow uprising played in the fate of the revolution as a whole [did as little to ensure] its outward success as the nearly bloodless outward defeat of the Petersburg march of January 22 [did to prevent] that event from becoming the day on which a great revolution was born. Would the defeat of the Moscow uprising become a call to advance the revolution or a call for absolutism to eradicate the revolutionary movement? That was the question that stood before the proletariat after the December crisis. The answer would decide the fate of the revolution for years to come. This moment was a crossroads in the path of the revolution.

The answer came in the form of the calling of the First Duma, condemning the revolution to defeat. The Duma was a parody of representation by the people and legislation by representatives. All real political power remained in the hands of absolutism, and the first attempt to wrest that power away had just ended in the defeat of the proletariat. By nature, such a Duma could only be a maneuver of the counterrevolution, a fort under whose protection the old powers could take time to rebuild their damaged batteries and close ranks. Were the proletariat to allow such a Duma to assemble, and were they to participate in it, that would have been to take part personally in liquidation, to call individual defeat total defeat, to treat the reaction's victory over the Moscow uprising as a victory over revolution, to halt the forward movement of the revolutionary struggle, and to start a retreat down the whole line.

Those politicians who have exchanged their initial role of advance guard leading the proletarian troops into battle for the far more comfortable role of "historians" of their own movement, historians possessed of twenty-twenty hindsight, point out self-assuredly that subsequent events proved the emptiness of the hope in further occurrences of mass uprising after the defeat in Moscow. And the course of the revolution was indeed upended, and the revolution was indeed destined to a long season of finding other ways to fight and leading an underground social life—a season of mustering the energy while underground to resume the subversive activity of distinguishing between classes and amassing new explosive material for future outbreaks. Without a doubt, such a turn could not have been prevented by Social Democracy, whatever its tactics. But those in the vanguard of the revolutionary army were completely correct in their judgments of the internal logic of the struggle, of the preconditions for its further development. At the turning point, they took every action they should have taken to stop the advances made from being undone. They endeavored to push the situation to the furthest point of revolutionary logic that it could achieve. They yielded only in the face of the revolution's undeniable downfall, and only when the inevitability of downfall became obvious—they did not throw down their weapons out of clever foresight or presentiment of defeat. These truths will constitute one of the most glorious models of truly revolutionary tactics in the history books of the revolution, and their brilliance may partially atone for the tragic errors later committed during the First Duma and after its dissolution.

This is the inner meaning of the boycott of the First Duma. The degree to which this means of struggle is revolutionary depends not on its technical aspects, if one may say so, but on the assemblage of particular tactical moments, on the political content of which the boycott is only the external surface.

This explains the state of depression that set in when the front ranks of the army of the proletariat were forced to acknowledge [it]; it was no wonder that countless members of the proletariat felt not enthusiastic but depressed and worried. That is, it was not fondness for the thunderous cry of "boycott" that caused Polish proletarians to display extraordinary passivity during the elections to the Second Duma. It was their knowledge that to participate in the elections was to recognize, openly and formally, the collapse of the revolution.

The lessons of three years cannot pass by with no effect, however. Social Democracy's first responsibility is to learn from history. Currently, in view of the evolution of Russia's social classes during the constitution of a state coup, in view of the lingering passivity of the working masses and the ever-stronger position of absolutism in domestic and international politics, to maintain offensive revolutionary tactics despite all this—that would be to lose oneself in quixotic futility. No serious politician can count on a mass revolutionary outbreak in the next few weeks or months. On the contrary, the more time passes, it becomes ever clearer that a long period of preparatory work may await us in the domain of organizing and raising the political awareness of the proletariat so that it can stand up to the tasks ahead when the revolution regains strength and matures in the midst of completely new surroundings. Clearly, then, the call to boycott the Duma under such conditions bears no relation to any general tactical guideline whatsoever; rather, it is completely at variance with the entirety of proletarian politics. A boycott under such conditions would be not the first salvo of an advancing army but a shot in the dark that can meet no response but a surprised echo. Such was the typical "passive resistance" of the Berlin National Assembly [in 1848], God rest their souls. Under the real conditions of the current environment, calls to dismiss the Social Democratic faction are not the solution [to the problems] of the First Duma, [since] the defeat of revolution is not a fleeting episode but marks a long, grim era. Following the natural course of events, hopes were again directed toward a new period of mass revolutionary struggle when the campaign of the liberals, which had pushed the proletarian campaign back from its initial plan of revolution in the First Duma, ended in a stunning fiasco. For the same reason, when Social Democracy resolutely called for an about-face by participating in the elections [to the Second Duma], it courageously asserted that this change in its operational basis was a "revolutionary tactic of the proletariat" [against] the miserable tactics of a spineless bourgeoisie; it was "the resistance of the calf before the butcher."

The call to boycott the Duma of the Black Hundreds is curious from at least one other perspective. The boycott is justified by the general counterrevolutionary character of the Duma, which allegedly does not allow Social Democratic envoys to undertake actions related to its campaign. But the reactionary tendencies of the great personages gracing the Tauride Palace does not fully capture their character, their essence. The definitive circumstance is that the Third Duma is no longer an assemblage of the counterrevolutionary cronies in government, it is an organ of the counterrevolution of all the bourgeois of Russia. In this consists the historical significance of the current Russian "parliament," and from this arises the need to bring the class struggle of the proletariat to the floor of this "parliament," however difficult and wearisome the conditions of that fight are.

III.

What may be most important, after all, is not the individual tactical error of the cry to recall the Social Democratic envoys in the Duma. It is the general psychological backdrop that made such a cry uniquely possible. At the base of the party faction that deemed it necessary to make a noise christened "Otzovism"* can be found a disbelief, albeit unconscious, in the future and in the objective guarantee that the revolution will be resurrected and won. Only such an implosion of spirit could have given rise to the need to cook up false calls to "be more revolutionary" and to fight with one other, instead of peacefully and steadily waging a truly revolutionary campaign among the proletarian mass using the uninterrupted stream of material produced by every day of Stołypinian rule and every step taken by the counterrevolutionary club they call the Third Duma. A sign of the shameful collapse of revolutionary spirit, this tendency requires resolute opposition from Social Democracy.

---

* Or "Recallism," from the Russian *otzovat*, "to recall."

The May Day Celebrations before the Decision*

After a series of attempts to regulate the May Day celebrations on a new basis, namely in connection with the question of support, the party faces a final decision. The Leipzig Party Congress† must find the final solution not only for the reason that the debates and experiments to date have had the most fatal effect on the fate of the May Day celebrations, as the whole world can see, but also because the Leipzig Party Congress is the last before the *International Socialist Congress in Copenhagen*.‡ In Leipzig, then, it is to be decided what position the representatives of the German class-conscious working class will adopt before the forum of the International on the May Day question: whether they will appear as supporters and preservers of the old fighting tactics and the tradition of the international proletariat on this question, or whether they will take the initiative to revise these tactics and abandon the May Day celebrations.

Anyone who notices the role of the May Day celebrations in various countries to date, as well as the mood that has prevailed at all international congresses on this issue, will hardly doubt that an initiative that in one way or another, directly or indirectly, would aim to abolish May Day celebrations is virtually certain of defeat in Copenhagen—even if this initiative itself may come from such a powerful and influential party as the German Social Democratic Party! In Copenhagen, therefore, it will be less a question of whether May Day will be maintained by the international proletariat in the way it has been up to now, than of what role the representation of the workers' movement in Germany should play in the ranks of the International; whether it will advance it, as it once did, as the leader in the revolutionary class struggle and serve the other fellow parties as a signpost, as a model, or whether in its timidity it will fall behind and be mistreated by others. The negotiations of the International Congress in Stuttgart§ have shown, and the events of the recent International Conference of Trade Union Centers¶ have confirmed, that the German working class, despite its numerical size and enormous organizational successes, is and will only remain the leader of the International if it advances ahead of all others

---

* This article was first published in *Leipziger Volkszeitung*, No. 210, September 11, 1909. It is translated by Manuela Kölke from Luxemburg's *Gesammelte Werke*, Vol. 2, pp. 274–8.
† The party congress of German Social Democracy in Leipzig took place from September 12 to 18, 1909.
‡ The International Socialist Congress in Copenhagen took place from August 28 to September 3, 1910.
§ The International Socialist Congress in Stuttgart took place from August 18 to 24, 1907.
¶ The International Conference of National Trade Union Centers was held in Paris from August 30 to September 1, 1909.

in the clarity of its purpose, firmness of its principles, and determination of its tactics. The position of the German delegation on the May Day question at the Copenhagen Congress will be of extraordinary importance for the relevance of German Social Democracy and the German trade unions, and consideration of this fact should primarily have a determining influence on the negotiations at the Party Congress in Leipzig.

Already now, the current situation urgently calls for clarification of the issue. We are faced with the fact that the most powerful proletarian organization in the world, after having reached the strength of 2 to 3 million politically organized and 2.5 million unionized members, as well as 3.25 million voters, is almost about to declare that it cannot carry out the decisions of the international congresses and that it must give up the May Day celebrations, even as they have been observed with increasing success in Germany for almost twenty years. It is obvious that this fact, combined with constant bickering about the May Day celebrations between party and trade unions in Germany in recent years—including such decisions as those made by the metalworkers,* the strongest trade union in Germany—must have a deeply depressing effect on the workers' movement in all countries. For all the proletarians of the International, who until now have looked with pride toward the strength of the German workers' movement and regarded it as the utmost goal to meet the German movement's strength of organization, the question must inevitably arise: Is it worthwhile, in the end, to do everything in one's power to achieve a similar power when, having only just reached this summit, there is such a palpable sense of one's own weakness and doubt in one's ability to tackle tasks that one had previously approached with vigor, courage, and faith in a much-weaker organization?

The opponents of May Day celebrations bring two different points of view into the field. Above all, the mettle of the May Day celebrations is yet to be tested, as a general strike has not even nearly been carried out in Germany.

However, the futile attempts to enforce strikes bring serious shocks, dangers, and struggles for the trade union organizations, which are completely useless in view of the impossibility of reaching the goal. Those who stubbornly point to the alleged failure of the May Day celebrations so far assume a perception of the May Day celebrations that contradicts all the observations and experiences of twenty years of practice. No sensible, thinking politician of the class struggle can expect the May Day celebrations to become an absolute general strike repeated every year with automatic regularity in all countries or even only in some, or in one country. Strangely enough, the defenders of the deliberate policy of installment payments and the small, step-by-step achievements are proving to substantiate

---

* At the Ninth General Assembly of the German Metalworkers' Union in Hamburg from May 31 to June 5, 1909, a resolution downplayed the significance of the May Day celebrations and left it to the members to take part in May Day. It was expressly emphasized that participation in the event could not be made compulsory for the members of the union.

the otherwise much-frowned-upon principle: all or nothing. Where May Day cannot be asserted as an absolute annual strike,* it should be dropped completely. But May Day is not a sophisticated trick of proletarian tactics, not a mechanical method of creating a sudden general strike on command. The main meaning of the May Day celebrations lies *in the pursuit* of this goal, in the *agitation* for the sake of this goal, in the *enlightenment* for the sake of this goal, in the fact that it gives us the opportunity every year to measure the educational power of our idea on the basis of the shifting progresses of strikes, to test the effectiveness of our means of agitation, to constantly feel the pulse of the class struggle.

As a living part of the class struggle, the May Day celebrations react to all vicissitudes, to all the economic and political cycles of the working class. Economic upswing or crisis, political election years, intensification of political party struggles, revival of wage struggles—all this is reflected every year in every country in the May Day celebrations, when the call for strikes takes on greater and lesser dimensions. And if the social conflict rises to the outbreak of a revolutionary period, then the May Day celebrations suddenly become—despite the weakness of the organizations—a physical and absolute strike, as it was in Russian Poland—in 1905 and partly still more in the following years. This year, the highest point of the counterrevolutionary victory in Russia was reflected in the lowest degree of the May Day celebrations in Russia in twenty years. Did this not prove the inner vitality of the May Day celebrations, its indissoluble connection with the general fate of the proletarian class struggle? In Austria, the period of the proletariat's stormiest struggles for universal, equal, and direct suffrage culminated in a series of brilliant May Day celebrations. In France, the strongholds of the Social Democratic Workers' Party† expressed their revolutionary sentiments through bloody May sacrifices in the 1890s. In Germany we have generally had a "silent period" in the last two decades; our entire public life suffers under the curse of leaden parliamentary stagnation, and Germany's entire domestic policy has come to a dead end. What a miracle that even in view of this, the May Day celebrations in Germany, despite all the slow progress, were not able to precipitate a sudden outbreak of general strikes! But to abandon them completely, to abandon them for the slogans of the eight-hour day and socialism, would mean to declare as much as publicly in advance: Germany will never come out of the present swamp of stagnation; in Germany, we will never experience a period of great open struggles for the goals of the proletariat!

---

* The word used by Luxemburg here and below in referring to May Day "strikes" is not *Streik* but *Arbeitsruhe*—literally, "rest from work." The latter does not connote a strike linked to specific demands in a local context or a general strike but a one-day event that takes the form of a demonstration.

† A reference to the French Workers' Party (POF), founded by Guesde and Paul Lafargue in 1880.

The trade union organizations fear the dangers of conflicts arising from the May Day celebrations, especially in the face of the strong coalitions of employers. But the current *Swedish general strike*[*] is a powerful reminder that the employers' coalitions are generating huge internal conflicts for us, whether we like it or not. But it is precisely the policy of the employers' associations that leads to a generalization of the conflict, meaning that a general gathering representing the whole proletariat class becomes such an inevitable thing that a general strike is the only possible resort. But isn't it in this case the wisest trade union policy to organize the most impressive May Day celebrations possible every year? Isn't this the best way to show the employers' associations the power and fighting position of the trade unions *every year*, which the Swedish proletariat now see themselves forced to do most urgently? It is neither conflict nor the massive struggles that represents a danger to the trade unions, but, rather, simply the fear of conflict. For nothing can strengthen the exuberance of the employers' coalitions more than a decision such as that of the metalworkers on the May Day celebrations, which betrays to the enemy their weakness and despair in advance.

If the Leipzig Party Congress wants to do justice to the situation in Germany, to the expectations of the International, to the lessons of the Swedish general strike, it must resound with [August] Bebel when he said in Dresden:[†] "Expropriation will prevail!"—with the clear message: The May Day celebrations will prevail!

---

[*] From August 4 to September 6, 1909, by a decision of the National Trade Union Center in Sweden, a general strike was carried out by all affiliated organizations. Participants included 75 percent of the workers employed in industry, crafts, and transport. This strike managed to fend off an attempt by the employers' associations to force the unions to agree to wage reductions through lockouts during the economic crisis.

[†] The Party Congress of German Social Democracy took place in Dresden from September 13 to 20, 1903.

The Funeral of the May Day Celebrations*

The agenda of this year's party congress† mainly includes a review of the party's work in its various fields of activity: parliamentary, organizational, and agitational. New tactical tasks or guiding theoretical questions and principles are not being negotiated, and the numerous motions on the various items on the agenda unfortunately also show, we must admit, that this is not a particularly vivid picture of intellectual work at the moment. However, one thing can easily make the Leipzig Party Congress a turning point in the development of the workers' movement: namely, the solution it will provide regarding the question of May Day. For we must be clear about this. The Leipzig Party Congress is called not to decide on this or that incidental detail in the implementation of the May Day celebrations, nor on this or that kind of support for the May victims, but on the cardinal question: Should May Day, as a key part—for decades—of the unbroken continuance of Social Democratic combat tactics in Germany and of the spread of socialist doctrine throughout the world, be maintained, or should it be finally abandoned? It is a piece of "revision" that here again is expected of the party, not a revision of its theoretical equipment, which in view of its hopelessness is a relatively more harmless pastime, but a piece of revision of practical activity, namely regarding one of the few methods of direct activity with the broadest base of masses.

In fact, we must honestly admit to the circles in the party and trade union officials who are working toward a smooth abolition of the May Day celebrations that, with their systematic, tireless work, they have for years already achieved a good part of their goal. For one would indeed have to be blind if one did not want to realize that the previous incessant arguments about the May Day celebrations, which have become a constant misery for the party congresses, have already contributed—and keep contributing in the most effective way—toward undermining the concept of the May Day celebrations for the broadest masses, to shatter the tradition, to cool the enthusiasm, to have a sobering, disappointing, confusing effect; that is to say, to have exactly the effect that the opponents of the May Day celebrations want to achieve. The purpose of the annual treatment of May Day celebrations at party congresses used to be to keep the idea of May Day alive for the masses, to constantly propagate it from the party's highest rostrum, but now it has turned into the annual undermining and compromising of May Day. The masterpiece of this tactic, however, was to put the question of support at the forefront of the entire May Day question and, on top of that, to

---

* This article was first published in *Vorwärts* (Berlin), No. 213, September 12, 1909. It is translated by Manuela Kölke from Luxemburg's *Gesammelte Werke*, Vol. 2, pp. 269–73.

† The Party Congress of German Social Democracy took place in Leipzig from September 12 to 18, 1909.

get the party executive to settle the question together with the other supreme body of the workers' movement, the General Commission of Trade Unions. The Party Executive Committee and the General Commission were given the dual task of reconciling the position of the majority of the party, which was resolutely directed toward the maintenance of the May Day celebrations, with the position of the trade union circles, which themselves were more or less openly directed toward the abolition of the May Day celebrations. At the same time, they were tasked with holding the May Day celebrations while ensuring in advance sufficient support for all possible victims of May Day. The fact that the Executive Committee and the General Commission could not, with the best will in the world, achieve this double squaring of the circle, must be understood by everyone upon closer reflection. These efforts to have one's cake and eat it too could, of course, only result in a series of more or less unsuccessful attempts at compromise, with the end result that "the party's 'problem child,'" as May Day is now happily called by friend and foe, will soon itself begin to suffer from the many experiments and operations.

The latest result of the negotiations of the Party Executive Committee and the General Commission presents itself as a miscarriage at first sight. Last year's agreement between the two highest authorities rejected the support of the victims of the May Day celebrations from the central coffers of the party and the trade unions and passed it on to the district coffers. The majority of the delegates in Nuremberg* declared this agreement null and void, in the correct knowledge that it would amount to an actual abolition of the May Day celebrations, since each respective district would not be able to bear the burden of supporting the May victims for the most part, but even more so, they would shy away, and the fear of this imposed responsibility would paralyze any possible momentum May Day might generate. Now the Party Executive Committee and the General Commission are proposing to support the victims of the May celebration from "regional" instead of district coffers. Apparently, this is a compromise that meets the wishes of the party majority in one regard, since the regional treasuries represent a middle step between district and central treasuries. In reality, the new solution is a big step in the opposite direction. Certainly, places and centers of the movement with their coffers exist, but what the "regions" should be, to which the costs of the May Day celebrations and the responsibility for them should be ascribed, remains a secret of the legislator. Not only do the coffers not yet exist on which to rest the material basis, not even the geographical and organizational units that are to form those coffers are at hand. By being rejected from the local as well as the central treasuries, the May Day celebrations are being handed over to a fantastic organization that is yet to be formed.

---

* The Party Congress of German Social Democracy in Nuremberg took place from September 13 to 19, 1908.

In the existing organizations of the political and economic workers' movement there is no place for the concerns about the celebration of May Day; a completely new organizational apparatus is yet to be created. Germany must first be divided into "regions," each locality must first create new commissions —of course on a dualistic basis—and the newly created districts must then create new coffers. In these "regions," the same party and trade union members are to be involved and the same funds as before are to be used, and only then can "the worthy celebration" begin. If someone wanted to make a malicious satire of a May Day decision for the sake of mocking May Day, they could not have had a better idea than this. It creates a whole new bureaucratic apparatus, in which it is unclear by whom and how it should actually be brought into being. Its dualistic basis is to be transplanted into the respective communes, which will lead to the same infertility of action as the previous May Day negotiations of the two highest authorities. The sluggishness of the apparatus rules out any momentum from the outset and, most importantly, the uniform celebration of May Day throughout the country. There is one more thing. The motion of the party executive does not say a single word about the strikes as the desired form of the May Day celebration. It should "ensure a worthy celebration." But what the "worthy celebration" consists of is left to interpretation, with a covert reference to the "consideration of professional and local conditions and the provisions of trade union organizations, as well as the decisions of the party congress." In other words, instead of the previous general and uniform decisions about strikes being the worthiest form possible of celebrating May Day, the arrangement of May Day celebrations is left to the free discretion of mixed commissions in each location and, where the provisions of the trade union organization (such as the metalworkers) conflict with the previous party decisions, it is left to the comrades on the ground to work their way out of these contradictions.

As tormented and contradictory as the proposals of the Party Executive Committee are, the Committee could not, with the best will in the world, achieve a more satisfactory result after having been confronted, together with the General Commission, with an unsolvable task. If, however, the party executive cannot be reproached for having failed to square the circle, then it is no less certainly the party's duty, having rejected the agreement before the Nuremberg Party Congress, to also *reject* the current one for the same and even better reasons. In determining the question of the May Day celebrations, the workers' movement, as for all questions, needs at least full *clarity*. It is necessary for the party to decide openly: Either it wants to adhere to the idea of the May Day celebrations as a rest from work—that is, in the form and in the sense in which it has been cultivated, propagated, and sanctified by the international proletariat for twenty years—in which case the May Day celebrations, as before, must not be made dependent on any question of forms of support. Or, if we want to abolish the celebration of May Day as a rest from work, then this must be stated clearly and unambiguously, because it means that the May Day celebration itself is actually abolished. In fact, the delegation of the May Day celebration to the newly invented "regional coffers" means its expulsion to the "fourth dimension"—that is, the funeral of the concept of May Day in its entirety. But the clear and open abolition of the May Day celebration would certainly have the advantage that it would have to put an immediate end to all misunderstandings, while also causing inevitable and fierce protest in the broadest circles of the 3-million-strong Social Democratic army.

It would in fact be a way of reacting to the recent slap in the face dealt by the reaction to the Hottentot [elections]* and the Schnaps Bloc,† to the new huge tax burden,‡ to the mockery and starvation of the masses—a reaction that the masses would be unlikely to understand. In a time of ever-intensifying and escalating contrasts, of ever bolder provocations by the class state, of ever more hopeless and sterile efforts for positive achievements and concessions from the ruling order—in such a time of strong and stormy winds, to voluntarily hand over such an outstanding weapon as the May Day celebrations would truly be, as a tactic, a strange contradiction to the traditions of German Social Democracy. It would mean giving away a singular method of shaking up the broad masses, of inspiring them, of winning them over to socialism and educating them in the idea of internationalism. That would be a retreat from the line of battle so far—and a very inglorious one at that. The current mood of broad sections of the population in Germany can be detected from the recent by-elections to the Reichstag,§ and from the pathetic mood of the bourgeois opponents themselves. What the masses now expect of us is certainly the consolidation, the intensification, of our fighting tactics, and by no means their weakening. The abandonment of the May Day celebrations would be a slap in the face of the masses that have been bled white and trampled underfoot by the reactionaries.

---

* "Hottentots" was a derogatory term used by European imperialists to refer to the Koikhoi peoples of southwest Africa. The 1907 federal elections in Germany came to be known at the time as the "Hottentot elections" because of the support they reflected for Germany's imperialist conquest of the region. The SPD lost over half of its seats in Parliament in the election, and the setback solidified the position of reformists within the party who wanted to mute opposition to (or in some cases openly support) German colonialism.

† During the debate on the Reich's financial reform in the summer of 1909, the kaiser replaced German chancellor Bernhard von Bülow with Theobald von Bethmann-Hollweg, leader of the so-called "Schnaps Bloc" or "Black-and-Blue Block" composed of conservatives and the Center Party.

‡ On July 10, 1909, the Reichstag adopted the financial reform against the votes of the Social Democrats, the National Liberals, and the liberal Free-Minded People's Party (Freisinnigen Volkspartei). Since four-fifths of the new taxes were indirect taxes, additional burdens were placed on the masses.

§ In the period from August 1, 1908, to July 31, 1909, fourteen by-elections for the Reichstag took place, in which the votes cast for the Social Democrats increased from 16 to 18 percent in relation to the Reichstag elections of 1907.

The Leipzig Party Congress will earn great merit both before us and before the international workers' movement if it succeeds in putting an end to this cruel game and decides unequivocally to maintain May Day, putting a stop with a strong hand to any further unnecessary experiments, which would only lead to the slow death of May Day.

Excerpts and Notes from Books and Studies on the English Revolution*

I.

guizot†
(1)
Cont. I. 1664–73
II. 1689–1714‡
NB 1. V.
(2)
Organiz[ation]. Democracy. Centralization.

---

* This manuscript is translated from the German by Jacob Blumenfeld and the Russian by Vladislav Hedeler, based on the text in Rosa Luxemburg, *Gesammelte Werke*, Vol. 7.1, pp. 237–62. In order to make the particular character of the source visible, abbreviations and incomplete sentences have been largely omitted. Words and passages crossed out by the author are indicated by a strikethrough. All insertions by the editors are in square brackets. The numbers in the text are mainly page references to the works on which Luxemburg is commenting. The manuscript is undated. It was probably written at different times, some beginning in the period 1907–1909, during which Luxemburg taught at the SPD party school in Berlin, others during World War I. There are some clues in Luxemburg's letters: On July 17, 1909, for example, she wrote to Kostja Zetkin that she had read Eduard Bernstein on the English Revolution and ordered François Guizot's work through Hans Kautsky. She wanted to read it because of the context of ongoing world events (see *Gesammelte Briefe*, Vol. 3 [Berlin: Dietz Verlag, 1984], p. 50). In November 1915, she read Guizot's *Histoire de la révolution d'Angleterre depuis l'avènement de Charles Ier jusqu'à sa mort* (History of the English Revolution) in German translation once more and noted that "English naval power and England's position in the world is virtually the work of the Revolution of 1649" (see *Gesammelte Briefe*, Vol. 5 [Berlin: Dietz Verlag, 1987], p. 87). And on August 13, 1917, she reported to Hans Diefenbach that she had worked through Guizot three times (ibid., p. 291). The concluding part of the manuscript consists of "Notes on Political Economy," which includes many substantive references to her main work, *The Accumulation of Capital: A Contribution to the Economic Theory of Imperialism*, which appeared in 1913, and to *The Accumulation of Capital; or, What the Epigones Have Made Out of Marx's Theory—An Anti-Critique*. The "Notes on Political Economy" will appear in the forthcoming Volume 2, Part B of the *Complete Works*.

† The excerpts and notes on the English Revolution of 1642 to 1660 are based mainly on the German translation of François Guizot, *History of the English Revolution to the Death of Charles the First*. See *Geschichte der Revolution in England von der thronbesteigung Karls I. bis zu seinem Tode* (Leipzig: F. Luden, 1850). Most of the page references in the excerpts and notes below on Guizot refer to theses or keywords to this book.

‡ This probably refers to other German translations of publications by Guizot, such as *Warum war die englische Revolution erfolgreich? Ein Diskurs über die Geschichte der englischen Revolution* (Why Was the English Revolution Successful? A Discourse on the History of the English Revolution) (Leipzig: Diskurs, 1850); *Geschichte der englischen Republik bis zum Tod von Cromwell* (History of the English Republic to the Death of Cromwell) (Leipzig: Diskurs, 1854); and *Geschichte von Richard Cromwell und die Restaurierung von Charles II* (History of Richard Cromwell and the Restoration of Charles II) (Leipzig: Diskurs, 1856).

[*On left margin:*] Ad 2. The *Swamp* continues the ideology of the official party: fetishism of organization as an end in itself.[*]
(3) Military situation. Offensives (1643–
(4) [King] Georg[e] I. 13–76 makes peace
(5) Parliamentarism. Decay. ——[†]
(6) Restoration
(7) Further perspectives: alternative
(8) The systematic tough resistance of Icherid & Co.[‡] Compare Guizot: [History of the English Revolution to the Death of Charles the First], p. 16, 17, 19.
(9) Process of decomposition outside and inside (ID [Independents?][§] as organized part of b[ourgeois] society)
(10) With regard to winning even more of to the 18 war.
(11) The Girondins[¶]
(12) Land redistribution (H + D K.K.)
NB Tactic of [King] George I is to act in the House of Commons just as he did *before* the Civil War, as if nothing had happened!!
(13) World war as civil process
Legitimists-party.[**] "P. Decrees" Guizot 86.
(14) La legalité at any price
Fanatics of unity
Split

(NB ad 2. [Oliver] Cromwell's army first served him to fight the king's power, in support of the republic, then to fight the Republicans and establish his sole rule.
The same with Napoleon's army. Full analogy with sd.)
Guizot 33

---

 * This refers to the moderate opposition around Karl Kautsky, Hugo Haase, and Georg Ledebour, among others, which Luxemburg often referred to as "the politics of the swamp." It refers specifically to the Social Democratic Working Group (SAG) and the Independent Social Democratic Party of Germany (USPD) founded in 1917. This is one of the only places in her writings in which she explicitly criticizes the "fetishism of organization as an end itself."
 † Deletion unreadable.
 ‡ Since Guizot's *Geschichte der englischen Revolution* reveals no entries for "Icherid," it is possible that Luxemburg meant to write "Ireland."
 § The Independents were one of the major tendencies supporting parliamentary governance during the English Revolution. The name derived from their advocacy of local congregational control of religious orders. Oliver Cromwell was their leading figure.
 ¶ The Girondins were a group of deputies during the French Revolution of 1789, many of whom were from the area of Gironde around Bordeaux, centered around the figure of J. P. Brissot. They opposed Parisian dominance as well as rising authoritarianism.
 ** During the English Civil War, those who defended the divine right of kings were called Royalists or Cavaliers. "Legitimist" was one of several terms used in France for those who supported the divine right of kings. Luxemburg's calling the seventeenth-century English Royalists "Legitimists" derives from Guizot's specifically French political perspective.

NB *Lensch* & Co, "The Greatest Rev. of World History"*
(NB The † End & Successes)
Nat lib., Freis. ‡ —Difference from England historically (surrender of the prince.)
Lord [Jacob] *Astley* was supposed to go to Oxford with his 3,000 men to join Charles, but was completely defeated by Sir Will[iam] Brereton & Colonel [Thomas] Morgan at Stow (Gloucestershire), Astley himself fell into their hands.§
Charles makes secret ties with [Henry] Vane¶ while at the same time offers to Parliament to dissolve his army and return to Whitehall. (April 1646)

[*On left margin:*] NB

Parliament's measures against the return of Charles. *State of siege in London.*
Fairfax** approaches in order to enclose Oxford.
April 27 Charles flees from Oxford to the Scottish camp in Kelham.
[William] Prynne†† 129, 154, 292, 420
Cleansing Parliament 355/356, 364, 401
Hamilton 136, 225
[Robert Devereux, Third Earl of] Essex 138, 274, 281, 297, 299
Negotiations of Parliament with Charles
(1) 1642   p. 194, 196ff. militia
(2) 1642   207, 9, 19
(3) 1642   217ff.
(4) March 1643   225,6 in Oxford (Earl of Northam)‡‡

---

* Paul Lensch published the brochure *Social Democracy: Its End and Its Successes* in Leipzig in 1916, which states, among other things: "On August 4 [1914] the party made a decision in its dark throes, which was tactically not without reservations and has also avenged itself on it, but which was all the more right in the higher sense of world historical development ... A new time and with it a new social ideal is taking hold: socialist society, but its sword is Germany" (pp. 134 and 175).
† Deletion unreadable.
‡ Deletion unreadable.
§ Jacob Astley was a Royalist commander during the English Civil War who was appointed governor of Plymouth by Charles I. He was captured at Stow-on-the-Wold on March 21, 1646, and was imprisoned until Charles I surrendered in Oxford in June 1646. William Brereton was the commander of the parliamentary army during the English Civil War; Thomas Morgan was a major general of the army and was appointed parliamentary governor of Gloucester in 1645.
¶ Vane was a close ally of Cromwell who had earlier served as the governor of the Massachusetts Bay Colony.
** Thomas Fairfax, Third Lord Fairfax of Cameron (1612–71), also known as Sir Thomas, was an English peer and politician who served as parliamentary commander in chief during the English Civil War.
†† Originally a firm supporter of Cromwell, Prynne opposed his Independents, which advocated local (as against national) control of religious matters.
‡‡ It seems Luxemburg is referring here to Robert Devereux, Third Earl of Essex, who commanded forces in Northam, Devon, against Charles I's army in the first three years of the English Civil War.

(5) August 1643 Proposals of the House of Lords
(6) November 1644   285ff., 239, 294ff.
(7) January 1645
[Thomas] Fairfax*   206, 229, 236, 238, 268, 270, 274, 295, 268, 270, 274, 295, 297, 299, 302, 307/8, 309, 320, 327
Parliamentary army   211, 269, 297
Cromwell   229, 230, 238, 274, 282, 289, 293, 295, 297, 301, 302, 319, 321, 321.
Reign of Presbyterians & co.   250ff.†
Charles' military commander   309, 325

1.

The War!
August 23, 1642, Charles officially planted his banner in *Nottingham*.
Headquarters of the Parliamentary Army was in *Northampton*, about 20,000 under Essex.
Charles moved from Nott. to *Shrewsbury*
Essex followed went to meet him.
September 23 he came to *Worcester* and stayed there for three weeks, idle.
Charles decided to march on London. Essex followed him.
October 23, first battle at Edgehill, Warwickshire. Both sides "won." [John] Hampden, [Denzil] Holles,‡ etc. pressed for another attack, but Essex§ refused.
Charles Essex moved his headquarters in Oxford, Essex in to *Warwick*, Charles first to Oxford, then to *Reading*, close to London, then to *Brentford*.
Neutrality Agreement of the two parties in the County of York and Chester.¶ Devonshire and Cornwallis** declared to stay out of the war. Nevertheless, the war also went on in all counties.

---

   * Fairfax was initially the military leader of the opposition to Charles I, but Cromwell, his former deputy, outmaneuvered him in a power struggle. Fairfax opposed the trial and execution of Charles I.
   † The Presbyterians adopted a more moderate stance against Charles I, in that they were in favor of a negotiated settlement with the monarchy, whereas the Independents under Cromwell sought its elimination.
   ‡ Denzil Holles was the outspoken leader of the Presbyterian "Peace Party" in the House of Commons during the civil wars and later became a baron and privy councilor after the Restoration. John Hampden was an early leader of the civil war; troops under his command scored an important victory at the Battle of Edgehill.
   § See p. 451 above for more on Robert Devereux.
   ¶ The Treaty of Neutrality was signed on September 29, 1642, by Fairfax for the Parliamentarians and Henry Bellasis for the Royalists, with the aim of avoiding civil war in Yorkshire.
   ** Luxemburg refers to this county as "Cornwallis." It has been uniformly referred to simply as "Cornwall" in English since the nineteenth century.

February 1643 The queen* returned from Holland with four ships of ammunition, weapons and crew and went to York.

March 1643 Negotiations in Oxford—smashed. The campaign began again. Hampden demanded the march against Oxford. But Essex besieged *Reading*, which surrendered after ten days. Hampden again demanded an attack against Oxford, Essex refused.

Meanwhile *Fairfax*, father & son, fought successfully against *Lord Newcastle*[†] in the north, Lord *Manchester*[‡] & *Cromwell* in the east, *Sir William Waller*[§] in the south and west.

Essex's army is boycotted by the safety committee (no clothing, food, etc.)

Cromwell formed a new cavalry of indignant peasants of the East (231)

June 19,1643 Battle of Chalgrove, [Prince] Rupert'[¶] beats the parliamentary army. Hampden wounded June 24.

Two months of defeats: Fairfax at the Atherton Moor; Sir John Hotham ready to hand Hull over to the Queen;[**] Lord [Francis] Willoughby[††] could not hold Lincolnshire against Lord Newcastle; ~~Lord~~ Sir W. Waller lost two battles in Cornwallis in a week. The cities of Dorchester, Weymouth, Portland, Barnstaple, Bedford, Taunton, Bridgewater, Bath surrendered without battle, Bristol on the first charge. [Henry] Wilmot and [Ralph] Hopton[‡‡] defeated the parliamentary soldiers at Roundway Down, Waller returned to London without soldiers. Essex did not move and advised the ~~parliam~~ House of Lords to ask Charles for peace.[§§]

Charles declared both houses of Parliament to be high traitors and null and void.

July 5, 1643 Both Houses then decided to ask the *Scots* for support.

---

   * Queen Henrietta Maria of France was the wife of Charles I. The March 1643 negotiations between Charles I and the Long Parliament were aimed at resolving the conflict between them, but they broke off by April 15 over Charles' demands for major concessions.

   † A reference to William Cavendish, generally referred to as the First Duke of Newcastle, who was appointed captain-general of Northern England by Charles I during the civil war.

   ‡ Edward Montagu, a commander of parliamentary forces in the early stages of the civil war who was for a time Cromwell's superior. He later supported the Presbyterians against Cromwell's Independents. Luxemburg is referring to p. 181, on which Guizot discusses the spread of Manchester's influence in popular opinion.

   § A commander of the parliamentary armies in the early stage of the civil war.

   ¶ Prince Rupert of the Rhine, Duke of Cumberland, was a German-British officer who commanded the royal cavalry. He was a nephew of Charles I.

   ** Hotham seized control of the town of Hull on behalf of the Parliamentarians in January 1642, which contained large stores of ammunition. In April he refused to allow Charles I and the queen to enter the town.

   †† Willoughby was a commanding officer of the time in the parliamentary army; he later became a Royalist.

   ‡‡ Wilmot and Hopton were Royalist commanders during the First English Civil War (1642–46).

   §§ The Battle of Atherton Moor (June 30, 1643) solidified the Royalists' hold of Yorkshire and forced the Parliamentarians into alliance with Scotland.

In the East a new army of 10,000 was formed under Lord Manchester (& Cromwell), *Hotham* was arrested & Lord *Fairfax* took his place in *Hull*.

August 1643 peace proposals of the Lords, rejected by the [House of] Commons with a narrow majority.

Charles had the plan to merge his army with the Lord Newcastle's before London, but Newcastle refused the order and did not want to leave Yorkshire. Charles had to change the plan and *besieged Gloucester* (Aug. 10, 1643)

Aug. 24 Essex went to *relieve Gloucester** (giving way to Parliament's only stronghold in the west and an obstacle in the union of royal troops in the north and west). After twenty-six days, besieged when Essex approached, Charles lifted the siege without a fight.

Essex went straight back to London, but Charles represented him in *Newbury*. Battle here on Sep. 20, 1643. Charles' army withdraws (his losses Lord Sunderland, Lord Carnarvon, *Lord Falkland*,† and seventeen other higher officials.) In the battle, the London militia distinguished themselves.‡

Essex moved to *Reading*.

Meanwhile, *Vane* concluded a Covenant with the *Scots*, which was confirmed on August 17 and September 25 [1643];§ 21,000 Scots were promised.

Sept. 26, Essex moved came to London, was welcomed in triumph, and submitted his resignation. This was not accepted and full supreme command was transferred to him.

Winter 1643/44 The main armies did not make develop any activity. Attempts of negotiations between Oxford and London. Counter-parliament in Oxford (1–4, 1644). Meanwhile, partial *victories* of the parliamentary armies.

Fairfax beat the Irish troops in the county of *Chester* near Nantwich.

2.

The *Scots* joined up in the north under the Earl of Leven. They were met by Newcastle. At his backside, however, *Fairfax* beat a significant corps of Royalists at *Selby*. Thus Newcastle had to station himself in York.

In the east, Lord Manchester and Cromwell formed *a new army* of 14,000 men.

To the south, Sir William *Waller* beat the Sir Ralph Hopton at *Alresford* in Hampshire. However, Rupert gained some advantages in *Nottingham* and Lancaster.

Demoralization in the Royal Army as a result of the defeats. In London, on the

---

* The siege of Gloucester occurred from August 10 to September 5, 1643.

† Henry Spencer, First Lord of Sunderland; Robert Dormer, First Earl of Carnarvon; and Lucius Cary, Second Viscount of Falkland, were all killed at the first Battle of Newbury in 1643 in fighting on behalf of Charles I.

‡ The Battle of Newbury resulted in a significant triumph for the Parliamentarians.

§ The Covenant was accepted by the Church of England on August 17, 1643, and by the English Parliament on September 25, 1643.

other hand, unification and streamlining of leadership: ("Committee of Both Kingdoms").* At the beginning of the campaign in 1644——† *five armies*:
(1) Scots under Leven‡
21,000
(2) Essex
10,500
(3) Fairfax
5–6,000
(4) W. Waller
5,100
(5) Manchester
14,000
Sum approx. 50,000

The campaign plan of the "Committee" for *1644* was this: Essex and Waller are to siege Oxford, while Fairfax, Manchester and Leven blockade York.

At the end of May *Oxford* was trapped with the help of *8,000 London militiamen* who joined up with Essex. Charles remained in Oxford without help: Prince Rupert was still in the north in *Lancaster*, Prince Maurice [of the Palatine]§ deep in the south in *Dorsetshire*, where he besieged the port city of *Lyme*, S̶i̶r̶ Lord Hopton was in *Bristol* and had to guard the city against parliamentary influences.

June 3, Charles escaped from Oxford with the Prince of Wales. The siege of Oxford was pointless. Essex decided to send *Waller* north to pursue Charles, and to go west (south?) himself, to relieve the besieged city of Lyme and subjugate the country. Waller acquiesced, but complained to the committee and the committee brought the matter before the House of Commons. They immediately ordered Essex to take over the pursuit of the king himself and to let Waller go west. *Essex disobeyed and continued the march.* The committee did not feel strong enough to take up the fight with him and gave in. Meanwhile, Waller pursued the *king* without result. He came back to Oxford a̶f̶t̶e̶r̶ ̶s̶e̶v̶-̶ ̶e̶n̶t̶e̶e̶n̶ ̶d̶a̶y̶s̶ on June 20 when he heard about the separation of the generals and took the offensive. He immediately ordered Prince Rupert to come to York's aid, going against London himself. Waller had to quickly turn around to shield London and offered *a battle on June 29 in Buckinghamshire* (near

---

* The Committee of Both Kingdoms became the military high command responsible for strategy during the civil wars.
† Deletion unreadable.
‡ Alexander Leslie, First Earl of Leven, was commander of the Scottish army from 1644 to 1646 that fought against Charles I.
§ Brother of Prince Rupert, who fought in the same army as his brother in support of their uncle Charles I at the Battle of Edgehill.

Cropredy Bridge), where he was *completely defeated*. Charles then swiftly headed southwest to pursue *Essex*, who now appeared in front of *Exeter*, where the queen was.

Meanwhile, the great *Battle of Marston Moor* ~~happened~~ took place on July 2, 1644, near York. Rupert, under Charles' order, moved ~~against~~ into York with 20,000, the parliamentary generals had given up the siege of York on the news of his advance, in order to stop ~~the~~ Rupert on his way. This failed, but Rupert followed the withdrawing parliamentary troops and at Marston Moor. ~~The~~ Complete victory of *Cromwell* ~~n. Manchester~~ [?] and the Independents (3,000 dead, 1,600 wounded ~~on~~ Royalists.)

After the ~~battle~~ defeat, *Newcastle* embarked at Scarborough to go to the Continent, Rupert went with the rest of his army to Chester and *York capitulated* on July 16.

Meanwhile, Essex went farther and farther west, taking *Lyme, Weymouth, Barnstaple, Tiverton, Taunton* (Dorsetshire and Devonshire) in three weeks. The queen fled [from] Exeter to Falmouth and embarked for France. In front of Exeter, Essex learned that Charles had beaten ~~against~~ Waller and was advancing against London. He called the War Council and they decided—nevertheless—to continue pushing toward *Cornwall*! Essex followed this decision and demanded reinforcements from London, since Charles turned against him in his back, food was also missing. The committee allegedly gave eager orders to Waller, [Sir Thomas] Myddelton,[*] Manchester, Essex to help, they promised, but did not move. Meanwhile, Charles tried twice in August to start *peace negotiations* with Essex.

3.

Essex turned him down. Meanwhile, he was more and more surrounded by ~~the~~ Charles' army, and demoralization developed in the army. Finally, he sent the *cavalry* under *Sir Will[iam] Balfour*,[†] to get through ~~g~~ between the enemy guards, suddenly left his army himself and fled with two officers to Plymouth, leaving command to [Philip] *Skippon*.[‡]

On *Sept. 1, 1644*, the rest of Essex's army surrendered, against the will of Skippon. ~~and Es~~

Essex sent a self-indictment from Plymouth to the ~~comm~~ Parliament, but Parliament accepted him with respect and goodwill, ordered Manchester and Waller to rush to Dorchester to his aid and provided him with weapons, etc., to organize the army again.

---

[*] Myddelton was a Welsh politician who supported the parliamentary cause in the early stage of the civil war; he later became a supporter of the restoration of the monarchy.

[†] Balfour was a Scottish general in the parliamentary forces.

[‡] Skippon was later appointed major general in Fairfax's army.

In the meantime, *Montrose*[*] had provoked an uprising in northern Scotland, *Aberdeen* and *Perth* had captured ~~Charles~~ and threatened Edinburgh. Using this diversion, *Charles* moved *against London*.

Parliament, however, had taken its measures. Manchester's, Waller's and Essex's troops covered London in the west. In addition, there were *five regiments of London militias* under [James] *Harington*[†] (Essex himself was ill in London).

October 27, 1644, Battle of Newbury, Essex of Manchester held supreme command. Victory seemed undecided, but Charles retired to *Oxford*, where he moved into his winter quarters on Oct. 30.

After the battle, *struggle between Cromwell and Manchester* because of the undecided outcome of the battle. Struggle of Presbyterians against Cromwell.

Dec. 21, 1645[‡] *Self-Denying Ordinance*[§]

NB *Reform of the Army* by the Independents. Jan. 1645 Negotiations at Uxbridge.

Campaign under Fairfax and Cromwell

In early May 1645, *Cromwell* won three battles between *Oxford and Worcester* and took *Bletchingdon*.

~~Ch~~ Fairfax headed west to relieve Taunton, which was encircled by the Prince of Wales. Charles, however, went north, liberated *Chester* (in connection with Ireland) and then threw himself to the east.

Fairfax and Cromwell were ordered to seize Oxford ~~to~~, but then *Cromwell* was sent to *Cambridge* to defend the East.

Meanwhile, Charles took *Leicester* by storm and *Taunton* was trapped again. *Fairfax* received orders to abandon Oxford and pursue Charles, *Cromwell* received ~~no apermanent~~ temporary appointment again.[¶]

At the urging of the frightened court in Oxford, Charles wanted to return there, but ~~recei~~ got in touch with ~~Crom~~ Fairfax and Cromwell's armies and

---

[*] James Graham, First Marquess of Montrose, was a Scottish nobleman who supported Charles I and commanded Irish Royalist auxiliaries in Scotland.

[†] Sir James Harington, Third Baronet of Ridlington, was a major general in the parliamentary army who fought at the Battle of Cropredy Bridge. Luxemburg gives his name as "Harrington"; he should not be confused with James Harrington, the major English political theorist who wrote on the English Civil War.

[‡] The actual date on which this occurred was December 19, 1644.

[§] The "Self-Denying Ordinance" was actually debated in December 1644, before being passed in Parliament on April 3, 1645. It "was engineered by Sir Henry Vane and the parliamentary 'War Party' to rid Parliament's armies of its aristocratic commanders, some of whom appeared reluctant to inflict a decisive military defeat on the king and were leaning toward the 'Peace Party' position of resolving the conflict through a negotiated settlement." See "British Civil Wars," Commonwealth and Protectorate Project, bcw-project.org. Luxemburg has made a slip of the pen in writing "December 21, 1645," at this point in the manuscript: Below she dates this same event more accurately to "Dec. 21, *1644*."

[¶] Luxemburg is referring to the Battle of Naseby, which occurred from June 1 to 14, 1645.

withdrew to *Leicester*. Here, he and Rupert decided to go face the parliamentary army and wage a battle.

June 1645 at Naseby (NW of Northampton.)
"The King's Cabinet Opened."*

In July, *Fairfax* headed west, beating *Goring* at Langport (*Somersetshire*) and soon trapping all the cavaliers in their castles.

Charles went from Naseby to *Wales* and remained idle. It was not until Rupert advised peace and the *Scots* came from the north to besiege *Hereford* that Charles rose up. He went to the shires of *Shrop*, *Stafford*, *Derby* and *Nottingham* and brought all the Cavaliers together to the shire of *York* in order to proceed to Montrose in Scotland. Meanwhile *Leslie* left Hereford with the Scottish cavalry and hurried after the king. His Cavaliers feared a battle and scattered, for the most part. Charles moved back to *Oxford* with the rest.

[*On left margin:*] Aug. 29, 45

After two days, he received news that *Montrose* was victorious, the Scots had been defeated by Baillie (for the seventh time) on *August 15* and *Bothwell, Glasgow, Edinburgh* had opened a~~the~~ gates for him.†

4.

Then Charles left Oxford and wanted first to relieve *Hereford*.‡ But the Scots gave up Hereford and quickly headed north on the mere news of Charles' approach. Charles then went to Wales to friends (Marquess of Worcester).§

Meanwhile, *Rupert* was besieged by *Fairfax* in *Bristol* and handed the city over on the first attack, almost without resistance. Rupert is dismissed from command. (He retires to Oxford.)

In the meantime, Charles was persecuted by the parliamentary army under Colonel General [Sydnam] *Poyntz*. He went to *Chester*, besieged by *Jones*, to relieve this last connection with Ireland. ~~Here~~ On the road, Charles ended up between *Poyntz* and *Colonel Jones*, was attacked and fled back to Wales.

---

* See Guizot, *History of the English Revolution*, p. 308.

† As at other points in the civil war manuscripts, Luxemburg's shortening of the nobles' titles could confuse the reader. In this sentence, "Glasgow, Edinburgh," she's referring to nobles with titles bearing these place names, rather than these localities themselves. "Opened the gates" is to be understood figuratively.

‡ This is the geographical location, not the name of a person.

§ Henry Somerset, First Marquess of Dorchester, was an important financier of the Royalists. After the Battle of Naseby in 1645, he gave refuge to Charles I at Raglan Castle in Wales. He was forced to surrender the castle the next year and died shortly thereafter.

Meanwhile, *Montrose* was also defeated on *Sept. 13, 1645*, by *Leslie* at the border of the two kingdoms.

Charles went to *Newark*. Lord [George] *Digby*, however, with the rest of his the Royal Army [went] north to bring assistance to *Montrose*. He was defeated at *Sherburne* by the parliamentary army. As Poyntz moved closer and closer to Hereford Newark, Charles fled back to *Oxford*.

Meanwhile, *Cromwell* and *Fairfax* h took one town after another in the west. The west was lost to Charles, and he had the Prince of Wales let be ferried ready to be ferried to the Continent.

Charles proposed three peace negotiations three times to Parliament, they were rejected.

Unveiling of Charles' agreement with the Irish and the Pope of August 20, war must go on.

Charles still had two troop corps: under Lord Hopton in Cornwall, under Lord Astley at the border of Wales.

Hopton was defeated by *Fairfax* on February 16, 1646, near *Torrington* and was pursued to the headland. The army was completely demoralized and the inhabit surrendered, against Hopton's will. The inhabitants wanted to surrender the Prince of Wales. He left with Hopton to the Isles of *Scilly*.

NB Problem of land redistribution
NB Republic dead in all life there
(ad 1. NL Role of the Germans in the H[and]B[ook])
Ad 13: The 1688 "Glorious Revolution" as an "act of *pure self-defense*." Guizot, p. 65,*
67. (86)
"a revolution both proud and humble"†

[*Adjacent:*] Exact analogy to the mindset of the center
General solution: K. around the polar powers [sic]
The same drama as in the beginning of the war.

Naulki frech [?] Then: just as the republic was fortified in France 1793–1871, it was also in 1640–59, that the Presbyterian Party, the Independents and the pressure of the Levellers successively secured the modest result that

---

* Luxemburg is referring perhaps to this sentence: "The time had come when the nation, thoroughly excited, only needed known, steady, influential leaders, who would resist, not as adventurers or mere sectaries, but in the name of the rights and interests of the whole country" (Guizot, *History of the English Revolution*, p. 65).

† In the Glorious Revolution of 1688–89, the opponents of royal absolutism in England won the power struggle that had been going on since the beginning of the seventeenth century with the House of Stuart. Since then, the monarch has been the bearer of state sovereignty only in conjunction with Parliament. See Guizot, *History of the English Revolution*, p. 65.

remained after the ~~rest~~ "Glorious Revolution" of 1688 for one to two centuries and which was far below what the Presbyterians had achieved.

Earlier attempts at recovery: The P[arty] Committee." Idea of George [Ledebour?]! Political "heads"

Apparently, there can be no "parties" in sd [Social Democracy] anymore, because it represents only one class. That's only true for ideology. The *theory* is homogeneous, based on a cl[ass]inter[est]. But reality has *stratifications* and *phases* in historical development, in which ours [?] from an organ[izational] member of civil society to its *antipode*.

[*On left margin:*]
NB Hangover idea: Abstention*
K[arl] K[autsky] 4. 8.
Friedrich Adler silence†

(NB The ~~Girondists and~~ Presbyterians appealed only to the legal conditions of Old England, to the Church of Scotland and similar "*prejudices*.")
(NB "In short, the discord was as great in Oxford as it was in London and all the more disastrous because it accelerated the movement in London but slowed it down in Oxford.")
Guizot, p. 259‡
Summa: An oppositional parliamentary party (everywhere)
NB (Difference from rev. People's Party)
Guizot

Charles I (1625–49) convened the Parliament in 1625.§ Requests money for the *war with Spain*. Parliament approves only a small tax and customs duties for only one year. However, it discussed and demanded the end of abuses: use

---

* See the remark by Franz Mehring on Kautsky's response to the SPD's capitulation to World War I in Luxemburg's article "Rebuilding the International" (1915): "In a polemic, Karl Kautsky said: 'I believed that the difficulties of the situation could best be avoided by abstaining. Since neither the majority nor the minority [of the SPD] agreed, it seemed to me at least worth considering making the decision conditional on the granting of guarantees.'" See Luxemburg, *Gesammelte Werke*, Vol. 4, p. 32. Kautsky was referring to a meeting of the Reichstag faction on August 3, 1914, which resulted in its voting for war credits for the German government.

† "The only politics befitting socialism during the war is 'Silence,' only when the peace bells ring does it begin to function again." See Friedrich Adler, "Die Sozialdemokratie in Deutschland und der Krieg," *Der Kampf* (Wien), Vol. 8, No. 1 (January 1915).

‡ Luxemburg is here quoting Guizot from the original: "In short, discord was as great at Oxford as at London, and far more fatal; for in London it precipitated, at Oxford it paralyzed the progress of things."

§ In the source: 1825.

of taxes, ~~religious persecutions,~~ church conditions, Papists, weakness of the navy, etc. NB Sir Robert Cotton's speech. p. 86* The House of Lords refused to sanction the decisions of the Commons, which remained firm. After four months, *dissolution of Parliament* p. 88.

[*On left margin:*] First Parl.

Charles tries to get by without Parliament. In the counties, "voluntary" loans ~~under~~ are attempted among rich citizens, the obstinate should be noted down. *Catholic persecutions* are ordered to win public opinion. The loans failed. The war (sea expedition against Cádiz) was miserable.†
Six months after the dissolution, Parliament was reconvened. The leaders of the opposition were removed (appointed as sheriffs of their counties). But Parliament went even further than the first one, putting the *Duke of Buckingham on trial* (February 21, 1626.)‡

[*On left margin:*] Second Parl.

In response, the king accused the Earl of Bristol of high treason,§ arrested two lords from the lower house and one from the upper house. G. p. 90. Parliament asserted their freedom. Parliament drew up a "general reprimanding presentation." (The draft of the "presentation" was publicly burned.) Then again, after four months, *dissolution of Parliament.* (June 15, 26)
Meanwhile, Charles also got tangled up in a *war with France* (expedition of [La] Rochelle to help the French Protestants).¶ Money became more and more necessary. *General forced loan*, port districts were instructed to equip ships. A *sermon* was ordered everywhere, proclaiming *blind obedience* to the king's

---

* Cotton's speech was directed against policies that debased the coinage in order to pay for military adventures and other extravagances. See *A Speech Made by Sir Robert Cotton, before the Lords of His Majesty's Most Honorable Privy-Council, at the Council-table: Being Thither Called to Deliver His Opinion Touching the Alteration of Coin* (London: The Horne, 1690).

† This was an effort by the English and Dutch in 1625 to seize the lucrative Spanish city of Cádiz. They failed to intercept the Spanish fleet and were forced to withdraw without obtaining any of their objectives.

‡ George Villiers, the Duke of Buckingham, was a close companion of Charles I during the early years of his reign. He was much disliked by Parliament, which tried to impeach him for a series of military misadventures and misappropriation of funds. Although he was not convicted, he was assassinated a year later.

§ John Digby, First Earl of Bristol, was sent to the Tower of London over his conflict with the Duke of Buckingham, one of Charles I's favorite courtiers. Later the king and Digby reconciled, and he remained a staunch loyalist during the English Revolution.

¶ In 1627, Charles I commissioned a fleet under the command of the Duke of Buckingham to attack the French Port of La Rochelle, a stronghold of Protestant Huguenots that he hoped to make use of in his conflict with Louis XIII of France. The English were soundly defeated by the French.

power. *Bishop of Canterbury* refused to give it, was dismissed and banished. Citizens who refused to sign the loan were drafted into the army or imprisoned. *Martial law* was proclaimed against the soldiers' debauchery. Noisy grumbling that this happened without parliament. [La] Rochelle's expedition failed. General ~~ung~~ excitement.

March 17, 1628, Parliament convened again. For the elections, prisoners are released and enthusiastically welcomed. Twenty-seven of them elected to Parliament. Parliament initially voted on an important *tax*, but did *not* yet give it the *force of law*. On the other hand, both houses met to work out a general *Petition of Rights*. The king offered to reaffirm and abide by the Magna Carta, the House of Lords ~~and~~ would have been satisfied with that. However, the Commons insisted on their demand, worked alone on the *petition* and submitted it to the Lords for approval. The Lords tried a *compromise amendment*. The Commons rejected it. The Lords had to comply. Charles tried to avoid it, but yielded. *The petition became law*. The *tax law* was also now definitively adopted.

[*On left margin:*] Third Parliament

Leaders of the Opp. in Third Parliament: Sir Edward Coke, Sir Thomas Wentworth, Sir John Eliot, Denzil Holles, Pym, etc. p. 95. G. 98.

Despite the adoption of the *Bill of Rights*,[*] the *practice* remained the same: Buckingham remained at the helm, customs duties were arbitrarily levied. The Commons worked out two new "remonstrances" in one week. The answer: *adjournment of Parliament*.

Two months later, *Buckingham was murdered*. From then on, Charles ruled as an absolutist. *Laud* became Bishop of London. Customs duties were forcibly collected. *Special courts* were in full activity. At the same time, betrayal: *Wentworth*[†] ~~(Straftebury)~~ Strafford appointed minister.[‡]

Second session of Parliament. It was determined that the publication of the Bill of Rights had been forged by the government and that an evasive wording of the king was added. G. 102 Charles demanded the granting of customs duties for the entire period of his government. Instead, the commons drew up complaints against the abuses. The speaker did not want to allow the vote

---

[*] A constitutional landmark act of 1689 setting out basic civil rights and who would inherit the crown.

[†] Thomas Wentworth, First Earl of Strafford, was one of the strongest supporters of Charles I. After the opponents of the king in Parliament had him tried for treason because of his policies when serving as Lord Deputy of Ireland, Charles reluctantly agreed to his execution.

[‡] The murder of George Villiers, First Duke of Buckingham, was a watershed moment in the revolution. It occurred on August 23, 1628.

and wanted to leave; he was forcibly detained, the hall closed from the inside and the king's messenger was not allowed in. *Dissolution of Parliament.**

1629–1640 Absolutism
Great trials against the incarcerated. Refusing to release them on bail. Refusal of the convicts to pay the fines. *Peace agreement with Spain and France.* Rule of Strafford—[William] Laud.† Arbitrary customs duties, monopolies and price-gouging foodstuffs, trade with public offices, mercenary justice, high fines, corruption (*Lord Mountnorris trial*)‡ G. 116. Defenselessness of the sea trade, piracy. Uncertainty of property (growth of royal forests 115). Deficit of finances. Favoring the Papists (Laud offered the cardinal's hat). Persecution of nonconformists.§ Emigration of these, as well as French, Dutch and German craftsmen. Strict *censorship* against writings of religious content—protest by the ecclesiastical courts! (G. 120) History and death of the *preacher Workman*¶ NB G. 127. Catholicization of the Anglican. Cults. Counter-reformation. Emigration of dissident sects (Brownists,** Independents) to America. *Ban on emigration* just as *Cromwell,* [*John*] *Pym,* [*Arthur*] *Haselrig and Hampden* had embarked.†† Emergence of a lot of new dissident sects. ~~since~~ *1636*: a flood of *pamphlets* (smuggled in from Holland). Severe persecutions because of them. *Trial against Prynne,* [*Henry*] *Burton and* [*John*] *Bastwick* (129).‡‡ *Trial against* [*John*] *Lilburne.*§§ *Hampden trial*¶¶ over twenty shillings of ship money. (132) *Uprising in Edinburgh* against the new liturgy

---

* Parliament was dissolved on March 2, 1629.
† Laud was archbishop of Canterbury from 1633 until his execution in 1645.
‡ Francis Annesley Valentia, or Lord Mountnorris, played a central role in the colonization of Ireland while serving as secretary of state under Charles I. He was brought to trial by Wentworth on the grounds of taking a percentage of revenue meant for the government for his private use. He was convicted, removed from office, and sent to prison in Dublin.
§ Nonconformists at the time referred to such dissident Protestants as Baptists and Congregationalists.
¶ John Workman was a minister who preached against the use of images in churches and consequently was imprisoned in 1633. When released from prison, he opened a school that Laud closed down; Workman is reported to have suffered severe mental illness before his death.
** Followers of Robert Browne, a Puritan Congregationalist leader who demanded separation from the Church of England.
†† Pym, Haselrig, and Hampden were among the Parliamentarians opposed to Charles I whom he attempted to arrest in 1642. They all fled, and the furor over their attempted arrest helped spark the English Civil War.
‡‡ Burton and Bastwick, both English Puritans, had their ears cut off by Laud, the archbishop of Canterbury, for writings that sharply criticized the Church of England.
§§ Lilburne was a leader of the Levellers, one of the most radical tendencies of the English Revolution. He coined the phrase "freeborn rights," meaning rights that cannot be denied to any individual. He was put on trial by Cromwell's followers for writing articles that criticized members of Parliament for living in luxury while common peopled starved. His writings have often been considered a direct source of the First Amendment to the US Constitution.
¶¶ Hampden, one of five opposition Parliamentarians that Charles I unsuccessfully tried to arrest in 1642, was put on trial for refusing to pay the tax that provided the money for shipbuilding.

(after the abolition of the Calv[inist] Reformation and reintroduction of the episcopate). *March 1, 1638, the Scottish Covenant* ~~ab~~ *created.*[*] (G. 136) War with Scotland. 1639[†] in Treaty of Berwick without result. Rebellion once more after Charles breaks his word. ~~Against the Scots~~

Convocation of the Parliament, April 13, 1640. Elections result in a very moderate majority. Demand of aid funds for the war against Scotland. The House of Commons wanted to discuss its complaints first. The House of Lords supported the king, but the lower house remained firm. *Dissolution of Parliament* after three weeks.

[*On left margin:*] Fourth Parl.

The second Scottish war began.[‡] Main funds from Ireland, from the Papists and through all kinds of oppressions, forced loans, monopolies, ship money, etc. Opposition members of Parliament were arrested and persecuted. The army sympathized with the Scots and did not want to fight "against brothers." Money was lacking. Charles wavered and ~~they~~ called for general elections *November 3, 1640, The Long Parliament* convened.[§]

[*On left margin:*] Fifth Parl.
ii.

The Long Parliament

Rule of the Presbyterian Party (1640–43)[¶]
Political reform

Before the Civil War. Split of parties. Parliament seizes power.

---

    * This is referred to by historians as the National Covenant.
    † In the original: 1839.
    ‡ The major factor behind what Luxemburg calls "the second Scottish war," which the subject literature more commonly refers to as the Bishops' Wars of 1639–40, is the long-standing conflict between the people of Scotland and the crown about liturgical and religious practice. This was exacerbated by Charles' imposition of a deeply unpopular liturgy on Scottish churches in July 1637. Matters came to a head when protesters signed the National Covenant in Scotland in February 1638. October 18, 1637, marked the intensification of the conflict about religious practice between ordinary Scottish people and Royalist liturgy was introduced to Scottish churches. This immediately sparked a women-led riot in St. Giles Kirk, Edinburgh, the principal church building in Scotland.
    § The Long Parliament convened from 1640 to 1660. It received its name from an act of Parliament that stipulated the body could only be dissolved by agreement of its members.
    ¶ In the source: 1840.

Immediately after ~~Sam~~ meeting, petitions were read out from all sides to investigate abuses and complaints. *Forty commissions.* ~~From~~ Farmers and citizens traveled to London in droves to bring complaints to parliament. *"Delinquent lists." G. 150.* Revival of public gatherings of sects, pamphlets. Nov. 11, 1640, *at Pym's request, Strafford was accused of high treason, and arrested, as was Laud.** ~~Because~~ Other ministers fled. Parliament seized power; *it suspended commissioners who took over the whole administration* and granted them funds for day-to-day business through *public loans.* The sentences against *Prynne, Burton, Bastwick, Leighton and Lilburne* were lifted, and they were released.

New law: *Parliament must* ~~conve~~ *assemble at least every three years* (with or against the king) and may not be adjourned or dissolved before fifty days, it elects the speakers itself.

[*On left margin:*] ~~Wotte~~ NB. Letter of Strafford to Charles I. 167.

Abolition of the Star Chamber,† the Northern Court [of Justice], the high ecclesiastical court‡ and *all special courts.* Various and conflicting petitions concerning the church structure. *Conflict of the sects* (156/7).

Ministry of Mediation was proposed and discussed. At the same time, Charles hatched a conspiracy in the army, which was betrayed and destroyed all mediation. *Trial of Strafford* NB 161–8. *Bill of attainder* Execution May 12, 1641. Charles gives his consent to everything.

The parliamentary party (Pym, Hampden, Holles) has to rely on the radical element of the Presbyterians ~~sects~~. Charles seeks to engineer a conspiracy in Scotland and goes there. Parliament adjourns, but leaves two commissions behind: one follows the king, the other, chaired by Pym, runs the London office. The intrigue in Scotland fails and is uncovered.

Catholic Royalist uprising in Ireland,§ bloody persecution of English Protestants. The House of Commons votes on a *general notice of appeal* against the government. This leads to an open *split between two parties*: moderate, Royalist (Lord Falkland, Hyde, [John] Colepeper, L. Holland, Palmer) and

---

* Laud, archbishop of Canterbury, was arrested at the same time as Wentworth and held at the Tower of London.

† The Star Chamber was the court made up of judges and privy councillors that grew out of the medieval king's council as a supplement to the regular justice of the common-law courts.

‡ This probably refers to the Court of High Commission, which was the supreme English ecclesiastical court. It was established by the crown in the sixteenth century as a means to enforce the laws of the Reformation settlement. It was finally dissolved by the Long Parliament in 1641; prior to then, the court was convened at will by the sovereign, and had near-unlimited power over civil as well as church matters.

§ The Irish rebellion of November 1, 1641, in which the Irish Catholic gentry rose against the Protestants in the name of liberty to worship for their country.

more radical (Pym, Hampden, Cromwell), which balance each other. p. 177.

Struggle of the parties begins. A Royalist party, half and half joined by the City,* demonstratively received Charles returning from Scotland.

The House of Commons adopts three laws:

(1) Citizens may only be enlisted into the army in the event of a foreign invasion of the country;

(2) The organization of the militia and the renewal of its generals shall be subject to the approval of Parliament;

(3) Clergymen are excluded from every civil office.

The streets are full of crowds and battles. *Cavaliers and Roundheads.*

The *twelve bishops* of the House of Peer, against whom the street crowds were usually directed, put resigned—after a meeting with Charles—from Parliament and declared all his acts unlawful in advance. They were placed in the tower by both chambers. The intrigues and conspiracies of the court with the Cavaliers increased the excitement. The House of Commons (of whom Charles had taken the guard) had *weapons* brought into the courtroom and kept the *militias of London* equipped.

Charles brings *charges of high treason* against L[ord] Kimbolton† of the upper house as well as *Hampden, Pym, Holles,* [William] *Strode* and [Arthur] *Haslerig*. NB 185.

Struggle for the immunity of the five members. *Charles' escape from London, January 10, 1642.*

The threat posed to the five members of Parliament became a signal of a general movement for Parliament. The House of Commons quickly adopted laws:

(1) No member may be arrested without his consent.;

(2) In an emergency, the Parliament may adjourn to any place;

(3) The country is in danger and a state of defense declared.

The House of Commons took possession of the Tower, Portsmouth, Hull and all strongholds and arsenals. The House of Lords half-reluctantly complies with the measures. p. 192.

Petition storm from all strata to provoke the House of Commons. 195 *Women's procession and petition*. Petitions demanded (1) reform of the church, (2) corporal punishment of the Papists, (3) oppression of the evil-minded, including the *House of Lords*. (In the upper house, there were [around] thirty Lords on the side of the People's Party)

The main concern of the House of Commons at this moment: *to get hold of the militia* in order to be equipped for the secret armaments of the Cavalier army. Charles prolonged it his reply. The upper house, intimidated, joined the lower house in the militia cause. At the same time, it excluded *the bishops* by a law.

---

* That is, the City of London.

† This is the trial and impeachment of Edward Montagu, Baron Kimbolton, for treason.

Charles accepted this law, but refused to hand over the militia. Meanwhile, the queen ~~went~~ traveled *to the Continent* to raise arms and money. The House of Commons demanded Charles' return to London. Instead he went to York. General excitement. Flood of writings, leaflets, journals all over the country. In parliamentary writings, *Hyde* and *Falkland* wrote responses for the king, which Charles himself copied at night in York and published on behalf of the Council of State.[†] The effect of these writings was great. The Royalist party strengthened. *The House of Commons resorted to vigorous repressive measures.*

April 23, 1642, *War openly breaks out* when Charles sought to seize Hull's arsenal with 300 cavaliers, and was rejected. *Thirty-two lords and over sixty members of Commons* traveled *to* York for Charles. The lower house ~~comma~~ ordered the *formation of militias*, forbade them from taking up arms by order of the king, moved the arsenal from Hull to London, took out a loan of £100,000 in the City and had Charles monitored. cf. p. 265.

Royalist Meeting on Heyworth-Moor (40 000), where the majority (peasants) accepted a petition in line with Parliament. p. 206.

The uprising in Ireland continued and became increasingly violent. Charles offered to suppress it himself; the House of Commons rejected it and gave supreme command of the fleet against Charles *A* Protest to Earl of Warwick. *Appeal to citizens to collect money for armaments: silverware,* wedding rings and hairpins of poor women. Charles' similar appeal and its failure.

Meanwhile, the ~~House of Commons~~ Parliament drafted *settlement proposals* and sent them to the king: ~~Peers~~ Appointment of new peers, education and marriage of royal children, appointment ~~of all~~ and dismissal of all senior officials, all military, earls and clergy ~~without consent~~ only with participation of Parliament. Parliament demanded total authority *(that is, instead of parliamentary regimes* ~~in the sense~~ *in present sense of direct rule of the Parliament as government). Charles' Reply.* NB 209: Sir Benjamin Rudyerd's warning speech before the start of the Civil War.[‡] Parliament confiscates *all state revenue.*

---

[*] Edward Hyde, First Earl of Clarendon, was loyal to Charles I but opposed his proposal to annul Parliament twice.

[†] Luxemburg uses "Staatsrat" at this point in the manuscript, to describe the monarchical-state institution led by Charles I, and whose name Charles used to lend legitimacy to his own positions. This is somewhat misleading, since the English Council of State is the name of the institution first appointed by the Rump Parliament on February 14, 1649, *after* the execution of Charles I. The body of courtiers through which Charles I enacted his autocratic rule is referred to as the Privy Council.

[‡] Rudyerd was a renowned poet, and also one of the major early financiers of colonialism in what would later become Nicaragua. In 1630, he became a co-incorporator of the Providence Company, established to fund a colony on Providence Island and on the Mosquito Coast. In a famous speech given as a member of Parliament in 1640, he stated, "I would desire nothing more than that we proceed with such moderation as the Parliament may be the mother of many more happy parliaments."

Comité of public safety. Formation of the army decreed (20,000 inf., fifteen squadrons of sixty horses). All leaders of Parliament as officers, Earl of Essex as general.

III.

The Long Parliament

The Civil War. A year of hesitation. Party struggles.

On August 23, 1642,* Charles officially ~~comm~~ called to arms under his banner in Nottingham. His army formed slowly and weakly, it finally amounted to 12,000 men. *Essex* had a committee of both houses in the camp with him and followed Charles idly. Charles marched on London. Here the whole population took part in preparations.

Oct. 23 Battle of Edgehill. NB Its course!† pp. 216, 218. Peace negotiations! *Battle at Brentford*, victory for Charles. London recruited *new militiamen* (4,000 from the city, many apprentices). Essex now had *24,000* men. There were always quarrels in his council between parliamentary leaders ~~his~~ who advised ~~rapid action~~ toward the offensive and all those officers who hesitated, distrusting the untrained militias. NB 219. The army mostly unsettled the party struggle, the ~~strug~~ resistance and belligerence of the Royalist party of the City. Negotiations again.

At the same time, the struggle between the two camps spread *to all counties*, which conscripted soldiers, imposed taxes and led battles all on their own. 222

Character of war. NB 222–3.

February 1643 the queen returned from Holland and began to work from York.

March 1643 negotiations again with the king.

Cromwell's peasant cavalry (1,000 men.) 231. Party struggles in Parliament. Waller's Conspiracy‡ (May 31, 43) Hampden's death, June 24, 43.

The state of Essex's army is poor. *Defeats*: ~~the~~ Fairfax, ~~etc.~~ W. Waller etc. *Big losses*. New training of *10,000 men* under *Manchester* and *Cromwell*. Parliament's energy. ~~Negotiations with Scotland.~~ Negotiations for peace once more ~~under~~ pressure proposed by the House of Lords. Peace petitions. Women's demonstration. Victory of the radical party in the lower house. (August 1643) Some of the Lords go over to the king. The ~~P~~ terrible situation of the war stifled

---

* In the source: 1842.

† Battle of October 23, 1642, in Warwickshire, in which both armies were close by—Essex had overtaken the king's army.

‡ Waller's Conspiracy is better known as the Rye House Plot of 1683, an attempt to assassinate Charles II during the Restoration.

once again the party struggle. Essex's army was increased to 14,000 (except for the two reserves of Manchester and Waller).

[*On left margin:*] (In the vote [around] 150 members in the House of Commons.)

NB Gloucester's siege as Gloucester's reply Aug. 10, 43, 244.*
Sept. 20, 43 First *Battle of Newbury*, ~~victory~~ bravura of the London militia. *Lord Falkland and his death.*
Alliance with Scotland (Aug. 25, 43) "Solemn league and Covenant" [p. 248] (political and religious). This won Parliament an army of *21,000 Scots*.

~~III The Long Parliament – Rise of the independent party, Disintegration of the Presbyterians. Analysis of the P~~

IV.

The Long Parliament

1643–44. Disintegration of the Presbyterian Party. War always undecided. Reform of the army.

~~An~~ Internal contradictions of Presbyterians: ecclesiastical Republicanism, political ~~er~~ moderate monarchism. G. 250ff. Suppression of sects, censorship.
Political reform, Presb. program, carried out until the end of 1643, mission completed. At the same time, war with Charles undecided. *Charles concludes a cease-fire with rebellious Ireland* Sept. 5, 43, and relocated the army to England against the Parliament. ~~At the sam~~ Royalist Counter-parliament opened in Oxford on Jan. 22, 1644, numbering forty-five Lords and 118 Commons members. On the same day, the ~~payout~~ roll call in Westminster resulted in twenty-two Lords and 280 Commons members, as well as one hundred Commons members who were absent on behalf of the Parliament. Charles had to adjourn his *Oxford Parliament on April 16.*
The 1643/44 campaign left the main armies without action, but the Parliament achieved a number of successes in the counties, strengthening and organizing itself.
To ensure that Parliament's measures were not known too quickly and were not too slow, NB a "*Committee of Both Kingdoms*" was formed out of seven Lords, fourteen Commons members and four Scottish commissioners, with the highest power over war, foreign policy, etc. [p. 248]

---

* A reference to the Battle of Edgehill of August 10 to September 5, 1643, between the Parliamentarian garrison headed by Gloucester and the king and his army. It ended with the withdrawal of Royalist forces.

At the beginning of the 1644 campaign, in May, the *entire parliamentary army* under this committee included over 55,000 men (21,000 Scots under Earl of Leven, 10,500 under Essex, 5,100 under Waller, 14,000 under Manchester (and Cromw.), and 5–6,000 under Fairfax. In addition, 8,000 London militiamen joined them. G. 269 NB Financial resources for their maintenance!

Siege of Oxford. Charles' escape. Defeat of Waller, Jun. 29.

Decisive Battle before York at *Marston Moor*, July 2, 44. Rupert with 20,000 and Newcastle with?* On the other side, Fairfax, Manchester and the Scots (about 40,000), escape of the Scots. *Decision by Cromwell's peasant cavalry. S First victory of the Independents and their strategy.* 3,000 dead and 1,600 wounded in the ~~Roal~~ Cavaliers. 274/5

Essex's defeat in Cornwallis. His resignation rejected from Parliament.

Montrose at the top of the high ~~Scot~~ countries in Scotland. Charles marches on London. *Battle* (second!) *at Newbury*, Oct. 27, 44.[†] Manchester's, Waller's and Essex's army (without Essex, who stayed in London), plus five regiments of London militias under Sir James Harington.[‡] Charles retreats to Oxford to his winter quarters.

Grumbling in London about the length and indecisiveness of the war, splitting of the army and friction among generals. *Cromwell's speech against the waiting tactics of the Presbyterians*, namely Lord Manchester against the Scots, against the House of Lords and against royalty. p. 282.

Attempts of the Presbyterians to overthrow Cromwell.

Negotiations at Uxbridge with the King.

Dec. 21, 1644 NB. "*Self-Denying Ordinance*" as a blow against the Presb. [p. 291f.]. Political escalation. *Trials against Laud*, etc. Five executions.

Reorganization of the army: An army of 21,000 men, Feb. 19, 45, under a general with full power: *Fairfax*. Essex's and Manchester's dismissal. NB "The horde of preaching peasants and craftsmen who ~~the~~ chased away famous officers and were commanded by leaders as unknown and inexperienced as themselves." 302. *Satirical songs of the Cavaliers.*

NB *Cromwell remains an officer* despite Self-Denying Ordinance.[§] His victories at Oxford, end of April 1644. (In addition, ~~Sir W~~ Brereton, ~~Sir S.~~ Myddleton and ~~Sir~~ Price remain with the army as exceptions).

---

* The Battle of Marston Moor, July 2, 1644; Luxemburg is referring here to Rupert, Prince of the Rhine, who fought with Newcastle.

† This is the Second Battle of Newbury.

‡ "Harrington" in the manuscript.

§ The Self-Denying Ordinance was an act passed by Parliament on April 3, 1645, that stipulated that all members of the body that were also members of the parliamentary army be required to resign from one or the other position within six weeks. It was passed as part of a debate on the need to create a professional army.

V.

The Long Parliament

IV The Independents' Army. Campaign 1645/46

Battle of Naseby, 13 June 45. Cromwell appointed again for three months. The Lords advise new negotiations. Cromwell and [Henry] Ireton, among others, on the other hand, *publicly read the King's letters in Guildhall* to the people. Publication of *"The King's Cabinet Opened"* 308. Effect: even more energetic armaments and warfare.

310 NB Disintegration in the Cavalier's army. The *"Clubman"*. Peasant rebellion against Cavaliers and the war. *Cromwell suppresses and outlaws them.* (319)

The House of Commons ~~co-opts itself~~ replenishes itself *with new elections.* 320. 130 members in the place of those who went over to Charles: some best Independent leaders (Fairfax, Ireton, Ludlow etc.). Thus, the *Independents are strengthened.* Resolutions: no more negotiations with Charles.

Cromwell's command extended for another four months.

Greater severity against royalists.

Sale of a large part of the goods of the bishops and state criminals.

Ban on giving pardon to an armed Irishman in England.

Conflict *with the Scots. Charles offers peace.* After that publication of *Charles' secret contract with Ireland* (of August 20, 1645.) 322. Continuation of the war inevitable. The king's army worn down. Escape of the Prince of Wales. Charles' secret negotiations with the Independents and his offer *to return to London. Parliamentary measures against it.* NB 326. Reign of Terror, siege of ~~Newark~~ Oxford. *Charles' escape from Oxford on April 27 and arrival in the* ~~to~~ *Scottish camp on* ~~April 27~~ *May 5, 46.*

VI.

The Long Parliament

Struggle of the Independents for political dominance = struggle between Parliament and army.

The biggest concern of the Independents ~~i~~ is to prevent the *fugitive king from connecting with the Presbyterians* (City). They are looking for a *break with the Scots.*

([John] *Milton's* struggle for freedom of conscience, freedom of the press and the right to divorce.)

Still *unsteady majority* of the Independents in the lower house, minority in the upper house.

NB 331 *The Municipal Council of the City* presents a favorable petition to *the Scots*, which is directed *against the sects* and demands their suppression. *The Lords* thank the council.

Presbyterians ruled *some regiments* left over from Essex's army (Major General Massey). The Independents pushed *through the* their *dissolution.* 331.

The lower house decided to pay off *the Scots* with £100,000 and *send them home.*

The Scots mistreat Charles as a prisoner. NB *The "controversy"* with Henderson (May 29 – July 16) *about his conversion to Presbyterianism!* [p. 333]

NB! p. 334. *July 23, Proposals of Parliament* (both Houses) delivered to the king: acceptance of the covenant, abolition of the Episcopal Church, relinquishment of command over army, fleet and militia to the chambers for twenty years, expulsion of seventy-one Royalists from amnesty, exclusion of *all* Royalists from all public offices.

All Presbyterians, Scots, the queen, the French court pressure Charles *to accept the conditions!* (Petitions from cities, including the City, *banned* only by Parliament.)

August 1, Charles' evasive answer and request *to be admitted into London.* (At the same time, Charles is still scheming with the Irish and the Pope). 333.

Triumph of the Independents.

Scots offer to leave England, but after everything they were already paid, they demand £700,000. The Independents *no* longer want to grant anything, the Presbyterians negotiate it down to £400,000 in two installments. In addition, immediate *loans* in the City, premised on the *sale of church property.* Big *fight with Scots* about Charles himself. Leaflets, conferences, etc. Hate against Scots. After Charles surrenders to Parliament, *the Presbyterians* hope *to be able to dissolve the army, the main pillar of the Independents.* Hence pressure on the Scots to hand Charles over and yield to them.

Hamilton's efforts to persuade Charles to accept the terms. *Charles' five-time demand to be heard personally in London.*

Jan. 1, 1647, The train of 200 boxes of £1000 silver *wage for the Scots* arrived in York (on thirty-six wagons, under cover of an infantry division). Dispute in Parliament as to whether Charles should be handed over to the infantry together with the receipt for the money or received formally by a deputation.

February 9–16, 47 Charles transferred to Holmby Castle.*

NB 19. 2. Resolution of the House of Commons to dissolve the army (with exclusion of troops against Ireland, for garrisons and for public safety). Triumph of the Presbyterians ([Denzil] Holles, Glynn, [Philip] Stapleton, [John] Maynard, Waller). Beginning of the struggle between Parliament and army.

---

* This is more commonly known as Holdenby House.

[*On left margin:*] Since then, declining influence of the Independents in Parliament.

The Independents (Cromwell, Ireton, Lambert, [Thomas] Harrison, [Robert] Hammond, [Thomas] Pride, Rich, [Thomas] Rainsborough—all the best officers)* began to complain in the army against the dissolution (insisting on the full payment of arrears, refusing the service against Ireland, sticking together).
(1) ~~Pleas~~ *Petition of fourteen officers to the Parliament*
(2) *Petition on behalf of all officers and soldiers* (full payment, pension for cripples and widows, no forced deployment against Ireland) no longer addressed to the Parliament but *to Fairfax*.
Parliament's resolution and threat against the "machinations in the army." [p. 344] Ban of petitions. Refusal ~~all~~ of the officers to go to Ireland without their (Independent) generals—Fairfax, Cromwell, etc.
(3) *Petition of 141 officers to Parliament*
(4) *Petition of eight cavalry regiments (soldiers) to go to Ireland*. Appearance of the three soldiers appear before Parliament. Presbyterian turmoil.

VII.

Cromwell to [Edmund] Ludlow: "These people will not rest until the army drags them out by their ears." (346)

[*On left margin:*] NB Prophecy!

Organization in the army. (346) The army as autonomous power. Open rebellion against the order to dissolve. ~~A~~
May 29, 47, letter from soldiers to Fairfax Open struggle. In London, the militia is taken away from the Independents. Presbyterian generals (Waller, Poyntz, [Edward] Massey) as well as officers of Essex's army ~~are preparing~~ as well as *the City* are preparing themselves ~~to attack~~ to form a counter-army. ~~Exception~~ Secret *negotiations between Parliament and the king* to bring him to London. NB 318/9
June 3, 47 Charles kidnapped by the army at Cromwell's order.
Incitement against Cromwell in Parliament. (354) Scene. June 10, 47, Cromwell leaves the lower house and presents himself openly as the head of the army.
The "humble presentation" of the army to Parliament with a political program. (354)

---

* A reference to the foundation of the New Model Army (functioning between 1645 and 1660) of Parliamentarians dissatisfied with the army during the civil war.

Parliament prepares for resistance: enlistment of recruits, alliance with the City, London in defensive position.

~~Demand~~ The army advances against London. Their demand to kick out eleven Presbyterian leaders (Holles, Stapleton, Maynard, Waller, Glynn, Massey, and others) from Parliament. *June 26, 47, these eleven "voluntarily"* ~~left tr~~ stepped down.

Parliament acquiesces to all the demands of the army.

! ~~Secret~~ Negotiations of Cromwell and the army with Charles. Their conditions p. 360, third refusal of Charles.

NB *Revolt of the Presbyterians* (City)* and citizens fight in London ~~(Since July 23, the army marches again against London. Meanwhile~~ in secret contact with Charles! (p. 364) Siege, invasion of the Parliament by the people. General demand (1) *The militia* should again be taken away from the Independents and placed under Presbyterian rule. ~~Parliament obeys~~ (2) Recalling the king. Parliament obeys. (Ludlow is the only one voting loudly against).

The army marches hastily on London (July 23, 47). Sixty members of both houses, including the two speakers (Lord Manchester and [William] Lenthall), *flee London toward the army in order to be protected from the mob.*

In London, the eleven Presbyterians return to Parliament, election of new speaker, recruitment of a new army, recalling the king. But the Independents worked hard. *The City soon submitted itself to the army* formally.

August 6, 47 Triumphal entry of the army into London. Presbyterian leaders flee. The sixty or more parliamentary members who fled the country were reinstated and Fairfax was appointed commander of the tower.

August 1647 The Independents take possession of authority. City, both houses and people comply.

Independents openly develop *the Republican program*. Radicalism in all areas. Leaflets and petitions on rationalism. Egalitarianism, communism. Sectarianism. (*Lilburne* continues in the tower!)

Charles at Hampton Court, Cromwell's intrigue with the king. Suspicions against Cromwell in the army. Lilburne's agitation against him. *Formation of the radical left in the army* (Rainsborough, Hewers, Harrison, Rob. Lilburne (brother), Scott among others).

Pamphlets. Fairfax enforces strict censorship. (373)

~~The intercepted Bri~~ "New Agents" chosen in the army. [p. 373] Oct. 9, 47, Declaration on behalf of five Cavalier regiments "The Situation of the Army":

Nov. 1, 47 "An Agreement of the People" (sixteen regiments) Political and Social Program (p. 375) *The Officers' Council in Putney.* 376.

Charles' intercepted letter to the queen.

Charles' escape from Hampton Court. Nov. 11, 47, to the Isle of Wight (with

---

* This is presumably the revolt of the Presbyterians in Kent, on May 29.

Cromwell's knowledge?) 383.

The Army assembly on goods. Nov. 15, 47, Death-sentence against the "insurgents." 384.

Parliament's vote of gratitude to Cromwell. (Ludlow protests)

Thereupon *reconciliation and harmony in the army* (general assembly in the headquarters) at the price of Charles' downfall.

Parliament's last proposal to Charles (the four Bills), his refusal.

Resolution of the two chambers (Jan. 15, 48) to govern from now on without the king. (390)

Royalist counter-demonstrations. Apprentices from the City! 394. *Reprisals, trials, censorship*, quartering of the army in London. 392. Ban on "riotous assembly," state of siege. *Uprising in Wales* (395). Scotland for Ch decides to set up a "danger committee" and 40,000 troops against the Republicans and sectarians. [p. 395]

The City demonstrates against the Republicans

April 28, 1648, The House of Commons decides

(1) Preservation of the monarchy and the House of Lords;
(2) Implementation of the proposals to Charles (in Hampton Court) "for establishing public peace." NB 396.

Cromwell seeks a compromise with the Presbyterians, rejected by them.

Cromwell's *proposal to the Council of Officers* to march to London and *drive out all the Presbyterians from Parliament* is rejected by Fairfax and others.

Armed uprising of royalist *Cavaliers* in London and in the counties, in the fleet. 398 Open religious and political counterrevolution. *Even the Presbyterians are afraid* of falling into the hands of the Cavaliers. Their vigorous measures in the House of Commons

(1) an against the Independents:
(May 6–24, 48) renewed negotiations with the king, command over the militia assigned to the City, death penalty against heresy and blasphemy.
(2) against the Cavaliers:

Banishment of the Papists from London, sale of the goods of delinquents, sale of the church estates, troops sent with Fairfax against the Cavaliers.

City fully satisfied, decides to live and die with the Parliament.

Fairfax, Cromwell and [John] Lambert along with the army crush the Cavaliers' revolt in fourteen days.

The Presbyterians in the House of Commons want to negotiate with Charles in London.

NB June 48. The eleven (June 26, 47) exiled representatives are recalled.

July 8, 48, Hamilton's invasion of England *with the Scots (14,000)*

NB The whole time: Presbyterians have Parliament in their hands, but the Independents have the *Derby House Committee*. This now directs all troops with Cromwell against the Scots. Cromwell is *completely destroys them in three great battles* and captures Hamilton.

Presbyterians fear Cromwell's victory. Attempts to overthrow him fail. Desperate *decision of Parliament to begin negotiations with the king* to bring peace at all costs. NB p. 408.

Fifteen commissioners go to the Isle of Wight. to

Sept. 18, 48 Beginning negotiations with Charles. He continues to scheme with France and Ireland and makes concessions only as a pretense to prepare his escape. *The scenes.* 410ff.

Negotiations extended three times. Voted five times that the king's concessions are insufficient. *Inconclusive.*

Republican petition storm. Renewal of the "*General Council of the Army*" Nov. 48 [p. 414f.]

Nov. 20 *The army demands* that the chambers bring Charles to justice, proclaim the sovereignty of the people, make the king electable by Parliament, equal suffrage and to close the Parliament until a new one is elected.

New flare-up of the Royalist uprising.

The House of Commons discussed the terms of the agreement with Charles.

Nov. 30, 48 King kidnapped by the army from the Isle of Wight and brought to Hurst Castle.

Outrage of the Presbyterians in the chamber. After a twenty-four-hour session, they vote on December 5, 48, with 140 votes against 104 that Charles' answers should be accepted as the basis for peace.

Dec. 6–7, 48 The army marches into London under Fairfax and Ireton, occupies Westminster and *expels 143 members of Parliament.* (The Chamber considered the army's proposals *with fifty votes against twenty-eight.* The twenty-eight left voluntarily.) N The Independents rule in the chamber. NB 423.

Dec. 7 Cromwell, back from the Scottish campaign, takes his place in the House of Commons. Ovation for him. He moves into the royal home in Whitehall.

The army introduces *a constitutional plan* and demands trial against Charles.

Dec. 23, 48 Charles transferred by the army from Hurst Castle to Windsor. (425)

Dec. 23, 48 Resolution of the Commons to bring Charles to trial. High Court of Justice of 150 commissioners.

The House of Lords (twelve Lords) unanimously reject the resolution.

The House of Commons decides to lead *without the Lords.* The High Court of Justice is reduced to *135.*

For the Court sessions (Jan. 8–19, 49.) only fifty-eight members appeared at the most.

Jan. 20, 49 Trial. Only sixty-nine (out of 135) members of the High Court were present had accepted as court.

January 22 Second trial day (the twenty-first was a Sunday) only sixty-two members of the court present (Fairfax stayed away).

Jan. 27 Judgment. By force and cunning, *fifty-nine signatures* of the judges brought together.

Jan. 30, 49 Execution (Jan. 30, 48 = Feb. 9, 49?) [p. 445f.]

Feb. 6, 49 Abolition of the House of Lords with forty-four against twenty-nine votes.

Feb. 7, 49 Abolition of monarchy. "Experience has shown and this House declares that the kingly office in this country is useless, burdensome and dangerous to the liberty, safety and public interest of the people. As a result, it is abolished from today on." [p. 447]

(1) How many negotiations between Parl[iament] and Charles? Their contents.
(2) Military action[s] of the Civil War. Training of the army.
(3) Role of the Scots in different phases.
(4) Petitions and their fates.
(5) Presence of the Parliament (both chambers).
6) History of the Presbyterian Party.
(7) " " of the Independents.
(8) Cromwell's role.
(9) Parliament's demands at various stages.

A Glossary of Personal Names

Adler, Friedrich (1879–1960), Austrian physicist and Social Democrat. A leading theoretician of the Austro-Marxist school; lecturer at the University of Zurich (1907–11); editor of the Swiss Social Democratic newspaper *Volksrecht* (1910–11); after that, secretary of the Social Democratic Party of Austria; assassinated Count Karl von Stürgkh, the Austrian prime minister, on October 21, 1916. He was a spokesperson for the left wing of the Social Democratic Party of Austria after 1914.

Akimov, Mikhail (1847–1915), conservative Russian politician, served as assistant prosecutor in Kiev in the early 1880s; minister of justice in Sergei Witte's government in 1906 and later chairman of the Imperial State Council.

Aksakov, Sergei (1791–1859), Russian writer and translator; colleague of Nikolai Gogol, Ivan Turgenev, and Leo Tolstoy; broke from classical forms in order to express themes of everyday life; best known for *A Family Chronicle* (1840), renowned for its detailed portrayal of the Russian nobility.

Alexander II (1818–81), Russian tsar from 1855 to 1881; initially pursued a cautious course of liberalization—for instance, the so-called Emancipation of the Serfs (1861) and the introduction of the zemstvo system; in 1863–64, ordered the crushing of the January Uprising in the Kingdom of Poland and in parts of Lithuania; assassinated in 1881 by the People's Will (Narodnaya Volya).

Alexander III (1845–94), Russian tsar from 1881 to 1894. An extremely conservative figure who came to power after the assassination (by a revolutionary) of his father, Alexander II. He reversed most of Alexander II's reforms and sought to centralize all power within the monarchy. Strongly supported the policies of Great Russian chauvinism and sought to destroy any autonomous existence for the many subject nationalities of the empire.

Alexeyev, S. N. (1878–1930), Russian socialist editor and writer of Social Democratic works, first in Odessa in 1904 and later in St. Petersburg; translated Karl Marx's *Poverty of Philosophy* into Russian.

Annesley, Francis (1585–1660), English politician, instrumental in promoting the English colonialization of Ireland; secretary of state of Ireland from 1616 to 1634; relieved of his posts on grounds of corruption.

Arago, François (1786–1853), French politician and mathematician; elected to the French Chamber of Deputies in 1830; facilitated the abolition of slavery in the French colonies in 1848. As provisional head of state of France in June 1848, presided over the violent crushing of the 1848 Revolution. He was forced out of power by the ascension of Napoleon III.

Astley, Jacob (1579–1652), a Royalist commander during the English Civil War who was appointed governor of Plymouth by Charles I. He was captured at

480   A GLOSSARY OF PERSONAL NAMES

Stow-on-the-Wold on March 21, 1646, and was imprisoned until Charles I surrendered at Oxford in June 1646.

Auer, Ignatz (1846–1907), German Social Democrat. Joined the Social Democratic Workers' Party of Germany (SDAP), also known as the "Eisenachers," in 1869; 1874, secretary of the party's Executive Committee; 1875, at the Gotha (Unity) Congress where the SDAP joined with Ferdinand Lassalle's General German Workers' Association (ADAV), elected as one of the secretaries of the SDAP; member of the Reichstag in the years 1877–78, 1880–81, 1884–87, and 1890–1907; in 1890 became secretary of the Executive Committee (Vorstand) of the SPD; an influential reformist from the mid-1890s onward.

Axelrod, Pavel B. (1850–1928), in the 1870s, a Narodnik; in 1883, a co-founder of the Emancipation of Labor Group, an early group of Russian Marxists led by Georgi Plekhanov; in 1900, an editor of *Iskra*; after 1903, one of the leading Mensheviks. Opposed the Bolshevik seizure of power; lived remaining years in exile.

Babeuf, François-Noël (Gracchus) (1760–97), French revolutionary and journalist, member of the "Conspiracy of the Equals" of 1796 that sought to replace the Directorate with a radical regime committed to the eradication of poverty and inequality. Participated in the Revolution of 1789; initially close to the Jacobins, but went on to advocate a more radical program of income redistribution and equality of property.

Bachem, Nicolaus Heinrich Julius (1845–1918), German lawyer, publisher, and politician associated with the Center Party. 1869 to 1914, editor in chief of *Kölnische Volkszeitung*, the leading Catholic newspaper in western Germany; 1877 to 1891, member of Prussian House of Representatives; major representative of anti-Semitism in Catholic Germany.

Bakunin, Mikhail (1814–76), Russian anarchist. Studied in Berlin, early 1840s, where he met a number of left-wing followers of Hegel, including Marx; participated in 1848 Revolutions in Germany and Austrian Empire; imprisoned in Russia and exiled to Siberia in 1850s. In 1868, he formed a secret society favoring anarchism in the First International, leading to conflict with Marx and others; between 1870 and his death, he wrote such classic anarchist works as *Statism and Anarchy* and *God and the State*.

Balfour, Sir William (1578–1660), Scottish general in the parliamentary army during the English Civil War; initially served as a military commander for Charles I but went over to the side of the parliamentary forces in the early 1840s and fought on their behalf at the Battle of Edgeville. He retired from military service upon the creation of the New Model Army.

Bastwick, John (1593–1654), English writer and physician. A leading voice of Presbyterianism, he wrote a series of works scathingly critical of Catholicism, such as *The Litany*. Served as a captain during the English Civil War; opposed the Levellers and the Independents.

Bax, Ernest Belfort (1854–1926), English socialist and historian. Turned toward socialism under the impact of the 1871 Paris Commune; studied under John Stuart Mill, 1870s; 1880, while in Germany, studied Kant and Hegel and produced the first English translation of Kant's *Prolegomena to Any Future Metaphysics*; in 1882, joined the Social Democratic Federation, one of England's first socialist groups; near the end of his life, he wrote a review of Marx's work that was at the time among the fullest discussions of his work available in English. At turn of the century, supporter of Eduard Bernstein and reformist socialism; supported World War I.

Bebel, Ferdinand August (1840–1913), German Social Democrat. Member of the Reichstag from 1867 to 1881 and 1883 to 1913; 1869, co-founded the SDAP; led the legal and illegal struggle of the party during the period of the antisocialist "exceptional" laws in Germany and contributed in a major way to the founding of the party's central organ, *Der Sozialdemokrat*; 1881–90, was a member of the regional parliament (*Landtag*) in the state of Saxony. From 1892 to 1913, was one of the two co-chairmen of the SPD; from 1889 on, a leading member of the Second International; and from 1900 on, a member of the International Socialist Bureau (ISB).

Bernstein, Eduard (1850–1932), German socialist politician and theoretician, initially a follower of Ferdinand Lassalle, joined the Marxist "Eisenachers" in the 1870s; 1890–1901, lived in exile in London; appointed literary heir of Marx's archives by Engels; regular contributor to *Die Neue Zeit*; from 1896 on, one of the major theoreticians of "revisionism," the view that Marxism should be revised and "modernized"; subject of Luxemburg's polemic in her *Reform or Revolution*; member of the German Reichstag 1902–1906 and 1912–18; in 1906, became a teacher at the SPD's school in Berlin; resigned from the SPD on pacifist grounds in 1914 and became a leading member of the Independent Social Democratic Party of Germany (USPD); rejoined the SPD in 1919.

Bethmann-Hollweg, Theobald von (1856–1921), German politician. Appointed to various administrative positions in the Prussian government from 1881; president of Brandenburg, 1899; from 1905 to 1907, he was prime minister of the interior, and from 1909 to 1917, chancellor of Germany. A strong proponent of German imperialism and expansionist policies that led to World War I, he favored the ethnic cleansing of Poles and other non-Germans from the empire; forced from power in July 1917.

Biedermann, Alfred (1866–1936), Polish industrial capitalist. Head of a major textile producing firm in Łódź, which he inherited from his father; worked closely with Juliusz Karol Kunitzer in fostering commercial and social interests of the national bourgeoisie in Congress Poland; during World War I moved to Germany and invested in the coal industry.

Bielecki, Marian (pseud. M. Kowieński) (1879–1910), Polish revolutionary theoretician; co-author of the PPS-Left's founding program, 1906; leading theoretician of the PPS-Left in subsequent years, writing a number of essays arguing for the peaceful assimilation of Jews into Polish society. Strongly opposed to Józef Piłsudski, he argued that a social revolution was imminent in Russia and that the fate of the Polish workers was bound up with that of the Russian working class.

Bismarck, Otto von (1815–98), Prussian-German statesman and first chancellor of Germany from 1871 to 1890. A member of the Junker landowning class and extreme nationalist and authoritarian, he was instrumental in Prussia's (and later Germany's) military expansion. He imposed the Antisocialist Laws against the workers' movement while trying to buy off sections of it by providing some social welfare protections.

Blanc, Louis (1811–82), French journalist, historian, and politician; reformist socialist who advocated national workshops, under government control, to ameliorate poverty and unemployment; in 1848, member of the Provisional Government; 1848–70, lived in England as an émigré; in 1871, elected to the French National Assembly; supported the reactionary regime of Adolphe Thiers and took a position against the Paris Commune of 1871; in 1876, became a member of the Radical Party.

Blanqui, Auguste (1805–81), French revolutionary, and co-founder, from 1831 on, of republican and socialist secret societies. After the failure of the May 1839 uprising, he was imprisoned in Paris until 1848; he was one of the radical speakers during the June Days uprising in 1848, leading to a further lengthy imprisonment. He departed as an exile to Belgium in 1865, from where he returned to France in 1869; part of the leadership of the Paris Commune for a short period in 1871, after which he was subsequently imprisoned until 1879, and published several theoretical works. As early as 1848, he was convinced that a dictatorship of the proletariat, supported by a relatively small group of armed workers, was possible—and viewed such a dictatorship as the start of socialism.

Block, Hans (1870–1953), German Social Democrat. A supporter of Karl Kautsky, he was opposed to the revisionist and reformist position adopted by Eduard Bernstein and others in the right wing of the SPD; 1905, appointed to editorial board of *Vorwärts*, the SPD's daily newspaper, at Luxemburg's insistence, replacing the older board led by reformist Kurt Eisner. Broke from SPD to join USPD, 1917, and rejoined the SPD in 1922 after refusing to join the Communist Party of Germany (KPD).

Bobrinsky, Alexei Alexandrovich (1852–1927), Russian conservative historian; presided over the St. Petersburg zemstvo assemblies in the late 1870s; represented the interests of the wealthy landed gentry as member of the Second Duma in 1907; chairman of the Union of Russian Nobility from 1905. Following the Bolshevik Revolution, lived in exile in France, remaining a staunch monarchist until the end.

Bogdanov, Alexander (1873–1928), Russian Marxist philosopher, scientist, and economist. Initially trained as a physician, joined the People's Will (Narodnaya Volya) as a youth; joined Bolshevik faction of RSDRP in 1903; 1904–1906 published three-volume philosophical work *Empiriomonism*, which sought to reconcile Marxism with recent discoveries in logical empiricism; led group of Bolsheviks opposed to participation in tsarist Duma (the Otzovists); clashed often with Lenin, who attacked him in his 1908 *Materialism and Empirio-Criticism*; expelled from Bolsheviks, 1909; abandoned active involvement in revolutionary politics after 1911; denounced Bolshevik seizure of power in 1917; 1918–20 became leading figure in proletarian art movement (Prolekult); arrested in 1923 for supporting opposition group, Worker's Truth.

Bömelburg, Theodor (1862–1912), German socialist and trade unionist; co-founded a local chapter of bricklayers' union in Bochum, 1886; 1891, founded Zentralverband der Maurer, the central trade union of German bricklayers; 1905, helped found an international association of bricklayers. After merging his union with industrial workers, he helped lead a massive strike in the building industry in 1910. A member of the Reichstag from 1905 to 1912, he consistently argued for keeping the trade unions independent of the SPD—a position sharply critiqued by Luxemburg.

Brandenburg, Count Friedrich Wilhelm (1792–1850), son of King Friedrich William II of Prussia. He was in the midst of a distinguished military career when, in an effort to quell the ongoing uprisings in 1848, he was called back to Berlin to succeed Ernst von Pfuel as Prussian prime minister.

Brereton, William (1604–61), English soldier and politician. Elected to Parliament in 1628, he opposed Charles I from 1640 on. Appointed commander in chief of the parliamentary army in March 1643, he overcame the Royalists at the First Battle of Middlewich, but was defeated at the Battle of Nantwich a year later and subsequently withdrew from military affairs.

Bringmann, August (1861–1920), German carpenter, writer, and trade unionist. Active in the Carpenters' Union from the mid-1880s, at the 1899 Trades Union Congress in Frankfurt he argued for a clear division of labor between the SPD and the unions, and took a strong position against participation in May Day demonstrations, on the grounds that trade unions should not engage in political activity. Author of *Geschichte der deutschen Zimmerer-Bewegung* (History of the German Carpenters' Movement).

Browne, Robert (c. 1550–1633), English theologian, leader of the Puritans, and one of the first Separatists (who advocated independence from the Church of England); widely considered the founder of Congregationalism. His followers were known at the time as "Brownists." Exiled to the Netherlands, upon his return to England near the end of his life he returned to the Anglican Church. Among his many works is *A Treatise of Reformation without Tarying for Anie*.

Bülow, Bernhard Heinrich Karl Martin von (1849–1929), German politician. Served as imperial chancellor and Prussian prime minister. During his tenure as chancellor (1900–1909), he became notorious for pursuing a highly imperialistic and aggressive foreign policy, which contributed to Germany's growing diplomatic isolation. Succeeded in concluding the Treaty of Björkö, a mutual defense agreement between Germany and Russia, on July 24, 1905; this, however, did not prevent Russia from moving closer to France politically. Domestically, his government rested on the support of the Conservatives, the National Liberals, and the centrists. He kept the Social Democrats out of any real power without directly repressing them as Bismarck did.

Bułygin, Alexander (1851–1919), Russian politician. Governor of Kaluga and Moscow, 1889 to 1902; right-hand man to the governor-general of Moscow, 1902 to 1905; minister of the interior from February 1905 to October 1905. Proposed the "Bułygin Constitution" of August 1905, which offered a purely advisory Duma (parliament) that excluded most of the populace rather than being a truly representative legislative assembly. Dissatisfaction with his efforts to appease the revolution through such measures led to a series of mass strikes in September and October 1905, whereupon he was fired by the tsar on October 17, 1905. Between 1913 and 1917, again held high-ranking positions within the tsarist regime. Executed by the Bolsheviks in 1919.

Burton, Henry (1578–1648), English religious reformer. A leading Puritan, imprisoned in 1637 for his attacks on the Church of England; his ears were cut off as punishment. Freed from prison in 1640, he was vindicated by an act of the House of Commons. Author of *Protestation Protested* (1641), a text that had an important impact on both the English Revolution (1640–60) and the Glorious Revolution of 1688.

Camphausen, Gottfried Ludolf (1803–90), German politician. Appointed minister of state during the 1848 Revolutions; a moderate liberal, he was forced from power during the June Days of 1848 by more conservative forces. After a brief tenure as a representative of the Frankfurt Parliament in 1848 and 1849, retired from politics and worked in the banking industry.

Cavaignac, Louis-Eugène (1802–57), French militarist and general. In 1830, supported the revolution that brought Louis Philippe to power; was stationed in Algeria from 1832–48, where he was instrumental in carrying out the French conquest of the region. Became de facto head of state in June 1848 and moved to violently crush the revolutionary forces on the streets of Paris; during the week of June 23 to 26, 1848, he was responsible for the deaths of thousands. He lost the subsequent presidential election to Louis Napoleon, who had him briefly imprisoned in 1851.

Cavendish, William (1593–1676), English general. Fought on the side of Charles I during the English Civil War; defeated at Marston Moor in 1644, he went into exile, returning in 1660 upon the restoration of the monarchy.

Chamisso, Adelbert von (1781–1838), German poet and botanist. Author of *Peter Schlemihl*, the story of a man who lost his shadow; wrote numerous satires and lyric poetry. Best known for his work in botany, he cataloged the native flora of Mexico and other regions.

Charles I (1600–49), King of England from 1625 to 1649, when he was executed at the end of the English Civil War by the forces allied with Oliver Cromwell.

Cherevanin, Fyodor Andreyevich (1869–1938), Russian revolutionary; joined the Social Democratic movement in Kharkov in the 1890s and became a member of RDSRP in 1900; from 1903 he was a leading Menshevik. Following the 1905 Revolution, he was a leader of the "Liquidationist" faction of the Mensheviks, which argued for abandoning underground and illegal activity. Supported World War I; headed the Economic Department of the Petrograd Soviet following the February 1917 Revolution; opposed the Bolshevik seizure of power, was associated with the left-wing Mensheviks around Martov in the 1920s. Arrested in 1930 and sentenced to five years in prison. Murdered during the purge of 1938.

Clemenceau, Georges Benjamin (1841–1929), French politician. A participant in the Paris Commune and leading spokesperson for French Radicalism before 1903, by 1906 he had become a forceful opponent of workers' movements; in 1906, appointed minister of the interior; president of France, 1906–1909 and 1917–20; an extreme chauvinist, especially in World War I, he supported the policy of "total war."

Cobden, Richard (1804–65), British liberal politician who worked closely with John Bright in leading the Anti–Corn Law League. A firm supporter of free trade, he opposed both the conservative landlords and the radical Chartist movement. He was a sharp critic of British foreign policy, arguing against excessive military spending and colonial domination; he especially opposed Britain's role in the First Opium War against China.

Coke, Edward (1552–1634), English jurist; served as speaker of the House of Commons in the 1580s, and later as chief justice of the Court of Common Pleas; in 1605, chief prosecutor of those arrested in the Gunpowder Plot; by 1616, became a leading figure in the opposition to the royal prerogative; wrote a series of highly influential legal works, such as *Institutes and Reports*, which famously declared that "a man's home is his castle," influencing the later writings of the Fourth and Fifth Amendments of the US Constitution.

Colepeper, John (1600–60), English politician; although initially inclined toward the position of religious reformers during the reign of Charles I, recoiled from the radicalism of the English Revolution and in 1642 served as chancellor of the Exchequer. Went into exile upon the execution of Charles I, returning to England shortly before his death.

Constans, Jean Antoine Ernest (1833–1913), French politician; served in various posts of the French colonial empire, beginning with being the first governor-general of French Indochina. Minister of the interior from 1880 to 1881, he later served as French ambassador to the Ottoman Empire.

Corday, Charlotte (1768–93), French political activist. During the French Revolution of 1789–92, supported the moderate Girondists; appalled by the radicalization of the revolution under Robespierre, she assassinated the outstanding revolutionary and editor of *L'Ami du peuple*, Jean-Paul Marat.

Cotton, Robert (1570–1631), English politician and antiquarian. Elected member of Parliament, 1601; in 1628, argued in defense of the rights of Parliament in *The Dangers Wherein the Kingdom Now Standeth, and the Remedye*. A supporter of King James I, he favored the impeachment of Francis Bacon. After leaving Parliament, devoted much of his time to attempting to form Britain's first national library; his Cottonian Library was one of the largest book collections ever assembled, later housed in the British Library.

Cromwell, Oliver (1599–1658), principle leader of the English Revolution of 1640s and 1650s. Underwent religious conversion to Puritanism in 1830s; member of Parliament from 1628; fought in the early stages of First English Civil War and soon emerged as a leading voice of opposition to Charles I; signed the king's death warrant in 1649; led the Commonwealth and ruled as lord protector of England from 1653 until his death. Widely condemned by many on the right as a dictator, he was heralded as a pathbreaking revolutionary by many on the left.

Cunow, Heinrich Wilhelm Carl (1862–1936), German economist, historian, sociologist, and ethnographer; one of the leading theoreticians of the Second International, edited the main theoretical journal of German Social Democracy, *Die Neue Zeit*, from 1917 to 1923; a teacher at the SPD's school from 1906, he wrote a number of influential works on the kinship structure of Australian aborigines, the Inca Empire, ancient technology, and the origin of marriage and the family; initially an opponent of revisionism, in 1914 he supported Germany's entry into World War I and moved to the right; in his last years, argued that socialism could be peacefully introduced through state intervention in the economy.

Dan, Fyodor Ilyich (orig. surname: Gurvitch) (1871–1947), Russian revolutionary, politician, and one of the Mensheviks' leading theoretical thinkers. Involved in Russia's Social Democratic movement from 1894 on; after the 1917 October Revolution, sharply criticized the Bolsheviks' seizure of power. He left the Soviet Union in 1922, and in 1923 was stripped of his Soviet citizenship. From 1941 until his death, he lived in the United States.

Danilevsky, Nikolai Yakovlevich (1822–85), Russian naturalist, historian, and ideologue of pan-Slavism. Originally a member of the leftist Petrashevsky Circle, he moved to the right and became a pan-Slavic nationalist; author of the influential book *Russia and Europe* (1868), which rejected efforts to "Westernize" Russia. A natural scientist, he was a strong opponent of Darwinism, arguing that evolution is guided by divine force.

Danton, Georges Jacques (1759–94), French lawyer and politician. Played a leading role in the French Revolution of 1789–93, particularly in preparing the popular uprising of August 1792; served as minister of justice after the fall of the monarchy; in April 1793, became a member of the Committee of Public Safety; at the end of 1793, argued for an end to the Jacobin dictatorship; executed at the beginning of April 1794 by order of Robespierre.

Daszyński, Ignacy (1866–1936), Polish socialist politician. In 1892 co-founded the Polish Social Democratic Party (PPSD), a forerunner of the Polish Socialist Party (PPS); from 1892 to 1919, was a leading spokesperson for the PPSD and PPS and a deputy in the Austro-Hungarian Parliament; to the left of Józef Piłsudski, as shown by preceding him in declaring the independence of Poland on November 7, 1918; elected to the Polish Parliament in 1919, where he served until 1930.

David, Eduard (1863–1930), German teacher and Social Democrat; in 1896, became a leading advocate of revisionism; 1896–97, edited *Plainzer Volkszeitung*; 1898–1908, served as a member of the lower house of Hesse; was a member of the staff and regular contributor to the revisionist organ *Sozialistische Monatshefte*. A member of the Reichstag from 1903 to 1918, he was a fervent supporter of German expansionism and strongly supported World War I.

Davidson, Georg (1872–1942), German socialist journalist and politician. From 1895 to 1905, translated numerous political works; from 1905 to 1910, served on the editorial board of SPD's newspaper *Vorwärts*, assuming his position at the end of 1905 at the suggestion of Luxemburg, who opposed its earlier reformist bent; from 1903 to 1919, was editor of *Der abstinente Arbeiter*. Was briefly a member of the workers' and soldiers' councils in 1918–19; in 1920, he was a member of the USPD. Arrested and jailed during the Nazi regime.

Desrousseaux, Alexandre-Marie (Bracke) (1861–1955), French philosopher and socialist. Taught ancient Greek philosophy at the University of Lille from 1887, and later at the Sorbonne; appointed director of its school of advanced studies in 1915. Converted to Marxism upon reading Marx's *Capital*, joined the French Section of the Workers' International in 1905; co-editor of *L'Humanité* until 1919. Member of Chamber of Deputies for the Socialist Party, 1928 to 1936; aided the underground during the German occupation in World War II; deported to Büchenwald concentration camp, but survived. Translated several works of Luxemburg, whom he met several times at congresses of the Second International, into French.

Devereux, Robert, Third Earl of Essex (1591–1646), one of the few Puritans in the House of Lords prior to the English Revolution, he served as chief commander of the parliamentary army in the early stages of the English Civil

War. After failing to defeat the forces of Charles I, he was replaced as chief commander by Oliver Cromwell in 1644. He died during a hunting accident.

Dickens, Charles (1812–70), English novelist and social critic. Widely renowned for his realist portrayal of social and political life during the Industrial Revolution; author of *Oliver Twist*, *A Tale of Two Cities*, *Great Expectations*, and many others.

Diefenbach, Hans (1884–1917), German physician. Sympathetic to German Social Democracy; wrote articles for *Neue Zeit*; Luxemburg's lover for several years prior to 1915; killed in action during World War I.

Digby, George (1612–77), English politician; member of House of Commons from 1640 to 1641; supported the Royalists during the English Revolution. Initially opposed to some policies of Charles I, he became a firm (if at times inconsistent) supporter and fought on his behalf at the Battle of Edgehill; served as secretary of state and privy councilor, 1643; defeated at Sherburn in 1645, went into exile in France, 1646. He returned to power during the Restoration, serving as secretary of state under Charles II.

Dmowski, Roman (1864–1939), Polish politician. Co-founded and led the nationalist and conservative party National Democracy, which opposed Germany's policies against Poles by allying itself with its main enemy, tsarist Russia. Sought to establish an independent Poland freed from non-Polish and non-Catholic elements; opposed those who sought a multinational Poland, including Józef Piłsudski; in the 1920s became sympathetic to fascism.

Dreyfus, Alfred (1859–1935), French Jewish officer. A victim of an anti-Semitic campaign launched against him in 1894 by conservative forces in the French government and military, he was accused of treason for allegedly spying for Germany; after being humiliated, stripped of his rank, and deported to Devil's Island, his conviction was overturned in 1899 following an international campaign on his behalf led by the French writer Émile Zola and others. His trial and persecution exposed the depth of anti-Jewish hatred in French society and the growing dangers facing Jews throughout Europe. While French socialists such as Jean Jaurès (as well as Luxemburg herself) came to Dreyfus' defense, others, such as Jules Guesde, abstained from doing so on the grounds that the attack on Dreyfus had "nothing to do with the working class."

Duncker, Franz Gustav (1822–88), German publisher and liberal politician. Publisher of *Berliner Volkszeitung* from 1853, one of the most widely read newspapers in Prussia; in the late 1850s, founded the publishing house that bears his name, issuing works by Lassalle, Marx, and many others; from 1868, was a member of the liberal-left Progressive Party that proclaimed a harmony of interests between workers and employees and opposed strikes; served as a member of the Prussian House of Representatives, 1861 to 1877. Together with Max Hirsch, headed the Hirsch-Dunckersche Gewerkvereine, a liberal trade union movement.

Durnovo, Pyotr Nikolayevich (1845–1915), Russian politician and bureaucrat. Graduate of the Imperial Naval School; director of police in 1884; assistant minister of interior in charge of post and telegraph, 1900; remained in this position until 1905, when appointed minister of the interior. Opposed closer ties to the United Kingdom and believed that relations with Germany should be a priority. At the outbreak of World War I, advised Nicholas II that its outcome would lead to a socialist revolution in Russia.

Düwell, Wilhelm (1866–1936), German socialist and communist trade unionist. A locksmith by profession, he became a leader of the German Metalworkers' Association in 1899; editor of *Arbeiterzeitung* (in Dortmund), 1900 to 1905. Opposed reformist and opportunist currents in the SPD and its trade union movement. From 1905 to 1912, he was an editor of *Vorwärts*, at Luxemburg's suggestion; in 1917, he broke from the SPD to join the USPD; became a member of the Communist Party of Germany in 1919.

Eisner, Kurt (1867–1919), German Social Democrat and political journalist. Editor of *Vorwärts* from 1899 to 1905, a role in which Luxemburg succeeded him after a dispute over the mass strike; from 1907 to 1910, was chief editor of *Fränkische Tagespost* in Nuremberg; advocated ethical-socialist views from a reformist perspective. Although he initially supported Germany's entry into World War I, in 1917 he became a member of the USPD; in 1918, he took part in preparing for and carrying out the November Revolution in Germany; in 1918 and 1919, he served as president of the short-lived Bavarian Socialist Republic. Assassinated by counterrevolutionaries on February 21, 1919.

Eliot, John (1592–1632), English politician; defended the rights of Parliament against James I's transgressions; later spoke out against illegal taxation imposed by Charles I, who imprisoned him in response. His voice, in defiance of his persecution, was an inspiration for many who launched the English Revolution.

Elm, Adolph von (1857–1916), German Social Democrat. Founder of a credit union associated with the German trade unions.

Fairfax, Thomas (1612–71), major figure in the English Civil War; served as commander in chief of the parliamentary army battling Charles I until superseded by Oliver Cromwell; as a result of the Battle of Naseby in 1645, became the effective military ruler of England. He opposed the trial and execution of Charles I, and increasingly fell out of favor with the political opposition; he later supported the Restoration and served under Charles II.

Fallières, Armand (1841–1931), French bourgeois politician, leader of the right-of-center section of the French republicans known as the Opportunist Republicans; an ally of Adolphe Thiers, he supported the violent suppression of the Paris Commune of 1871; from 1880 to 1883 and in 1885, served as minister of the interior, and briefly as prime minister in 1883; president of the French Senate from 1899 to 1906.

Favre, Jules Claude Gabriel (1809–80), French bourgeois politician. A leader of the Reformist republican opposition to Napoleon III from the 1850s, held the office of foreign minister in the Government of National Defense and in the government of Adolphe Thiers, who crushed the Paris Commune.

Fischer, Richard (1855–1926), German socialist politician and editor. Initially worked as a typesetter in Switzerland, where he joined the socialist movement, in the early 1870s; became editor of *Berliner Freien Presse* in 1878; returned to Switzerland during the Antisocialist Laws in Germany, becoming a leading figure of the SPD in exile. In 1902, became a member of the German Reichstag; founded and managed the SPD's publishing house, Vorwärts, from the late 1890s to 1922. A revisionist who often opposed Luxemburg's positions, he avidly supported Germany's entry into World War I.

Fourier, François-Marie-Charles (1772–1837), French utopian socialist and radical defender of democracy, women's emancipation, and gay rights; his writings were a major influence on the young Marx, who held his work in high regard throughout his life. Marx refers to Fourier's work numerous times in the *Grundrisse* and *Capital*.

Fredro, Aleksander (1793–1876), Polish romantic poet and playwright; wrote numerous comedies about the Polish nobility as well as children's stories, such as *The Monkey in the Bath*. Viewed himself as a disciple of the French playwright Molière. The Polish director Andrzej Wajda adapted his comedy *The Revenge* as a film in 2002.

Frohme, Karl Franz Egon (1850–1933), German Social Democrat. Member of the Reichstag, 1881–1924; editor of *Hamburger Echo* and co-editor of *Sozialistische Monatshefte*. A part of the revisionist wing of the SPD, he clashed often with Luxemburg over his rejection of the mass strike and revolutionary action. Supported Germany's entry into World War I and opposed the 1917 Russian Revolution.

Gambetta, Léon (1838–82), French bourgeois politician. An anti-monarchist, he nevertheless supported the suppression of the Paris Commune; during the Commune, he fled Paris in a hot-air balloon; elected to the Chamber of Deputies in 1879. He generally supported the interests of the lower middle class and petty bourgeoisie.

Gapon, Georgi Apollonovich (1870–1906), Russian Orthodox priest and activist. Popular with the working class; led a march in January 1905 to petition the tsar for social reforms, leading to Bloody Sunday, when troops fired on the crowd. Although he had earlier worked closely with government-controlled organizations, the revolution and his subsequent exile radicalized him; traveled to Western Europe in 1905, where he had lengthy discussions with Social Democrats such as Plekhanov and Lenin; drew close to the Socialist Revolutionary Party (SR); upon his return to Russia at the end of 1905, reportedly entered into discussions with the tsarist government, whereupon he was arrested, tried, and executed by the SR as a traitor.

Gelfand, Israel Lazarevich (pseud.: Alexander Parvus) (1867–1924), Russian revolutionary. In 1890s, active in the German Social Democratic movement; 1895–96, editor of the *Leipziger Volkszeitung*; 1896–98, chief editor of the *Sächsische Arbeiter-Zeitung* in Dresden; in 1902, together with Julian Marchlewski, founded a publishing house in Munich for progressive international literature; 1898–1905, produced a newsletter entitled *Aus der Weltpolitik* (From the World Political Scene); worked closely with Trotsky in formulating the theory of permanent revolution, 1904; during the 1905 Revolution in Russia, a member of the St. Petersburg Workers' Council (Soviet); helped produce the newspaper *Nachalo*; 1906–1909, served on the editorial staff of the *Arbeiterzeitung* in Dortmund. Supported Germany's entry into World War I; in 1915, founded Social Sciences Publishers (Verlag für Sozialwissenschaft) and edited the weekly *Die Glocke*. After the Bolshevik Revolution in Russia in 1917, he offered to assist the Bolsheviks, but Lenin turned him down.

Georgiyevsky, Eulogius (1868–1946), Russian Orthodox Christian bishop and politician. A virulent anti-Semite and Great Russian chauvinist, he worked with the tsarist regime to suppress movements for national self-determination in Ukraine and eastern Galicia. Bishop of the Russian Orthodox Church, 1903; representative in the Russian Duma, 1907; Bishop of Kholm, 1912 to 1914, and of Volhynia, 1914 to 1919. Went into exile in Western Europe in the early 1920s, where he headed the Russian Orthodox Church Outside Russia (ROCOR).

Goethe, Johann Wolfgang von (1749–1832), German poet, prose writer, dramatist, and naturalist. Renowned for *Faust*, *Sorrows of Young Werther*, and many other works; the foremost representative of nineteenth-century German classicism and romanticism. Was one of Luxemburg's favorite writers.

Gogol, Nikolai (1809–52), Ukrainian novelist. One of the greatest voices of nineteenth-century literature, whose work was deeply admired by Luxemburg. His portrayal of the corruption and hypocrisy permeating everyday life in the Russian Empire had an enormous influence on generations of readers throughout Europe and the Americas. Author of *Dead Souls* and *The Overcoat*.

Golovin, Fyodor Alexandrovich (1867–1937), Russian politician and landowner. In 1904, a leader of the Union of Zemstvo-Constitutionalists, representing landowners' interests. In 1905, co-founded the Constitutional Democratic Party (or Cadets); following the Bolshevik Revolution, he held a number of administrative positions in the Soviet government. In 1937 he was arrested by the secret police and executed.

Górski, Ludwik (1818–1908), Polish political activist and agronomist. In the late 1840s, pioneered the use of progressive farming techniques; 1856, founded the Agricultural Society, an organization devoted to the advancement of the interests of rural landowners; from 1864 to 1904, was leader of the Earth

Credit Society. During the 1905 Russian Revolution, defended the interests of the conservative landed gentry, opposing wide-ranging land reform.

Graham, James (1612–50), Scottish nobleman who assumed command of Irish Royalist auxiliaries in Scotland and won several important battles in Tippermeur, Inverlochy, and Kilsyth during the English Civil War.

Groussier, Arthur (1863–1957), French socialist. Joined France's first socialist party, the Federation of the Socialist Workers of France, in the 1880s; in 1890, became a member of the Revolutionary Socialist Workers' Party, a pro-syndicalist group; in 1905, joined the French Section of the Workers' International. Member of the Chamber of Deputies from 1893 to 1924. Author of *La Convention collective de travail* (The Collective Agreement of Labor, 1913).

Gualbert, Giovanni (985–1073), Catholic monk and founder of the Vallumbrosan Order, cenobite monks who emphasized communal life instead of hermetic isolation. Originally a Benedictine monk, he was a critic of simony and materialism within the Catholic Church. According to tradition, in his earlier life he was consumed with worldly pleasures and sought vengeance against the murderer of his brother; upon finding the culprit on Good Friday, he forgave him when the man outstretched his arms to him in the form of a cross. He was canonized in 1193.

Guchkov, Alexander Ivanovich (1862–1936), conservative Russian politician; in October 1906 became leader of the Union of October 17, or Octobrists, which advocated a limited constitutional monarchy while defending the interests of the landed aristocracy. Served as chairman of the Third Duma in 1910; was voted out of the Duma 1912; raised objections to the Tsarina Alexandra's relations with Rasputin, leading to his estrangement from the tsar; served as war minister in the Provisional Government of 1917; supported Lavr Kornilov and other counterrevolutionary forces later in 1917; died in exile.

Guesde, Jules (Mathieu-Basile) (1845–1922), French socialist and journalist. Jailed for opposition to Franco-German War of 1871; originally a follower of Mikhail Bakunin, broke from anarchism and in 1879 became founder of the French Workers' Party (POF); in 1890s, represented the "state-collectivist" tendency in the French working-class movement. Later, evolved into a reformist and supported World War I.

Guizot, François (1787–1874), French historian and statesman. The guiding hand of France's domestic and foreign policy between 1840 and 1848, he defended the interests of finance capital and big business. A voluminous writer and historian, he wrote a series of works on the English Revolution that was carefully studied by Luxemburg.

Haase, Hugo (1863–1919), German lawyer and politician. Joined the Social Democratic movement in the early 1890s; 1894–1910, city councilor in

Königsberg; member of the Reichstag in 1897–1906 and 1912–18; 1911–16, co-chairman of the SPD (with Friedrich Ebert); 1912–15, chairman of the SPD's Reichstag group; in 1914 opposed voting for war credits but did not break party discipline by making his views public; 1916, member of the Executive Committee of the Social Democratic Working Group (Arbeitsgemeinschaft); 1917, one of the chairmen of the USPD; 1918, member of the Council of People's Representatives. Assassinated by a monarchist in 1919.

Hammond, Robert (1621–54), English soldier and politician. An officer in the New Model Army of Oliver Cromwell during the English Revolution; took part in many battles, including the Battle of Naseby. He took initial custody of Charles I after the latter surrendered to him in 1647; in 1654 he was elected to the House of Commons, while playing a relatively minor role in the Commonwealth; assigned by Cromwell to reorganize the judicial system in Ireland.

Hampden, John (1594–1643), English politician. A major figure in opposition to Charles I during the English Revolution, he rose to fame as a result of being put on trial in 1637 for refusing to pay taxes on shipping that the monarchy used to raise extra funds. His unconstitutional arrest (along with Denzil Holles, John Pym, and William Strode) in 1642 helped spark the English Civil War. Died a year later of wounds inflicted in the Battle of Chalgrove.

Hansemann, David Justus (1790–1864), a German bourgeois liberal who was appointed minister of finance by Gottfried Ludolf Camphausen, a banker who served as minister of state beginning on March 29, 1848. Their efforts to strike a compromise between the monarchy and the radicals inside and outside of the National Assembly ultimately proved fruitless. Marx viewed them as spineless compromisers.

Hansemann, Ferdinand von (1861–1900), Prussian politician. From his youth, a member of various right-wing German nationalist organizations; a large landowner in Poznań, he harbored intense hatred of Poles and sought their removal from German-controlled areas; from 1894 to 1900, he was active in the German Eastern Marches Society, which advocated the ethnic cleansing of the area of non-Germans. The group proved influential in the later formation of Nazi ideology.

Harington, James (1607–80), English politician. Served as major-general in the parliamentary army during the English Civil War; he was a judge at the trial of Charles I that decided upon his execution. Forced into exile during the Restoration.

Harrison, Thomas (1616–60), English politician. Fought in the parliamentary army during the English Civil War; joined Cromwell's New Model Army in 1645; elected to the Long Parliament, 1646; in 1649 signed the death penalty for Charles I. After the Restoration he was found guilty of regicide and was one of the last people in England to be hanged, drawn, and quartered.

Haselrig, Arthur (1601–61), English politician. One of five members of the parliamentary opposition whose attempted illegal arrest by officers of Charles I helped spark the English Revolution; led military forces against the monarchy during the First English Civil War; victor at the Battle of Cheriton, considered a turning point in the war. Broke with Oliver Cromwell over his objection to one-man rule during the Commonwealth; imprisoned during the Restoration.

Heinzel, Juliusz (1834–95), German manufacturer. Instrumental in the industrialization of Łódź, with his founding of a mechanical weaving mill for textiles in the 1870s. It became the largest facility making products from wool in Poland.

Helbertówna, Albertyna, (1889–1906), Polish revolutionary. At the age of sixteen, took part in the PPS Combat Organization's attempted assassination of Georgi Skalon. She was caught and executed, along with twenty-year-old Zofia Owczarkówna.

Hirsch, Max (1832–1905), German economist and politician. Traveled extensively through North Africa and the Middle East in the 1850s, publishing an important study of economic conditions in Algeria in 1857; upon return to Germany, worked with Franz Duncker to establish a left-liberal trade union movement that proclaimed a harmony of interests between workers and employees.

Holles, Denzil (1599–1680), English politician and writer. One of five members of the parliamentary opposition whose attempted illegal arrest by officers of Charles I helped spark the English Revolution; member of Parliament, 1640; together with John Pym, authored the Grand Remonstrance, a series of grievances presented to Charles I in 1641; as a leader of the Presbyterian Party, he came into increasing conflict with Cromwell's Independents, leading the army to draw up charges against him, which eventually forced him into exile. He later took on a leading role in facilitating the Restoration.

Hopton, Ralph (1596–1652), English politician and soldier. Fought on the Royalist side during the First English Civil War; advisor to Charles I; went into exile in 1646; served as advisor to Charles II during the Second English Civil War of 1648–49; insisted on recognizing no accepted religious institution other than the Anglican Church, which led him to fall out with Charles II over his decision to recognize Presbyterianism.

Horwitz, Maksymilian (pseud.: Henryk Walecki) (1877–1937), Polish revolutionary socialist; member of PPS-Left from 1906 and founding member of the Communist Party of Poland (KPP), 1918; Central Committee member of KPP, 1918–20, 1923–24. From 1921 an official of the Third International. Arrested and executed along with tens of thousands of Polish communists by Stalin in 1937.

Hotham, John (1589–1645), English politician and soldier. Member of

Parliament, 1620; in 1639 refused to pay tax on shipping, in a rebuke to Charles I's effort to raise revenue, and joined the parliamentary opposition to the king. In 1862 he took control of Hull and refused to allow Charles I to enter the town. He was captured, along with his son, in 1643 and executed on orders of the king in 1645.

Hyde, Edward, First Earl of Clarendon (1609–74), English politician and historian. Served as chief advisor to Charles I and later as lord chancellor under Charles II. He was a moderate Royalist who initially favored constitutional monarchy, but had moved to the right by 1842 out of concern that Parliament was demanding too much power. After the end of the First English Civil War, he went into exile, returning in 1660 upon the restoration of the monarchy. After falling out with Charles II in 1667, he again went into exile, where he devoted himself to writing *The History of the Rebellion*, considered one of the most important studies of the period.

Iglesias, Pablo (1850–1925), Spanish socialist. Member of the Spanish Socialist Workers' Party; member of the ISB, the administrative arm of the Second International.

Ireton, Henry (1611–51), English general. Headed the parliamentary army for a period during the English Civil War; fought at the Battle of Edgehill in 1642; a son-in-law and close follower of Oliver Cromwell. Member of Parliament, 1645; opposed radical tendencies like the Levellers in favor of a constitutional monarchy. Accompanied Cromwell on his invasion of Ireland; led the bloody siege against the Irish town of Limerick, 1651; died of the plague shortly thereafter.

Izvolsky, Alexander (1856–1919), Russian diplomat. Russia's ambassador to the Vatican, late 1890s; ambassador in Japan, 1899, during which time he argued for Russo-Japanese cooperation; Russian foreign minister, 1906–10; engineered Russia's alliance with Britain in 1907; ambassador to France in 1910. Supported the allied invasion of Russia following the Bolshevik Revolution.

Jacoby, Johann (1805–77), German Jewish liberal politician. Published a series of works calling for the emancipation of the Jews; active during the 1848 Revolutions and served in the Prussian National Assembly and Frankfurt Parliament, becoming famous for telling the king of Prussia, "It is the misfortune of kings that they will not listen to the truth." Fled to Stuttgart after dissolution of the Frankfurt Parliament and fought to proclaim a German Republic; later became a leading critic of Bismarck and joined the SPD; in 1874, he was elected to the Reichstag as an SPD delegate.

Jaurès, Jean (1859–1914), French socialist and historian. Deputy in the National Assembly for several electoral periods from 1885 on, and a resolute opponent of war. In 1904, he founded the newspaper *L'Humanité*, remaining its editor in chief until he was assassinated in Paris on July 31, 1914.

Jogiches, Leo (pseud. Jan Tyszka) (1867–1919), Polish Social Democrat born in Vilnius. A newspaper publisher and one of the leading political figures in the SDKP (later SDKPiL), which he co-founded in 1893. He was Luxemburg's most important political and personal companion. In the period 1903–12, he became the most important ideological figure in the SDKPiL. Following his imprisonment in Warsaw from March 1906 to March 1907, he lived for various periods in Kraków, Switzerland, and Finland—but principally in Berlin. In 1911, he broke with Lenin over the question of the organizational unity of the RSDRP. From 1912 on, he lost influence in the SDKPiL, in the wake of a split in the party precipitated in part by the Bolsheviks. During World War I in Germany, he was one of the leading figures of the Spartacus Group. In prison in Berlin from March to November 1918, he became one of the leading figures in the newly renamed Spartacus League after his release, co-founding the Communist Part of Germany (KPD) soon after. In March 1919, he was arrested in Berlin and subsequently murdered in Moabit Prison.

Kamenev, Lev (1883–1936), Russian revolutionary. Joined RSDRP in 1901; became a follower of Lenin a year later; in 1908, along with Grigory Zinoviev, was one of the main proponents of Lenin's position within the Bolsheviks. Initially opposed Lenin's decision to seize power in October 1917; along with Stalin and Zinoviev, formed a block to oppose Trotsky in the early 1920s; in 1925, Kamenev broke with Stalin and demanded his removal as general secretary; submitted to Stalin by the early 1930s and was arrested, tried, and executed in 1936.

Kant, Immanuel (1724–1804), major European philosopher, wrote extensively on epistemology, ethics, logic, anthropology, and politics; leading representative of German transcendental idealism.

Karpiński, Franciszek (1741–1825), Polish romantic poet. His most famous works are "Bóg się rodzi, moc truchleje" (God is Born, Power Trembles) and "Kiedy ranne wstają zorze" (When the Morning Lights Arise).

Kasprzak, Marcin (1860–1905), Polish revolutionary, socialist, and Social Democrat. Active in the Polish and German workers' movement from 1881, with organizational activities that included facilitating Luxemburg's flight to Zurich. In 1892, he was accused by the PPS of working together with the Russian secret service. These allegations were only withdrawn in the summer of 1905, shortly before Kasprzak's execution. From 1903, he had close political contact with Leo Jogiches and Luxemburg, and took on the role for the SDKPiL of distributing the illegal party press inside the Kingdom of Poland. In 1904, he was sent into the Kingdom of Poland, on Jogiches' instigation, to build up illegal printshops. This led him into being caught in a trap in Warsaw in April 1904—during his arrest four tsarist policemen were killed, and Kasprzak took responsibility. Sentenced to death in September 1905 by a military court, he was executed in the Warsaw Citadel.

Katkov, Mikhail Nikoforovich (1818–87), Russian conservative publisher and politician; originally a liberal, he befriended such figures as Alexander Herzen and Mikhail Bakunin and associated with followers of Hegel while in Berlin in the early 1840s. In the 1850s he supported calls for Polish self-determination, but strongly opposed the Polish National Uprising of 1863 and became a leading figure in right-wing Russian nationalism. He published numerous journals and newspapers, including *Russkii Vestnik* and *Moskovskie Vedomosti*. He was the leading figure of Russian conservatism at the end of the nineteenth century.

Kautsky, Karl (1854–1938), German Marxist theoretician and the leading figure, from the 1890s to World War I, of German Social Democracy and the Second International. In 1882, he co-founded the journal *Die Neue Zeit* and was its chief editor until 1917. An ally of Luxemburg in the revisionist debate of 1898, she broke with him in 1910 as he moved closer to reformism with his "strategy of attrition"; in 1917 co-founded the USPD; became a fierce critic of the Bolshevik Revolution after 1917; returned to the SPD in 1920, when much of the USPD's membership joined the German Communist Party.

Kautsky, Hans (nickname: Igel) (1864–1937), professor of art. Painter at the Royal Theater of Prussia; brother of Karl Kautsky.

Kaznakov, Nikolai Nikolaevich (1856–1929), Russian general. Headed the cavalry of the Russian Imperial Army during the Russo-Turkish War of 1877–78; at the outbreak of World War I, served as commander in chief of the Russian army but was replaced for incompetence within a year; went into exile following the Russian Revolution of 1917.

Kelles-Krauz, Kazimierz (pseud: Michał Luśnia-Krauz) (1872–1905), Polish socialist and sociologist. Leading Marxist theoretician in the PPS. Provided a Marxist and class struggle–based reasoning for the party program of re-establishing Poland as an independent state. Lived as an émigré in Paris, Brussels, and Vienna from 1892 on.

Kempner, Stanisław Aleksander (1857–1924), Polish publicist and economic scientist. He shared many of Eduard Bernstein's views regarding economics, especially concerning the importance of marginal utility theory. He belonged to the so-called progressive camp and founded the newspaper *Gazeta Handlowa* in 1904, which turned into the *Nowa Gazeta* at the start of 1906, and was published under his editorship until 1918. After 1918, he continued to be active as a publicist and journalist in Poland.

Kennemann, Hermann (1815–1910), German politician. Co-founded the German Eastern Marches Society, a far-right and racist organization devoted to the ethnic cleansing of eastern Germany of Poles; his ideas proved of importance in later Nazi ideology. He lived and organized in the area around Poznań.

Khomiakov, Nikolai Alexeyevich (1850–1925), Russian lawyer and politician; graduate of Faculty of Law at Moscow Imperial University, 1874; went on to become a leading figure of the Octobrists and chairman of the Third Duma following the 1905 Revolution. Favored the convening of a land assembly to address the problems facing the peasantry.

Kokovtsov, Vladimir Nikolayevich (1853–1943), count and Russian politician; finance minister between February 1904 and October 1905, and again from May 1906 to the start of 1914. Lived as an émigré in France from 1918 on.

Kościuszko, Tadeusz (1746–1817), leader of the 1794 national uprising in Poland and a hero in the American War of Independence. On the one-hundredth anniversary of the uprising, celebrations were held throughout Russian-, German-, and Austrian-occupied parts of Poland. Hopes that the commemorations might result in a mass uprising failed to materialize.

Koszutska, Maria (pseud: Wera Kostrzewa) (1876–1939), Polish socialist and communist. Member of the PPS from 1902, and of the PPS-Left from 1906. In December 1918, she co-founded the KPRK (later known as the KPP). Arrested in the Soviet Union in 1937, she perished in a prison camp during Stalin's purge of the Polish communists.

Kowieński, M., see Bielecki, Marian.

Krahelska-Filipowicz, Wanda (1886–1968), Russian revolutionary. Joined PPS Combat Organization, 1905; along with Zofia Owczarkówna and Albertyna Helbvertówna, attempted to assassinate Georgi Skalon, governor-general of Warsaw, in 1906; escaped arrest by fleeing to Austria-Hungary. She later became a Catholic socialist activist and a major figure in Poland's underground resistance to the Nazis, saving hundreds of Jews from arrest and extermination; co-founded the Polish Council to Aid Jews (known as Żegota), an underground resistance organization during the German occupation.

Kramář, Karel (1860–1937), Czech politician. Leader of the Young Czech Party, which advocated autonomy, then independence from the Austro-Hungarian Empire. Imprisoned during World War I; upon his release in 1918 he headed the National Committee, which proclaimed independence. A conservative nationalist and antisocialist, he served as first prime minister of Czechoslovakia in 1918; he was a member of the National Assembly until 1937.

Kunert, Fritz (1850–1931), German Social Democrat. From 1888 to 1889, member of the Berlin City Council; 1889, editor of *Schlesischen Nachrichten*; member of the Reichstag, 1896–1907 and 1909–18. Although initially favoring voting for war credits at the outbreak of World War I, he broke from the SPD and joined the USPD in 1917; he was a member of the National Assembly in 1918 and 1919, during which time he argued for the abolition of government benefits for religious institutions and a strict separation of church and state. He refused to join the USPD majority that joined the KPD in 1920, rejoining the SPD in 1922.

Kunitzer, Juliusz Karol (1843–1905), Polish industrial capitalist. In the 1870s formed the Kunitzer & Meyer Company in Łódź, a center of textile manufacturing; over the ensuing decades it became one of the largest industrial enterprises in Congress Poland. He treated his workers with great brutality and contempt, often denying them wages and violently breaking strikes; in September 1905 he was assassinated by members of the PPS.

Lafargue, Paul (1842–1911), French physician; socialist; member of the First International; together with Jules Guesde, leader of the POF; leading propagandist of Marxism in the French and international workers' movements; son-in-law of Karl Marx, married to Marx's daughter Laura; author of *The Right to Be Lazy*.

Lambert, John (1619–84), English general and politician. A major figure in Cromwell's campaign in Scotland in 1650; served in various posts afterward in the Protectorate; author of the highly influential work *Instrument of Government*, which sought to codify a constitution for England based on a separation of powers between executive, legislative, and judicial branches. Returned to the army in 1659 to resist the Restoration; upon their defeat, was imprisoned for the remaining twenty-four years of his life.

Lamoricière, Christophe Léon Louis Juchault de (1806–65), French imperialist. Sent to Algeria as a soldier in 1830, participated in its conquest and colonization; after assuming other positions in the military, appointed governor-general of Algeria in 1845; opposed those among the French occupation authorities who argued for a war of extermination against the Arab populace. An opponent of Napoleon III, he was arrested in 1851 and stripped of his posts.

Lassalle, Ferdinand (1825–64), writer and political organizer, major figure in the formation of German socialist movement. Participant in the 1848 Revolution; 1849–62, maintained connections with Marx, who ultimately broke from him for being "a future workers' dictator"; in 1863, co-founded the Allgemeine Deutscher Arbeiterverein (General Union of German Workers), which for many years was the largest socialist organization in Germany. Lassalle's followers merged with the "Eisenachers," the purported followers of Marx, in 1875, despite Marx's strong objections, voiced in his *Critique of the Gotha Program*. Lassallean ideas and approaches continued to influence German Social Democracy for decades afterward.

Laud, William (1573–1645), English prelate. Archbishop of Canterbury, 1633; sought to impose doctrinal and organizational uniformity upon the Anglican Church, which further fueled opposition to the policies of Charles I. After falling out with the king in 1645, he was imprisoned and executed.

Ledebour, Georg Theodor (1850–1947), Social Democratic politician and journalist. From 1890 to 1895, contributor to *Vorwärts*; 1897–1900, editor of the *Sächsische Arbeiter-Zeitung* in Dresden; member of the Reichstag, 1900–18; in 1916, member of the Executive Committee of the Social Democratic "Working Group" (Arbeitsgemeinschaft); in 1917, a co-founder of the USPD, to whose Central Committee he belonged until March 1919. Worked closely with Karl Liebknecht to overthrow the reformist government of Friedrich Ebert in 1919; a critic of the Bolshevik monopolization of power, he refused to join the KPD when most members of the USPD did so in 1920, and instead helped found the "Second-and-a-Half International" and lead the Socialist Worker's Party of Germany (SAPD) in opposition to the SPD and KPD. Fled to Switzerland upon Hitler's seizure of power.

Leder, Jan (1867–94), Polish revolutionary. A locksmith by occupation, joined the Polish socialist movement as a youth in the 1880s; 1889, founded the Union of Polish Workers (ZRP) along with Julian Marchlewski; led numerous strikes in and around Warsaw; in the early 1890s organized workers in Łódź, and led a massive march for the eight-hour workday on May Day 1891. Arrested by tsarist police in October 1891 and imprisoned in the notorious Warsaw Citadel; died of tuberculosis shortly after being released from prison.

Leder, Zdzisław (real name: Władysław Feinstein) (1880–1938), Polish Social Democrat, communist, and publicist. Became close to the SDKPiL during 1901–1902, took on leading party functions from 1904. Based in Kraków from February 1904, and from there made regular journeys to the Kingdom of Poland. Worked as an editor for *Czerwony Sztandar* in 1905–1906, a period in which his stays in the Kingdom became longer and more regular. Imprisoned from October 1906 to August 1908 in Warsaw Citadel, he lived in exile in Berlin, Zurich, and Paris after his release. In 1911, he retired from active party life, and in 1912, due to the split within the SDKPiL, he withdrew from politics. From 1915 to 1918 in Switzerland, he obtained his PhD. In November 1918, he returned to Warsaw, where he was a co-founder of the Communist Party of Poland (initially known as the KPRP, later as the KPP). After being arrested in Poland, he moved to Moscow in 1921, from where he carried out Comintern functions, with periods in Berlin, until 1924. After that, he did several stints abroad working for the Comintern or as a Soviet diplomat, including periods in Italy, France, and Great Britain. Commissioned by the Comintern in 1929 to write an extensive pamphlet about the life and work of Leo Jogiches, the resulting work was subsequently rejected, and only published in 1976 (by Feliks Tych in Poland). Arrested in Moscow in 1937, he was sentenced to eight years in a prison camp. He died in 1938, en route to the Gulag.

Legien, Karl (1861–1920), German trade unionist and Social Democrat. Originally a wood turner, joined SPD in 1885; 1887, chairman of the German Association of Turners; 1891–1919, chairman of the General Commission of German Trade Unions; president of the International Federation of Trade Unions, 1913–19; member of the Reichstag, 1893–98 and 1903–20; part of the reformist wing of the SPD, strongly opposed endorsement of the mass strike; enthusiastically supported Germany's role in World War I; during the war, argued for the expulsion of antiwar opponents from SPD (which he termed the "Jewish gang"). In 1920, mobilized a general strike against the rightist Kapp Putsch.

Leimpeter, Johann (1867–1923), German Social Democrat and trade unionist. Editor of *Bergarbeizeitung* from 1901 to 1906; wrote a pamphlet entitled *The Social Democratic Party and the Trade Unions* in opposition to Luxemburg's *Mass Strike*.

Lenin, Vladimir Ilyich (1870–1924), Russian revolutionary; from 1903 on, leader of the Bolsheviks; worked closely with Luxemburg, especially immediately after the 1905 Revolution, though differed with her on many issues; after the Bolshevik Revolution of 1917, he was the leader of the revolutionary government of Soviet Russia.

Lensch, Paul Albert (1873–1926), German Social Democrat. 1900–1902, editor of the *Freie Presse für Elsass-Lothringen* in Strasbourg; 1902–1907, contributor to *Leipziger Volkszeitung* and, until 1913, its chief editor; member of the Reichstag, 1912–18; a proponent of the views of the German left until 1914; during World War I, evolved into supporter of militarism; in the November Revolution of 1918–19, he was a delegate from the Council of People's Representatives to the army high command.

Lenthall, William (1591–1662), English politician. Speaker of the House of Commons, 1640–59; won renown for standing up to Charles I and refusing to disclose the whereabouts of five leading opposition members of Parliament that the king sought to arrest. Although close to Cromwell and the Independents, he preferred a constitutional monarchy; during the Restoration he was banned from public life.

Lesche, Friedrich (1863–1933), German socialist politician and trade unionist. A carpenter, he joined the SPD in 1883 and served as member of the Reichstag, 1903–1907 and 1920–25. Reformist in political orientation, he fostered the development of credit bureaus managed by trade unions.

Lessner, Frederick (1825–1910), early colleague-in-arms of Marx and Engels. Member of the Communist League, participated in the 1848–49 Revolution. Later became a Social Democrat; actively involved in politics in Britain from the 1880s on.

Liebknecht, Karl (1871–1919), co-founder of the SPD (with August Bebel); later co-founded, with Luxemburg, the Spartacus League and the German Communist Party. Trained as a lawyer, he was famous for his defense of socialist leaders, and later for refusing to accede to the SPD's voting of war credits in August 1914. Liebknecht was arrested with Luxemburg in 1919 and summarily tortured and executed by the Friekorps.

Liebknecht, Wilhelm (1826–1900), German Social Democrat, philologist, and publicist; close confidant of Marx. Together with August Bebel, he co-founded the SDAP, known colloquially in German as the "Eisenachers," and acted as one of this organization's chief political figures. After joining together in 1875 with the General German Workers' Association—known colloquially as the "Lassalleans"—this party was named the Socialist Workers' Party, subsequently changed in 1890 to the Social Democratic Party of Germany (SPD). He agreed with Marx and Engels' position that the Polish workers' movement had to fight for the re-establishment of Poland, a viewpoint at odds with the SDKPiL party program.

Lilburne, John (1614–57), English revolutionary. A leader of the Levellers during the English Civil War, a radical current advocating social equality, freedom of expression, and popular sovereignty. Fought in the English Civil War against the forces of Charles I, including at the Battle of Edgehill; resigned from the army in 1645 over the refusal of Cromwell and his followers to allow for freedom of religious expression. His radical and democratic ideas proved enormously influential upon later democrats and revolutionaries.

Lityński, Alfred (pseud: F. Zaorski) (1880–1945), Polish zoologist and hydrobiologist, active with the PPS from 1905 to 1910. Organized a students' strike at Dorpat University in 1901, for which he was expelled; after being imprisoned, he lived in exile from 1902 to 1905; returned to Poland in 1905 and served as editor of the journal of the PPS-Left, signing his articles pseudonymously. He withdrew from political activity in 1910 in favor of scientific pursuits, and was a strong advocate of ecology and protection of the natural environment; served as editor of *Zakopane* magazine, 1913–14. Fought with the Polish Legion in World War I; from 1924–38, he was a professor at the University of Warsaw; main areas of research were the hydrobiology of lowland lakes. During World War II he lived in the countryside and composed his most famous book, *General Hydrobiology*.

Loubet, Émile François (1838–1929), French politician. A moderate republican who advocated social reforms such as secular education while at the same time promoting France's imperialist expansion overseas. Member of the Chamber of Deputies, 1876; member of the French Senate, 1885; prime minister of France, 1891; president of France, 1899–1906. Played a major role during the Dreyfus affair, ultimately annulling Alfred Dreyfus' ten-year jail sentence.

Louis XVI (1754–93), king of France from 1774 to 1792; attempted to impose some reforms in the early part of his reign, such as the abolition of serfdom, but resisted deeper calls for change and was deposed as a result of the French Revolution of 1789. In 1793, he was tried and executed by the National Convention for his covert support for the foreign invasion of France.

Louis Philippe I (1773–1850), king of France from 1830 to February 1848, for the period of government known as the July Monarchy; subsequently emigrated to England.

Ludlow, Edmund (1617–92), English politician and soldier. Fought in the parliamentary army against Charles I during the English Civil War and served as second in command of Cromwell's forces that invaded Ireland in 1649. He was one of the signatories of the order to execute Charles I. He fell out with Cromwell after he opposed his appointment as lord protector; the latter responded by arresting him. Lived in exile during the Restoration but returned to England in 1688, during the Glorious Revolution.

Lunacharsky, Anatoly Vasilievich (1875–1933), Ukrainian-born Russian Marxist and cultural critic; member of RSDRP, joined the Bolsheviks during the 1903 split with the Mensheviks; influenced by ideas of Fichte and Nietzsche; broke from the Bolsheviks in 1908 in support of Alexander Bogdanov's position; founded a school in Capri, Italy (along with Maxim Gorky), for Russian socialist workers; founded the Circle for Proletarian Culture in Paris, 1913; opposed World War I; rejoined Bolsheviks in July 1917. After the Bolshevik Revolution, he became commissar of enlightenment (equivalent of minister of culture), 1917–29. Four years later, he was purged by Stalin.

Luśnia-Krauz, Michał, see Kelles-Krauz, Kazimierz.

Malakhov, Nikolai Nikolayevich (1827–1908), Russian general; commander of the Moscow Military District from February 1905 to January 1906.

Marat, Jean-Paul (1744–93), French revolutionary. A doctor, physicist, and political journalist, he published the outstanding newspaper of the French Revolution of 1789–92 *Ami du Peuple*; he was a leader of the Jacobin Club and of "the Mountain" in Parliament, and the foremost defender of workers' rights among the Jacobins.

Marchlewski, Julian (pseuds.: J. Karski, Johannes Kämpfer) (1866–1925), Polish Social Democrat; 1889, co-founded the ZRP; emigrated to Switzerland in 1893; helped produce the Social Democratic newspaper *Sprawa Robotnicza* together with Rosa Luxemburg, Leo Jogiches, and Adolf Warski; 1893, co-founded the SDKP (which in 1900 became the SDKPiL); in 1896, moved to Germany; in 1898, became a contributor to *Sächsische Arbeiter-Zeitung* in Dresden and to *Neue Zeit*; undertook the editorship of *Przegląd Robotnyczy* in 1900. In 1902, together with Alexander Parvus, he founded, in Munich, a publishing house for progressive international literature; also in 1902, he became a member of the staff of the *Leipziger Volkszeitung*, for which he edited periodically until 1913. Belonged to the German left. In 1913–14, together with Luxemburg and Franz Mehring, edited *Sozialdemokratische Korrespondenz*; in 1915, edited *Wirtschaftliche Rundschau*. Co-founded the Spartacus Group. In 1916–18, he interned in Havelberg, following which he succeeded in reaching Moscow by way of Petrograd; he returned to Berlin in January 1919.

Martov, Julius (born Yuly Osipovich Tsederbaum; pseud.: Ignotus) (1873–1923), Russian revolutionary. In 1895, took part, together with Lenin, in organizing the St. Petersburg League of Struggle for the Emancipation of the Working

Class; 1896, arrested and sentenced to three years of internal exile; after that, served as a member of the editorial board of *Iskra*. From 1903 on, he was a leading Menshevik. From 1908 to 1911, edited *Golos Sotsial-Demokrata*; opposed World War I as an imperialist war and worked with Trotsky in publishing *Nashe Slovo*; took part in the Zimmerwald Conference in 1915 and the Kienthal Conference in 1916; leader of the Left-Mensheviks, he critically supported the Bolsheviks while opposing their suppression of democracy; supported the Red Army during the Russian Civil War.

Massey, Edward (c. 1619–74), English soldier and politician. Member of the House of Commons, 1646; fought in the parliamentary army in the early stages of the First English Civil War; a Presbyterian, he opposed Cromwell's Independents and supported the Royalists from 1651; became a member of Parliament during the Restoration.

Maurice, Prince of the Palatinate (1621–52), German prince who fought on the side of the Royalists during the English Civil War; the son of Anne of Denmark (daughter of King James I of England) and Frederick V of Palatine (a principality in southwestern Germany), he served in the armies of the Netherlands and Sweden before leading regiments in defense of his uncle, Charles I. After winning a series of battles, he was defeated at the Battle of Naseby in 1645. He thereupon sailed to the West Indies, where he was lost at sea during a storm near the Virgin Islands.

Mazzini, Giuseppe (1805–72), Italian nationalist politician. Leader of Italy's movement for national independence from the 1830s, initially in the form of the Young Italy society; in 1848, leader of the short-lived Italian Republic; spent much of the next two decades in exile; worked closely with Garibaldi in obtaining unity of Italy. A bitter enemy of socialism and the labor movement, he supported the crushing of the Paris Commune of 1871.

Mehring, Franz (1846–1919), German historian, literary scholar, and political journalist; leading German socialist; 1891–1913, contributor to *Neue Zeit*; from 1892 until 1895 was head of the association Freie Volksbühne; 1902–1907, chief editor of *Leipziger Volkszeitung*; 1906–11, instructor in history at the SPD's Central Party School in Berlin; a leading representative of the German left; in 1913–14, together with Luxemburg and Julian Marchlewski, edited *Sozialdemokratische Korrespondenz*, and in April 1915, together with Luxemburg, the first issue of the journal *Die Internationale*; belonged to the International Group (Spartacus Group), later renamed the Spartacus League; 1917, member of the Prussian House of Deputies; co-founder of the German Communist Party.

Mickiewicz, Adam (1798–1855), Polish national poet. Born and raised in Lithuania, where he remained until the outbreak of the November Uprising. In 1831 he moved to Germany, from where he sought in vain to join those fighting inside the Kingdom of Poland. Lived from 1832 in exile in Paris, where he wrote the Polish national epic *Pan Tadeusz* (1834), which became the poetic work most quoted by Luxemburg. From 1841 he was intermittently one of the leading intellectual figures of Polish messianism, and, in the context of the Revolutions of 1848, became open to more radical societal themes, including an idiosyncratic version of socialism. He died from cholera in Constantinople, where he was attempting, with French support, to gather together Polish and Jewish units for the Crimean War against Russia.

Mikhailovsky, Nikolai (1842–1904), Russian sociologist and Populist; editor of the publication *Otechestvennye Zapiski*, in which he argued that Marx's *Capital* stipulates that countries such as Russia needed to endure an extended period of capitalist development before being ready for socialism—a claim that Marx rejected in a famous letter to the publication. Mikhailovsky rejected the application of Darwinian principles of evolution to society and argued that the social organization of the Russian peasantry was more advanced than those of Western Europe.

Millerand, Alexandre (1859–1943), French politician. Leading representative of the French Independent Socialists; 1899–1902, minister of trade in the bourgeois cabinet of Waldeck-Rousseau; in 1904, expelled from the French Socialist Party for participating in a capitalist government. Subjected to a series of sharp critiques by Luxemburg.

Milyukov, Pavel (1859–1943), Russian politician and historian. Co-founder of the Cadets in October 1905. From 1907, member of the Third Duma, leading the Cadet faction in that parliament. Foreign minister after the February Revolution in 1917. On the side of the Whites after the October Revolution 1917. In November 1918 he left for Turkey, and from there to exile in Western Europe—first in England, and from 1920 in France. He wrote numerous studies about the Russian Revolutions of 1905 and 1917. He was a staunch opponent of Hitler during World War II, and supported the Soviet Union in that war from 1941.

More, Thomas (1478–1535), English philosopher and statesman; an important figure in Renaissance humanism; coined the term "utopia." A religious conservative, he defended the traditions of the Catholic Church against the claims of Luther and other Protestants. Opposed to King Henry VIII's break from the Papacy, he was tried and executed on trumped-up charges of treason.

Morgan, Thomas (1604–79), Welsh soldier. Fought in the English Civil War with the parliamentary army against Charles I, helped defeat one of the last Royalist armies and served as a major general in Scotland. He ended his career supporting the Restoration.

Mozart, Wolfgang Amadeus (1756–91), composer. One of the greatest figures of classical music of the eighteenth century.

Müntzer, Thomas (c. 1489–1525), German theologian and revolutionary. Leader of the German Peasants' War of 1525, which opposed both the

Catholic Church and nobility supporting Martin Luther, considered by Marx and Engels the most important popular upsurge in German history prior to the 1848 Revolution.

Myddelton, Thomas (1624–63), English politician. Member of Parliament, 1646; supported the parliamentary army during the civil war, but as a political moderate opposed Cromwell and the Independents; in 1659 he took up arms on behalf of Charles II and returned as a member of Parliament during the Restoration.

Nansen, Fridtjof (1861–1930), Norwegian scientist and explorer. Headed the team that traversed the interior of Greenland in 1896, reaching the northernmost latitude of any European explorer of the time. The techniques he pioneered in the use of equipment and clothing were employed by subsequent explorers of the Arctic and Antarctic regions. Later studied and wrote on zoology, neuroscience, and oceanography; in 1905 and 1906 became a leading exponent of Norway's independence from Denmark; 1921, appointed high commissioner for refugees of the League of Nations; winner of the Nobel Peace Prize, 1922.

Napoleon I (1769–1821), emperor of France from 1804 to 1815. Rising through the ranks of the military during the French Revolution, he seized control of France and initiated a series of wars against reactionary European powers known as the Napoleonic Wars. Initiated a series of legal reforms, with the Napoleonic Code, which laid the foundation of modern-day France. Died in exile in St. Helena.

Napoleon III (1808–73), first president of France from 1848 to 1851, and emperor of France from 1851 to 1870; presided over the extension of French control of Algeria, the building of the Suez Canal, and France's seizure of Senegal and parts of Indo-China; decisively defeated in Franco-Prussian War of 1870, he was captured and later retired in England.

Nechayev, Sergei (1847–82), Russian revolutionary. As a young student, worked as an assistant to the historian Mikhail Pogodin; active in the radical student movement of the late 1860s; author of *Catechism of a Revolutionary*, which advocated a total commitment to revolutionary terror to awaken the masses; Marx issued a powerful denunciation of him during his work in the First International. Arrested in 1872, spent the last decade of his life in prison.

Nicholas I (1796–1855), emperor of Russia from 1825 until his death. Among Russia's most reactionary rulers, he ruled through brutal autocratic power. Fostered Russian nationalism and repressed the rights of Russia's many national minorities. His crushing of the Hungarian Revolution of 1848 earned him the enmity of democrats and Free Thinkers throughout Europe.

Nicholas II (1868–1918), emperor of Russia from 1894 to 1917; forced to abdicate by the February Revolution. Presided over Russia during its defeat in the Russo-Japanese War of 1904–1905 and the revolution that followed; led

Russia into World War I, in which 4 million of his countrymen perished. His regime was marked by severe repression and anti-Semitic pogroms as well as political corruption. He was executed by the Bolsheviks during the Russian Civil War.

Owczarkówna, Zofia (1886–1906), took part in the PPS Combat Organization's attempted assassination of Georgi Skalon. She was caught and executed along with the youngest of the group, sixteen-year-old Albertyna Helbertówna.

Owen, Robert (1771–1858), Welsh social reformer, leading figure in utopian socialism; manager of a textile mill, he became a sharp critic of the inhumanity of capitalist industrialization and a leading figure in the cooperative movement. Although initially a follower of English liberals like Jeremy Bentham, he embraced socialism and became a firm critic of the free market; argued for the creation of freely associated townships based on common ownership, which he applied in creating New Harmony, Indiana; also established an equitable labor exchange, in which distribution of the products of labor was effected by use of labor notes instead of money.

Palacký, František (1798–1876), Czech historian and politician. During the 1848 Revolutions, adopted a left-liberal position as chairman of the Slav Congress in Prague; served as deputy to the Austrian Imperial Diet, 1848–49; advocated a federation of autonomous areas inhabited by Slavs that would remain part of the Austrian Empire.

Parvus, Alexander, see Gelfand, Israel Lazarevich.

Pfannkuch, Wilhelm (1841–1923), German Social Democrat. In 1863, became a member of the ADAV; member of the Reichstag 1884–87, 1898–1906, and 1912–18; 1893, co-founder of the German Woodworkers' Union; 1894, member of the SPD Executive Committee and, in 1917, secretary of the Executive Committee; from 1900, a city councilor in Berlin; supported World War I and German imperialism.

Pfuel, Ernst Heinrich Adolf von (1779–1866), Prussian general and politician. Military commander who led the suppression of the revolutionary uprising in Posen in March 1848; served as prime minister and war minister of Prussia from September to October 1848.

Piłsudski, Józef (1877–1935), Polish politician and military officer. Member of PPS from 1892, and from 1895 to 1906 de facto leading party member. Arrested in 1900, and subsequently fled from the Kingdom of Poland in 1901. After the outbreak of the Russo-Japanese War in February 1904, attempted to win Japanese support for a Polish uprising. From 1906, was a leading member of the Revolutionary Faction of the PPS; after the defeat of the revolution in 1905–1906, he focused on a future war between Russia on one side and Germany and Austro-Hungary on the other. After the outbreak of World War I, founded the Polish Military Organization. Later, during the years of the Stalinist terror, this was used as a scapegoat for Polish communists to be persecuted and murdered in the Soviet Union. In 1916 he separated from the PPS for good. Following his imprisonment in Germany from 1917 to November 1918, he became a formative and leading figure in the Republic of Poland. Between 1918 and 1922, his official title was provisional chief of state; in May 1926 he carried out a coup d'état, while preserving, at least at a formal level, certain democratic procedures such as parliamentary elections.

Plekhanov, Georgi (1856–1918), Russian revolutionary and Marxist theoretician; originally a Populist, he became an avowed Marxist in the early 1880s and established, in 1883, the Emancipation of Labor Group. Author of many books on politics, economics, and philosophy, he coined the term "dialectical materialism"; leader of the Menshevik faction of the RSDRP from 1903; one of the only party leaders not to return to Russia during the 1905 Revolution, he sharply opposed the Bolsheviks on the basis of an economic determinist and unilinear evolutionist understanding of historical development; a strong supporter of World War I, he sharply opposed the Bolshevik seizure of power as well as left-wing Mensheviks such as Julius Martov; left Russia following the October Revolution.

Pobedonostsev, Konstantin (1827–1907), Russian conservative politician. Leading apologist for tsarist absolutism and anti-Semitism during the reigns of Alexander II, Alexander III, and Nicholas II; 1880, procurator of the Holy Synod, the leading body of the Orthodox Church; 1881, author of "Alexander's Manifesto," which affirmed the absolute power of the tsar; placed in charge of the universities in order to curb dissent, 1899; survived an assassination attempt by a revolutionary socialist, 1901; ordered Tolstoy's excommunication, 1901. Authored the notorious anti-Semitic "May Laws" that banned Jews from owning land and engaging in a range of occupations; a virulent enemy of democracy who opposed even the mildest of reforms.

Pogodin, Mikhail (1800–75), Russian historian. Propagated the view that the Russian state was originally established by Varangians (or Vikings) from Scandinavia. A pan-Slavic nationalist, he argued for the political and social unity of the Slavic people; co-edited *Moskvityanin*, a major organ of right-wing Slavic nationalism. He was a fierce opponent of liberal reformists such as Alexander Herzen.

Potretsov, Alexander (pseud.: Starover) (1869–1934), Russian Social Democrat. Joined the ranks of Russian Marxists in the early 1890s after having first been a Populist; member of St. Petersburg League of Struggle for the Emancipation of the Working Class, 1896; emigrated in 1900 and took part in the founding of the newspapers *Iskra* and *Zarya*; after the 1903 Congress of the RSDRP, he was a leading Menshevik. Returned to Russia during the 1905 Revolution, where he edited such Menshevik newspapers as *Nachalo* and *Nevskii Golos*; a prominent theoretician of the "Liquidators" following the defeat of the Revolution. A strong supporter of Russia's involvement in World War I, he insisted on its continuation after the February 1917 Revolution; left the RSDRP in 1918 and allied with counterrevolutionary political currents; emigrated from Russia in 1925; died in exile in France.

Poyntz, Sydnam (1607–63), English soldier. Fought in the Thirty Years' War on the side of Spain, rising to the rank of major general; returned to England, 1645, and joined the parliamentary army during the English Civil War. His forces defeated Charles I at the Battle of Rowton Heath. In 1647, was involved in the conflict between Parliament and Cromwell's New Model Army; defeated by Cromwell's forces, he fled to the Netherlands and later migrated to Virginia.

Poznański, Izrael (1833–1900), Polish Jewish businessman. Established a complex of textile mills in Łódź in the middle and late nineteenth century, making him one of the wealthiest and most powerful capitalists in Congress Poland.

Pride, Thomas (1610–58), English soldier and revolutionary. Worked as a drayman in London; joined the parliamentary army at the outbreak of the English Civil War; later became a colonel in Cromwell's New Model Army; in 1648, his troops expelled members of the House of Commons who sought a negotiated settlement with Charles I, known as "Pride's Purge." Knighted by Cromwell, served in Parliament as one of his closest followers. During the Restoration his corpse was exhumed and hung in public display in Tyburn.

Purishkevich, Vladimir Mitrofanovich (1870–1920), Russian politician. An extreme political reactionary, helped found the Union of the Russian People in 1905 that carried out violent attacks against leftists, Jews, and other national minorities. Infamous for a series of anti-Semitic speeches made while a delegate in the Second, Third, and Fourth Dumas; in 1908, formed the Union of Archangel Michael, an ultra-nationalist organization; involved in the murder of Rasputin, 1916; arrested by a Soviet court shortly after the Bolshevik Revolution, he was granted amnesty and joined the counterrevolutionary White Armies; died of typhus.

Puttkamer, Robert von (1828–1900), German politician. Served as conservative minister of the interior in Germany; enforced Bismarck's Antisocialist Law and forcibly suppressed strikes during the 1870s and 1880s.

Pym, John (1584–1643), English politician. Member of Parliament, 1621; major figure in parliamentary opposition to Charles I; 1641, helped draft the Grand Remonstrance, a list of grievances issued against the king; among five members of Parliament that Charles I sought to arrest in 1642 who helped spark the English Civil War.

Rainsborough, Thomas (1610–48), English soldier. Office of the Royal Navy, commanding the *Swallow*, in 1643; in 1645, commanded a regiment in Cromwell's New Model Army and fought at the Battle of Naseby; member of

Parliament, 1646, supported the demands of the Levellers for universal suffrage and religious toleration. Died at the Battle of Doncaster.

Rejtan, Tadeusz (1742–80), Polish politician. Member of the Polish Sejm (parliament), 1773; fought to prevent the first partition of Poland between Austria, Russia, and Prussia; at a famous session of the Sejm debating whether or not to accept the partition, he bared his chest and laid down in front of a doorway to stop other members from leaving the chamber during the debate. Withdrew from politics after the Partition; died by suicide.

Rexhäuser, Ludwig (1863–1914), German Social Democrat and trade unionist; 1896–1910, editor of *Korrespondenz für Deutschlands Buchdrucker und Schriftgiesser*; a proponent of reformist views, he denied the need for revolutionary class struggle; expelled from the SPD.

Robespierre, Maximilien François Marie Isidore de (1758–94), French statesman. One of the most prominent figures in the French Revolution; elected to the States-General in 1789, as leader of the Jacobins and at the head of the Committee for Public Safety; presided over the Reign of Terror.

Roland-Holst, Henriette (1869–1952), Dutch socialist and author. Broke from the Second International over its reformist tendencies, 1909; tried unsuccessfully to gain Luxemburg's support in doing so. Member of the Communist Party of Holland from 1918 to 1927. Author of a short biography of Luxemburg.

Rosenfeld, Kurt (1877–1943), German lawyer. From 1906 to 1910 worked as an instructor in civil law at the SPD's Central Party School in Berlin; in 1910, became a city council member in Berlin; 1917, became a member of the USPD.

Rousseau, Jean-Jacques (1712–78), French philosopher. One of the leading figures of the French Enlightenment, author of *Discourse on Inequality*, *The Social Contract*, and *Émile*.

Rudyerd, Benjamin (1572–1658), English poet and politician. Close friend of poet Ben Johnson and other writers of the period; 1618, appointed surveyor of the Court of Wards; 1621, member of Parliament; initially a supporter of James I, he assumed a moderate position in the disputes between Charles I and Parliament, while becoming increasingly critical of many of the king's policies; member of Cromwell's Long Parliament, yet maintained friendly relations with many Royalists; he opposed the trial and imprisonment of Charles I. Arrested by the New Model Army in 1648 and withdrew from politics thereafter.

Rupert, Prince (1619–82), German-British militarist. Son of Elizabeth, daughter of Friedrich V of Palatine (in southwest Germany), and James I of England; fought for the Dutch against Spain in the early 1640s as well as in the Thirty Years' War; 1642, appointed commander of the Royal Cavalry and was one of Charles I's most prominent Cavaliers. Defeated at Marston Moor, he proceeded to surrender Bristol. Exiled from England after his defeat; served under King Louis XIV of France in the 1650s and returned to England during the Restoration.

Saint-Just, Louis Antoine de (1767–94), French revolutionary. Prominent Jacobin during French Revolution, member of National Convention, 1792; spearheaded the execution of King Louis XVI; leader of the Committee of Public Safety that presided over the Reign of Terror; played a pivotal role in drafting the Constitution of 1793. Executed upon the overthrow of his close friend and political ally Robespierre.

Saint-Simon, Claude Henri de Rouvroy (1760–1825), French political theorist and philosopher; advocated a form of statist socialism based on utilizing the power of modern industry; his advocacy of science as the key to progress helped pave the way for positivism. He was not a revolutionary, appealing instead to the agents of existing society to implement such ideals as full employment, social equality, and meritocracy.

Sarrien, Ferdinand (1840–1915), French politician. Leader of the left-of-center Radical Party; served as prime minister of France from March to October 1906.

Scheibler, Karl Wilhelm (1820–81), German industrialist; originally from Belgium, he moved to Russian-occupied Poland in 1848 and helped establish the textile industry in the city of Łódź, building a series of factories and businesses. He became very wealthy during the 1860s, when he managed to obtain supplies of cotton for his factories that were unavailable to other industrialists.

Schiller, Friedrich (1759–1805), German poet, historian, playwright, and philosopher. One of the most outstanding representatives of the German Enlightenment, he made important contributions on aesthetics, ethics, and the meaning of human emancipation. His distinction between overcoming the divide between "formal drive" and "sensuous drive" through the realization of the "play drive" anticipated later utopian thinkers and had an especially important impact on the thought of such twentieth-century critical theorists as Herbert Marcuse.

Singer, Paul (1844–1911), German Social Democrat. Member of SDAP, 1869; 1883–1911, city councilor in Berlin; 1886, member of the SPD Executive Committee, and in 1890, one of the co-chairmen of the SPD; opposed to aspects of revisionism but far more opposed to the semi-anarchist views of "the Young Ones" (*die Junge*) who were expelled from the SPD in 1895; became a member of the ISB in 1900.

Skalon, Georgi (1847–1914), Russian general. From 1905 until his death, he was governor-general of Warsaw and commander in chief of the Warsaw Military District. In August 1906, he survived an attempt carried out by the military wing of the PPS to assassinate him by bombing his carriage.

Skippon, Philip (c. 1600–60), English soldier and naturalist. Commanded troops of the New Model Army during the English Civil War.

Skrzynecki, Jan Zygmunt (1787–1860), Polish general. Commander in chief of the Polish forces during the November Uprising of 1830; at the Battle of Ostrołęka he failed to resolutely confront the Russian forces, which crushed the uprising.

Słowacki, Juliusz (1809–49), Polish romantic poet. Considered one of the most important voices of nineteenth-century Polish literature; author of such works as *Kordian* and *Testament mój*. He participated in the 1830 November Uprising; after its defeat, he lived the rest of his life in exile.

Sombart, Werner (1863–1941), German economist and sociologist, leading figure in the "Young Historical School" of empirical-based social theory. Studied under Gustav von Schmoller and later befriended such figures as Max Weber and Carl Schmitt. An avowed Marxist in his early years, his major works are *Modern Capitalism* and *Why There Is No Socialism in the United States*, a highly influential work that promoted the myth of American exceptionalism. By the 1930s he had moved to the right and supported a corporativist fusion of state power and economic development.

Somerset, Henry (1577–1646), English aristocrat. Royalist supporter of Charles I during the English Revolution; lent huge sums of money to the king; after the Battle of Naseby, Charles I sought refuge at his castle in Raglan; a year later, he was forced to surrender the castle to the revolutionaries, ending the civil war in Wales. Died while under arrest by parliamentary forces.

Sosnkowski, Kazimierz (1885–1969), Polish politician, general, and linguist. Joined the PPS in 1905; February 1906, attended the Seventh Congress of the PPS; member of Piłsudski's Revolutionary Faction, 1906–1909; arrested and imprisoned during World War I, he was released in 1918 and became deputy minister for military affairs in the Second Polish Republic, 1920–23; he distanced himself from Piłsudski in 1926 over criticism of his military coup. Appointed commander of a section of the Polish army during Hitler's invasion of 1939; fled to France, where he became president-in-exile of Poland; resigned from Polish government in 1941; initially opposed the Polish national insurrection of 1944, incurring the wrath of Churchill, whom he accused of sacrificing Polish independence for the sake of maintaining relations with the USSR. Lived the rest of his life in Canada.

Spasowicz, Włodzimierz (1829–1906), Polish lawyer. Professor at St. Petersburg University, 1850s; resigned his position in defense of students persecuted for opposing the tsarist regime. Served in legal defense of Sergei Nechayev and of many other leftists and revolutionaries of the period. Advocated Polish national autonomy; founded the newspaper *Kraj* and wrote for Polish journal *Atheneum*.

Spencer, Henry (1620–43), English nobleman. Fought in the First English Civil

War on behalf of Charles I, including at the Battle of Edgehill; killed by a cannonball at the Battle of Newbury shortly afterward.

Stadthagen, Arthur (1857–1917), German Social Democrat and lawyer. From 1889–1917, city councilor in Berlin; 1890–1917, member of the Reichstag; 1893–1916, contributor to and editor of *Vorwärts*; before World War I, defended the views of the German left; after 1914, adhered to the centrist forces, and in 1917, became a member of the USPD.

Stalin, Joseph (1878–1953), Russian dictator. A native of Georgia, joined the RSDRP while leading strikes there in 1901; active during the 1905 Revolution with the Bolsheviks and assumed a number of important administrative posts following the October Revolution of 1917; in the mid-1920s consolidated total power, and in the 1930s imposed a program of rapid industrialization that cost the lives of tens of millions; his imposition of a totalitarian state resulted in the extermination of most of the leadership of the 1917 Revolution.

Stapleton, Philip (1603–47), English politician. Member of the House of Commons, 1640; supported Parliament in its conflict with Charles I and fought with the parliamentary army in the battles of Edgehill and Newbury. A moderate, he opposed the arrest and imprisonment of Charles I, seeking a negotiated settlement of the conflict; under threat of arrest by Cromwell, died while attempting to leave England.

Stołypin, Pyotr (1862–1911), Russian politician. In 1906, became minister of the interior, and subsequently Russian prime minister, a position he held until the end of his life. He used brutal methods to crush the revolution of 1905–1906. He subsequently carried out a program of agrarian reform. He died after an assassination that was carried out against him, with the tsar's knowledge, in Kiev.

Straszewicz, Ludwik (1857–1913), Polish journalist and publisher. Worked with Ludwik Warynski and other Polish socialists; arrested in 1879 for distributing illegal literature. Expelled from Russian-occupied Poland, lived in Western Europe and came under the influence of the school of August Comte. Published Polish journal *Atheneum* and co-edited *Kraj* with Włodzimierz Spasowicz; lived in St. Petersburg from 1888; in 1905, grew close to the Cadets and co-founded the Party for Realpolitik (Stronnictwo Polityki Realnej), a left-of-center reformist current.

Ströbel, Heinrich (1869–1944), German journalist and poet. Joined the SPD in 1889; wrote for various socialist publications, including *Vorwärts*. In 1900, at Luxemburg's insistence, he became its main editor. Member of Prussian House of Representatives from 1908 to 1918; opposed World War I on pacifist grounds and joined the USPD in 1917; served as Prussian prime minister following the German Revolution of 1918. Returned to the SPD in 1920 when much of it joined the KPD; member of Reichstag, 1924–32. Emigrated to Switzerland in 1933.

Strode, William (1598–1645), English politician. Member of House of Commons, 1624–45; one of five members of the body that Charles I tried to illegally arrest in 1642, helping to spark the English Civil War; supported the Great Remonstrance of 1641 and opposed any compromise with the king; fought on the side of the parliamentary army at the Battle of Edgehill, 1642.

Struve, Pyotr (1870–1944), Russian political economist and writer; became a leading figure among the Legal Marxists in the 1890s; argued that Russia could and should endure an extended period of capitalist industrialization before being ready for socialism; as he later admitted, "socialism never roused the slightest emotion in me"; by 1900 he had moved to the right and made a transition to liberalism; in 1905 became founder of the liberal Constitutional Democratic Party; supported Russia's entry into World War I and moved further to the right, becoming a severe critic of the Russian Revolution in 1917 and supporter of the White counterrevolutionary armies.

Svyatopolk-Mirsky, Pyotr Danilovich (1857–1914), Russian politician. Minister of the interior, 1904, after the assassination of Vyacheslav von Plehve. Presided over massacre of Bloody Sunday on January 22, 1905; denied authorizing shooting of the demonstrators, but was generally blamed for it; retired from political life shortly thereafter.

Świętochowski, Aleksander (1849–1938), Polish writer, publicist, and, during the 1870s and 1890s, a leading figure in what became known as Warsaw Positivism. In the revolutionary period of 1905–1906, he was a leading representative of the "progressive camp," and attempted to represent enlightened liberalism in public debate, including through support for women's suffrage. This did not, however, prevent him making a name for himself as an opponent of the revolution. After the revolution's defeat, Świętochowski included anti-Semitic motifs in his politics, which culminated in an all-out campaign to sway public opinion against the SDKPiL, and against Luxemburg and Jogiches as two of their leading figures.

Sytin, Ivan Dmitiyevich (1851–1934), Russian publisher; highly regarded by writers and intellectuals, including Tolstoy and Gorky. His printing house on Pyatnitskaya Street was one of the main stages of activity during the street uprising in Moscow in December 1905. His property was later expropriated by the Bolsheviks. Decided against going into exile; lived until the end of his life in the small Moscow apartment that was left to him. Today, this houses a museum to him as a publisher.

Taaffe, Eduard (1833–95), Austrian politician. Originally associated with the Liberals in the 1860s, he subsequently moved to the right; prime minister of Austria, 1867–70 and in 1879; remembered best for his electoral reform bill of 1882, which increased the size of the electorate.

Thiers, Adolphe (1797–1877), French politician and historian; served as prime minister of France in 1836, 1840, and 1848. An opponent of Napoleon III, he returned to power in the national elections of February 1871 and sued for peace with the Germans. Forced to flee Paris during the Commune of 1871, he directed the government forces that broke through the city defenses, resulting in the slaughter of tens of thousands of communards. Following his brutal repression of the Commune, he became president of France, only to be forced from power in 1873 by opposition from the monarchists.

Tidemann-Seeheim, Heinrich von (1840–1922), German politician. Cofounder of the German Eastern Marches Society, a racist group devoted to securing the ethnic cleansing of Poles and other minorities from the German Empire. Its ideas were influential in the development of Nazi ideology.

Tirard, Pierre Emmanuel (1827–93), French politician. Member of Chamber of Deputies, 1876; minister of agriculture and commerce, 1879–81; prime minister of France, 1889–90.

Tolstoy, Leo (1828–1910), Russian writer of the realist school. Pacifist and social reformer, influential among generations of Russian writers and activists. One of Luxemburg's favorite writers, whom she repeatedly praised for his incisive and profound treatment of social and personal relations.

Trotsky, Leon (1879–1940), Russian revolutionary. Joined socialist movement, 1897; initially a supporter of the Mensheviks, following 1903 split in the RSDRP; led St. Petersburg Soviet during the 1905 Revolution, the most important in the empire; published *Nachalo*, a paper that was influential in the 1905 Revolution; moved closer to the Bolsheviks during the February 1917 Revolution, joining them later in 1917 and becoming people's commissar of foreign affairs, 1917–18, head of the Red Army; leader of Left Opposition to Stalin, 1923; expelled from USSR, 1927; founded Fourth International, 1938; murdered while in exile in Mexico by agents of Stalin.

Vaillant, Édouard (1840–1915), French socialist politician. Following studies in Germany, returned to Paris at the outbreak of the Franco-Prussian War; participant in the revolts against the Government of National Defense, 1870–71. A supporter of the creation of the Paris Commune, he ran, unsuccessfully, as a revolutionary socialist candidate for National Assembly in 1871. Following the suppression of the uprising, fled for Great Britain, where he remained until 1880; returned to France following the declaration of general amnesty; elected to the Chamber of Deputies, 1893.

Vandal, Albert (1853–1910), French historian. Author of several books on Napoleon and his influence, including a three-volume work on his invasion of Russia.

Vane, Henry (1613–62), English politician. A Puritan seeking religious freedom, he moved to Boston in 1635, where he spoke out against the persecution of fellow reformer Anne Hutchinson; as governor of the colony, he directed wars of extermination against the First Nations people of the area. Returned to England in the 1640s, where he joined the parliamentary opposition to

Charles I; opposed to the radical ideas of the Levellers, he worked closely with Cromwell from 1647; appointed to Council of State after the abolition of the monarchy. Fell out with Cromwell over his insistence that Parliament have political primary over the army; arrested and beheaded by Charles II shortly after the Restoration.

Villiers, George (1592–1628), English politician. As Duke of Buckingham and admiral of the Royal Navy, was virtual ruler of England in the last years of the reign of James I and the first years of Charles I. In 1625, organized the attack on the Spanish port of Cádiz that ended in a complete disaster. These and other failures in political and military affairs led Charles I to dismiss him from his posts in government. He was later stabbed to death by a naval officer. His arrogant and shortsighted policies are often cited among the reasons for growing discontent at the time with the monarchy.

Voltaire (François-Marie Arouet) (1694–1778), French writer and philosopher. A major figure of the French Enlightenment; his criticism of established religion and suppression of freedom of thought made him one of the most influential figures in the history of early modern France.

Waldeck-Rousseau, René (1846–1904), French politician. Minister of the interior, 1881 and 1883–85; in 1884 sponsored the legislation that made trade unions legal; in 1899, during the upheavals associated with the Dreyfus Affair, he headed a government of national defense, which for the first time included a socialist.

Walecki, Henryk, see Horwitz, Maksymilian.

Waller, William (1597–1668), English soldier and politician. Fought for Bohemia in the early stages of the Thirty Years' War; member of Parliament, 1640; colonel in the parliamentary army at the outbreak of First English Civil War. Due to winning numerous victories in southern England, earned the appellation "William the Conqueror" before being defeated in Lansdown and Roundway Down; faced with these defeats, he was one of the first to propose the formation of the New Model Army. A Presbyterian, he opposed Cromwell's Commonwealth and was imprisoned numerous times between 1649 and 1659.

Warski, Adolf (born Jerzy Warszawski) (1868–1937), Polish Social Democrat and communist. Co-founded the SDKP in Zurich in 1893, and from then on was one of Luxemburg's closest Polish colleagues. Resident in the Kingdom of Poland from March 1905 during the Revolution of 1905, and, parallel to this, one of the SDKPiL's most important publicists of the whole revolutionary period; participated in the RSDRP's Fourth Party Congress in Stockholm in April 1906, at which the SDKPiL united with the RSDRP. Arrested in June 1906 in Warsaw; escaped, arrested again at the end of 1906; sentenced to exile, fled in May 1907, and reached Russia. Arrested in St. Petersburg in April 1908, and again sentenced to exile, he fled again, first to Western

Europe in December 1908, and later to Galicia. From 1912 to 1916, he was challenged in his leadership role due to factional struggles inside the SDKPiL; from 1913, strengthened his campaign for the SDKPiL and the PPS-Left to unite on both political and organizational levels. Participated in the conferences in Zimmerwald (1915) and Kienthal (1916). Returned in May 1916 to a Warsaw occupied by German troops; May 1916, arrested and subsequently imprisoned in Havelberg until the end of 1917, after which he returned to Warsaw. At the end of 1918, co-founded the Communist Party of Poland (KPRP, later the KPP). From 1926 to 1929, he was a deputy in the Sejm; from 1929, an employee in the Marx-Engels Institute in Moscow, where he wrote two important studies on the background of the conflict between Lenin and Luxemburg on the question of nationalities, and on the history of the SDKPiL. In 1937 he was arrested in Moscow, and subsequently executed.

Weber, Maximilian Karl Emil (1864–1920), German sociologist. A founding figure in sociology, thanks to such influential works as *The Protestant Ethic and the Spirit of Capitalism* and *Economy and Society*; Luxemburg studied and criticized his work in her lectures at the SPD party school from 1907 to 1914; a supporter of World War I, he voiced strong opposition to Luxemburg's effort to promote a German socialist revolution in 1918–19.

Wentworth, Thomas (1593–1641), English politician. Member of Parliament, 1614; allied during reign of James I with George Villiers; strong supporter of centralized monarchy, became privy counsellor in 1629 and lord deputy of Ireland 1632; became chief advisor to Charles I, 1639, earning many political enemies. In 1640 censored by Parliament for "tyrannical behavior" while governing Ireland; although initially defended from the charges by Charles I, the king assented to the sentence of death passed against him by Parliament for fear of further antagonizing his political opponents.

Wermuth, Karl (1878–1951), German journalist. Joined the SPD at the turn of the twentieth century; from 1906 to 1914, co-editor (along with Luxemburg and several others) of *Vorwärts*.

Wielopolski, Aleksander Ignacy Jan-Kanty (1803–77), Polish politician. Fought for a politics of reaching a political settlement with Russia in order to re-establish wide-reaching autonomy for the Kingdom of Poland. In 1862, negotiated with the Kingdom of Poland's military government for a civilian government, and in 1862–63 led the latter. The outbreak of the January Uprising of 1863 destroyed his political hopes.

Wilhelm II (1859–1941), German kaiser and king of Prussia from 1888 to 1918. Forced from power by German Revolution of November 1918; died in exile in the Netherlands.

Willoughby, Francis (c. 1614–66), English politician and soldier. A Presbyterian, he joined the opposition to Charles I in the early 1640s and fought in the parliamentary army. Disturbed by the increasingly radical direction of the revolution, he became a Royalist and was accused of treason by Parliament in 1647; he fled England and worked alongside supporters of Charles I in the Netherlands. During the Restoration he was made governor of Barbados by Charles II, in 1666; died in a hurricane in the Caribbean.

Wilmot, Henry (1612–58), English aristocrat. A Royalist who fought on behalf of Charles I during the English Revolution; defeated William Waller at Roundway Down in 1643 and Cropredy Bridge in 1644; after a dispute with Prince Rupert, was relieved of his command and went into exile in France, where he became a major advisor to Charles II. After failing to spark a Royalist uprising through an attack on Marston Moor in 1655, again went into exile.

Windisch-Grätz, Alfred Candidus Ferdinand (1787–1862), member of the Bohemian noble Windisch-Grätz family. Served during the Napoleonic Wars; noted for his suppression of the 1848 Revolutions in the Austrian Empire. An avowed reactionary, he crushed the March revolt in Vienna as well as the Czech uprising of June 1848 with brute force, earning him the enmity of Social Democrats and revolutionaries.

Windthorst, Ludwig (1812–91), German politician. Member of the Diet of the Kingdom of Hannover 1849; for many years a supporter of Hannover's independence and opponent of Prussian domination; minister of justice in Hannover 1851 and 1862. With Hannover's incorporation into the German Empire in 1871, became leader of the Catholic Center Party, which opposed Bismarck's discriminatory policies against minorities; Bismarck considered him his main political opponent in the last years of his rule. The Center Party opposed the aims of the Social Democratic movement and competed with it for support among the working class.

Witte, Sergei (1849–1915), Russian politician and entrepreneur. Pushed through the construction of the Trans-Siberian Railway during his period as finance minister, 1893–1903. From October 1905 to April 1906, prime minister of Russia, after which he withdrew from public life.

Workman, John (1590–1640), an English minister who preached against images in churches and consequently was imprisoned in 1633. When released from prison he opened a school, subsequently shut down by Archbishop William Laud; Workman went mad and died.

Zaorski, F., see Lityński, Alfred.

Zasulich, Vera (1849–1919), Russian revolutionary. Initially a supporter of revolutionary terror, she seriously wounded Colonel Theodore Trepov, governor of St. Petersburg, in an assassination attempt in 1878; she was acquitted in a famous trial and went into exile in Switzerland; a convert to Marxism, she worked closely with Plekhanov and the Emancipation of Labor Group; wrote a famous letter to Marx in 1881 asking if Russia was destined to endure a stage of capitalism before being able to reach socialism; became a leading figure of Menshevism after split in the RSDRP in 1903; moved to the right, supported World War I, and opposed the Bolshevik seizure of power in 1917; she died after returning to Russia from exile.

Zetkin, Konstantin "Kostja" (1885–1980), son of Clara Zetkin, a key feminist organizer in the SPD and close friend of Rosa Luxemburg. Zetkin and Luxemburg were lovers between 1907 and 1915. After World War II he moved to the United States, where he was a practicing physician until 1957, when he and his wife retired to Canada.

Zhelyabov, Andrei Ivanovich (1851–81), Russian revolutionary. Expelled from Novorossiysk University in Odessa 1871 for agitating for democratic rights; 1873, joined the Tchaikovsky Circle, a Russian literary society close to the Narodniks (or Populists); by the late 1870s, argued for the necessity for violent revolt to bring down the regime. Active with the Land and Liberty (Zemlya i Volya) organization among the peasantry; a leading advocate of revolutionary terror, he was involved in the effort to assassinate Tsar Alexander II. He was executed in April 1881, even though he had been arrested before the assassination occurred.

Zinoviev, Grigori (1883–1936), well-known leader of the Bolesheviks; after the revolution served as chair of the Comintern and chair of the Petrograd Soviet until 1926. He was removed from Soviet leadership by Stalin and put on trial in 1936 (part of the Trial of Sixteen), which resulted in his execution.

Zubatov, Sergei (1864–1917), Russian police official. Joined the revolutionary movement as a youth, but soon abandoned the cause and became an informant for the tsarist regime; starting in 1896, headed Moscow office of the Okhrana, the secret police; fostered the promotion of pro-government trade unions, known as *zuvbatovshchina*, to control the workers' movement. Forced from his position as police chief in 1903 by Interior Minister Vyacheslav von Plehve in response to his failure to curb massive workers' strikes; committed suicide in 1917 upon hearing of Nicholas II's abdication.

Index

absolutism, xix, xxx, 4, 8, 14–15, 32–4, 45, 47, 79–80, 83, 85, 100–101, 105–6, 109–17, 121–6, 131, 133–8, 140–6, 148–9, 164–5, 176–7, 179–80, 183, 205, 208, 210–12, 220, 230–1, 233–4, 240–3, 269–71, 293, 303–4, 306, 308–9, 314, 319, 325–6, 337, 339, 343–4, 357, 361–3, 368, 375–7, 379–87, 391–2, 401–8, 432–3, 435–7, 459, 462–3, 508
Adler, Friedrich, 460, 479
adventurism, 179, 245, 314, 415–16
affordable housing, 42
Africa, xxxiii, 26, 51, 362, 446, 494
agitate, 113–14. *See also* organize
agriculture, 60, 234, 515
    agrarian question, 199, 319, 394
    agrarian movements, 376
    agricultural workers, 102, 218, 234, 245–6
Akimov, Mikhail, 395, 479
Aksakov, Sergei, 402, 479
Alexander II (Russia), 170, 328, 479, 508, 519
Alexander III (Russia), 479, 508
Alexandrovsky [Alexandrowski] barracks, 19
Alexeyev, S. N., 396–7, 399, 479
Algeria, 14, 484, 494, 499, 506
Alsace-Lorraine, 359
Altona, 193
America, xxxiii, 26, 31, 35, 164, 361–2, 369, 423, 463, 491. *See also* United States
Amsterdam, 3, 273
anarchism, 179, 193, 195–8, 265–7, 317, 416, 480, 492
    anarcho-communism, 193, 196
    anarcho-socialist, 265–6
    anarcho-syndicalists, 265–7
ancien régime, 242, 404
Annesley, Francis, 463, 479
anti-Semitism, 19, 73, 290, 316, 320, 396, 480, 488, 507–9, 514. *See also* Black Hundreds; Jews
Aquarium Theater, 18
Arago, François, 160, 479
Armenians, xvi, 36
army/armies, 17–21, 25–6, 28–9, 31–2, 34–5, 37–8, 49–52, 55, 77–9, 84, 89, 105, 107, 109–10, 112, 114, 116, 120, 122–3, 125–8, 136–7, 140–4, 158, 160–2, 171, 176–7, 208, 210, 219, 234, 238, 241, 253, 271, 276, 295, 304–5, 321, 340, 353, 367, 375, 380, 394, 412, 415, 424–5, 431, 434–7, 446, 450–9, 462, 464–6, 468–77, 480, 483, 487, 489, 493–5, 497, 499, 501–6, 509–10, 512–17
    abolition, 51, 424
    proletariat/peoples' army, 49, 51, 120, 123, 126, 140–1, 295, 305, 321, 367, 394, 412, 436–7, 446
    dragoons, 17, 19, 21, 142
    military, xxi, 37, 39, 45, 47, 49–50, 53, 56, 87–8, 97, 104, 106–7, 109, 113, 125, 131, 138, 140, 142–3, 156, 158, 162, 181, 193, 206–7, 209–10, 213–14, 219, 222, 271, 283, 293, 297, 353, 357, 370, 388, 395–6, 404, 411–14, 424, 434, 450, 452, 455, 457, 461, 467, 477, 480, 482–3, 485, 488–9, 494, 496, 499, 503, 506–7, 511–12, 516–17
art, 36, 43, 123, 363, 483, 497
artisans, 13, 25, 30, 56, 87–8, 92, 110
Asia, 26, 164, 362
assassination, xx, 107, 170, 411, 414, 479, 494, 507–8, 511, 513–14, 518–19
assembly, xxiii–xxv, 13, 15, 35, 37, 46–7, 66, 79, 85, 93, 100–101, 105, 115, 135, 173, 177, 183, 189–92, 205–7, 209–10, 212, 216–17, 220, 223, 233, 239, 248–9, 251–2, 264, 269, 275–6, 278, 280, 283, 302, 304–5, 311, 313, 354, 381–2, 386, 388–9, 432, 437, 440, 475, 482, 484, 493, 495, 498, 515
    Constituent, xxv, 101, 173, 177, 183, 189–92, 276, 311, 381
    constitutional, 101, 115, 388
    legislative (French Revolution), 13, 388
    National (1848), 304–5, 432, 493
Astley, Jacob, 451, 459, 479
Auer, Ignatz, 273, 480
Australia, 26, 369
Austria, 14, 30, 32–3, 39–40, 105, 164, 191, 227, 276, 294, 300, 347, 353, 356, 362, 395, 400–401, 414, 423, 434, 441, 479, 498, 510, 514

Austria-Hungarian Empire, 85, 227, 276, 300, 395, 414, 423, 434, 498
Austrian Empire, 164, 398, 433, 480, 507, 518
Austrian parliament, 84, 434
Austrian Social Democratic Party, 128. *See also* political parties
autocracy, 21, 183, 196, 276, 407
Axelrod, Pavel, 312, 315, 480

Babeuf, François-Noël, 389, 480
Babeufism, 389
Babruysk, 213
Bachem, Nicolaus Heinrich Julius, 428, 480
Bakhmut, 137, 218
Baku, 36, 202, 205, 207–208, 213, 224, 226, 228, 376
Bakunin, Mikhail, 193–5, 480, 492, 497
Bakuninist, 193
Balfour, Sir William, 456, 480
ballot, 41, 153
banditry, 412–14, 416
barricades, xvii, 222
Bashmakov, Alexander, 396
Bastwick, John, 463, 465, 480
Battle of June [1848], 13
Battle of Tsushima, 403
Batumi, 202, 204–5, 207
Bavaria, 28, 319
Bax, Ernest Belfort, 297, 481
Bebel, August, 201, 256, 264–5, 274, 337–8, 442, 481, 501
Berezina, 340
Berlin, ix, xi, xiii, xxiv, 3, 84, 101, 105, 126, 150, 155, 244, 251, 259, 263, 265, 267, 273, 275, 277, 281, 289, 304, 307, 352, 408, 417–18, 423, 433, 437, 443, 449, 480–1, 483, 496–8, 500, 503–4, 507, 510–11, 513
Berlin Zeughaus, 304
Bernstein, Eduard, xviii, 3, 72, 197, 242, 266, 316, 352, 449, 481–2, 497
Beskidy, 141
Bethmann-Hollweg, Theobald von, 446, 481
Białystok, 23, 77–8, 127, 196, 218
Biedermann, Alfred, 291, 481
Bielecki, Marian, 327–8, 481, 498. *See also* Kowieński, M
Bismarck, Otto von, 150, 185, 197, 285, 310, 361, 428, 482, 484, 495, 509, 518
Black Hundreds, 73, 79, 141, 148, 166, 184, 190, 377, 396, 403, 437. *See also* anti-Semitism; pogroms
Black lives, xvi
Black reparations, 170
Blanc, Louis, ix, 51, 147, 328, 482
Blanqui, Auguste, xxvii, 7, 147, 169–71, 482
Blanquism, vii, xxviii, 7, 169–73
Blanquist, xxvii, 7, 170–4
Block, Hans, 275, 482
Bloody Sunday, xxii, 78, 276, 490, 514
Bobrinsky, Alexei Alexandrovich, 398, 482
Boers, 51
Bogdanov, Alexander, 193, 427, 483, 503
Bohemia, 359, 400, 434, 516
Bolshevik(s), xx, xxiv, xxvi–xxviii, xxxi–xxxii, 79, 99, 152, 169–74, 181, 190, 193, 302, 304, 307, 310, 314–17, 375, 385, 427, 431, 480, 482–6, 491, 495–7, 500–501, 503–4, 507–9, 513–15, 519. *See also* Russian Social Democratic Labor Party (RSDRP)
Bolshevism, xxvii, 172
Bömelburg, Theodor, 197, 274, 483
bourgeois, xxiv, xxvi–xxxi, 4, 7–8, 13–16, 24, 30–1, 33, 36, 41–5, 55, 58, 65, 69–73, 83, 85, 91–7, 99–103, 108, 110, 116–20, 122–3, 128–9, 131, 137, 139–40, 142–51, 156–7, 159–61, 163, 166, 169, 171, 175–7, 179–80, 183–4, 186, 190–1, 196, 208–9, 211–12, 231–2, 236–7, 239–43, 246, 248–50, 252–3, 255–6, 269–70, 279–80, 283–4, 294–5, 297, 300–308, 311–12, 314–21, 329, 332, 336–7, 342, 344, 349, 351–2, 354, 357, 361, 363–4, 366, 369, 373, 376–81, 384, 386–93, 405–8, 412, 415–16, 423–4, 427–9, 438, 446, 489–90, 493, 505
  democracy, xxvi, 15, 100, 209, 241, 246, 270, 301–3, 357
  intellectuals, xxiv, 4, 69, 110, 118, 122, 131, 336, 384
  liberalism, xxvi, 177, 179, 208, 301–2, 311–12, 318, 352, 366, 377–8, 380–1, 387, 390–2
  parties, 91–4, 96, 99, 103, 123, 166, 183–4, 241, 294, 300, 307, 314, 317, 377, 380, 427–9. *See also* political parties
  revolutions, 14–16, 65, 108, 116, 139, 146–7, 180, 241–3, 246, 305–6, 308, 377–9, 387–91
  rule, xxx, 30–1, 388, 393

society, xxiv, 13–16, 58, 93, 95, 101, 117, 119–20, 128, 140, 144, 148, 177, 183, 190–1, 208, 212, 241, 243, 248, 255, 294–5, 301–2, 311, 318–19, 363–4, 373, 388–90, 392, 408, 412, 416, 423–4
Bourgeoisie, vii, xxiv–xxvi, xxix, xxxi, 3–4, 7, 9, 13–16, 24, 26, 30, 32–5, 37, 39–44, 46–7, 59, 69–73, 76, 80, 83–4, 91–7, 99–101, 103, 105–6, 113, 116–17, 119, 121–3, 128, 131, 133, 135, 139, 141, 143–8, 151, 153–6, 159, 161–7, 171, 173, 175–7, 179–80, 183, 186, 191–2, 212, 241, 243, 269–71, 276, 279, 284–5, 293–5, 297, 301, 303–4, 306–8, 310–11, 313–14, 317–20, 330–4, 336, 338–9, 342, 348, 358, 362, 369, 371, 377–9, 383–6, 388–94, 399, 403–4, 406–7, 412–13, 423–4, 432–3, 437, 481, 490
  European, 69, 403
  French, 35, 69–70, 147, 163, 165–6, 391
  German, 7, 69, 243, 285, 320, 404, 433
  industrial, 13, 311, 369, 371
  liberal, xxvi, xxix, 147, 175–7, 192, 308, 314, 377, 383, 388
  modern, 13
  Polish, vii, 33–4, 37, 69–73, 94–5, 153, 166, 334, 338–9, 342, 358, 406–7
  Russian, 71, 270–1, 306, 319, 377, 392
boycott, 91–3, 190–1, 310, 385, 432, 434–7. *See also* Duma
Brandenburg, Count Friedrich Wilhelm, 432, 481, 483
Brereton, William, 451, 470, 483
Bringmann, August, 267, 280, 483
Britain, 236, 485–6, 495, 500–501, 515
brotherhood, 62, 77, 133, 399, 425
Browne, Robert, 463, 483
Bülow, Bernhard Heinrich Karl Martin von, 446, 484
Bund, 170, 317, 320, 358. *See also* Jews
Bundesrat, 284
burghers, 44–5, 147, 389
Burton, Henry, 463, 465, 484
Bułygin Constitution, 78, 484
Bułygin, Alexander, 40, 78–9, 94, 133–4, 136, 149, 219, 276, 484

Cadets, 151–4, 171–2, 175, 190–1, 271, 308–10, 377, 383–6, 391, 403, 428, 491, 505, 513. *See also* Constitutional Democratic Party

Camphausen, Gottfried Ludolf, 304, 484, 493
Canut Revolts, 164
capital, 5, 15–16, 25, 29, 33, 39, 44, 46, 49, 55–61, 77, 87–8, 102, 111, 115–19, 121, 132–3, 138, 157, 160–1, 163–4, 167, 180, 209–12, 225–6, 232–4, 236, 241–3, 245, 289–90, 297, 334, 340, 361–2, 369–70, 372, 375, 386, 395, 412, 492
capitalism, xvi, xxiv, xxvii, xxxi–xxxiii, 13–15, 24, 26–7, 30–1, 35–6, 46, 49, 51, 57–8, 70, 144, 167, 183, 194, 208, 210, 214–15, 294, 318, 334, 336, 350, 357–8, 362–4, 369, 402, 407, 409, 412, 423, 425, 512, 517–18
  abolition of, 26, 31
  class rule in, 15
  development of, xxvii, 4, 105, 189, 232, 236, 238, 241–3, 246, 306, 335, 337–9, 348–9, 358, 361–4, 376, 387, 390, 406, 505
  finance, 5, 13
  law of value, xxxiii
capitalists, 4, 24–6, 28–30, 33, 39–41, 47, 49–52, 55–62, 88–9, 102, 116, 118, 123, 156–7, 164, 166, 290, 369–72, 509
child labor, 424
children, xi, 19–20, 25, 38, 42, 48–9, 52–3, 56–61, 71, 162, 186, 207, 269, 331, 424, 467, 490
Carniola, 276
Caucasus, 36, 77, 79, 95, 132–3, 138, 140, 202, 204, 208–9, 218, 330, 356
Cavaignac, Louis-Eugène, 13, 159–60, 166, 484
Cavendish, William, 453, 484
censorship, 96, 134, 186, 463, 469, 474–5. *See also* freedom of the press
central authority, 29, 267
Central Committee, 172, 221, 224, 299, 306–7, 330, 333, 430, 494, 500
Chamisso, Adelbert von, 349, 368, 485
Charles I (England), 451–5, 457–8, 460–3, 465, 467, 472, 479–80, 483–6, 488–9, 493–5, 499, 501–5, 509–10, 512–14, 516–18
Charles II (England), 449, 468, 488–9, 494–5, 506, 516, 518
Chartists, 194, 424
Chechnya, 205
Cheka, 171

Chemnitz, 276
Cherevanin, Fyodor Andreyevich, 378, 392, 485
Cherkasy, 217
China, xxxiii, 27, 403, 485, 506
Chișinău, 214
Christianity, 27–28
class, viii, xv, xviii–xx, xxii–xxxiii, 3–5, 7–9, 13–16, 23–53, 55–9, 62–3, 68–73, 76–80, 83–5, 88–107, 109–23, 126–9, 132–9, 144–50, 155–6, 161, 164, 166–7, 169, 171–3, 175–7, 179–81, 183, 189, 193–6, 199–201, 203–4, 206, 208–12, 215, 218, 220, 222–3, 225–7, 230–4, 236–54, 257, 259, 261, 265–7, 269, 271–3, 275–280, 282–4, 293–5, 297, 299–307, 310–21, 327–8, 330–40, 342–4, 347–52, 354, 357–8, 360–1, 363–9, 371–2, 376–80, 382–4, 386–94, 403, 406–7, 412–13, 415–18, 423–5, 427–31, 433–42, 446, 460, 482, 488, 490, 492, 497, 504, 508, 510, 518
  consciousness, xxiii–xxiv, 15–16, 94, 103, 112, 114, 117–20, 133, 135, 200, 203, 210–12, 239, 241, 272, 297, 302, 327, 388
  struggle, viii, xxx–xxxi, 4, 7, 13, 15, 37, 57, 92–3, 99–100, 106–7, 110–12, 114–16, 119–21, 127–8, 133, 135–6, 144–5, 149, 164, 171–2, 180, 183, 189, 195, 200–201, 220, 222–3, 225, 227, 236–8, 242–3, 247–8, 250, 252–4, 257, 259, 261, 265–7, 273, 277, 279–80, 282, 293–5, 297, 299, 301–3, 305–6, 312–13, 315, 321, 327, 333–8, 340, 343–4, 348–51, 354, 360, 364–5, 368–9, 377, 379, 389–93, 403, 413, 415, 417, 423–5, 427, 429–31, 438–41, 497, 510
Clemenceau, Georges, 297, 485
clergy, 39, 44, 48, 141, 155, 389, 399, 402, 406, 467
Cobden, Richard, 72, 485
Coke, Edward, 462, 485
Colepeper, John, 465, 485
colonialism, 362, 446, 467
colonies, 57, 361–2, 479
Committee of Socialist Revolutionaries (Moscow), 17
communal, xxix, 27, 41–43, 402, 492
communism, xxxi–xxxii, 13, 196, 474
Communist Party of Germany (KPD), xii, xvi, xxxv, 482, 489. See also political parties
Communist Workers' Party of Poland (KPRP), 23, 326, 500, 517. See also political parties
confinement, 58, 61. See also pregnant
congresses, iv, vii–viii, xii, xviii–xx, xxviii, 3, 38–9, 41, 43, 49, 170, 191, 194, 197–198, 201, 208, 215, 223, 231, 244, 258, 260, 263–7, 272–4, 299–321, 325–6, 347–8, 352, 354, 357, 366, 368, 396, 398, 408, 417, 424, 439–40, 442–5, 447, 480–1, 483, 499, 507–9, 512, 516. See also Austrian Social Democratic Party; political parties; Russian Social Democratic Labour Party; Social Democratic Party of Galicia and Silesia; Social Democratic Party of Germany; Social Democracy of the Kingdom of Poland and Lithuania
Congress of Vienna, 191. See also Congress Poland
Congress Poland, xix, 191, 231, 481, 499, 509
Constans, Jean Antoine Ernest, 297, 485
Constantinople, 401–3, 505
constitutions, xxxi, 13, 31, 35, 44, 78, 87, 96, 101, 131, 134, 150, 165, 176–7, 183, 185, 189, 312, 344, 349, 381, 384–5, 389–90, 393, 405, 433, 437, 463, 484–5, 499, 511
Constitutional Democratic Party (Russia), 151, 271, 310, 491, 514. See also Cadets
constitutional monarchy, xxxi, 13, 35, 37–8, 97, 147, 151, 300, 305, 377, 386–8, 391, 393, 492, 495, 501
consumer associations, 4–5
Copenhagen, 439–40
Corday, Charlotte, 414, 486
Cossacks, 17, 19, 21, 34, 76, 83, 85, 92, 94, 97, 142, 186, 205
Cotton, Robert, 53, 213, 290, 461, 486, 511
Council of Workers' Delegates, 17, 219, 376
counterrevolution, viii, xxi, xxix, 83, 94, 131, 136, 141–2, 144–5, 173, 222, 289, 297, 304–5, 377–9, 382–3, 385–6, 388, 391, 393, 395, 397, 399, 401–7, 409, 412–14, 427, 430, 432–3, 436, 438, 475
crime, 21, 46, 79–80, 122, 141, 163, 182, 184, 200, 230, 370–1, 389, 412–14, 434
Crimean War, 143–4, 505
crisis, xv–xvi, 13, 25–7, 85, 96–7, 149, 193,

204, 300, 305, 334, 371–2, 408, 412–13, 423–4, 429, 433, 436, 441–2
Croats, 400, 405, 433
Cromwell, Oliver, 449–54, 456–7, 459, 463, 466, 468, 470–1, 473–7, 485–6, 488–9, 493–5, 499, 501–4, 506, 509–10, 513, 516
culture, 34, 36–7, 369–70, 372–3, 396, 400, 404, 503
Cunow, Heinrich, 275, 486
Czech nationalists, 433–4
Czechs, 289, 405, 433–4
Czemierniki, 186
Czerwony Sztandar [Red Flag], xxiii, 17, 65, 69, 75, 83, 87, 91, 95, 99, 105, 115, 131, 151, 155,
169, 175, 179, 183, 189, 202, 500
Częstochowa, 23, 77–8, 127, 132, 222

Dąbrowa, 77–8, 89, 103, 117, 119, 121, 126–7, 132, 222
Danilevsky, Nikolai, 401, 486
Danton, Georges, 244, 487
Daszyński, Ignacy, 17, 98, 128, 487
David, Eduard, ix, 194, 242, 249, 264, 266, 304, 487, 493
Davidson, Georg, 275, 487
Delft, 3
democracy, vii–viii, xi–xii, xv–xix, xxii, xxiv, xxvii–xxxi, xxxv, 4–5, 15–17, 23, 26, 31, 34, 36–8, 40–1, 43–9, 51–3, 55–6, 58–63, 65–7, 72–3, 75–6, 78–80, 87–9, 91–3, 95–100, 103–5, 108, 110–13, 115–24, 127–9, 134–5, 137–8, 142, 144, 148–9, 152–4, 169, 171–3, 179, 183–7, 189–92, 194–6, 201, 205–6, 208–10, 217, 227–9, 232, 234, 237–42, 244–54, 256–61, 263, 265–6, 273–84, 289, 299–304, 306–8, 310, 312–16, 318–19, 326, 328, 330, 332, 338–9, 341, 344, 347, 351–4, 356–9, 364–5, 368, 376, 382, 384–7, 390, 394, 397, 399, 406–7, 414–17, 428–31, 436–40, 442–4, 446, 449, 451, 460, 486, 488, 490, 497, 499, 504, 508
civil rights, 37, 231, 462
democratic republic, xxv–xxvii, xxix–xxxii, 4, 31, 147–8, 150, 196, 276, 348, 387
equality/equal rights, 34, 36, 40, 44–5, 48–9, 62, 155, 248–9, 257–8, 266, 390, 392, 399, 480, 502, 511
political rights, 35, 37, 45, 49, 63, 100, 105, 133, 155–6, 195–7, 233, 245, 272–73, 276
universal suffrage, xxvi, 201, 227, 244, 264, 270, 276, 282, 294, 300, 302, 313, 510
demonstrators, 17, 125, 127, 276, 293, 304, 514
despotism, 32, 47, 75, 81, 109, 111, 134, 230, 246, 291, 308
Desrousseaux, Anexandre-Marie (Bracke), 297, 487
Devereux, Robert, Third Earl of Essex, 451–2, 487
dialectical thought, 308
Dickens, Charles, 198, 488
Die Einigkeit [Unity], 266
Die Gleichheit [Equality], 293
die Junge, 338, 511
Diefenbach, Hans, 449, 488
Digby, Georges, 459, 461, 488
disabled, xv, 43
discrimination, 43, 257, 293. *See also* racism
Dmowski, Roman, 72–3, 97, 184–6, 372, 397–8, 404, 406–8, 488
Dnipropetrovsk, 205. *See also* Jekaterinoslaw
domination, xxiii, xxxiii, 30–1, 269, 330, 400, 485, 518
Dorpat, 214, 502
Dresden, 76, 274, 276, 442, 491, 499, 503
Dreyfus, Alfred, xix, 316, 429, 488, 502, 516
Duma, vii–viii, xxviii–xxxi, 78–80, 83–5, 87, 89, 91–4, 96–7, 99, 103, 133–4, 144, 149, 151–3, 165–6, 172, 174–7, 190–2, 199, 216, 219, 221, 224, 270–1, 276, 305–6, 309–10, 312, 318, 344, 375, 377, 379–87, 389, 391–3, 396–9, 403, 427–8, 430–2, 434–8, 482–4, 491–2, 498, 505, 509
First, 152, 175, 190, 199, 270–1, 309, 375, 380–2, 385–6, 432, 434, 436–7
Second, 310, 375, 377, 381–6, 430, 432, 437, 482
Third, 375, 382–383, 385–7, 392–3, 396, 398, 403, 427–8, 430–2, 438, 492, 498, 505
Duncker, Franz Gustav, 252, 488, 494
Duokhobors, 32
Durnovo, Pyotr Nikolayevich, 94, 131, 145, 489
Dutch railroad workers, 226
Düwell, Wilhelm, 275, 489
Dzierżyński, Feliks, 171

Dzwon Polski [The Polish Bell], 153–4, 185. See also Praca Polska

East Elbian Junkers, 245
Eastern Marches Society, 185, 493, 497, 515
economic struggle, 37, 100–101, 120–2, 126, 204, 206–7, 209–12, 214, 218, 221, 223, 225–7, 230–5, 239, 248, 251, 254, 278, 289, 337, 382
  education, 29, 42, 44, 47, 51–3, 62, 77, 87–8, 145, 195, 224, 283, 307, 362, 467, 502
  eight-hour workday, xxx, 56–8, 75, 77–8, 88–9, 101, 120, 132–3, 148, 167, 186, 207, 209, 213, 215, 218, 235, 295, 298, 311, 424, 441, 500
Eisenachers, 480–1, 499, 502. See also Social Democratic Workers Party (SDAP)
Eisner, Kurt, 197, 274, 482, 489
Ekaterinhof Garden, 203
El Dorado, England, 232
elections, 32, 35, 37–41, 43–4, 46, 49, 79–80, 83, 85, 87, 91–4, 98–100, 105, 134, 144, 149, 152–3, 156, 201, 216, 219, 221, 223, 244–5, 251, 276, 294–5, 302, 306, 312, 344, 383, 389, 434, 437, 446, 462, 464, 471, 508, 515
  boycotts, 91, 93, 190, 385, 432. See also Duma
  laws, 37, 39, 100, 190, 375, 383, 385
  rights, 31, 38–41, 147
Eliot, John, 462, 489
Elm, Adolf von, 244, 266, 275, 489
employers' associations, 442
employment of children, 59. See also child labor
Engels, Friedrich, xix, 24–26, 165, 169, 173, 193–6, 248, 270–1, 284–5, 308, 329, 331, 333, 335, 337, 339, 401, 501–2, 506
England, 23–4, 31, 33, 35, 105, 144, 194, 232, 253, 308, 337, 361, 403, 412, 449, 451, 453–4, 459–60, 463, 469, 471–2, 475, 481–6, 489, 494, 499, 502–6, 509–11, 513, 515–16, 518
English Revolution, 450–1, 453, 457, 463, 479–80, 484–6, 489, 492–5, 502–5, 509, 512, 514, 516. See also Glorious Revolution
  Long Parliament, 453, 464–5, 468–9, 471, 493, 510
enlightenment, xxiv, xxxii, 510–11

entrepreneurs, 30, 58–61, 203, 216, 219, 226, 289, 291
Erfurt Program, xxiv, 313
estates, 29, 35, 44–5, 219, 412, 475
Europe, xi, xxvi, xxxii–xxxiii, 13–14, 16, 26–7, 30, 45, 76, 105, 108, 141, 164, 195, 200, 216, 233, 270, 278, 289, 292, 301, 304, 306, 314, 327, 329, 331, 333, 340, 343, 347, 356–7, 361–2, 388–9, 401–2, 405, 408, 412, 423, 486, 488, 490–1, 505–6, 513, 516
exploitation, 23–6, 29–30, 33, 36–7, 44, 46, 48, 52–3, 56, 58, 61–2, 77, 80, 84–5, 88–9, 102, 110, 116–21, 145, 156–7, 163–4, 167, 186, 214, 241–2, 246, 248, 252, 297, 326, 362, 370, 373, 425

factories, 4, 17, 23–6, 28, 44, 49, 55–60, 77, 88, 102–3, 114, 118, 163, 205–7, 209, 212–15, 219, 235, 242, 289–92, 326, 372, 511
Fairfax, Thomas, 451–9, 468, 470–1, 473–6, 489
faith, 27, 48, 71, 131, 257, 313, 335–6, 378, 402, 416, 440
Falcon, 88, 186. See also Sokół
Fallières, Armand, 403, 489
farms, 56, 59, 87, 110
fascism, xxxiii, 488
Faubourg Saint-Antoine, 158, 162
Favre, Jules Claude Gabriel, 389, 490
Feinstein, Władysław, 155, 500. See also Leder, Zdzisław
feudalism, xxvii, 13, 30, 144, 155, 302
Finland, xx, 175, 193, 218, 271, 496
Finns, xvi, 36
First International, xxxv, 68, 194, 293, 480, 499, 506. See also International Workingmen's Association
First Proletariat Party (Poland), 331. See also Second Proletariat Party; political parties
Fischer, Richard, 417–18, 490
Fourier, Charles, 24, 27, 490
Fourmies, 293
Fraktion Drehscheibe (National Liberals), 366
France, xix, 14–15, 23–4, 31, 33, 35, 44, 53, 105, 108, 116–17, 144, 147, 155, 159, 161, 163–4, 169–170, 239, 241, 264–5, 270, 293–4, 297, 302, 304, 308, 319, 337–8, 344, 353, 389–90, 412–13, 423–4, 429, 431, 441,

450, 453, 456, 459, 461, 463, 476, 479, 482, 484–5, 488, 492, 495, 498, 500, 502, 505–6, 509, 511–12, 514–16, 518. *See also* French Revolutions
Fredro, Aleksander, 331, 490
free trade, 72, 485
freedom, vii, xv, xxiii–xxiv, xxvi, xxix–xxx, 14–15, 32–8, 44–9, 51, 66, 68, 71–3, 75–80, 85, 87–8, 93–8, 102, 105–6, 109, 111–12, 116–17, 121, 131–7, 144–5, 151, 153, 155, 157–8, 164, 166–7, 177, 184, 186, 189, 205, 207, 209, 217, 220, 233, 241, 244, 270–1, 281, 299, 302, 309, 316, 329, 331, 334, 336–8, 340, 347, 351, 356, 359–60, 370–1, 376, 381–2, 392–3, 399, 406, 413, 427, 461, 471, 502, 515–16
  of critique, 68
  of conscience, xxiv, 41, 47–8, 85, 125, 159, 165, 408, 414, 471
  of assembly, xxiii–xxiv, 15, 35, 46–7, 66, 85, 93, 100, 105, 135, 205, 275, 302, 313, 381
  of speech, 35, 47, 94, 157, 205, 209, 281, 381–2
  of the press, xxiii–xxiv, xxvi, 15, 35, 46–47, 66, 79, 105, 134–135, 186, 209, 270, 381–382. *See also* censorship
  political freedom, xxx, 14, 32–3, 38, 44–5, 47, 49, 75–7, 87–8, 105–6, 109, 116, 121, 132–7, 144–5, 155, 164, 205, 217, 220, 241, 329, 331, 334, 337–8, 347, 351, 376, 381, 393
  republican freedoms, 37, 164
  right of association, 15, 201, 209, 224, 226, 233–5, 246, 257, 270
  right of coalition, 15
  voting rights, 32, 39, 41, 47
Freikorps, xii
French Revolutions, xix, xxvii, 7, 13–14, 16, 19, 27, 30, 32, 35, 69–70, 75, 105, 144, 147, 155–6, 163–6, 169, 191, 193, 198, 227, 243, 265, 270, 273, 293, 297, 310–11, 316, 321, 332, 338, 340, 353, 363, 371, 388–91, 394, 403, 412, 414, 423–4, 429, 431, 441, 450, 461, 463, 472, 479–80, 482, 484–90, 492, 495, 499, 502–3, 505–6, 510–11, 514–16
  Committee of Public Safety (French Revolution), 388, 487, 511
  February Revolution 1848, 13, 155–67, 332

  July Revolution 1830, 13, 156, 479, 484
  Paris Commune 1871, xxvi, 76, 147, 164, 310, 332, 337, 340, 389, 390, 481, 482, 485, 489, 490, 504, 515
Frohme, Karl Franz Egon, 244, 275, 490

Galicia, xxxv, 32, 85, 95, 128, 276, 348, 356, 396, 491, 517
gallows, 375, 382, 398–9, 403, 412–16
Gambetta, Léon, 390, 490
Gapon, Georgi Apollonovich, 209, 216, 490
Gazeta Polska [The Polish Gazette], 97
Gelfand, Israel Lazarevich, 174, 491, 507
General Commission of Trade Unions (Germany), 199, 259, 276–7, 500. *See also* political parties
General German Workers' Association (ADAV), 480, 502, 507. *See also* political parties
Gotha Unity Congress 1875, 480. *See also* Social Democratic Workers' Party
general strike, viii, xvii, 17, 77, 95–6, 115, 117, 119, 131, 134–9, 165, 193–5, 202–12, 214–16, 218–24, 226, 231, 263–4, 266, 273–7, 279, 293–4, 299–300, 365, 435, 440–2, 501. *See also* mass strike
gentry, 33, 71, 76, 83–4, 87, 89–90, 96–7, 106, 133, 140, 145, 155–6, 191, 212, 379, 383–5, 465, 482, 492
Georgia, 202, 205, 513
Georgiyevsky, Eulogius, 396, 491
German Peasants' War, 27, 319–20, 505
German Progressive Party (Deutsche Fortschrittspartei), 310. *See also* political parties
Germany, vii, xi–xiii, xv–xvii, xxiii, xxix, xxxv, 14–16, 23, 25, 27–8, 30–1, 33, 35, 41, 44, 47, 53, 73, 76, 99–103, 105, 108, 116–17, 164, 185, 195, 197–201, 215, 221, 223, 226–7, 230, 232–6, 239–41, 243–7, 249–50, 252–4, 256, 258–60, 263–7, 269–70, 272–80, 282–3, 285, 294–5, 297, 299–305, 307–8, 310, 313, 316, 318–20, 329, 337–8, 353–4, 356, 361, 381, 395, 404, 408, 413, 417–19, 423–4, 428, 432, 439–43, 445–6, 450–1, 480–2, 484, 486, 488–91, 494, 496–7, 499–500, 502–4, 507–10, 515
Hamburg mass strikes 1905–06, 76, 223, 227, 278, 281, 284, 300

labor unions, 215, 235, 236, 237, 243, 249, 250, 252, 253, 255, 257, 273
militarism, 353–4
parliament (Reichstag), 84, 201, 244–5, 252, 275, 283–4, 295, 301–2, 352, 361, 428, 446, 460, 480–1, 483, 487, 490, 493, 495, 498–501, 507, 513
   Social Democracy, xxiv, 72, 100, 103, 185, 195, 201, 242, 256, 273, 279, 299, 300, 306, 310, 313, 315, 316, 338, 352, 354, 365, 429, 440, 446, 486, 488, 497, 499. See also Social Democratic Party of Germany; Social Democracy
   working class in/proletariat, xxxv, 32, 102, 105, 230, 232–6, 239–40, 243–7, 254, 258, 260, 272–3, 276, 278–80, 283, 299–303, 305–6, 310, 338, 354, 418, 439–40, 480, 496, 499, 502
Geyer, 292
Girondins, 450
Glorious Revolution (England), 459–60, 484, 503
Goethe, Johann Wolfgang von, 312, 491
Gogol, Nikolai, 20, 431, 479, 491
Golovin, Fyodor, 310, 491
Goniec [The Herald], 153, 407
Górski, Ludwik, 406, 491
Graham, James, 457, 492
Graz, 276
Greece, 27
Groussier, Arthur, 297, 492
Gualbert, Giovanni, 336, 492
Guchkov, Alexander, 385, 492
guerrilla war, 235, 413
Guesde, Jules (Mathieu-Basile), xix, 316, 389–90, 441, 488, 492, 499
Guesdists, xix, 316, 344
guilds, 28
Guizot, François, 449–50, 453, 458–60, 492
Głos Warszawski, 397

Haase, Hugo, 450, 493
hakatyści, 185. *See also* Ostmarkenverein
Hamburg, 76, 193, 223, 227, 275–6, 278, 281, 284, 297, 300, 440
Hamburger Echo, 275, 281, 490
Hammond, Robert, 473, 493
Hampden, John, 452–3, 463, 465–6, 468, 493
Hansemann, Ferdinand, 185, 304, 493
Hapsburgs, 340, 401

Harington, James, 457, 470, 493
Harrison, Thomas, 473–4, 493
Haselrig, Arthur, 463, 494
health, 25, 28, 42, 56, 58–62, 118, 167, 269, 342
Heine, Wolfgang, 352
Heinzel, Juliusz, 290–1, 494
Helbertówna, Albertyna, 414, 494, 507
Hirsch, Max, 252, 297, 488, 494
historical dialectic, 196, 206, 319, 376
historical materialism, 198, 308, 328, 335
HKT-ists, 185. *See also* Ostmarkenverein
Holland, 239, 453, 463, 468. *See also* Netherlands
Holles, Denzil, 452, 462, 465–6, 472, 474, 493–4
homeless, 43
Hopton, Ralph, 453–5, 459, 494
Horwitz, Maksymilian, 330, 494, 516
hospitals, 37, 43
Hotham, 453–4, 495
human society, 14, 26–7, 44, 49, 63
humanity, 8, 26–8, 46, 76, 111, 118–19, 197, 350, 414
Hungary, 164, 227, 304, 356, 395, 414, 423, 434
   Hungarian Revolution, 164, 506
hunger, 24, 30, 53, 61, 79, 146, 156, 160–1, 164, 269, 413, 424
Hungertarif, 283
Hyde, Edward, First Earl of Clarendon, 465, 467, 495

Iglesias, Pablo, 297, 495
imperialism, xii, xxiii, xxxiii, 401–4, 449, 481, 507
Indigenous peoples, 51, 112
insurance, 59–61, 88, 119
intelligentsia, 4, 69, 79, 84, 110, 118, 122, 128, 131, 135, 140–1, 144, 151, 183, 191, 241, 325, 336–9, 341, 383–4, 386, 399, 406
International Conference of Trade Union Centers, 439. *See also* trade unions
international solidarity, 292, 297
International Workingmen's Association, xxxv, 117, 194, 293. *See also* First International
Alliance of Socialist Democracy, 194
Ireland, 362, 450, 457–8, 462–5, 467, 469, 471–3, 476, 479, 493, 495, 503, 517

INDEX 529

Ireton, Henry, 471, 473, 476, 495
Irish, 362, 454, 457, 459, 465, 472, 492, 495
Italy, 14, 31, 35, 164, 239, 264, 308, 336, 361, 400, 412, 423, 500, 503-4
Ivanovo, 214, 218
Izvolsky, Alexander, 395-6, 495

Jacobin, 13, 388, 392, 413, 480, 487, 503, 510-11
Jacobinism, 388-9
Jacoby, Johann, 428, 495
jacquerie, 319
Japan, xiii, 35, 51, 112, 143, 164, 204, 403, 408, 495
Japanese War, 34, 96, 204, 308, 353, 403
Jaurès, Jean, xix, 316, 488, 495
Jekaterinoslaw, 205, 207, 217. See also Dnipropetrovsk
Jelisawetgrad, 205. See also Kropyvnytskyi
Jena, 144, 201, 244, 263-4, 274-5, 281, 284, 299-300, 365
Jena Resolution, 201, 263-4, 275
Jews, 36, 47-8, 79, 141, 289, 325, 330, 358, 369, 414, 482, 488, 495, 498, 508-9. See also anti-Semitism; Bund; pogroms
Jogiches, Leo, xi, xviii, 17, 23, 117, 128, 155, 171, 325-6, 496, 500, 503, 514
judiciary, 29, 177, 361, 380
July Revolution (1830), 13
June Days uprising (1848), vii, 15, 147, 155, 157, 159, 161, 163-7, 303, 311, 337, 398, 424, 479, 482, 484, 518

Kamenev, Lev, 193, 496
Kant, Immanuel, 8, 342, 481, 496
Karpiński, Franciszek, 339, 496
Kasprzak, Marcin, 78, 222, 496
Katkov, Mikhail Nikoforovich, 402, 497
Kaunas, 214. See also Kowno
Kautsky, Karl, xxiii, 3-5, 7-9, 265-6, 274-5, 278, 330, 339, 362, 449-50, 460, 482, 497
Kaznakov, Nikolai Nikolaevich, 371-2, 412, 497
Kelles-Krauz, Kazimierz, 357, 497, 503. See also Luśnia-Krauz, Michał
Kempner, Stanisław Aleksander, 69, 336, 372, 497
Kennemann, Herman, 185, 497
Kharkiv, 214, 218
Khmelnytskyi, 217

Khomiakov, Nikolai, 396, 497
Kiev, 78-9, 132, 140, 205, 207, 213, 217-18, 273, 280, 479, 513
Kirovo, 205
Kirovograd, 205
Kishinev, 214
knout, 343, 398, 400-403, 407
Kokovtsov, Vladimir, 385, 498
Komissarovsky school, 18
Königsberg trial, 245
Kościuszko, Tadeusz, 342, 498
Koszutska, Maria, 325, 498
Kowieński, M, 327, 329-31, 340, 347, 351, 353, 481, 498. See also Bielecki, Marian
Kowno, 214. See also Kaunas
Krahelska-Filipowicz, Wanda, 414, 498
Kramář, Karel, 395-8, 498
Kremlin, 19
Kropyvnytskyi, 205-6, 218. See also Jelisawetgrad
Kunert, Fritz, 275, 498
Kunitzer, Juliusz Karol, 291, 481, 498
Kuokkala, 193
Kur'yer [Courier], 307. See also Pis'mo pyatoe
Kurier Warszawski [The Warsaw Courier], 69, 169, 399
Kurjer Polski [The Polish Courier], 399, 408

L'Humanité [Humanity], 403, 487, 495
labor protection legislation, 424
Lafargue, 70-1, 441, 499
Lambert, John, 473, 475, 499
Lamoricière, Christophe Léon Louis Juchault de, 160, 499
Land and Liberty Party, 170, 191, 519. See also Zemlya i Volya
Lassalle, Ferdinand, 25, 101, 150, 176, 301, 310, 385, 480-1, 488, 499
Laud, William, 462-3, 465, 470, 499, 518
law, xi, xvii, xxiv, xxvi-xxvii, xxxiii, 4, 9, 28-9, 34-41, 43-6, 48-9, 52, 56, 58-9, 61-2, 79, 83-5, 88, 92-4, 96, 100-103, 127, 131, 139, 142, 146-7, 176-7, 190, 198, 210, 215, 219, 222, 227, 230, 237, 270, 275-6, 278-9, 281, 283-4, 294, 310, 313, 325, 338, 355, 359, 375, 383, 385, 398, 401, 403, 412, 432, 434, 462, 465-7, 481-2, 485, 490, 495, 497, 499, 508-10
Le Rappel [The Recall], 390

Le Socialisme [Socialism], 423
leadership, xi–xii, xviii, xxvi, xxix, 195, 199, 202–3, 209, 223, 227–31, 238, 240–1, 254, 257–60, 265, 276–7, 282, 318–19, 348, 357, 382, 389, 424, 455, 482, 513, 517, 519
League of Struggle for the Emancipation of the Working Class, 203, 231, 508
Ledebour, Georg, 450, 460, 499
Leder, Jan, 117, 500
Leder, Zdzisław, 155, 500. *See also* Feinstein, Władysław
Legal Marxists, 208, 514
Legien, Karl, 263–4, 500
legislature, 29, 37, 85, 381–2
Leimpeter, Johann, 280, 501
Leipzig, 8, 76, 276, 439–40, 442–3, 447, 449, 451
Leipziger Volkszeitung [Leipzig Peoples' Newspaper], 3, 7, 263, 269, 281, 439, 491, 501, 503–4
Lenin, Vladimir Ilyich, xx–xxi, xxiv, xxvi–xxviii, xxxi–xxxii, 170, 172–3, 193, 206, 307, 310, 315, 317, 357, 427, 483, 490–1, 496, 501, 503, 517
Lensch, Paul Albert, 451, 501
Lenthall, William, 474, 501
Lesche, Friedrich, 275, 501
Lessner, Frederick, 70, 501
liberalism, xxvi–xxvii, 72, 171, 177, 179, 208, 212, 221, 246, 270–1, 301–2, 308–12, 313, 315, 318–19, 320, 352, 366, 377–8, 380–5, 387, 390–2, 402, 403, 428, 434, 437, 446, 484, 507, 514
Liebknecht, Karl, xii, 245, 357, 500–501
Liebknecht, Wilhelm, 274, 359, 501
Liepāja, 219
Lilburne, John, 463, 465, 474, 502
liquidationists, 430
Lithuania, vii, xi, xviii, xxx, xxxv, 17, 23, 32, 34, 36–7, 77, 89, 133, 171, 190–1, 209, 217, 289, 330, 342, 356, 391, 397–8, 479, 496, 504
Lithuanians, 36, 356, 358
Lityński, Alfred, 329, 502, 518. *See also* Zaorski, F.
Livonia, 77, 79, 89, 95, 132–3, 137, 212, 220, 222
local economy, 28, 37, 42
lockout, viii, 215, 217, 219, 229, 245, 289–92, 294, 297, 370, 372, 375, 442

Łódź, viii, 23, 77–8, 117, 122, 127, 132, 213–14, 217–18, 222, 228, 231, 289–93, 369–73, 376, 414, 416, 481, 494, 498, 500, 509, 511
Loubet, Emile, 316, 502
Louis XVI, 155, 502, 511
Louis Philippe I, 166, 502
Ludlow, Edmund, 471, 473–5, 502
Lunacharsky, Anatoly Vasilievich, 427, 503
Luśnia-Krauz, Michał, 329, 357, 497, 503. *See also* Kelles-Krauz, Kazimierz
Lviv, 128, 399
Lyon, 24, 164, 424

Mainz, 249, 264
Malakhov, Nikolai Nikolayevich, 19, 503
Manchester liberalism, 72
Manchuria, 112, 140
Mandatory leave, 58. *See also* confinement; pregnancy
Marat, Jean-Paul, 414, 486, 503
Marchlewski, Julian, xxix, 23, 117, 155, 325, 491, 500, 503–4
markets, 9, 50, 113, 406
Martial law, 79, 83, 85, 92, 94, 96, 131, 398, 403, 434, 462
Martov, Julius, 317, 430, 485, 503, 508
Marx, Karl, xix, xxv–xxvi, xxix–xxxii, 7, 24–6, 65, 68, 70–1, 139, 150, 165, 169, 193–8, 237, 248, 256, 270–1, 301–5, 307–10, 315, 320, 331, 333, 335, 338, 340, 350, 357, 360, 400–402, 405, 432–3, 449, 479–81, 487–8, 490, 493, 499, 501–2, 505–6, 517–18
  Communist Manifesto, 25–6, 97, 129, 165, 248, 303, 307–9, 333–4, 344
  Capital, 7, 256, 331, 487, 490, 505
  Eighteenth Brumaire of Louis Bonaparte, 65, 139
  Grundrisse, 490
Marxism, xvi, xxvii, 195–7, 208, 255, 277, 308, 312, 314–16, 321, 358, 377–8, 390, 481, 483, 487, 499, 518
mass strike, xvii, 149, 175, 196, 202–3, 209, 219–35, 237–40, 242, 244–5, 247, 259, 271, 276, 278, 282, 300, 391, 484
  anarchist theory of, 194, 197–8, 211, 273, 299
  demonstration strikes, 221–4
  economic strikes, xvii, 115–21, 126, 129, 166, 209, 211, 221, 225

general strike, St. Petersburg, 203
Mass Strike, Political Party, and the Trade Unions, xi, xii, xvii, xx, xxii, 193–261
practice of, vii–viii, xi–xii, xvii–xviii, xx–xxiii, xxv, 16, 76–79, 110, 113, 126, 128, 131–4, 193–205, 207–9, 211, 213, 215, 217–31, 233–7, 239–45, 247, 249, 251, 253, 255, 257, 259, 261, 263–5, 271–9, 281–3, 285, 299–300, 341, 380, 435, 489–90, 500–501
Austria, 227
Germany, 198, 201, 221, 223, 234, 239–40, 244, 274–5, 277–8, 282
Hamburg, 227
Russia, xvii, 77, 79, 110, 132–4, 149, 193, 196–7, 199, 202–3, 208–9, 219–22, 224–6, 228–32, 235, 241–2, 244, 247, 272, 274–5, 283, 341, 380, 484
Sweden, 227
militant strikes, xvii, 221, 223
partial strikes, xvii, 113, 207, 221, 231
rail workers' strike, 79
practice of, vii–viii, xi–xii, xvii–xviii, xx–xxiii, xxv, 16–17, 31, 47, 62, 76–9, 88, 95–6, 103–4, 110, 113, 115–22, 124, 126, 128–9, 131–41, 143–5, 149, 165–7, 172, 175, 186, 192–245, 247, 249, 251–3, 255, 257, 259, 261, 263–6, 271–9, 281–3, 285, 289, 291, 293–4, 297, 299–300, 302, 304, 308–9, 311, 313, 341, 365, 370–1, 380, 382, 391, 424, 435, 440–2, 445, 483–4, 488–90, 493, 499–502, 509, 513, 519
masses, xvi–xvii, xxii–xxiv, xxvii, xxxii, 26, 31, 44, 67–8, 106–8, 110, 113–14, 121–7, 137–8, 150–2, 164, 169–72, 182, 195, 198, 200, 207, 209–10, 218, 224, 228–31, 248, 251, 253, 256–7, 260, 265, 272, 278, 294–5, 307, 315, 337, 375–6, 378, 380, 393, 418, 434, 443, 446, 506
Massey, Edward, 472–4, 504
material conditions, xxvi, xxx–xxxi, 198, 350
materialism, 32, 143, 198, 308, 328, 335, 378, 388, 483, 492, 508
Maurice, Prince of the Palatinate, 455, 504
May Day, viii, xvii, 122, 128, 197, 218, 222–223, 229, 280, 293–5, 297–8, 328, 336–9, 356, 417–19, 423–5, 439–47, 483, 500
Mazzini, Giuseppe, 340, 504
Mehring, Franz, xii, 460, 503–4

Mensheviks, xx, xxvi–xxvii, xxix, 79, 99, 152, 170, 172, 174, 190, 275, 307, 310, 312, 315, 320, 347, 375, 377–9, 385–6, 390, 430, 480, 485–6, 503–4, 508, 515. *See also* Russian Social Democratic Labor Party
Menshinstvo, 275
Merchants, 30, 71, 89, 362
Mickiewicz, Adam, 341, 395, 399, 504
Middle Ages, 28, 30, 44
Mikhailovsky, Nikolai, 411, 505
militarism, xii, xv, 26, 50, 88, 142, 198, 245, 308, 353–4, 501
military court, 45, 411–14, 496
Millerand, Alexandre, 429, 505
Milyukov, Pavel, 384–5, 505
Molva, 20
monarchy, xxxi, 13, 21, 31, 35, 37–8, 87, 97, 147, 150–1, 155, 163, 193, 243, 300, 304–5, 325, 353, 377, 386–8, 391, 393, 452, 456, 475, 477, 479, 484, 487, 492–5, 501–502, 516–17
Montagnards, 13
Moravia, 276
More, Thomas, 27, 505
Morgan, Thomas, 451, 505
Morozov, 213
Moscow, vii, 16–17, 19–21, 79, 89, 95, 99, 132, 135, 137–8, 140–4, 149, 153, 196, 212–13, 217–18, 220, 226, 232, 299–300, 308, 329, 332, 340, 375–8, 380–1, 396, 425, 427, 431, 435–6, 484, 497, 500, 503, 514, 517, 519
Mozart, Wolfgang Amadeus, 351, 505
Municipal, 4, 41–3, 213–14, 252, 472
Müntzer, Thomas, 27, 319, 505
Muscovites, 89
Myddelton, Thomas, 456, 506
Mykolaiv, 205. *See also* Nikolaev
Myśl Socjalistyczna [Socialist Thought], 327, 329, 342, 347–9, 353–4, 356, 360, 362, 365, 367

Nacha Zariia [Our Charge], 430
Nakhichevan, 36
Nansen, Fridtjof, 336, 506
Napoleon I (France), 77, 108, 144, 155, 191, 332, 340, 353, 388, 450, 479, 484, 490, 499, 506, 514–15
Napoleon III (France), 353, 479, 490, 499, 506, 514

Napoleonic Wars, 13, 506, 518
Naprzód, 128
Narodniks, 196, 328, 378, 519
Narodowcy, 183, 328
National Democracy (Poland), 70, 73, 83–5, 87–9, 92–3, 95–8, 103, 117, 119, 124, 131, 153–4, 183–7, 189–90, 192, 328, 332, 344, 354, 397–9, 406–8, 488. *See also* political parties
National Workers' Committee, 117
nationalism, vii, xii, xix, xxii, 72–3, 87–8, 95–6, 98, 121, 123, 128, 152–4, 183, 185–7, 191–2, 325–8, 330–1, 339–44, 349, 352–3, 357–8, 360, 362, 366–8, 376, 395–6, 398, 404, 407–9, 415–16, 433–4, 482, 486, 493, 497–8, 504, 506, 508–9
  autonomy, 23, 36–7, 70, 83–5, 87, 96, 101, 132, 152–4, 170, 172, 189, 192, 354, 356, 367, 380, 398–9, 406, 424, 498, 512, 517
  independence, xix, 33–4, 39, 71, 106, 132, 183, 189, 192, 251, 257–8, 304, 316, 325–8, 330–1, 340, 342–3, 347, 349, 351–2, 354–5, 357–8, 360–3, 365, 367, 371, 397, 401, 406, 433, 483, 498, 504, 506, 512, 518
  self-determination, xvi, xix–xx, xxiii, 23, 73, 327, 357, 491, 497
  solidarity, 83–4, 87, 348
  struggles, 333, 359, 362
national question, xii, xvi, 332, 359, 363–4, 405
nationalization, 4
nations, 14, 23, 27, 34, 36, 62, 270, 357, 360–2, 400, 403, 425, 506, 515
navy, 78–9, 140, 380, 461, 509, 516
Nechayev, Sergei, 399, 506, 512
Neglinka, 18
Netherlands, 35, 164, 362, 412, 483, 504, 509, 517–18. *See also* Holland
Neue Rheinische Zeitung [New Rhenish Newspaper], 303–5, 309, 400, 432–3
Nicholas I (Russia), 402, 506
Nicholas II (Russia), 134, 203, 300, 342, 375, 489, 506, 508, 519
Nikolaev, 205, 207, 214, 217–19. *See also* Mykolaiv
Ninth General Assembly of the German Metalworkers' Union, 440
Nizhny Novgorod, 204, 217–18

nobility, xxi, 30, 32–5, 37, 40, 43–5, 47, 50, 155, 164, 348, 358, 389, 405–6, 479, 482, 490, 506
North America, 26
November Uprising (1831), 97, 106, 341, 504, 512
Novoye Vremya [The New Times], 190, 398
Nowa Gazeta [The New Gazette], 69, 497
Nowiny [The News], 70
Nyi Soyuz [The Labor Union], 217

obshchina, 402
October Days (1905), 216, 276, 300, 435
October Manifesto (1905), 212, 300, 377
Octobrists, 97, 377, 383–7, 391, 492, 498
Odessa, 78–9, 132, 138, 140, 205–7, 214, 217–19, 224, 226, 232, 479, 519
Okhrana, 206, 519
Old Triumph Square, 18
Olizar, Count, 397–8
Omladina trial, 434
oppression, xxvi, 27, 29–32, 34, 36, 44, 47–8, 51, 62, 77, 80–1, 103, 110, 186, 245, 308, 362, 372, 375, 464, 466
Orel, 213
organize, 4, 31, 35, 46–7, 57, 88, 91–2, 102, 112–14, 124, 135, 143, 164, 275, 314, 371–2, 424, 442, 456. *See also* agitate
Oriental despotism, 230, 246
orthodoxy, 47, 401–2
Ostmarkenverein, 185. *See also* hakatyści; HKT-ists
Osvobozhdenie [Liberation], 208
Ottensen, 193
Owczarkówna, Zofia, 414, 494, 498, 507
Owen, Robert, 24, 27, 507

Palace of the Tsars, 209
Palacký, František, 400, 507
Paris, xxvi, 13, 15–16, 23, 76, 107, 126, 147, 155–6, 158, 161, 164–6, 169, 183, 244, 297, 310–11, 331–2, 337, 340–2, 356, 389–90, 403, 409, 413, 423–4, 439, 481–2, 484–5, 489–90, 495, 497, 500, 503–4, 515
Paris battle (1848), 15
Paris Commune (1871), xi, xxvi, 76, 147, 164, 310, 332, 337, 340, 353, 361, 389–90, 413, 424, 459, 481–2, 485–6, 489–90, 492, 501, 504, 515, 518–19. *See also* French Revolutions

parliamentarianism, 196, 201, 215, 232, 239, 303, 312–15, 354, 366
parliamentary period, 15, 195, 237, 248
parliamentary rule, 16, 279
Parnowski regiment, 19
Party for Realpolitik, 399, 406–8, 513. *See also* political parties
Party of October 30, 97
Parvus, Alexander, xxviii, 174, 491, 503, 507
passive resistance, 91, 271, 309, 432–4, 437
peaceful demonstrations, 124–5
Peaceful Regeneration group (1905), 391
peasantry/peasants, xxi, xxv, xxviii–xxix, xxxi–xxxii, 9, 20, 25, 27, 30, 32, 40, 45–6, 51, 75–6, 79, 84–5, 87–9, 96–7, 111, 153, 173, 190–1, 196, 317–20, 330, 338–9, 342, 361, 371, 378–80, 383, 393–4, 396, 453, 467, 470, 498, 505, 519
    peasant movements, xxviii, 181, 319–20, 394
pensions, 61, 220, 224, 473
People's Will (Narodnaya Volya) Party, xxvii, 75, 170, 173, 328, 331, 479, 483. *See also* political parties
permanent revolution, xxi, xxviii, 174, 491
Persia, 403
Petersburg (St./Saint), xxi, xxviii, 16, 20–1, 75, 77, 79, 81, 83–4, 89, 110, 115, 120, 132–5, 138, 142, 176, 190, 202–4, 206, 208–10, 213–14, 216–19, 222–4, 226, 228–9, 231–2, 276, 289, 299–300, 307, 309, 335, 341, 376, 380, 395–7, 399, 404, 425, 427, 431, 435, 479, 482, 491, 503, 508, 512–13, 515–16, 518
Petersburg massacre (1905), xxi, 77, 133–4, 202
Petersburg Soviet, xxviii, 300, 515
petty bourgeois/bourgeoisie, xxv, xxxi, 9, 13–15, 33–4, 40–1, 44, 83–4, 92, 96–7, 105, 119, 123, 135, 146–7, 171, 173, 180, 183, 191, 211, 241, 301, 311, 317–18, 330–1, 334, 338–9, 342, 358, 384, 386, 388, 391, 393–4, 406, 412, 490
Pfannkuch, Wilhelm, 307, 507
Pfuel, Ernst Heinrich Adof von, 432, 483, 507
Pí y Margall, Francisco, 193
Pis'mo pyatoe, 307. *See also Kur'yer* [Courier]
Piłsudski, Józef, xix, 73, 106, 128, 325–7, 348, 482, 487–8, 507, 512

Plekhanov, Georgi, xx, xxvii, 169–70, 172–4, 307–8, 310, 314, 316, 318, 321, 430, 480, 490, 508, 518
Pobedonostsev, Konstantin, 402, 508
Pogodin, Mikhail, 401–2, 506, 508
pogroms, 79, 141, 381, 396, 404, 507. *See also* Black Hundreds; Jews
Poland, vii, xi, xiii, xviii–xix, xxii, xxx, xxxv, 17, 23, 31–4, 36–7, 51–2, 62, 66–7, 69–73, 76–7, 79, 81, 83–4, 87, 95, 97–9, 101–2, 106, 109–12, 116–17, 122, 126, 128, 131–3, 138, 140–1, 144, 148, 151–4, 164, 171, 183–6, 189–92, 209, 217, 220, 222, 231, 281, 289–90, 293, 304, 314, 325–31, 333, 336–44, 347–50, 352, 354–60, 362–4, 367, 369, 376–7, 391, 393–4, 397–400, 404–8, 411–12, 414–15, 418, 441, 479, 481, 488, 494, 496–500, 502, 504, 507–13, 516–17
    autonomy for, 83–4, 153, 399
    Circle, 83–4, 152–4, 190–1
    culture in, 369–70
    Duma Group, 397
    Kingdom of, vii, xi, xviii, xxx, xxxv, 17, 23, 32–4, 37, 70, 73, 117, 128, 171, 189, 191, 217, 231, 289, 348, 399, 479, 496, 500, 504, 507, 516–17
    nobility in, 32, 34, 358, 490
    national question in, 96, 352, 354–5, 358–60, 365, 367, 398, 404, 408
    Poles, xvi, 18, 32, 34, 36, 47, 65, 73, 185, 289, 369, 396–400, 405–6, 408, 481, 488, 493, 497, 515
    Sejm, 38, 85, 191–2, 357, 365, 433–4, 510, 517
    working class in/proletariat, xxx, xxxv, 32–4, 37, 63, 78, 83–5, 111, 117, 119, 129, 185–6, 189, 293, 314, 326–7, 331, 333–4, 339–42, 344, 347, 349–51, 353, 355, 358, 364, 393, 406, 482, 500, 502–3
police, xv, 18, 23, 28–9, 36, 45–7, 60, 62, 92, 94, 97, 99, 102, 113, 122, 151, 171, 176–7, 198–9, 206, 208–10, 216–17, 226, 231, 257, 276, 278–9, 293, 297, 370, 372, 405, 423, 434, 489, 491, 500, 519
Polish Social Democratic Party of Galicia and Silesia (PPSD), 128, 487
Polish Socialist Party (PPS), xviii–xix, xxxv, 23, 33, 66–8, 98, 106, 111, 115, 121–3, 127–8, 179, 183, 189–91, 325–32, 334–45, 347–60, 362, 365–8, 411,

Polish Socialist Party (PPS) (*continued*)
  414–16, 481–2, 487, 494, 496–9, 502,
  507–8, 511–12, 517
  PPS Combat Organization, 326, 414, 494,
    498, 507. *See also* PPS-Revolutionary
    Faction (FR)
  PPS-Left, 325–7, 329–30, 347, 350, 416,
    481–2, 494, 502, 517
  PPS-Revolutionary Faction (FR), 326. *See
    also* PPS Combat Organization
  Seventh Congress, 512
  Tenth Congress (Cieszyn) 1908, 347–8,
    354, 366, 368
Polish Sport Association, 399. *See also* Sokół
political liquidation, 325
political parties, vii, xi–xii, xvii–xviii, xxii–
  xxiii, xxv, xxxii, 31, 92–3, 97, 179, 193,
  195, 197, 199, 201, 203, 205, 207, 209, 211,
  213, 215, 217, 219, 221, 223, 225, 227, 229,
  231, 233, 235, 237, 239, 241, 243, 245, 247,
  249, 251, 253, 255, 257, 259, 261, 308,
  310, 319, 332, 363–4, 441. *See also* Social
  Democracy
political power, xxx, 4–5, 7, 9, 30–1, 34,
  63, 99–100, 106, 121, 249, 314, 365, 378,
  380–1, 386, 392, 435–6
political revolution, xxviii, 105, 111, 119–20,
  123, 177, 230, 377, 394
political struggle, 30–2, 35, 57, 94, 106, 109,
  111, 120, 122, 126, 129, 149, 181, 194–7,
  201, 206, 215, 225–7, 229, 231–2, 235, 237,
  241, 246–9, 256, 289, 294, 299, 313, 330,
  343, 428, 433
Polska Praca [Polish Labor], 97
Poltava, 214, 217
populist, 170, 196, 328, 331, 505, 508, 519
Potemkin/Potemkim rebellion, 78–9, 149,
  219
Potretsov, Alexander, 430, 508
poverty, 13, 25–6, 29, 35, 39, 52; 61, 96–7,
  160, 163, 233, 292, 375, 412, 479–80, 482
Poyntz, Sydnam, 458–9, 473, 509
Poznański Corporate Groups, 292
Poznański, Izrael, 290–2, 509
Praca Polska, 153. *See also Dzwon Polski*
  [The Polish Bell]
Prague, 76, 276, 395–6, 398, 400, 402, 434,
  507
Pravitel'stvennyi Vestnik, 396
Prawda, 70

praxis, 195, 197, 249–50, 256, 333
pregnant, 58. *See also* confinement;
  mandatory leave
press, iv, xxii–xxiv, xxvi, 5, 15, 35, 46–7,
  65–6, 79, 96–7, 100, 105, 118, 128, 131,
  134–5, 151, 184–6, 196, 209, 217, 220, 227,
  251, 257–8, 270, 275, 283–4, 289, 310, 320,
  358, 381–2, 397, 399, 403–4, 407, 429–30,
  471, 496
  bourgeois/capitalist, 118, 128, 184
  freedom of, xxiii–xxiv, xxvi, 15, 35, 46–7,
    66, 79, 105, 134–5, 186, 209, 270, 381–2.
    See also censorship
  liberal, 151
  reactionary, 5, 131, 184, 186
  socialist, xxii, 5
prison, 28–9, 45, 47, 70–1, 75, 105, 131,
  151–2, 163, 176, 193, 199, 217, 226, 269,
  281, 283, 285, 375, 413, 463, 484–5, 496,
  498, 500, 506, 518
  Berlin Women's, 281
  Draft Bill on Forced Labor in, 283
private entrepreneurship, 9
private property, xxvi, xxx, 24, 26, 29, 44, 49,
  110, 164, 319, 412–13
Progressive Democracy/Progressive
  Democratic Party (Poland), 69–70, 73,
  91, 153, 171, 184, 190, 344, 377. *See also*
  political parties
Progressive Union (Poland), 70. *See also*
  political parties
proletarian consciousness, xxiii, 66–7
proletariat, xi, xvii, xxii–xxxii, 3–5, 8–9,
  13, 15–16, 26–7, 30–5, 37, 47, 52, 56–9,
  63, 65–7, 70, 76–81, 83–5, 91–4, 99–107,
  110–2, 114–23, 126–9, 131–50, 156, 159,
  161, 163–7, 169–73, 175, 179–81, 183,
  186, 189, 191–2, 194–8, 200–203, 205–6,
  208–12, 215, 218–21, 224–8, 230–44,
  246–8, 260, 264–5, 270–4, 276, 278–80,
  283, 293–5, 297–321, 326–8, 330–44,
  347–55, 358, 360, 363–4, 366–8, 370–3,
  375–80, 383–94, 403, 406–7, 409, 412–13,
  415–16, 424–5, 427–33, 435–9, 441–2,
  445, 482. *See also* working class
  conquest of political power by, xxviii,
    xxxii, 4, 9, 15, 30, 304, 317, 388–90
  dictatorship of, xxvii–xxix, xxxi–xxxii, 16,
    31, 63, 99, 103, 147, 173, 246, 304, 317,
    377, 387, 393, 482

INDEX 535

English, 194
European, xxviii, 279
French, 265, 310, 316, 321, 332, 389, 431
German, xxxv, 32, 102, 105, 230, 232–6, 239–40, 243–7, 254, 258, 260, 272–3, 276, 278–80, 283, 299–303, 305–6, 310, 338, 354, 418, 439–40, 480, 496, 499, 502
international, xxxi, 15, 120, 273, 298, 306, 393, 439, 445
lumpenproletariat, 73, 148, 196, 208, 210, 412–16
modern, 13, 16, 210, 241, 425
Polish, xxx, xxxv, 32–4, 37, 63, 78, 83–5, 111, 117, 119, 129, 185–6, 189, 293, 314, 326–7, 331, 333–4, 339–42, 344, 347, 349–51, 353, 355, 358, 364, 393, 406, 482, 500, 502–3
revolutionary, xxx, 80, 91–2, 96–7, 100, 127, 136, 141–3, 165, 180, 182–3, 186, 199, 207–8, 212, 271, 301, 329, 370, 386–7, 391–2, 403, 413, 415–16, 435
Russian, xvii, xxx, 15, 32, 34, 37, 51, 89, 101–2, 111, 165, 224, 227, 230, 232, 239, 274, 298, 305, 321, 328, 376, 378, 392, 482
Swedish, 442
Proskurov, 217
prostitution, 26, 413
Prussia/Prussian, xxxv, 33, 40, 47, 144, 147, 185, 191, 198, 245, 257, 265, 275–6, 278, 300, 305, 329, 337, 347, 352–3, 361, 365, 384, 386, 389, 404, 432, 480–4, 488, 493, 495, 497, 504, 506–7, 510, 513, 515, 517–18
Przedświt [Proletariat], 326, 352, 356–8
Przegląd Robotniczy [Workers' Review], 155, 165
Przegląd Socjaldemokratyczny [Social Democratic Review], 325, 347, 369, 375, 395, 411, 427
Przegląd Tygodniowy [The Weekly Review], 70
Purishkevich, Vladimir, 372, 428, 509
Putilov, 208–9, 224
Puttkamer, Robert von, 198, 509
Pym, John, 462–3, 465–6, 493–4, 509

racism, xv. *See also* discrimination; slavery
Rainesborough, Thomas, 509

rebellion, 33, 73, 76, 78, 113, 140–1, 155, 163, 175, 293, 314, 330, 348, 352, 360–2, 376, 412, 464–5, 471, 473, 495
reformism, xi, xviii, 497
reformist, xvi, 249, 265, 280, 327, 446, 480–2, 487, 489–90, 492, 500–501, 508, 510, 513
social reform, vii, xxi, 3–5, 24, 70, 170, 245, 352, 490, 502
Rejtan, Tadeusz, 357, 408, 510
religion, 27, 38, 43, 47–9, 516
religious persecution, 48, 461
republic, xxv–xxvii, xxix–xxxii, 4, 13, 15, 31, 34–8, 87, 101, 106, 115–16, 141, 147–8, 150–1, 155–6, 158, 162–4, 166, 196, 207, 270, 276, 293, 311, 313, 327, 330, 340, 347–9, 356, 360, 376, 382, 387–90, 392–3, 400, 424, 429, 449–50, 459, 489, 495, 504, 508, 512
Reval, 214, 223. *See also* Tallinn
Revolution (1917), xxxi, 485, 509, 513, 515
Revolutionary Tribunal, 388
revolutionism, 179, 432
revolutions, xii, xvi, xxvi, xxviii–xxix, xxxii–xxxiii, 14–16, 30, 45, 65, 77, 85, 108, 114, 139, 144, 146–7, 156, 158, 227–8, 232, 241–3, 271, 282, 304, 306, 312, 329, 388–9, 391–3, 480, 484, 495, 505, 507, 518
bourgeois, xxiv, xxvi–xxxi, 4, 7–8, 13–16, 24, 30–1, 33, 36, 41–5, 55, 58, 65, 69–73, 83, 85, 91–7, 99–103, 108, 110, 116–20, 122–3, 128–9, 131, 137, 139–40, 142–51, 156–7, 159–61, 163, 166, 169, 171, 175–7, 179–80, 183–4, 186, 190–1, 196, 208–9, 211–12, 231–2, 236–7, 239–43, 246, 248–50, 252–3, 255–6, 269–70, 279–80, 283–4, 294–5, 297, 300–308, 311–12, 314–21, 329, 332, 336–7, 342, 344, 349, 351–2, 354, 357, 361, 363–4, 366, 369, 373, 376–81, 384, 386–93, 405–8, 412, 415–16, 423–4, 427–9, 438, 446, 489–90, 493, 505
European, xxviii–xxix, xxxii, 28, 69–70, 113–14, 214, 230, 232, 239, 241, 279, 289, 315, 336–7, 347, 353, 357, 360, 362, 392, 402–3, 405, 408, 446, 496, 506
modern, xii, xxiv, xxxv, 3–4, 8, 13–16, 28, 33, 76, 105, 108, 145–6, 194, 196, 199, 209–11, 214, 231–2, 240–1, 246, 252, 265, 299, 301, 310, 352, 355–6, 358–64,

536 INDEX

revolutions (*continued*)
  modern (*continued*), 376, 387, 389, 392, 400, 403, 423, 425, 506, 511–12, 516
  people's, xxvii, 13, 20, 28, 44, 46, 49, 51–3, 62, 75, 80, 106, 108, 124, 126, 142, 147, 157, 165–6, 170, 173, 175, 177, 257, 269, 278, 283, 328, 331, 376, 408, 446, 460, 466, 479, 483, 493, 501, 515
  proletarian, xxii–xxiii, xxv–xxxii, 4, 7, 9, 15–16, 25–6, 28, 30, 34, 39–42, 51, 56–61, 65–7, 71, 75–6, 80–1, 85, 92, 94, 99–102, 104, 107, 109, 111, 117–18, 123, 125–7, 129, 131, 137–9, 145–6, 149, 156, 162, 164–5, 175, 177, 189, 192, 197, 200–201, 204, 206, 209–11, 221–5, 228–9, 231, 237–8, 240–3, 247–9, 252–5, 258–61, 264–5, 269, 277–80, 289, 293–5, 297, 299–300, 302–3, 305–8, 310–11, 313, 317, 319–20, 333–4, 336, 338, 340–1, 344, 347, 351–2, 360, 364, 367, 370–2, 381, 387, 389–93, 412, 415, 423, 427–30, 432–8, 440–1, 483, 503
  social revolution, vii, 3–5, 7–9, 16, 164, 193–4, 196–7, 327, 379, 482
  socialist, xi, xv–xix, xxii, xxiv–xxvi, xxviii, xxx–xxxi, xxxiii, xxxv, 3–5, 7–8, 15–17, 23–31, 33–4, 36, 44, 49, 66–7, 71, 77, 79, 93, 99, 101, 106–10, 112–13, 115, 118, 120–3, 126, 129, 132, 137–8, 147–8, 152, 163–4, 166, 170–1, 173, 177, 179, 181, 185–7, 190–4, 196, 265–7, 273, 275, 279–80, 284, 293, 297, 299, 303, 310, 313, 316, 319–20, 326–9, 331–44, 347, 349–50, 354–8, 362–6, 375–9, 382, 387, 392–3, 413–15, 417, 429–31, 434, 439, 443, 451, 479, 481–3, 487–92, 494–505, 508, 510–11, 513, 515–17
Rexhäuser, Ludwig, 280, 510
Riga, 78, 132, 141, 214
Robespierre, Maximilien François Marie Isidore de, 388, 409, 486–7, 510–11
Robotnik [The Worker], 106, 341, 357, 359
Rosenblatt, 292
Rosenfeld, Kurt, 281, 510
Rothschild oil refinery, 202
Rousseau, Jean-Jacques, 8, 429, 510, 516
Rudyerd, Benjamin, 467, 510
Rupert, Prince, 453–6, 458, 470, 510, 518
rural, xxxi, 40–2, 47, 52, 55, 76, 79, 83, 87–8, 110–13, 119, 123, 134–5, 140, 149, 164, 181, 210–12, 234, 241, 295, 318, 375, 390, 393–4, 425, 492
Russia, vii–viii, xi–xiii, xv–xxii, xxiv–xxxiii, xxxv, 13–17, 20–1, 23, 31–4, 36–7, 40, 42, 45, 51–3, 55, 62, 66, 70–3, 76–7, 79, 81, 83–5, 87, 89–90, 94–9, 101–2, 106–13, 116, 121, 123, 126, 128–9, 131–4, 138, 140–1, 143–4, 148, 151–3, 164–6, 169–75, 181, 183, 185–6, 189–93, 195–7, 199–217, 219, 221–35, 237–47, 251, 263–5, 269–76, 278–80, 283, 289–90, 293–5, 297–301, 303, 305–16, 318–21, 325–31, 333–44, 347–9, 351–3, 356–8, 364–6, 368–70, 375–82, 384–7, 390–409, 411, 413–16, 418, 423, 427–8, 430–2, 435, 437–8, 441, 449, 479–80, 482–92, 495–8, 501, 503–19.
  See also Russian Social Democratic Labor Party
  Empire, xvi, xix, xxi, 14, 20, 175, 289, 356, 403, 406, 416, 491
  imperialism, 401, 404
  Imperial Guard, 97
  Imperial Navy, 376
  Kronstadt rebellion, 79, 140, 218–19, 376
  liberalism, 270, 308–10
  proletariat, xxvi, xxx, 15–16, 32, 34, 84, 106, 129, 165, 189, 203, 224, 227–8, 230–1, 235, 239, 241, 243, 264, 270–2, 274, 279, 295, 298–9, 301, 305–13, 315, 321, 341, 377–8, 392
  Revolution 1905–1906, vii, xii, xv–xvii, xix, xxi, xxiv, xxvi, xxix, xxxii, 13–16, 23, 70, 73, 83, 89, 128, 151, 152, 172, 186, 192–3, 195–7, 199–202, 215, 221–2, 224–5, 230, 240–1, 243–7, 263–4, 269–72, 276, 283, 294, 297, 300–301, 303, 306, 312, 317, 320–1, 325, 327, 364–5, 370, 391, 399, 403, 405, 406, 415, 423, 485, 490, 491–2, 497, 498, 501, 505, 508, 513, 514, 515
  Russo-Japanese War, 34, 96, 353
  Social Democracy, viii, xx, xxiv, xxvii, xxxv, 23, 170, 172, 206, 221, 224, 231, 279, 299, 303, 306–8, 312–13, 315–16, 347, 377, 379, 382, 384, 386–7, 390, 431–2
  Sveaborg rebellion, 376
Russian Social Democratic Labor Party (RSDRP), xx, xxviii, xxxv, 23, 99, 170, 279, 299, 310, 312, 316, 385, 427, 430, 483, 496,

503, 508–9, 513, 515–16, 518. *See also* political parties
  Brussels (second) Congress 1903, 170, 508
  London Congress 1907, vii, xii, xx, xxviii, 299–321
  Stockholm Congress 1906, 312
  Sweden (fourth) Congress 1906, 170, 312
Russkoye Slovo [Russian Word], 20
Ruthenia/Ruthenians, 36, 190, 356

Sächsische Arbeiterzeitung [The Workers Newspaper of Saxony], 199, 359
Sadovaya, 18
Saint-Just, Louis Antoine de, 388, 511
Saint-Simon, Claude Henri de Rouroy, 24, 511
sailors' revolts, 219, 376
Samara, 213, 217
Saratov, 204, 217–18
Sarrien, Ferdinand, 297, 511
Saxony, 199, 276, 300, 359, 481
Scheibler, Karl, 290–1, 392, 511
Schiller, Friedrich, 7–8, 197, 261, 312, 511
schools, 29, 36–7, 43, 48, 52–3, 77, 145, 253, 396
Second International, xviii, 25, 67, 189, 313, 403, 424, 481, 486–7, 495, 497, 510
  Amsterdam 1904, 273
  Copenhagen 1910, 439, 440
  London Congress 1896, 357
  Stuttgart 1907, 417, 439
  Zurich Congress 1893, xviii, 273
Second Proletariat Party, 117, 331. *See also* First Proletariat Party; political parties
security, 45, 230, 423
serfdom/serfs, 26–7, 30, 44–5, 60, 144, 211, 371, 479, 502
Sevastopol, 79, 140, 143
Shusha, 36
Siberia, 47, 126, 132–3, 209, 399, 480
Silberstein, 292, 372, 392
Singer, Paul, 284, 297, 511
Skalon, Georgi, 83, 85, 94, 97, 399, 404, 411–12, 414, 494, 498, 507, 511
Skippon, Philip, 456, 512
Skrzynecki, Jan Zygmunt, 340, 512
slavery, xxiv, 5, 226, 233, 291, 425, 479. *See also* racism
Slavic Commission, 396–7
Slavic culture, 396, 404

Slavophilism, 405
Slovenia, 276
Smolensk, 217
Social Democracy of the Kingdom of Poland (SDKP), xi, xviii, 23, 117, 171, 496, 503, 516. *See also* political parties
Social Democracy of the Kingdom of Poland and Lithuania (SDKPiL), xi, xviii–xx, xxxv, 17, 23, 33, 128, 155, 171, 189, 289, 325–7, 355, 415, 496, 500, 502–3, 514, 516–17. *See also* political parties
  Zakopane (Fifth) Congress 1906, 217
Social Democratic Party of Austria, 227, 479. *See also* political parties
Social Democratic Party of Galicia and Silesia (PPSD), xxxv, 128, 487. *See also* political parties
Social Democratic Party of Germany (SPD), xi–xii, xvii–xix, xxiii–xxiv, xxxv, 251, 256, 263, 266, 274–5, 279, 283–4, 295, 313, 338, 352, 446, 449, 460, 480–3, 486–7, 489–90, 493, 495, 497–8, 500–502, 504, 507, 510–11, 513, 517, 519. *See also* political parties
  Dreseden Congress, 1903, 442
  Jena Congress 1905, vii, 201, 244, 263, 267, 299. *See also* Jena Resolution
  Leipzig Congress 1909, 439, 440, 442-3, 447
  Mannheim Congress, 1906, vii, 263, 417
  Nuremburg Congress 1908, 417, 445
  Stuttgart Congress 1898, 352
Social Democratic Workers Party (SDAP), 231, 441, 480–1, 511. *See also* Eisenachers; General German Workers' Association; political parties
Social Democracy, vii–viii, xi, xvi–xix, xxii, xxiv, xxvii–xxviii, xxx, xxxv, 4, 15, 17, 23, 26, 31, 34, 36–8, 40–1, 43–9, 51–3, 55–6, 58–63, 65–7, 72, 75–6, 78–80, 91–3, 98–100, 103–5, 108, 110–13, 115–18, 120–4, 127–9, 134–5, 137–8, 142, 144, 148–9, 152, 154, 169, 171–3, 179, 183, 185, 189, 191, 194–6, 201, 205–6, 208–10, 217, 227–9, 232, 234, 237–40, 242, 244–54, 256–61, 263, 265 6, 273–84, 289, 299–301, 303, 306–8, 310, 312–16, 318–19, 326, 330, 338, 344, 347, 352, 354, 356–9, 364–5, 368, 376, 382, 384–7, 390, 394, 414–17, 428–31, 436–40, 442–4, 446, 451,

Social Democracy (*continued*), 460, 486, 488, 497, 499. *See also* Austrian Social Democratic Party; political parties; Russian Social Democratic Labor Party; Social Democratic Party of Galicia and Silesia; Social Democratic Party of Germany; Social Democracy of the Kingdom of Poland and Lithuania
social-patriotism, xix, 23, 325–8, 338, 340, 342–4, 347, 353–4, 357–9, 361, 366–8, 414, 416
Socialism, xi, xxi, xxiv–xxxiii, 3, 9, 15–16, 26–8, 30–1, 47, 63, 67, 70–1, 76, 78, 98, 103, 111, 116, 120, 147–8, 163–5, 167, 171, 173, 185, 193, 196, 205, 226, 250, 256, 270, 285, 289, 303, 306, 311, 315–16, 320–1, 327, 333–5, 337, 339, 341, 343–4, 349–50, 354–5, 357, 360, 363–5, 367–8, 402, 414, 423, 429, 441, 446, 460, 481–2, 486, 504–5, 507, 511–12, 514, 518
  Antisocialist Laws, 198, 237, 279, 283–4, 294, 338, 482, 490, 509
  inequality/social inequality, xv, 26–7, 36, 44–5, 49, 156, 163, 480, 510
  scientific, 67, 226, 250, 303, 315, 320, 333–5, 350
  transition to, xxviii–xxix, xxxi, 16, 305
  utopian, 15, 24, 27, 132, 147–8, 170–1, 183, 189, 236, 314, 319, 326–7, 334, 337, 342, 350, 354–5, 362, 388–9, 407, 415, 434, 490, 507, 511
Socialist International. *See* Second International
Socialist Reading Association in Amsterdam, 3
Socialist Revolutionary Party in Russia (SR), xxxv, 79, 106–7, 152, 173, 196, 490–1. *See also* political parties
Sokół, 186. *See also* Polish Sport Association
Sokoł case, 399
soldier(s), xx, 18–21, 37, 50, 106, 108–12, 123, 131, 139, 142–3, 146, 156, 158–62, 181–2, 218–19, 222, 264, 304, 353, 381, 453, 462, 468, 473, 483, 487, 493–5, 499, 502, 504–5, 509, 512, 516–17
Sombart, Werner, 255–6, 512
Somerset, Henry, 458, 512
Sosnkowski, Kazimierz, 348, 512
Sosnowiec, 117, 213–14

South Africa, 51
Spain, 31, 193, 362, 460, 463, 509–10
Spartacus/Spartakus, xii, xxix, 369, 496, 501, 503–4
Spasowicz, Włodzimierz, 399, 512–13
Spencer, Henry, 454, 512
spontaneity, xii, xxi–xxii, 27, 77, 122, 137, 179, 215, 223, 228, 278, 293, 430
St. Petersburg. *See* Petersburg
Stadthagen, Arthur, 275, 513
Stalin, Joseph, xxix, 202, 402, 494, 496, 498, 503, 513, 515, 519
Stalinism, xxx, xxxiii
Stapleton, Philip, 472, 474, 513
Steinert, 291
Stołypin, Pyotr, 175, 185, 375, 383, 396–9, 403–5, 513
Strastnoi Square, 18
Straszewicz, Ludwik, 399, 404, 408, 513
Ströbel, Heinrich, 275, 513
Strode, William, 28, 466, 493, 514
Struve, Pyotr, 208, 310, 344, 403, 514
students, 21, 53, 78, 304, 502, 512
Svet [The World], 396
Sweden, 170, 227, 442, 504
Świętochowski, Aleksander, vii, 69–73, 153, 372, 514
Switzerland, xi, 31, 35, 51, 117, 490, 496, 500, 503, 513, 518
Sytin, Ivan Dmitrievich, 20, 514
Słowacki, Juliusz, 395, 512
Słowo [The Word], 124, 184, 186, 397, 407
Słowo Polskie [The Polish Word], 124
Słowo Warszawskie [The Warsaw Word], 397

Taaffe, Eduard, 294, 434, 514
tactics, vii, xviii, xxi, xxxii, 19, 66, 91–2, 94, 99–104, 108, 123, 125, 127, 151–2, 171, 174, 179, 195, 215, 229–30, 240, 244–5, 247, 266, 273–5, 278, 282, 299, 301–3, 305–8, 310–12, 314–15, 321, 326, 332, 337–9, 342–3, 352, 354, 360, 364, 369, 377, 380, 383–4, 414–16, 427–30, 432, 434, 436–7, 439–41, 443, 446, 450, 470
Tallinn, 214. *See also* Reval
Targowica, 405
tariffs, 37, 53–5, 84, 88–9, 227, 330, 339, 356
Tatu, 214

INDEX 539

Tauride Palace, 176, 438
taxes/taxation, 27, 29–30, 53–5, 88–9, 446, 489
Tbilisi, 205, 207, 213, 218, 222, 224
telegraph, 18, 20, 79, 132, 135, 140, 145, 224, 269, 396, 489
terrorism, xx, 78, 99, 106–7, 112, 123, 147, 170, 196, 279–80, 370, 388, 414–16, 424, 430, 471, 506–7, 510–11, 518–19
textile industry, 203, 214, 289–90, 292, 341, 511
textile workers, viii, 23, 203–4, 219, 224, 233, 240, 289, 291–2
Thiers, 389, 482, 489–90, 514
Third Republic, 13, 389–90
Tiflis, 205, 218
Tikhoretsk, 205
Tirard, Pierre Emmanuel, 297, 515
Tobolsk, 132
Tolstoy, Leo, 20, 479, 508, 514–15
Tomsk, 132
Trade and Industry Party (Russia), 212. *See also* political parties
trade unions, vii, xi–xii, xvii, xxii–xxiii, xxv, xxxv, 5, 15, 47, 76, 88, 193, 195, 197, 199, 201, 203, 205, 207, 209, 211, 213, 215, 217, 219, 221, 223, 225, 227, 229, 231, 233, 235, 237, 239, 241, 243, 245, 247, 249, 251, 253, 255, 257, 259, 261, 263–6, 273, 276–7, 284, 354, 371, 375, 417–18, 440, 442, 444, 483, 489, 500–501, 516, 519. *See also* labor unions
  Central Union of Masons, 274
  Cologne (Fifth) Congress 1905, 197–8, 201, 223, 263, 274
  Frankfurt Congress 1899, 483
  Free Association of German, xxxv, 266
  General Commission of (Germany), 199, 259, 276–7, 500
  International Conference of National Centers (Paris) 1909, 439
  leaders in, 198, 200, 235–7, 243, 247, 249–56, 260
  labor unions, xvii, 88, 102, 149, 197–201, 204, 206, 209–10, 215–18, 221, 223–4, 226, 231–7, 239–40, 243, 246–61
  Ninth General Assembly of the German Metalworkers' (Hamburg) 1909, 440
  Saint Petersburg Labor Union Combine 1906, 217, 231

Union of Polish Workers, xxxv, 117, 500, 503 Union of Printing Workers, 280
Union of Workers, 171
Trotsky, Leon, xxi, xxiv, xxviii, 70, 174, 491, 496, 504, 515
Trudoviks, 152, 190–1
tsarism, xxvi, xxix, xxxi, 20, 32, 47, 70–1, 75–7, 79–80, 102, 134–8, 141, 143–4, 147, 152–3, 176–7, 180, 183–4, 192, 204, 220, 245, 347, 357, 386, 405–6
Tsushima navy, 403
Turkey, 144, 359, 400–401, 403, 505
Tverskoy Street, 18
Tyrol, 276

Ukraine, xvi, 73, 132, 141, 330, 356, 396, 491
Ultimatists, 431
unemployment, 13, 57, 85, 123, 156, 163–4, 167, 204, 208, 226, 412–13, 482
unification, 170, 259, 334, 343, 347, 361, 455
Union of Polish Workers, xxxv, 117, 500, 503
Union of Printing Workers (Lithuania), 280
Union of the Russian Nation, 377. *See also* Black Hundreds
Union of Workers, 171
United States, x, xv–xvi, 35, 360–2, 423, 486, 512, 519. *See also* America
Urals, 137
urban, 40–2, 47, 52, 54–6, 73, 83, 88, 110, 112, 119, 123–4, 134, 140, 149, 153, 181, 212, 232, 235, 241–2, 251, 375, 383–4, 394

Vaillant, Edouard, 265, 515
Vandal, Albert, 412–13, 515
Vane, Henry, 451, 454, 457, 515
vanguard party, xxii, xxviii, 195, 224, 228, 233, 235, 238, 240, 293, 303, 306, 308–9, 318, 321, 370, 393, 436
Vienna, 70, 76, 84, 105, 126, 128, 191, 231, 276, 304, 395–6, 433–4, 497, 518
Villiers, George, 462, 516–17
Vilnius, 23, 77, 218
violence, xx, 21, 24, 29–30, 46, 51, 73, 91, 94, 113, 122, 124–5, 136–7, 145, 161–2, 175, 245–6, 281, 284–5, 378, 433
Vladicaucasus Railroad, 205
Vladikavkav, 205
Vladimirov, General, 395, 398, 404
Vladivostok, 79, 213, 219

Vogtland, 233
Voltaire, François-Marie Arouet, 8, 516
Voronezh, 217
Vorwärts, 3, 244, 251, 263, 265, 274–5, 278, 281, 289, 417, 443, 482, 487, 489–90, 499, 513, 517
vote, 31, 38–41, 79, 83–5, 92, 97, 144, 153, 197, 201, 223, 244–5, 251, 275, 278, 283–4, 295, 365, 383, 385, 446, 462, 465, 469, 475–7
Vyborg Manifesto, 309

wage slavery, 5
wages, 5, 25, 32, 54, 57, 92, 99, 203–5, 207, 211, 213–14, 218–19, 224, 226–7, 232–3, 255, 291, 293, 499
Walecki, Henryk, 106, 325, 330, 340, 342–3, 348, 494, 516
Waller, William, 453–7, 468–70, 472–4, 516, 518
Wandsbek, 193
war, 13, 35, 50–1, 108, 143–4, 320, 389, 452, 455, 457–8, 464, 506, 515, 518
Warsaw Constitution, 349
Warsaw Russian Club, 396
Warski, Adolf, 23, 155, 325, 503, 516
Waryński, Ludwik, 331
weapons, xx, 18–20, 50–1, 95, 97, 106–9, 112, 114, 123, 143, 157–8, 161, 304, 307, 415, 429, 436, 453, 456, 466
weavers, 24, 203, 424
Weber, Maximilian Karl Emil, 213, 256, 512, 517
Weltanschauung/en, 258, 273, 279
Wentworth, Thomas, 462–3, 465, 517
Wermuth, Karl, 275, 517
Western Europe, xxvi, xxxii, 30, 45, 105, 108, 200, 216, 278, 314, 327, 329, 331, 356, 362, 408, 412, 490–1, 505, 513, 516
Wielopolski, Aleksander Ignacy Jan-Kanty, 399, 405–6, 517
Wilhelm II (Germany), 227, 316, 517
Willoughby, Francis, 453, 517
Wilmot, Henry, 453, 518
Windisch-Grätz, Alfred Candidus Ferdinand, 402, 518
Windthorst, Ludwig, 428, 518

Winter Palace, 75, 202, 396
Witte, Sergei, 94, 145, 175, 370, 377, 479, 518
Wojnarowska, Cezaryna, 23
women, xi, xv, 19–20, 27, 38, 47, 49, 56, 58–62, 71, 78, 158–9, 161–2, 207, 236, 266, 281, 310, 413–14, 424, 464, 466–8, 490, 514
workers' insurrection, 300
workers' revolution, 77, 115–16, 123, 128, 132–3, 135, 139–40, 144, 175, 180, 329
workers' subjective agency, xxvii
working class, xviii–xix, xxii, xxiv–xxxii, 3–5, 7–9, 13–16, 23–6, 28–35, 37–46, 48–53, 55–7, 59, 62–3, 68, 76–9, 83, 88, 91, 93–4, 96–104, 107, 109–11, 115–17, 119–23, 126, 133–7, 145–50, 155, 161, 164, 166, 173, 176, 183, 189, 194, 196, 200–201, 203–4, 206, 208, 215, 218, 223, 225–6, 230–3, 236–9, 242, 246–9, 251, 257, 259, 265, 269, 273, 275–6, 280, 283, 293–4, 297, 299, 301, 303–4, 315–16, 321, 328, 332–3, 336, 340, 348, 357, 364, 371, 376, 382, 390, 392–3, 412, 415–16, 418, 424, 429, 431, 434, 439, 441, 482, 488, 490, 504, 508, 518.
See also proletariat
Workman, John, 463, 518
World Labor Day, 297

Zakopane, 217
Zakopane Magazine, 502
Zaorski, F., 329, 502, 518. *See also* Lityński, Alfred
Zasulich, Vera, 402, 518
Zemlya i Volya, 170, 519. *See also* Land and Liberty
Zemstvo Liberalism, 212
Zetkin, Clara, xii, 352, 519
Zetkin, Kostja, xii, 352, 449, 519
Zhelyabov, Andrei Ivanovich, 170, 519
Zinoviev, Grigori, 193, 496, 519
Zinovievsk, 205
Zollparlament, 361
Zollverein, 361
Zubatóv, Sergei, 206, 519
Zurich, xi, xviii, 23, 155, 273, 479, 496, 500, 516